Foundation

MATHEMATICS
GCSE for AQA
Student Book

Karen Morrison, Julia Smith, Pauline McLean, Rachael Horsman and Nick Asker

CAMBRIDGE
UNIVERSITY PRESS

University Printing House, Cambridge CB2 8BS, United Kingdom

Cambridge University Press is part of the University of Cambridge.

It furthers the University's mission by disseminating knowledge in the pursuit of education, learning and research at the highest international levels of excellence.

www.cambridge.org
Information on this title:
www.cambridge.org/9781107448049 (Paperback)
www.cambridge.org/9781107449800 (1 Year Online Subscription)
www.cambridge.org/9781107449770 (2 Year Online Subscription)
www.cambridge.org/9781107447950 (Paperback + Online Subscription)

© Cambridge University Press 2015

First published 2015

Printed in the United Kingdom by Latimer Trend

A catalogue record for this publication is available from the British Library

ISBN 978-1-107-44804-9 Paperback
ISBN 978-1-107-44980-0 1 Year Online Subscription
ISBN 978-1-107-44977-0 2 Year Online Subscription
ISBN 978-1-107-44795-0 Paperback + Online Subscription

Additional resources for this publication at www.cambridge.org/ukschools

Approval message from AQA

This textbook has been approved by AQA for use with our qualification. This means that we have checked that it broadly covers the specification and we are satisfied with the overall quality. Full details of our approval process can be found on our website.

We approve textbooks because we know how important it is for teachers and students to have the right resources to support their teaching and learning. However, the publisher is ultimately responsible for the editorial control and quality of this book.

Please note that when teaching the GCSE Mathematics (8300) course, you must refer to AQA's specification as your definitive source of information. While this book has been written to match the specification, it cannot provide complete coverage of every aspect of the course.

A wide range of other useful resources can be found on the relevant subject pages of our website: www.aqa.org.uk

Contents

Note

The colour of each chapter corresponds to the area of maths that it covers:

- ●   Number
- ●   Algebra
- ●   Ratio, proportion and rates of change
- ●   Geometry and measures
- ●   Probability
- ●   Statistics

Introduction

This book has been written by experienced teachers to help build your understanding and enjoyment of the maths you will meet at GCSE.

Each chapter opens with a list of skills that are covered in the chapter. The **real-life applications** section describes an example of how the maths is used in real life.

All chapters build on knowledge that you will have learned in previous years. You may need to revise some topics before starting a chapter. To check your knowledge, answer the questions in the **Before you start ...** table. You can check your answers using the free answer booklet available at **www.cambridge.org/ukschools/gcsemaths-studentbookanswers**. If you answer any questions incorrectly, you may need to revise the topic from your work in earlier years.

The chapters are divided into sections, each covering a single topic. Some chapters may cover topics that you already know and understand. You can use the **Launchpad** to identify the best section for you to start with. Answer the questions in each step. If you find a question difficult to answer correctly, the step suggests the section that you should look at.

Throughout the book, there are features to help you build knowledge and improve your skills:

 This means you may need a calculator to work through a question.

 This means you should work through a question without using a calculator.

 This shows the question is from a past exam paper.

Tip

Tip boxes provide helpful hints.

Calculator tip

Calculator tips help you to use your calculator.

Learn this formula

Learn this formula boxes contain formulae that you need to know.

Key vocabulary

Important maths terms are written in green. You can find what they mean in **Key vocabulary** boxes and also in the **Glossary** at the back of the book.

Did you know?

Did you know? boxes contain interesting maths facts.

WORK IT OUT

Work it out boxes contain a question with several worked solutions. Some of the solutions contain common mistakes. Try to spot the correct solution and check the free answer booklet available at **www.cambridge.org/ukschools/gcsemaths-studentbookanswers** to see if you're right.

WORKED EXAMPLE

Worked examples guide you through model answers to help you understand methods of answering questions.

Some chapters contain a **Problem-solving framework**, which sets a problem and then shows how you can go about answering it.

Checklist of learning and understanding

At the end of a chapter, use the **Checklist of learning and understanding** to check whether you have covered everything you need to know.

Chapter review

You can check whether you have understood the topics using the **Chapter review,** which contains questions from the whole chapter.

A booklet containing answers to all exercises is free to download from the maths pages at **www.cambridge.org/ukschools/gcsemaths-studentbookanswers**.

You can find more resources, including interactive widgets, games and quizzes on **GCSE Mathematics Online**.

Working with integers

In this chapter you will learn how to …

- use formal written methods to calculate with positive and negative integers.
- perform operations in the correct order based on mathematical conventions.
- recognise inverse operations and use them to simplify and check calculations.

 For more resources relating to this chapter, visit GCSE Mathematics Online.

Using mathematics: real-life applications

Everyone uses numbers on a daily basis often without really thinking about them. Shopping, cooking, working out bills, paying for transport and measuring all rely on a good understanding of numbers and calculation skills.

 Tip

You probably already know most of the concepts in this chapter. They have been included so that you can revise them if you need to and check that you know them well.

"Number puzzles and games are very popular and there are mobile apps and games available for all age groups. I use an app with my GCSE classes where they have to work in the correct order to solve different number puzzles."

(Secondary school teacher)

Before you start …

KS3	You should be able to add, subtract, multiply and divide positive and negative numbers.	**1**	Copy and complete each statement to make it true. Use only <, = or >. **a** $2 + 3 \;\square\; 4 - 7$ **b** $-3 + 6 \;\square\; 4 - 7$ **c** $-1 - 4 \;\square\; 20 \div -4$ **d** $-6 \times 2 \;\square\; -7 - (-5)$
KS3	You should know the rules for working when more than one operation is involved in a calculation (BODMAS).	**2**	Spot the mistake in each calculation and correct the answers. **a** $3 + 8 + 3 \times 4 = 56$ **b** $3 + 8 \times 3 + 4 = 37$ **c** $3 \times (8 + 3) \times 4 = 130$

KS3	You should understand that addition and subtraction, and multiplication and division are inverse operations.	**3**	Identify the inverse operation by choosing the correct option.
			
			a $14 \times 4 = 56$
			  A $56 \times 4 = 14$ B $14 \div 4 = 56$ C $56 \div 4 = 14$
			b $200 \div 10 = 20$
			  A $200 \div 20 = 10$ B $200 = 10 \times 20$ C $10 \times 200 = 2000$
			c $27 + 53 = 80$
			  A $80 = 4 \times 20$ B $80 - 27 = 53$ C $80 + 27 = 107$

Find answers at: cambridge.org/ukschools/gcsemaths-studentbookanswers

Assess your starting point using the Launchpad

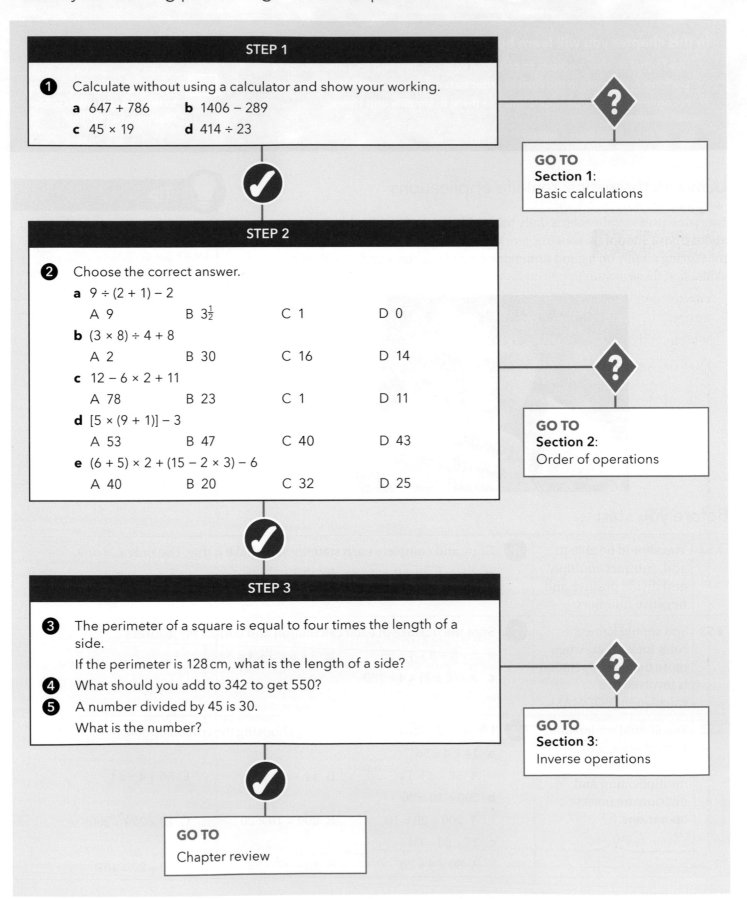

STEP 1

❶ Calculate without using a calculator and show your working.

a 647 + 786   **b** 1406 − 289

c 45 × 19   **d** 414 ÷ 23

GO TO
Section 1:
Basic calculations

STEP 2

❷ Choose the correct answer.

a 9 ÷ (2 + 1) − 2

A 9   B 3½   C 1   D 0

b (3 × 8) ÷ 4 + 8

A 2   B 30   C 16   D 14

c 12 − 6 × 2 + 11

A 78   B 23   C 1   D 11

d [5 × (9 + 1)] − 3

A 53   B 47   C 40   D 43

e (6 + 5) × 2 + (15 − 2 × 3) − 6

A 40   B 20   C 32   D 25

GO TO
Section 2:
Order of operations

STEP 3

❸ The perimeter of a square is equal to four times the length of a side.

If the perimeter is 128 cm, what is the length of a side?

❹ What should you add to 342 to get 550?

❺ A number divided by 45 is 30.

What is the number?

GO TO
Section 3:
Inverse operations

GO TO

Chapter review

Section 1: Basic calculations

You will not always have a calculator so it is useful to know how to do calculations using mental and written strategies.

It is best to use a method that you are confident with and always **show your working**.

When a question asks you to find the:

- **sum**, you need to add
- **difference**, you need to subtract the smaller number from the larger number
- **product**, you need to multiply
- **quotient**, you need to divide.

Tip

Some examination papers will not allow you to use your calculator.

WORK IT OUT 1.1

Look at these calculations carefully.

Discuss with a partner what methods these students have used to find the answer.

Which method would you use to do each of these calculations? Why?

① $489 + 274$

$$400 + 200 \rightarrow 600$$
$$80 + 70 \rightarrow 150$$
$$9 + 4 \rightarrow \underline{13}$$
$$\underline{763}$$

② $284 - 176$

$$\begin{array}{r} 2\overset{7}{\cancel{8}}\overset{1}{\cancel{4}} \\ - 176 \\ \hline 108 \end{array}$$

③ 29×17

$$= 30 \times 17 - 17$$
$$= 3 \times 170 - 17$$
$$= 510 - 17$$
$$= 493$$

④ 15×62

$$\begin{array}{ll} = 30 \times 31 & 310 \\ = 930 & 310 \\ = 3 \times 310 & \underline{310} \\ & 930 \end{array}$$

⑤ 207×47

×	200	0	7
40	8000	0	280
7	1400	0	49

$$9400 + 0 + 329$$
$$= 9729$$

⑥ $2394 \div 42$

$$\begin{array}{r} 2394 \\ - 1680 \quad ㊵ \\ \hline 714 \\ - 420 \quad ⑩ \\ \hline 294 \\ - 210 \quad ⑤ \\ \hline 84 \\ - 84 \quad ② \\ \hline 0 \quad 57 \end{array}$$

$$42 \times 10 = 420$$
$$42 \times 20 = 840$$
$$42 \times 40 = 1680$$
$$42 \times 5 = 210$$
$$42 \times 2 = 84$$

Find answers at: cambridge.org/ukschools/gcsemaths-studentbookanswers

Problem-solving strategies

The problem-solving framework below outlines the steps that you can take to break down most problems to help you solve them.

Follow these steps each time you are faced with a problem to help you become more skilled at problem solving and more able to self-check.

These are important skills both for your GCSE courses and for everyday life.

Problem-solving framework

Sally had a budget of £60 to buy items.
Sally bought:

a table for £32 and

a bench for £18.

She spent £12 to repair them.

She then sold the two items for £69.

How much profit did she make?

Steps for solving problems	What you would do for this example
Step 1: Work out what you have to do. Start by reading the question carefully.	Find the profit.
Step 2: What information do you need? Have you got it all?	Cost of items = £32 + £18 Cost of repairs = £12 Selling price = £69
Step 3: Is there any information that you don't need?	You don't need to know her budget. You just need to know how much she spent. Many problems contain extra information that you don't need to test your understanding.
Step 4: Decide what maths you can do.	Profit = selling price – cost
Step 5: Set out your solution clearly. Check your working and make sure your answer is reasonable.	Cost = £32 + £18 + £12 = £62 Profit = £69 – £62 = £7 Sally made £7 profit.
Step 6: Check that you have answered the question.	Yes. You needed to find the profit and you have found it.

EXERCISE 1A

Solve these problems using written methods.

You **must** show your working.

1 A pack of pens cost £3.90 for three.
Nola bought fifteen pens.

    a i How much did she pay in total?

      ii What is the cost per pen?

    b How many packs of pens did Nola buy? Why do you need to know this?

    c What operation would you do to find the total cost? Why?

    d How would you work out the cost per pen?

    e Does a price of £1.50 per pen seem reasonable?

2 A pair of jeans costs £34.
A scarf costs £9.50.
A top costs £20.

    Sandra saved £100 to buy these items.
How much money does she have left?

3 How many 16-page brochures can you make from 1030 pages?

4 Jason can type 48 words per minute.

    a How many words can he type in an hour and a half?

    b Approximately how long would it take him to type 2000 words?

5 At the start of a year the population of Greenside Village was 56 309.

    During the year:

    617 people died,

    1835 babies were born,

    4087 people left the village

    and 3099 people moved into the village.

    What was the population at the end of the year?

6 The Amazon River is 6448 km long.

    The Nile River is 6670 km.

    The Severn River is 354 km long.

    a How much longer is the Nile River than the Amazon River?

    b How much shorter is the Severn River than the Amazon River?

7 What is the result when you combine the sum of 132 and 99 with the product of 36 and 127?

8 Find the result when the difference between 8765 and 3087 is added to the result of 1206 divided by 18.

Tip

You don't always need to write something for the first few steps in the problem-solving framework, but you should still consider these steps mentally when approaching a problem in order to help you decide what to do. You should **always** show how you worked to solve the problem.

Did you know?

The Severn is the longest river in the UK.

Find answers at: cambridge.org/ukschools/gcsemaths-studentbookanswers

Key vocabulary

integers: whole numbers in the set $\{\ldots, -3, -2, -1, 0, 1, 2, 3, \ldots\}$; when they have a negative or positive sign they can be referred to as **directed numbers**.

Tip

You will be expected to work with negative and positive values in algebra, so it is important to make sure you can do this early on in your GCSE course.

Working with positive and negative integers

When doing calculations involving positive and negative **integers**, you need to remember the following:

- Adding a negative number is the same as subtracting the number:
  $4 + -3 = 1$
- Subtracting a negative number is the same as adding a positive number:
  $5 - -3 = 8$
- Multiplying or dividing the same signs gives a positive answer:
  $-4 \times -2 = 8$ and $\frac{-4}{-2} = 2$
- Multiplying or dividing different signs gives a negative answer:
  $4 \times -2 = -8$ and $\frac{-4}{2} = -2$

EXERCISE 1B

1 Calculate:

a $12 - 5 + 8$ b $-3 - 4 - 8$ c $3 + 5 - 6$

d $-2 - 8 + 5$ e $14 - 3 - 9$ f $9 - 3 - 4$

g $-34 + 18 - 12$ h $25 - 19 - 42$ i $-9 - (-7)$

j $-3 - (-10)$ k $-4 - (-12)$ l $8 - (-9)$

m $9 - (-8)$ n $-3 - 8 - (-9)$ o $-12 + 4 - (-8)$

2 Calculate:

a $-2 \times -4 \times -4$ b $-4 \times 3 \times -6$ c $-3 \times -4 \times 3$

d $-4 \times -8 \times 3$ e $3 \times 6 \times -4$ f $12 \times 2 \times -3$

g $1 \times -1 \times 10$ h $-3 \times -8 \times 9$ i $24 \div 3$

j $-24 \div 3$ k $-28 \div 2$ l $-48 \div -6$

m $-300 \div -10$ n $400 \div -40$ o $42 \div -7$

p $-22 \div -22$ q $-33 \div 11$ r $-27 \div -3$

s $45 \div -9$ t $-64 \div -8$

3 Calculate:

a $\frac{-40}{5}$ b $\frac{-28}{-4}$ c $\frac{30}{-5}$ d $\frac{12}{-2}$

e $\frac{65}{-5}$ f $\frac{-48}{-6}$ g $\frac{-330}{-10}$ h $\frac{-400}{40}$

i $\frac{-63}{7}$ j $\frac{-60}{-20}$ k $\frac{60}{-6}$ l $\frac{-36}{6}$

4 The final score in a card game is worked out by allocating points to each card as follows:

Hearts +2   Diamonds –3   Clubs +4   Spades –5

a A player is left holding 3 diamonds, 2 hearts, a spade and 4 clubs. Choose the correct score from the following options.

    A 16   B 11   C 6   D –6

b Choose the card combination that will give the score closest to 0.

    A 2 diamonds   B 2 hearts, 1 diamond

    C 2 clubs, 1 spade   D 2 diamonds, 1 spade

5 Apply the operations in the first row to the given number to complete each table.

a

	– 10	× –2	+ 4	÷ –2	– 8	+ 1
–5						

b

	× –4	÷ –5	+ 8	– 3	× 2	– 9
10						

c

	– 10	× –2	+ 4	÷ –2	– 8	+ 1
0						

6 Here are some bank transactions.

Calculate the new balance in each case.

a Balance of £230.
Withdraw £100.

b Balance of £250.50.
Withdraw £300.

c Balance of –£450.
Deposit £900.
Withdraw £300.

d Balance of –£100.
Deposit £2000.
Withdraw £550.

Tip

Your bank balance is how much money you have in your account. Taking money out is a withdrawal. Putting money in is a deposit.

7 In 2010, there was an oil spill from a well in the Gulf of Mexico.
The opening of the oil well was 5000 feet below sea level.
The oil well itself extended to a depth of 13 000 feet.

Express the answers to these questions as positive or negative numbers.

a How deep was the deepest part of the oil well below the sea bed?

b How far did oil travel from the bottom of the well to reach the surface of the water?

c The oil company estimated that they were losing money at the rate of $15 000 000 per day. Use an integer to express the money lost after:

i one week   **ii** thirteen weeks.

Tip

Feet is a standard unit of **imperial** measurement for length. The metric measurement for length is metres. You will learn about **metric** measurements in Chapter 21.

8 Here is a set of integers.

–8, –6, –3, 1, 3, 7

a Write down two numbers with a difference of 9.

b Write down three numbers with a sum of 1.

c Write down two numbers whose product is –3.

d Write down two numbers which, when divided, will give an answer of –6.

9 One more than –6 is added to the product of 7 and 6 less than 3.

What is the result?

10 The temperature in Inverness is 4 °C at 7 pm at night.

By 2 am the same night, it has dropped by 12 degrees.

a What is the temperature at 2 am?

b What is the average hourly change in the temperature?

c By noon the next day, the temperature is 7 °C.

How many degrees warmer is this than it was at 2 am?

Find answers at: cambridge.org/ukschools/gcsemaths-studentbookanswers

Section 2: Order of operations

Jose posted this calculation on his wall on social media.

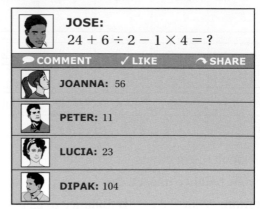

JOSE:
$24 + 6 \div 2 - 1 \times 4 = ?$

💬 COMMENT   ✓ LIKE   ↷ SHARE

JOANNA: 56

PETER: 11

LUCIA: 23

DIPAK: 104

Which one of Jose's friends (if any) do you think is correct? Why?

There is a set of rules that tell you the order in which you need to work when there is more than one operation.

The order of operations is:

1   Do any operations in brackets first.
2   If there are any '**powers of**' or '**fractions of**' in the calculation, do them next.
3   Do division and multiplication next, working from left to right.
4   Do addition and subtraction last, working from left to right.

Brackets

Brackets are used to group operations. For example:

$(3 + 7) \times (30 \div 2)$

When there is more than one set of brackets, work from the **innermost set** to the **outermost set**.

Tip

Many people remember these rules using the letters **BODMAS** (or sometimes BIDMAS).

Brackets

Of ('powers of' or 'fractions of', in BIDMAS I stands for indices)

Divide and/or **M**ultiply

Add and/or **S**ubtract

WORKED EXAMPLE 1

Work out $2((4 + 2) \times 2 - 3(1 - 3) - 10)$.

$2((4 + 2) \times 2 - 3(1 - 3) - 10)$

Highlight the different pairs of brackets to help if you need to.

$2((4 + 2) \times 2 - 3(1 - 3) - 10)$
$= 2((6) \times 2 - 3(-2) - 10)$
$= 2(6 \times 2 - 3 \times -2 - 10)$

The red highlighted brackets are the innermost, so do the calculations inside these brackets first. There are two lots, so work from left to right. **Note** that you can leave −2 inside brackets if you prefer because 3(−2) is the same as 3 × −2.

$2(6 \times 2 - 3 \times -2 - 10)$
$= 2(12 - -6 - 10)$
$= 2(8)$
$= 2 \times 8$
$= 16$

Yellow highlighted brackets are next. Do the multiplications first from left to right, then the subtractions from left to right.

Different styles of bracket can be used to make it easier to identify each pair.

For example, the following different types of brackets have been used below: ( ), [ ], { }.

$\{2 - [4(2 - 7) - 4(3 + 8)] - 2\} \times 8$

Other symbols can also be used to group operations.

For example:

Fraction bars: $\dfrac{5 - 12}{3 - 8}$

Roots: $\sqrt{16 + 9}$

These symbols are treated like brackets when you do a calculation.

Tip

$\dfrac{5 - 12}{3 - 8}$ is the same calculation as $(5 - 12) \div (3 - 8)$.

WORK IT OUT 1.2

Which of the solutions is correct in each case?

Find the mistakes in the incorrect option.

	Option A	Option B
1	$7 \times 3 + 4$ $= 21 + 4$ $= 25$	$7 \times 3 + 4$ $= 7 \times 7$ $= 49$
2	$(10 - 4) \times (4 + 9)^2$ $= 6 \times 16 + 81$ $= 96 + 81$ $= 177$	$(10 - 4) \times (4 + 9)^2$ $= 6 \times (13)^2$ $= 6 \times 169$ $= 1014$
3	$45 - [20 \times (4 - 3)]$ $= 45 - [20 \times 1]$ $= 45 - 21$ $= 24$	$45 - [20 \times (4 - 3)]$ $= 45 - 20 \times 1$ $= 45 - 20$ $= 25$
4	$30 - 4 \div 2 + 2$ $= 26 \div 2 + 2$ $= 13 + 2$ $= 15$	$30 - 4 \div 2 + 2$ $= 30 - 2 + 2$ $= 30$
5	$\dfrac{18 - 4}{4 - 2}$ $= \dfrac{18}{2}$ $= 9$	$\dfrac{18 - 4}{4 - 2}$ $= \dfrac{14}{2}$ $= 7$
6	$\sqrt{36 \div 4} + 40 \div 4 + 1$ $= \sqrt{9} + 10 + 1$ $= 3 + 11$ $= 14$	$\sqrt{36 \div 4} + 40 \div 4 + 1$ $= \sqrt{9} + 40 \div 5$ $= 3 + 8$ $= 11$

Calculator tip

Most modern calculators are programmed to use the correct order of operations. Check your calculator by entering $2 + 3 \times 4$. You should get 14.

If a calculation is written with brackets, you need to enter the brackets into the calculator to make sure it does these first.

Find answers at: cambridge.org/ukschools/gcsemaths-studentbookanswers

EXERCISE 1C

1 Choose the correct answer.

a $18 + 2 \times -3 + 5 - 2 =$

A 18   B 53   C 0   D 15

b $-5 \times 8 \div 2 \times -2 - 6 \times -3 =$

A −12   B −22   C −58   D 58

2 Calculate the following:

Show the steps in your working.

a $5 \times 10 + 3$ **b** $5 \times (10 + 3)$ **c** $2 + 10 \times 3$

d $(2 + 10) \times 3$ **e** $23 + 7 \times 2$ **f** $6 \times 2 \div (3 + 3)$

g $10 - 4 \times 5$ **h** $12 + 6 \div 2 - 4$ **i** $3 + 4 \times 5 - 10$

j $18 \div 3 \times 5 - 3 + 2$ **k** $5 - 3 \times 8 - 6 \div 2$ **l** $7 + 8 \div 4 - 1$

m $\dfrac{15 - 5}{2 \times 5}$ **n** $(17 + 1) \div 9 + 2$ **o** $\dfrac{16 - 4}{4 - 1}$

p $17 + 3 \times 21$ **q** $48 - (2 + 3) \times 2$ **r** $12 \times 4 - 4 \times 8$

s $15 + 30 \div 3 + 6$ **t** $20 - 6 \div 3 + 3$ **u** $10 - 4 \times 2 \div 2$

3 Check whether these answers are correct.

If the answer is wrong, work out the correct answer.

a $12 \times 4 + 76 = 124$ **b** $8 + 75 \times 8 = 698$

c $12 \times 18 - 4 \times 23 = 124$ **d** $(16 \div 4) \times (7 + 3 \times 4) = 76$

e $(82 - 36) \times (2 + 6) = 16$ **f** $(3 \times 7 - 4) - (4 + 6 \div 2) = 12$

4 Use the numbers listed to make each number sentence true.

a $\square - \square \div \square = \square$ 0, 2, 5, 10

b $\square - \square \div \square = \square$ 9, 11, 13, 18

c $\square \div (\square - \square) - \square = \square$ 1, 3, 8, 14, 16

d $(\square + \square) - (\square - \square) = \square$ 4, 5, 6, 9, 12

Section 3: Inverse operations

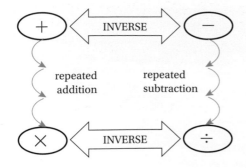

The four operations, add, subtract, multiply and divide, are related to each other.

Operations are inverses of each other if one undoes (cancels out) the effect of the other.

- Adding is the inverse of subtracting, for example, add 5 is undone by subtract 5.

- Multiplying is the inverse of dividing, for example, multiply by 2 is undone by divide by 2.

- Taking a square root is the inverse of squaring a number, for example, 4^2 is undone by $\sqrt{16}$.

- Taking the cube root is the inverse of cubing a number, for example, 2^3 is undone by $\sqrt[3]{8}$.

When you add a number to its inverse, the answer is always 0, for example,

$1 + -1 = 0$

−1 is known as the **additive inverse** of 1.

When you multiply a number by its inverse, the answer is always 1.

$2 \times \frac{1}{2} = 1$

$\frac{1}{2}$ is known as the **multiplicative inverse** of 2.

Inverse operations are useful for checking the results of your calculations.

For example, is $4320 - 500 = 3820$ correct?

Check by doing the inverse operation, that is, adding 500 back to the result to see if you get 4320.

$3820 + 500 = 4320$, so the original calculation is correct.

EXERCISE 1D

1 Find the additive inverse of each of these numbers.

a 5 **b** 2 **c** 100

d −3 **e** −16 **f** −12

2 By what number would you multiply each of these to get an answer of 1?

a 5 **b** 10 **c** −3

d $\frac{1}{3}$ **e** 9 **f** $\frac{1}{9}$

3 Use inverse operations to check each calculation.

Correct those that are wrong. (You can correct the question or the answer.)

a $6172 - 3415 = 2757$ **b** $488 - 156 = 322$ **c** $219 - 361 = -142$

d $264 + 469 = 723$ **e** $4019 + 217 = 4235$ **f** $617 + 728 = 1345$

g $512 \div 4 = 43$ **h** $672 \div 12 = 56$ **i** $1274 \div 15 = 85$

j $3840 \div 30 = 128$ **k** $30 \times 125 = 3770$ **l** $214 \times 8 = 1732$

m $\sqrt{900} = 30$ **n** $\sqrt{15\,625} = 120$ **o** $400^2 = 16\,000$

4 Use inverse operations to find the missing values in each of these calculations.

a $\square + 217 = 529$ **b** $\square + 388 = 490$ **c** $\square - 218 = 182$

d $121 \times \square = -605$ **e** $-6 \times \square = 870$ **f** $\square \div 40 = 5400$

5 Which operation can be used to check that $500 \times 38 = 19\,000$?

A $19\,000 - 500$ B $1900 \div 5$

C $190 \div 5$ D $19\,000 \div (500 + 38)$

Tip

The multiplicative inverse of a number is also called its **reciprocal**. For example, $\frac{1}{3}$ is the reciprocal of 3.

Tip

You will use inverse operations to solve equations and when you deal with functions, so it is important that you understand how they work.

Checklist of learning and understanding

Basic calculations

- Written methods are important for when you do not have a calculator.
- You can use any method as long as you show your working.
- Negative and positive numbers can be added, subtracted, multiplied and divided as long as you apply the rules to get the correct sign in the answer.

Order of operations

- In maths there is a conventional order for working when there is more than one operation:
  - Always work out brackets (or other grouping symbols) first,
  - then powers,
  - multiply and/or divide next,
  - then add and/or subtract.

Inverse operations

- An inverse operation undoes the previous operation.
- Addition is the inverse of subtraction.
- Multiplication is the inverse of division.
- Squaring is the inverse of taking the square root.

For additional questions on the topics in this chapter, visit GCSE Mathematics Online.

Chapter review

 1 Choose the correct answer.

a What is the first operation you would do in this calculation:
$4 \times [20 \div (5 - 3)] - 8 + 2$?

A +   B −   C ×   D ÷

b To make the statement $5 - 3 \times 8 - 6 \div 2 = 2$ correct, you would need to insert brackets as follows:

A $5 - (3 \times 8) - 6 \div 2 = 2$

B $5 [- 3 \times (8 - 6)] \div 2 = 2$

C $(5 - 3) \times 8 - 6 \div 2 = 2$

D $(5 - 3) \times (8 - 6) \div 2 = 2$

2 Look at the grid at the top of the next page. These are the solutions to a cross-number puzzle.

The clues are all calculations that involve using the correct order of operations.

Write a set of clues that would give these results.

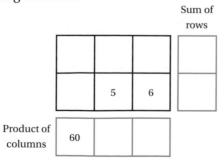

The crossword-number grid contains:

Row 1: ¹2 ²7 ³3
Row 2: ⁴1 4 8 ⁵6 ⁶1 9 7 ⁷4
Row 3: ⁸3 0 7 5
Row 4: ⁹4 ¹⁰9 ¹¹3 2 7 ¹²2 ¹³4
Row 5: 2 1 8
Row 6: 0 ¹⁴4 ¹⁵2 5 ¹⁶2 6
Row 7: ¹⁷4 1 ¹⁸7 1 0
Row 8: ¹⁹2 3 ²⁰3 ²¹2 0 4 ²²9 0
Row 9: ²³7 9 4 1 ²⁴7 9

3 Use integers and operations to write ten different questions that give an answer of −17.

4 On a page of a magazine there are three columns of text.

Each column contains 42 rows.

In each column row there is an average of 32 letters.

Approximately how many letters are there on a page?

5 A stadium has seats for 32 000 people.

There are 125 seats in a row.

How many rows are there in the stadium?

6 This grid follows two rules.

Rule 1: The sums of each row are equal.

Rule 2: The products of each column are equal.

			Sum of rows
5	32	80	117
96	15	6	117
Product of columns 480	480	480	

The grid below follows the same two rules.

Work out the missing numbers.

			Sum of rows
	5	6	
Product of columns 60			

(3 marks)

© AQA 2013

7 Two numbers have a sum of −15 and a product of −100.
What are the numbers?

8 The sum of two numbers is 1, and their product is −20.
What are the numbers?

9 Jenna's bank account was overdrawn.
Then she deposited £1000.
Her new balance is £432.
By how much was her account overdrawn to start with?

2 Collecting, interpreting and representing data

In this chapter you will learn how to ...

- work out the properties of a large set of data from a sample of the data, and understand the limitations of sampling.
- interpret and construct appropriate tables, charts and graphs.
- choose the best form of representation for data and understand the appropriate use of different graphs.

 For more resources relating to this chapter, visit GCSE Mathematics Online.

Using mathematics: real-life applications

We live in a very information-rich world. Knowing how to construct accurate graphs and how to interpret the graphs we see is important. Many graphs in print and other media are carefully designed to influence what we think by displaying the data in particular ways.

> **Tip**
>
> The key to displaying data is to choose the graph or chart that clearly shows what the data tells us without any further explanation.
>
> Getting the scale and labelling right makes a big difference when creating graphs and charts.

"When we have data, we need to display it so that our message has the maximum impact."
(Newspaper editor)

Before you start ...

KS3	You need to be able to sort and categorise data.	**1**	What would be suitable categories for a set of adult heights ranging from 1.39 m to 1.85 m?
KS3	You need to be able to use scales properly.	**2**	**a** What is each division on this scale: 200 300 **b** A scale between 0 and 100 has four divisions. Which numbers should go alongside each division?
KS3	You need to be able to measure and draw angles to create pie charts.	**3**	**a** Measure these angles: **b** Draw an angle of 72° accurately.

Find answers at: cambridge.org/ukschools/gcsemaths-studentbookanswers

Assess your starting point using the Launchpad

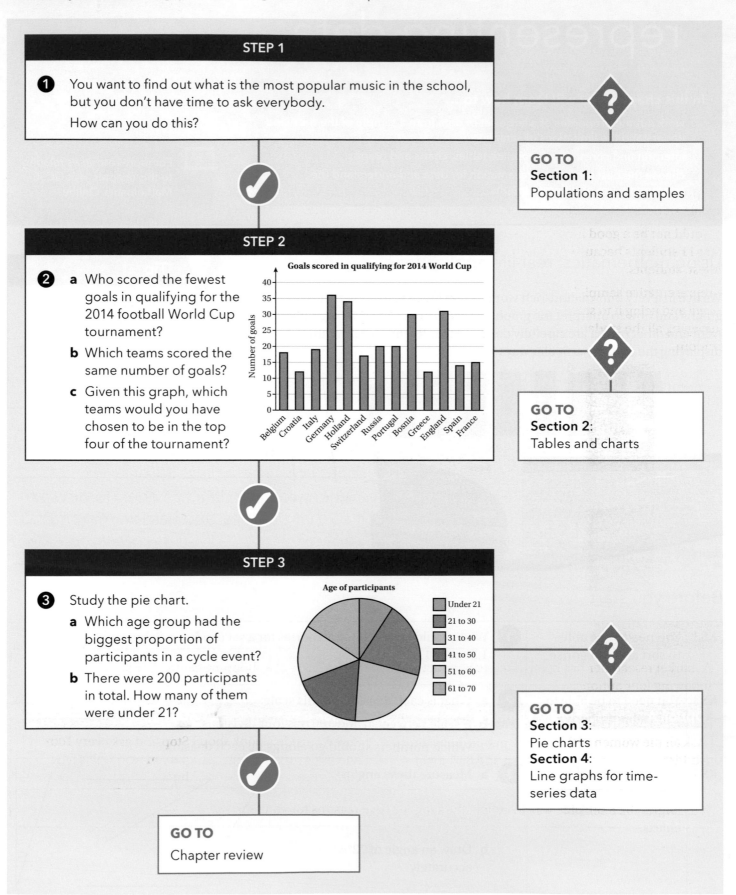

STEP 1

1 You want to find out what is the most popular music in the school, but you don't have time to ask everybody.

How can you do this?

?

GO TO
Section 1:
Populations and samples

STEP 2

2 **a** Who scored the fewest goals in qualifying for the 2014 football World Cup tournament?

b Which teams scored the same number of goals?

c Given this graph, which teams would you have chosen to be in the top four of the tournament?

Goals scored in qualifying for 2014 World Cup

Number of goals

Belgium, Croatia, Italy, Germany, Holland, Switzerland, Russia, Portugal, Bosnia, Greece, England, Spain, France

?

GO TO
Section 2:
Tables and charts

STEP 3

3 Study the pie chart.

a Which age group had the biggest proportion of participants in a cycle event?

b There were 200 participants in total. How many of them were under 21?

Age of participants

Under 21
21 to 30
31 to 40
41 to 50
51 to 60
61 to 70

?

GO TO
Section 3:
Pie charts
Section 4:
Line graphs for time-series data

GO TO
Chapter review

Section 1: Populations and samples

A statistical **population** is a set of individuals or objects of interest.

For example, a school wants to find the mean height of students to decide what size of equipment to buy for the gymnasium.

In this example, the population would be all the students in the school.

In a large school it would be impractical to measure each student's height. It is more likely that the researcher would choose some of the students as a **sample** of the population.

The sample needs to be a **representative sample** to provide useful data.

A representative sample would come from measuring a mix of male and female students from different years, to get a good spread of the data.

It would not be a good idea to measure just the Year 7 students, or just the Year 11 students because the sample would only be the shortest, or the tallest, students.

A representative sample can be created by taking a factor that is unrelated to age and using it to select the students. This can be done, for example, by surveying all the students whose first name begins with a letter drawn at random.

Key vocabulary

population: the name given to a data set

sample: a small set of data from a population

representative sample: a smaller quantity of data that represents the characteristics of a larger population

"I collect data on behalf of my company so that they can find out how likely people are to buy new products. We use quota sampling in our work. This involves choosing people with particular characteristics. For example, I might only be interested in teenage boys who play video games." *(Market researcher)*

WORK IT OUT 2.1

A market researcher has been asked to conduct a sample of shoppers at a shopping centre. She suggests the following four options.

Option A	Option B	Option C	Option D
Ask all the women with children.	Ask people between 8 am and 8.30 am.	Stand outside a book shop and ask everyone who comes out.	Stop and ask every 10th person who walks past her.

What would be a sensible way to collect the sample? Give reasons for your answer.

EXERCISE 2A

1 Which of these would be a good way to collect a sample? Give reasons for your answers.

A Selecting all the odd numbered houses in a street.

B Calling people on their home telephones during the day.

C Selecting everybody who is wearing trainers.

D Calling the person whose name is at the top of each page of the phone book.

E Drawing a series of names from a hat.

2 A market research company wants to find out how many people are likely to buy a new baby food.

a Suggest a good place to conduct a survey of young parents.

b Of the people asked, 35 of the 50 parents said they would be interested.

How many parents would you expect to be interested in a population of 1000 parents?

3 A gym owner wants to know how many treadmills to buy.

She asks every member whose surname begins with an 'S' whether they will use a treadmill.

a In her sample of 28, 15 members say 'yes'.

There are 300 members overall.

What is a sensible number of machines to buy?

b Does she really need this many machines?

c Suggest a better way of sampling her members to make sure she gets a realistic number of machines.

4 At the end of 2012 there were 28.7 million cars on the roads of Great Britain.

Surjay and his friends conduct a random survey of the cars passing the school.

They discover that of the 50 cars recorded, 3 had a sun roof, 1 had a faulty exhaust and 4 had chips on the windscreen.

Use this information to estimate how many cars in Great Britain have:

a sun roofs   **b** faulty exhausts   **c** chips on the windscreen.

Section 2: Tables and charts

Using tables to organise data

When you have many pieces of data you can use a table to organise them and make them simpler to work with.

A frequency table is used to collect or record data. The table shows the 'frequency' of an event, or how often it happens.

For example, the number of goals scored by each of the 20 Premiership teams one weekend was as follows:

5	1	3	0	1	2	4	1	1	2
0	3	1	0	0	4	0	1	3	0

In a frequency table these results would look like this:

Number of goals scored	Tally	Frequency
0	ⅢⅢ I	6
1	ⅢⅢ I	6
2	II	2
3	III	3
4	II	2
5	I	1

Tip

You will work with frequency tables again in Chapters 19 and 24 when you learn about probability.

Using bar charts to display data

The data in the frequency table above can be shown on a bar chart.

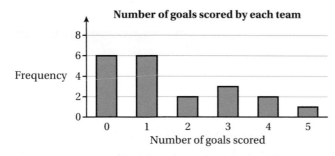

The chart has a title, a scale on the left and accurately drawn bars.

There is a gap between each bar and each one is labelled.

Bar charts are used to display **discrete data**.

The number of goals scored by each team is discrete data because it can only have certain values. It must be a whole number as you can't score $\frac{1}{2}$ a goal or 2.34 goals.

Sometimes it is helpful to sort data into categories.

For example, pairs of shoes in a cupboard could be categorised into 'brown shoes', 'black shoes', etc. Each piece of data can only be in one category. This is known as **categorical data**.

Key vocabulary

discrete data: data that can be counted and can only have certain values

categorical data: data that has been arranged in categories

Number of goals scored by each team

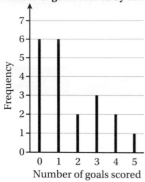

A vertical line chart is very similar to a bar chart but the number of pieces of data in each category is represented by a line rather than a bar, as shown in the line chart in the margin.

This data could also be shown using a pictogram.

In a pictogram for this data a symbol could be used to represent either each goal or a number of goals.

In this example each ball represents two goals:

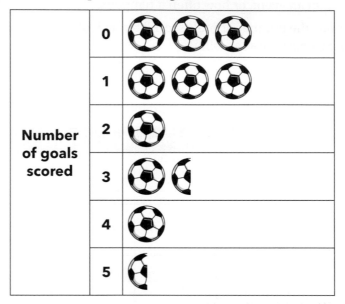

A pictogram should always have a key to indicate what the symbol represents.

WORK IT OUT 2.2

Ramiz records the number of mistakes he makes in a series of maths tests.

2   3   1   3   4   2   0   3   2   6   1   1   3   2   4   2

Which graph or chart best shows this data? What is wrong with the other two?

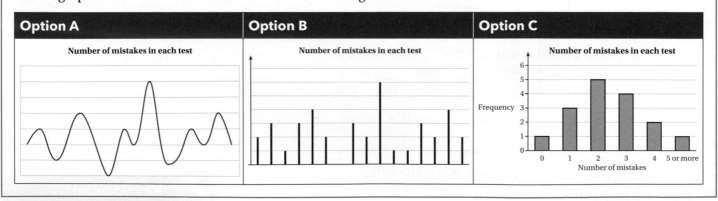

Option A	**Option B**	**Option C**
Number of mistakes in each test	Number of mistakes in each test	Number of mistakes in each test

Tip

In Chapter 3, you will learn about scatter diagrams. Scatter diagrams are useful for showing relationships between different sets of data.

It is not always possible to say that one type of graph is better than another. The type of graph you draw depends on what data you have collected.

These guidelines can help you choose an appropriate graph for different kinds of data.

- Use bar charts or vertical line charts for discrete data that can be categorised.
- Use a pie chart or a composite bar chart if you want to compare different parts of the whole or show proportions in the data.
- Use a line graph for numerical data when you want to show trends (changes over time).

EXERCISE 2B

1 In an extended family of 30 members, 10 have blond hair, 9 have black hair, 6 have brown hair and 5 have grey hair.

Draw a vertical line graph to show this information.

2 The table below shows the percentages of people who use a particular mode of transport to get to work.

Mode of transport	Percentage
car	36
bus	27
cycle	19
walk	18

Show this information in a bar chart.

3 30 students were asked how many times in the last week they had visited the snack shop. Their responses were:

1 2 1 2 1 5 1 3 2 1 2 1 3 2 1 2 0 2 3 2 0 2 0 1 2 0 0 3 1 2

a Draw a frequency table for this data.

b Present this information on a suitable graph.

4 Construct a bar chart for the data in this table.

Favourite holiday destination	UK	Spain	France	USA	Greece
Frequency	9	15	17	12	8

5 A group of students were asked to choose their favourite snacks. The results are in the table below.

Favourite snack	Number of students
fruit	6
crisps	8
chocolate bar	9
pizza slice	12
cookie	7

Draw a pictogram to show these results.

Find answers at: cambridge.org/ukschools/gcsemaths-studentbookanswers

6 The graph shows the number of goals scored in football matches.

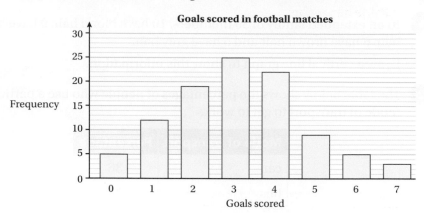

What is the total number of games played? Choose from the options below.

A 90   B 95   C 100   D 110

7 The chart below shows the monthly rainfall in Lowestoft in 2012.

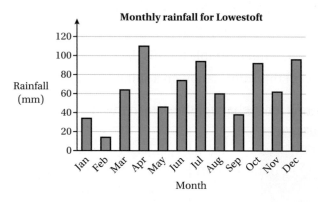

a State which month had the heaviest rainfall.

b Estimate the amount of rain that fell in April.

c State which month was the driest.

d Spring is March, April and May. Estimate how much rain fell during spring.

e The average annual rainfall for Lowestoft is approximately 575 mm.

Was 2012 a wetter or drier year than average? Give a reason for your answer.

8 Jenny is carrying out a survey of the sort of snacks bought from a shop outside her school.

She writes down the items that people buy:

Chocobar	Apple	NRG drink	Juicebar	Crisps	NRG drink	Chocobar	NRG drink	Juicebar
Juicebar	Crisps	Cheese puffs	Gum	Cheese puffs	Fruit chews	NRG drink	NRG drink	Chocobar
Chocobar	Juicebar	Chocobar	Crisps	Chocobar	Gum	Chocobar	Cheese puffs	Crisps
Cheese puffs	Crisps	NRG drink	Fruit chews	NRG drink	Cheese puffs	NRG drink	Juicebar	Gum
NRG drink	Chocobar	Apple	NRG drink	Chocobar	Juicebar	Crisps	Chocobar	Cheese puffs
Gum	Fruit chews	Gum	Crisps	Apple	Crisps	Fruit chews	Fruit chews	Fruit chews
Juicebar	Crisps	Cheese puffs	Fruit chews	Gum	Cheese puffs	Fruit chews	Crisps	Cheese puffs

a Suggest how Jenny could have been better organised before she started her survey.

b Use Jenny's data to create a table to show what was bought in the shop.

c Jenny gets extra marks if she categorises her data.

Adjust your table so that the data is classified in an appropriate way.

Multiple and composite bar charts

A multiple bar chart is useful when you want to compare data for two or more groups.

For example, this chart compares shoe sizes of male and female students in Year 9. The chart shows the data for male and female students in pairs.

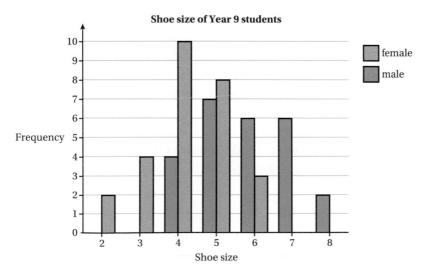

Notice that:

- the chart has a key to show what each colour bar represents
- the two bars for male and female students who wear each size touch each other, but there is an equal space between each pair of bars.

Composite bar charts are used to show parts of a whole.

The total height of each bar represents a total amount. The length of the bar is divided into parts that show each category's share of the total amount.

To interpret a composite bar chart you need to work out what each bar represents and then do a calculation to find the fraction or percentage of the total that each part represents.

WORKED EXAMPLE 1

This composite bar chart shows the amount of water used by three different households over a four-month period.

a What does each bar show?

b State which household used the greatest amount of water in month 1.

c Describe the trend in water use for the Ozbek household over this period.

d One household had a leaking pipe in this period.

Can you work out from the chart which household this was and when it happened?

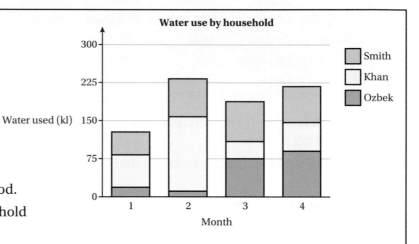

a The top of each bar shows the total water used by three households in a month. Each coloured segment shows the fraction of the total used by each household.

> The key tells you that each colour represents a household.
>
> The vertical scale shows the amount used.
>
> The horizontal scale indicates that this is per month.

b The Khan household.

> The yellow section is bigger than the other two.

c In months 1 and 2 the Ozbek household used very little water. In month 3 the amount of water it used increased quite dramatically and in month 4 it went up a little more.

> You can see this trend by looking only at the coloured section representing the Ozbek family. It increases in height as the water use increases.

d It is most likely the Khan household as they had a massive jump in consumption in month 2. However, it could be the Ozbek household as well. If their water pipe started leaking in month 3 and wasn't fixed, it could account for the big increase in their consumption.

> You can't really tell this for sure, but you can look at the month-to-month changes to try to work it out.

EXERCISE 2C

1 Study the bar chart.

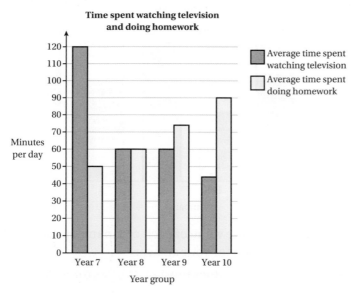

a What two sets of data are shown on this chart?

b Describe the trend in the amount of time spent watching TV as students move into higher grades.

c Describe what happens to the amount of time spent on homework as TV watching time decreases.

d How much time do Year 10 students spend on average each day:

  i doing homework?   **ii** watching TV?

2 Naresh runs a computer company. He keeps a record of his costs and his income for four large projects in a year.

He drew this chart to compare his costs and his income for each project.

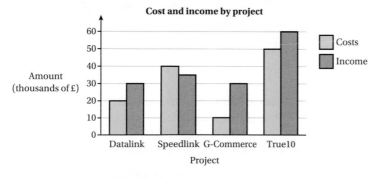

a Which project brought in most money?

b Which project brought in least money?

c Which project had the highest costs?

d Which project had the lowest costs?

e Which project gave Naresh the biggest profit?
(Remember, profit = income – cost)

f On which project did Naresh lose money? Give a reason for your answer.

g How much profit did Naresh make altogether?

 Find answers at: cambridge.org/ukschools/gcsemaths-studentbookanswers

3 This composite bar chart shows the proportions in sales for four different companies.

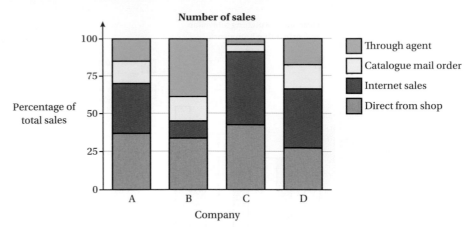

a Can you work out the value of each company's total sales from this chart? Give a reason for your answer.

b State which company does most of its sales direct from the shop.

c State which company makes the least of its sales through agents.

d State which company makes almost half of its sales over the internet.

e State what fraction of Company A's sales are done over the internet.

f Describe the breakdown of sales by type for Company D.

4 The bar chart shows the results in geography for six students in their mock and actual exams.

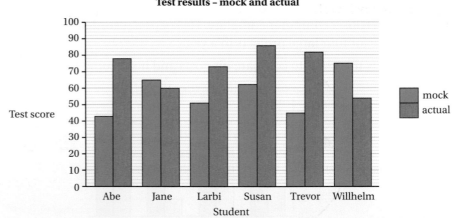

a Who achieved the highest score on their mock exam?

b Who achieved the highest score on their actual exam?

c Who made the biggest improvement from the mock to the actual exam?

d What was similar about Jane and Willhelm's results in these exams.

Section 3: Pie charts

A pie chart is useful for displaying data when you are interested in the relative sizes or the proportions of the data.

Pie charts are always circular, so the sum of the angles at the centre must always be 360°.

When drawing pie charts that have data as percentages, each 1% will be represented by 3.6° because 360° ÷ 100 = 3.6°.

In this example, data has been collected that shows where students in a class live:

Area where students live	Frequency	Percentage (%)
Reepham	12	40.0
Whitwell	6	20.0
Booton	3	10.0
Cawston	2	6.7
Salle	7	23.3

There are 30 students altogether.

Each percentage is worked out by dividing the number of students by the total number of students and multiplying by 100. For example, for Reepham,

$\frac{12}{30} \times 100 = 40\%$.

The pie chart below shows this data:

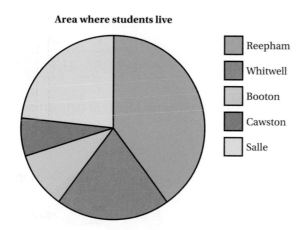

Area where students live

- Reepham
- Whitwell
- Booton
- Cawston
- Salle

WORK IT OUT 2.3

These are the results from a survey of how many minutes late 20 trains were on a particular day:

1 0 2 0 3 1 5 4 1 3 6 4 3 5 2 4 3 2 2 4

Which of the pie charts best shows this information? Write down what is wrong with the other two pie charts.

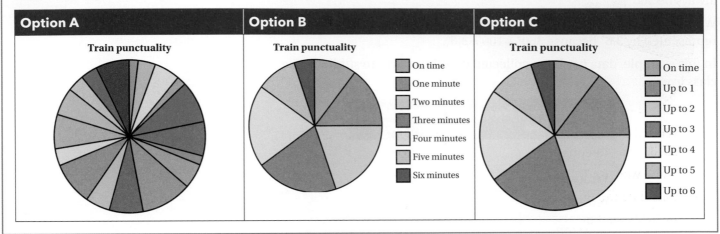

Option A	Option B	Option C

EXERCISE 2D

1 Draw a pie chart to represent this data:

Electricity generation	Proportion used (%)
gas	28.0
other fuels	2.6
coal	39.0
nuclear	19.0
renewables	11.4

2 The pie charts below show the population of two different countries by age.

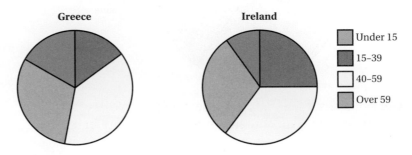

a Write down two differences between Greece and Ireland.

b Which country has the biggest number of over 59s?

c There are more under 15s in Ireland than Greece.

Is this statement true or false?

3 The Department for Transport maintains data for the different types of vehicles on the road in the UK. Data for vehicles other than cars is shown for 1994 and 2013.

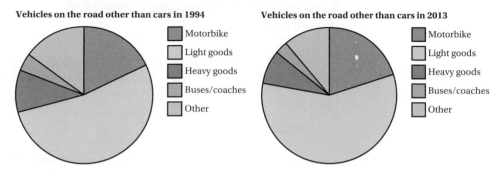

Vehicles on the road other than cars in 1994   Vehicles on the road other than cars in 2013

- Motorbike
- Light goods
- Heavy goods
- Buses/coaches
- Other

a Write down two differences between the proportions for 1994 and 2013.

b There were 6.075 million vehicles other than cars on the road in 2013.

  Calculate the number of light goods vehicles there were.

c In 2013, what percentage of vehicles other than cars were motorbikes?

d Which of the following statements is true?

  A There are more motorbikes on the road in 1994.

  B The proportion of heavy goods vehicles is greater in 1994 than in 2013.

  C Buses and coaches are a bigger proportion of vehicles other than cars in 2013 than in 1994.

  D There are more buses and coaches on the road in 1994 than in 2013.

4 This pie chart shows the favourite leisure activity of 72 students.

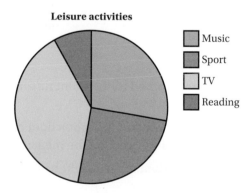

Leisure activities

- Music
- Sport
- TV
- Reading

a Use a protractor to measure the sector for music. Use this measurement to work out how many students prefer music.

b State which activity is the most popular.

c How many students prefer reading?

5 This data shows the destinations of students leaving a sixth-form college:

Destination	College A	College B
higher education	32	46
further education	45	72
employment	28	31
gap year	12	24
unemployment	15	22

Create two pie charts and use them to argue that one college is more successful than the other.

Section 4: Line graphs for time-series data

Line graphs are useful for showing how data changes over time.

When time is one of the variables it is always plotted on the horizontal axis of the graph.

For example, the temperature at a weather station is recorded at midday every day. Data showing change over time like this is called time-series data.

Monday	15 °C
Tuesday	17 °C
Wednesday	18 °C
Thursday	21 °C
Friday	16 °C
Saturday	20 °C
Sunday	14 °C

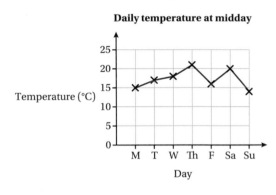

Each of the points on the line is joined to the point next to it by a straight line (for example, Mon, 15 °C is joined to Tues, 17 °C).

The type of data in this graph is called **continuous data** because it can take any numerical value (within a range) and can be measured.

Another example of continuous data is the height of students in your class.

Key vocabulary

continuous data: data that can have any value

Problem-solving framework

The average temperature each month in Alicante is as follows:

Jan 17 °C	Feb 18 °C	Mar 20 °C	Apr 21 °C	May 24 °C	Jun 28 °C
Jul 30 °C	Aug 31 °C	Sep 29 °C	Oct 25 °C	Nov 20 °C	Dec 18 °C

Display this data to show how the temperature changes through the year.

Steps for solving problems	What you would do for this example
Step 1: If it is useful to have a table, draw one.	<table><tr><th>J</th><th>F</th><th>M</th><th>A</th><th>M</th><th>J</th><th>J</th><th>A</th><th>S</th><th>O</th><th>N</th><th>D</th></tr><tr><td>17°C</td><td>18°C</td><td>20°C</td><td>21°C</td><td>24°C</td><td>28°C</td><td>30°C</td><td>31°C</td><td>29°C</td><td>25°C</td><td>20°C</td><td>18°C</td></tr></table>
Step 2: Identify what you have to do.	We need to choose a suitable means of displaying the data and then draw it.
Step 3: Start working on the problem using what you know.	We know that a time-series graph shows changes over time, so will be a good visual way of showing how the temperature varies. Choose a suitable scale and plot each point on the axes using the table. Join the points to make a line. **Monthly average temperature for Alicante**
Step 4: Check your working and that your answer is reasonable.	Check the shape of the graph. Does it get warmer in the summer and colder in the winter? Are there any unexpected sharp increases or decreases?
Step 5: Have you answered the question?	Yes, the graph shows how the temperature changes through the year.

EXERCISE 2E

1 **a** Construct a time-series graph for the average temperature (in °C) in a particular city from the data given in the table below.

Month	Jan	Feb	Mar	Apr	May	Jun	Jul	Aug	Sep	Oct	Nov	Dec
Average temp (°C)	15.2	16.5	17.2	19.1	19.6	20.1	22.2	24.1	21.3	19.3	17.6	16.6

b Use the time-series graph to write a brief description of how the average temperature varies in this particular city.

2 The table below gives the annual profit (in £million) of a company over a ten-year period. Construct a time-series graph of the information.

Year	Year 1	Year 2	Year 3	Year 4	Year 5	Year 6	Year 7	Year 8	Year 9	Year 10
Profit (£million)	2.2	1.8	2.3	1.2	0.6	1.1	2.2	3.1	3.7	4.2

3 The table below gives the number of teeth extracted at a dentist's surgery each month for a year.

Month	Jan	Feb	Mar	Apr	May	Jun	Jul	Aug	Sep	Oct	Nov	Dec
Number of teeth	54	47	49	60	41	45	36	11	38	42	32	22

a Represent this information on a time-series graph.

b Briefly describe how the number of teeth extracted each month changed over the year.

c Why might the number of teeth extracted fall during August?

4 The table below gives the position of a particular five-a-side football team in a league of 10 teams at the completion of each week throughout the season.

Round	1	2	3	4	5	6	7	8	9
Position	2	3	5	7	6	5	6	7	5
Round	10	11	12	13	14	15	16	17	18
Position	5	4	5	3	4	3	3	4	3

a Represent this information on a time-series graph.

b Describe the progress of the team throughout the season.

5 The data in the table shows the value of sales at a service station on a main road over a period of three years. Each quarter represents three months (a quarter) of the year. The quarters are labelled 1 to 12 in the corresponding time-series graph shown below.

Sales quarter	Sales (£thousand)
Quarter 1	64
Quarter 2	82
Quarter 3	83
Quarter 4	65
Quarter 5	77
Quarter 6	89
Quarter 7	96
Quarter 8	58
Quarter 9	79
Quarter 10	92
Quarter 11	101
Quarter 12	66

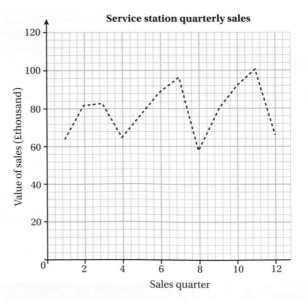

a In which quarter of each year is the value of sales highest?

b In which quarter of each year is the value of sales lowest?

c Compare the sales figures for the first quarter of each year. Are the sales figures improving from one year to the next?

6 The table below gives the number of garden sheds sold each quarter during 2012–2014.

Number of sales

Year \ Quarter	Q1	Q2	Q3	Q4
2012	27	32	56	41
2013	33	35	65	45
2014	38	41	72	51

a Represent this information on a time-series graph.

b Describe how the shed sales have altered over the given time period.

c Does it appear that sheds sales are seasonal?

7 Study the following graph.

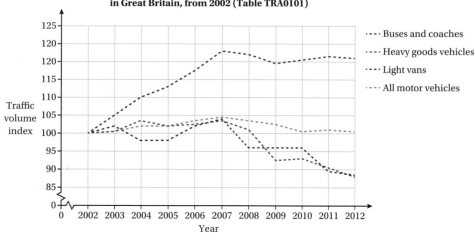

Road traffic by vehicle type (commercial and public service vehicles) in Great Britain, from 2002 (Table TRA0101)

a Describe the trend in numbers of light vans.

b Describe what has happened to the total number of motor vehicles.

c Suggest why the number of heavy goods vehicles might have decreased. Can this be answered by just using the graph?

8 This graph shows how the water level in a pond varies from month to month.

a When is the lowest depth of water?

b Suggest what might have happened in July.

c When does the water level drop most rapidly?

d How much water is in the pond in May?

e Find the difference in depth between August and September.

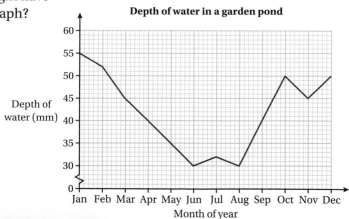

Depth of water in a garden pond

Checklist of learning and understanding

Sampling

- A sample is a representative group chosen from a population.

Tables and charts

- A frequency table is a method of organising data by showing how often a result appears in the data.
- Data can be displayed using a number of different charts and graphs.
- All charts and graphs should be clearly labelled and scaled, and have a title.
- Vertical line charts and bar charts are a good way of showing discrete data, where the height of each bar or line indicates the frequency.
- Pictograms are an interesting visual way of displaying discrete data.
- Pie charts are used to compare categories of the same data set.

Line graphs

- Line graphs for time-series data show trends and changes over time.

For additional questions on the topics in this chapter, visit GCSE Mathematics Online.

Chapter review

1 Bonita takes a representative sample to find out how students travel to school.

    a Suggest two ways in which she could do this.

    b Bonita asks a representative sample of 50 students and gets the following results:

car	15
walk	17
bus	6
taxi	7
bike	5

There are 600 students in the school in total. What is a sensible estimate of the total number of students who walk to school?

2 Kimberley surveys her classmates to find their favourite pizza topping. The results are shown in the table below.

cheese and tomato	5
seafood	8
meat	2
roast vegetable	6
pepperoni	7

Choose a suitable scale and draw a pictogram to represent this data.

3 Josh and Ben are comparing how much money they spend each month.

a Draw suitable charts of the data to compare the proportions of money they spend.

b Write two sentences comparing their spending habits.

Expenditure per month (£)	Josh	Ben
rent	840	450
food	250	300
transport	350	160
savings	250	40
entertainment	110	250

4 The pie chart shows information about the number of magazines sold in four countries.

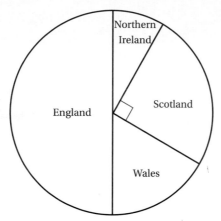

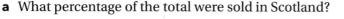

a What percentage of the total were sold in Scotland? *(2 marks)*

b Make one comparison of the sales in England with the sales in the other countries. *(1 mark)*

c 30 000 magazines were sold in Wales.

How many magazines were sold in total? *(3 marks)*

© AQA 2013

5 The table shows the profits for two companies for each quarter of a two-year period.

a Use the data to plot a suitable graph to compare how the profits change.

b Which company is the most successful?

c Which is the biggest change between quarters?

d Which of the following statements is true?

A Company B's sales are always better than Company A's.

B Company A's sales never exceed £198 000.

C Company B's sales are more consistent than Company A's.

D Both companies' sales are better in the 4th quarter of 2014 than in the 1st quarter of 2013.

Company profits (£)	Company A	Company B
1st quarter 2013	134 820	125 912
2nd quarter 2013	138 429	189 355
3rd quarter 2013	140 721	130 969
4th quarter 2013	131 717	156 548
1st quarter 2014	103 746	219 357
2nd quarter 2014	197 028	151 296
3rd quarter 2014	187 883	249 216
4th quarter 2014	168 414	102 158

Find answers at: cambridge.org/ukschools/gcsemaths-studentbookanswers

3 Analysing data

In this chapter you will learn how to …

- calculate and compare averages and ranges for ungrouped and grouped data.
- recognise when data are being misrepresented.
- plot and interpret scatter diagrams and use them to describe correlation and predict results.
- identify outliers.

 For more resources relating to this chapter, visit GCSE Mathematics Online.

Using mathematics: real-life applications

Analysing large sets of data enables financial and insurance companies to make predictions about what might happen in the future. Car insurance premiums are worked out according to typical or 'average' behaviour of large groups of people.

 Tip

Knowing how to calculate averages and measures of spread gives us tools to compare different sets of data. Make sure you know what these are and when to use the different measures.

"We group drivers together by age and gender and use statistics to find typical driving behaviour for each group. Young drivers have more accidents, so their insurance costs more." *(Insurance broker)*

Before you start …

KS3	You should remember how to find the mean, median, mode and range of a set of data.	**1** Find the mean, median, mode and range of the following sets of data. Give your answers to one decimal place. **a** 2, 4, 2, 7, 3, 5, 4, 2, 3, 1 **b** 40, 20, 30, 60, 50, 10
KS3	You should be able to plot coordinates on a set of axes.	**2** Write down the coordinates of points A, B and C on the line.
KS3	You should be able to recognise whether a gradient is positive or negative.	**3** Look at the graph in question 2. **a** What is the gradient of the graph? **b** What is the equation of the line?

Assess your starting point using the Launchpad

STEP 1

1 Three sets of data are shown in this table.

A	10	5	9	10	8	12	7
B	3	4	5	6	6	10	12
C	7	10	11	14	18		

a Find the median of Set C.

b Which data set has a mode of 10?

c Which set of data has the smallest mean?

d Which data set does not have a mode?

e How would the mode, median and mean of Set B change if we added the value 14 to the set?

2 The frequency table shows the ages of a group of students visiting a museum.

a What is the modal age?

b What is the mean age of the students in this group?

Age (years)	14	15	16	17
Frequency	23	17	13	9

c What is the range of ages in the group?

?

GO TO
Section 1:
Averages and range

STEP 2

3 This graph appeared in a newspaper article. Give a reason why this graph could be misleading.

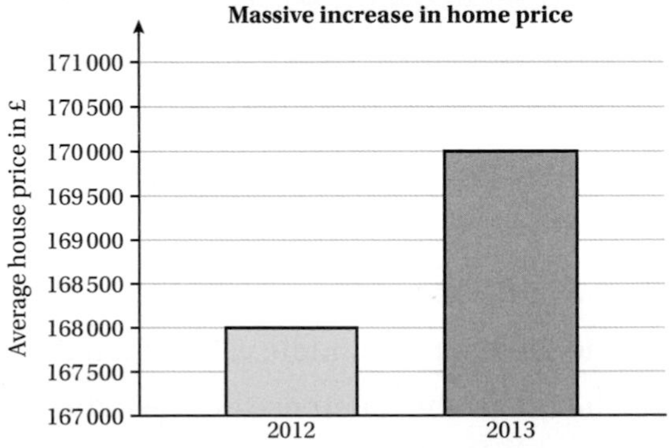

Massive increase in home price

Average house price in £

171 000
170 500
170 000
169 500
169 000
168 500
168 000
167 500
167 000

2012   2013

?

GO TO
Section 2:
Misleading graphs

GO TO
Step 3:
The Launchpad continues on the next page …

Launchpad continued ...

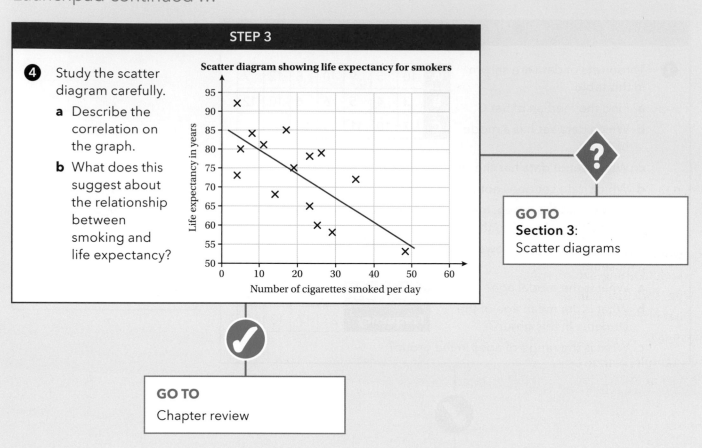

STEP 3

④ Study the scatter diagram carefully.

a Describe the correlation on the graph.

b What does this suggest about the relationship between smoking and life expectancy?

Scatter diagram showing life expectancy for smokers

Life expectancy in years

Number of cigarettes smoked per day

GO TO
Section 3:
Scatter diagrams

GO TO
Chapter review

Section 1: Averages and range

In statistics you are often asked to give a single value that summarises the data and tells you something about it.

Four different values are used to summarise data, as follows:

- the mean: $\dfrac{\text{sum of values}}{\text{number of values}}$
- the mode: the value with the highest frequency
- the median: the middle value when the values are arranged in size order
- the range: the difference between the highest value and the lowest value.

These are all called **summary statistics**.

The mean, median and mode are all types of averages, or measures of central tendency.

The range is a measure of spread or dispersion. The range is useful for finding out whether the mean is distorted or not.

To describe and compare two sets of data, calculate the averages and range and write a few sentences to summarise what you notice.

Tip

The mode can also be referred to as the modal value.

Choosing the correct type of average

The type of average that you choose depends on the situation and what you want to know.

The mean is useful when you want to know a typical value. If the data values are very spread out (they have a big range) then the mean will not be typical.

For example, the manager in a company earns £20 000 per month. Her nine employees earn £2000 each per month. This gives a mean salary of £3800, which is not typical.

In this situation, the median salary is £2000 and the modal salary is £2000. Both are more representative than the mean.

When the data is not numerical, you have to use the mode as the average.

The mode is most useful when you need to know which item is most common or most popular.

You would use the mode when you wanted to show:
- which clothing size was bought most often
- what shoe size is most common
- what brand of mobile phone is the most popular.

The type of average you choose can affect how you see the data.

For example, Jeanne asks her friends how many takeaways they have had in the past month. These are their answers:

> 1   1   2   1   3   26   1

She works out the mean number of takeaways:

$$\frac{1 + 1 + 2 + 1 + 3 + 26 + 1}{7} = \frac{35}{7} = 5$$

The mean suggests that Jeanne's friends have had an average of 5 takeaways each in the past month.

But that is not a very representative average and it does not give the typical number of takeaways.

The mean number of takeaways is high because one friend had many more than the others.

Jeanne doesn't think the mean is a good average, so she finds the median:

> 1   1   1   1   2   3   26

This gives her an average of 1 takeaway. That seems more typical of the sample.

The mode is also 1 because most people have had only one takeaway.

The median and the mode are more representative averages and they are not affected by outliers in the data, so they are better averages to use in this case.

Tip

Modal salary means the salary which is the mode, or the one that occurs most often.

Tip

A very high or a very low value in a set of data is called an outlier. If there is an outlier then the mean will not be a typical value.

WORKED EXAMPLE 1

Babak has developed a website and is monitoring how many hits it receives per hour.

In the first 48 hours it receives the following numbers of hits per hour (arranged in numerical order):

100	105	106	106	107	107	108	110	117	118
135	137	145	148	148	148	153	155	157	159
162	171	171	179	183	183	185	185	189	199
201	203	204	209	216	220	223	224	224	227
229	230	231	233	234	235	237	238		

1 Find the following summary statistics:

a the mean, the median and the mode **b** the range.

a Mean of the data:

$\frac{8394}{48} = 174.88$ hits

> Find the mean of the data by finding the total number of hits, then dividing this total by the number of hours.

Median of the data is halfway between the 24th and the 25th data values

$= \frac{179 + 183}{2} = 181$ hits

> Arrange all the data values in numerical order and the median is the middle value if you have an odd number of data values, or halfway between the two middle values if you have an even number of data values.

The value 148 is the mode because it occurs three times.

> Find the mode by identifying the piece of data that appears most often.

b The range = 238 − 100 = 138

> Calculate the range by subtracting the smallest data value from the largest data value.

2 Babak is trying to sell advertising on his website.

Write a sentence he could use about the number of hits his site is receiving.

There is a consistent hit rate of over 100 hits per hour with 175 hits per hour on average.

> Write a sentence that summarises the key data.

3 Babak compares his data to a similar website run by his colleague Delia.

Delia's data set has the following data values:

mean = 180 hits   median = 140 hits   mode = 135 hits   range = 200

What can Babak say to compare the two sets?

Although the mean of the hits is a bit higher for Delia's set, the median is much lower.
This shows that the mean of Delia's hits is influenced by a few high values, but usually the number of hits is lower.

> Compare and contrast the two data sets, looking for differences and similarities.

Delia's data show a wider range, which means that the data is more spread out and therefore less consistent.

> Make a statement about how spread out or consistent the data is.

Analysing grouped data

Data is sometimes grouped together before it is analysed.

The groups are known as class intervals. They do not overlap.

For example:

When you have grouped data in a frequency table, it is not possible to calculate exact values for the mean, median, mode and range because you don't know the individual values.

However, you can identify the modal and median classes from the table.

Marks scored	Frequency
0–9	6
10–19	6
20–29	4
30–39	5
40–50	9
Total	30

- The modal class is the class interval that has the most elements, not the individual value that appears the most. In the table above the modal class is 40–50 marks.

- To estimate the median of grouped data, find the class interval in which the middle value occurs. It is only possible to say that the median is within that group. In the table there are 30 values and the middle value is between the 15th and 16th values, so it must fall in the class 20–29 marks.

Estimating the mean of a frequency distribution

To estimate the mean of grouped data, first find the midpoint of each class interval.

The midpoint is found by adding the lowest and highest possible values for each class interval and dividing by 2.

Multiply each midpoint by the frequency for each class interval.

Find the total of these values, and divide by the total number of values you have.

WORKED EXAMPLE 2

Ben goes fishing and records the masses of the fish he catches in this table:

a Complete the table.

b Find the modal class.

c Estimate the mean, the median and the range.

Mass, m (kg)	Frequency	Midpoint	Midpoint × frequency
$2 \leqslant m < 4$	5		
$4 \leqslant m < 6$	8		
$6 \leqslant m < 8$	4		
$8 \leqslant m < 10$	9		
$10 \leqslant m < 12$	3		

Continues on next page …

a Completed table:

Mass, m (kg)	Frequency	Midpoint	Midpoint × frequency
$2 \leqslant m < 4$	5	3	15
$4 \leqslant m < 6$	8	5	40
$6 \leqslant m < 8$	4	7	28
$8 \leqslant m < 10$	9	9	81
$10 \leqslant m < 12$	3	11	33

> Find the midpoint between the upper and lower value in each class interval.
>
> Multiply this number by the frequency to complete the right-hand column of the table.

b The modal class is $8\,\text{kg} \leqslant m < 10\,\text{kg}$.

> The modal class is the one that has the largest frequency.

c The mean:
Total of midpoint × frequency values is 197.
The sum of the frequencies is 29 so the estimated mean is $\frac{197}{29} = 6.79\,\text{kg}$

> The mean is an estimate because you have used an approximate value, the midpoint.

The median class: there are 29 values, so the middle value is value number 15.
The median value falls in the class $6\,\text{kg} \leqslant m < 8\,\text{kg}$.
The range: $12 - 2 = 10\,\text{kg}$.

> The median class is found by finding the class in which the median value sits.

EXERCISE 3A

1 A small set of data has a mean of 5, a mode of 5 and a median of 5.
Which of these data sets would give this result?

A 3, 4, 5, 6, 7   **B** 5, 4, 3, 5, 5,6

C 5, 4, 3, 6, 7, 5   **D** 1, 2, 5, 5, 1, 6, 8

2 A company keeps a record of how many days each employee is absent from work each year.
The results are in the table below.

Days absent, d	Frequency	Midpoint	Midpoint × frequency
$0 \leqslant d < 5$	15		
$5 \leqslant d < 10$	23		
$10 \leqslant d < 15$	19		
$15 \leqslant d < 20$	12		
$20 \leqslant d < 25$	6		
Total			

a Copy and complete the table.

b Use the information to find the modal class.

c Estimate the mean, the median and the range.

3 The scores from a game of darts are given in the table.

89	11	57	25	55	78
28	35	15	90	83	38
57	37	28	14	36	40
74	59	57	9	18	70
25	18	22	2	37	53
74	61	79	53	87	46
30	29	4	90	83	77

a Choose suitable class intervals and group the data.

b Using your work in **a**, estimate the mean, the median and the range of the scores.

c Is it sensible to estimate the range?

d What is the modal group?

4 The heights, in centimetres, of some members of a club are given in the table.

1.68	1.68	1.58	1.72	1.58	1.75	1.89
1.84	1.55	1.65	1.66	1.84	1.55	1.81
1.47	1.55	1.58	1.66	1.55	1.61	1.68
1.57	1.57	1.69	1.65	1.75	1.55	1.73
1.64	1.85	1.53	1.65	1.77	1.66	1.75
1.75	1.59	1.88	1.82	1.62	1.69	1.67
1.63	1.66	1.84	1.77	1.52	1.84	1.53

a Use group intervals of every 5 cm, starting with the group $1.45\,\text{cm} \leqslant h < 1.50\,\text{cm}$, to draw a grouped frequency table.

Estimate the mean and the median.

b What is the modal class?

c Use class intervals of every 10 cm, starting with the class $1.40\,\text{cm} \leqslant h < 1.50\,\text{cm}$, to draw a new grouped frequency table. Estimate the mean and the median.

Write down the effect that the new group intervals have on your estimates of the mean and the median.

5 Thirty runners complete a marathon race. Their times are given below (to the nearest minute):

2 hours 45 minutes, 3 hours 25 minutes, 3 hours 46 minutes, 4 hours 15 minutes, 5 hours 8 minutes, 4 hours 49 minutes, 4 hours 18 minutes, 3 hours 38 minutes, 3 hours 43 minutes, 3 hours 5 minutes, 2 hours 55 minutes, 4 hours 23 minutes, 4 hours 25 minutes, 3 hours 39 minutes, 3 hours 20 minutes, 4 hours 1 min, 3 hours 33 minutes, 4 hours 6 minutes, 5 hours 11 minutes, 2 hours 51 minutes, 4 hours 35 minutes, 3 hours 19 minutes, 4 hours 47 minutes, 4 hours 28 minutes, 5 hours 5 minutes, 4 hours 19 minutes, 2 hours 46 minutes, 3 hours 18 minutes, 3 hours 53 minutes, 4 hours 35 minutes.

  a Group the data into suitable class intervals.

  b Find the modal class.

  c Estimate the mean, the median and the range.

6 The mass of fruit produced by a farm is recorded in the table below.

Mass of produce, m (kg)	Frequency	Midpoint of class interval	Midpoint × frequency
$200 \leqslant m < 250$	15		
$250 \leqslant m < 300$	11		
$300 \leqslant m < 350$	13		
$350 \leqslant m < 400$	7		
$400 \leqslant m < 450$	2		
$450 \leqslant m < 500$	2		
$500 \leqslant m < 550$	2		
Total			

  a Calculate an estimate of the mean mass of the fruit.

  b In which interval does the median lie?

Comparing two or more sets of data

Statistical measures allow us to compare sets of data and make decisions about them.

One measure on its own does not give enough information about the whole set. Think about the following:

Set A might have a similar mean value to Set B, but the median is lower than the median of Set B.

This shows us that there are a few higher values in Set A that have made the mean higher, but that more of the values are low.

For example, Set A {1, 1, 1, 7, 10} has a median of 1; whereas Set B {2, 2, 4, 5, 7} has a median of 4. Note that both sets have a mean of 5.

One set might have a higher mean than the other, but the range of the data might be much wider.

This shows us that many of the values are very different from the mean or the median.

For example, Set C {1, 4, 8, 12, 15} has a mean of 8 and a range of 14; whereas Set D {1, 3, 3, 3, 5} has a mean of 3 and a range of 4.

EXERCISE 3B

1 The results from two maths tests are given.

A	35	68	55	52	49	63	61	69	35	53
B	47	34	71	41	60	44	57	74	67	64

For each test, calculate the mean, median, mode and range to compare the two sets of data.

2 Two cricketers are having an argument about who has had the best season.

They have both batted 15 times, and the number of runs they have scored in each innings is given in the table.

Ahmed	27	16	36	27	55	35	51	38	44	17	41	53	7	43	48	49
Bill	2	30	44	11	26	32	13	46	40	44	0	45	15	34	14	24

a Compare and describe their records.

b Who do you think has had the best season? Write down your reasons.

3 Yusuf has recorded the time it takes him to get home on two different buses. His results are given in the table.

Bus 127	17	17	21	23	19	20	19	18	21	22	19	22	21	20
Bus 362	23	26	20	15	15	20	26	19	18	15	16			

Which bus route should he use? Give reasons for your answer.

Does it matter that he has more data about the 127 bus?

4 A factory needs to choose between two machines for bottling soft drinks.

Data about how many bottles each machine fills per hour is given in the table.

Machine A	Bottles, b	Frequency	Machine B	Bottles, b	Frequency
	$200 \leqslant b < 250$	36		$200 \leqslant b < 250$	16
	$250 \leqslant b < 300$	48		$250 \leqslant b < 300$	58
	$300 \leqslant b < 350$	59		$300 \leqslant b < 350$	63
	$350 \leqslant b < 400$	61		$350 \leqslant b < 400$	78
	$400 \leqslant b < 450$	21		$400 \leqslant b < 450$	15

Use estimates of the mean, the median and the range along with the modal group to decide which machine the factory should choose.

5 The following statement in a newspaper seems to be incorrect.

According to latest figures, half the population weighs more than 70 kg. The 'average' person weighs 80 kg.

Can you give an example of a sample of five people with mean weight of 70 kg and median weight of 80 kg?

6 According to the Office of National Statistics, the 'average' price of a house in the UK in July 2014 was £272 000.

a What would be the best type of average to measure house prices?

Give a reason for your answer.

b Give an example of when using the mean as a measure of central tendency would be the most useful.

c Give two examples when using the mode as a measure of central tendency is the most useful.

Section 2: Misleading graphs

One of the advantages of using graphs is that they show information quickly and visually.

Graphs can also be misleading because most people don't look at them very closely.

When you look carefully at a graph you might find that it has been drawn in a way that gives a misleading impression.

When you look at a graph, think about:

- the scale and whether or not it has been exaggerated in any way to give a particular impression
- whether or not the scale starts at 0, as this can affect the information shown and give us a misleading impression
- whether bars or pie charts have 3D sections which make some parts look much bigger than others
- whether the scales are labelled and whether or not the graph has a title
- whether the source of the data is given.

Here are some examples of misleading graphs.

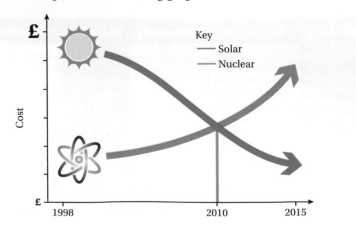

This graph seems to suggest that the price of solar energy is dropping quickly while the cost of nuclear power is increasing.

There are no values on the cost scale, so it is not possible to decide whether that is really true.

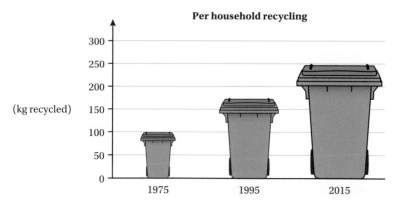

Per household recycling

This graph of household recycling uses proportion to mislead.

The scale shows that the amount of recycled material has increased from 100 kg to 250 kg, so 2.5 times more material is recycled.

The bin is about six times bigger, so it makes it look like much more is recycled.

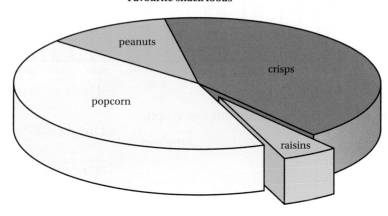

Favourite snack foods

Drawing the pie chart in this orientation and with the sectors 3D makes it look like raisins are just as popular as peanuts and that popcorn is more popular than crisps.

The real figures show that 5% chose raisins and 11% chose peanuts, so the green sector represents less than half of the blue sector.

The other two sectors each represent 42% but they don't look the same size in the pie chart.

EXERCISE 3C

1 Identify the errors in this graph.

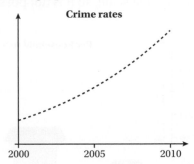

2 Write down reasons why this graph is misleading.

Suggest why someone might have drawn the graph like this.

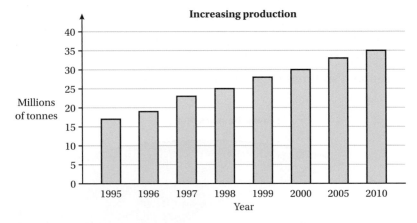

3 Write down what is wrong with this graph.

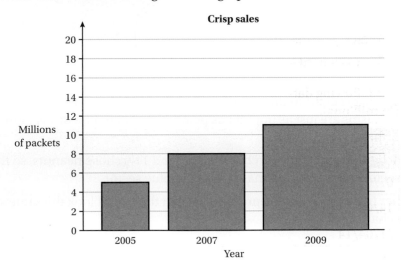

4 Look carefully at the graph below.

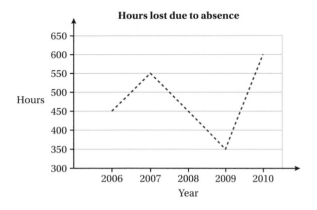

a What is misleading about this graph?

b Suggest why it might have been drawn this way.

5 The same data as in question 4 have been presented in this 3D graph.

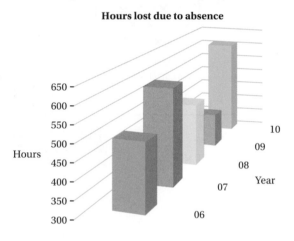

a Which year has the most days lost, 2006 or 2008?

b Why is it hard to tell?

6 The following data shows viewing figures for different TV programmes (in millions).

Week beginning	*Britain's Got Talent*	*The Crimson Field*	*Gogglebox*
07/04/14	10.03	6.89	2.75
14/04/14	8.45	6.31	3.37
21/04/14	8.63	6.25	3.48
28/04/14	8.45	6.01	3.47
05/05/14	8.58	6.33	3.54

Choose one of the TV programmes and create a graph that shows how well it has performed. You can use any type of graph, but you must not change the numbers.

Section 3: Scatter diagrams

Key vocabulary

bivariate data: data that is collected in pairs

correlation: relationship or connection between data items

A scatter diagram is used to show whether or not there is a relationship between two sets of data collected in pairs. Data that is collected in pairs is called **bivariate data**.

For example, you could record the number of hours different students spend studying and the results they get in a test.

This would give two pieces of data for each student: time spent studying and their result.

In bivariate data, both sets of data are numerical, so each pair of data can be plotted as a point using coordinates on a pair of axes, (x, y).

Once you have plotted the data, you can look for a pattern to see whether there is a **correlation** between the two variables.

These diagrams show the typical patterns of correlation and what they mean.

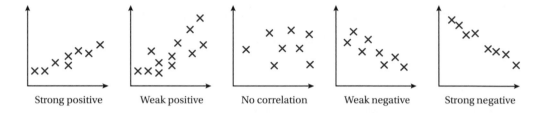

Strong positive   Weak positive   No correlation   Weak negative   Strong negative

WORKED EXAMPLE 3

Nick says people who are good at maths are also good at science.

Use this data to draw a scatter diagram and comment on whether the graph supports Nick.

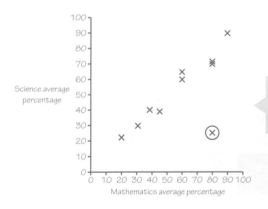

Maths average (%)	Science average (%)
20	22
32	30
45	39
38	40
60	60
80	70
80	72
90	90
80	25
60	65

Look at the distribution of the points to see if there is a general pattern.

The points slope up towards the right, so there is a positive correlation between maths achievement and science achievement. The graph seems to support Nick.

Decide whether there is a positive correlation (as one quantity increases, so does the other) or a negative correlation (as one quantity increases the other decreases).

In the graph from Worked Example 3, maths is on the horizontal axis and science is on the vertical axis.

Science is the **dependent variable** in this case.

Nick's statement is that science achievement is dependent on whether or not you are good at maths. Maths is the independent variable so it goes on the horizontal axis.

One dot (circled on the graph) is far away from the others and doesn't seem to fit the pattern.

It shows a student with a high mark for maths but a low mark for science.

This point is an **outlier** in this set of data.

It is important to understand that *correlation is not causation*. This means that although there might be a relationship between two variables, you cannot be certain that the change in one is the reason for the change in the other. One does not necessarily cause the other.

Key vocabulary

dependent variable: the variable that is being measured in an experiment

outlier: data value that is much larger or smaller than others in the same data set

Lines of best fit

A line of best fit is used to show a general trend on a scatter diagram.

This is a straight line drawn on the graph passing as close to as many points as possible.

This is the line of best fit for the scatter diagram in Worked Example 3. Note that the circled point, which is an outlier, has not been included in the plotting of this line.

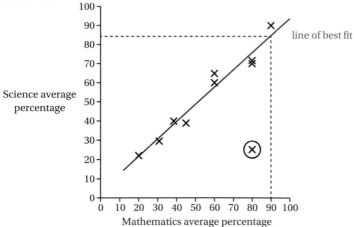

You can use the line of best fit to make predictions based on the data collected.

For example, if you wanted to predict the science results for a student who got 90% for maths, by using the line you find this is 84%. This is shown by the dotted line on the diagram. The same method can be used to predict the maths score for any other science score.

EXERCISE 3D

1 Draw a scatter diagram for the following data and draw a line of best fit.

Time spent on homework (min)	10	25	38	65	84	105	135	158
TV viewing time (min)	60	55	50	20	30	15	10	8

State the type of correlation.

2 Draw a scatter diagram to show the relationship between car engine size and fuel economy (miles per gallon):

Car fuel economy (miles per gallon)	64	60	59	58	55	49	47	42
Car engine size (litres)	1.1	1.3	1.4	1.6	1.8	2.0	2.5	3.0

3 Mike writes down the number of ice creams he sells and the maximum temperature each day for a week.

Ice creams sold	86	89	45	69	84	25	78
Maximum temperature (°C)	25	26	19	23	25	15	21

a Draw a scatter diagram to show the correlation between ice cream sales and the temperature.

b Suggest any other factors that might affect sales of ice cream.

4 During a census the number of people living in each house on a street is recorded.

House number	1	3	5	7	9	11	13	15	17	19	21
Number of residents	1	5	1	4	2	5	6	3	5	3	6

a Draw a scatter diagram to show this data.

b State what kind of correlation this shows.

5 The table below shows the athlete's height and the height jumped by the last 10 men's high jump world record holders.

	Athlete height (m)	Height jumped (m)
Sotomayor	1.95	2.45
Sjöberg	2.00	2.42
Paklin	1.91	2.41
Povarnitsyn	2.01	2.40
Jianhua	1.93	2.39
Wessig	2.00	2.36
Mögenburg	2.01	2.35
Wszola	1.90	2.35
Yashchenko	1.93	2.34
Stones	1.96	2.32

  a Draw a scatter diagram showing this data.

  b Is there a correlation between the height of the jumper and the height he jumped?

  c Which one of the following statements is true?

   A The shortest man jumps the smallest height.

   B The tallest man jumps the highest height.

   C All men over 2 m tall can jump higher than those under 2 m tall.

   D Paklin can jump the same distance above his own height as Sotomayor.

Outliers

Outliers are data values that lie outside the normal range for a set of data.

It can be difficult to decide when it is reasonable to disregard an outlier, but if it is an obvious error then the value is usually just ignored.

However, outliers can't be ignored just because they spoil a pattern.

Outliers will have an impact on calculating the mean and the range of a set of data, but less so when finding the median and the mode.

On a scatter diagram an outlier will be a point that is away from the main scatter of points, or might fit the line of best fit but be at an extreme value.

Find answers at: cambridge.org/ukschools/gcsemaths-studentbookanswers

WORKED EXAMPLE 4

A coach records the 100-metre times of her 10 athletes at the start and the end of a week of intense training.

Nine of the athletes improve by a mean of 0.2 second, but one athlete is 2 seconds slower.

Can the coach claim to be making an impact on her athletes?

Yes, the coach is making an impact on the athletes. The mean would show a reduced performance, because the single athlete's performance has reduced by much more than the others have improved. The athlete with reduced performance is an outlier, and her performance might be affected by ill health.

Answer the question directly – is the coach making an impact?

Give reasons and justify why this is the case.

Suggest an explanation for the outlier.

EXERCISE 3E

1 Which one of the following statements is correct?

A An outlier is the biggest number in a data set.

B An outlier is a value that is significantly different from the rest in a data set.

C An outlier is the smallest number in a data set.

D In the data set 5, 6, 7, 10, 12, 15, the value 15 is an outlier.

2 Some students' scores in a test are given below:

54   50   47   42   54   44   36   37   45   36   55   55   52   85   39

a Work out the mean score in the test.

b Work out the range.

c What is the median score?

d What is the median without the outlier?

e Work out the mean without the outlier.

3 The maths and English exam scores for a set of students are given below:

English	49	42	46	44	53	41	64	14	44	53	55	42
Maths	46	47	43	45	49	48	69	39	33	46	53	44

a Plot the scores on a scatter diagram.

b Draw a line of best fit on your scatter diagram.

c Identify any outliers.

4 The time taken to travel by train from Norwich to London in minutes is recorded for 20 journeys:

| 109 | 129 | 98 | 106 | 109 | 156 | 128 | 98 | 99 | 113 |
| 126 | 99 | 105 | 110 | 126 | 98 | 106 | 114 | 122 | 107 |

On a normal day the journey should take between 95 and 115 minutes, depending on the number of stops at stations.

a Work out the mean journey time.

b The train company claim that the mean journey time is 111 minutes on a normal day.
Is this right?

 Checklist of learning and understanding

Averages and range

- The mean, the median and the mode are all measures of central tendency. They can be found precisely for populations that are ungrouped and have to be estimated for grouped data.
- The range is a measure of spread. It can be found precisely for ungrouped data and has to be estimated for grouped data.

Misleading graphs

- The way that data is presented in graphs can be misleading. Watch out for uneven scales and for graphs that show increases by using areas that exaggerate these increases.

Scatter diagrams and correlation

- Scatter diagrams can be used to look for correlations in bivariate data. A correlation is a relationship, such as one quantity increasing as another decreases. Some bivariate data has no correlation.
- Correlation does not mean causation. In other words, identifying a relationship does not necessarily mean that a change in one data set is causing the change in the other.
- Outliers are pieces of data that sit outside the pattern or expected result. They can be ignored if they are an obvious error, but otherwise should be considered and reasons given.

For additional questions on the topics in this chapter, visit GCSE Mathematics Online.

Chapter review

1 A learner windsurfer would typically sail in a wind speed of 7–18 knots, but an expert would prefer to sail at speeds above 30 knots.

a The data in the following table is wind speed in knots measured at the same time each day for two lakes. From the data, decide which lake is best for beginners and which is best for experts.

Use measures of central tendency and spread to support your argument.

Wind speed on first lake (knots)	0	21	33	13	20	11	35	3	5	3	31
	28	19	19	22	26	40	40	4	25	21	26
Wind speed on second lake (knots)	15	11	19	11	10	19	23	25	10	18	10
	16	23	15	15	20	22	10	13	11	18	18

b Which of these statements is true about the data?

A 0 is an outlier.

B We can ignore values above 35 knots as they are outliers.

C All data must be considered to support the argument.

D The second lake is always windier than the first lake.

2 Study the two line graphs.

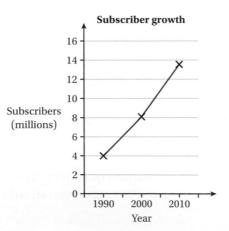

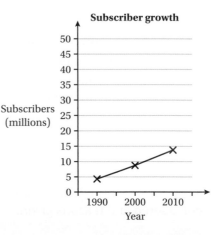

a These two graphs show the same data. Give reasons why they look different.

b Which graph would you use if you were a mobile phone service provider who wanted to suggest that there had been a huge increase in subscribers over this period? Give reasons for your answer.

c Who might find the other graph useful? Why?

3 Data for the price of chocolate bars and their mass is given in the table.

Price of chocolate bar	45p	80p	£1.50	£3.00	£5.00	£10
Mass of bar	35 g	80 g	175 g	320 g	540 g	1 kg

   a Plot the data on a scatter diagram and draw a line of best fit.

   b State what type of correlation there is.

4 The pay of 100 students with Saturday jobs was recorded.

Pay (£x)	Number of students
$0 < x \leqslant 10$	2
$10 < x \leqslant 20$	44
$20 < x \leqslant 30$	41
$30 < x \leqslant 40$	1
$40 < x \leqslant 50$	2
$50 < x \leqslant 60$	4
$60 < x \leqslant 100$	6
	Total = 100

   a How many were paid more than £30?   *(1 mark)*

   b How many were paid £5 or less?

   Choose your answer from the following options.

       0   1   2   Cannot tell   *(1 mark)*

   c Work out the class interval that contains the median.   *(1 mark)*

© AQA 2012

4 Properties of integers

 For more resources relating to this chapter, visit GCSE Mathematics Online.

Using mathematics: real-life applications

People use numbers and basic calculations on a daily basis. A market stall holder has to quickly calculate the cost of a customer's order; a logistics manager has to order stock and divide the supplies so that they are never over- or under-stocked. There are many applications of basic calculation.

 Tip

You probably know most of the concepts in this chapter. They have been included so you can revise them if you need to and check that you know them well.

"Counting in multiples saves quite a bit of time. If I know that each shelf has 15 boxes and each box contains 5 reams of paper, then I know straightaway that I have 75 reams on each shelf without having to count each ream."

(Logistics manager)

Before you start ...

KS3	You should be able to recognise and find the factors of a number and to list multiples of a number.	**1** If these are the factors, what is the number? **a** 1, 5, 25 **b** 1, 2, 3, 6 **c** 1, 11 **2** If these are all multiples of a number, what is the number? **a** 8, 10, 12, 14 **b** 18, 21, 27, 33 **c** 5, 20, 35, 60
KS3	You should know the first few prime numbers, square numbers and cube numbers.	**3** Which of the numbers in the box are: **a** prime numbers? **b** square numbers? **c** cube numbers? 0, 1, 2, 3, 4, 5, 6, 7, 8, 9, 10, 11, 12, 13, 14, 15, 16, 17, 18, 19, 20
KS3	You will need to be able to express a number as a product of its prime factors.	**4** Match each number to the product of its prime factors. **a** 450 **b** 180 **c** 120 **d** 72 A $2 \times 2 \times 2 \times 3 \times 3$ C $2 \times 2 \times 3 \times 3 \times 5$ B $2 \times 2 \times 2 \times 3 \times 5$ D $2 \times 3 \times 3 \times 5 \times 5$

Assess your starting point using the Launchpad

STEP 1

1 True or false?

a 1 is the smallest prime number.

b If you square 7 you get 14.

c 8 is the cube of 2.

d Any whole number that ends in 1 is an odd number.

e 33, 43 and 53 are prime numbers.

f 7, 14 and 21 are factors of 7.

2 There is one incorrect number in each set.

Work out what the set is and find the incorrect number.

a 20, 22, 24, 26, 28, 29, 30   **b** 11, 22, 33, 44, 56, 66

c 1, 2, 3, 4, 8, 12   **d** 27, 30, 33, 36, 39, 41

e 1, 2, 3, 4, 6, 9, 12, 18, 24, 36   **f** 12, 24, 48, 60, 72, 86

g 2, 3, 5, 7, 9, 11, 13, 17, 19

GO TO
Section 1:
Types of numbers

STEP 2

3 Choose the correct product of prime factors for each number.

a 48   A $2 \times 2 \times 2 \times 3 \times 3$ B $2 \times 2 \times 2 \times 2 \times 3$

b 100   A $2 \times 2 \times 5 \times 5$ B $2 \times 5 \times 5$

GO TO
Section 2:
Prime factors

STEP 3

4 Given that $72 = 2 \times 2 \times 2 \times 3 \times 3$ and $120 = 2 \times 2 \times 2 \times 3 \times 5$, choose the correct answers.

a The HCF of 72 and 120 is:

A 360   B 12   C 24   D 5

b The LCM of 72 and 120 is:

A 30   B 2   C 120   D 360

GO TO
Section 3:
Multiples and factors

GO TO
Chapter review

Section 1: Types of numbers

Defining mathematical terms

Make sure you remember the correct mathematical terms for the different types of numbers shown in the table.

Mathematical term	Definition	Example
odd number	A whole number that cannot be divided exactly by 2; it has a remainder of 1.	1, 3, 5, 7, …
even number	A whole number that can be divided exactly by 2 (no remainder).	0, 2, 4, 6, 8, …
prime number	A whole number greater than 1 that can only be divided exactly by itself and by 1. (It has only two factors.)	2, 3, 5, 7, 11, 13, 17, 19, …
square number	The product when an integer is multiplied by itself. For example, $2 \times 2 = 4$, so 4 is a square number.	1, 4, 9, 16, …
cubed number	The product when an integer is multiplied by itself twice. For example, $2 \times 2 \times 2 = 8$, so 8 is a cube number.	1, 8, 27, 64, …
root $\sqrt{}$	The number that produces a square number when it is multiplied by itself is a square root. The number that produces a cubed number when it is multiplied by itself and then by itself again is a cube root.	The square root of 25 is 5. $\sqrt{25} = 5$ $(5 \times 5 = 25)$ The cube root of 8 is 2. $\sqrt[3]{8} = 2$ $(2 \times 2 \times 2 = 8)$
factor (also called divisor)	A number that divides exactly into another number, without a remainder.	Factors of 6 are 1, 2, 3 and 6. Factors of 7 are 1 and 7. Factors of 25 are 1, 5 and 25.
multiple	A multiple of a number is found when you multiply that number by a whole number. Times tables are really just lists of multiples.	Multiples of 3 are 3, 6, 9, 12, … Multiples of 7 are 7, 14, 21, …
common factor	A common factor is a factor shared by two or more numbers. The number 1 is a common factor of all numbers.	Factors of 6 are 1, 2, 3 and 6. Factors of 12 are 1, 2, 3, 4, 6 and 12. 1, 2, 3 and 6 are common factors of 6 and 12.
common multiple	A common multiple is a multiple shared by two or more numbers.	Multiples of 2 are 2, 4, 6, 8, 10, 12, … Multiples of 3 are 3, 6, 9, 12, … 6 and 12 are common multiples of 2 and 3.

 Did you know?

Mathematicians use the following arguments to define zero as an even number:

- When divided by two, it results in two equal answers (zero); and there is no remainder.
- In a list of consecutive numbers, an even number has an odd number before and after it, i.e. −1 and 1 are either side of zero.
- When an even number is added to another even number it will give an even result, but when added to an odd number it will give an odd result. When zero is added to any number, the result is the number you started with.
- Numbers that end in 0 are even.
- It is the next number in a pattern of even numbers: 8, 6, 4, 2, …

EXERCISE 4A

1 Here is a set of numbers.

1	2	3	4	5	6	7	8	9	10
11	12	13	14	15	16	17	18	19	20
21	22	23	24	25	26	27	28	29	30

Write down the numbers from the box that are:

a odd   **b** even   **c** prime   **d** square

e cube   **f** factors of 24   **g** multiples of 3   **h** common factors of 8 and 12

i common multiples of 3 and 4.

2 Which of the following options is both a prime **and** a factor of 12?

A 2   B 4   C 6   D 12

3 Write down:

a the next four odd numbers after 207

b four **consecutive** even numbers between 500 and 540

c the square numbers between 20 and 70

d the factors of 23

e four prime numbers greater than 15

f the first ten cube numbers

g the first five multiples of 8

h the factors of 36.

Key vocabulary

consecutive: following each other in order and without a gap. For example, 1, 2, 3 or 35, 36, 37.

4 Write down whether the following results will be odd or even.

a The sum of two odd numbers.

b The sum of two even numbers.

c The difference between two even numbers.

d The square of an odd number.

e The product of an odd number and an even number.

f The cube of an odd number.

Place value

Consider the number 222 222.

Each of the 2s in the number has a different place value.

The place value tells you the value of the digit. The underlined 2 in the number above has a value of 2 thousands or 2000.

Hundred thousands 100 000	Ten thousands 10 000	Thousands 1000	Hundreds 100	Tens 10	Ones/units 1
2	2	2	2	2	2

Each column in the place-value table is ten times the value of the place to the right of it.

EXERCISE 4B

1 For each set of numbers, rewrite the numbers in order from smallest to biggest.

   a 432   456   348   843   654

   b 606   660   607   670   706

   c 123   1231   312   1321   231

   d 12 700   71 200   21 700   21 007

2 Write down the value of the 5 in each of these numbers.

   a 35   **b** 534   **c** 256

   d 25 876   **e** 50 346 987   **f** 1 532 980

   g 5 678 432   **h** 356 432   **i** 56 987 089

3 What is the value of 7 in the number 307 642?

   Choose from the following options.

   A 70 000   B 7000   C 700   D 7

4 For each set of digits, write down:

   i the biggest number you can make

   ii the smallest number you can make.

   Use each digit only once in each number.

   a 4, 0 and 6   **b** 5, 7, 3 and 1   **c** 1, 0, 3, 4, 6 and 2

Section 2: Prime factors

Key vocabulary

prime factor: a factor which is also a prime number

If a factor of a number is a prime number it is called a **prime factor**.

Every integer greater than 1 can be written as a product of its prime factors.

Finding the prime numbers that multiply together to make a given number is known as **prime factorisation**.

You can find the prime factors of a number by **repeatedly dividing by prime numbers**, or by using **factor trees**.

Tip

Remember that 1 is **not** a prime number because it only has one factor, and 2 is the only even prime number. It will help you work faster if you learn to recognise all the prime numbers up to 100.

WORKED EXAMPLE 1

Express 48 as a product of its prime factors:

a by division   **b** by using a factor tree.

a

$$2 \times 2 \times 2 \times 2 \times 3$$

> Divide by prime numbers.
>
> Start with the lowest divisor that is prime; always try 2 first. Continue dividing, moving to higher prime numbers as necessary.

b

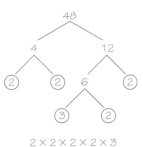

$$2 \times 2 \times 2 \times 2 \times 3$$

> Write the number as a product of any two of its factors. Keep doing this for the factors until you cannot divide a factor anymore, that is, until you get to a prime factor.

Even if you do the division in a different order and split the factors differently in the factor tree, you will always get the same result for a given number.

You get the same result with both methods because a whole number can only be expressed in terms of its prime factors in one way. This is called the **unique factorisation theorem**.

Here are three ways of finding the prime factors of 280.

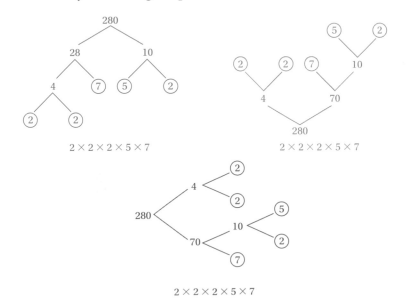

Tip

The **unique factorisation theorem** in mathematics states that each number can be written as a product of prime factors in one way only. It means that different numbers cannot have the same product of prime factors.

Writing a number as a product of its prime factors is known as **prime factor decomposition**.

You have seen the product of factors in expanded form, but you can write them in a more efficient way using powers, called the index form, as shown in the margin.

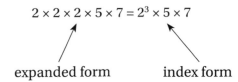

$$2 \times 2 \times 2 \times 5 \times 7 = 2^3 \times 5 \times 7$$

expanded form   index form

 Find answers at: cambridge.org/ukschools/gcsemaths-studentbookanswers

EXERCISE 4C

1 Write down the prime numbers in each set.

a 1, 2, 3, 4, 5, 6, 7, 8, 9, 10

b 50, 51, 52, 53, 54, 55, 56, 57, 58, 59, 60

c 95, 96, 97, 98, 99, 100, 101, 102, 103, 104, 105

2 How should you express 96 as a product of its prime factors?

Choose from the following options.

A 32×3 B 3×2^5 C 2×48 D $1 \times 2^5 \times 3$

3 Express each of the following numbers as a product of its prime factors.

Write your final answers in index form.

a 36   **b** 65   **c** 64   **d** 84

e 80   **f** 1000   **g** 1270   **h** 1963

4 A number is expressed as $2^3 \times 3^3 \times 5$.

a What is the number?

b Could it be any other number?

Give a reason for your answer.

Section 3: Multiples and factors

The lowest common multiple (LCM)

The lowest common multiple (LCM) of two or more numbers is the smallest number that is a multiple of all the given numbers.

To find the LCM, list the multiples of the given numbers until you find the first multiple that appears in all the lists.

Tip

The notation M_4 means multiples of 4.

F_4 means factors of 4.

WORKED EXAMPLE 2

Find the LCM of 4 and 7.

$M_4 = 4, 8, 12, 16, 20, 24, 28, 32, \ldots$ List the multiples of 4.

$M_7 = 7, 14, 21, 28, \ldots$ List the multiples of 7.

Stop listing at 28 as it appears in both the lists.

LCM of 4 and 7 is 28.

The highest common factor (HCF)

The highest common factor of two or more numbers is the largest number that is a factor of all the given numbers.

To find the HCF, list all the factors in each number, and pick out the highest number that appears in all the lists.

WORKED EXAMPLE 3

Find the HCF of 8 and 24.

$F_8 = \underline{1}, \underline{2}, \underline{4}, \underline{8}$

> List the factors of 8.

$F_{24} = \underline{1}, \underline{2}, 3, \underline{4}, 6, \underline{8}, 12, 24$

> List the factors of 24.
> Underline the common factors.

HCF of 8 and 24 is 8.

> The highest underlined number in both lists is the HCF.

Tip

The LCM is used to find the lowest common denominator when you add or subtract fractions.

The HCF is useful for cancelling fractions. You will use these terms again in Chapter 7 to factorise algebraic expressions.

With word problems, you need to work out whether to use the LCM or HCF to find the answers.

- Problems involving the LCM usually include repeating events. You might be asked how many items you need to 'have enough' or when something will happen again at the same time.
- Problems involving the HCF usually involve splitting things into smaller pieces or arranging things in equal groups or rows.

Finding the HCF and LCM using prime factors

When you work with larger numbers you can find the HCF and LCM by writing the numbers as products of prime factors, that is, by prime factorisation.

Once you have done that you can use the factors to quickly find the HCF and LCM.

Tip

Use the letters to help you remember what to do. LCM requires the **L**argest set of **M**ultiples.

WORKED EXAMPLE 4

Find the HCF and LCM of 72 and 120.

a HCF of 72 and 120.
$72 = \underline{2} \times \underline{2} \times \underline{2} \times \underline{3} \times 3$
$120 = \underline{2} \times \underline{2} \times \underline{2} \times \underline{3} \times 5$

> First express each number as a product of prime factors. Underline the common factors.

$2 \times 2 \times 2 \times 3 = 24$
HCF of 72 and 120 is 24.

> Write down the common factors and multiply them out.

b LCM of 72 and 120.
$72 = \underline{2} \times \underline{2} \times \underline{2} \times \underline{3} \times \underline{3}$
$120 = 2 \times 2 \times 2 \times 3 \times \underline{5}$

> First express each number as a product of prime factors. Underline the largest set of multiples of each factor across **both** lists. Here, 2 appears three times in each list, so underline one set of them. 3 appears twice in the first list, but only once in the second, so underline the top set of 3s. 5 only appears in the bottom list, so underline it there.

$2 \times 2 \times 2 \times 3 \times 3 \times 5 = 360$
LCM of 72 and 120 is 360.

> Write down each set of underlined multiples and multiply them out.

Find answers at: cambridge.org/ukschools/gcsemaths-studentbookanswers

EXERCISE 4D

1 **a** What is the LCM of 5, 3 and 2?

Choose from the following options.

A 30　　　　B 15　　　　C 10　　　　D 6

b Which number is not a factor of 42?

Choose from the following options.

A 6　　　　B 7　　　　C 8　　　　D 14

2 Find the LCM of the numbers given.

a 9 and 18　　**b** 12 and 18　　**c** 15 and 18　　**d** 24 and 12

e 36 and 9　　**f** 4, 12 and 8　　**g** 3, 9 and 24　　**h** 12, 16 and 32

3 Find the HCF of the numbers given.

a 12 and 18　　**b** 18 and 36　　**c** 27 and 90　　**d** 12 and 15

e 20 and 30　　**f** 19 and 45　　**g** 60 and 72　　**h** 250 and 900

4 Find the LCM and the HCF of the following numbers by using prime factors.

a 27 and 14　　**b** 85 and 15　　**c** 96 and 27　　**d** 53 and 16

e 674 and 72　　**f** 234 and 66　　**g** 550 and 128　　**h** 315 and 275

5 A roll of red fabric is 72 metres long.

A roll of yellow fabric is 90 metres long.

Sian wants to cut equal lengths of red and yellow fabric with as little waste as possible.

What is the longest possible length the pieces can be?

6 Every 30th shopper gets a £10 voucher.
Every 120th shopper gets a free meal.

How many shoppers must there be before one receives both a voucher and a free meal?

7 Amanda has 40 pieces of fruit and 100 sweets.

She gives each student an equal number of pieces of fruit and an equal number of sweets.

What is the largest possible number of students in her class?

8 Samir and Li walk in opposite directions around a track.

They start at the same point at the same time.

It takes Samir 5 minutes to walk round the track.

It takes Li 4 minutes.

How long will it be before they meet again at the starting point?

9 Lana cycles every 2nd day.
Pete cycles every 3rd day.
Karen cycles every 4th day.
Anna cycles every 5th day.

They all cycle on 1 January this year.

a After how many days will they all cycle on the same day again?

b How many times a year will they all cycle on the same day?

10 Mr Abbot has three pieces of ribbon of different lengths:

2.4 m   3.18 m   4.26 m

He wants to cut the ribbons into pieces that are all the same length, with the least possible waste.

What is the greatest possible length for the pieces?

11 One warning light flashes every 20 seconds.

Another warning light flashes every 30 seconds.

They flash together at 4.30 pm.

When will they next flash at the same time?

Checklist of learning and understanding

Types of numbers

- Even numbers are multiples of 2, odd numbers are not.
- Factors are numbers that divide exactly into a number.
- Prime numbers have only two factors, 1 and the number itself.
- Square numbers are the product of a number and itself ($n \times n$).
- Cube numbers are the product of a number multiplied by itself twice ($n \times n \times n$).
- The value of a digit depends on its place in the number.

Prime numbers

- If a factor is a prime number it is called a prime factor.
- Whole numbers can be written as the product of their prime factors.
- You find the prime factors by:
  - repeated division by prime numbers (starting from 2 and working upwards)
  - using a factor tree and breaking down factors until they are prime factors.

Find answers at: cambridge.org/ukschools/gcsemaths-studentbookanswers

Multiples and factors

- The lowest common multiple (LCM) of two numbers can be found by:
  - listing the multiples of both numbers and selecting the lowest multiple that appears in both lists
  - finding the largest set of multiples of each of the prime factors and multiplying them together.
- The highest common factor (HCF) of two numbers can be found by:
  - listing the factors of both numbers and selecting the highest factor that appears in both lists
  - finding the common prime factors and multiplying them together.

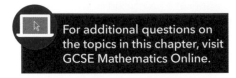 For additional questions on the topics in this chapter, visit GCSE Mathematics Online.

 Chapter review

1 Complete the crossword puzzle provided by your teacher.

Clues

Across

1 The times tables are examples of these.

2 Whole numbers divisible by 2.

3 Another word used for factor.

4 Numbers in the sequence 1, 4, 9, 16, …

5 An even prime number.

6 The result of a multiplication.

Down

a $n \times n \times n$ is the __ of *n*.

b Numbers with only two factors.

c Whole numbers that are not exactly divisible by 2.

d Number that divides into another with no remainder.

e HCF of 12 and 18.

2 Is 149 a prime number?

Give reasons for your answer.

3 Which number is both a factor and a multiple of 12?

Choose from the following options.

A 12　　　　B 24　　　　C 4　　　　D 3

4 Find the HCF and the LCM of 20 and 35 by listing the factors and multiples.

5 **a** Write 36 as the product of prime factors.

Give your answer in index form. *(3 marks)*

b Work out the Highest Common Factor (HCF) of 36 and 81. *(2 marks)*

© AQA 2013

6 Express 800 as a product of prime factors.

Give your final answer in index form.

7 Work out the HCF and LCM of the following by prime factorisation.

a 72 and 108 **b** 84 and 60

8 Jo jumped 2 steps at a time on a flight of stairs.

Mo jumped 3 steps at a time.

Jenny jumped 4 steps at a time.

They started together on the bottom step.

What is the first step they will **all** jump on together?

5 Working with fractions

In this chapter you will learn how to …

- recognise equivalence between fractions and mixed numbers.
- carry out the four basic operations on fractions and mixed numbers.
- work out fractions of an amount.

For more resources relating to this chapter, visit GCSE Mathematics Online.

Using mathematics: real-life applications

Nurses and other medical support staff work with fractions, decimals, percentages, rates and ratios every day. They calculate medicine doses, convert between different systems of measurement and set the patients' drips to supply the correct amount of fluid per hour.

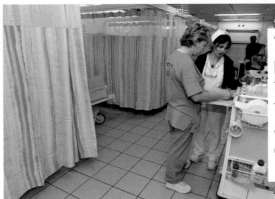

"We have to record how much fluid patients drink when they are recovering from surgery. So for example, if we give the patient a 300 ml glass of orange juice and they only drink $\frac{2}{3}$ of it, we have to work out that they have taken in 200 ml of fluid."

(Nurse)

Before you start …

KS3 Ch 4	Check that you can find common factors of sets of numbers.	**1** From this set of numbers, choose numbers that have: 18 24 27 28 30 32 36 **a** a common factor of 9. **b** common factors 2 and 3. **c** common factors 3, 4, and 12. **d** common factors of 3 and 6.
KS3 Ch 4	Find the lowest common multiple of sets of numbers.	**2** Choose the lowest common multiple of each set of numbers. **a** 5 and 10 A 15 B 50 C 10 D 20 **b** 8 and 12 A 12 B 96 C 36 D 24 **c** 2, 3 and 5 A 1 B 30 C 10 D 6
KS3 Ch 1	Know the correct order for performing operations (BODMAS).	**3** Which calculation is correct in each pair? Why?

	Student A	**Student B**
a	$-3 - 2 \times -6 - 4 = 5$	$-3 - 2 \times -6 - 4 = 50$
b	$-60 \div 5 + 3 \times -4 - 8 = 28$	$-60 \div 5 + 3 \times -4 - 8 = -32$
c	$13 - 2 \times -6 - 5 \times 4 = 80$	$13 - 2 \times -6 - 5 \times 4 = 5$

Assess your starting point using the Launchpad

STEP 1

1 Which fraction does not belong in each set?

a $\dfrac{3}{15}, \dfrac{1}{5}, \dfrac{6}{30}, \dfrac{5}{35}, \dfrac{4}{20}$

b $\dfrac{4}{7}, \dfrac{8}{14}, \dfrac{12}{21}, \dfrac{9}{16}, \dfrac{52}{91}$

c $\dfrac{22}{10}, \dfrac{11}{4}, 2\dfrac{3}{4}, \dfrac{33}{12}, 2\dfrac{18}{24}$

GO TO
Section 1:
Equivalent fractions

STEP 2

2 Each calculation contains a mistake.

Find the mistake and write the correct answer.

a $\dfrac{2}{3} + \dfrac{3}{4} = \dfrac{5}{7}$

b $\dfrac{4}{5} - \dfrac{9}{10} = \dfrac{1}{10}$

c $\dfrac{2}{7} \times \dfrac{4}{5} = \dfrac{6}{35}$

d $30 \div \dfrac{1}{2} = 15$

GO TO
Section 2:
Using the four operations
with fractions

STEP 3

3 Which is greater in each pair?

a $\dfrac{5}{8}$ of 40   or $\dfrac{3}{5}$ of 60

b $\dfrac{3}{4}$ of 240   or $\dfrac{7}{10}$ of 300

c $\dfrac{1}{4}$ of $\dfrac{1}{2}$ or $\dfrac{1}{2}$ of $\dfrac{3}{4}$

GO TO
Section 3:
Fractions of quantities

GO TO
Chapter review

Find answers at: cambridge.org/ukschools/gcsemaths-studentbookanswers

Tip

It doesn't matter what number you use as long as the numerator and denominator are multiplied by the same number. What you are really doing is multiplying by 1 because any number divided by itself is equal to 1.
$\frac{4}{4} = 1$, $\frac{5}{5} = 1$ and $\frac{x}{x} = 1$.

Key vocabulary

common denominator: a number into which all the denominators of a set of fractions divide exactly

Tip

You can use the LCM of the denominators to find a common denominator, but any common denominator works (not just the lowest).

Section 1: Equivalent fractions

Fractions tell you what share you have of a quantity.

Fractions that look different can be describing the same share.

For example, the fractions $\frac{1}{4}$ and $\frac{2}{8}$ are equivalent.

You can find equivalent fractions by multiplying or dividing the numerator and denominator by the same number.

For example:

Dividing like this is known as simplifying or reducing the fraction to its lowest terms.

When you give an answer in the form of a fraction, you should give it in its simplest form.

When you are asked to compare fractions that look different, you might need to find a **common denominator** so that you can tell whether they are equivalent.

WORKED EXAMPLE 1

a Is $\frac{5}{6}$ equivalent to $\frac{7}{8}$?

b Is $3\frac{3}{4}$ equivalent to $\frac{45}{12}$?

a $\frac{5}{6} = \frac{20}{24}$ and $\frac{7}{8} = \frac{21}{24}$

$\frac{5}{6} \neq \frac{7}{8}$

Write both fractions with the same denominator.

When the fractions have the same denominator it is easy to see whether they are equivalent or not.

It is also easy to tell which one is bigger or smaller.

b $3\frac{3}{4} = \frac{15}{4}$

$\frac{15}{4} = \frac{45}{12}$

So the fractions are equivalent.

Write the mixed number as an improper fraction.

Write $\frac{15}{4}$ with a denominator of 12, or write $\frac{45}{12}$ with a denominator of 4.

EXERCISE 5A

1 Copy and complete each statement to make a pair of equivalent fractions.

a $\dfrac{3}{4}=\dfrac{\square}{44}$ **b** $\dfrac{1}{3}=\dfrac{1000}{\square}$ **c** $\dfrac{1}{2}=\dfrac{\square}{300}$ **d** $\dfrac{-2}{5}=\dfrac{-18}{\square}$

e $\dfrac{-6}{-10}=\dfrac{42}{\square}$ **f** $\dfrac{\square}{5}=\dfrac{36}{20}$ **g** $\dfrac{4}{3}=\dfrac{28}{\square}$ **h** $\dfrac{10}{14}=\dfrac{50}{\square}$

2 List five fractions that are equivalent to each of these fractions.

a $\dfrac{5}{7}$ **b** $\dfrac{4}{5}$ **c** $\dfrac{12}{8}$ **d** $\dfrac{-5}{-3}$

3 Write each mixed number as an improper fraction in its simplest form.

a $2\frac{1}{3}$ **b** $3\frac{1}{3}$ **c** $5\frac{2}{8}$ **d** $4\frac{6}{12}$

e $2\frac{14}{21}$ **f** $1\frac{12}{36}$ **g** $2\frac{30}{50}$ **h** $3\frac{35}{45}$

4 Rewrite each fraction as an equivalent mixed number.

a $\dfrac{12}{5}$ **b** $\dfrac{7}{3}$ **c** $\dfrac{8}{5}$ **d** $\dfrac{-11}{5}$

e $\dfrac{12}{11}$ **f** $\dfrac{13}{9}$ **g** $\dfrac{-9}{-4}$ **h** $\dfrac{21}{9}$

5 a Which fraction is greater than $\dfrac{5}{8}$?

Choose from the following options.

    A $\dfrac{1}{2}$ B $\dfrac{2}{3}$ C $\dfrac{5}{9}$ D $\dfrac{6}{12}$

b Which fraction is smaller than $\dfrac{2}{3}$?

Choose from the following options.

    A $\dfrac{3}{2}$ B $\dfrac{3}{4}$ C $\dfrac{2}{5}$ D $\dfrac{20}{30}$

c What is the simplest form of $\dfrac{24}{32}$?

Choose from the following options.

    A $\dfrac{2}{3}$ B $\dfrac{6}{5}$ C $\dfrac{3}{4}$ D $\dfrac{14}{16}$

6 Work out whether the following pairs of fractions are equivalent (=) or not (≠).

a $\dfrac{2}{5}$ and $\dfrac{3}{4}$ **b** $\dfrac{2}{3}$ and $\dfrac{3}{4}$ **c** $\dfrac{3}{8}$ and $\dfrac{5}{12}$ **d** $\dfrac{2}{11}$ and $\dfrac{1}{10}$

e $\dfrac{3}{5}$ and $\dfrac{9}{15}$ **f** $\dfrac{10}{25}$ and $\dfrac{4}{10}$ **g** $\dfrac{6}{24}$ and $\dfrac{5}{20}$ **h** $\dfrac{11}{9}$ and $\dfrac{121}{99}$

7 Reduce the following fractions to their simplest form.

a $\dfrac{3}{15}$ **b** $\dfrac{4}{6}$ **c** $\dfrac{25}{100}$ **d** $\dfrac{-5}{-10}$

e $\dfrac{4}{12}$ **f** $\dfrac{7}{21}$ **g** $\dfrac{36}{24}$ **h** $\dfrac{60}{100}$

i $\dfrac{-14}{21}$ **j** $\dfrac{18}{27}$ **k** $\dfrac{-15}{-21}$ **l** $\dfrac{18}{42}$

8 Write each set of fractions in ascending order.

a $\dfrac{3}{5}, \dfrac{1}{4}, \dfrac{9}{4}, 1\frac{3}{4}, \dfrac{4}{7}$ **b** $\dfrac{5}{6}, \dfrac{3}{4}, \dfrac{11}{3}, \dfrac{19}{24}, 2\frac{2}{3}$ **c** $2\frac{3}{7}, \dfrac{1}{7}, \dfrac{7}{7}, \dfrac{8}{14}, \dfrac{10}{21}, \dfrac{13}{7}$

Section 2: Using the four operations with fractions

Multiplying fractions

Look at this rectangle. It has been divided into 12 smaller squares, or twelfths.

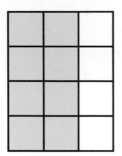

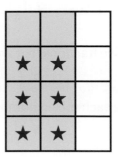

$\frac{2}{3}$ of this rectangle is blue.　　　$\frac{3}{4}$ of the $\frac{2}{3}$ have been marked with a star ★.

From the diagram you can see that $\frac{3}{4}$ of $\frac{2}{3}$ is 6 of the original 12 parts.

$$\frac{3}{4} \text{ of } \frac{2}{3} = \frac{3}{4} \times \frac{2}{3} = \frac{6}{12}$$

The example above gives you a general rule for multiplying fractions.

To multiply fractions, multiply the numerators and then multiply the denominators.

If possible, cancel before you multiply to make the calculations easier.

Tip

You can cancel before you multiply to make it easier to work out the answers.

WORKED EXAMPLE 2

Calculate　　**a** $\frac{3}{4} \times \frac{2}{7}$　　**b** $\frac{5}{7} \times 3$　　**c** $\frac{3}{8} \times 4\frac{1}{2}$

a $\frac{3}{4} \times \frac{2}{7} = \frac{3 \times 2}{4 \times 7}$

$= \frac{6}{28}$

$= \frac{3}{14}$

> Multiply numerators by numerators and denominators by denominators.
>
> Give the answer in its simplest form.

b $\frac{5}{7} \times 3 = \frac{5 \times 3}{7 \times 1}$

$= \frac{15}{7}$

$= 2\frac{1}{7}$

> Think of a whole number as a fraction with a denominator of 1.
>
> $\frac{15}{7}$ cannot be simplified further but it can be written as a mixed number.

c $\frac{3}{8} \times 4\frac{1}{2} = \frac{3}{8} \times \frac{9}{2}$

$= \frac{27}{16}$

$= 1\frac{11}{16}$

> Rewrite the mixed number as an improper fraction.
>
> $\frac{27}{16}$ cannot be simplified but it can be written as a mixed number.

Adding and subtracting fractions

To add or subtract fractions they must have the same denominators.

Find a common denominator and then find the equivalent fractions before you add or subtract the numerators.

WORKED EXAMPLE 3

Simplify   **a** $\frac{1}{2}+\frac{1}{4}$ **b** $2\frac{1}{2}+\frac{5}{6}$ **c** $2\frac{3}{4}-1\frac{5}{7}$

a $\frac{1}{2}+\frac{1}{4}$

$=\frac{2}{4}+\frac{1}{4}$

$=\frac{3}{4}$

Write $\frac{1}{2}$ as its equivalent of $\frac{2}{4}$. Use 4 as a common denominator.

Add the numerators.

b $2\frac{1}{2}+\frac{5}{6}$

$=\frac{5}{2}+\frac{5}{6}$

$=\frac{15}{6}+\frac{5}{6}$

$=\frac{20}{6}$

$=\frac{10}{3}$ or $3\frac{1}{3}$

Rewrite mixed number as improper fraction.

Find a common denominator.

Add the numerators.

Simplify the answer.

c $2\frac{3}{4}-1\frac{5}{7}$

$=\frac{11}{4}-\frac{12}{7}$

$=\frac{77}{28}-\frac{48}{28}$

$=\frac{29}{28}$ or $1\frac{1}{28}$

Rewrite mixed numbers as improper fractions.

Find a common denominator.

Subtract the numerators.

Simplify the answer.

Tip

Think of $\frac{3}{7}$ and $\frac{2}{7}$ as 3 lots of 7ths and 2 lots of 7ths. If you combine them, you have 5 lots of 7ths, or $\frac{5}{7}$

You never add the denominators.

Dividing fractions

To divide one fraction by another fraction you multiply the first fraction by the **reciprocal** of the second fraction.

To understand why this works, look at the example below.

$\frac{9}{10}\div\frac{1}{2}$ is the same as the fraction $\dfrac{\frac{9}{10}}{\frac{1}{2}}$

Multiply the numerator and the denominator by 2, to get rid of the fractional denominator.

$\dfrac{\frac{9}{10}}{\frac{1}{2}}=\dfrac{\frac{9}{10}\times\frac{2}{1}}{\frac{1}{2}\times\frac{2}{1}}=\frac{9}{10}\times\frac{2}{1}=\frac{18}{10}=\frac{9}{5}$

You can do this calculation faster by just inverting the fraction you are dividing by:

$\frac{9}{10}\div\frac{1}{2}$ is the same as $\frac{9}{10}\times\frac{2}{1}$

Key vocabulary

reciprocal: the value obtained by inverting a fraction. Any number multiplied by its reciprocal is 1.

Tip

To find the reciprocal of a fraction you invert it. So, the reciprocal of $\frac{3}{4}$ is $\frac{4}{3}$ and the reciprocal of $\frac{7}{4}$ is $\frac{4}{7}$. The reciprocal of a whole number is a unit fraction. For example, the reciprocal of 3 is $\frac{1}{3}$ and the reciprocal of 12 is $\frac{1}{12}$.

Find answers at: cambridge.org/ukschools/gcsemaths-studentbookanswers

WORKED EXAMPLE 4

Simplify   **a** $\dfrac{3}{4} \div \dfrac{1}{2}$ **b** $1\dfrac{3}{4} \div 2\dfrac{1}{3}$ **c** $\dfrac{6}{7} \div 3$

a $\dfrac{3}{4} \div \dfrac{1}{2}$

$= \dfrac{3}{4} \times \dfrac{2}{1}$ ◁ Multiply by the reciprocal of $\dfrac{1}{2}$.

$= \dfrac{6}{4}$

$= \dfrac{3}{2}$ or $1\dfrac{1}{2}$ ◁ Simplify the answer.

b $1\dfrac{3}{4} \div 2\dfrac{1}{3}$

$= \dfrac{7}{4} \div \dfrac{7}{3}$ ◁ Convert mixed numbers to improper fractions.

$= \dfrac{\cancel{7}}{4} \times \dfrac{3}{\cancel{7}}$ ◁ Multiply by the reciprocal of $\dfrac{7}{3}$.
Cancel the 7s.

$= \dfrac{3}{4}$

c $\dfrac{6}{7} \div 3$

$= \dfrac{6}{7} \times \dfrac{1}{3}$ ◁ Multiply by the reciprocal of 3.

$= \dfrac{6}{21}$

$= \dfrac{2}{7}$ ◁ Simplify the answer.

The rules for order of operations and negative and positive signs also apply to calculations with fractions.

EXERCISE 5B

1 Calculate:

a $\dfrac{3}{4} \times \dfrac{2}{5}$ **b** $\dfrac{1}{5} \times \dfrac{1}{9}$ **c** $\dfrac{5}{7} \times \dfrac{1}{5}$ **d** $\dfrac{7}{10} \times \dfrac{2}{3}$

e $\dfrac{4}{7} \times \dfrac{3}{8}$ **f** $\dfrac{6}{11} \times \dfrac{-5}{6}$ **g** $\dfrac{3}{4} \times 24$ **h** $\dfrac{4}{9} \times \dfrac{8}{10}$

i $\dfrac{3}{8} \times \dfrac{4}{9}$ **j** $\dfrac{7}{25} \times \dfrac{3}{4}$ **k** $1\dfrac{1}{2} \times -10$ **l** $1\dfrac{4}{5} \times -6$

m $1\dfrac{2}{7} \times 3\dfrac{1}{2}$ **n** $4\dfrac{1}{11} \times -3\dfrac{1}{8}$ **o** $\dfrac{7}{25} \times \dfrac{7}{9}$ **p** $3\dfrac{1}{3} \times 9\dfrac{2}{5}$

2 Simplify:

a $\dfrac{1}{5} \times \dfrac{3}{8} \times \dfrac{-5}{9}$ **b** $\dfrac{2}{3} \times \dfrac{3}{4} \times \dfrac{4}{5}$ **c** $\dfrac{1}{2} \times \dfrac{2}{3} \times \dfrac{4}{11}$

d $\dfrac{5}{8} \times \dfrac{3}{7} \times \dfrac{2}{3}$ **e** $\dfrac{4}{25} \times \dfrac{-3}{5} \times \dfrac{-7}{8}$ **f** $\dfrac{9}{20} \times \dfrac{10}{11} \times \dfrac{1}{12}$

3 Simplify:

a $\frac{2}{7} + \frac{1}{2}$ b $\frac{1}{2} + \frac{1}{4}$ c $\frac{1}{4} + \frac{3}{8}$ d $\frac{5}{6} + \frac{6}{10}$

e $\frac{5}{8} - \frac{1}{4}$ f $\frac{7}{9} - \frac{1}{3}$ g $\frac{3}{4} + \frac{2}{5}$ h $\frac{3}{4} - \frac{1}{3}$

i $\frac{4}{5} - \frac{1}{3}$ j $\frac{4}{5} - \frac{3}{10}$ k $\frac{3}{4} + \frac{1}{6}$ l $\frac{4}{9} - \frac{1}{4}$

m $\frac{2}{3} - \frac{3}{10}$ n $\frac{7}{8} - \frac{3}{5}$ o $\frac{1}{4} - \frac{1}{5}$ p $\frac{13}{2} - \frac{8}{5}$

4 Simplify:

a $2\frac{3}{4} + 2\frac{1}{2}$ b $1\frac{3}{4} - 1\frac{1}{3}$ c $2\frac{7}{8} + 1\frac{3}{5}$ d $3\frac{7}{10} + 2\frac{9}{11}$

e $4\frac{3}{4} + 1\frac{5}{6}$ f $8\frac{2}{5} - 3\frac{1}{2}$ g $7\frac{1}{4} - 2\frac{9}{10}$ h $9\frac{3}{7} - 2\frac{4}{5}$

i $6\frac{3}{5} - 1\frac{11}{13}$ j $2\frac{11}{20} - 1\frac{9}{10}$ k $8 - 2\frac{3}{4}$ l $9\frac{3}{5} - 7\frac{1}{2}$

5 a Which expression is equivalent to $\frac{2}{3} \div \frac{1}{4}$?

Choose your answer from the following options.

A $\frac{2}{3} \times \frac{1}{4}$ B $\frac{3}{2} \times \frac{1}{4}$ C $\frac{2}{3} \times \frac{4}{1}$ D $\frac{3}{2} \times \frac{4}{1}$

b Which expression is equivalent to $\frac{5}{8} \div 3\frac{3}{4}$?

Choose the correct answer from the options below.

A $\frac{1}{8}$ B $\frac{1}{6}$ C $\frac{1}{4}$ D $\frac{1}{3}$

6 Simplify:

a $\frac{1}{4} \div \frac{1}{4}$ b $\frac{1}{2} \div \frac{1}{4}$ c $\frac{1}{5} \div \frac{2}{7}$ d $\frac{-6}{7} \div \frac{2}{5}$

e $\frac{1}{8} \div \frac{7}{9}$ f $\frac{2}{11} \div \frac{-3}{5}$ g $\frac{5}{9} \div \frac{3}{7}$ h $\frac{-5}{12} \div \frac{-1}{2}$

i $\frac{3}{4} \div -2\frac{1}{3}$ j $2\frac{1}{2} \div \frac{2}{5}$ k $3\frac{1}{5} \div 2\frac{1}{2}$ l $1\frac{7}{8} \div 2\frac{3}{4}$

7 Calculate:

a $4 + \frac{2}{3} \times \frac{1}{3}$ b $2\frac{1}{8} - (2\frac{1}{5} - \frac{7}{8})$ c $\frac{3}{7} \times (\frac{2}{3} + 6 \div \frac{2}{3}) + 5 \times \frac{2}{7}$

d $2\frac{7}{8} + (8\frac{1}{4} - 6\frac{3}{8})$ e $\frac{5}{6} \times \frac{1}{4} + \frac{5}{8} \times \frac{1}{3}$ f $(5 \div \frac{3}{11} - \frac{5}{12}) \times \frac{1}{6}$

g $(\frac{5}{8} \div \frac{15}{4}) - (\frac{5}{6} \times \frac{1}{5})$ h $(2\frac{2}{3} \div 4 - \frac{3}{10}) \times \frac{3}{17}$ i $(7 \div \frac{2}{9} - \frac{1}{3}) \times \frac{2}{3}$

Tip

Remember that the rules for order of operations apply to fractions as well. Simplify brackets first, then powers, then multiplication and/or division, then addition and/or subtraction. When there is more than one set of brackets, work from the inner ones to the outer ones.

EXERCISE 5C

1 A petrol tank holds 55 litres and is $\frac{3}{4}$ full.

How many litres are in the tank?

Choose your answer from the options below.

A $13\frac{3}{4}$ B $18\frac{1}{3}$ C $41\frac{1}{4}$ D $73\frac{1}{3}$

2 Nicci buys a 4 kg packet of nuts and raisins, and she notices that $\frac{3}{8}$ of the contents are raisins.

How many kilograms of nuts were there in the packet?

3 It takes $\frac{3}{4}$ of an hour to climb 50 steps.

How long does it take to climb 460 steps at this speed?

Choose your answer from the options below.

A $10\frac{4}{15}$ hours   B $6\frac{9}{10}$ hours   C $\frac{15}{4}$ hours   D $6\frac{1}{2}$ hours

4 Jo eats 8 packets of crisps each week. Nick eats $1\frac{3}{4}$ times as many packets.

How many packets do they eat altogether?

5 Kevin is a deep-sea diver.

He spends:

$9\frac{3}{4}$ minutes swimming to a wreck

$12\frac{5}{6}$ minutes exploring the wreck

and $3\frac{5}{6}$ minutes examining corals.

How much time has he spent underwater in total?

6 At a conference, $\frac{5}{12}$ of the people are from Britain.

$\frac{3}{16}$ are from India.

$\frac{7}{24}$ are from Brazil.

The rest are from Malaysia.

a What fraction of the people at the conference are from Malaysia?

b Which country has most people at the conference?

c Which country has the fewest people at the conference?

d The Indian delegation leaves the conference a day before everyone else. What fraction of the original number of people is left?

7 In a café, $\frac{1}{4}$ of the customers order coffee and $\frac{2}{5}$ order tea.

The rest of the customers order juice.

a What fraction of the customers order hot drinks?

b What fraction of the customers order juice?

8 A litre carton of milk is $\frac{3}{4}$ full.

Sandra uses $\frac{1}{3}$ of a litre to make breakfast.

What fraction of a litre is left?

9 Mrs Smith spends $\frac{1}{4}$ of her wages on rent and $\frac{2}{5}$ on other expenses.
What fraction does she have left?

10 There are $1\frac{3}{4}$ cakes left over after a party.
These are shared out equally among 6 people.
What fraction of a cake does each person get?

11 A container holds $5\frac{2}{3}$ litres of juice.
Each cup in a set holds $\frac{2}{15}$ of a litre.
How many cups will the container fill?

12 Nico buys 6 trays of chicken pieces for his restaurant.
Each tray contains $2\frac{1}{2}$ kg of chicken.
Each chicken meal he serves uses $\frac{3}{8}$ kg of chicken.
How many chicken meals can he serve?

Section 3: Fractions of quantities

When you see the word 'of' in a fraction problem, replace it with × and do the multiplication as you would normally.

For example, half of £50 is the same as $\frac{1}{2} \times 50 = \frac{50}{2} = 25$

WORKED EXAMPLE 5

Lisa makes 220 phone calls in a month.
$\frac{4}{5}$ of the calls are for business.
How many business calls did she make?

$\frac{4}{5} \times \frac{220}{1} = \frac{880}{5} = 176$ calls $\qquad$ Multiply by $\frac{4}{5}$ to get the answer.

Expressing one quantity as a fraction of another

The numerator in a fraction tells you how many parts of the whole quantity you are dealing with.

The denominator represents the whole quantity.

So, the fraction $\frac{3}{5}$ means you are dealing with 3 parts of the 5 parts that make up the whole.

Find answers at: cambridge.org/ukschools/gcsemaths-studentbookanswers

To write a quantity as a fraction of another quantity make sure the two quantities are in the same units and then write them as a fraction and simplify.

WORKED EXAMPLE 6

a What fraction is 20 minutes of 1 hour?

b Express 35 centimetres as a fraction of a metre.

a 20 minutes is the part of the whole, so it is the numerator.

The hour is the whole, so it is the denominator.

20 minutes is part of 60 minutes: $\frac{20}{60} = \frac{2}{6} = \frac{1}{3}$

20 minutes is $\frac{1}{3}$ of an hour.

> Decide which time is the numerator and which is the denominator.
>
> You cannot form a fraction using one unit for the numerator and another for the denominator, so you need to convert the hour to minutes.

b 35 cm is the part of the whole, so it is the numerator.

The metre is the whole, so it is the denominator.

35 cm is part of 100 cm: $\frac{35}{100} = \frac{7}{20}$

35 cm is $\frac{7}{20}$ of a metre.

> You cannot use centimetres and metres in the same fraction, so you convert 1 m to 100 cm.

EXERCISE 5D

1 Calculate:

a $\frac{3}{4}$ of 12　　b $\frac{1}{3}$ of 45　　c $\frac{2}{9}$ of 36　　d $\frac{3}{8}$ of 144

e $\frac{4}{5}$ of 180　　f $\frac{1}{3}$ of 96　　g $\frac{1}{2}$ of $\frac{3}{4}$　　h $\frac{1}{3}$ of $\frac{3}{10}$

i $\frac{4}{9}$ of $\frac{3}{14}$　　j $\frac{1}{4}$ of $2\frac{1}{2}$　　k $\frac{3}{4}$ of $2\frac{1}{3}$　　l $\frac{5}{6}$ of $3\frac{1}{2}$

2 Choose your answer from the options given.

a What is $\frac{7}{12}$ of 768?

　A 64　　　B $109\frac{7}{12}$　　　C 448　　　D $537\frac{1}{2}$

b How many minutes is $\frac{3}{2}$ of $2\frac{3}{10}$ hours?

　A 204 min　　B 205 min　　C 206 min　　D 207 min

3 Calculate the following quantities.

a $\frac{3}{2}$ of £28　　　　　b $\frac{3}{5}$ of £210　　　　c $\frac{2}{5}$ of £30

d $\frac{2}{3}$ of £18　　　　　e $\frac{1}{2}$ of 3 cups of sugar　f $\frac{1}{2}$ of 5 cups of flour

g $\frac{1}{2}$ of $1\frac{1}{2}$ cups of sugar　h $\frac{3}{4}$ of $2\frac{1}{3}$ cups of flour　i $\frac{2}{3}$ of $1\frac{1}{2}$ cups of sugar

j $\frac{2}{3}$ of 4 hours　　　k $\frac{1}{3}$ of $2\frac{1}{2}$ hours　　　l $\frac{3}{4}$ of 5 hours

m $\frac{1}{3}$ of $\frac{3}{4}$ of an hour　n $\frac{2}{3}$ of $3\frac{1}{2}$ minutes　　o $\frac{3}{15}$ of a minute

4 Express the first quantity as a fraction of the second.

a 12p of every £1

b 35 cm of a 2 m length

c 12 mm of 30 cm

d 45 minutes per 8 hour shift

e 5 minutes per hour

f 150 m of a kilometre

g 45 seconds of 30 minutes

h 575 ml of 4 litres

5 James earns £18 000 per year. His friend Samir earns £24 000 per year.

What fraction of Samir's salary does James earn?

6 The area of the floor in a room is 12 m².

Pete buys a rug that is 110 cm wide and 160 cm long.

What fraction of the area of the floor will be covered by this rug?

7 In a Year 10 group, $\frac{1}{3}$ of the students like maths. Of those who like maths, $\frac{1}{3}$ also like music.

What fraction of the Year 10 group likes music?

8 Jess spent $1\frac{3}{5}$ hours online in four days.

If she spends the same amount of time online each day, how many minutes does she spend online?

Checklist of learning and understanding

Equivalent fractions

- Fractions that represent the same amount are called equivalent fractions.
- You can change fractions to their equivalents by multiplying the numerator and denominator by the same value or by dividing the numerator and denominator by the same value (simplifying).

Operations on fractions

- To add or subtract fractions, find equivalent fractions with the same denominator.
- Add or subtract the numerators once the denominators are the same. Do not add or subtract denominators.
- To multiply fractions, multiply numerators by numerators and denominators by denominators.
- To divide fractions, multiply by the reciprocal of the divisor.

Fractions of a quantity

- The word 'of' means multiply.
- A quantity can be written as a fraction of another as long as they are in the same units. Write one quantity as the numerator and the other as the denominator and simplify.

Find answers at: cambridge.org/ukschools/gcsemaths-studentbookanswers

Chapter review

1 What fraction is equivalent to $3\frac{60}{72}$?

Choose your answer from the options below.

A $\frac{138}{72}$ B $\frac{180}{72}$ C $\frac{23}{60}$ D $\frac{23}{6}$

2 Simplify:

a $\frac{15}{90}$ **b** $\frac{195}{230}$ **c** $4\frac{18}{48}$

3 Write each set of fractions in ascending order.

a $\frac{8}{9}, \frac{4}{5}, \frac{5}{6}, \frac{3}{7}$ **b** $2\frac{2}{5}, \frac{23}{7}, 1\frac{3}{5}, \frac{16}{9}$

4 Evaluate:

a $\frac{7}{5} + \frac{3}{8}$ **b** $\frac{7}{5} \times \frac{3}{8}$ **c** $\frac{7}{5} \div \frac{3}{8}$ **d** $3\frac{1}{7} + 2\frac{2}{5}$

e $3\frac{1}{15} - 1\frac{3}{5}$ **f** $\frac{1}{7}$ of $3\frac{3}{12}$ **g** $\frac{2}{7} \times \frac{8}{18} \div 3$ **h** $28 \div \frac{3}{4}$

5 Simplify:

a $\left(\frac{3}{8} \div \frac{13}{4}\right) + \left(\frac{5}{9} \times \frac{3}{5}\right)$ **b** $2\frac{2}{3} \times \left(8 \div \frac{4}{7} + \frac{7}{8}\right)$

6 Express $425\,\text{g}$ as a fraction of $2\frac{1}{2}\,\text{kg}$.

7 Sandy has $12\frac{1}{2}$ litres of water.

How many bottles containing $\frac{3}{4}$ litre can she fill?

8 A surveyor has to divide a $15\,\text{km}^2$ area of land into equal plots each measuring $\frac{1}{2}\,\text{km}^2$.

How many plots can she make?

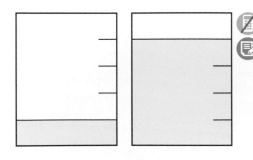

9 When a jug is $\frac{1}{5}$ full of water it weighs 250 grams.

When the same jug is $\frac{4}{5}$ full of water it weighs 550 grams.

How much does the jug weigh when it is empty?   *(4 marks)*

© AQA 2013

10 A fruit drink is made by mixing concentrated squash with water. $\frac{7}{9}$ of the fruit drink is water.

How many litres of water will there be in 15 litres of the fruit drink?

11 Andy uses 2 cups of flour to make 12 muffins.

How many cups of flour would he need to make 20 muffins?

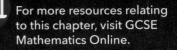

In this chapter you will learn how to …

- express decimals as fractions and fractions as decimals.
- convert decimals to fractions and fractions to decimals.
- order fractions and decimals.
- carry out the four basic operations on decimals without using a calculator.
- solve problems involving decimal quantities.

For more resources relating to this chapter, visit GCSE Mathematics Online.

Using mathematics: real-life applications

Food technologists analyse the contents of different raw and prepared foods to work out what they contain and how much there is of each ingredient. For example, how much water, protein and fat there is in a cut of meat. They use decimal fractions to give the quantities correct to tenths, hundredths or even smaller parts of a gram.

> Tip
>
> You might already know most of the concepts in this chapter. They have been included so that you can revise concepts if you need to and check that you know them well.

"The laws about labelling food are fairly strict. Manufacturers need to state exactly what is in their product and give exact amounts of different ingredients so I have to measure things very accurately."

(Food technologist)

Before you start …

KS3	You need to be able to work confidently with place value.	1	130.098 0.0398 300.098 0.98308 19.308 Choose the number from the box that has a 3 in the: **a** hundreds position **b** hundredths position **c** tenths position **d** thousandths position **e** tens position.
KS3	Check that you can compare decimal fractions and order them by size.	2	Fill in <, = or > between each pair of decimal fractions. **a** 0.65 ☐ 0.7 **b** 0.08 ☐ 0.01 **c** 0.8 ☐ 0.85 **d** 2.87 ☐ 0.99 **e** 4.230 ☐ 4.23
KS3	You need to know the fractional equivalents of some common decimals.	3	Make equivalent pairs by matching the decimals in the top row of the box with the fractions in the bottom row of the box.

a 0.25	**b** 0.375	**c** 0.4	**d** 0.75	**e** 0.5	**f** 0.025
$\frac{2}{5}$	$\frac{3}{4}$	$\frac{45}{90}$	$\frac{1}{40}$	$\frac{4}{16}$	$\frac{3}{8}$

Find answers at: cambridge.org/ukschools/gcsemaths-studentbookanswers

Assess your starting point using the Launchpad

STEP 1

1 Write a decimal that is between:

    a 2.15 and 2.16

    b 2.155 and 2.156

    c 0.6753 and 0.6754

2 Write the red digit in each number as a fraction with a denominator of 10, 100 or 1000.

    a 3.0987

    b 12.342

    c 0.8865

3 Which is greater in each pair?

    a 3.14 or $3\frac{1}{4}$

    b 0.78 or $\frac{8}{9}$

    c $\frac{10}{11}$ or 0.99

GO TO
Section 1:
Review of decimals and fractions

STEP 2

4 Choose the correct answer for each calculation.

Calculation	Possible answers		
a 24 − 2.35	A 2.165	B 216.5	C 21.65
b 19.5 − 3.45	A 16.5	B 1.605	C 16.05
c 2.25 × 3	A 675	B 67.5	C 6.75
d 18.32 × 4	A 732.8	B 73.28	C 7.328
e 7.488 ÷ 6	A 1.248	B 12.48	C 124.8
f 58.35 ÷ 3	A 0.1945	B 1.945	C 19.45

GO TO
Section 2:
Calculating with decimals

GO TO
Chapter review

Section 1: Review of decimals and fractions

The table shows the results of the men's 4 × 100 m relay final at the 2010 Commonwealth Games in New Delhi.

Five teams completed the race.

Team	Time (seconds)
Australia	39.14
Bahamas	39.27
England	38.74
India	38.89
Jamaica	38.79

Comparing decimals

To write the times in order from fastest to slowest, compare the whole number parts of each time first. If those are the same, compare the decimal parts.

England, India and Jamaica ran the relay in 38 seconds and a fraction of a second.

To decide first, second and third places, you need to look at the decimal parts.

Here are the times written in a place value table.

	Tens	Ones/units	.	Tenths	Hundredths
England	3	8	.	7	4
India	3	8	.	8	9
Jamaica	3	8	.	7	9

Start by comparing the tenths, and then the hundredths.

India has the highest number in the tenths place so India came third.

England and Jamaica both have 7 in the tenths place so compare the hundredths.

England has 4 in the hundredths and Jamaica has 9. This means that England was faster.

The places were: England (1st), Jamaica (2nd) and India (3rd), followed by Australia then the Bahamas.

 Tip

Remember you are comparing winning times, so you are looking for the smallest fraction of a second as this is the fastest time. The greater the fraction, the slower the team ran.

Converting decimals to fractions

England ran the relay in 38 seconds and $\frac{74}{100}$ of a second.

Tens	Ones/units	.	Tenths	Hundredths
3	8	.	7	4

The fraction can be simplified further: $\frac{74}{100} = \frac{37}{50}$

Any decimal can be converted to a fraction in this way. For example:

$$0.6 = \frac{6}{10} = \frac{3}{5} \qquad 0.25 = \frac{25}{100} = \frac{1}{4} \qquad 0.375 = \frac{375}{1000} = \frac{3}{8}$$

Converting fractions to decimals

Fractions can be converted to decimals. There are different methods of doing this and you should choose the method that is easiest for the fraction involved.

Method 1: Equivalent fractions with denominators of 10, 100, 1000, and so on.	**Method 2:** Pen and paper division.	**Method 3:** Calculator division.
Express $\frac{61}{125}$ as a decimal. $$\frac{61}{125} = \frac{122}{250} = \frac{244}{500} = \frac{488}{1000}$$ $$\frac{61}{125} = 0.488$$ This method works well if the denominator is a factor of 10, 100 or 1000.	Express $\frac{5}{8}$ as a decimal. Work out $5 \div 8$ using division.	Express $\frac{2}{3}$ as a decimal. Input $2 \div 3$ on your calculator. 0.666666666 The 6s continue forever (they recur) show this by writing the answer as $0.\dot{6}$. **Tip** Remember you write a dot above the first and last digit of the recurring numbers if more than one digit recurs.

Tip

When you have to compare and order ordinary fractions you can convert them all to decimals and compare them easily using place value. This is often quicker than changing them all into equivalent fractions with a common denominator.

EXERCISE 6A

1 Which of the following decimals is equivalent to $\frac{6}{24}$?

    A 0.12   B 0.25   C 0.3   D 0.144

2 Write each of the following decimals as a fraction in its simplest form.

    a 0.6   **b** 0.84   **c** 1.64   **d** 0.385   **e** 0.125

    f 1.08   **g** 0.875   **h** 0.008   **i** 3.064   **j** 0.333

3 Convert the following fractions to decimals without using a calculator.

    a $\frac{3}{5}$ **b** $\frac{3}{4}$ **c** $\frac{18}{25}$ **d** $\frac{19}{20}$ **e** $\frac{34}{50}$

    f $\frac{110}{250}$ **g** $\frac{89}{200}$ **h** $\frac{76}{500}$ **i** $\frac{185}{20}$ **j** $\frac{145}{50}$

    k $\frac{11}{6}$ **l** $\frac{3}{8}$ **m** $\frac{9}{4}$ **n** $\frac{8}{9}$ **o** $\frac{19}{8}$

4 Use a calculator to convert the fractions from $\frac{1}{9}$ to $\frac{8}{9}$ into decimals.

    a What pattern do you notice?

    b What is the mathematical name for this type of decimal?

    c Repeat this for the fractions from $\frac{1}{6}$ to $\frac{5}{6}$.

    d Convert $\frac{1}{11}$ and $\frac{2}{11}$ to decimals.

    e Predict what $\frac{3}{11}$ and $\frac{4}{11}$ will be if you convert them to decimals.
        Check your prediction using a calculator.

5 Arrange the following sets of numbers in order from largest to smallest.

    a 5.2, 5.29, 8.62, 4.92, 4.09   **b** 7.42, 0.76, 0.742, 0.421, 3.219

    c 14.3, 14.72, 14.07, 14.89, 14.009   **d** 0.23, 0.26, 0.273, 0.287, 0.206

    e 0.403, $\frac{1}{2}$, $\frac{2}{3}$, 0.68, 0.45, $\frac{5}{11}$ **f** $\frac{7}{9}$, $\frac{3}{8}$, 0.625, 0.88, 0.718

6 Copy and fill in the boxes using < , = or > to make each statement true.

    a 13.098 ☐ 13.099   **b** 0.312 ☐ 0.322   **c** $\frac{5}{6}$ ☐ 0.84

    d 0.375 ☐ $\frac{3}{8}$ **e** 2.05 ☐ $\frac{205}{1000}$ **f** $\frac{3}{5}$ ☐ 0.7

    g $\frac{2}{5}$ ☐ 0.35   **h** $\frac{18}{25}$ ☐ 0.67   **i** $\frac{1}{3}$ ☐ 0.37

7 Write a decimal fraction that is between each pair of decimals.

    a 3.135 and 3.136   **b** 0.6645 and 06646   **c** 4.998 and 4.999

8 The lengths of some roller coaster rides are given in the table.

Roller coaster	Length of ride (km)
The Beast	2.243
California Screaming	1.851
Formula Rossa	2.0
Fujiyama	2.045
Steel Dragon	2.479
The Ultimate	2.268

a Which is the longest roller coaster?

b Which is the shortest roller coaster?

c Is the Steel Dragon longer or shorter than $2\frac{1}{2}$ km?

d Which roller coasters are longer than $2\frac{1}{4}$ km?

e Write the lengths in order from longest to shortest.

Section 2: Calculating with decimals

You need to be able to add, subtract, multiply and divide decimals without using a calculator.

Estimating and reasoning

When you calculate with decimals it is useful to estimate the answer.

An estimate helps you decide whether your solution is reasonable and whether you have the decimal point in the correct place.

EXERCISE 6B

For each of the following problems:

Write down your estimate of the answer.

Write down what you did to estimate your answer.

1 The masses of some coins are given below.

7.1 g   6.6 g   8.1 g   9.5 g

a What is the approximate difference in mass between the heaviest and lightest coins?

b Find the approximate total mass of the four coins.

c What is the approximate total mass of a £1 coin and two 10p coins?

d Jan has five £1 coins in his pocket. Approximately how much do they weigh altogether?

e Xena has a packet of 50p coins that weighs 162 grams.

Approximately how many coins are in the packet?

f Do ten 10p coins weigh more or less than six £1 coins?

g Ana has twenty 2p coins. Ben has twenty 10p coins.

What is the approximate difference in the mass of the two sets of coins?

2 A bottle of medicine contains 0.375 litre and costs £2.55.

a Is it possible to buy two bottles for £5?

b About how many litres of medicine fills 5 bottles?

c Estimate how many bottles are filled with 1 litre of the medicine.

d Tanja has to take 15 ml of the medicine twice a day.

Approximately how long will the bottle last?

e Nina buys two bottle of the medicine and pays with a £20 note.

Estimate how much change she should get.

f In one day, the pharmacy sold 23 bottles of this medicine.

Write down whether this makes up more or less than 5 litres of medicine in total.

g What is the approximate cost per 100 ml of the medicine?

3 Compare your work with a partner.

a Write down what you did to estimate the answers.

How did you use rounding and approximation?

How did you decide what to do?

b Look at your answers.

Did you get the same estimates? If not, is one estimate closer than the other?

Give reasons why this is.

Adding and subtracting decimals

Add or subtract decimals in columns by lining up the places and decimal points.

WORKED EXAMPLE 1

Calculate:

a 12.7 + 18.34 + 3.087   **b** 399.65 − 245.175

a
```
  12.7
  18.34
+  3.087
 34.127
```
Make sure you line up the decimal points and the place values correctly or you will get the wrong answer.

b
```
  399.650
− 245.175
  154.475
```
Write an 0 as a place holder here.

 Find answers at: cambridge.org/ukschools/gcsemaths-studentbookanswers

Multiplying and dividing decimals

Andy made the following notes about multiplying and dividing decimals when he was studying for exams at the end of last year.

- When multiplying or dividing by a power of 10 (10, 100, 1000, etc):

  Move the digits as many places to the left as the number of zeros when multiplying.

  Move the digits as many places to the right as the number of zeros when dividing.

- When multiplying decimal fractions by decimal fractions:

  Ignore the decimal points and multiply the numbers.

  Place the decimal point in the answer so it has the same name number of digits after the decimal point as there were altogether in the multiplication problem.

- When dividing by a decimal:

  Make the divisor a whole number by multiplying the divisor and the dividend (number you are dividing into) by the same power of 10.

  Then divide as normal, keeping the decimal point in the answer directly above the decimal point in the number you are dividing.

EXERCISE 6C

1 Work with a partner.

   a Read through Andy's summary notes.

   b Provide one or two examples for each summary point using numbers to show what he means.

   c Write your own summary point for dividing a decimal by a whole number.

   Include two examples that show what you mean.

2 Use a place value chart and provide some examples to show why you can multiply and divide decimals in the way Andy has summarised.

EXERCISE 6D

1 Which of the following is a sensible estimate for the calculation 16.34×1.8?

   A 24.75　　　　　B 30　　　　　C 35　　　　　D 40

2 Estimate the answer then calculate:

   a $0.8 + 0.78$　　　　　**b** $12.8 - 11.13$　　　　　**c** $0.8 + 0.9$

   d $15.31 - 1.96$　　　　　**e** 2.77×8.2　　　　　**f** 9.81×3.5

3 Evaluate without a calculator:

a $12.7 + 18.34 + 35.01$ **b** $12.35 + 8.5 + 2.91$ **c** $6.89 - 3.28$

d $34.45 - 12.02$ **e** $345.297 - 12.39$ **f** $56 + 8.345 - 34.65$

g $27.4 + 9.01 - 12.451$ **h** 0.786×100 **i** 54.76×2000

j 1.234×0.65 **k** 87.87×2.34 **l** $1.83 \div 61$

m $0.358 \div 4$ **n** $5.053 \div 0.62$ **o** $31.72 \div 0.04$

4 The world record for the men's 4×100 m relay is 36.84 seconds (Jamaica, 2012).

The Commonwealth Games record is 37.58 seconds (Jamaica, 2014).

a What is the time difference between the world record and the Commonwealth Games record?

b In the 2014 Commonwealth Games, the English team won silver and ran the relay in 38.02 seconds.

How much slower is this than the Commonwealth record?

c Each of the four runners in a relay runs 100 m.

Calculate the average time taken to run 100 m during the world record winning race.

d Does each runner take the same amount of time? Give reasons for your answer.

5 Nadia makes a dish that requires 1.5 litres of cream.

She has four 0.385 litre cartons of cream.

Does she have enough cream?

6 Jai takes a multivitamin every morning.

He calculates that if he takes one tablet every day for a week he will take in:

1166.69 g of vitamin C,

54.6 mg of boron, and

257.95 mg of calcium.

Work out how much of each ingredient there is in a tablet.

7 The Chetty household uses about 25.75 kilowatt-hours of electricity per day.

Calculate how much they will use in:

a one week **b** one year (not a leap year).

When working with decimals you need to make sure that your answer is reasonable and sensible in the context.

For example, if you get an answer of £15.987, it makes sense to round it to £15.99 because we don't have coins smaller than 1p (a hundredth of a pound).

Problem-solving framework

Salman had £20 to go and see an exhibition.

His train ticket cost £6.35.

The ticket for the exhibition was £8.00.

He bought an exhibition booklet for £2.50.

He spent £1.55 on a snack.

How much money did he have left?

Steps for solving problems	What you would do for this example
Step 1: Work out what you have to do. Start by reading the question carefully.	The words 'how much does he have left' tell you that you need to find the change. So you have to add up what Salman spent and then subtract it from the money he had.
Step 2: What information do you need? Have you got it all?	You need the starting amount and how much he spent. You have that information.
Step 3: Is there any information that you don't need?	You don't need to know where he went or what he spent the money on. That detail is unnecessary.
Step 3: Decide what maths you can use.	You can add up the amounts he spent. You can then subtract the total spending from £20.
Step 4: Set out your solution clearly. Check your working and that your answer is reasonable.	$\begin{array}{r} 6.35 \\ 8.00 \\ 2.50 \\ + 1.55 \\ \hline 18.40 \\ 20.00 \\ - 18.40 \\ \hline 1.60 \end{array}$
Step 5: Check that you have answered the question.	Salman has £1.60 left over.

EXERCISE 6E

You may use a calculator in this exercise.

1 Sandra has £87.50 in her purse.

She buys two jumpers that cost £32.99 each.

How much money does she have left? Choose from the options below.

A £21.52   B £30.00   C £54.51   D £153.48

2 George travels from York to Oxford by car.

His odometer (device that measures distance) reads 123 456.8 km when he leaves York and 123 642.7 km when he arrives in Oxford.

How far did he travel? Give your answer in km.

3 A container holds 5.67 litres of juice.

How many cups containing $\frac{2}{15}$ of a litre each does this fill?

4 Find 0.75 of 2400.

5 Sheldon wants to place fence posts 0.84 m apart along his boundary fence.

The fence is 60 metres long.

How many posts does he need?

6 Jamil bought 6.65 litres of petrol at £1.29 per litre.

What is the total cost of the petrol?

7 Toni earns £28 650 per year.

  a How much is this per day? Remember there are 365.25 days in a year.

  b How much is this per five-day week? Give your answer to two decimal places.

  c If Toni is paid the amount in part **b** every week for 52 weeks of a year, will she earn more or less than the original total? Give a reason for your answer.

 Checklist of learning and understanding

Decimals and fractions

- You can express decimals as fractions by writing them with a denominator that is a power of ten and then simplifying them. For example, $0.4 = \frac{4}{10} = \frac{2}{5}$

- You can change fractions to decimals by dividing the numerator by the denominator. For example, $\frac{3}{4} = 3 \div 4 = 0.75$

- Changing ordinary fractions to decimals makes it easier to compare their sizes using place value.

Calculations with decimals

- Pen and paper methods are important in the non-calculator exam paper.
- You can use any method as long as you show your working.
- Decimals can be added and subtracted by lining up the places and the decimal points.
- Decimals can be multiplied like whole numbers. You need to insert the decimal point so there are the same number of decimal places in the answer as there were altogether in the numbers being multiplied.
- Decimals can be divided by making the divisor a whole number (multiply both numbers by a power of ten to do this). Then divide as normal, keeping the decimal point in the answer directly above the decimal point in the number you are dividing.

 For additional questions on the topics in this chapter, visit GCSE Mathematics Online.

Chapter review

1 Arrange each set of numbers in order from smallest to largest.

   a 4.2, 4.8, 4.22, 4.97, 4.08

   b 2.96, 2.955, $2\frac{46}{50}$, $2\frac{9}{25}$, 2.12

   c $\frac{3}{4}$, 0.86, $\frac{4}{5}$, 0.78, $\frac{5}{6}$, 0.91

2 Here are four rods.   A   B   C   D

   a Which rod is the longest?   3.4 m $3\frac{1}{4}$ m   3.35 m   3.1 m

         Not drawn accurately

         (1 mark)

   b Work out the total length of rod C and rod D.   *(1 mark)*

   c Which three rods have a total length of 10 metres?   *(2 marks)*

         © *AQA 2013*

3 Convert each fraction to a decimal and insert <, = or > to compare them.

   a $\frac{3}{5}\,\square\,\frac{12}{30}$ **b** $\frac{5}{6}\,\square\,\frac{7}{11}$ **c** $\frac{2}{9}\,\square\,\frac{1}{3}$

4 Write each as a fraction in its simplest form.

   a 0.88   **b** 2.75   **c** 0.008

5 **a** Increase $\frac{2}{5}$ by 2.75   **b** Reduce 91.07 by half of 42.8

   c Divide 4 by 0.125   **d** Multiply 0.4 by 0.8

6 **a** Add 4.726 and 3.09   **b** Subtract 2.916 from 4.008

   c Multiply 8.76 by 100   **d** Divide 18.07 by 1000

   e Multiply 4.12 by 0.7   **f** Simplify $\frac{32.64}{2.4}$

7 Jarryd and Kate have £16 each. Jarryd spends 0.416 of his money and Kate spends $\frac{4}{15}$ of hers.

   Who has the most money left? How much more?

8 Mike had a 0.75 litre tin of varnish. He used half of the tin on his desk and 0.3 of the tin on a small table.

   What fraction of the varnish was left over?

7 Basic algebra

In this chapter you will learn how to ...

- use algebraic notation and write algebraic expressions.
- simplify and manipulate algebraic expressions.
- use common factors to factorise expressions.
- use algebra to solve problems in different contexts.

 For more resources relating to this chapter, visit GCSE Mathematics Online.

Using mathematics: real-life applications

Algebra lets you describe and represent patterns using concise mathematical language.

This is useful in many different careers including accounting, navigation, building, plumbing, health, medicine, science and computing.

"You are unlikely to think about algebra when you watch cartoons or play video games, but animators use complex algebra to program the characters and make objects move." *(Games designer)*

Before you start ...

KS3	You need to understand the basic conventions of algebra.	**1** Choose the correct way to write each of these.
		
		 a $n \times n$
		
		     A $2n$ B n^2 C 2^n D $2(n)$
		
		 b c multiplied by 3 and then added to 5
		
		     A $3c + 5$ B $3(c + 5)$ C $c + 15$
		
		 c n squared and then multiplied by 2
		
		     A $2n^2$ B $(2n)^2$ C $4n^2$

KS3	You should be able to substitute numbers for letters and evaluate expressions.	**2** **a** Evaluate the following expressions for $n = 5$ and $n = -5$. **i** $3n + 4$ **ii** $3(n + 4)$ **b** What is the value of $\dfrac{(2 + 4)^2}{6}$?
Ch 4	You should be able to find the highest common factor in a group of terms.	**3** Write down the HCF of: **a** $12xy$ and $18y^2$ **b** $45x$ and $50xy$

Find answers at: cambridge.org/ukschools/gcsemaths-studentbookanswers

Assess your starting point using the Launchpad

STEP 1

1 Use the correct notation and conventions to write each statement as an algebraic expression.

a Multiply n by 3 and add 4 to the result.

b Subtract 4 from n and multiply the result by 3.

c Multiply n squared by 4, add 3 and divide the result by 2.

GO TO
Section 1:
Algebraic notation

STEP 2

2 Simplify these expressions by collecting like terms.

a $3a + 2b + 2a - b$ **b** $4x + 7 + 3x - 3 - x$

c $4a^2 + 8ab - 10a^2 - 5ab$

GO TO
Section 2:
Simplifying expressions

STEP 3

3 Expand and simplify:

a $m(n - p)$ **b** $3(x + 5) + 4(x + 2)$ **c** $2z(z + 4) - z(z + 5)$

GO TO
Section 3:
Expanding brackets

STEP 4

4 Complete the following.

a $3x + 12 = \square(x + 4)$ **b** $5x + 10y = \square(x + 2y)$

c $x^2 - 3x = \square(x - 3)$ **d** $ab - ac = a(\square - \square)$

e $-x + 7x^2 = -x(\square\square\square)$

5 Factorise each expression.

a $2x + 4y$ **b** $-3x - 9$ **c** $5x + 5y$

GO TO
Section 4:
Factorising expressions
Section 5:
Solving problems using algebra

GO TO
Chapter review

Section 1: Algebraic notation

In algebra you use letters to represent unknown numbers.

For example: $x + y = 20$

The letters can represent many different values so they are called **variables**.

Letters and numbers can be combined and linked together with operation signs to form **expressions** such as $5a^3 - 2xy + 3$.

This expression has three **terms**.

The sign belongs with the term that follows it.

Terms should always be written in the simplest way:

You write $a \times b$ as ab and $5 \times z$ as $5z$

$2 \times h$ is written as $2h$

$x \times x \times y$ is written as x^2y

$4x \div 3$ is written as $\dfrac{4x}{3}$

$(x + 4) \div 2$ is written as $\dfrac{x + 4}{2}$

The symbol $\equiv$ means exactly the same as, or identical to. The following are examples of **identities**.

$a \times b \equiv ab$ and $5 \times z \equiv 5z$

$a \div b \equiv \dfrac{a}{b}$ and $5 \div z \equiv \dfrac{5}{z}$

Key vocabulary

variable: a letter representing an unknown number

expression: a group of numbers and letters linked by operation signs

term: a combination of letters and/or numbers

identity: an equation that is true no matter what values are chosen for the variables

Tip

When you have numbers and letters in a term, the number is written first and the letters are usually written in alphabetical order.

So, you write $5x$ not $x5$ and $3xy$ not $3yx$.

EXERCISE 7A

1 **a** Write down whether each of the following is true or false.

   i $2n \equiv n + 2$ **ii** $2n \equiv n + n$ **iii** $2n \equiv n^2$ **iv** $2n^2 \equiv (2n)^2$

  b What is the value of n other than $n = 0$ where $2n = n^2$?

2 A number x is squared and divided by 3.

How is this written?

Choose from the following options.

A $\dfrac{3}{x^2}$ B $\dfrac{2x}{3}$ C $3x^2$ D $\dfrac{x^2}{3}$

3 Write the algebraic expression for:

  a x multiplied by 3 and added to y multiplied by 7

  b 4 subtracted from x squared and the result multiplied by 5

  c x cubed added to y squared and the result divided by 4

  d 6 added to x and the result multiplied by 4, then minus y

  e x multiplied by itself and then divided by 2.

4 Match each statement to the correct algebraic expression.

a Take a number and multiply it by 3, then add 2 to it.	**i**	$\dfrac{6+x}{2}$
b Take a number and add 3 to it, then double it.	**ii**	$3x+2$
c Take a number, multiply it by itself, then add 3 to it.	**iii**	$5(x-4)$
d Add 6 to a number, then divide it by 2.	**iv**	$9x^2$
e Subtract 4 from a number and multiply the result by 5.	**v**	x^2+3
f Square a number, then multiply it by 9.	**vi**	$2x^2-3x^3$
g Square a number and multiply it by 2, then subtract the same number cubed and multiplied by 3.	**vii**	$2(x+3)$

5 Use algebra to write these in their simplest form.

a $2 \times 3a$　　　　　　**b** $4b \times 5$　　　　　　**c** $d \times (-9)$

d $4a \times 3b$　　　　　　**e** $5c \times 2d$　　　　　　**f** $-3m \times 4n$

g $-2p \times (-3q)$　　　　**h** $a \times a$　　　　　　**i** $m \times m$

j $2a \times 4a$　　　　　　**k** $-3a \times 5a$　　　　　**l** $-2m \times (-4m)$

m $7a \times 8ab$　　　　　**n** $-6cd \times (-2de)$　　**o** $2a \times 2a \times 2a$

6 Rewrite each division using algebraic conventions. Simplify them where possible.

a $15x \div 5$　　　　　　**b** $27y \div 3$　　　　　　**c** $24a^2 \div 8$

d $7 \times 15p \div 21$　　　**e** $24x \div (8 \times 3)$　　　**f** $18y \div (6 \times 2)$

g $-18x^2 \div 9$　　　　　**h** $-16a^2 \div (-4)$　　　**i** $15 \div (3 \times n \times n)$

7 Write each of the following in its simplest form.

a $2 \times 5n$　　　　　　**b** $p \times q$　　　　　　**c** $a \times (b+c)$

d $(x+y) \div z$　　　　　**e** $n^2 \times n^3$　　　　　**f** $p^3 \times p$

8 Write expressions to represent the perimeter and area of each shape:

a

b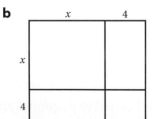

c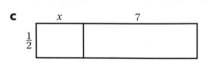

d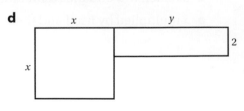

9 A man is x years old.

    a How old will he be ten years from now?

    b How old was he ten years ago?

    c His daughter is a third of his age. How old is his daughter?

Substituting values for unknowns

You can work out the value of an expression if you are told what the letters represent. Working out the value of an expression is called evaluating.

For example, if you know that $x = -2$, then you can work out that:

    $2x + 1 = 2 \times -2 + 1 = -4 + 1 = -3$

Tip

When you substitute values into a term, such as $2y$, you need to remember that $2y$ means $2 \times y$.

So, if $y = 6$, you need to write $2y$ as 2×6 and not as 26.

WORKED EXAMPLE 1

Given that $a = -2$ and $b = 8$, evaluate:

a ab **b** $3b - 2a$ **c** $2a^3$ **d** $2(a + b)$

a $ab = a \times b$
$\quad\quad = -2 \times 8$
$\quad\quad = -16$

In algebra ab is the way we write $a \times b$. To evaluate, replace the letters with the values given and complete the calculation.

Be careful to make sure that the sign of the final answer is correct.

b $3b - 2a = 3 \times b - 2 \times a$
$\quad\quad\quad\quad = 3 \times 8 - 2 \times -2$
$\quad\quad\quad\quad = 24 - (-4)$
$\quad\quad\quad\quad = 28$

Expand the expression and evaluate by substituting values given for the letters a and b.

Be careful with negative signs:

$2 \times -2 = -4$

$-(-4) = 4$

The final answer is $24 + 4 = 28$

c $2a^3 = 2 \times a^3$
$\quad\quad = 2 \times (-2)^3$
$\quad\quad = 2 \times -8$
$\quad\quad = -16$

Expand the expression and make the given substitution for the value of a.

Be careful when cubing a negative value:

$(-2)^3 = -2 \times -2 \times -2 = 4 \times -2 = -8$

d $2(a + b) = 2 \times (a + b)$
$\quad\quad\quad\quad = 2 \times (-2 + 8)$
$\quad\quad\quad\quad = 2 \times 6$
$\quad\quad\quad\quad = 12$

Remember to do the calculation in brackets first.

Tip

Evaluate means to calculate the value of. This word is often used in examination questions.

Tip

Substitution is an important skill. You will need to substitute values for letters when you work with formulae for perimeter, areas and volumes of shapes and when you solve problems involving Pythagoras' theorem.

EXERCISE 7B

1 Given that $x = 3$ and $y = 6$, evaluate these expressions.

a $2x + 3y$ b $3x + 2y$ c $10y - 2x$ d $x + 2y$

e $6x + y$ f $5x - 5y$ g $2xy$ h $\frac{1}{2}xy$

2 Find the value of each expression when $a = -2$ and $b = 5$.

a $-5ab + 10$ b $-3ab - 6$ c $\frac{10}{b}$ d $\frac{400}{a}$

e $\frac{6}{a} - \frac{15}{b}$ f $\frac{15}{b} - \frac{24}{2a}$ g $8 - 2a + 2b$ h $7a - 4 + 2b$

3 An expression has two terms. One term is a number and the letter x and the other term a number and the letter y.

Write two different expressions in x and y, with two terms that evaluate to 37 for given values for x and y. Show by substitution:

a That the values for x and y can be both positive.

b That the values for x and y can be both negative.

Section 2: Simplifying expressions

Adding and subtracting like terms

Like terms have exactly the same letters or combination of letters and powers.

You can simplify expressions by adding or subtracting like terms.

$3a$ and $4a$ are **like** terms.

$3a + 4a = 7a$

$7xy$ and $2xy$ are **like** terms.

$7xy - 2xy = 5xy$

$5x^2$ and $3x^2$ are **like** terms.

$5x^2 - 3x^2 = 2x^2$

$5ab^2$ and $2a^2b$ are **not like** terms so $5ab^2 - 2a^2b$ cannot be simplified further.

When an expression contains many different terms you might be able to simplify it by collecting and combining like terms.

Tip

You should always give an answer in its simplest form, even if the question does not ask you to.

WORKED EXAMPLE 2

Simplify $2x - 4y + 3x + y$

$2x - 4y + 3x + y = 2x + 3x - 4y + y$

> Rearrange the terms so like terms are together.
>
> Keep the signs with the terms they belong to.

$= 5x - 3y$

> Combine the like terms.
> Remember $y = 1y$.

Multiplication and division

WORKED EXAMPLE 3

Simplify   **a** $5 \times 4a$ **b** $2x \times 6y$ **c** $2a^2 \times 7ab$ **d** $12a \div -4$

              e $\dfrac{6x^2}{2}$ **f** $\dfrac{-8xy}{-16}$ **g** $\dfrac{12ab^2}{36ab}$

a $5 \times 4a = 20a$

b $2x \times 6y = 12xy$ Multiply numbers by numbers and write letters in alphabetical order.

c $2a^2 \times 7ab = 14a^3b$ $a^2 = a \times a$, so $a^2 \times a = a \times a \times a = a^3$

d $12a \div -4 = \dfrac{12a}{-4} = -3a$ Write the division as a fraction and reduce it to its lowest terms.

e $\dfrac{6x^2}{2} = 3x^2$ Reduce to lowest terms.

f $\dfrac{-8xy}{-16} = \dfrac{xy}{2}$ Reduce to lowest terms.

g $\dfrac{12ab^2}{36ab} = \dfrac{b}{3}$ Write the numerator as b not $1b$ by convention.

EXERCISE 7C

1 Say whether each of these are like or unlike terms.

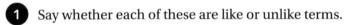

   a $4a$ and $3b$ **b** $5b$ and $-3b$ **c** $3b$ and $9b$

   d $4p$ and $6p$ **e** $8p$ and $-4q$ **f** $5a$ and $6b$

   g $7mn$ and $3mn$ **h** $4ab$ and $-2ab$ **i** $-6xy$ and $-7x$

   j $9ab$ and $3a$ **k** $9x^2$ and $6x^2$ **l** $6a^2$ and $-7a^2$

2 Simplify:

   a $9x + 4y - 4y - 3x + 5y$ **b** $3c + 6d - 6c - 4d$

   c $2xy + 3y^2 - 5xy - 4y^2$ **d** $2a^2 - ab^2 + 3ab^2 + 2ab$

   e $5f - 7g - 6f + 9g$ **f** $7a^2b + 3a^2b - 4a^2b$

   g $6mn^3 - 2mn^3 + 8mn^3$ **h** $3st^2 - 4s^2t + 5s^2t + 6st^2$

3 Copy and complete:

   a $2a + \square = 7a$ **b** $5b - \square = 2b$

   c $8mn + \square = 12mn$ **d** $11pq - \square = 6pq$

   e $4x^2 + \square = 7x^2$ **f** $6m^2 - \square = m^2$

   g $8ab - \square = -2ab$ **h** $-3st + \square = 5st$

Find answers at: cambridge.org/ukschools/gcsemaths-studentbookanswers

4 **a** Simplify $3a + 4b + 4a - 3b$.

Choose your answer from the following options.

A $7ab + 8ba$ B $7a + b$ C $6a + 8b$ D $7a + 7b$

b Simplify $7ab \times 2a$.

Choose your answer from the following options.

A $14ab$ B $9a^2b$ C $14ab^2$ D $14a^2b$

c Simplify $\dfrac{6ab}{4b^2}$

Choose your answer from the following options.

A $3ab$ B $3b$ C $3ab^2$ D $\dfrac{3a}{2b}$

5 Copy and complete:

a $8a \times \square = 16a$ **b** $9b \times \square = 18b$

c $8a \times \square = 16ab$ **d** $5m \times \square = 15mn$

e $3a \times \square = 12a^2$ **f** $6p \times \square = 30p^2$

g $-5b \times \square = 10b^2$ **h** $4m \times \square = 12m^2n$

6 Rewrite each expression in its simplest form.

a $7 \times 2x \times -2$ **b** $4x \times 2y \times 2z$ **c** $2a \times 5 \times a$

d $ab \times bc \times cd$ **e** $-4x \times 2x \times -3y$ **f** $\dfrac{1}{4x} \times 4y \times -y$

g $-9x \div 3$ **h** $-24y \div 2x$ **i** $18x^2 \div 6$

7 Simplify:

a $\dfrac{4x}{6}$ **b** $\dfrac{3a}{9}$ **c** $\dfrac{-12m}{18}$ **d** $\dfrac{14p}{21}$

e $\dfrac{22x^2}{33}$ **f** $\dfrac{15xy}{20}$ **g** $\dfrac{12ab}{a}$ **h** $\dfrac{2xy}{6xy}$

Key vocabulary

expanding: multiplying out an expression to get rid of the brackets

Tip

Remember that $2(a + b)$ means $2 \times (a + b)$.

In algebraic notation you don't write the multiplication sign.

Tip

Pay careful attention to the rules for multiplying negative and positive numbers when you multiply out.

Section 3: Expanding brackets

You might need to multiply to remove brackets before you can simplify an expression.

Removing brackets is called **expanding** the expression.

To expand an expression such as $2(a + b)$ you multiply each term inside the bracket by the value outside the bracket.

$$2(a + b) = 2 \times a + 2 \times b$$
$$= 2a + 2b$$

$$-2(a + b) = -2 \times a + (-2 \times b)$$
$$= -2a - 2b$$

WORKED EXAMPLE 4

Expand   **a** $3x(y + 2z)$ **b** $-2x(4 + y)$ **c** $-(3x - 2)$

a $3x(y + 2z) = 3x \times y + 3x \times 2z$

> Remove the brackets and multiply each of the terms inside the brackets by $3x$.

$\qquad\qquad\quad = 3xy + 6xz$

> Write each of the two terms in the standard simplified form. In algebra we write number and letters next to each other to mean multiplication.

b $-2x(4 + y) = -2x \times 4 + (-2x \times y)$
$\qquad\qquad\ = -8x - 2xy$

> Expand the brackets and multiply out the two terms formed. Remember the rules for multiplying different signs.

c $-(3x - 2) = -1 \times 3x + (-1 \times -2)$
$\qquad\qquad = -3x + 2$

> The value in front of this bracket is –1 so each term in the bracket is multiplied by –1 when the brackets are removed.
>
> Remember the rules for multiplying different signs.

The distributive law states that

$\quad a(b + c) \equiv ab + ac$

So:

$\quad 3(2x - 4) \equiv 6x - 12$

and

$\quad 2x(x - 5) \equiv 2x^2 - 10x$

Both sides of these expressions are identical no matter what the value of the variable so you can use the $\equiv$ symbol.

If two algebraic expressions are identical, the values calculated will be equal for any numbers substituted for the variables.

Identical expressions are called identities. See key vocabulary in Section 1.

WORKED EXAMPLE 5

Use substitution to work out if $(a + b)^2 \equiv a^2 + b^2$ is an identity.

Let $a = 1$ and $b = 2$.

> Choose small values to make your calculations as simple as possible.

$(a + b)^2 = (1 + 2)^2 = (3)^2 = 9$

> Substitute a and b into the left-hand side of the identity.

$a^2 + b^2 = 1^2 + 2^2 = 1 + 4 = 5$

> Substitute a and b into the right-hand side of the identity.

$9 \neq 5$

> The expressions are not identical.

Tip

Remember an identity is true for all values.

Expanding and simplifying

When you have expanded an expression it might contain like terms.

Add or subtract like terms to simplify the expression further.

You should always give an answer in its simplest form.

EXERCISE 7D

1 Which identity is correct?

A $2(y-1)-y \equiv 3y-2$ B $2(y-1)-y \equiv 2y-2$

C $2(y-1)-y \equiv y-2$ D $2(y-1)-y \equiv y-1$

2 Some of these expansions are incorrect.

Check each one and correct those that are wrong.

a $4(a+b) = 4a+b$ **b** $5(a+1) = 5a+6$

c $8(p-7) = 8p-56$ **d** $-3(p-5) = -3p-15$

e $a(a+b) = 2a+ab$ **f** $2m(3m+5) = 6m^2+10m$

g $-6(x-5) = 6x+30$ **h** $3a(4a-7) = 12a^2-7$

i $4a(3a+5) = 12a^2+20a$ **j** $3x(2x-7y) = 6x^2-21y$

3 Expand and simplify:

a $2(c+7)-9$ **b** $(a+2)+7$ **c** $5(b+3)+10$

d $2(e-5)+15$ **e** $3(f-4)-6$ **f** $2a(4a+3)+7a$

g $5b(2b-3)+6b$ **h** $2a(4a+3)+7a^2$ **i** $3b(3b-5)-7b^2$

4 Expand and simplify:

a $2(y+1)+3(y+4)$ **b** $2(3b-2)+5(2b-1)$

c $3(a+5)-2(a+7)$ **d** $5(b-2)-4(b+3)$

e $x(x-2)+3(x-2)$ **f** $2p(p+1)-5(p+1)$

g $3z(z+4)-z(3z+2)$ **h** $3y(y-4)+y(y-4)$

5 The expression in each box is obtained by adding the expressions in the two boxes directly below it.

	$9x+14y$	
$5x+5y$		$4x+9y$
$2x+y$	$3x+4y$	$x+5y$

Copy and complete these two pyramids.

a

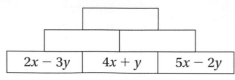

$2x-3y$	$4x+y$	$5x-2y$

b

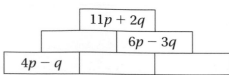

	$11p+2q$	
		$6p-3q$
$4p-q$		

6 Give reasons why the following expressions are **not** identities.

a $a + a$ and a^2

b $3x + 4 - x + 2$ and $2x + 2$

c $(m + 2)^2$ and $m^2 + 4$

d $\dfrac{x + 4}{3}$ and $x + 1$

Section 4: Factorising expressions

Factorising is the inverse of expanding.

When you factorise an expression you use brackets to write it as a product of its factors.

To factorise $5x + 35$ you find the highest common factor of the terms.

The highest common factor (HCF) of $5x$ and 35 is 5.

The number 5 is written outside the brackets and the remaining factors are written in the brackets:

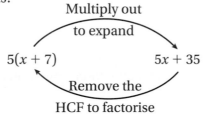

$5(x + 7)$ $5x + 35$

Multiply out to expand

Remove the HCF to factorise

> **Tip**
>
> The highest common factor (HCF) can be a number or a variable. It might also be a negative quantity.

WORKED EXAMPLE 6

Factorise each expression.

a $10a + 15b$
$10a + 15b = 5(2a + 3b)$

> HCF of 10 and 15 is 5. There are no common variables.

b $-2x - 8 = -2(x + 4)$

> HCF of -2 and -8 is -2.

c $3x^2 - 6xy = 3x(x - 2y)$

> HCF is $3x$.

d $3(m + 2) - n(m + 2) = (m + 2)(3 - n)$

> This looks like an expansion, but you are asked to factorise!
> $(m + 2)$ is common to both terms, so it is the HCF.

EXERCISE 7E

1 Factorise each expression.

a $2x + 4$

b $12m - 18n$

c $3a - 3b - 6$

d $xy - xz$

e $5xy - 15xyz$

f $14ab - 21bc$

g $pq - pr$

h $x^2 - x$

i $18abc - 12ac$

j $2x^2 - 4xy$

k $2x^2y - 4xy^2$

l $-6a - 12$

m $-3a - 9$

n $-xy - 5x$

o $-x^2 + 6x$

> **Tip**
>
> You will learn other methods of factorising expressions in Chapter 16 when you deal with binomials and quadratic equations.

2 Factorise:

a $7x - xy + x^2$

b $2xy + 4xz + 10x$

c $10x - 5y + 15z$

d $x(x - 2) + 5(x - 2)$

e $a(a - 7) - (a - 7)$

f $(x - 3) - 3(x - 3)$

 Find answers at: cambridge.org/ukschools/gcsemaths-studentbookanswers

Section 5: Solving problems using algebra

Read through this example to see how algebra can be used to generalise situations and solve problems.

WORKED EXAMPLE 7

Write down an expression for the sum of any three consecutive numbers.

Let the first number be n.
The next number must be 1 more than n, so let it be $n + 1$
The third number is 1 more than $n + 1$, so let it be $n + 1 + 1 = n + 2$
Sum of three consecutive numbers
$= n + n + 1 + n + 2$
$= 3n + 3$

> This gives you a general rule for finding the sum of any three consecutive numbers, when the first number, n, is known.

> Try it out.
> What is the sum of the three consecutive numbers starting at 205?

$3 \times 205 + 3 = 615 + 3 = 618$

> Substitute 205 for n in $3n + 3$.

Check: $205 + 206 + 207 = 618$

> Check your answer.

Expressions like this are very useful for programmed operations and repeated calculations involving different starting numbers.

EXERCISE 7F

1 Write down whether the following statements are true or false.

  a The expression $3z^2 + 5yx - z^2 - 6yx$ simplified is $2z^2 - 11xy$.

  b If you expand the brackets $2p(3p + q)$ you get the expression $6p^2 + 2pq$.

  c This is a correct use of the identity symbol: $4(a + 1) \equiv 4a + 4$.

  d $\frac{4}{x}$ always has the same value as $\frac{x}{4}$.

  e x squared and added to 7 with the result divided by 3 is $\frac{x^2 + 7}{3}$.

2 In a magic square the sum of each row, column and diagonal is the same.

State whether the following is a magic square. You must show your working.

$m - p$	$m + p - q$	$m + q$
$m + p + q$	m	$m - p - q$
$m - q$	$m - p + q$	$m + p$

3 **a** Write an expression for each missing length in this rectangle.

b Write an expression for P, the perimeter of the rectangle.

c Given that $a = 2.1$ and $b = 4.5$, calculate the area of the rectangle.
(Area = length × breadth.)

Tip

Opposite sides of a rectangle are equal in length.

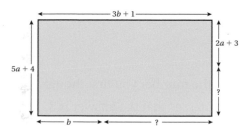

4 **a** The area of a rectangle is $2x^2 + 4x$.

If the length is $2x$, what is the width?

b The perimeter of a rectangle is $2x^2 + 4x$.

If the width is $2x$ units, what is the length?

5 Draw two diagrams representing areas to prove that $(3x)^2$ and $3x^2$ are different.

6 In the following pyramids, the number in each cell is made by adding the numbers in the two cells beneath it.

Copy and complete the diagrams.

Write each expression as simply as possible. The first entry in part **a** has been completed in red.

a

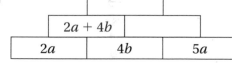

b

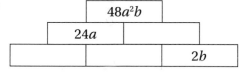

c

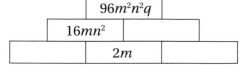

7 **a** Paul plays a 'think of a number game' with his friends.

He predicts what their answer will be.

These are the steps he tells his friends to follow:

Think of a number.

Double it.

Add 6.

Halve it.

Take away the number you first thought of.

Paul then guesses that the answer is 3.

Use algebra to show why Paul will always guess correctly.

b Make up a 'think of a number' problem of your own.

Use algebra to check that it will work and to see which number you end up with.

Try it out with another student to check that it works.

 Checklist of learning and understanding

Algebraic notation

- You can use letters (called variables) in place of unknown quantities in algebra.
- An expression is a collection of numbers, operation signs and at least one variable.
- Each part of an expression is called a term.
- To evaluate an expression you substitute numbers in place of the variables.

Simplifying expressions

- Like terms have exactly the same variables.
- Expressions can be simplified by adding or subtracting like terms.

Expanding brackets

- You can multiply and divide unlike terms.
- If an expression contains brackets you multiply them out and then add or subtract like terms to simplify it further.

Factorising

- Factorising involves putting brackets back into an expression.
- If terms have a common factor, write it in front of the bracket and write the remaining terms in the bracket as a factor. You can check by multiplying out.

Solving problems

- Algebra allows you to make general rules that apply to any number. This is useful in problem solving.

Chapter review

 For additional questions on the topics in this chapter, visit GCSE Mathematics Online.

1 Simplify where possible:

   a $12x - 7x$ **b** $4a - 12b - 3a + 4b$ **c** $5xy \times z \times 2 + 8xyz$

2 **a** Simplify fully $6x + 4y - x - 7y$ *(2 marks)*

   b Matt knows the value of a is 6 or 7 and the value of b is 4 or 5.

     Work out the largest and smallest possible values of $3a - 2b$

                                                                   (4 marks)

                                                                 © AQA 2013

3 The expression $7(x + 4) - 3(x - 2)$ simplifies to $a(2x + b)$. Work out the values of a and b.

4 Check whether each expression has been fully simplified. If not, give it in its simplest form.

   a $5(g + 2) + 8g$ $5g + 10 + 8g$

   b $4z(4z - 2) - z(z + 2)$ $15z^2 - 10z$

   c $-5ab \times (-3bc)$ $15ab^2c$

   d $\dfrac{18x^1}{3x}$ $\dfrac{6x^1}{x}$

5 Multiply out the brackets and simplify $2(3a - 1) + 4(b - 4)$.

   Choose your answer from the following options.

   A $9ab - 18$ B $5a + 4b - 6$ C $6a + 4b - 18$ D $6a + 4b + 18$

6 The nth even number is $2n$. The next even number after $2n$ is $2n + 2$.

   a Give a reason why this is.

   b Write an expression, in terms of n, for the next even number after $2n + 2$.

   c Show algebraically that the sum of any three consecutive even numbers is always a multiple of 6.

7 Work out by substitution whether the following pairs of expressions are identities.

   a $5(x + 3)$ and $5x + 3$ **b** $-3(m - 2)$ and $-3m - 6$

   c $4(y - 3) + 2(y + 4)$ and $6y - 4$

Find answers at: cambridge.org/ukschools/gcsemaths-studentbookanswers

8 Properties of polygons and 3D objects

In this chapter you will learn how to ...

- use the correct geometrical terms to talk about lines, angles and shapes.
- recognise and name common 2D shapes and 3D objects.
- describe the symmetrical properties of various polygons.
- classify triangles and quadrilaterals and use their properties to identify them.

 For more resources relating to this chapter, visit GCSE Mathematics Online.

Using mathematics: real-life applications

Many people use geometry in their jobs and daily lives. Artists, craftspeople, builders, designers, architects and engineers use shape and space in their jobs, but almost everyone uses lines, angles, patterns and shapes in different ways every day.

- Diverging
- Merging
- Crossing

"I use a CAD package to plot lines and angles and show the direction of traffic flow when I design new road junctions."

(Civil engineer)

Before you start ...

KS3	You should be able to use geometrical terms correctly.	**1** Choose the correct labels for each diagram. 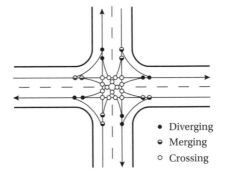 base vertex acute angle point edge right angle height face
KS3	You need to be able to recognise and name different types of shapes.	**2** **a** Identify three different shapes in this diagram and use letters to name them correctly. **b** ABCE is one face of a solid with 8 faces. What type of solid could it be? 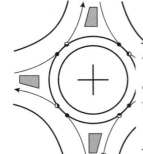

Assess your starting point using the Launchpad

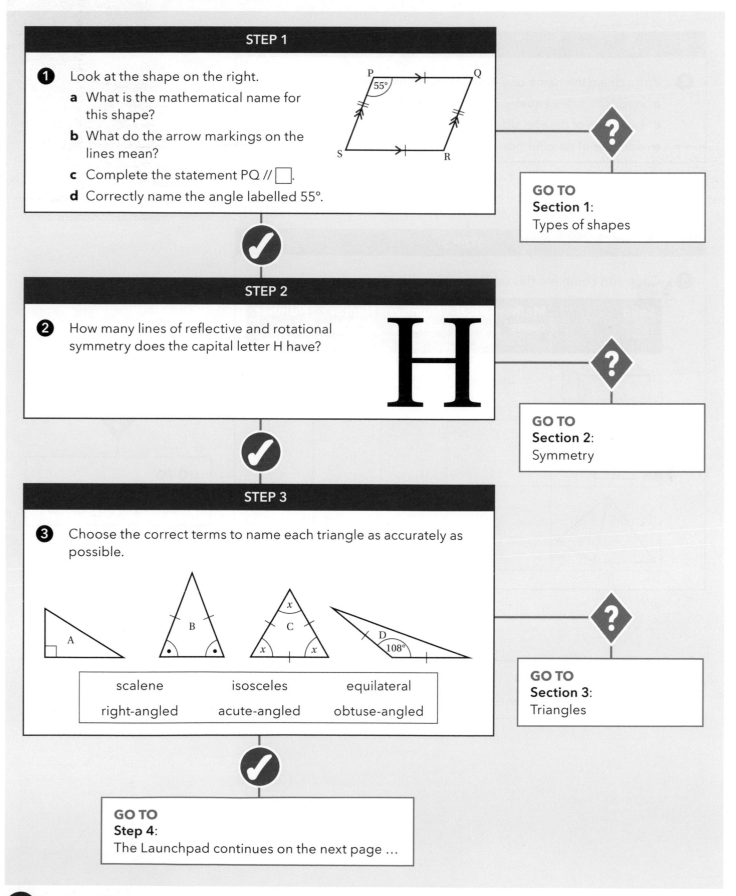

STEP 1

❶ Look at the shape on the right.

a What is the mathematical name for this shape?

b What do the arrow markings on the lines mean?

c Complete the statement PQ // ☐.

d Correctly name the angle labelled 55°.

GO TO
Section 1:
Types of shapes

STEP 2

❷ How many lines of reflective and rotational symmetry does the capital letter H have?

GO TO
Section 2:
Symmetry

STEP 3

❸ Choose the correct terms to name each triangle as accurately as possible.

| scalene | isosceles | equilateral |
| right-angled | acute-angled | obtuse-angled |

GO TO
Section 3:
Triangles

GO TO
Step 4:
The Launchpad continues on the next page …

Find answers at: cambridge.org/ukschools/gcsemaths-studentbookanswers

Launchpad continued …

STEP 4

4 Write down the name of a 4-sided shape that has:
   a opposite sides equal
   b all sides equal
   c two pairs of parallel sides
   d four equal angles
   e one pair of parallel sides only
   f no parallel sides.

GO TO
Section 4:
Quadrilaterals

STEP 5

5 Copy and complete this table.

Solid	Mathematical name	Number of faces	Number of edges	Number of vertices
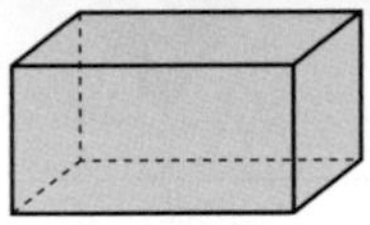				
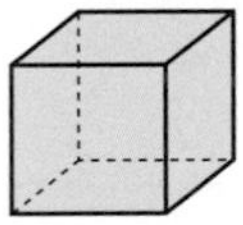				
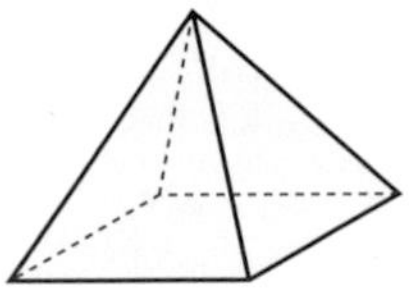				

GO TO
Section 5:
Properties of 3D objects

GO TO
Chapter review

Section 1: Types of shapes

Flat shapes are called **plane shapes** or two-dimensional (2D) shapes.

A **polygon** is a closed plane shape with three or more straight sides.

Circles and ellipses (ovals) are plane shapes, but they do not have straight sides, so they are not classified as polygons.

A **regular polygon** has:

- all sides of equal length
- all interior angles of equal size
- all exterior angles of equal size.

The equilateral triangle above is a regular polygon.

If a polygon does not have equal sides and equal angles it is called an **irregular polygon**.

The rectangle above is an irregular polygon because its sides are not all equal.

Key vocabulary

plane shape: a flat, two-dimensional shape

polygon: a closed plane shape with three or more straight sides

regular polygon: a polygon with equal straight sides and equal angles

irregular polygon: a polygon that does not have equal sides and equal angles

Polygons

Polygons can be named according to the number of sides they have:

Name of polygon	Number of sides	Regular polygon	Irregular polygon
triangle	3		
quadrilateral	4		
pentagon	5		
hexagon	6		
heptagon	7		
octagon	8		
nonagon	9		
decagon	10		

 Find answers at: cambridge.org/ukschools/gcsemaths-studentbookanswers

Tip

3D means an object has three dimensions or measurements: length, breadth and height.

Key vocabulary

polyhedron: a solid shape with flat faces that are polygons

Tip

You will deal with solids and their properties in more detail in Section 5.

Solids

Solids are three-dimensional (3D) shapes with length, breadth and height.

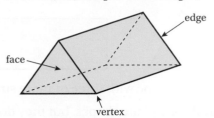

A solid such as the triangular prism above can also be called a **polyhedron**.

Polyhedra are solid shapes with flat faces that are polygons.

Cylinders, spheres and cones are not polyhedra. They are solids with a curved surface.

EXERCISE 8A

1 Write down the mathematical name for each of the following shapes.

   a A plane shape with three equal sides.

   b A polygon with five equal sides.

   c A polygon with six vertices and six equal angles.

   d A plane shape with eight equal sides and eight equal internal angles.

2 Give a real-life example of where you might find each of the following.

   a A regular octagon.   **b** A cube.

   c A regular quadrilateral.   **d** An irregular pentagon.

Perpendicular and parallel lines

Perpendicular lines meet at right angles (90°).

The symbol ⊥ means 'perpendicular to'.

In the diagram, AB ⊥ CD.

The shortest distance from a point to a line is the perpendicular distance between them.

Lines are parallel if they are equidistant along their length.

The symbol // means 'parallel to'.

Small arrow symbols are drawn on lines to indicate that they are parallel to each other.

When there is more than one pair of parallel lines in a diagram, each pair is usually given a different set of arrow markings.

In this diagram, AB // DC, AD // HG and EF // HC.

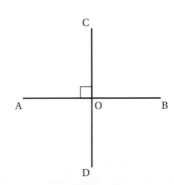

Perpendicular Lines

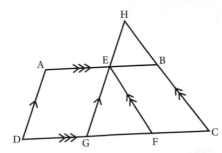

Sides and angles

Shapes are labelled using capital letters on each vertex.

The letters are usually written in alphabetical order as you move round the shape.

This shape would be called △ABC.

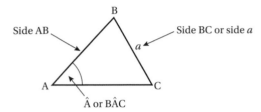

Each side of this triangle can be named using the capital letters on the vertices: AB, BC and CA.

The angles can be named in different ways.

The angle at vertex A can be named A, BAC or CAB.

Symbols can be used to label angles. For example, ∠BAC or BÂC.

Sometimes single letters are used to name the sides.

In this example, side BC can also be called side *a* because it is opposite to angle A.

This convention is often used when you work with Pythagoras' theorem and in trigonometry which both explore angle sizes and lengths of sides in triangles.

Marking equal sides and angles

Small lines can be drawn on the sides of a shape to show whether the sides are equal or not.

Sides that have the same markings are equal in length.

Curved lines and symbols such as dots or letters can be used to show whether angles are equal or not.

Angles that are equal have the same marking, symbol or letter.

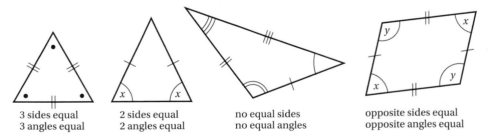

3 sides equal
3 angles equal

2 sides equal
2 angles equal

no equal sides
no equal angles

opposite sides equal
opposite angles equal

EXERCISE 8B

1 Read each clue in Column A. Match it to a term in Column B.

	Column A	Column B
a	A shape that has two fewer sides than an octagon.	decagon
b	A shape that has two sides more than a triangle.	hexagon
c	A shape with four sides.	equilateral triangle
d	An 8-sided shape.	two-dimensional
e	A figure that has length and height.	pentagon
f	A closed plane shape with all sides x cm long and all angles the same size.	quadrilateral
g	A 10-sided figure.	square
h	Another name for a regular 4-sided polygon.	regular polygon
i	The more common name for a regular 3-sided polygon.	octagon

2 Look at this diagram.

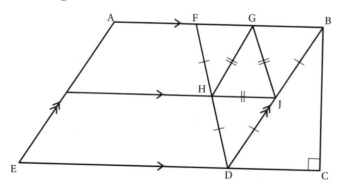

Write down whether the following statements are true or false.

a AF // EC.
b △BFD is isosceles.
c CE ⊥ BC.
d AE // BD.
e ABCE is a regular polygon.
f GB // BC.
g In △DHJ, angle H = angle J = angle D.
h △GHJ is a regular polygon.

3 Draw and correctly label a sketch of each of the following shapes.

a A triangle ABC, with angle B = angle C and side AB ⊥ AC.
b A regular four-sided polygon DEFG.
c Quadrilateral PQRS such that PQ // SR but PQ ≠ SR and ∠PSR = ∠QRS.

Section 2: Symmetry

Reflection symmetry

If you can fold a shape in half to create a mirror image (**reflection**) on either side of the fold the shape has reflection symmetry.

The fold is known as the **line of symmetry**.

Each half of the shape is a reflection of the other half so this type of symmetry is also called line symmetry.

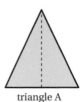 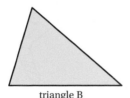

triangle A   triangle B

Triangle A has reflection symmetry. The dotted line is the line of symmetry.

Triangle B is not symmetrical. You cannot draw a line to divide it into two identical parts.

A shape can have more than one line of symmetry.

For example, a regular pentagon has five lines of symmetry.

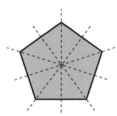

Lines of symmetry can be horizontal, vertical or diagonal.

Rotation symmetry

A shape has **rotation symmetry** if you rotate it around a fixed point and it looks identical in different positions.

The order of rotation symmetry tells you how many times the shape will look identical before it returns to the starting point.

If you have to rotate the shape a full 360° before it appears identical again then it has an order of rotation symmetry of 1 and it does **not** have rotation symmetry.

A square has an order of rotation symmetry of 4 around its centre.

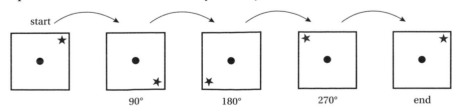

start   90°   180°   270°   end

The star shows the position of one vertex of the square as it rotates.

Key vocabulary

reflection: an exact image of a shape about a line of symmetry (mirror line)

line of symmetry: a line that divides a plane shape into two identical halves, each the reflection of the other

Tip

The line of symmetry is sometimes called the mirror line. If you place a small mirror on the line of symmetry you will see the whole shape reflected in the mirror.

Key vocabulary

rotation symmetry: symmetry by turning a shape around a fixed point so that it looks the same from different positions

Tip

You will deal with reflections in mirror lines and rotations about a fixed point again in Chapter 31 when you deal with transformations using coordinates.

 Find answers at: cambridge.org/ukschools/gcsemaths-studentbookanswers

The symbol below is the national symbol for the Isle of Man.

It has an order of rotation symmetry of 3 about its centre.

EXERCISE 8C

1 Write down which of the dotted lines in each figure are lines of symmetry.

a

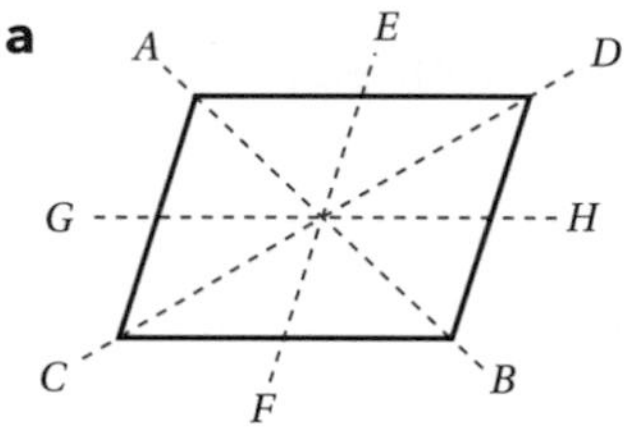

b

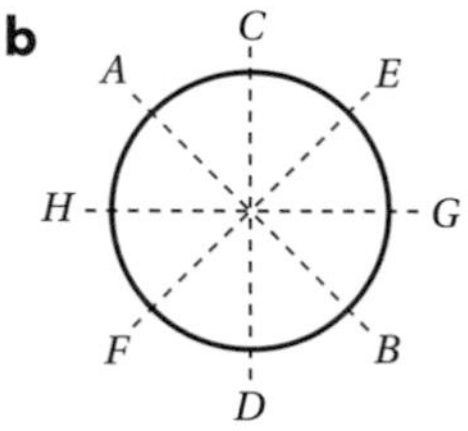

c

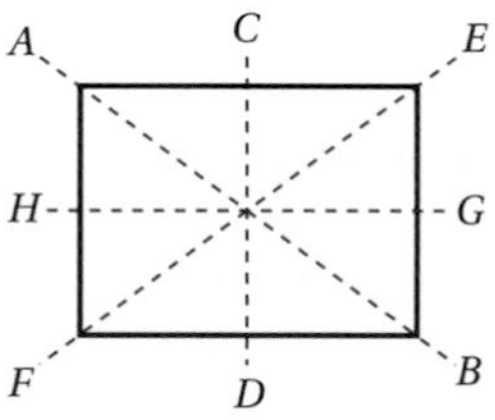

d

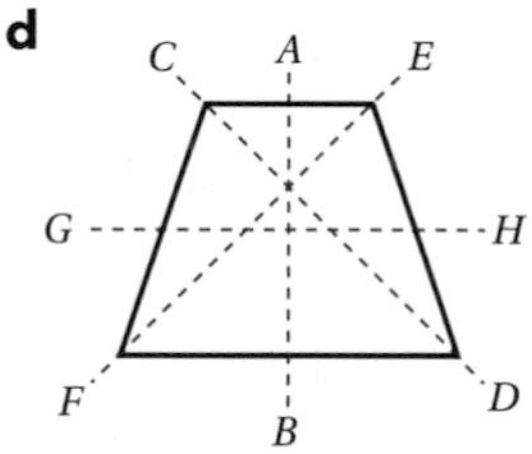

2 How many lines of reflective symmetry does an equilateral triangle have?

Choose from the following options.

A 0   B 3   C 1   D 2

3 Investigate and work out the number of lines of symmetry and the order of rotation symmetry of each shape.

Copy and complete the table to summarise your results.

Shape	Number of lines of symmetry	Order of rotation symmetry
square		
rectangle		
isosceles triangle		
equilateral triangle		
parallelogram		
regular hexagon		
regular octagon		
regular decagon		

4 Give an example of a shape that has rotation symmetry of order 3 but which is not a triangle.

5 Write down which of the following letters has rotation symmetry.

C   H   A   R

6 Describe the symmetry in this design in as much detail as possible.

7 Find and draw five examples of metal alloy rim designs for cars.

For each one, state its order of rotation symmetry.

8 Find and sketch five different symmetrical designs or logos that you can find in your environment.

Label your sketches to indicate how the design is symmetrical.

Section 3: Triangles

The table below summarises the properties of different types of triangles.

Type of triangle	Properties
Scalene	No equal sides.
	No equal angles.
	No line of symmetry.
	No rotation symmetry (or rotation symmetry of order 1).
Isosceles	Two equal sides.
	Angles at base of equal sides are equal.
	One line of symmetry.
	Line of symmetry is perpendicular height.
	No rotational symmetry (or rotation symmetry of order 1).
Equilateral	All sides equal.
	Three equal angles, each of 60°.
	Three lines of symmetry.
	Rotation symmetry of order 3.
Acute-angled 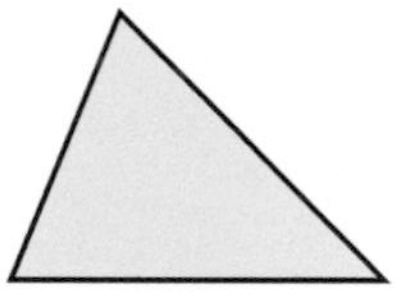	All angles are less than 90° (acute).
Right-angled 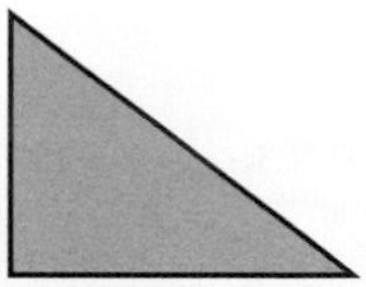	One angle is a right angle (90°).
Obtuse-angled 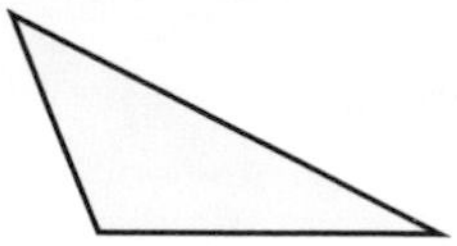	One angle is greater than 90° (obtuse).

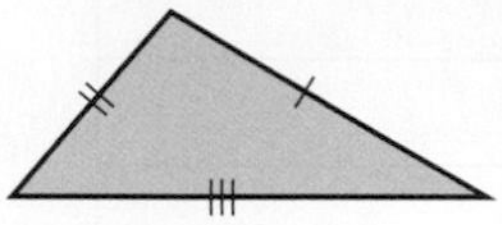

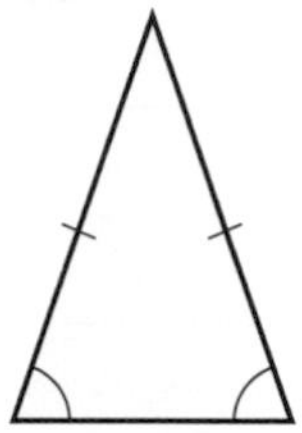

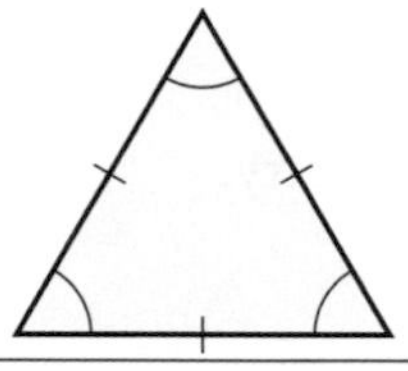

Triangles can be more than one type.

For example, triangle MNO below is right-angled and an isosceles triangle.

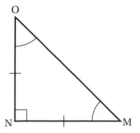

Angle properties of triangles

The angles inside a triangle are called interior angles.

The three interior angles of any triangle always add up to 180°.

If you extend the length of one side of a triangle you form another angle outside the triangle.

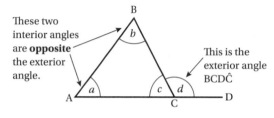

These two interior angles are **opposite** the exterior angle.

This is the exterior angle BCD̂C

Angles formed outside the triangle are called exterior angles.

The exterior angle is equal to the sum of the two interior angles that are opposite it.

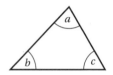  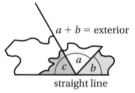

$a + b$ = exterior

straight line

Using the properties of triangles to solve problems

You can use the properties of triangles to solve problems involving unknown angles and lengths of sides.

Problem-solving framework

Triangle ABC is isosceles with perimeter 85 mm.

AB = BC and AC = 25 mm. Angle ABC = 48°.

Find:

a the length of each equal side

b the size of each equal angle.

Steps for solving problems	What you would do for this example	
Step 1: Work out what you have to do. Start by reading the question carefully.	You need to use the properties of isosceles triangles and the given information to find the length of two sides and the size of two angles.	
Step 2: What information do you need? Have you got it all?	Draw a labelled sketch to see whether you have the information you need.	
Step 3: Decide what maths you can use.	Use the values you already have to make equations to find the missing values.	
Step 4: Set out your solution clearly. Check your working and that your answer is reasonable.	**a** Perimeter = AC + AB + BC $\qquad\qquad$ = 85 mm So, 85 = 25 + AB + BC 85 − 25 = AB + BC 60 = AB + BC But AB = BC, so AB = BC = 30 mm Check: 30 + 30 + 25 = 85.	**b** Let each equal angle be x. 48° + 2x = 180° (angle sum of triangle) 2x = 180° − 48° 2x = 132° x = 66° Check: 66 + 66 + 48 = 180
Step 5: Check that you've answered the question.	Each equal side is 30 mm long. Each equal angle is 66°.	

Tip

You will use these properties often when you deal with trigonometry in Chapter 36.

In many questions you will have to find the size of unknown angles before you can move on and solve the problem.

EXERCISE 8D

1 Without measuring, write down the type of triangle in the diagram.

Give a reason for your answer.

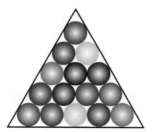

2 Choose the correct type of triangle from the options given.

A obtuse-angled scalene

B right-angled isosceles

C acute-angled isosceles

D obtuse-angled isosceles

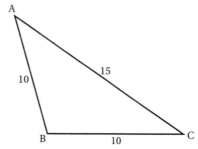

3 Identify which of these triangles are not possible.

Give reasons for your answers.

a An isosceles triangle with an obtuse angle.

b A scalene triangle with two angles > 90°.

c A scalene triangle with three angles, 34°, 64° and 92°.

d An obtuse-angled equilateral triangle.

e An isosceles triangle with side lengths 6.5 cm, 7 cm and 7.5 cm.

4 Two angles in a triangle are 67° and 45°.

What is the size of the third angle?

A 68°   B 136°   C 90°   D 112°

5 A triangle has two angles of 38° and 104°.

a What is the size of the third angle?

b What type of triangle is it?

6 Find the size of angles *a* to *e* in the diagrams.

Show your working and give mathematical reasons for any deductions you make.

  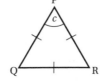 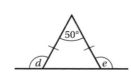

Isosceles triangle DEF, with DE = EF, has a perimeter of 50 mm. Find the length of EF if:

a DF = 15 mm

b DE = $\sqrt{13}$.

Section 4: Quadrilaterals

You need to know the names and basic properties of the quadrilaterals shown in the table.

Key vocabulary

adjacent: next to each other. In shapes, sides that intersect each other are adjacent.

bisect: to divide exactly into two halves

Quadrilateral		Properties
trapezium		• One pair of opposite sides are parallel.
kite		• Two pairs of **adjacent** sides are equal. • Diagonals are perpendicular. • One diagonal **bisects** the other. • One diagonal bisects the angles.
parallelogram		• Both pairs of opposite sides are parallel. • Both pairs of opposite sides are equal. • Both pairs of opposite angles are equal. • Diagonals bisect each other.
rhombus		As for parallelogram, plus: • All sides are equal. • Diagonals bisect at right angles. • Diagonals bisect the angles.
rectangle		As for parallelogram, plus: • All angles are 90°. • Diagonals are equal in length.
square		As for a rectangle, plus: • All sides are equal. • Diagonals bisect at right angles. • Diagonals bisect the angles.

Using the properties of quadrilaterals to solve problems

You can use the given or marked properties of a quadrilateral to identify and name it.

You should always state what properties you are using to justify your answer.

WORKED EXAMPLE 1

A plane shape has two diagonals.

The diagonals are perpendicular.

a Write down what shape(s) this could be.

b The diagonals are not the same length. Write down what shape(s) it could not be.

a Two diagonals means that the shape is a quadrilateral.
Only the square, rhombus and kite have diagonals that intersect at 90°.
The shape could be a square, a rhombus or a kite.

b Of the three shapes, only the square has diagonals that are equal in length.
Therefore the shape could not be a square.

> Take a systematic approach by working through the properties of quadrilaterals. By a process of elimination you can work through to identify which shape it might be.

The angle sum of quadrilaterals

All quadrilaterals have only two diagonals. If you draw in one diagonal you divide the quadrilateral into two triangles.

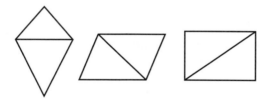

The interior angles of a triangle add up to 180°.

Therefore, the interior angles of a quadrilateral are equal to $2 \times 180° = 360°$.

You can use this property together with the other properties of quadrilaterals to find the size of unknown angles.

WORKED EXAMPLE 2

Find the size of unknown angles x and y.

a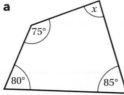

b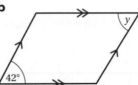

a $75° + 80° + 85° + x = 360°$
$240° + x = 360°$
$x = 360° - 240°$
$x = 120°$

> Shape is a quadrilateral, angles of a quadrilateral add up to 360°.
>
> Solve equation for x.

b $y = 42°$

> Shape is a parallelogram, so the opposite angles are equal.

EXERCISE 8E

1 A quadrilateral has:
- two pairs of equal parallel lines
- opposite angles are equal, and
- the diagonals bisect each other.

Name the shape from the options below.

A Rhombus   B Kite   C Trapezium   D Parallelogram

2 Identify the quadrilateral(s) from the description in each part.

a All angles are equal.

b Diagonals are equal in length.

c Two pairs of sides are equal and parallel.

d No sides are parallel.

e The only regular quadrilateral.

f Diagonals bisect each other.

3 You can identify a quadrilateral by considering its diagonals.

Copy and complete this table.

Shape	Diagonals are equal in length	Diagonals bisect each other	Diagonals are perpendicular
rhombus			
parallelogram			
square			
kite			
rectangle			

4 What is the most obvious difference between a square and a rhombus?

5 Millie says that quadrilateral ABCD has all four sides the same length.

Elizabeth says it must be a square.

Is Elizabeth correct? Give a reason for your answer.

6 A kite has one angle of 47° and one of 133°. What sizes are the other two angles?

7 State whether each statement is always true, sometimes true or never true.

Give a reason for each of your answers.

a A square is a rectangle.　　**b** A rectangle is a square.

c A rectangle is a rhombus.　　**d** A rhombus is a parallelogram.

e A parallelogram is a rhombus.

Section 5: Properties of 3D objects

The flat surfaces of a solid are called faces. Two faces meet at the edge of a solid.

Three or more faces meet at a point called a vertex. (The plural of vertex is vertices.)

A solid with flat faces and straight edges is a polyhedron.

Cubes, cuboids, prisms and pyramids are all types of polyhedra.

Cubes and cuboids

Cubes and cuboids are box-shaped polyhedra.

They have six faces, twelve edges and eight vertices.

A cube has **congruent** square faces.

A cuboid has rectangular faces.

All cubes are cuboids, but not all cuboids are cubes.

Prisms

A prism is a 3D shape with two congruent, parallel faces.

If the prism is sliced parallel to one of these faces the cross-section will always be the same shape.

The parallel faces of a prism can be any shape.

If the prism is a polyhedron all of the other faces are rectangular.

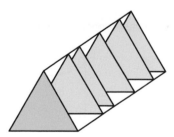

> ### 💡 Tip
>
> You need to know the properties of the basic polyhedra and other 3D solids.
>
> You will use these properties to draw plans, elevations and nets of solids in Chapter 20 and you will apply them when you solve problems relating to volume and surface area in Chapter 23.

> ### 🔑 Key vocabulary
>
> **congruent**: identical in shape and size

Prisms are named according to the shape of their parallel faces.

Pentagonal prism	**Hexagonal prism**	**Octagonal prism**
2 pentagonal faces	2 hexagonal faces	2 octagonal faces
5 rectangular faces	6 rectangular faces	8 rectangular faces

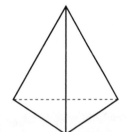 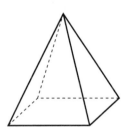 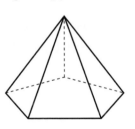 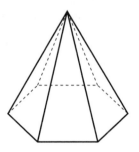

A cube is a square prism and a cuboid is a rectangular prism.

Pyramids

A pyramid is a polyhedron with a base and triangular faces which meet at a vertex (sometimes called the apex of the pyramid).

Pyramids are named according to the shape of their base.

Triangular pyramid   **Square pyramid**   **Pentagonal pyramid**   **Hexagonal pyramid**

The number of sides of the base tells you how many triangular faces the pyramid has.

Other solids

Cylinders, cones and spheres are also 3D shapes.

They do not have straight edges or flat faces that are polygons so they are not polyhedral.

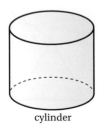  

cylinder   cone   sphere

EXERCISE 8F

1 Sketch an example of each of the following solids.

a A tall thin cylinder.

b A cube.

c A rectangular prism.

d An octagonal pyramid.

e A prism with a parallelogram-shaped cross-section.

2 A solid has 8 vertices, 12 edges and 6 faces.

Name the solid from the options below.

A Triangular-based pyramid   B Cylinder

C Cube   D Hexagonal prism

3 Write down the difference between a sphere and a circle.

4 Compare a cone and a cylinder. Write down how they are similar and how they are different.

5 Name two solids that have six flat faces.

6 Copy and complete this table.

3D shape	Faces	Vertices	Edges
cube			
cuboid			
triangular pyramid			
square pyramid			
triangular prism			
hexagonal prism			

7 In total how many faces, edges and vertices does the tower have?

Checklist of learning and understanding

Types of shapes

- Polygons are closed plane shapes with straight sides.
- Triangles, quadrilaterals, pentagons and hexagons are all polygons.
- Circles and ovals are plane shapes, but they are not polygons.

Symmetry

- Shapes have reflection symmetry if they can be folded along a line of symmetry to produce two identical mirror images.
- Shapes have rotation symmetry if they fit on to themselves more than once during a 360° rotation.

Triangles

- Triangles are 3-sided polygons.
- Triangles can be classified and named using their side and angle properties.
- The sum of the interior angles of a triangle is 180°.

Quadrilaterals

- Quadrilaterals are 4-sided polygons.
- Quadrilaterals can be classified and named using their side, angle and diagonal properties.
- The sum of the interior angles of a quadrilateral is 360°.

Properties of 3D objects

- 3D shapes are solids with length, breadth and height.
- Polyhedra are solids with flat faces and straight edges.
- Prisms and pyramids are polyhedral.
- Cylinders, cones and spheres are 3D shapes but they are not polyhedral.

Chapter review

 For additional questions on the topics in this chapter, visit GCSE Mathematics Online.

1 Write down whether the following statements are true or false.

   a A slice of pizza can be accurately described as a triangle.

   b A triangular pyramid has 4 vertices, 4 faces and 6 edges.

   c A pair of lines that are equidistant and never meet are described as being perpendicular.

2 Describe the symmetrical features of a regular hexagon as fully as possible.

3 Find the missing angles in this trapezium.

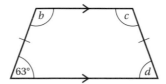

4 Decide whether the missing angle in the diagram is a right angle. Give a reason for your answer.

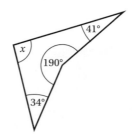

5 Spot the mistakes in this table and correct them.

3D shape	Faces	Edges	Vertices
a square-based pyramid	5	5	5
b triangular prism	9	9	9
c cube	12	6	8
d sphere	2	2	1

Find answers at: cambridge.org/ukschools/gcsemaths-studentbookanswers

6 Look at the shape below.

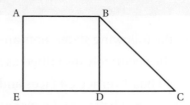

Complete the sentences by choosing the correct words from the box.

parallel	perpendicular	reciprocal	acute	congruent
reflective symmetry	reflex	obtuse	parallelogram	
obtuse	trapezium	kite	right angle	rotational symmetry

a AB is _____ to DC

b AE is _____ to AB

c ABCE is called a _____

d Angle EDB is a _____

e Angle ABC is _____

f Shape ABCE has no lines of _____

7 Look at the diagram of the building.

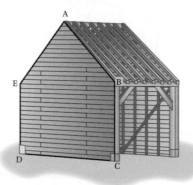

a Which side lengths are parallel?

b Which side lengths are perpendicular?

c How many lines of reflective symmetry does this shape have?

d What rotational symmetry does it have?

8 Look at the diagram of the rhombus.

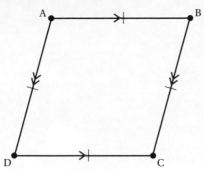

  a How many lines of symmetry does it have?

  b What rotational symmetry does it have?

  c At what angle do the diagonals cross each other?

  d What do the angles ABC and BCD add to?

9 **a** The diagram shows a letterbox.

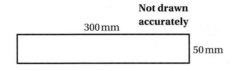

Not drawn accurately

300 mm

50 mm

  Which of these parcels will fit through the letterbox?

  Circle Yes or No for each parcel.

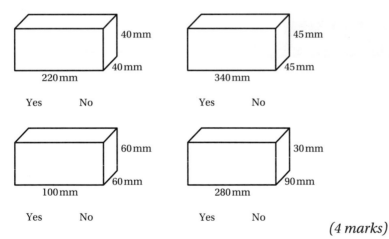

40 mm
40 mm
220 mm

Yes   No

45 mm
45 mm
340 mm

Yes   No

60 mm
60 mm
100 mm

Yes   No

30 mm
90 mm
280 mm

Yes   No

(4 marks)

  b Pat wants a letterbox that all four of the parcels will fit through.

  What is the width and height of the smallest letterbox possible?

(3 marks)

© AQA 2013

Find answers at: cambridge.org/ukschools/gcsemaths-studentbookanswers

9 Angles

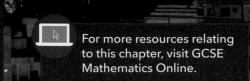

For more resources relating to this chapter, visit GCSE Mathematics Online.

Using mathematics: real-life applications

People who work in many varied and unrelated jobs rely on an understanding of angles and how shapes fit with others in their daily work. These include designers, architects, opticians and tree surgeons among others.

> "I had to work quite carefully with the 360 degrees around the centre to place each of the 32 pods correctly on the London Eye." *(Structural engineer)*

Before you start …

KS3 Ch 1	You should be able to use inverse operations to make 180° and 360°.	**1** Copy and complete. **a** $180° - 96° = \square$ **b** $180° - 116° = \square$ **c** $360° - 173° = \square$ **d** $360° - 55° - 97° = \square$
KS3 Ch 8	You need to know and apply the basic properties of triangles and quadrilaterals.	**2** Use the marked properties to name each polygon as accurately as possible.  **3** What can you say about angles x and y in **c**? Why?
KS3 Ch 31	You need to know how to use a protractor to measure angles.	**4** Measure the following angles. **a** **b**

Assess your starting point using the Launchpad

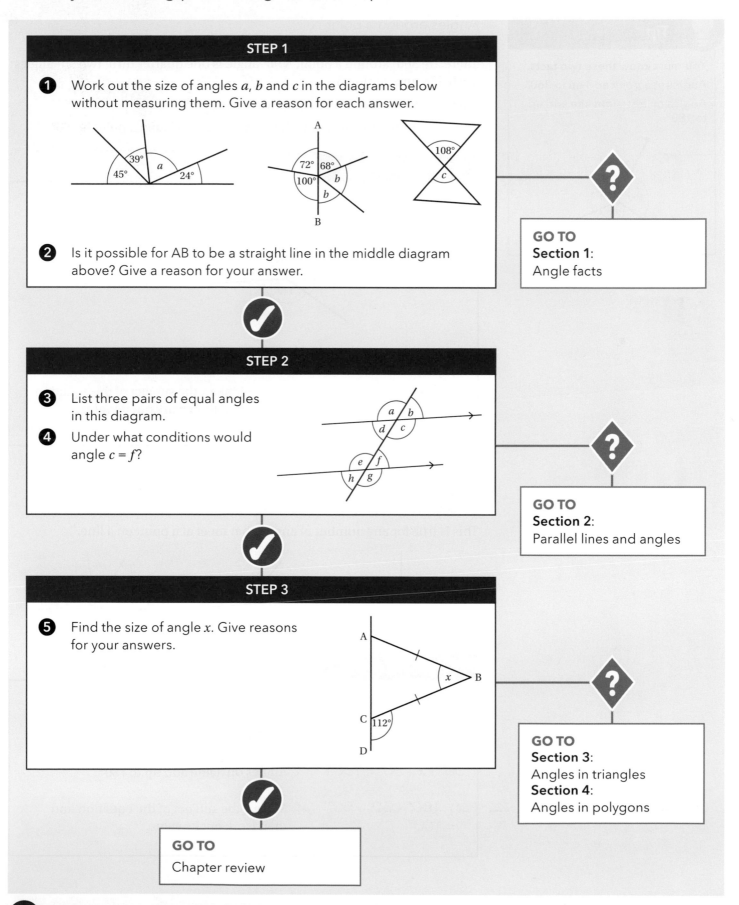

STEP 1

1 Work out the size of angles *a*, *b* and *c* in the diagrams below without measuring them. Give a reason for each answer.

2 Is it possible for AB to be a straight line in the middle diagram above? Give a reason for your answer.

GO TO
Section 1:
Angle facts

STEP 2

3 List three pairs of equal angles in this diagram.

4 Under what conditions would angle *c* = *f*?

GO TO
Section 2:
Parallel lines and angles

STEP 3

5 Find the size of angle *x*. Give reasons for your answers.

GO TO
Section 3:
Angles in triangles
Section 4:
Angles in polygons

GO TO
Chapter review

Find answers at: cambridge.org/ukschools/gcsemaths-studentbookanswers

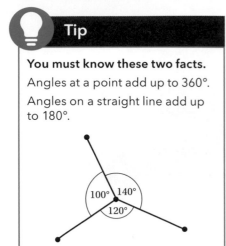

Tip

You must know these two facts.

Angles at a point add up to 360°.

Angles on a straight line add up to 180°.

Section 1: Angle facts

Angles around a point

There are 360° around a point. A 90° angle is one quarter turn, two 90° angles are half a turn, and so on.

There are four quarter turns around a point. $4 \times 90° = 360°$

This rule applies to any point. The sum of angles around a point is 360°.

WORKED EXAMPLE 1

Find the size of x.

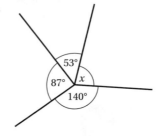

$87° + 53° + x + 140° = 360°$ ◁ Angles round a point add up to 360°.

$x = 360° - 140° - 53° - 87°$
$\quad = 360° - 280°$
$\quad = 80°$

Make x the subject of the equation and then work out its value.

Angles on a straight line

Angles on a straight line add up to 180°.

This is true for any number of angles that meet at a point on a line.

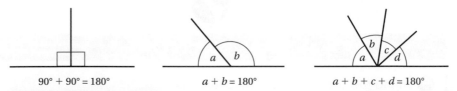

$90° + 90° = 180°$　　　　$a + b = 180°$　　　　$a + b + c + d = 180°$

WORKED EXAMPLE 2

Work out the size of x.

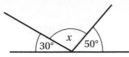

$30° + x + 50° = 180°$ ◁ Angles on a line add up to 180°.

$x = 180° - 30° - 50°$
$\quad = 100°$

Make x the subject of the equation and then work out its value.

Vertically opposite angles

When two lines cross, or intersect, they form four angles.

The angles *a* and *b* are vertically opposite each other and the angles *x* and *y* are vertically opposite each other.

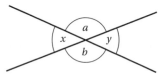

Vertically opposite angles are equal.

$a = b$

$x = y$

EXERCISE 9A

1 Three angles meet at a point.
Two angles are obtuse and are 120° and 96° respectively.
Choose the correct option for the size and type of the third angle.

A Obtuse angle of 144°   B Acute angle of 36°

C Reflex angle of 216°   D Obtuse angle of $\sqrt{144°}$

2 Which of the following statements is correct?

A Angles around a point always add up to 180°.

B Angles on a straight line always add up to 180°.

C Vertically opposite angles always add up to 180°.

3 Calculate the size of the angles marked *x*.

a
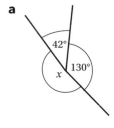

b
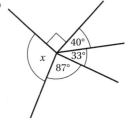

c
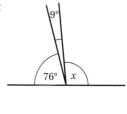

d What type of angle is *x* in each case?

4 Find the marked angles in each diagram. Give reasons for any deductions you make.

a Find *x* and *y*.
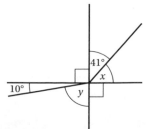

b Find *x*.
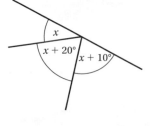

c Find *p*.
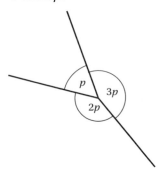

5 Give a reason why AE cannot be a straight line.

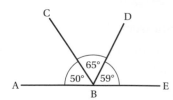

6 Calculate the size of the marked angles in each figure.

The lines are straight lines but the diagrams are not to scale.

Show your working and give reasons for any deductions you make.

a   **b**

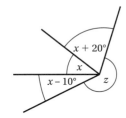

7 In the diagram, $x = 50°$.

Find the size of angle z.

8 Three angles meet at a point.

a What is the size of the acute angle?

b What is the size of the reflex angle?

c What is the size of the obtuse angle?

9 Work out the size of angle x.

Key vocabulary

transversal: a straight line that crosses a pair of parallel lines

Section 2: Parallel lines and angles

A line intersecting two or more parallel lines is called a **transversal**.

When a transversal intersects with parallel lines, it creates pairs of angles.

"When I'm designing and making clothes I need to be able to cut on the bias (at a given angle) and also bisect angles to add darts and fit sleeves." *(Fashion designer)*

Corresponding angles

Corresponding angles formed between a transversal and each parallel line are equal.

When a transversal crosses two parallel lines, there are four pairs of corresponding angles.

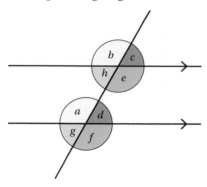

 Key vocabulary

corresponding angles: angles that are created at the same point of the intersection when a transversal crosses a pair of parallel lines

The corresponding angle pairs are:

$a = b$ $c = d$ $e = f$ $g = h$

Alternate angles

Alternate angles on opposite sides of the transversal on parallel lines are equal.

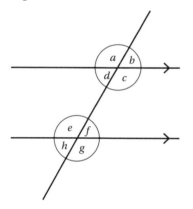

 Key vocabulary

alternate angles: the angles on parallel lines on opposite sides of a transversal

The alternate angle pairs are:

$a = g$ $b = h$ $c = e$ $d = f$

This table summarises the facts you need to know about the angles associated with parallel lines.

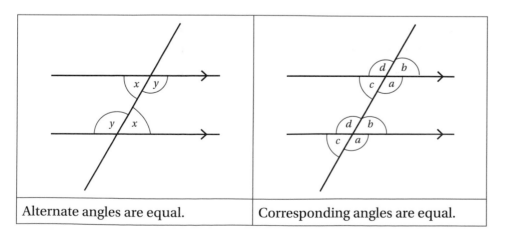

Alternate angles are equal.	Corresponding angles are equal.

EXERCISE 9B

1 Which of the following is the correct definition of a transversal?

A a pair of lines that are always an equal distance apart and never meet

B a pair of lines that meet at a right angle

C a straight line that crosses a pair of parallel lines

D a straight line that bisects a set of perpendicular lines

2 Find the size of the missing angles *a*, *b*, *c* and *d*.

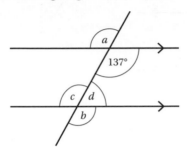

3 Find the sizes of the angles marked *x* and *y*.

Choose the correct answer from the following options.

A $x = 130°$ and $y = 130°$ B $x = 130°$ and $y = 50°$

C $x = 50°$ and $y = 130°$ D $x = 50°$ and $y = 50°$

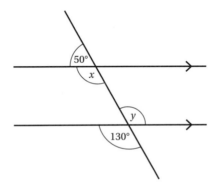

4 In the diagram, the two poles are parallel to each other.

Find the angle *x*.

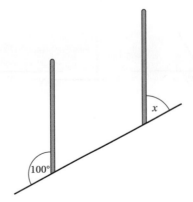

5 Find the size of the missing angles *a*, *b* and *c*.

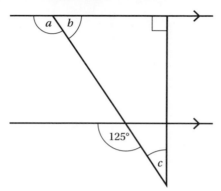

6 Find the size of angles *x* and *y*.

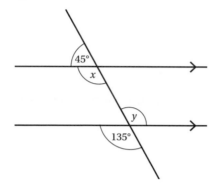

7 Find the size of the missing angles.

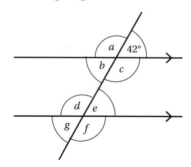

8 Find the size of ∠CEG.

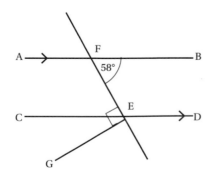

9 Find the size of ∠DCF.

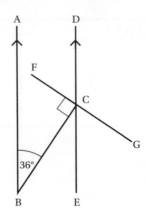

Section 3: Angles in triangles

Angle sum of a triangle

In the diagram, a line parallel to one side of the triangle has been drawn.

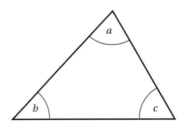 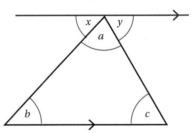

Tip

Make sure you know the differences between an equilateral triangle, a right-angled triangle, an isosceles triangle and a scalene triangle. Look back at Chapter 8 if you need to revise the properties of these triangles.

Using the properties of angles and parallel lines, you can prove that $a + b + c = 180°$

$x + a + y = 180°$ (Angles on a line sum to 180°.)

But: $x = b$ and $y = c$ (Alternate angles are equal.)

Substitute b for x and c for y and you prove that $a + b + c = 180°$.

The angle sum of a triangle is 180°.

The exterior angle is equal to the sum of the opposite interior angles

The exterior angle of a triangle is equal to the sum of the two opposite interior angles.

There are different ways to prove this using mathematical principles.

The worked example shows one way.

WORKED EXAMPLE 3

Show that $a + b = x$, and hence prove that the exterior angle of any triangle is equal to the sum of the opposite interior angles.

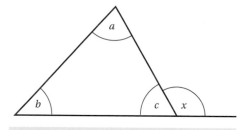

$c + x = 180°$ Angles on a line add to 180°.
$\therefore c = 180° - x$

$a + b + c = 180°$ Angles within a triangle add to 180°.
$\therefore c = 180° - (a + b)$

But, $c = (180° - x)$ Proven above.
So, $180° - (a + b) = 180° - x$
$\therefore a + b = x$

> **Tip**
>
> Always give reasons for any statements you make based on known facts.

EXERCISE 9C

1 A scalene triangle has two angles of 67° and 73°.

Which of the following is the third angle?

A 70°   B 40°   C 220°   D 67°

2 Calculate the size of the missing angles.

a

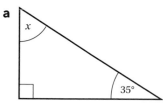

b

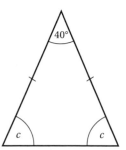

3 Find the size of the angles marked x and y.

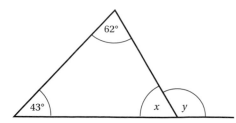

Find answers at: cambridge.org/ukschools/gcsemaths-studentbookanswers

4 Find the size of the angles marked *a* and *b*.

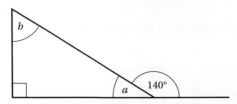

5 Find the size of the angles marked *x*, *y* and *z*.

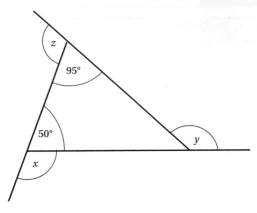

6 Work out the sizes of the angles marked *a*, *b* and *c*. Give reasons to justify your answers.

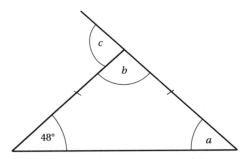

7 Calculate the size of *x*.

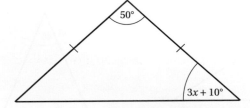

8 An isosceles triangle has one angle of 74°.

What could the size of the other two angles be?

Find both possible answers.

Section 4: Angles in polygons

These basalt columns are formed naturally when lava cools.

The end faces are mostly hexagonal.

The angle sum of a polygon

This is a regular hexagon.

It has six **interior angles** that are all equal.

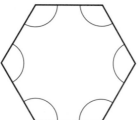

The diagonals divide the hexagon into four triangles.

So the sum of the interior angles of a hexagon is $4 \times 180° = 720°$.

The hexagon is regular, so the six interior angles are equal in size.

$720° \div 6 = 120°$, so, each interior angle is 120°.

For any polygon, the sum of the interior angles = $180(n - 2)$, where n is the number of sides.

Work through the investigation in Exercise 9D to understand how this rule is derived.

EXERCISE 9D

1 Draw the following polygons and divide them into triangles by drawing diagonals from one vertex as with the hexagon above.

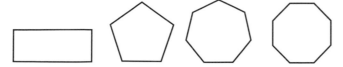

2 Predict how many triangles you could form if you did the same for a ten-sided and twenty-sided polygon.

 Find answers at: cambridge.org/ukschools/gcsemaths-studentbookanswers

3 Copy and complete this table using your results.

Number of sides in polygon	3	4	5	6	7	8	10	20
Number of triangles	1			4				
Angle sum of interior angles	180°			720°				

4 What is the relationship between the number of sides in a polygon and the number of triangles you can form in this way?

5 If a polygon has *n* sides, how many triangles can you form in this way?

6 Write a rule for finding the angle sum of a polygon:

a in words

b in general algebraic terms for a polygon of *n* sides.

7 Use your rule to find the angle sum of a polygon with 12 sides.

8 How could you find the size of each angle of a regular 12-sided polygon?

WORK IT OUT 9.1

Three students attempted to calculate the size of the interior angles in a regular pentagon.

Which is the correct solution?

What mistakes have been made by the other students?

Option A	Option B	Option C
There are three triangles within the pentagon. $3 \times 180° = 540°$ Five angles in a pentagon. $540° \div 5 = 108°$ Interior angle = 108°	There are five triangles in a pentagon. $5 \times 180° = 900°$ $900° \div 5 = 180°$ Interior angle = 180°	There is a trapezium and a triangle inside the pentagon. $360° + 180° = 540°$ There are five angles inside the pentagon including the central 360° which gives a total of 900°. Interior angle = $900° \div 5 = 180°$

The sum of exterior angles of a polygon

Each interior angle of a hexagon is 120°.

By extending each side, you can form six **exterior angles**.

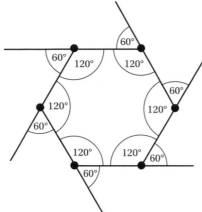

The sum of exterior angles is always 360°.

The total of the exterior and interior angles of a polygon is $n \times 180°$ where n is the number of sides of the polygon. Remember that angles on a straight line add to 180° and the exterior and interior angles are supplementary.

In the case of a hexagon this is $6 \times 180° = 1080°$

The sum of the interior angles $= 4 \times 180° = 720°$

The difference between the sum of the total angles 1080° less the sum of the interior angles 720° is the sum of the exterior angles. This equals 360°. To calculate the size of one exterior angle in a regular shape, divide 360° by the number of sides.

Exterior angle of a regular polygon $= \dfrac{360°}{n}$, where n is the number of sides.

You can use these rules to find the angle sum of any polygon.

If the polygon is regular, you can also calculate the size of each interior and exterior angle.

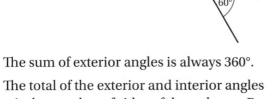

WORKED EXAMPLE 4

For a regular ten-sided polygon, find:

a the sum of the interior angles

b the size of each interior angle.

Use the general term for the sum of interior angles, where n is the number of sides in the polygon and/or the total number of interior angles.

a Angle sum = $180(n - 2) = 180(8) = 1440°$

b In a ten-sided figure $n = 10$.
There are 10 interior angles,
so one angle $= \dfrac{1440}{10} = 144°$

EXERCISE 9E

1 Copy and complete the following table.

Regular polygon	Sum of interior angles	Size of interior angle	Size of exterior angle
triangle			120°
quadrilateral		90°	
pentagon			
		120°	60°
heptagon			

2 In a regular octagon what is the size of each interior angle?

Choose from the following options.

A 110° B 180° C 135° D 120°

3 Calculate the sum of interior angles of a polygon with:

a 9 sides **b** 12 sides **c** 25 sides.

4 A regular polygon has 15 sides. Find:

a the sum of the interior angles **b** the sum of the exterior angles

c the size of an interior angle **d** the size of an exterior angle.

5 A regular polygon has an interior angle that is three times the size of the exterior angle.

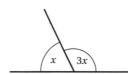

a What is the size of each exterior angle?

b What is the size of each interior angle?

c What is the name of the regular polygon?

6 Find the size of the angle marked x in each of the following polygons.

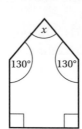
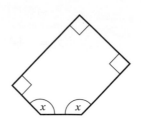
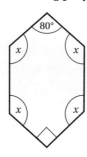

Checklist of learning and understanding

Basic angle facts

- Angles around a point sum to 360°.
- Angles on a straight line sum to 180°.
- Vertically opposite angles are equal.

Angles associated with parallel lines

- Corresponding angles are equal.
- Alternate angles are equal.

Geometric proofs

- Using properties of alternate and corresponding angles, you can show that the three interior angles of any triangle sum to 180°.
- Using the angle sum of triangles and properties of angles at a line and at a point, you can find the interior and exterior angles of any polygon.

 Chapter review

For additional questions on the topics in this chapter, visit GCSE Mathematics Online.

1 Select the correct size for the marked angle in each diagram.

a

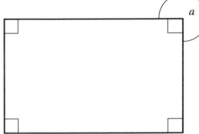

b

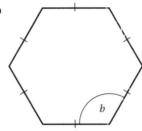

c

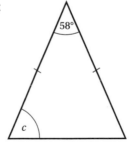

d

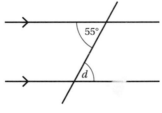

e

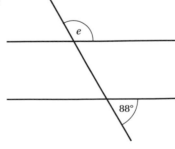

f

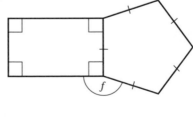

| 270° | 92° | 120° | 162° | 61° | 55° |

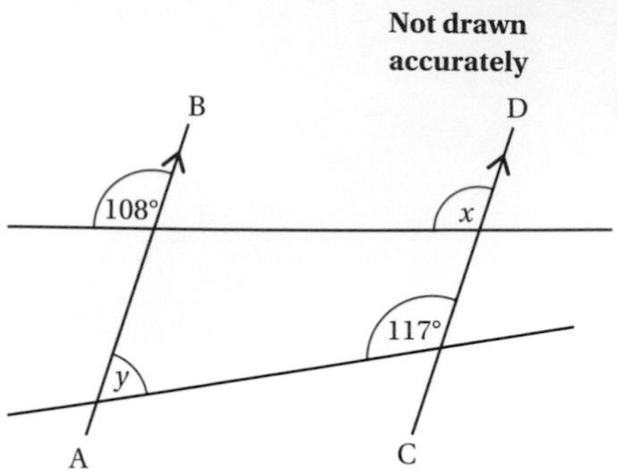

Not drawn accurately

2 AB is parallel to CD.

  a Write down the size of angle x.

    Give a reason for your answer. *(2 marks)*

  b Work out the size of angle y. *(2 marks)*

© AQA 2013

3 Is this a straight line? Give a reason for your answer.

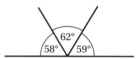

4 The interior angle of a regular polygon is 108°.

What type of polygon is it?

5 The angles are marked on the diagram.

Calculate $p + q + r + s + t$.

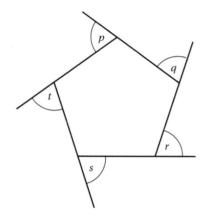

6 Work out the size of angles x and y.

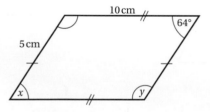

7 Work out the size of angle x.

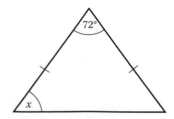

8 In this irregular hexagon, calculate the value of *z*.

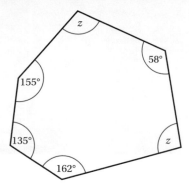

9 This diagram shows part of a regular polygon. The interior angle is 144°.

  a Calculate the number of sides of the polygon.

  b What is the name given to this polygon?

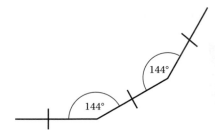

10 Calculate the exterior angle of a regular decagon.

11 Show mathematically why the sum of the exterior angles of any polygon is 360°.

12 Find the values of the angles marked *x* and *y*.

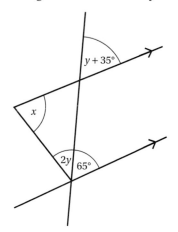

13 Work out the size of angle *x*.

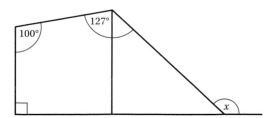

Find answers at: cambridge.org/ukschools/gcsemaths-studentbookanswers

10 Perimeter

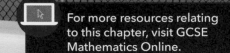
Using mathematics: real-life applications

Working out the amount of fencing needed for a field, or the number of tiles needed to edge a swimming pool, or the number of perimeter security cameras needed to secure an area, all require the calculation of a perimeter.

"Security cameras in a car park are only effective if they can see all round the perimeter of the car park."

(Security camera technician)

Before you start ...

Ch 8	You must be able to recognise and name some common polygons.	**1** Match each name to the correct shape. octagon pentagon hexagon **a** **b** **c**
KS3	You must be able to convert between basic metric units.	**2** Convert: **a** 5 km into m **b** 12 km into cm **c** 8500 mm into m **d** 4.8 m to mm.
KS3	You need to know and use the correct names of circle parts.	**3** True or false? **a** The diameter of a circle is twice the length of the radius. **b** The diameter of a circle is always shorter than the radius. **c** The angles at the centre of a circle add up to 180°.
KS3	You should be able to change the subject of a formula.	**4** Make l the subject of the formula $P = 2(l + w)$. **5** Make r the subject of the formula $P = \pi r + 2r$.

Assess your starting point using the Launchpad

STEP 1

1 A football pitch is 90 m long and 55 m wide.

What is the distance around the pitch?

2 Calculate the perimeter of each shape.

a

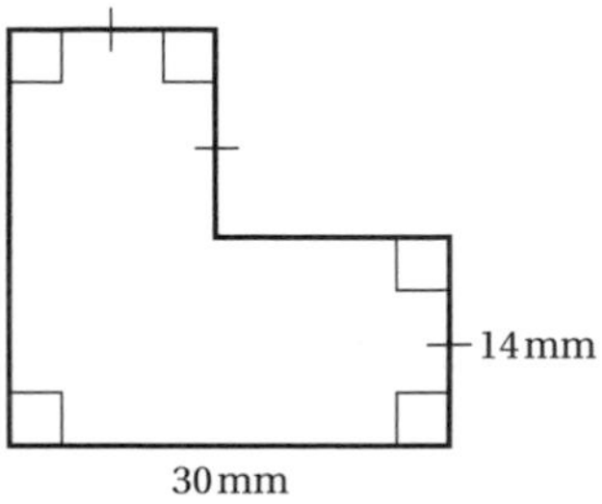

14 mm

30 mm

b

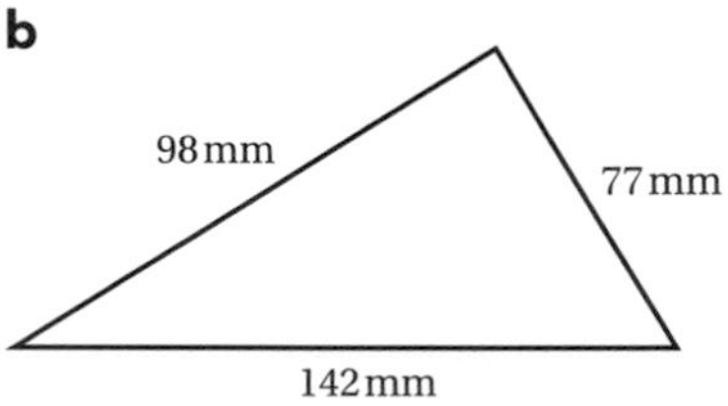

98 mm

77 mm

142 mm

3 A square has a perimeter of 169 mm. What is the length of a side?

4 A rectangle with a length of 4 cm, has a perimeter of 150 mm. Calculate the width of the rectangle. (Pay attention to the units.)

GO TO
Section 1:
Perimeter of simple and composite shapes

STEP 2

5 Work out the circumference of each circle. Use exact values of π and give your answers to two decimal places.

a

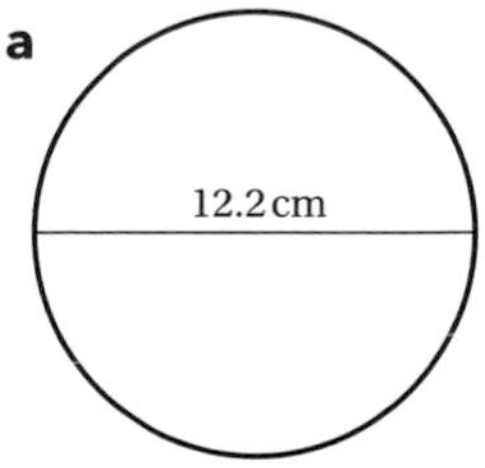

12.2 cm

b

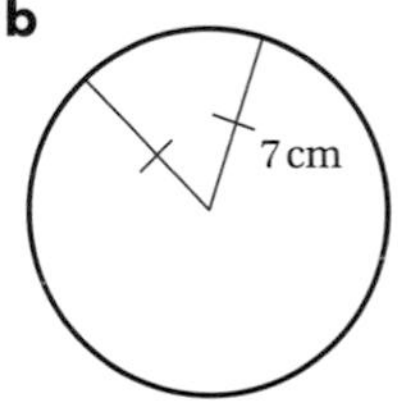

7 cm

6 Work out the diameter of a circle to the nearest centimetre, given that its circumference is 37.7 cm (to one decimal place).

7 What is the perimeter of a semicircular rug of radius 1.6 m? Give your answer to two decimal places.

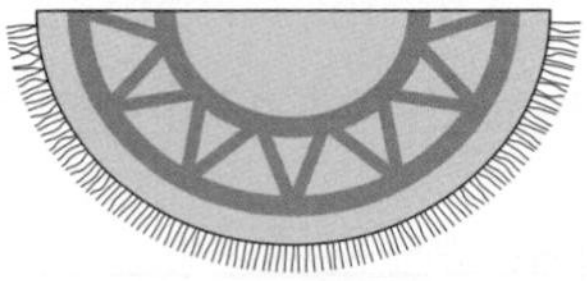

GO TO
Section 2:
Circumference of a circle
Section 3:
Problems involving perimeter and circumference

GO TO
Chapter review

Find answers at: cambridge.org/ukschools/gcsemaths-studentbookanswers

Key vocabulary

perimeter: distance around the boundaries (sides) of a shape

Tip

Composite shapes are shapes that are made up of two or more basic shapes, for example, a rectangle joined to a triangle. Sometimes you will see them referred to as **compound shapes**.

Section 1: Perimeter of simple and composite shapes

The **perimeter** of a shape is the total distance around the boundaries of the shape. To calculate the perimeter of a shape:

- find the lengths of all the sides, making sure they are in the same units
- add the lengths together.

Tip

The perimeter must include **all** the lengths. You can use what you know about the properties of shapes to deduce missing lengths.

WORKED EXAMPLE 1

Find the perimeter (P) of this T-shaped piece of cardboard.

All angles are right angles and all dimensions are in centimetres.

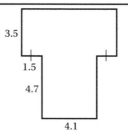

Start by working out the lengths of the missing sides.

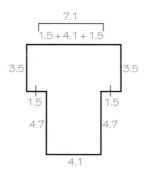

$P = 7.1 + 3.5 + 1.5 + 4.7 + 4.1 + 4.7 + 1.5 + 3.5$
  $= 30.6$

Add up the side lengths.

In shapes with parallel sides:

perimeter = sum of one pair of parallel sides + sum of the other pair of parallel sides,

so you can work it out quickly by finding the total length of each and doubling.

In this example the horizontal sides are 7.1 cm long and the vertical sides are 8.2 cm long, so

$P = 2(7.1 + 8.2) = 30.6 \text{ cm}$

Using formulae to find perimeter

The properties of different polygons can be used to derive formulae for calculating the perimeter without adding up all the sides.

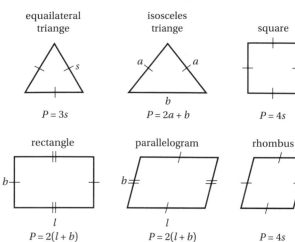

equailateral triangle
$P = 3s$

isosceles triangle
$P = 2a + b$

square
$P = 4s$

rectangle
$P = 2(l + b)$

parallelogram
$P = 2(l + b)$

rhombus
$P = 4s$

Tip

You might remember some of these formulae from KS3. You do not need to memorise them, but you must be able to apply and manipulate them.

For **regular polygons** you only need the length of one side to find the perimeter.

Multiply the side length by the number of sides.

Each side length of this regular hexagon is 6 cm so the perimeter is: $6\,\text{cm} \times 6 = 36\,\text{cm}$.

Tip

Writing a general expression is a way of showing the quantity of something when the actual numbers are not known. Numbers can be substituted into the expression to find the unknown quantity.

WORKED EXAMPLE 2

Write an expression for the perimeter of this shape in terms of x.

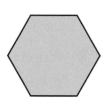

$$\text{Perimeter} = x + (x + 5) + x + (x + 10)$$
$$= 4x + 15$$

The perimeter is calculated by adding the side lengths around the outside of the shape. In this example the lengths are given in algebraic terms. Add the algebraic terms by collecting like parts.

Tip

Simplifying expressions by collecting like terms is covered in Chapter 7.

EXERCISE 10A

1 What is the perimeter of an equilateral triangle of side length 10 cm?

2 A yard is fully enclosed by a fence of lengths 12 m, 4.7 m, 354 cm, 972 cm. What is the perimeter of the yard?

3 The perimeter of a square patio is 64 m.

What length is the side of the patio? Choose your answer from the options below.

A 8 m   B 10 m   C 12 m   D 16 m

Find answers at: cambridge.org/ukschools/gcsemaths-studentbookanswers

4 Write expressions for the perimeter of these shapes.

   a An equilateral triangle, side length a.

   b A rectangle, width x and length y.

   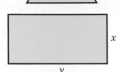

   c A regular octagon, side length z.

5 What is the perimeter of the triangle, in terms of x?
   Choose from the options below.

   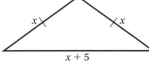

   A $x^3 + 5$ B $\dfrac{3x + 5}{2}$ C $3x + 5$ D $1.5x + 5$

6 Work out the perimeter of this shape.
   Each side length is 10 cm.

   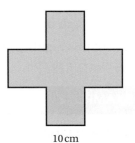

   10 cm

7 This pattern is made by joining identical hexagons together.

   If the side length of each hexagon is 8 cm, what is the perimeter of this shape?

   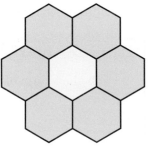

8 Each side length of this tiling pattern is 15 cm.
   Work out its perimeter.

   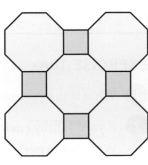

9 **a** Give reasons why the formulae for calculating the perimeter of a rectangle and a parallelogram and those for a square and a rhombus are the same.

   b Give a reason why is there no formula for finding the perimeter of a trapezium.

10 A field has dimensions as shown on the diagram.

A fence is put up around the field.

The fence consists of upright posts and four strands of wire, as shown.

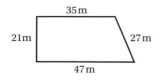

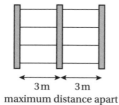

a Find the total length of wire needed for the fencing.

b The fence posts are placed 2.8 metres apart.

Work out how many posts are needed.

(Assume there is no gate, only a style to get over the fence. You will need to add 4 extra posts as they are unlikely to fit exactly in each corner.)

c Each post costs £2.39 and the wire costs £1.78 per metre.

Calculate the cost of the fencing.

Finding lengths when the perimeter is known

You can calculate missing side-lengths of shapes if you know the perimeter and have enough information about the shape.

For example, if you know a regular hexagon has a perimeter of 72 cm, you can deduce that each of the six equal sides is 12 cm long because 72 cm ÷ 6 = 12 cm.

In other shapes you can substitute known values into the formula and solve for the unknown length.

WORKED EXAMPLE 3

What is the length of a rectangle of perimeter 20 cm and width 5.5 cm?

$P = 2(L + W)$
$P = 20, W = 5.5$

Think about the information you have.

$$20 = 2L + 2(5.5)$$
$$20 = 2L + 11$$
$$20 - 11 = 2L$$
$$9 = 2L$$
$$L = 4.5 \, cm$$

Substitute the values into the formula and solve for L.

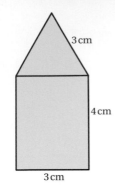

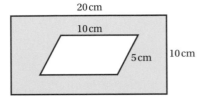

Perimeter of composite shapes

Composite shapes are formed by combining shapes or by removing parts of a shape.

For example, this shape is made up of a rectangle and a triangle.

To find the perimeter, add up the side lengths around the outside boundary of the shape.

The perimeter is: $4 + 3 + 3 + 4 + 3 = 17\,\text{cm}$

This rectangle has a parallelogram cut out of it.

The perimeter of the shape must include all of the boundaries, so in examples like these, you must include the outer and inner boundaries of the shape.

$$P = 2(20 + 10) + 2(10 + 5)$$
$$= 2(30) + 2(15)$$
$$= 60 + 30$$
$$P = 90\,\text{cm}$$

WORK IT OUT 10.1

This shape was made by combining five identical squares with sides of 6.5 cm with four identical equilateral triangles.

Which calculation will result in the correct perimeter? Why?

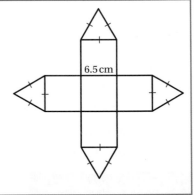

Option A	Option B	Option C
$P = 16 \times 6.5$ $= 104\,\text{cm}$	$P = 20 \times 6.5$ $= 130\,\text{cm}$	$P = 24 \times 6.5$ $= 156\,\text{cm}$

EXERCISE 10B

1 Copy and complete the table to find the missing values.

Perimeter	Length	Width
rectangle ABCD $P = 242\,\text{mm}$	77 mm	
parallelogram MNOP $P = 200\,\text{mm}$		55 mm
rhombus CDEF $P = 12.25\,\text{cm}$		
square PQRS $P = 47.28\,\text{cm}$		

2 Calculate the perimeter of each shape.

a

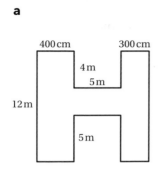

400 cm 300 cm
4 m
5 m
12 m
5 m

b

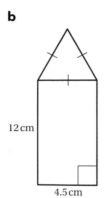

12 cm
4.5 cm

c

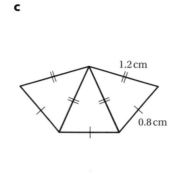

1.2 cm
0.8 cm

d

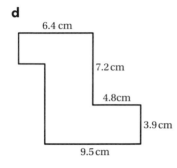

6.4 cm
7.2 cm
4.8 cm
3.9 cm
9.5 cm

e

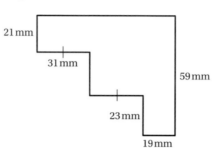

21 mm
31 mm
23 mm
59 mm
19 mm

3 Petra has the following mosaic tiles:

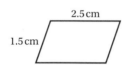
2.5 cm
1.5 cm

2.5 cm

2.5 cm
2.5 cm

2.5 cm
3 cm 3 cm
4 cm

She arranges the tiles to make these shapes.

a

b

c

d

e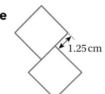
1.25 cm

f

Use the dimensions above to find the perimeter of each shape.

4 The end of a maze consists of a regular pentagon with side length 5 m.

A child runs round this 3 times.

How far has she run in total? Choose from the options below.

A 15 m   B 25 m   C 75 m   D 750 m

5 A rectangular allotment has a perimeter of 25 metres.

The length of one side is 6.8 metres.

How wide is the allotment?

Section 2: Circumference of a circle

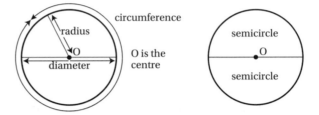

The perimeter of a circle is called its **circumference (C)**.

The **radius** (r) is the distance from the centre to the circumference.

The diameter (d) is a line through the centre of the circle. The diameter is twice the radius (2r).

When you divide the circumference of a circle by its diameter you get a constant ratio of approximately 3.142.

$\pi = \dfrac{C}{d}$ This ratio is called pi and the symbol π is used to represent it.

This ratio can be rearranged to give two formulae for finding the circumference of any circle.

Key vocabulary

radius: (plural **radii**): distance from the centre to the circumference of a circle. The radius is half of the diameter of the circle.

 Learn this formula

$C = \pi d$

where C = circumference and d = diameter.

Since the diameter is twice the length of the radius, the formula can also be written in terms of r.

$C = 2\pi r$

where r = radius.

Pi has no exact decimal or fractional value (it is an irrational number).

When you do calculations involving pi you might need to give rounded or approximate answers.

Your calculator can work with exact values of π but you might be given an approximate value of pi to use in a problem.

Problem-solving framework

Racing wheelchairs can travel at speeds of up to 45 mph and can cost up to £20 000.

The rear wheels of a chair have a diameter of 70 cm.

The hand wheels have a radius of 20 cm.

a Find the difference in circumference between the two wheels.

b Find the number of revolutions that the rear wheels will make over a 100 m race.

Steps for solving problems	What you would do for this example
Step 1: What have you got to do?	Find the difference in circumference between the two wheels, and find the number of revolutions (turns) that the rear wheels will make over 100 m.
Step 2: What information do you need?	Diameter (d) of rear wheel = 70 cm Radius (r) of hand wheel = 20 cm Length of race = 100 m Circumference formula: $C = \pi d$ or $2\pi r$
Step 3: What information don't you need?	The speed of the wheelchair and its cost are irrelevant.
Step 4: What maths can you use?	Circumference of rear wheel = $\pi d = \pi \times 70 = 219.9$ cm (to 1 dp) Circumference of hand wheel = $2\pi r = 2 \times \pi \times 20 = 125.7$ cm (to 1 dp) Difference in circumference = $219.9 - 125.7 = 94.2$ cm Change the units so that they are the same: $100\,\text{m} = 100 \times 100\,\text{cm} = 10\,000\,\text{cm}$ Number of revolutions made by rear wheel = $10\,000 \div 219.9 = 45.5$ (to 1 dp)
Step 5: Have you used all the information? At this point you should check to make sure you have calculated what was asked for in the question.	All relevant information used ✓ Calculated part **a** ✓ Calculated part **b** ✓
Step 6: Is it correct?	Used diameter for rear wheel ✓ Used radius for hand wheel ✓ Converted cm into m correctly ✓

Find answers at: cambridge.org/ukschools/gcsemaths-studentbookanswers

Knowing the circumference of a circle means that you can calculate the diameter and/or the radius.

WORKED EXAMPLE 4

A circle has a circumference of 200 cm.

Calculate the diameter of the circle to one decimal place.

$$C = \pi d$$
$$200 = \pi \times d$$

Using the equation for the circumference of a circle, fill in the parts you are given, using the value of π as 3.14 unless you are told otherwise.

$$200 \div \pi = d$$
$$d = 63.7 \text{ cm (to 1 dp)}$$

Rearrange the formula to find the diameter.

Tip

If you are asked to find r and use $C = \pi d$, remember to divide d by 2 to get r.

EXERCISE 10C

1 Use the ⊞ key on your calculator to calculate the circumference of each circle.

Give your answer to two decimal places where necessary.

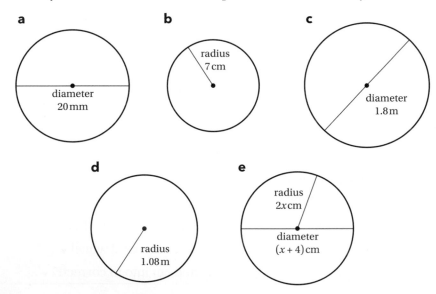

a

diameter
20 mm

b

radius
7 cm

c

diameter
1.8 m

d

radius
1.08 m

e

radius
2x cm

diameter
($x + 4$) cm

2 The circumference of a circle is 94.2 cm.

What is its diameter? Use $\pi = 3.14$

Choose your answer from the following options.

A 295.8 cm   B 60 cm   C 30 cm   D 3.14 cm

3 A car rim has a diameter of 42 cm. Calculate the circumference of the rim.

4 A plastic toy consists of 36 coils of plastic.

The diameter of one coil is 55 mm.

What length of plastic is needed to make the toy?

5 Nate has a square piece of metal with sides of 8.5 cm.

He needs to cut out a round disc from the square with a radius of at least 4 cm.

  a Draw a rough sketch to show this piece of metal.

  b Calculate the circumference of the disc with a radius of 4 cm.

  c When he cuts the disc out, Nate finds the diameter is actually 8.3 cm.

  What is the circumference of the disc?

  d What is the perimeter of the piece of metal left after cutting out a disc of:

  i radius 4 cm?   **ii** diameter 8.3 cm?

6 Find the diameter, to two decimal places, of a circle with a circumference of:

  a 20 mm   **b** 15.2 cm.

7 A round CD has a circumference of 36.33 cm.

Find the radius of the CD to the nearest millimetre.

8 A round cake has a circumference of 77 cm.

The cake is displayed on a square plate.

What is the smallest possible side length of a plate the cake will fit on, without it hanging over the edge?

9 The minute hand of a clock is 75 mm long.

How far will the tip of the hand travel in one hour?

Give your answer to the nearest centimetre.

Find answers at: cambridge.org/ukschools/gcsemaths-studentbookanswers

Tip

The term circumference is only used to describe the distance around a whole circle. When you deal with distance around parts of a circle you talk about the perimeter.

Sectors of a circle

A sector is a 'slice' of a circle.

The perimeter of a sector is formed by two radii and a section of the circumference called an arc.

Perimeter of a sector = radius + radius + arc length.

To find the perimeter of a sector you have to work out the length of the arc.

The angle at the centre of a circle is a fraction of 360°. You can express this as $\frac{x}{360}$.

The arc length is a fraction of the circumference. To find the length of the arc, use the size of the angle and the circumference of the circle.

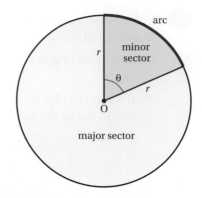

$$\text{Arc length} = \frac{x}{360} \times \pi d \qquad \text{or} \qquad \text{Arc length} = \frac{x}{360} \times 2\pi r$$

$$\underset{\text{fraction}}{\nearrow} \qquad \underset{\text{circumference}}{\nwarrow} \qquad\qquad \underset{\text{fraction}}{\nearrow} \qquad \underset{\text{circumference}}{\nwarrow}$$

WORKED EXAMPLE 5

Find the length of the arc in each of these circle sectors.

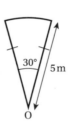 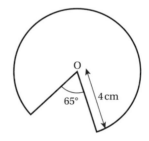

a Arc length $= \frac{30}{360} \times 2\pi r$

$= \frac{1}{12} \times 2 \times \pi \times 5$

$= 2.62\,\text{m (to 2 dp)}$

> Use $2\pi r$ here as you have been given the radius.

b $360° - 65° = 295°$

Arc length $= \frac{295}{360} \times 2 \times \pi \times 4$

$= 20.59\,\text{cm (to 2 dp)}$

> The angle inside the sector is not given. Work it out using angles round a point.

The semicircle and quarter-circle (quadrant) are special cases.

- In a semicircle, the angle at the centre is 180° and the arc length is half the circumference.
- In a quarter-circle, the angle at the centre is 90° and the arc length is a quarter of the circumference.

EXERCISE 10D

1 Find *l* in each of the following circles.

a

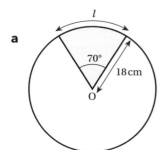

b

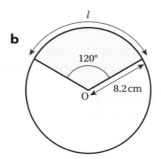

c

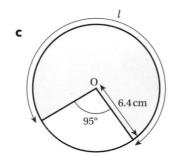

d

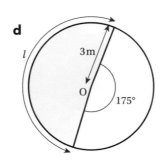

2 Find the perimeter of each shape.

a

b

c

d

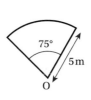

e

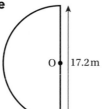

f

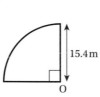

Section 3: Problems involving perimeter and circumference

In this section you are going to combine what you have learned about perimeter and circumference to solve problems involving composite shapes.

To work with irregular and composite shapes, divide them up into known shapes to make it easier to do the calculations.

WORKED EXAMPLE 6

The diagram shows a baseball field which is $\frac{1}{4}$ of a circle.

Calculate the perimeter of the field to the nearest metre.

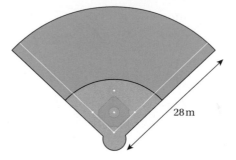

28 m

Circumference of whole circle =
$2\pi r = 2 \times \pi \times 28$.

> The basis of this calculation is the formula relating to circles: circumference and arc length.

Arc length of $\frac{1}{4}$ circle $= \dfrac{C}{4}$

$\qquad\qquad = \dfrac{2 \times \pi \times 28}{4}$

$\qquad\qquad = 43.98\,\text{m}$

> The arc length is a portion of the circumference of a circle.

Perimeter $= 2r +$ arc length

$\qquad\quad = 2 \times 28 + 43.98$

$\qquad\quad = 56 + 43.98$

$\qquad\quad = 99.98\,\text{m}$

Perimeter $= 100\,\text{m}$, to the nearest metre

> The perimeter in this case consists of the arc length added to two radii (plural of radius).

WORK IT OUT 10.2

This is a plan of a children's play area.

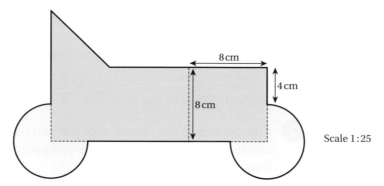

8 cm

4 cm

8 cm

Scale 1 : 25

Edging is to be placed around the curved edges of the sandpits.

Using $\pi = 3.14$, work out the total length of edging required.

Which of the answers below is the correct answer?

What mistakes have been made in the other workings?

Option A	Option B	Option C
Circumference of a circle = $\pi d = 2\pi r$	Circumference of a circle = $\pi d = 2\pi r$	Circumference of a circle = $2\pi d = \pi r$
$r = 4$ cm	$r = 4$ cm	$r = 4$ cm
$C = 2 \times 3.14 \times 4$ $= 3.14 \times 8$ $= 25.12$ cm	$C = 2 \times 3.14 \times 4$ $= 3.14 \times 8$ $= 25.12$ cm	$C = 2 \times 3.14 \times 8$ $= 3.14 \times 16$ $= 50.24$ cm
Scale 1 : 25 So, actual circumference of circle = 25.12×25 $= 628$ cm $= 6.28$ m	Only $\frac{3}{4}$ of the sandpit needs edging: $\frac{3}{4} \times 25.12$ cm $= 18.84$ cm	Only $\frac{3}{4}$ of the sandpit needs edging: $\frac{3}{4} \times 50.24$ cm $= 37.68$ cm
Two sandpits so total edging required = $6.28 \times 2 = 12.56$ m	Two sandpits: $18.84 \times 2 = 37.68$ cm of edging Scale 1 : 25 So actual amount of edging required: $37.68 \times 25 = 942$ cm $= 9.42$ m	Two sandpits: $37.68 \times 2 = 75.36$ cm of edging Scale 1 : 25 So actual amount of edging required: $75.36 \times 25 = 1884$ cm $= 18.84$ m

Tip

Perimeter can be worked out by measuring lengths, or by using lengths from a scale diagram.

Find answers at: cambridge.org/ukschools/gcsemaths-studentbookanswers

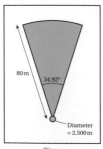

Discus

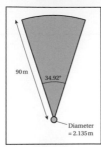

Hammer throw

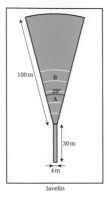

Javelin

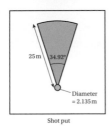

Shot put

EXERCISE 10E

The diagram shows the shape and dimensions of different throwing event field areas used in competitions, such as discus.

Use the information on the diagram to answer questions 1 to 4.

1 Calculate the length of the white line painted around the outside of:

  a the discus area

  b the hammer throw area.

2 Competitors in the discus, shot put and hammer throw have to remain inside a marked circle while the equipment is in their hands (before they throw it).

  a Which sport has the largest marked circle?

  b What is the circumference of the circle in the discus throwing cage?

  c In shot put and hammer throw, a raised edge is built around the circumference of the starting circle.

  The edge is 10 cm wide.

  Calculate its inner and outer circumference.

3 Calculate the perimeter of the event space for javelin.

4 The curved measurement lines on each event space are 10 m apart.

  Using the javelin field, calculate the length of the lines marked A and B.

5 The radius of the Earth is approximately 6378.1 km at the Equator.

  Calculate the approximate distance around the Equator. Give your answer to two decimal places.

6 A pizza has a circumference of 94 cm.

  What is the side length of the smallest cardboard box it will fit into? Choose your answer from the following options.

  A 94 cm   B 29.94 cm   C 14.97 cm

7 Find the perimeter of this symmetrical logo.

  Use a ruler and protractor to measure and find the dimensions you need.

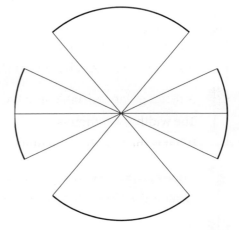

Checklist of learning and understanding

Perimeter
- Perimeter is the total distance around the boundaries of a shape.
- You can calculate perimeter by adding the lengths of the sides or by applying a formula based on the properties of the shape.

Circumference
- The perimeter of a circle is called its circumference (C).
- $C = \pi d$ or $C = 2\pi r$
- A sector is a part of a circle between two radii. You can find the arc length of a sector by working out what fraction of a circle the sector represents.

Chapter review

For additional questions on the topics in this chapter, visit GCSE Mathematics Online.

1 What is the formula for the circumference of a circle?

Choose from the options below.

A $\frac{1}{2}bh$ B $2\pi r$ C πr^2 D $\frac{4}{3}\pi r^3 h$

2 The perimeters of these two shapes are equal.

What is the side length of the square?

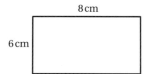

3 A jar of jam has a diameter of 12 cm.

What is the smallest circumference of the gift box tube needed for it to fit into? Use $\pi = 3.14$

4 What is the circumference of the centre circle of a football pitch that has a radius of 9.15 m? Use $\pi = 3.14$

5 The perimeter of a regular pentagon is 90 cm.

Work out the length of each side.

6 Drew has a piece of ribbon that is 0.5 m long. She wants to tie a bow around a present in a tube that has a diameter of 10 cm.

Will she have enough ribbon? Use $\pi = 3.14$

7 A rectangular vegetable plot has a perimeter of 50 metres.

The width is 6.5 metres.

What is the length of the plot?

8 An irrigator in a field can water a circular area of radius 14.5 m.

What is the circumference of the area that can be irrigated? Use $\pi = 3.14$

9 A pizza has a diameter of 28 cm. It is placed in a cardboard box.

Calculate the perimeter of the smallest box that it will fit into.

10 The perimeter of this square is 48 cm.

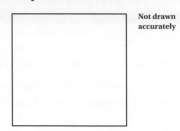

Not drawn accurately

Semicircles are joined to two sides of the square.

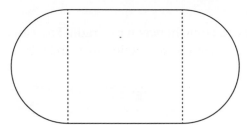

Work out the perimeter of this shape.

(4 marks)

© AQA 2013

11 Calculate the perimeter of the shape shown in the margin.

Give your answer to one decimal place.

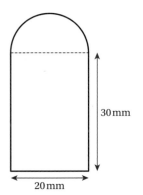

30 mm

20 mm

12 The diagram shows some staging for a concert.

Stage 1   Stage 2   Stage 3

The main stage is a circle of diameter 6 m.

The smaller stages can be made by splitting up a main stage into smaller pieces.

The curved edges of the staging pieces have a patterned edge.

a Work out the length of the patterned edging on the stage sections shown in the diagram.

b A safety rubber strip is to be applied along all the edges of the staging.

Work out the total length of strip required for the three stage sections shown in the diagram.

11 Area

In this chapter you will learn how to ...

- apply formulae to find the area of different shapes, including circles and parts of circles.
- use appropriate formulae to calculate the area of composite shapes.

 For more resources relating to this chapter, visit GCSE Mathematics Online.

Using mathematics: real-life applications

Ordering the right quantity of turf for a sports field, preparing detailed floor plans, and working out how much fertiliser is needed to treat a field crop all require knowledge and calculation of areas.

 Did you know?

The area of farmland is often given in acres or hectares. An acre was traditionally the area of farmland that could be ploughed in one day by oxen. In the metric system, the acre was replaced by the hectare. 1 hectare = 10 000 m²

"Fertiliser application rates are normally given in kilograms per hectare. One hectare is an area of 100 m × 100 m or 10 000 m². Applying too much or too little fertiliser to an area can have disastrous results on the crops." *(Farmer)*

Before you start ...

Ch 8	You should remember the properties of quadrilaterals.	**1** Use the marked properties to name the quadrilaterals correctly. **a** **b** **c**

KS3 Ch 4	You should be familiar with square numbers and square roots.	**2** Calculate:
		   a 5^2 **b** 2×10^2 **c** $3^2 + 4^2$
		
		3 Find the number that is squared to give each of these.
		   a 144 **b** 10 000 **c** 0.25

KS3	You need to be able to convert between square units of measurement.	**4** Complete these: **a** $5\,m^2 = \square\,cm^2$ **b** $\square\,cm^2 = 87\,000\,mm^2$ **c** $4\,km^2 = \square\,m^2$

Find answers at: cambridge.org/ukschools/gcsemaths-studentbookanswers

Assess your starting point using the Launchpad

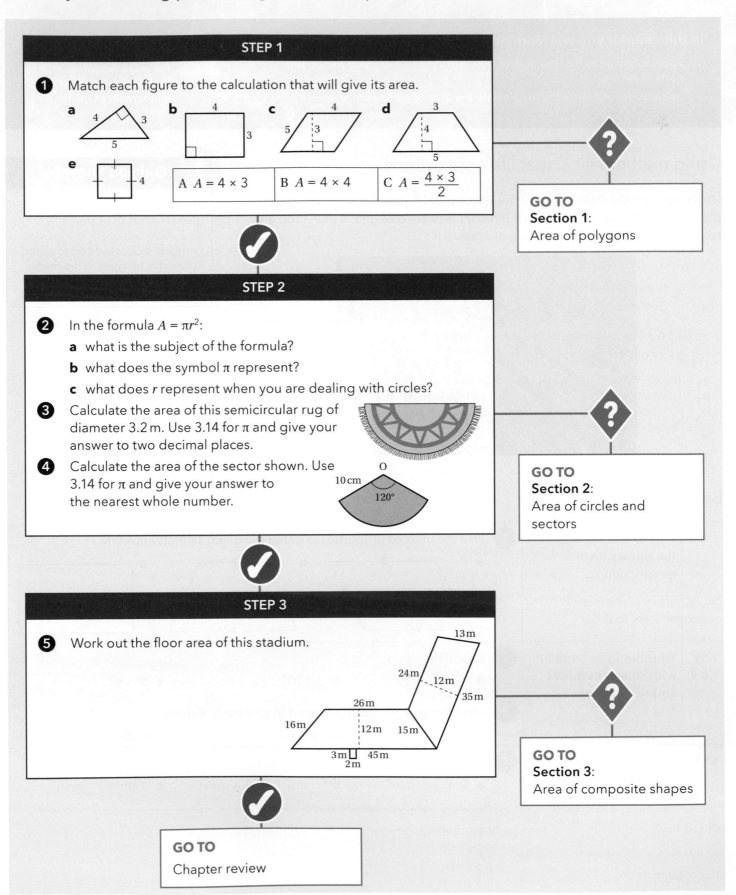

STEP 1

1 Match each figure to the calculation that will give its area.

a

b   4

c   4

d   3

e   4

A $A = 4 \times 3$ B $A = 4 \times 4$ C $A = \dfrac{4 \times 3}{2}$

GO TO
Section 1:
Area of polygons

STEP 2

2 In the formula $A = \pi r^2$:

  a what is the subject of the formula?

  b what does the symbol π represent?

  c what does r represent when you are dealing with circles?

3 Calculate the area of this semicircular rug of diameter 3.2 m. Use 3.14 for π and give your answer to two decimal places.

4 Calculate the area of the sector shown. Use 3.14 for π and give your answer to the nearest whole number.

O

10 cm

120°

GO TO
Section 2:
Area of circles and sectors

STEP 3

5 Work out the floor area of this stadium.

13 m

24 m

12 m

35 m

26 m

16 m

12 m   15 m

3 m   45 m

2 m

GO TO
Section 3:
Area of composite shapes

GO TO
Chapter review

Section 1: Area of polygons

The **area** of a plane shape is the amount of space it takes up.

Area is always given in square units. Common units are mm² (square millimetres), cm² (square centimetres), m² and km².

Area of rectangles and squares

The formula for finding the area of a rectangle is:

area = length × width

$A = lw$

In a square, the length and width are equal, so the formula is:

area of the square $= l \times l = l^2$

$A = l^2$

You can change the subject of area formulae to find unknown lengths if you know the area and the other lengths.

> **Tip**
>
> You will learn more about how to change the subject of a formula in Chapter 22.

WORKED EXAMPLE 1

A rectangle of area 45 cm² has one side 9 cm long.
How long is the other side?

$A = l \times w$
$45 = 9 \times w$
$\frac{45}{9} = w$
$5 = w$
The other side is
5 cm long.

> Use either l or w in this case as you don't know which it is.
>
> Divide each side by 9 to get w on its own.

Area of a triangle

You can show that the area of any triangle is half the area of a rectangle by drawing in a rectangle.

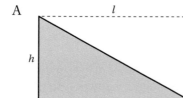

$b = l$
$h = w$

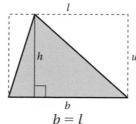

$b = l$
$h = w$

Figure A shows a right-angled triangle. Figure B shows a scalene triangle.

In both diagrams the areas of the shaded and unshaded parts are equal.

Area of rectangle $= l \times w$

Area of triangle $= \frac{1}{2} \times l \times w$

Find answers at: cambridge.org/ukschools/gcsemaths-studentbookanswers

The length l is equal to the base of the triangle and w is equal to the height of the triangle, so

$$\text{area of triangle} = \tfrac{1}{2} \times \text{length of its base} \times \text{its height}$$

This gives a formula for the area of any triangle.

⊞ Learn this formula

Area of a triangle $= \tfrac{1}{2} \times$ base $\times$ perpendicular height

$$= \tfrac{1}{2} \times b \times h$$

You can use any side of a triangle as the base.

The height must be perpendicular to the side that you are using as its base.

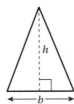 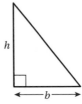 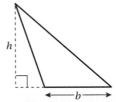

WORKED EXAMPLE 2

Calculate the area of each triangle.

a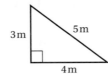

b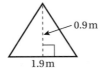

c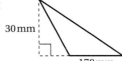

a Area $= \tfrac{1}{2} \times b \times h$

$= \tfrac{1}{2} \times 4 \times 3$

$= \tfrac{1}{2} \times 12$

> In a right-angled triangle the two shorter (perpendicular) sides can be used as the base and height.

$= 6\,\text{m}^2$

> Remember to include the units in the answer.

b Area $= \tfrac{1}{2} \times b \times h$

$= \tfrac{1}{2} \times 1.9 \times 0.9$

$= \tfrac{1}{2} \times 1.71$

$= 0.855\,\text{m}^2$

> Use the side marked 1.9 as the base because the height is perpendicular to it.

c Area $= \dfrac{bh}{2}$

$= \dfrac{(170 \times 30)}{2}$

$= \dfrac{5100}{2}$

$= 2550\,\text{mm}^2$

> This is the same formula but expressed differently. Multiplying by $\tfrac{1}{2}$ is the same as dividing by 2.

Tip

The order of the multiplication is not important:

$\tfrac{1}{2} \times 4 \times 3 = \tfrac{1}{2} \times 12 = 6$

$\tfrac{1}{2} \times 4 \times 3 = 2 \times 3 = 6$

 Did you know?

Two triangles that look completely different might still have the same area.

These two triangles are equal in area.

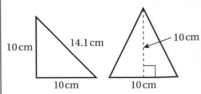

EXERCISE 11A

1 How might each of the following people use area calculations in their jobs? For each one, give examples of the shapes they would work with most often and the formulae they might need.

a House painter   **b** Mosaic artist   **c** Gardener

d Dressmaker   **e** Carpet layer

2 Choose the correct answer from the given options.

a What is the area of a rectangular field with length 24 m and width 17 m?

A $82\,\text{m}^2$ B $204\,\text{m}^2$ C $408\,\text{m}^2$ D $408\,\text{m}^3$

b What is the area of a triangle with perpendicular height x cm and base y cm?

A $x^2y^2\,\text{cm}$ B $(x+y)\,\text{cm}^2$ C $\frac{1}{2}(xy)\,\text{cm}^2$ D $xy\,\text{cm}^2$

3 Calculate the area of each triangle.

a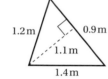

b

4 The area of a triangle is $36\,\text{m}^2$.

Its perpendicular height is 6 m.

Work out the length of its base.

5 Work out the total area of the kite shown in the margin.

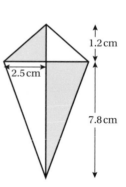

6 A triangle has a base of 3.6 m and a height of 50 cm. (Remember 100 cm = 1 m)

What is its area? Give your answer in square metres.

7 A triangle of area $0.125\,\text{m}^2$ has a base 25 cm long.

What is its height in centimetres?

8 The mast on this small boat is 2.7 m tall.

The smaller sail extends $\frac{2}{3}$ of the way up the mast.

Calculate the total area of the sails.

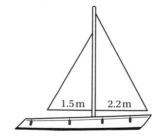

Find answers at: cambridge.org/ukschools/gcsemaths-studentbookanswers

Area of a parallelogram

The base of this parallelogram is b and the **perpendicular height** is h.

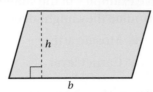

By removing a triangle from one end and joining it to the other end, you can form a rectangle.

The parallelogram and rectangle have the same area.

Tip

You must use the perpendicular height and not the slant height.

Learn this formula

Area of a parallelogram = base × perpendicular height
$$= b \times h$$

WORKED EXAMPLE 3

Calculate the area of the parallelogram.

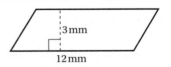

Area $= b \times h$
$= 12 \times 3 = 36 \, \text{mm}^2$

Substitute into the area formula.

Don't forget to add the units.

WORK IT OUT 11.1

A parallelogram is made by combining a rectangle and two right-angled triangles like this.

Which of these options will give the correct area?

What is wrong in the other two calculations?

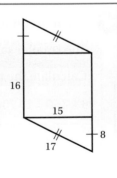

Option A	Option B	Option C
$A = bh$	$A = bh$	$A = bh$
$= 16 \times 17$	$= 24 \times 17$	$= 24 \times 15$

Area of a trapezium

A **trapezium** has parallel sides a and b, and perpendicular height h.

If you join two trapezia you can form a parallelogram.

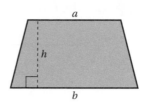

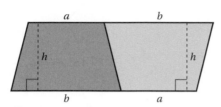

The parallelogram has a base of length $a + b$, and perpendicular height h.

Area of a parallelogram = base × perpendicular height

So area = $(a + b) \times h$

Each trapezium is half the area of the parallelogram.

 Learn this formula

Area of a trapezium = $\frac{1}{2} \times (a + b) \times h$, where a and b are the lengths of the parallel sides and h is the perpendicular height

WORK IT OUT 11.2

A solar farm is being built in a field.

Each solar panel measures 98 cm by 150 cm.
A total of 500 panels are installed on the field.
What is the total area of panels being used, in m²?
(Remember 1 m² = 10 000 cm²)

Which of the answers below is correct?

What errors were made in each of the others?

Answer A	Answer B	Answer C
Area of one panel:	Area of one panel:	Area of one panel:
$98 \times 150 = 14\,700\,\text{cm}^2$	$\frac{1}{2} \times (98 \times 150) = 7350\,\text{cm}^2$	$98 \times 150 = 14\,700\,\text{cm}^2$
$1\,\text{m}^2 = 10\,000\,\text{cm}^2$	$1\,\text{m}^2 = 10\,000\,\text{cm}^2$	$1\,\text{m}^2 = 100\,\text{cm}^2$
1 panel = $14\,700 \div 10\,000 = 1.47\,\text{m}^2$ 500 panels = $1.47\,\text{m}^2 \times 500$ $= 735\,\text{m}^2$	1 panel = $7350 \div 10\,000 = 0.735\,\text{m}^2$ 500 panels = $0.735\,\text{m}^2 \times 500$ $= 367.5\,\text{m}^2$	1 panel = $14\,700 \div 100 = 147\,\text{m}^2$ 500 panels = $147\,\text{m}^2 \times 500$ $= 73\,500\,\text{m}^2$

Find answers at: cambridge.org/ukschools/gcsemaths-studentbookanswers

EXERCISE 11B

1 Use the formula $A = bh$ to calculate the area of each parallelogram.

a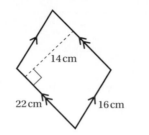
12 cm
5 cm

b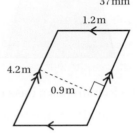
19 mm
37 mm

c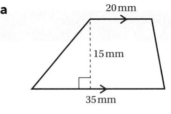
14 cm
22 cm   16 cm

d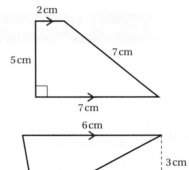
1.2 m
4.2 m
0.9 m

2 Use the formula $A = \frac{1}{2}(a + b)h$ to calculate the area of each trapezium.

a
20 mm
15 mm
35 mm

b
2 cm
7 cm
5 cm
7 cm

c
16 cm
3 cm
5 cm
19 cm

d
6 cm
3 cm
1 cm   4 cm

3 The area of this rectangle is 96 cm².
Work out its length.

8 cm
l

4 The area of a parallelogram is 40 cm².
Its perpendicular height is 10 cm.
Work out the length of its base. Choose from the options below.

A 2 cm   B 4 cm   C 8 cm   D 10 cm

5 The area and one other measurement is given for each shape.
Use the given information to find the unknown length in each shape.

a
24 cm²
h
8 cm

b
b
289 cm²   17 cm

c
a
132 cm²   14 cm
16 cm

d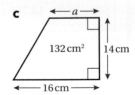
15 cm
75 cm²
b

e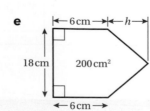
6 cm h
18 cm   200 cm²
6 cm

6 Amira grows organic vegetables.

The area of land available in one field is shown on the plan.

a Calculate the area of the available land.

b Amira lays down 25 kg of soil and 10 kg of compost per square metre of land.

Work out how much soil and compost she will need.

c There is a gate 2 m wide along the 22 m boundary.

The rest of the land needs to be fenced.

Work out the total amount of fencing needed.

[Plan shows: top edge 22 m, left side 10 m with right angle, "Land available", right side 18 m, bottom 30 m]

Section 2: Area of circles and sectors

Calculator tip

Use the π key of your calculator to find the area and circumference of circles unless you are given an approximate value to use for π.

Leave the value you get on the display for the next step and only round off to the required number of places when you have a final value.

The area of a circle is calculated using the formula:

Learn this formula

Area of a circle, $A = \pi r^2$ where r = radius of the circle

If you are given the diameter, d, of the circle you can still use this formula by remembering that:

$$r = \frac{1}{2}d$$

WORKED EXAMPLE 4

Calculate the area of this circle to two decimal places.

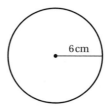

[Circle with radius 6 cm]

$A = \pi r^2$

$= \pi \times 6 \times 6$

$= 113.0973355\,cm^2$

$= 113.10\,cm^2$ (to 2 dp)

> Substitute the value for the radius into the formula for the area.
>
> Don't forget to add the units.
>
> Round to 2 decimal places.

When you know the area of a circle you can find the length of a radius (or the diameter).

WORKED EXAMPLE 5

Calculate the radius of a circle with area 50 cm².

$A = \pi r^2$

$50 = \pi \times r^2$ — Substitute the value for the area into the formula.

$r^2 = \dfrac{50}{\pi}$ — Rearrange the equation to make r^2 the subject.

$r = \sqrt{\dfrac{50}{\pi}}$ — Solve for r.

$= 3.989422804$ cm — Don't forget to add the units.

$= 3.99$ cm (to 2 dp) — Round to 2 decimal places.

Tip

If you are asked to find the diameter (*d*), remember it is twice the radius (2 × *r*).

Area of a sector

A sector is a fraction of the area of the whole circle.

To find the area of a sector you need to know what fraction the sector is of the circle.

You find this by dividing the sector angle by 360.

In the diagram the fraction of the area of the whole circle is $\dfrac{\theta}{360}$.

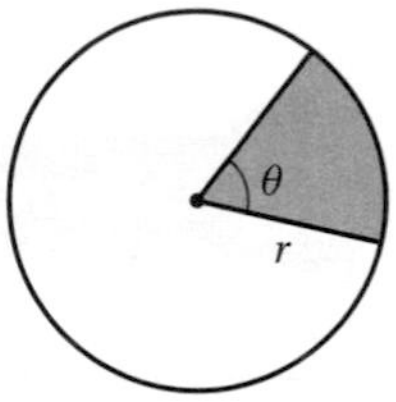

So, area of sector of circle = $\dfrac{\theta}{360} \times$ area of circle

Area of a circle = πr^2

area of sector of circle = $\dfrac{\theta}{360} \times \pi r^2$

Remember:

A semicircle is half a circle, so its area is half the area of a circle ($\dfrac{\pi r^2}{2}$).

A quarter-circle is one quarter of a circle, so its area is one quarter of the area of a circle ($\dfrac{\pi r^2}{4}$).

Tip

You also did this to find the arc length in Chapter 10.

WORKED EXAMPLE 6

Calculate the area of the sector shown.

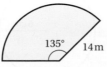

135°   14 m

Area of sector of circle = $\dfrac{\theta}{360} \times \pi r^2$

$= \dfrac{135}{360} \times \pi \times r^2$ — Substitute the value of θ into the formula.

$= 0.375 \times \pi \times 14^2$ — Substitute for r.

$= 230.90706$ m² — Add the units and round to 2 decimal places.

$= 230.91$ m² (to 2 dp)

EXERCISE 11C

1 Calculate the area of a circle with a diameter of 20 m. Take π as 3.14.

Choose your answer from the options below.

A $314 \, m^2$ B $1256 \, m^2$ C $62.8 \, m^2$ D $31.4 \, m^2$

2 Find the area of each circle in the diagram.

Use a value of 3.14 for π and give your answers to two decimal places.

a 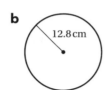 9 cm   **b** 12.8 cm   **c** 14 cm   **d** 21.3 cm

3 Use the formula $A = \dfrac{\theta}{360} \times \pi r^2$ to find the area of each sector of these circles.

a 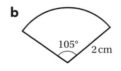 53°   18 mm   **b** 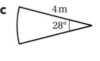 105°   2 cm   **c** 4 m   28°   **d** 122°   19 mm

4 Find the difference in area between these two sectors of a circle.

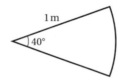 1 m   40°   50 cm   80°

5 A pizza has a diameter of 14 cm.

  a Calculate the area of the pizza.

  b The pizza is served on a round plate with about 1 cm space around the edge.

    Estimate the area of the plate.

6 A pair of sunglasses has circular lenses each 6.4 cm in diameter.

  a What is the total area of the tinted surface of the lenses?

  b What is the circumference of the smallest round frame that each lens can fit into?

7 The area for discus at an international event has the dimensions shown in the diagram in the margin.

  a Calculate the area of the grass in the landing zone.

  b Calculate the area of the starting circle in the throwing cage.

8 A circular disc has a circumference of 75.398 mm.

Use this information to find the area of the disc.

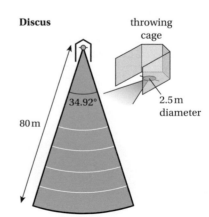

Discus   throwing cage

34.92°   2.5 m diameter

80 m

Section 3: Area of composite shapes

You can find the area of composite shapes in different ways.

Addition of parts

- Divide the figure into smaller known shapes whose areas can be found directly.
- Calculate the area of each part separately.
- Add the areas of all the parts to find the total area.

For example:

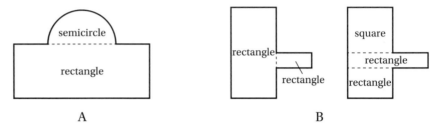

A   B

Figure A can be divided into a rectangle and a semicircle.

Figure B can be divided in different ways. The first way requires fewer calculations.

Subtraction of parts

When one figure is 'cut out' of another you have to find the area of the larger figure and subtract the area of the cut-out part.

For example, in the diagram on the right:

    shaded area = area of square – area of circle

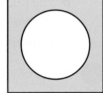

In some cases, you can find the area by viewing the figure as part of a larger known shape and subtracting the parts that have been 'removed'.

For example, to work out the area of the diagram on the right:

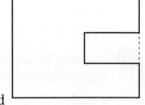

You can work out the area of the large rectangle (made by drawing the dotted line) and subtract the smaller cut-out rectangle from it.

You could also find the area by addition, but you would need to do more calculations.

EXERCISE 11D

1 Find the total area of each of these shapes. Show all your working.

a
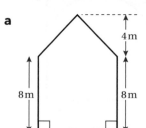

b
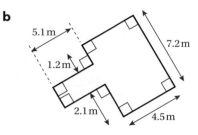

c
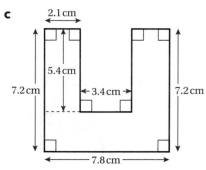

d
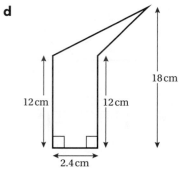

e
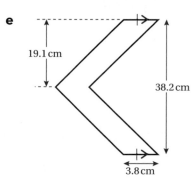

f
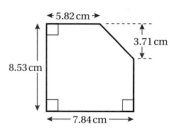

g
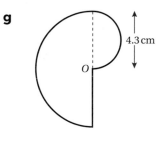

h
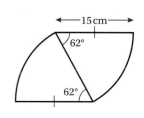

2 Find the area of the shaded part of each figure.

a

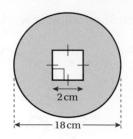

b

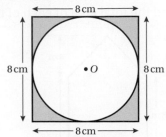

c

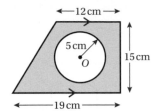

d

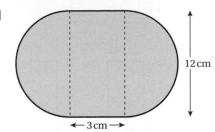

e

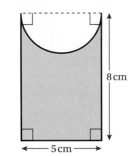

f

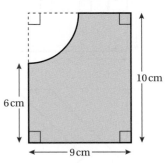

g

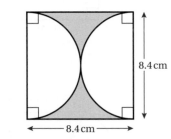

h

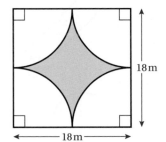

3 Here is a composite shape.

Calculate its area.

Choose the correct answer from the options given below.

A $65\,\text{cm}^2$ B $52.5\,\text{cm}^2$

C $31\,\text{cm}^2$ D $50\,\text{cm}^2$

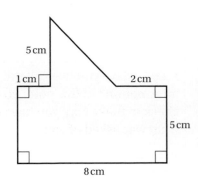

Problem-solving framework

Perimeter, circumference and area are often combined with other calculations in problem-solving situations.

A garden pond has a radius of 5 m.

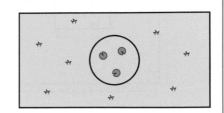

a The pond needs netting across the top and some edging all around the water's edge.

Calculate the quantities of **i** netting and **ii** edging required.

b The pond lies in a rectangular lawned area of width 15 m and length 20 m.

Grass seed is required for the lawn. What area must the grass seed cover?

Steps for solving problems	What you would do for this example
Step 1: What have you got to do?	**a i** find the area of netting needed for the pond. **ii** find the circumference of the pond to work out the amount of edging needed. **b** find the area of lawn needing grass seed.
Step 2: What information do you need?	Radius, r, of pond = 5 m Dimensions of lawn: 15 m × 20 m Area of circle, $A = \pi r^2$ Circumference of circle, $C = 2\pi r$ Use 3.14 as the value for π. Area of rectangle = length × width
Step 3: What information don't you need?	The netting will fit exactly on the top of the pond; need to mention that this is the minimum area of netting required.
Step 4: What maths can you use?	Area of pond = πr^2 = 3.14 × 5 × 5 = 78.5 m^2 A minimum of 78.5 m^2 of netting is required. Circumference of pond = $2\pi r$ = 2 × 3.14 × 5 = 31.4 m 31.4 m of edging is required for the pond. Rectangular lawn area = 15 × 20 = 300 m^2 Area for seeding = 300 – 78.5 (area of pond) = 221.5 m^2 Area of lawn needing grass seed is 221.5 m^2.
Step 5: Have you used all the information? At this point you should check to make sure you have calculated what was asked of you.	All information used. ✓ Calculated part **a i**. ✓ Calculated part **a ii**.✓ Calculated part **b**. ✓
Step 6: Is it correct?	Given radius of pond, so used $C = 2\pi r$ to calculate circumference. ✓ Used $A = \pi r^2$ to calculate area of pond. ✓ Squared the radius before multiplying by π. ✓ Used $A = l \times w$ to calculate area of rectangular lawn ✓ The correct units used. ✓

Find answers at: cambridge.org/ukschools/gcsemaths-studentbookanswers

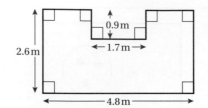

EXERCISE 11E

1 How many rectangular tiles 20 cm by 30 cm would you need to tile the area shown in the margin?

2 The net of a cylinder is shown below.

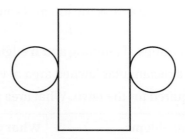

The rectangle has dimensions 10 cm × 16 cm.

Each circle has a radius of 2.55 cm.

Using 3.14 as an approximate value of π, calculate the surface area of the cylinder.

3 The diagram shows a circular mirror that has a mirrored centre and a decorative metal border.

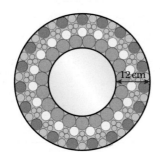

The border measures 12 cm across.

The width of the border is $\frac{4}{5}$ of the radius of the whole mirror.

a Calculate the area of the whole mirror.
(Use 3.14 as an approximate value of π.)

b Calculate the area of the metal border.

4 A piece of icing is rolled out into the shape of a square.

The largest circle that can be cut out of the square has a radius of 11 cm.

Find the difference between the area of the circular icing and the area of the square.

5 The diagram shows a sandpit at the end of a lawn.

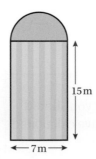

A cover is placed over the sandpit.

What is the area that needs to be covered?

6 A circular photo frame has a plastic surround.

The width of the plastic surround is 8 cm.

The diameter of the complete photo frame is 28 cm.

Calculate the area available for the photo.

7 The shapes have the same area.

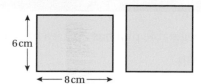

What is the side length of the square?

8 Guy is paid £0.15 for every square metre of grass he cuts.

How much would he be paid for cutting the grass in this garden?

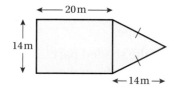

9 A stained glass window is a semicircle with radius 30 cm.

Calculate:

a the perimeter of the window

b the area of glass in the window.

Checklist of learning and understanding

Area of polygons

- Area is the amount of space occupied by a plane shape. Area is always given in square measurements.
- Area can be calculated using formulae.

Rectangle	Square	Triangle	Parallelogram	Trapezium
$A = lw$	$A = l^2$	$A = \frac{1}{2}bh$	$A = bh$	$A = \frac{1}{2}(a + b)h$

Area of circles and sectors

- Area of a circle $= \pi r^2$
- Area of a sector of a circle is a fraction of the area of the whole circle.
- Area of a sector $= \dfrac{\theta}{360} \times \pi r^2$

Composite shapes

- The area of a composite shape can be found by splitting it into known smaller shapes.
- Areas of smaller shapes can be calculated separately and added to find the total area.
- The area of a given shape can be subtracted from the area of a known shape to find the total area.

For additional questions on the topics in this chapter, visit GCSE Mathematics Online.

 Chapter review

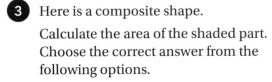

1 A rectangular vegetable plot has an area of $100\,\text{m}^2$.

The width is $6.5\,\text{m}$.

What is the length of the plot?

2 The net of a square-based pyramid is shown in the margin.

Each square is of side length $5\,\text{cm}$.

The triangles have a perpendicular height of $4.3\,\text{cm}$.

Calculate the surface area of the square-based pyramid.

3 Here is a composite shape.

Calculate the area of the shaded part. Choose the correct answer from the following options.

A $8\,\text{cm}$ B $8\,\text{cm}^2$

C $12\,\text{cm}^2$ D $12\,\text{cm}$

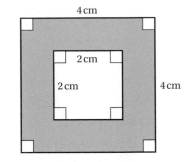

4 A square flower bed has a side length of $3\,\text{m}$.

It sits exactly in the middle of a rectangular lawned area of side length $5\,\text{m}$ and width $450\,\text{cm}$.

Calculate the area of lawn.

5 These steps can be used to work out the area of a circle.

Step 1   Square the radius

Step 2   Multiply by 3.14

a Use these steps to work out the area of a circle, radius $5\,\text{cm}$. *(2 marks)*

b The area of a circle is known.

Write down the steps to work out the radius. *(2 marks)*

© AQA 2013

6 An irrigator in a field waters a circular crop within a radius of $14.5\,\text{m}$.

What is the total area of the crop?

7 Calculate the area of the shape shown on the right. Give your answer in cm^2.

8 Calculate the area of the shape below.

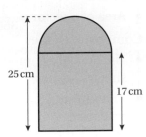

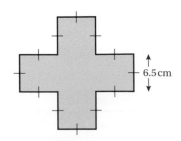

12 Rounding and estimation

Using mathematics: real-life applications

When you read that 34 000 people attended a festival, the actual number is likely to be slightly less or slightly more than that. When you roughly estimate what you spent over the weekend, look at an object and guess it is about $2\frac{1}{2}$ m long or say things like, 'I live about 15 kilometres from school' you are estimating and using approximate values.

"I round off the prices to the nearest pound and keep a mental running total of the costs of things I put in my trolley so I know that I am not over-spending."

(Consumer)

Before you start ...

KS3 Ch 1, 4	You should be able to use rounding to quickly estimate the answers to calculations.	**1** Use rounded values to estimate and decide whether each answer is correct without doing the calculation. **a** $312 - 56 = 256$ **b** $479 \times 17 = 3142$ **c** $350 + 351 - 96 = 798$	
KS3 Ch 6	You should be able to calculate with decimals and estimate to decide whether an answer is reasonable.	**2** State whether each statement is true or false. **a** $5.8 \times 6.72 \approx 42$ **b** $3.789 + 234.6 \approx 4 + 230$ **c** $0.00432 + 3.55 \approx 4$ **d** $4 \times \pi \approx 12$	
KS3 Ch 6	You need to be able to work confidently with decimals and place value.	**3** Write the number halfway between: **a** 3.0 and 5.0 **b** 3.5 and 3.6 **c** 0.02 and 0.07	

Assess your starting point using the Launchpad

STEP 1

1 Round each value to the degree of accuracy specified.

    a 86 to the nearest 10.   **b** 1565 to the nearest 1000.

    c 134.1234 to 2 decimal places.   **d** 19.999 to 1 decimal place.

    e 1235.26 to 1 significant figure.

    f 234 650 034 to 3 significant figures.

2 The length of a metal component is found to be 0.937 cm.

    What is its length to the nearest millimetre?

3 The cost of a phone call is given as £5.15932.

    a What is this amount truncated to the nearest penny?

    b What is this amount rounded to two decimal places?

GO TO
Section 1:
Approximate values

STEP 2

4 Estimate the cost of 12 packets of seeds at £1.36 each.

5 A litre of petrol costs £1.89.

    Approximately how many litres of petrol can you get for £20?

6 Use rounding to find an approximate answer to each calculation.

    a $\dfrac{784 + 572}{109}$ **b** $(2.099)^2$ **c** $\dfrac{3.802 + 7.52}{3.29}$

GO TO
Section 2:
Approximation and estimation

STEP 3

7 A piece of wire is 10 m long, to the nearest metre.

    Copy and complete the following statement to show the longest and the shortest possible lengths that this wire could be.

    $\square \leqslant 10\,\text{m} < \square$

GO TO
Section 3:
Limits of accuracy

GO TO
Chapter review

Section 1: Approximate values

In daily life we often use approximate values.

For example, you are more likely to say 'about £10' than to say 'exactly £10 and 24 pence.'

Approximation allows you to use numbers in a more convenient form by writing them in a simpler, but less accurate way.

Rounded values

Numbers can be **rounded** to:

- the nearest whole number or place (tens, hundreds or thousands)
- a particular number of decimal places
- a particular number of significant figures.

To round a number to a given place, first find the specified place.

If the digit to the right is 5 or greater, you round up. If it is less than 5, you round down.

This rule applies to whole numbers and decimals whether you are rounding to given places or to significant figures.

Rounding whole numbers

Consider the number 456 744. It can be rounded to different places. Depending on the value of the digit to the right of the digit you are rounding to, the number may be rounded up or down.

To the nearest ten 456 744 rounds down to 456 740.

To the nearest hundred 456 744 rounds down to 456 700.

To the nearest thousand 456 744 rounds up to 457 000.

You may be told to round numbers to a given **degree of accuracy**.

Tip

≈ means approximately equal to

= means exactly equal to

Key vocabulary

rounding: writing a number with zeros in the place of some digits

degree of accuracy: the number of places to which you round a number

Tip

If you are asked to give your answer to a certain degree of accuracy, remember to only round the final answer. You should not round any numbers in steps in your working.

EXERCISE 12A

1 Choose the correct approximation of each animal's weight.

	Weight of an animal		Rounded to	Approximation (choose from A or B)	
a	cow	635 kg	nearest 10 kg	A 630 kg	B 640 kg
b	horse	526 kg	nearest 100 kg	A 500 kg	B 600 kg
c	sheep	96 kg	nearest 10 kg	A 90 kg	B 100 kg
d	dog	32 kg	nearest 10 kg	A 30 kg	B 40 kg
e	cat	5.2 kg	nearest 10 kg	A 0 kg	B 10 kg

 Find answers at: cambridge.org/ukschools/gcsemaths-studentbookanswers

2 **a** Round each value to the nearest whole number.

   i 54.8   **ii** 10.6   **iii** 9.4   **iv** 12.3

   b Round each value to the nearest 10.

   i 26   **ii** 57.5   **iii** 111.1   **iv** 35 814

   c Round each value to the nearest 100.

   i 458   **ii** 5732   **iii** 2389   **iv** 35 814

   d Round each value to the nearest 1000.

   i 2590   **ii** 176   **iii** 35 814   **iv** 66 876

   e Round the following to the nearest hundred thousand.

   i 123 456   **ii** 1 234 567   **iii** 12 354 642   **iv** 123 456 789

   f Round the following to the nearest million.

   i 545 000   **ii** 555 000   **iii** 14 354 642   **iv** 546 267 789

3 **a** A food bill is £27.60. How much is this to the nearest pound?

   b There are 27 students in a class. What is this to the nearest ten students?

   c I have £175 saved up. What is this to the nearest £100?

   d A kite is made from 167 cm of material. Approximately how many metres is used?

   e The population of the United Kingdom is 63 793 234.

   Sue says this is 63.7 million to the nearest hundred thousand people.

   She is not correct. What mistake has she made?

Tip

The same rules for rounding apply to decimals but you leave off any digits after the required decimal place.

Rounding decimals

In calculations you will often get answers with many more decimal places than you need.

You will usually be told to give your answers to a specific number of decimal places.

WORKED EXAMPLE 1

Round: **a** 54.149 to one decimal place   **b** 0.8751 to two decimal places   **c** 0.10024 to three decimal places.

a 54.149   There is a 1 in the first decimal place, the next digit is 4, so round down.

   54.1   Leave the 1 unchanged and take off the digits to the right of it.

b 0.8751   There is a 7 in the second decimal place, the next digit is 5.

   0.88   Round 7 up to 8 and take off the digits to the right of it.

c 0.10024   There is a 0 in the third decimal place, the next digit is 2.

   0.100   Leave the 0 unchanged and take off the digits to the right of it.

   The answer 0.100 is the same as 0.1, but you write the two zeros to show that the number is rounded to three decimal places.

Suitable levels of accuracy

Sometimes, you have to decide what to round to.

This will depend on the number of decimal places required by the situation or problem.

If the situation involves whole quantities, you round to the nearest whole number. It does not make sense to talk about 5.45 bricks or 9.05 tins of paint.

If the question involves money, then you always round to two decimal places. An answer of £4.56896 would be rounded to £4.57.

In mathematical or scientific calculations you usually work to a higher degree of accuracy than when you describe real-life quantities.

If you are working with small values you might round them to tens, if you are working with large numbers you might round to the nearest ten thousand or million.

When you calculate with decimals or significant figures you normally round to no more than the number of places in the original values.

EXERCISE 12B

1 Round 13.68952 to one decimal place.

Choose the correct answer from the options below.

A 13.5   B 13.6   C 13.7   D 14

2 Round each number to:

  i 1 dp   **ii** 2 dp   **iii** 3 dp

a 4.52638   **b** 25.25637   **c** 125.61738

d 0.537921   **e** 32.3972

3 Write each value to two decimal places.

a 19.86903   **b** 302.0428   **c** 0.292

d 0.20528   **e** 21 245.8449   **f** 0.0039

g 0.0972   **h** 0.9999999   **i** 99.997

4 Round each value to a suitable level of accuracy. Give reasons for your decisions.

a A large dog weighs 24.4872 kg.

b To calculate a circumference, I use the value
$\pi = 3.14159265358979323846\ldots$

c Dan's car can travel 13.7895 km per 1.0000987 litres of petrol.

d My share of a phone bill is £14.09876

Significant figures

When you work with values with many digits or decimal places it is useful to **round to significant figures (sf)**.

The first **significant figure** in a number is the first non-zero digit when you read the number from left to right. All digits that follow are significant.

For example:

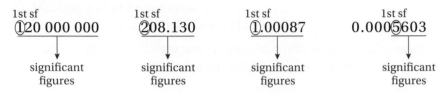

To round a number to a given number of significant figures:

- read the number from left to right and mark the first non-zero digit
- count the required number of significant figures from there to find the rounding place
- look at the digit to the right of this; if it is 5 or more round up, if it is less than 5 leave the digit unchanged
- use 0 as a place holder to fill any gaps between the rounding place and the decimal point (if there is one)
- leave off any digits past your rounding place if they are after the decimal point.

Key vocabulary

round to significant figures (sf): round to a specified level of accuracy from the first significant figure

significant figure: the first non-zero digit when you read a number from left to right

Tip

One significant figure does not mean that you will have only one digit in the answer. The number 12 756 is 10 000 to one significant figure, not 1.

WORKED EXAMPLE 2

Write each number to the given number of significant figures.

a 308 000 000   (to 2 sf)

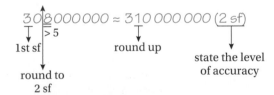

Include the zeros.

31 is not the same as 310 000 000.

b 476.372   (to 4 sf)

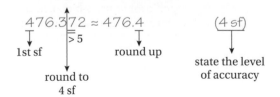

Ignore digits after the specified place if they are decimals.

Continues on next page …

Write each number to the given number of significant figures.

c 2531.8   (to 2 sf)

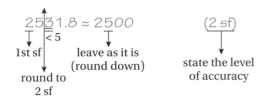

Replace digits before the decimal point with zeros.
Ignore digit after the decimal point.

d 0.00436   (to 1 sf)

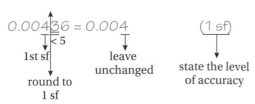

Ignore digits to the right.

EXERCISE 12C

1   **a**   Round each value to one significant figure.

     i 789   **ii** 3874   **iii** 69 356   **iv** 0.0456

  b   Write each value to 2 sf.

     i 789   **ii** 3145   **iii** 0.003325   **iv** 0.0007499

  c   Express each number to 3 sf.

     i 789   **ii** 46 712   **iii** 0.004214   **iv** 753 413

  d   Round each value to 2 sf.

     i 37.673   **ii** −4127   **iii** 3.0392   **iv** 1 999 000

  e   Write these to 3 sf.

     i 37.673   **ii** −4127   **iii** 3.0392   **iv** 1 999 000

2   Give reasons why it is more useful to round a value such as 0.000134567 to two significant figures than to two decimal places.

3   **a** $\pi \approx 3.1415926$

     What is this to 3 sf?

     Choose from the following options.

     A 3.142   B 3.14   C 3.00   D 3.141

  b   The density of a gas is 1.234 kg/m³. What is this to 2 sf?

  c   The speed of light is 299 792 458 m/s. What is this to 2 sf?

  d   The acceleration due to gravity at the Earth's surface is 9.806 65 m/s². What is this to 3 sf?

Tip

Rounding numbers to a given number of decimal places means that you start the rounding at the decimal point.

Rounding numbers to significant figures means you start at the first significant figure which can be before or after the decimal point.

Truncation

Key vocabulary

truncation: cutting off all digits in a decimal after a certain point without rounding

Tip

When you calculate with rounded or truncated values your results will not be completely accurate. You will learn more about this in *Section 3*.

Truncated means 'cut off'.

A decimal can be **truncated** by cutting off all the digits past a given point without rounding.

You will not generally use truncation to approximate values for calculation. However, you need to be aware that your calculator display will often give you a truncated rather than rounded value.

You can see this if you enter 2 ÷ 3. The display may show 0.66666666666

The fraction $\frac{2}{3}$ can be expressed as the recurring decimal $0.\dot{6}$. So the calculator is showing a truncated value.

If you enter $\frac{20}{3}$ your screen will show either 6.6666666666 or 6.6666666667

The first value is truncated, the second is rounded to 10 decimal places.

EXERCISE 12D

1 Truncate each number after the second decimal place.

   a 37.673   **b** −4.1275   **c** 3.0392   **d** 0.997

2 Truncate each number after the third significant figure.

   a 4.52638   **b** 25.25637   **c** 125.61738

   d 0.537921   **e** 32.397   **f** 200.6127

3 A bill of £20 is split equally between three people.

   What would each person pay? What method of approximation is most useful for deciding?

Did you know?

Truncation is used in statistics. A truncated mean is an average worked out by discarding (cutting off) very high or very low values in the data.

Section 2: Approximation and estimation

An **estimate** is a very useful tool for checking whether your answer is sensible.

If your estimate and your actual answer are not similar, then you may have made a mistake in your calculation.

For estimating an approximate answer you can generally round to one significant figure (1 sf).

Key vocabulary

estimate: an approximate answer or rough calculation

"I estimate measurements and prices to give customers a fairly accurate quote telling them what a building job will cost."

(Builder)

WORKED EXAMPLE 3

Estimate the value of $\dfrac{8.3 \times 536}{2.254 \times 9.612}$

$$\frac{8.3 \times 536}{2.254 \times 9.612} \approx \frac{8 \times 500}{2 \times 10}$$

Start off by rounding each number to 1 sf.

$$\approx \frac{4000}{20}$$

$$\approx 200$$

If you work out this problem using a calculator, the answer is actually 205.34 (to 2 dp).

Comparing this with your estimate tells you that your calculated answer is reasonable.

Tip

The symbol ≈ means approximately equal to.

WORK IT OUT 12.1

A group of four friends is travelling to a festival. They split the cost of everything between them.

The costs are as follows:

  tent hire, £86.50

  travel, 140 mile round trip with petrol costing roughly 20p per mile

  camping entry at £44 per night for three nights.

Three of them estimate how much they will each have to pay.

Which is the best estimate?
Why is it better than the others?

Estimate A	Estimate B	Estimate C
The cost of tent hire is roughly £90, which is £22.50 per person split between four.	The tent hire is roughly £100 which is £25 per person.	The tent hire is roughly £80, which is £20 each.
Petrol costs roughly £28 (140 × £0.20) which is £7 per person.	The petrol is roughly 150 × £0.20, which is £30, so split four ways this is £7.50.	Petrol is about 100 × £0.20 = £20, so £5 per person.
The camping ticket costs are £44 × three nights or roughly £120, which is £30 per person.	The camping costs about £50 × 3 = £150, which is about £40 each.	Camping cost is about £40 × 3 = £120 for three nights, so about £30 each.
So, total cost per person is £22.50 + £7 + £30 = £59.50	Total cost is approximately £25 + £7.50 + £40 = £72.50	Total cost is approximately £20 + £5 + £30 = £55

EXERCISE 12E

1 Estimate the following by rounding each number to 1 sf.

   a 111.11×3.6 **b** 378×1.07 **c** 0.99×16.7 **d** -13.6×0.48

   e $\pi \times (5.3)^2$ **f** 4.8×12.5 **g** $\dfrac{192}{17.2}$ **h** $\dfrac{58.38}{0.5185}$

2 Estimate the value of 937×26.

Choose your answer from the following options.

   A 2700   B 19 000   C 24 362   D 27 000

3 Which calculation would provide the best estimate? Choose from the options given.

   a 186×9.832 A $\;200 \times 10$ B $\;190 \times 9$ C $\;190 \times 10$

   b $15.76 \div 7.6$ A $\;15 \div 7$ B $\;16 \div 8$ C $\;16 \div 7$

4 Estimate the following by rounding each number to 1 sf.

   a $\dfrac{82.65 \times 0.4654}{42.4 \times 2.53}$ **b** $\dfrac{16.96 + 3.123}{16.9 - 6.432}$

   c $\dfrac{879 \div 43.6}{2.36 \times 0.23}$ **d** $\dfrac{976.9 \div 492.9}{21.6 \div 43.87}$

5 Estimate the following.

   a $\sqrt{\dfrac{3.2 \times 4.05}{0.39 \times 0.29}}$ **b** $\sqrt{\dfrac{4.1 \times 11.9}{7.9 \times 0.25}}$

6 Shafiek runs a cross-country race at an average speed of 6.25 m/s.

   a Estimate how far he will have run after 6 minutes.

   b Assuming he runs at a constant speed, estimate how long it takes him to cover 1467 m.

7 Look at the calculator display answers for each calculation.

Use estimation to state whether the answer is sensible.

   a $3 \times \pi \times 5^2$ `125.6637061`

   b 5×8.9 `445`

   c 50×8.9 `445`

   d 3×192.5 `57.75`

   e $\dfrac{\sqrt{86}}{2.8 \times 16.18}$ `0.204697565`

   f $0.0253 \div 0.45$ `56.222222222`

8 A parallelogram has an area of 54.67 cm².

The base of the parallelogram is 7.9 cm long.

When a student tries to find the height on his calculator, he gets a result of 69 202 531.

This is clearly wrong. Give the correct height, accurate to two significant figures.

Section 3: Limits of accuracy

Even with very accurate measuring instruments, quantities such as mass, length and capacity cannot be measured exactly.

However, the rules of rounding mean the measurement has to fall within certain limits.

A piece of wood that is 47 cm to the nearest centimetre, could be anything from 46.5 cm up to, but not including 47.5 cm long.

You can see this on the number line:

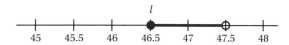

If the length was less than 46.5 cm, it would have been rounded down to 46 cm.

If it was 47.5 cm, it would have been rounded up to 48 cm.

If we let l represent the length of the piece of wood, the possible measurements can be expressed as

$46.5 \text{ cm} \leqslant l < 47.5 \text{ cm}$

For any measurement correct to a given level of accuracy, the exact value lies in a range half a unit below and half a unit above the measurement.

This range of possible values is known as the **error interval**.

Example	Error interval
0.5 rounded to 1 dp	$0.45 \leqslant x < 0.55$
0.65 rounded to 2 dp	$0.645 \leqslant x < 0.655$
0.7663 rounded to 4 dp	$0.76625 \leqslant x < 0.76635$
15 rounded to 2 sf	$14.5 \leqslant x < 15.5$
320 to 2 sf	$315 \leqslant x < 325$
2.32 rounded to 2 dp	$2.315 \leqslant x < 2.325$

Tip

It can be helpful to draw a number line to work out the upper and lower limits of a value.

Tip

$\leqslant$ means 'less than or equal to'
$\leqslant$ means 'greater than or equal to'
$<$ means 'less than'
$>$ means 'greater than'

Key vocabulary

error interval: the difference between the highest possible value and the lowest possible value

EXERCISE 12F

1 The following lengths were measured to the nearest millimetre.

Write down an error interval for each one using inequality notation. Let the length be L in each case.

a 4.9 cm   b 12.520 m   c 43.0 cm   d 29 mm

2 a There are 36 litres of petrol in a car's tank, to the nearest litre.

What is the least possible volume of petrol in the tank?

Choose from the following options.

A 35 litres   B 35.5 litres   C 36 litres   D 36.5 litres

b A length of wood is 1.4 m to the nearest centimetre. Is it possible for the wood to be 137 cm long?

c The weight of a stone is 43.4 kg to the nearest tenth of a kilogram. What is the least and greatest weight it could be?

Find answers at: cambridge.org/ukschools/gcsemaths-studentbookanswers

3 Verna buys 9-carat gold for £10.66 per gram and platinum for £33.46 per gram.

a Use this information to complete the table.

Mass of a piece of jewellery	Maximum value of gold (to nearest penny)	Maximum value of platinum (to nearest penny)
18 g (to nearest g)		
18 g (to nearest 0.1 g)		
18 g (to nearest 0.01 g)		

b Using your data, give reasons why jewellers tend to use scales that are accurate to a hundredth of a gram to weigh the metal they use to make jewellery.

Checklist of learning and understanding

Approximate values

- When you round to a specified place, if the number following is 5 or above, then the original number goes up to the next number. If it is not more than 5, then the number stays the same.
- Rounding to a given number of significant figures (sf) specifies the number of digits, starting from the first non-zero digit, that is used to express a number. The first significant figure is the first number that is not zero as you read the number from left to right.
- Truncating a decimal number means removing all digits after a specified number of decimal places and expressing the number that remains without rounding.

Estimation

- Complex calculations can be estimated without using a calculator by using approximations of each term in the calculation to make a simple calculation.
- Visual estimation techniques can also be used to approximate sizes and measurements.

Level of accuracy

- Measurement is really approximation within a range of limits. It can be expressed using inequality notation ($\leqslant, <, \geqslant, >$).

Chapter review

For additional questions on the topics in this chapter, visit GCSE Mathematics Online.

1 State whether each of the following is true or false.

	Original number	Approximation	Answer
a	123.456	rounded to 2 dp (2 decimal places)	123.456
b	123.456	rounded to 1 sf (1 significant figure)	120.000
c	123.456	rounded to 1 dp (1 decimal place)	123.5
d	123.456	rounded to 4 sf (4 significant figures)	123.5
e	123 456.789	truncated to 1 dp (1 decimal place)	123 456.8

2 Leona says she is 24 years old to the nearest year.

What is the youngest age she could be and the oldest age she could be?

3 The population of a town is given as 425 000 to the nearest 1000.

Write down the maximum the population could be.

4 A plasterer uses this method to work out how much she charges (£).

Calculate the area to be plastered in square metres.

Round this value to the nearest whole number.

Multiply by 10.

Add 30.

A rectangular ceiling measures 7.6 m by 2.4 m.

How much does she charge? *(5 marks)*

© AQA 2013

5 A charity raised £43 000 to the nearest £10.

What is the highest amount of money that they could have raised?

Choose the correct answer from the options below.

A £42 996   B £43 004   C £43 004.99   D £43 005

6 A camping field measures 45 m by 30 m to the nearest metre.

What is the maximum perimeter of the field?

7 There are 140 people at a party, to the nearest 10 people.

Write down the maximum number of people there could be at the party.

8 A length of rope measures 90 cm, rounded to the nearest centimetre.

State the possible range of values for its length.

Find answers at: cambridge.org/ukschools/gcsemaths-studentbookanswers

13 Percentages

In this chapter you will learn how to ...

- work interchangeably with fractions, decimals and percentages.
- calculate a percentage of an amount.
- express a quantity as a percentage of another.
- increase and decrease amounts by a given percentage.
- solve problems involving percentage change.

For more resources relating to this chapter, visit GCSE Mathematics Online.

Using mathematics: real-life applications

Percentages are often used in daily life to express fractions. For example, you might see adverts claiming that 76% of pets prefer a particular brand of food or that 90% of dentists recommend a particular type of toothpaste. Sale price-reductions, discounts and interest rates are usually given as percentages.

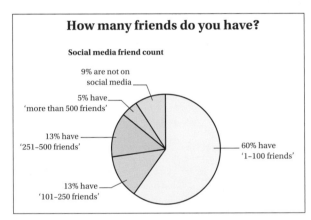

How many friends do you have?

Social media friend count

- 9% are not on social media
- 5% have 'more than 500 friends'
- 13% have '251–500 friends'
- 60% have '1–100 friends'
- 13% have '101–250 friends'

"Statistics in the media are often reported as percentages. This makes it easier to understand, but percentages can also be misleading – 60% sounds like a lot, but it could just mean 3 out of 5 people interviewed."

(Statistician)

Before you start ...

KS3 Ch 6	You need to be able to confidently multiply and divide by 100.	**1** Where should the decimal place go in each answer? **a** $210 \div 100 = 21$ **b** $21 \div 100 = 21$ **c** $0.24 \times 100 = 24$ **d** $0.024 \times 100 = 24$
Ch 5	You need to be able to cancel to express fractions in simplest terms.	**2** Match the fractions in box A to their equivalents in box B. | Box A	Box B
---	---
$\frac{16}{36}$ $\frac{15}{35}$ $\frac{30}{36}$	$\frac{1}{4}$ $\frac{3}{4}$ $\frac{1}{3}$
$\frac{9}{36}$ $\frac{39}{52}$ $\frac{13}{39}$	$\frac{5}{6}$ $\frac{3}{7}$ $\frac{4}{9}$	
KS 3 Ch6	You should be able to express any percentage as a decimal.	**3** Are the following statements true or false? **a** $20\% = 0.02$ **b** $25\% = 1.4$ **c** $3\% = 0.3$ **d** $12.5\% = 0.125$ **e** $1.25\% = 0.125$

Assess your starting point using the Launchpad

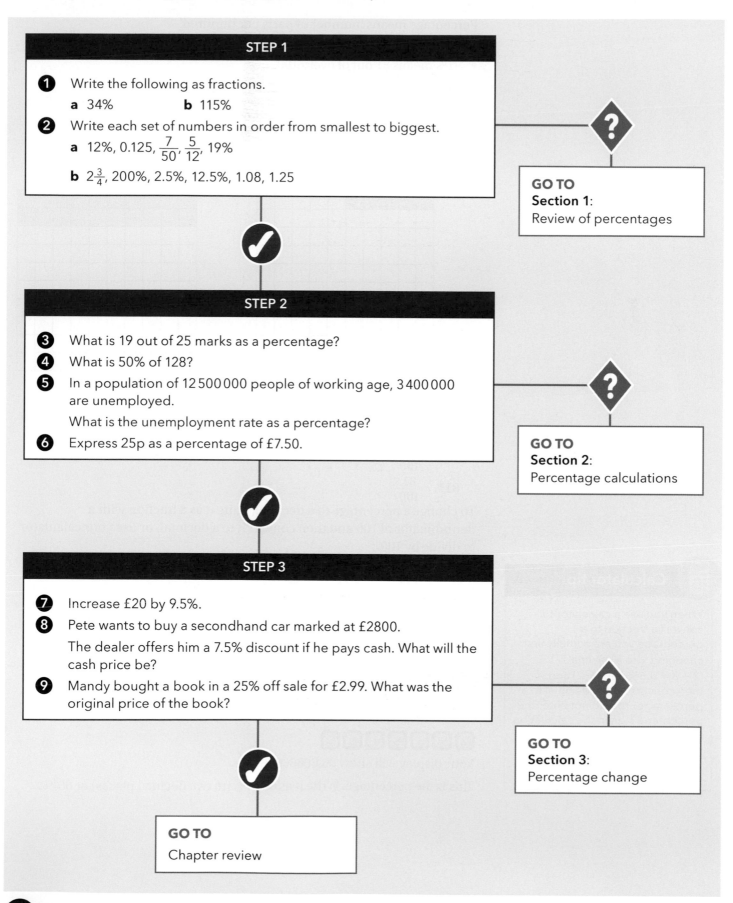

STEP 1

1 Write the following as fractions.
   a 34%   **b** 115%

2 Write each set of numbers in order from smallest to biggest.
   a 12%, 0.125, $\frac{7}{50}$, $\frac{5}{12}$, 19%

   b $2\frac{3}{4}$, 200%, 2.5%, 12.5%, 1.08, 1.25

GO TO
Section 1:
Review of percentages

STEP 2

3 What is 19 out of 25 marks as a percentage?

4 What is 50% of 128?

5 In a population of 12 500 000 people of working age, 3 400 000 are unemployed.
   What is the unemployment rate as a percentage?

6 Express 25p as a percentage of £7.50.

GO TO
Section 2:
Percentage calculations

STEP 3

7 Increase £20 by 9.5%.

8 Pete wants to buy a secondhand car marked at £2800.
   The dealer offers him a 7.5% discount if he pays cash. What will the cash price be?

9 Mandy bought a book in a 25% off sale for £2.99. What was the original price of the book?

GO TO
Section 3:
Percentage change

GO TO
Chapter review

Find answers at: cambridge.org/ukschools/gcsemaths-studentbookanswers

Section 1: Review of percentages

Percentage means 'number of parts per hundred'.

- 92% means 92 out of every 100.
- 81% means 81 out of every 100.

Percentages, fractions and decimals

Percentages, fractions and decimals are different ways of showing a part of a whole.

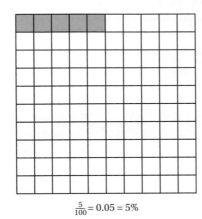 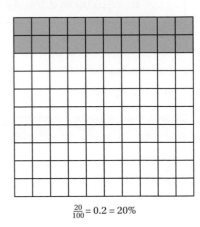

$$\frac{5}{100} = 0.05 = 5\%$$ $$\frac{20}{100} = 0.2 = 20\%$$

To convert a percentage to a fraction, write the fraction with a denominator of 100. Then simplify the fraction.

$$92\% = \frac{92}{100} = \frac{23}{25}$$

$$81\% = \frac{81}{100}$$

To change a percentage to a decimal, write it as a fraction with a denominator of 100 and then convert it to a decimal, or use your calculator to divide by 100.

$$92\% = \frac{92}{100} = 0.92 \qquad 92 \div 100 = 0.92$$

$$81\% = \frac{81}{100} = 0.81 \qquad 81 \div 100 = 0.81$$

To change a fraction to a percentage, you can write it as an equivalent fraction with a denominator of 100. For example:

$$\frac{1}{2} = \frac{50}{100} = 50\% \qquad \text{Do not simplify, write the fraction of 100 as a percentage.}$$

You can also use a calculator. For example:

to convert $\frac{2}{3}$ to a percentage, enter

Your display will show 66.666666667

This is the percentage. Write it as 66.67% (to two decimal places) or $66\frac{2}{3}\%$.

Calculator tip

When you use a calculator to convert a fraction to a percentage you are actually first changing $\frac{2}{3}$ to a decimal ($2 \div 3 = 0.6666666667$) and then converting the decimal to a percentage. You do not enter the percentage sign in the calculation because the values you are entering are not percentages. The percentage is the answer you get.

To change a decimal to a percentage, write it as a fraction with a denominator of 100 or use your calculator to multiply it by 100.

$$0.3 = \frac{3}{10} = \frac{30}{100} = 30\% \qquad 0.3 \times 100 = 30\%$$

$$0.025 = \frac{0.25}{10} = \frac{2.5}{100} = 2.5\% \qquad 0.025 \times 100 = 2.5\%$$

$$3.75 = \frac{37.5}{10} = \frac{375}{100} = 375\% \qquad 3.75 \times 100 = 375\%$$

Comparing percentages, fractions and decimals

When you have to compare a mixed set of percentages, fractions and decimals you can compare them by changing them all to percentages.

Some common conversions:

Fraction	Decimal	Percentage
$\frac{1}{2}$	0.5	50%
$\frac{1}{4}$	0.25	25%
$\frac{3}{4}$	0.75	75%
$\frac{1}{3}$	$0.\dot{3}$	$33\frac{1}{3}\%$
$\frac{2}{3}$	$0.\dot{6}$	$66\frac{2}{3}\%$

WORKED EXAMPLE 1

Write the following in ascending order.

$35\%, \frac{1}{3}, 0.38, \frac{2}{5}, \frac{2}{7}$

35%

$\frac{1}{3} \times 100 = 33.33\%$

$0.38 \times 100 = 38\%$

$\frac{2}{5} \times 100 = 40\%$

$\frac{2}{7} \times 100 = 28.57\%$

Convert all the fractions and decimals to percentages. Then put them in order, from the smallest to the largest.

The order is: $\frac{2}{7}, \frac{1}{3}, 35\%, 0.38, \frac{2}{5}$

Remember to use the original fractions when you write the answer, not the percentages you have changed them to.

 Tip

You can also change all the values to decimals or equivalent fractions to compare them.

EXERCISE 13A

1 **a** Choose the value that is equivalent to $\frac{7}{200}$.

A 7%   B 35%   C $\frac{3}{200}$ D $3\frac{1}{2}\%$

b What is the decimal equivalent of 0.08%? Choose from the options below.

A 80   B 0.08   C 0.008   D 0.0008

c Which symbol will make this statement true?
Choose from the options below.

$\frac{3}{20} \square 12\%$

A <   B >   C =   D ≡

 Find answers at: cambridge.org/ukschools/gcsemaths-studentbookanswers

2 Express the following as percentages.

Use fractional ($32\frac{1}{2}\%$) or decimal (2.5%) percentages where you need to.

a $\dfrac{5}{100}$ b $\dfrac{27}{50}$ c $\dfrac{11}{25}$ d $\dfrac{17}{20}$

e $\dfrac{1}{2}$ f $\dfrac{2}{3}$ g $\dfrac{5}{8}$ h $\dfrac{92}{50}$

i 0.3   j 0.04   k 0.47   l 1.12

m 2.07   n 2.25   o 0.035   p 0.007

3 Write each of the following percentages as a common fraction in its simplest terms.

a 25%   b 80%   c 90%   d 12.5%

e 50%   f 98%   g 60%   h 22%

4 Write the decimal equivalent of each percentage.

a 82%   b 97%   c 45%   d 28%

e 0.05%   f 0.08%   g 0.006%   h 0.0007%

i 125%   j 300%   k 7.28%   l 9.007%

5 State whether the following are true or false.

a $\dfrac{3}{5} > 70\%$ b $\dfrac{7}{9} < 83\%$ c $\dfrac{1}{3} = 30\%$ d 67% > 0.666

6 **a** The number of students in a school who have wi-fi at home is 93.5%.

What percentage do not?

b Two-thirds of all the SIM cards sold in a mobile phone shop are pre-paid.

What percentage are not pre-paid?

c The decimal fraction of computer users who back up their work every day is 0.325.

What percentage do not?

7 Zack spends:

- 24.7% of a day playing computer games
- 0.138 of the day doing homework, and
- $\dfrac{3}{8}$ of the day playing sport.

What percentage of the day does he spend doing all other activities?

8 What percentage of each pie chart is shaded?

a 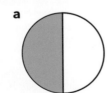   b 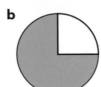   c   d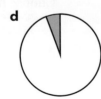

9 Write each of the following sets in order from smallest to largest.

a $\frac{1}{20}$, 30%, 0.1, $\frac{3}{5}$, 0.8%

b 0.75, 57%, 0.88, $\frac{1}{4}$, 0.15

c $\frac{2}{3}$, 0.75, 60%, $\frac{9}{100}$, 0.25

d $\frac{3}{7}$, 0.43, 45%, 0.395, $\frac{4}{9}$

e $\frac{5}{6}$, 80%, $\frac{19}{25}$, 55%, 49.3%

10 A media company states that 83.5% of its customers read the news online every day.

What fraction of the customers is this?

11 Lara pays 0.06 as a decimal fraction of her salary into her credit card account.

What percentage of her salary is this?

12 During one shift at work, Sandy spent $\frac{9}{20}$ of his time texting on his phone.

What percentage of the shift was he not texting?

13 Angie gets the following marks for three maths assignments: $\frac{31}{40}$, $\frac{27}{30}$ and $\frac{13}{15}$.

a In which test did she get the best marks?

b What is the mean result for the three assignments? Give your answer as a percentage.

Section 2: Percentage calculations

WORK IT OUT 13.1

9% of 400 is 36.

Which of the following methods will give you the correct answer?

Give reasons why the other methods won't work.

Method A	Method B	Method C	Method D	Method E
$\frac{9}{100} \times 400$	$\frac{400}{9} \times 36$	0.009×400	9×400	$\frac{9}{400} \times 100$

To find a percentage of an amount you have to multiply by the percentage.

Unless you use a calculator, you have to write the percentage as a fraction (with a denominator of 100) or a decimal.

WORKED EXAMPLE 2

What is 12% of 700?

Using fractions

$$\frac{12}{100} \times \frac{700}{1} = 84$$

Write the percentage as a fraction with a denominator of 100 and then cancel.

Using decimals

$$\frac{12}{100} = 0.12$$

$$0.12 \times 700$$
$$= 0.12 \times 100 \times 7$$
$$= 12 \times 7$$
$$= 84$$

Divide by 100 to convert the percentage to a decimal and then multiply.

Using a calculator

Answer is: 84

Enter the calculation correctly and write the answer.

Calculator tip

Make sure you know how to use the button on your calculator.

You might need to enter '12% × 700' or '700 × 12%' (some calculators will work both ways).

On some calculators you need to press the = but on others you might not have to.

Check how your calculator works by finding 12% of 350. The answer should be 42.

You do need to enter the percentage sign in these calculations because one of the values you are working with is a percentage.

EXERCISE 13B

1 Calculate:

   a 5% of 250   **b** 9% of 400   **c** 20% of 120

   d 65% of 4500   **e** 12% of 75   **f** 75% of 360

   g 32% of 50   **h** 110% of 60   **i** 150% of 90

2 Calculate, giving your answers as mixed numbers or decimals as necessary.

   a 19% of £50   **b** 60% of 70 kg   **c** 45% of 35 cm

   d 90% of 29 kg   **e** $3\frac{1}{2}$% of £400   **f** 2.6% of 80 minutes

   g 7.4% of £1000   **h** 3.8% of 180 m   **i** $9\frac{2}{3}$% of 600 litres

Tip

Remember your answer will have a unit not a percentage sign. You are not working out a percentage here, you are working out how much a given percentage of a quantity is.

3 Anya got 85% for a test that was out of 80 marks.

What was her mark out of 80?

4 Choose the correct option in each part.

   a A substance is 99.5% fat free. How many grams of fat would there be in 250 g of the substance?

     A 248.75 g   B 125 g   C 12.5 g   D 1.25 g

   b In a crowd of 75 242 people, 62% were female. How many females is this?

     A 4665.4   B 12 136   C 46 650   D 1213.6

5 A salesperson at a mobile phone shop estimates that about 3% of phones come back for some sort of repair in the first week.

The shop sells 180 phones.

How many can they expect to come back for repairs in the first week?

6 In an area, 46% of residents do not read the local paper, the rest do read it.

There are a total of 2450 residents in the area.

How many people:

   a don't read the paper?   **b** read the paper?

7 Of 240 trains arriving at King's Cross, 2.5% arrived early and 13.8% arrived late.

How many trains were on time?

8 A tablet computer is advertised for sale for £899 excluding VAT.

VAT was increased from 17.5% to 20% before Narea bought it.

How much would she have saved if she had bought it when VAT was 17.5%?

9 In a garden 7.5% of the 620 m² area is set aside for growing tulips.

The rest is used to grow vegetables.

How many square metres of land is used to grow:

   a tulips?   **b** vegetables?

Find answers at: cambridge.org/ukschools/gcsemaths-studentbookanswers

10 The population of a town increases by about 24.8% each summer.

The population of the town is normally 12 760.

How many people arrive during the summer?

11 Eighteen-carat gold contains 18 parts pure gold per 24 parts.

Nine-carat gold contains 9 parts pure gold per 24 parts.

  a Work out the percentage of pure gold in 9-carat and 18-carat gold.

  b Naz buys an 18-carat gold ring that weighs 7.3 grams.

    How much pure gold does it contain?

  c Vishnu buys a 9-carat gold pendant that has a mass of 16.3 grams.

    How much pure gold does it contain?

Tip

You expressed one quantity as a fraction of another in Chapter 5. Read through that work again if you cannot remember how to do this.

Expressing one quantity as a percentage of another

You write one quantity as a percentage of another quantity by writing the first quantity as a fraction of the other and then multiplying by 100 to get a percentage.

The two quantities must be in the same units before you write them as a fraction.

WORK IT OUT 13.2

Brian has run 1500 m of a 5 km race when he gets a cramp in his foot.

What percentage of the race has he completed at this stage?

Which of these two students has got the correct answer? Why is the other one wrong?

Student A	Student B
$\dfrac{1500}{5} \times 100$	$\dfrac{1500}{5000} \times 100$
$= 300 \times 100$	$= \dfrac{3}{10} \times 100$
$= 300\%$	$= 30\%$

Tip

When you convert quantities to get them to the same unit you can avoid decimal values by choosing the smaller units (for example, making both units metres in this example rather than making them both kilometres).

EXERCISE 13C

1 In each part, express the first amount as a percentage of the second.
Give your answer to two decimal places (if necessary).

a 400 m of 5 km	**b** 45 m of 3 km
c 150 m of 1 km	**d** 8 cm of 2 m
e 14 mm of 4 cm	**f** 19 cm of 3 m
g 25p of £4	**h** 66p of £3.50
i 20 seconds of a minute	**j** 25 seconds of 1.5 minutes
k 750 g of 23 kg	**l** 800 g of 1.5 kg
m 4 days of a week	**n** 3 days of 6 weeks
o 800 kg of 3 tonnes	**p** 8.4 tonnes of 50 000 kg
q 500 mm of 2 m	**r** 90 mm of 14 cm
s 350 ml of 2 litres	**t** 5 ml of 0.5 litres

2 What is 30p as a percentage of £2?
Choose from the options below.

A 1500%   B 85%   C 15%   D 6.66%

3 Angelika got 19 out of 24 for an assignment.
Nina got 23 out of 30.
Which of the two girls got the highest percentage mark?

4 In a local election there were 5400 registered voters.
Of these, 3240 voted.
What was the voter turnout? Give your answer as a percentage.

5 Mel improved his running time for the 400 m race by 3 seconds.
His previous running time was 50 seconds.
What is his percentage improvement?

6 Kenny had a box of 40 chocolates.
He ate 32 of them.
What percentage of the chocolates is left?

7 Sylvia keeps a record of how many tennis sets she wins.
In the past month she won 19 out of 27 sets.
What percentage of the sets did she lose?

8 The world record for the longest kiss is 58 hours, 35 minutes and 58 seconds.
It was set at a three-day event.
What percentage of the three-day event was the kiss?

Find answers at: cambridge.org/ukschools/gcsemaths-studentbookanswers

9 Read the label and answer the questions.

a Calculate the combined percentage of fat and sugar in a serving.

b What percentage of a serving is sodium?

Nutritional values	
(Per 30 g serving)	
Carbohydrates	19 g
(of which sugars)	6.2 g
Fat	3.8 g
Sodium	93 mg

Section 3: Percentage change

You will often see changes (increases or decreases) in amounts expressed as percentages.

For example, you might read that the price of petrol is to increase by 5.5% or that the cost of mobile broadband has decreased by 15% over the past year.

Increasing or decreasing an amount by a percentage

Tip

You can express any % increase or decrease as a multiplier.

To increase a number by x%, multiply it by $1 + \frac{x}{100}$.

To decrease a number by x%, multiply it by $1 - \frac{x}{100}$.

WORK IT OUT 13.3

A school population of 650 students increased by 12% last year.

At the same time, the registration fee of £120 decreased by 15%. Work out:

a the new student population   **b** the new registration fee.

Look at these examples to see how different students solved these problems.

Which method seems simpler to you?

Could you use your calculator to do these calculations? How?

Student A	**Student B**
650 increased by 12%	650 increased by 12%
12% of $650 = \frac{12}{100} \times 650$ $= 78$ $650 + 78 = 728$ There are now 728 students.	Old population = 100% New population = old + increase = $100\% + 12\% = 112\%$ $112\% = \frac{112}{100} = 1.12$ $1.12 \times 650 = 728$ The new student population is 728.
£120 decreased by 15% 15% of $120 = \frac{15}{100} \times 120$ $= 18$ £120 − £18 = £102 The new registration fee is £102.	£120 decreased by 15% £120 − £18 = £102 The new registration fee is £102. **% / £** 10 / 12 5 / 6 15 / 18

EXERCISE 13D

1 Increase each amount by the given percentage.

    a £48 increased by 14%   **b** £700 increased by 35%

    c £30 increased by 7.6%   **d** £40 000 increased by 0.59%

    e £90 increased by 9.5%   **f** £80 increased by 24.6%

2 The number 1500 is increased by 120%. What is the result?

Choose from the options below.

    A 300   B 1620   C 1800   D 3300

3 Decrease each amount by the given percentage.

    a £68 decreased by 14%   **b** £800 decreased by 35%

    c £90 decreased by 7.6%   **d** £20 000 decreased by 0.59%

    e £85 decreased by 9.5%   **f** £60 decreased by 24.6%

4 A salesperson earns £130 plus 1.5% of the value of sales.

£20 000 worth of goods were sold.

Calculate the salesperson's earnings.

Choose your answer from the options below.

    A $1.5 \times £20\,000$ B $130 + 1.5 \times £20\,000$

    C $130 + 0.15 \times £20\,000$ D $130 + 0.015 \times £20\,000$

5 A building cost £125 000 to build.

It increased in value by $3\frac{1}{2}\%$.

What is the building worth now?

6 Jack earns £3125 per month.

He receives a pay increase of 3.8%.

What are his new monthly earnings, to the nearest pound?

7 Sharon earns £25 per shift.

Her boss says she can either have £7 more per shift or a 20% increase.

Which is the bigger increase?

8 The membership of a sports club increased by 26% one year.

There were 284 members the previous year.

How many members do they have now?

9 Sammy bought £2500 worth of shares.

At the end of the first month their value had decreased by 4.25%.

At the end of the second month the value of the shares had gone up 1.5% from the previous month.

Work out the value of the shares at the end of each month.

10 Amira earns £25 000 per year plus 12% commission on any sales she generates.

She sells £145 250 worth of goods in one year.

Calculate her annual earnings.

Finding original values

If you know the percentage by which an amount has increased or decreased, you can use it to find the original amount.

Problems involving original values are often called reverse or inverse percentages.

When you work with these problems you need to remember that you are dealing with percentages of the original values.

Tip

Undoing a 10% decrease is not the same as just increasing the sale price by 10%. If you add 10% to the sale price of £108 you will get £118.80 which is **not** the right answer.

WORKED EXAMPLE 3

A shop is offering a 10% discount on all sale goods.

Jesse paid £108 for a bike in the sale.

What was the original price of the bike?

$$90\% \text{ of } x = £108$$
$$\therefore \frac{90}{100}x = 108$$
$$\therefore 90x = 100 \times 108$$
$$\therefore 90x = 10\,800$$
$$\therefore x = \frac{10\,800}{90}$$
$$\therefore x = 120$$

If the cost is reduced by 10% then you are actually paying 90%. If you let the original amount be x, you can write an equation and solve it to find x.

The original price was £120.

Check that you have answered the question.

WORKED EXAMPLE 4

Sameen sells her shares and receives £3450. This gives her a profit of 15%.

What did she pay for the shares originally?

$$1.15x = 3450$$
$$x = \frac{3450}{1.15}$$
$$x = 3000$$

She paid £3000 for the shares.

15% profit means an increase of 15%, so the selling price = 115% or 1.15 of the cost. If you let the cost price be x, you can write an equation and solve it to find x.

$$£3000 \times 1.15 = £3450$$

Check this by increasing £3000 by 15%.

EXERCISE 13E

1 Find the original values if:

  a 25% is £30   **b** 8% is 120 grams

  c 120% is 800 kg   **d** 115% is £2000

2 What is the original price of an item sold for £140 in a 25% off sale?

Choose your answer from the options below.

  A £175   B £245.50   C £186.67   D £560

3 VAT of 20% is added to most goods before they are sold.

The prices given here include VAT.

Work out the net cost of each item (cost before VAT is added).

  a Necklace £1200   **b** Camera £145.50

  c Painting £865   **d** Boots £54.99

4 Misha paid £40 for a DVD box set in a 20% off sale.

What was the original price of the DVD set?

5 A camera is sold for £87.

The shop makes a 45% profit.

What is the cost price of the camera?

Choose your answer from the following options.

  A £60   B £56.13   C £47.85   D £39.15

6 In a school 240 students are in Year 10.

This is 20% of the school population.

  a How many students are there in total in the school?

  b How many students are in all the other years put together at this school?

7 Sarita's pay increased by 15%.

Her new pay is £172.50.

What was her pay before the increase?

8 Nine-carat gold is 37.5% pure gold.

A piece of nine-carat gold jewellery is tested and found to contain 97.5 grams of pure gold.

What is the total weight of the piece of jewellery?

9 Julia is training for a marathon and she reduces her weight by 5%.

She weighs 58 kg at the end of her training.

What did she weigh at the start?

10 In an ultramarathon, 310 runners completed the course within the cut-off time.

This represents 62% of the runners.

How many runners started the race?

 Find answers at: cambridge.org/ukschools/gcsemaths-studentbookanswers

Checklist of learning and understanding

Review of percentages

- Percentage means 'parts per hundred'.
- To convert a percentage to a fraction, write the percentage with a denominator of 100 and simplify.
- To convert percentages to decimals divide by 100.
- To order a mixture of fractions, decimals and percentages, change them all to percentages or decimals.

Percentage calculations

- To find a percentage of an amount, express the percentage as a fraction over 100 and then multiply the fraction by the amount.
- To express one quantity (quantity A) as a percentage of another quantity (quantity B), make sure the units are the same and then calculate $\frac{\text{quantity A}}{\text{quantity B}} \times 100$.

Percentage change

- To increase or decrease an amount by a percentage, find the percentage amount and add or subtract it from the original amount.
- Or, use a multiplier: to increase an amount by $x\%$, the multiplier is $(1 + \frac{x}{100})$; to decrease an amount by $x\%$, the multiplier is $(1 - \frac{x}{100})$.
- To find an original value when you know the percentage increase or decrease and the new amount, make an equation and use reverse percentages to solve for x.

For additional questions on the topics in this chapter, visit GCSE Mathematics Online.

Chapter review

1   **a**   Choose the value that is equivalent to 4.5%.

A $4\frac{5}{100}$ B $\frac{45}{100}$ C $\frac{450}{100}$ D $\frac{45}{1000}$

    b   What is the decimal equivalent of 500%?

Choose from the following options.

A 50 000.0   B 5.0   C 0.05   D 0.005

2   Write the following percentages as fractions in their simplest form.

a 25%   **b** 30%   **c** 3.5%

3   Express each of these as a percentage.

a $\frac{1}{20}$ **b** $\frac{1}{8}$ **c** $\frac{8}{15}$

d 0.5   **e** 1.25   **f** 0.005

4   The value of an investment increased from £120 000 to £124 800.

What percentage increase is this?

5   The population of New Orleans was 484 674 before Hurricane Katrina.

Afterwards, the population was found to have decreased by 53.9%.

What was the population afterwards?

6 Customers at a shop who spend £100 or more can pay by these methods.

    A 12 payments. Each payment is 10% of the cost price.

    B 24 payments. Each payment is 6% of the cost price.

    C 36 payments. Each payment is 4% of the cost price.

Which method is the cheapest?

You must show your working.   *(3 marks)*

© AQA 2013

7 Shaz works 30 hours per week.

She increases this by 12%.

How many hours does she now work per week?

8 Express:

  a 3 hours as a percentage of a day

  b 750 metres as a percentage of 2 km.

9 The price of a plane ticket was reduced by 8% to £423.20.

What was the original price of the ticket?

10 Niall sold some shares for £1147.50 and made a 35% profit.

What did he pay for the shares?

Find answers at: cambridge.org/ukschools/gcsemaths-studentbookanswers

14 Powers and roots

In this chapter you will learn how to …

- use positive and negative powers to represent numbers in index notation.
- calculate with powers and roots.
- apply the rules for multiplying and dividing indices.

 For more resources relating to this chapter, visit GCSE Mathematics Online.

Using mathematics: real-life applications

Interior designers use square units to work out the area of floors to be tiled and walls to be painted. They then work out how much paint to buy and use the size of tiles (also in square units) to work out how many are needed.

 Calculator tip

Make sure you know which buttons to use to evaluate different powers and find different roots of numbers.

"I'm pretty good at estimating in square units. I can usually look at a room and guess the area of the floor and walls quite accurately. Tiles are harder, I do rough sketches on squared paper to help me work out how many tiles of a particular size are needed to cover a floor area."

(Interior designer)

Before you start …

Ch 1	You should be able to quickly add and subtract pairs of integers mentally.	**1** Choose the correct sign: <, = or >. **a** $-3 + -3 \;\square\; 4 + 2$ **b** $6 - 7 \;\square\; 3 - 4$ **c** $4 - (-5) \;\square\; -3 + -6$ **d** $-2 + 6 \;\square\; 9 - 5$

Ch 1	You need to be able to find the squares, cubes, square roots and cube roots of numbers.	**2** Choose the correct answer.
		
		a The area of a square with sides of 3 cm.
		   A $6\,\text{cm}^2$ B $9\,\text{cm}^2$ C $12\,\text{cm}^2$
		b $\sqrt[3]{27}$
		   A 9 B 5.2 C 3
		c $\sqrt{810\,000}$
		   A 9 B 90 C 900

Ch 5	You need to be able to find the reciprocal of a number or fraction.	**3** Find the reciprocal of each number. Choose from the values in the box. $\quad\boxed{\dfrac{12}{1} \quad \dfrac{4}{3} \quad \dfrac{1}{12} \quad \dfrac{7}{5} \quad \dfrac{5}{7}}$ **a** $\dfrac{3}{4}$ **b** 12 **c** $1\frac{2}{5}$

Assess your starting point using the Launchpad

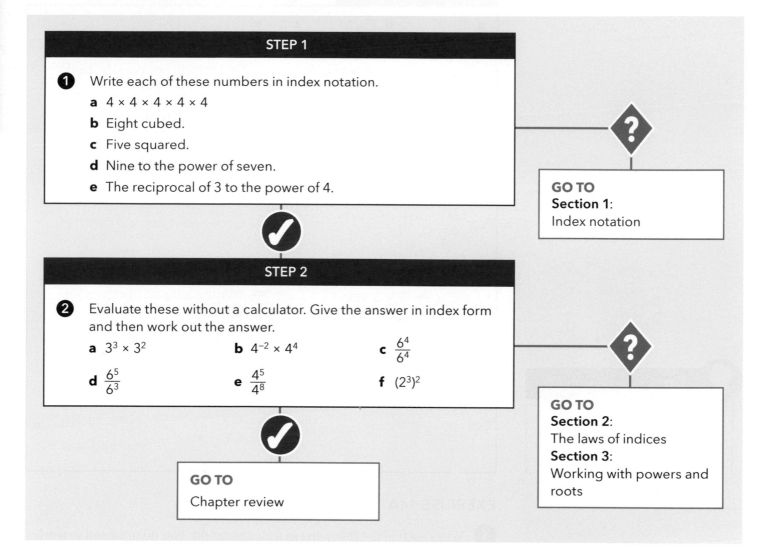

STEP 1

1 Write each of these numbers in index notation.

a $4 \times 4 \times 4 \times 4 \times 4$

b Eight cubed.

c Five squared.

d Nine to the power of seven.

e The reciprocal of 3 to the power of 4.

GO TO
Section 1:
Index notation

STEP 2

2 Evaluate these without a calculator. Give the answer in index form and then work out the answer.

a $3^3 \times 3^2$ **b** $4^{-2} \times 4^4$ **c** $\dfrac{6^4}{6^4}$

d $\dfrac{6^5}{6^3}$ **e** $\dfrac{4^5}{4^8}$ **f** $(2^3)^2$

GO TO
Section 2:
The laws of indices
Section 3:
Working with powers and roots

GO TO
Chapter review

Section 1: Index notation

You use powers to write repeated multiplications in a shorter form.

For example: $6 \times 6 = 6^2$ and $5 \times 5 \times 5 = 5^3$

$$5^3$$

This is the index.
The index can also be
called the power.

This is the base.

The **index** tells you how many times the base number is multiplied by itself.

$4^3 = 4 \times 4 \times 4$

$7^4 = 7 \times 7 \times 7 \times 7$

$9^{12} = 9 \times 9 \times 9 \times 9 \times 9 \times 9 \times 9 \times 9 \times 9 \times 9 \times 9 \times 9$

When you write a number using an index you are using **index notation**.

7^4 is in index notation.

When you write the multiplication out in full you are using expanded form.

$7 \times 7 \times 7 \times 7$ is in expanded form.

Key vocabulary

index: a power indicating how many times a base number is multiplied by itself. The plural of index is indices.

index notation: writing a number as a base and index, for example 2^3

Tip

Any number to the power of 1 stays as the same number so you don't usually write powers of 1.

 Find answers at: cambridge.org/ukschools/gcsemaths-studentbookanswers

WORKED EXAMPLE 1

a $3^4 - 2^4$ **b** $3^2 \times 3^3$ **c** $3^5 \div 3^2$

a $3^4 - 2^4$

> You cannot subtract these in index form because the bases are not the same.

$= 3 \times 3 \times 3 \times 3 - 2 \times 2 \times 2 \times 2$

> Write each term in expanded form.

$= 9 \times 9 - 4 \times 4$

> Multiply mentally. You can do this in pairs.

$= 81 - 16$
$= 65$

b $3^2 \times 3^3$

$= 3 \times 3 \times 3 \times 3 \times 3$
$= 9 \times 9 \times 3$
$= 81 \times 3$
$= 243$

> Write each part in expanded notation.

c $3^5 \div 3^2$

$= \dfrac{3 \times 3 \times 3 \times 3 \times 3}{3 \times 3}$
$= 9 \times 3$
$= 27$

Tip

In Section 2 you will learn how to use the laws of indices to simplify expressions in index form without having to expand them.

EXERCISE 14A

1 Write each of the following in index notation. You do not need to work out the value.

a $4 \times 4 \times 4$ **b** $3 \times 3 \times 3 \times 3 \times 3 \times 3$

c $7 \times 7 \times 7 \times 7$ **d** $9 \times 9 \times 9$

e $5 \times 5 \times 5 \times 5 \times 5$ **f** $12 \times 12 \times 12$

g $18 \times 18 \times 18 \times 18 \times 18 \times 18 \times 18$

h $11 \times 11 \times 11 \times 11 \times 11 \times 11 \times 11 \times 11 \times 11$

i nineteen to the power of eight

j 23 to the power of 6

k eleven multiplied by itself 14 times

l nine multiplied by itself 8 times

2 Write each expression in expanded form. Don't work out the answers.

a 3^4 b 9^3 c 4^5 d 8^3

e 5^6 f 3^8 g 23^5 h 51^4

i 72^5 j 203^3 k 121^4 l 100^5

3 Which value is equivalent to 15^3?

Choose your answer from the options below.

A 45 B 225 C 3375 D 15 000

4 Evaluate each expression without using a calculator.

a 2^3 b 6^2 c 1^8 d 8^3

e 10^4 f 10^6 g $2^3 - 1^5$ h $1^6 + 7^2$

i $2^4 \times 2^2$ j $2^4 + 4^2$ k $2^3 \times 2^4$ l $3^3 \times 3^3$

m $2^4 \div 2^3$ n $4^5 \div 4^3$ o $7^2 \times 10^3$ p 7×10^6

q $2 \times 10^2 + 3 \times 10^3$ r $6^2 \times 10^6$

Index notation on your calculator

Most calculators have one key to square a number:

Your calculator is also likely to have a key that allows you to enter any other powers quickly and easily. It might be y^x or x^y or a^b

To enter 13^4, you press

You will get a result of 28 561.

EXERCISE 14B

1 What is the value of $1^4 + 5^2$?
Choose your answer from the options below.

A 11 B 14 C 26 D 29

2 Use your calculator to evaluate the following.

a 4^6 b 12^3 c 8^5 d 7^4

e 15^3 f 10^4 g 28^2 h 25^3

3 Use a calculator to find the value of each expression.

a $12^3 - 2^8$ b $20^4 - 15^2$ c $15^3 \times 15^2$

d $3^{12} + 3^4$ e $3^6 + 2^8$ f $35^3 \div 5^3$

4 Copy each statement and fill in < or > to make each one true.

a $4^6 \square 6^4$ b $10^3 \square 3^{10}$ c $4^9 \square 9^4$

d $15^2 \square 2^{15}$ e $9^8 \square 8^9$ f $2^{10} \square 10^2$

Zero and negative indices

In this table, each value is $\frac{1}{10}$ of the value above it.

For example, $10^6 \div 10 = 10^5$

Index notation	Expanded form	Value
10^6	$10 \times 10 \times 10 \times 10 \times 10 \times 10$	$1\,000\,000$
10^5	$10 \times 10 \times 10 \times 10 \times 10$	$100\,000$
10^4	$10 \times 10 \times 10 \times 10$	$10\,000$
10^3	$10 \times 10 \times 10$	$1\,000$
10^2	10×10	100
10^1	10	10
10^0	$10 \div 10$	1
10^{-1}	$1 \div 10$	$\frac{1}{10}$
10^{-2}	$\frac{1}{10} \div 10$	$\frac{1}{100}$
10^{-3}	$\frac{1}{100} \div 10$	$\frac{1}{1000}$
10^{-4}	$\frac{1}{1000} \div 10$	$\frac{1}{10\,000}$

> ### Tip
>
> Remember that you use reciprocals to change fraction divisions into multiplications.
> $\frac{1}{10} \div 10 = \frac{1}{10} \times \frac{1}{10} = \frac{1}{100}$

The pattern in the table gives us two very important facts about indices.

Any number with an index of 0 is equal to 1: $a^0 = 1$
(Except for 0^0 which is undefined.)

For example, $5^0 = 1$ and $7^0 = 1$.

Any number with a negative index is equal to its reciprocal with a positive index: $a^{-m} = \frac{1}{a^m}$

For example, $4^{-2} = \frac{1}{4^2}$ and $5^{-3} = \frac{1}{5^3}$

EXERCISE 14C

1 How would you write 4^{-2} with a positive index?

Choose from the options below.

A $\frac{2^2}{2}$ B $\frac{2}{2^2}$ C $\frac{1}{4^2}$ D $\frac{4^2}{-1}$

2 Write each of the following using positive indices only.

   a 2^{-1} **b** 3^{-1} **c** 4^{-1}

   d 3^{-2} **e** 4^{-3} **f** 3^{-5}

   g 3^{-4} **h** 6^{-6} **i** 34^{-5}

3 Express the following with negative indices.

a $\frac{1}{3}$　　　　　**b** $\frac{1}{5}$　　　　　**c** $\frac{1}{7}$

d $\frac{1}{3^2}$　　　　**e** $\frac{1}{4^5}$　　　　**f** $\frac{1}{2^6}$

g $\frac{1}{7^2}$　　　　**h** $\frac{1}{10^5}$　　　**i** $\frac{1}{2^2}$

j $\frac{1}{12^3}$　　　**k** $\frac{1}{10^4}$　　　**l** $\frac{1}{3(2)^2}$

4 Copy each of these statements and fill in = or ≠ to make them true.

a $10^{-1} \square \frac{1}{10}$　　　**b** $6^0 \square 1$　　　**c** $6^{-1} \square \frac{1}{6}$

d $10^{-2} \square \frac{2}{10}$　　　**e** $6^{-3} \square \frac{1}{6^3}$　　　**f** $10^0 \square 1$

g $6^{-4} \square \frac{1}{6^4}$　　　**h** $\frac{1}{10^4} \square 10^{-4}$　　　**i** $\frac{1}{6^3} \square \frac{3}{6}$

Section 2: The laws of indices

The laws of indices show you how to multiply and divide powers without writing them out in expanded form.

Law of indices for multiplication

To multiply two numbers in index notation you add the indices.

$a^m \times a^n = a^{m+n}$

This law works for all indices, including negative indices.

For example, $2^3 \times 2^{-2} = 2^{3+(-2)} = 2^1 = 2$

Law of indices for division

To divide two numbers in index notation you subtract the indices.

$a^m \div a^n = a^{m-n}$

This law works for all indices, including negative indices.

$2^2 \div 2^4 = 2^{2-4} = 2^{-2}$

You can understand how this works by looking at the expanded notation:

$2^2 \div 2^4 = \frac{2 \times 2}{2 \times 2 \times 2 \times 2}$

If you cancel you get $\frac{1}{2 \times 2}$

$\frac{1}{2^2}$ is equal to 2^{-2}

Law of indices for powers of indices

To find the power of a power you multiply the indices.

$(a^m)^n = a^{mn}$

This law works for all indices, including negative indices.

$(3^2)^3 = 3^{2 \times 3} = 3^6$

$(4^3)^{-4} = 4^{(3)(-4)} = 4^{-12}$

You can understand how this works by looking at the expanded notation:

$(3^2)^3$ means 3^2 to the power of 3, which is $3^2 \times 3^2 \times 3^2$

$3^2 \times 3^2 \times 3^2 = 3 \times 3 \times 3 \times 3 \times 3 \times 3 = 3^6$

EXERCISE 14D

1 Simplify. Leave your answers in index notation.

a $2^4 \times 2^3$

b $10^2 \times 10^5$

c $4^3 \times 4^3$

d 5×5^6

e $2^4 \times 2^7$

f $3^2 \times 3^{-4}$

g $2^{-2} \times 2^5$

h $3^0 \times 3^2$

i $2 \times 2^3 \times 2^{-5}$

j $3^2 \times 3^2 \times 3$

k $10^2 \times 10^{-3} \times 10^2$

l $10^0 \times 10^{-2} \times 10^2$

2 Simplify. Leave your answers in index notation.

a $6^4 \div 6^2$

b $10^5 \div 10^2$

c $6^5 \div 6^3$

d $6^3 \div 6^5$

e $10^3 \div 10^5$

f $3^{10} \div 3^0$

g $3^8 \div 3$

h $10^4 \div 10^4$

i $\dfrac{5^4}{5^{-2}}$

j $\dfrac{10^6}{10^{-4}}$

k $\dfrac{3^{-2}}{3^{-3}}$

l $\dfrac{2^0}{2^3}$

3 Simplify each expression. Give your answers in index notation.

a $(2^2)^3$

b $(2^3)^3$

c $(2^4)^2$

d $(10^2)^2$

e $(10^2)^3$

f $(10^4)^2$

g $(2^4)^{-3}$

h $(10^{-2})^2$

i $(10^2)^{-3}$

j $(3^4)^{-2}$

k $(2^3)^0$

l $(2^2 \times 2^3)^2$

4 Say whether each statement is true or false. If it is false, write the correct answer.

a $3^3 \times 3^5 = 3^8$

b $3^8 \div 3^2 = 3^4$

c $10^8 \div 10^2 = 10^6$

d $(3^3)^2 = 3^6$

e $121^0 = 1$

f $4^5 \times 4^2 = 4^7$

g $3^{10} \div 3^2 = 3^5$

h $(4^2)^4 = 4^8$

i $(3^2)^0 = 1$

Section 3: Working with powers and roots

Powers and roots are used every day in many different occupations.

Builders, painters and decorators need to work out areas using square units (powers of 2 and square roots). Volume calculations use cube units (powers of 3 and cube roots).

Bankers and accountants who do calculations involving growth rates or decay rates use different powers and roots and many science formulae rely on being able to work with powers and roots.

Powers of 2, 3, 4, 5 and 10

It is useful to recognise the first few powers of 2, 3, 4 and 5. This can help you to work out their roots as well.

It is also useful to know these powers of 10:

$10^3 = 1000$

$10^6 = 1$ million

EXERCISE 14E

1 Draw up a table like this one.

Base \ Index	−3	−2	−1	0	1	2	3	4	5
2	$2^{-3} = \frac{1}{8}$	$2^{-2} =$	$2^{-1} = \frac{1}{2}$	$2^0 = 1$	$2^1 = 2$	$2^2 = 4$	$2^3 =$	$2^4 = 16$	$2^5 =$
3									
4									
5									

  a Use a calculator to work out the missing values in the table. Some powers of two have been done as an example.

  b Compare the positive and negative values for the same index. What do you notice?

  c Compare the powers of 2 with the powers of 4. What do you notice?

  d How can you decide quickly that a number is a power of 5?

Roots

Finding the square root of a number involves working out what number multiplied by itself gives you the value under the root sign.

$$5^2 = 25 \text{ and } \sqrt{25} = 5$$

For any other roots, the number in front of the root sign tells you how many times the number has to be multiplied by itself.

$$2^3 = 8 \text{ and } \sqrt[3]{8} = 2$$

Finding the root of a number is the inverse of working out the power of the number.

$$2^4 = 16 \text{ and } \sqrt[4]{16} = 2$$

You know this is correct because $2 \times 2 \times 2 \times 2 = 16$.

EXERCISE 14F

1 Three of the statements are incorrect. Which one is correct?

A $10^2 > 2^{10}$ B $4^2 = 2^4$ C $3^2 = 2^3$ D $6^2 > 2^6$

2 Use the table that you completed in Exercise 14E to decide whether each statement is true or false.

a $2^4 = 4^2$ b $2^5 > 3^5$ c $2^0 = 5^0$

d $2^1 = 2^{-1}$ e $3^4 > 4^3$ f $4^4 < 3^4$

g $5^2 = 2^5$ h $3^5 > 5^3$ i $2^{-3} > 3^{-2}$

j $3^{-3} = \dfrac{1}{27}$ k $5^{-1} = 4^{-1}$ l $2(2^{-1}) = 1$

3 Use your table to work these out without using a calculator.

a $\sqrt{25}$ b $\sqrt[3]{8}$ c $\sqrt[4]{256}$

d $\sqrt[3]{125}$ e $\sqrt[5]{243}$ f $\sqrt[3]{64}$

g $\sqrt[3]{8} + \sqrt[4]{625}$ h $\sqrt{2500}$ i $\sqrt[5]{32} + \sqrt[4]{81}$

j $\sqrt[3]{27\,000}$ k $\sqrt[4]{160\,000}$ l $\sqrt[5]{3125} \times \sqrt[4]{625}$

Solving problems involving powers and roots

Knowing that squaring or cubing numbers and finding their root are inverse operations can help you to solve problems involving area and volume.

WORKED EXAMPLE 2

Mr Jones paves a courtyard 4 m long and 4 m wide with square paving slabs.

Each paving slab covers an area of $0.25\,\text{m}^2$.

a What are the dimensions (length and breadth) of the slabs?

b How many slabs will he need for his courtyard?

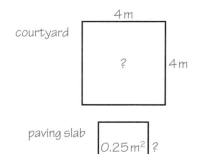

In problems like this it helps to make a sketch and to label it with the information you are given.

a Length of side of slab = L

$L^2 = 0.25\,\text{m}^2$

$L = \sqrt{0.25}\,\text{m}^2 = 0.5\,\text{m}$

Length and breadth of slab is 0.5 m

Use a letter to represent the unknown length.

You know the area of the slab so you can make an equation. Remember 'area = length squared'.

Take the square root of each side of the equation.

b Courtyard area = $4 \times 4 = 16\,\text{m}^2$

Area of one paving slab = $0.25\,\text{m}^2$

$\dfrac{16}{0.25} = 64$ paving slabs

Divide the total area by the area of one slab to work out how many Mr Jones will need.

EXERCISE 14G

1 Find the lengths of the sides of each of these square areas:

a Area = 64 cm²

b Area = 0.09 cm²

c Area = 0.16 m²

d Area = 1600 mm²

2 Jagriti has 900 square mosaic tiles. Is it possible to arrange them to make a perfect square?

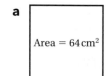

3 **a** The volume of a cube is 216 cm³.

What is the length of each edge? Choose from the options below.

A 6 cm   B 14.7 cm   C 24 cm   D 72 cm

b A box can hold 24 cuboids of volume 256 cm³.

What is the volume of the box? Choose from the options below.

A 216 cm³   B 256 cm³   C 624 cm³   D 6144 cm³

4 Sandy has a square piece of plastic with sides of 140 cm.

Is the plastic big enough to cover a square table with an area of 1.69 m²?

5 Mr Khan tiles a square floor of length 3.5 m.

The square tiles he uses each have an area of 1024 cm².

a Work out the area of the floor.

b Work out the length of one side of each tile.

c How many tiles does he need to tile the floor? Show your working.

d Mr Khan buys 15% more than he needs in case of breakages. The tiles come in boxes of eight.

How many boxes of tiles does he buy?

e The tiles cost £23.50 per box. How much will it cost Mr Khan to buy the tiles he needs (including the 15% extra)?

small

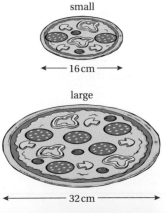

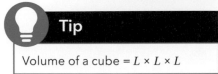

6 Nisha and Spencer buy pizzas. The pizzas come in small or large size.

The small pizza has a diameter of 16 cm and the large one has a diameter of 32 cm.

Nisha says that two small pizzas will give the same amount of pizza as one large one. Spencer disagrees.

a Use the formula, area $= 3.14 \times (\frac{1}{2} \times \text{diameter})^2$, to work out the area of each pizza to two decimal places. State whether Nisha is correct.

b What happens to the area of the pizza when you double the diameter?

7 Work out the length of the sides of each of these cubes.

a

volume = 125 cm³

b

volume = 64 cm³

c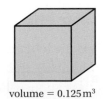

volume = 0.125 m³

Tip

Volume of a cube $= L \times L \times L$

8 This box is 4 cm long and 4 cm wide with a volume of 24 cm³.

Work out the depth of the box.

9 Sandy received an inheritance of £2500.

She wants to invest it for ten years in an account that offers 5% interest.

a To work out how much money she will have after ten years she uses the formula:

value of future investment = original amount $\times (1.05)^{10}$

How much money will Sandy have after ten years?

b Sandy decides to spend £500 of her inheritance and puts the rest of the money into this account.

Work out how much she will have after ten years in her investment.

10 Pam took a mortgage of £55 000 to buy a flat.

She uses this formula to work out how much she will repay over a 20-year period:

total amount paid = mortgage amount $\times (1.04)^{20}$

a Work out how much her mortgage will cost if she takes 20 years to repay it.

b The power of 20 in the formula represents the number of years over which it is to be repaid.

Work out what the total amount paid would be if Pam paid her mortgage off in 15 years.

c How much would she save by paying her mortgage off over the shorter period?

Checklist of learning and understanding

Index notation

- Numbers can be expressed as powers of their factors using index notation.
  - ○ $2 \times 2 \times 2 \times 2$ can be written in index notation as 2^4
  - ○ The 4 is the index (also called the power) and it tells us how many times the base (2) must be multiplied by itself.
- Any number to the power of 0 is equal to 1: $a^0 = 1$
- A negative index can be written as a reciprocal fraction with a positive index: $a^{-m} = \dfrac{1}{a^m}$

Laws of indices

- Multiplication: $a^m \times a^n = a^{m+n}$
- Division: $\dfrac{a^m}{a^n} = a^{m-n}$
- Raising a power: $(a^m)^n = a^{mn}$

Working with powers and roots

- Finding the root of a number is the inverse of raising the number to a power. For example, $4^2 = 16$ and $\sqrt{16} = 4$
- Powers and roots are useful for solving problems related to area, volume and future value of investments.

Find answers at: cambridge.org/ukschools/gcsemaths-studentbookanswers

For additional questions on the topics in this chapter, visit GCSE Mathematics Online.

Chapter review

1 Which expression is the smallest?

A 20^3 B 4^5 C 5^4 D 13^3

2 Write each number in index form.

a $8 \times 8 \times 8 \times 8 \times 8$ **b** three cubed

c nine squared **d** fourteen to the power of five

3 Write each expression in expanded form and work out the answer.

a 4^4 **b** 9^3 **c** $(4^3 - 3^3) \times 13^2$

4 Write these expressions in order from smallest to largest.

a $3^4, \sqrt{81}, 10^2, 4^3, 2 \times \sqrt{121}$ **b** $4^5, 5^4, 10^3, 96^0, 3^2, 20^2$

5 Write these numbers with positive indices.

a 3^{-3} **b** 2^{-10} **c** 5^{-2}

6 Simplify each expression by writing it as a single power of 4.

a $4^2 \times 4^2$ **b** $4^6 \times 4^{-3}$ **c** $4^7 \div 4^3$

d $4^3 \div 4^5$ **e** $(4^3)^2$ **f** $(4^{-2})^2$

7 Evaluate. Check your answers with a calculator.

a $\sqrt{121}$ **b** $\sqrt{0.25}$ **c** $\sqrt[3]{125}$

d $\sqrt[5]{32}$ **e** $\sqrt[4]{81}$ **f** $\sqrt{\dfrac{1}{4}}$

8 Find the length of each side of a cube of volume $0.027\,\text{m}^3$.

9 $\dfrac{V}{30} = \sqrt{h}$. Find V when $h = 25$.

10 $P - y = x^2$. Find P when $x = 2$ and $y = 8$.

11 Electricians use the formula $V = \sqrt{PR}$ to work out the voltage, V in volts, where P is the power in watts and R is the resistance in ohms.

Calculate the voltage when $P = 2000$ watts and $R = 24.2$ ohms.

12 a Copy and complete this table.

3^0	3^1	3^2	3^3	3^4	3^5	3^6	3^7
1	3	9			243	729	2187

(2 marks)

b $729 \times 2187 = 1\,594\,323$

and $1\,594\,323 = 3^x$

Use the table to work out the value of x. *(1 mark)*

c Use the table, or otherwise, to work out $\dfrac{2187}{9}$

Give your answer as a power of 3. *(1 mark)*

© AQA 2013

15 Standard form

 For more resources relating to this chapter, visit GCSE Mathematics Online.

Using mathematics: real-life applications

The study of stars, moons and planets involves huge numbers. Astronomers use standard form to write or type very large quantities. This makes it easier for them to compare the quantities and it allows them to calculate with and without calculators. The Sun has a mass of 1.988×10^{30} kg. This is a number with 27 zeros and it would be clumsy and impractical to have to write it out each time you wanted to use it.

"In astronomy we work with very large and very small numbers. There are 100 000 000 000 000 000 000 000 known stars alone! Imagine having to write this number out in full every time you wanted to use it! It is much easier to write 1×10^{23}."

(Astronomy student)

Before you start …

Ch 6	You should be able to calculate efficiently with decimals.	**1** Evaluate these without using a calculator.	
		a $2.9 + 5.8$ **b** $12.5 - 3.8$ **c** 4.5×1.5 **d** $4.5 \div 0.3$	
Ch 12	You need to be able to round numbers to a given number of significant figures.	**2** Choose the correct answer.	
		a 507 000 000 rounded to 2 sf. A 50 700 B 510 000 000	
		b 1.098 rounded to 3 sf. A 1.10 B 1.09	
		c 0.00625 rounded to 1 sf. A 0.6 B 0.006	
Ch 14	You should know how to apply the laws of indices.	**3** State whether the following are true or false. If the answer is false, work out the correct one.	
		a $x^5 \times x^3 = x^8$ **b** $x^{-3} \times x^4 = x$ **c** $\dfrac{x^4}{x^5} = x$ **d** $\dfrac{x^{-4}}{x^2} = x^{-6}$	

 Calculator tip

Make sure you know how your calculator deals with powers and that you have it in the correct mode to do calculations involving powers.

 Find answers at: cambridge.org/ukschools/gcsemaths-studentbookanswers

Assess your starting point using the Launchpad

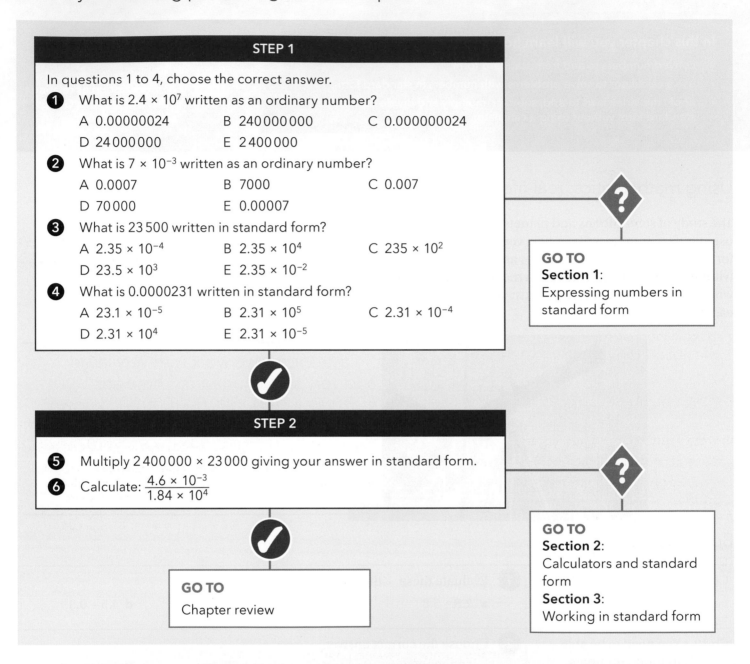

STEP 1

In questions 1 to 4, choose the correct answer.

1 What is 2.4×10^7 written as an ordinary number?

A 0.00000024   B 240 000 000   C 0.000000024

D 24 000 000   E 2 400 000

2 What is 7×10^{-3} written as an ordinary number?

A 0.0007   B 7000   C 0.007

D 70 000   E 0.00007

3 What is 23 500 written in standard form?

A 2.35×10^{-4} B 2.35×10^4 C 235×10^2

D 23.5×10^3 E 2.35×10^{-2}

4 What is 0.0000231 written in standard form?

A 23.1×10^{-5} B 2.31×10^5 C 2.31×10^{-4}

D 2.31×10^4 E 2.31×10^{-5}

GO TO
Section 1:
Expressing numbers in standard form

STEP 2

5 Multiply $2\,400\,000 \times 23\,000$ giving your answer in standard form.

6 Calculate: $\dfrac{4.6 \times 10^{-3}}{1.84 \times 10^4}$

GO TO
Chapter review

GO TO
Section 2:
Calculators and standard form
Section 3:
Working in standard form

Section 1: Expressing numbers in standard form

Writing out very large or very small numbers takes time and you might make mistakes when doing calculations.

Standard form is a way to write these numbers in a simpler way using powers of 10.

Remember			
$10^2 = 100$	one hundred	$10^5 = 100\,000$	one hundred thousand
$10^3 = 1000$	one thousand		
$10^4 = 10\,000$	ten thousand	$10^6 = 1\,000\,000$	one million

A number is in standard form when it is written as a product (×) of a number and a power of 10.

The number must be greater than or equal to 1 and smaller than 10.

For example, 2×10^2 and 1.2×10^{-2} are both in standard form.

Look at the patterns in this table.

$1.5 \times 10^0 =$	1.5	Remember $n^0 = 1$
$1.5 \times 10^1 =$	15	$1.5 \times 10^{-1} = 0.15$
$1.5 \times 10^2 =$	150	$1.5 \times 10^{-2} = 0.015$
$1.5 \times 10^3 =$	1 500	$1.5 \times 10^{-3} = 0.0015$
$1.5 \times 10^4 =$	15 000	$1.5 \times 10^{-4} = 0.00015$
$1.5 \times 10^5 =$	150 000	$1.5 \times 10^{-5} = 0.000015$
$1.5 \times 10^6 =$	1 500 000	$1.5 \times 10^{-6} = 0.0000015$

The index (power of ten) gives you important information.

- Multiplying by 10^4 means you are multiplying by 10 000 so the digits move four places to the left on a place value table.
- Multiplying by 10^{-4} means you are dividing by 10 000 so the digits move four places to the right on a place value table.

Tip

In the UK we use the term standard form for numbers in the form $A \times 10^n$, where $1 \leqslant A < 10$. This notation is also called scientific notation.

Writing a number in standard form

To write a number in standard form:

- Place the decimal point after the first non-zero digit.
- Find the power of 10 needed to move the digits back to their original position.
- Write the number as a decimal multiplied by a power of 10.

Tip

As numbers increase in size the digits move left (+) on a place value table and as numbers decrease in size the digits move right (-) on a place value table.

WORKED EXAMPLE 1

a Express 416 000 in standard form.

416000

$\overset{\frown}{4}.1\ 6$

$\overset{\textcircled{4}}{1}\ 6\ 0\ 0\ 0.$

Find the number between 1 and 10.

Work out how many places the digits need to move to get back to the original number.

$416000 = 4.16 \times 10^5$

The digits need to move five places to the left (+), so the power of ten is 5.

Continues on next page ...

b Express 0.0037 in standard from.

0.0037

3.⑦ 〰

0.0 0 3 ⑦

| Find the number between 1 and 10. |

| Work out how many places the digits need to move to get back to the original number. |

3.7×10^{-3}

| The digits need to move three places to the right (−), so the power of ten is −3. |

$0.0037 = \dfrac{37}{10\,000}$

| You can also work like this. Convert the decimal to a fraction. |

$= \dfrac{3.7}{1000}$

| Divide the top and bottom by 10 to get a numerator between 1 and 10. |

$= 3.7 \times 10^{-3}$

| Look at the number of zeros in the denominator to find the index. As the original number is less than 1, the index must be negative. |

EXERCISE 15A

1 Choose the correct power of 10 to complete the following statement.

$1.25 \times \square = 0.0125$

A 10 B 10^2 C 10^{-1} D 10^{-2}

2 Express each of the following in standard form.

a 321 000	**b** 1340	**c** 40 050
d 3 010 000	**e** 0.08	**f** 0.0001
g 32 000 000	**h** 910 000	**i** 0.000031255
j 0.00000024152	**k** 0.00305	**l** 0.201
m 34 000	**n** 0.00034	**o** 0.009
p 2.45	**q** 0.000426	**r** 0.426

3 Express each of the following quantities in standard form.

a The population of the Earth is more than 7 000 000 000.

b The distance from the Earth to the Moon is approximately 240 000 miles.

c There are about 37 000 000 000 000 cells in your body.

d Some cells are about 0.0000002 of a metre in diameter.

e The surface area of the Earth's oceans is about 140 million square miles.

f An angstrom is a unit of measure. One angstrom is equivalent to 0.0000000001 of a metre.

g Humans blink on average about 6 250 000 times per year.

h A dust particle has a mass of about 0.000000000753 kg.

Converting from standard form to ordinary numbers

To convert numbers from standard form to ordinary numbers or decimals you need to look at the powers and move the digits the correct number of places to the left or right.

WORKED EXAMPLE 2

Write as ordinary numbers.

a 3.25×10^5 **b** 2.07×10^{-5}

a 3.25×10^5

Move the digits 5 places to the left (+).

Fill in the correct number of zeros.

$3.25 \times 10^5 = 325\,000$

b 2.07×10^{-5}

$2.0\,⑦\,\rightsquigarrow$

$0.0\,0\,0\,0\,2\,0\,⑦$

Move the digits 5 places to the right (−).

Fill in the correct number of zeros.

$2.07 \times 10^{-5} = 0.0000207$

Remember to write the 0 before the decimal point as well.

EXERCISE 15B

1 Which number is equivalent to 1.4×10^7?

Choose the correct option below.

A 0.00000014   B 140 000 000   C 14 000 000   D 1 400 000

2 Express each of the following as an ordinary number.

a 1.4×10^2 **b** 4.8×10^4 **c** 2.9×10^3

d 3.25×10^2 **e** 3.25×10^{-1} **f** 3.67×10^5

g 4.5×10^7 **h** 2.13×10^{-2} **i** 3.209×10^4

j 3.46×10^{-3} **k** 1.89×10^{-4} **l** 7×10^{-7}

m 1.03×10^{-2} **n** 1.025×10^{-3} **o** 2.09×10^{-5}

3 Write each quantity out in full as an ordinary number.

  a The area of the Atlantic Ocean is 3.18×10^7 square miles.

  b The space between tracks on a DVD disc is 7.4×10^{-4} mm.

  c The diameter of the silk used to weave a spider's web is 1.24×10^{-6} mm.

  d There are 3×10^9 possible ways to play the first four moves in a game of chess.

  e A sheet of paper is about 1.2×10^{-4} m thick.

  f The distance between the Sun and Jupiter is about 7.78×10^8 km.

  g The Earth is about 1.5×10^{11} km from the Sun.

  h The mass of an electron is about $9.109\,382\,2 \times 10^{-31}$ kg.

Section 2: Calculators and standard form

You can use a scientific calculator to enter calculations in standard form.

The calculator will also give you an answer in standard form if it has too many digits to display on the screen.

Entering standard form calculations

You will need to use the $\boxed{\times 10^x}$, $\boxed{\text{Exp}}$ or $\boxed{\text{EE}}$ button on your calculator.

These are known as the exponent keys and they all work in the same way, even though they may look different on different calculators.

When you are using the exponent function key of your calculator you don't have to enter the $\times 10$ part. The function automatically includes that part.

Use your own calculator to work through this example. You should get the same result even if your function key is different to the one in the example.

> **Tip**
>
> Exponent is another term for power.

> **Calculator tip**
>
> Calculators work in different ways and you need to understand how your own calculator works. Make sure you know what buttons to use to enter standard form calculations, how to read and make sense of the display and how to convert your calculator answer into decimal form.

WORKED EXAMPLE 3

Use your calculator to calculate:

a 2.134×10^4 **b** 3.124×10^{-6}

a 2.134×10^4

Enter: $\boxed{2}\,\boxed{.}\,\boxed{1}\,\boxed{3}\,\boxed{4}\,\boxed{\times 10^x}\,\boxed{4}\,\boxed{=}$

Answer is: 21 340

b 3.124×10^{-6}

Enter: $\boxed{3}\,\boxed{.}\,\boxed{1}\,\boxed{2}\,\boxed{4}\,\boxed{\text{Exp}}\,\boxed{+/-}\,\boxed{6}\,\boxed{=}$

Answer is: 0.000003124

> Use the correct key for your calculator to enter the negative 6.

Making sense of the calculator display

The answer your calculator displays will depend on the calculator you use. Here are two ways in which calculators display answers in standard form:

$$5.98\text{E}-06$$ This is 5.98×10^{-6}

$$2.56\text{E}24$$ This is 2.56×10^{24}

To give the answer in standard form, read the display and write the answer correctly.

To give the answer as an ordinary number, apply the rules you know to convert it from standard form to ordinary form.

EXERCISE 15C

1 Enter each of these numbers into your calculator using the correct function key. Write down what appears on the display.

a 4.2×10^{12} **b** 1.8×10^{-5} **c** 2.7×10^6

d 1.34×10^{-2} **e** 1.87×10^{-9} **f** 4.23×10^7

g 3.102×10^{-4} **h** 3.098×10^9 **i** 2.076×10^{-23}

2 A calculator display gives an answer of $7.4\text{E}-04$

What is this as an ordinary number? Choose the correct answer below.

A 0.00074   B 74 000   C 0.0074   D 7400

3 Here are ten different calculator displays giving answers in exponential form.

Write each answer correctly in standard form.

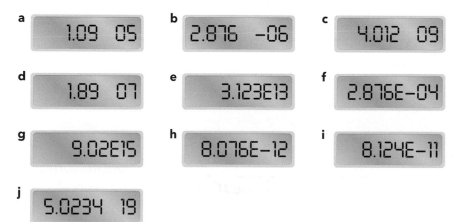

a $1.09 \quad 05$ **b** $2.876 \quad -06$ **c** $4.012 \quad 09$

d $1.89 \quad 07$ **e** $3.123\text{E}13$ **f** $2.876\text{E}-04$

g $9.02\text{E}15$ **h** $8.076\text{E}-12$ **i** $8.124\text{E}-11$

j $5.0234 \quad 19$

Significant figures

Tip

Look back at Chapter 12 if you need to remind yourself about how to round numbers to a given number of significant figures or decimal places.

When you work with standard form, you will often be asked to give the answers in standard form to a given number of significant figures.

- 0.003 is to 1 significant figure.
- 0.01 is to 1 significant figure.
- 0.10 is to 2 significant figures.

A zero after a non-zero digit is significant.

EXERCISE 15D

1 Write $(0.0125)^5$ in standard form, to three significant figures.

Choose from the options below.

A 0.12×10^5 B 0.12×10^{-5} C 3.05×10^{10} D 3.05×10^{-10}

2 Use your calculator to do these calculations. Give your answers in standard form to three significant figures.

a 4216^6

b $(0.00009)^4$

c $0.0002 \div 2500^3$

d $65\,000\,000 \div 0.0000045$

e $(0.0029)^3 \times (0.00365)^5$

f $(48 \times 987)^4$

g $\dfrac{4525 \times 8760}{0.000020}$

h $\dfrac{9500}{0.0005^4}$

i $\sqrt{5.25} \times 10^8$

j $\sqrt[3]{9.1} \times 10^{-8}$

Section 3: Working in standard form

Writing numbers in standard form allows you to use the laws of indices to calculate quickly without using a calculator.

Multiplying and dividing numbers in standard form

Tip

Remember:

$n^x \times n^y = n^{x+y}$ $\dfrac{n^x}{n^y} = n^{x-y}$

When you multiply powers of ten, you add the indices.

When you divide powers of ten, you subtract the indices.

WORKED EXAMPLE 4

Do these calculations without using a calculator. Give your answers in standard form.

a $(3 \times 10^5) \times (2 \times 10^6)$ **b** $(2 \times 10^{-3}) \times (3 \times 10^{-7})$ **c** $(2 \times 10^3) \times (8 \times 10^7)$

d $\dfrac{2.8 \times 10^6}{1.4 \times 10^4}$ **e** $\dfrac{4 \times 10^8}{9 \times 10^5}$

a $(3 \times 10^5) \times (2 \times 10^6)$

This is the same as:
$3 \times 2 \times 10^5 \times 10^6$

$= 6 \times 10^{5+6}$ | Add the indices.

$= 6 \times 10^{11}$ | Write the answer in standard form.

b $(2 \times 10^{-3}) \times (3 \times 10^{-7})$

This is the same as:
$2 \times 3 \times 10^{-3} \times 10^{-7}$

$= 6 \times 10^{-3+-7}$

$= 6 \times 10^{-10}$

c $(2 \times 10^3) \times (8 \times 10^7)$

This is the same as:
$2 \times 8 \times 10^3 \times 10^7$

$= 16 \times 10^{3+7}$

$= 16 \times 10^{10}$ | But 16 is greater than 10 so this is not in standard form.

$= 1.6 \times 10 \times 10^{10}$ | If you think of 16 as 1.6×10 you can change it to standard form.

$= 1.6 \times 10^{11}$

d $\dfrac{2.8 \times 10^6}{1.4 \times 10^4} = \dfrac{2.8}{1.4} \times \dfrac{10^6}{10^4}$

$= 2 \times 10^{6-4}$ | Subtract the indices to divide the powers.

$= 2 \times 10^2$

e $\dfrac{4 \times 10^8}{9 \times 10^5} = \dfrac{4}{9} \times \dfrac{10^8}{10^5}$

$= 0.44 \times 10^3$ | 0.44 is smaller than 1 so this is not standard form.

$= 4.4 \times 10^{-1} \times 10^3$ | If you think of 0.44 as 4.4×10^{-1} you can change it to standard form.

$= 4.4 \times 10^2$

Find answers at: cambridge.org/ukschools/gcsemaths-studentbookanswers

Problem-solving framework

You need to be able to solve problems involving numbers in standard form.

Read through this example.

The number of bacteria that can fit on to a piece of skin of area $1\,\text{mm}^2$ is approximately 1.5×10^{14}

A person's index fingertip has an approximate area of $3.75 \times 10^2\,\text{mm}$.

How many bacteria could fit on to it?

Give your answer in standard form and as an ordinary number.

Steps for solving problems	What you would do for this example
Step 1: Work out what you need to do.	Find the number of bacteria that will fit on to an area larger than the one given.
Step 2: Look for information that will help you.	Area of a fingertip is $3.75 \times 10^2\,\text{mm}$. Number of bacteria that can fit on to $1\,\text{mm}^2 = 1.5 \times 10^{14}$
Step 3: What maths can you use?	Multiply the number of bacteria by the area: $1.5 \times 10^{14} \times 3.75 \times 10^2 = 1.5 \times 3.75 \times 10^{14} \times 10^2$ $= 5.625 \times 10^{16}$
Step 4: Set out the solution clearly, making sure you have answered the original question.	$5.625 \times 10^{16} = 56\,250\,000\,000\,000\,000$ bacteria The answer is given in both of the forms required.

EXERCISE 15E

1 The answer to a calculation is given as 7×10^3.

Which of the following calculations produces this answer?

A $(7 \times 10^5) \div (7 \times 10^3)$ B $(7 \times 10^8) \div (1 \times 10^5)$

C $(1 \times 10^8) \div (7 \times 10^5)$ D $(0.7 \times 10^6) \div (1 \times 10^3)$

2 Simplify, giving the answers in standard form.

a $(2 \times 10^{13}) \times (4 \times 10^{17})$ **b** $(1.4 \times 10^8) \times (3 \times 10^4)$

c $(1.5 \times 10^{13}) \times (1.5 \times 10^{13})$ **d** $(0.2 \times 10^{17}) \times (0.7 \times 10^{16})$

e $(9 \times 10^{17}) \div (3 \times 10^{16})$ **f** $(8 \times 10^{17}) \div (4 \times 10^{16})$

g $(1.5 \times 10^8) \div (5 \times 10^4)$ **h** $(2.4 \times 10^{64}) \div (8 \times 10^{21})$

3 Simplify, giving the answers in standard form.

a $(2 \times 10^{-4}) \times (4 \times 10^{-16})$ **b** $(1.6 \times 10^{-8}) \times (4 \times 10^{-4})$

c $(1.5 \times 10^{-6}) \times (2.1 \times 10^{-3})$ **d** $(11 \times 10^{-5}) \times (3 \times 10^2)$

e $(9 \times 10^{17}) \div (4.5 \times 10^{-16})$ **f** $(7 \times 10^{-21}) \div (1 \times 10^{16})$

g $(4.5 \times 10^8) \div (0.9 \times 10^{-4})$ **h** $(11 \times 10^{-5}) \times (3 \times 10^2) \div (2 \times 10^{-3})$

4 Carry out these calculations without using your calculator. Leave the answers in standard form.

a $(3 \times 10^{12}) \times (4 \times 10^{18})$ **b** $(1.5 \times 10^6) \times (3 \times 10^5)$

c $(1.5 \times 10^{12})^3$ **d** $(1.2 \times 10^{-5}) \times (1.1 \times 10^{-6})$

e $(0.4 \times 10^{15}) \times (0.5 \times 10^{12})$ **f** $(8 \times 10^{17}) \div (3 \times 10^{12})$

g $(1.44 \times 10^8) \div (1.2 \times 10^6)$ **h** $(8 \times 10^{-15}) \div (4 \times 10^{-12})$

5 The speed of light is approximately 3×10^8 metres per second. How far will the light travel in:

a 10 seconds?   **b** 20 seconds?

c 10^2 seconds?   **d** 2×10^3 seconds?

6 An average human being blinks approximately 6.25×10^6 times per year.

a How often does an average human blink in five years? Give your answer in standard form and as an ordinary number.

b There are approximately 7.2×10^9 people on the planet. Calculate the total number of blinks in a year.

7 A sheet of paper is 1.2×10^{-4} m thick.

a Work out the height (in metres) of a stack of 500 sheets of this paper.

Give your answer in standard form and as an ordinary number.

b How many millimetres high is the stack of paper?

Adding and subtracting in standard form

When you want to add or subtract numbers in standard form you can rewrite them as ordinary numbers to do the calculation. You can then convert your answer back to standard form.

Calculator tip

If you are using a calculator you don't need to rewrite the numbers. You just need to enter the calculation correctly.

WORKED EXAMPLE 5

Calculate $6 \times 10^{-3} - 3 \times 10^{-4}$

$6 \times 10^{-3} - 3 \times 10^{-4}$
$= 0.006 - 0.0003$
$= 0.0057$
$= 5.7 \times 10^{-3}$

Remember to write the numbers so the place values line up:

$$
\begin{array}{r}
0.0060 \\
- \underline{0.0003} \\
\underline{0.0057}
\end{array}
$$

EXERCISE 15F

1 Carry out these calculations without using a calculator. Give your answers in standard form.

   a $(3 \times 10^8) + (2 \times 10^8)$ **b** $(3 \times 10^{-3}) - (1.5 \times 10^{-3})$

   c $(1.5 \times 10^5) + (3 \times 10^6)$ **d** $(6 \times 10^7) - (4 \times 10^6)$

   e $(4 \times 10^{-4}) + (3 \times 10^{-3})$ **f** $(5 \times 10^{-3}) - (2.5 \times 10^{-2})$

2 A length of 1.5×10^3 mm is cut from a wire 2.5×10^4 mm long.

How much is left? Choose from the options below.

   A 1×10^1 mm   B 1×10^7 mm   C 2.35×10^4 mm   D 2.35×10^7 mm

3 The Pacific Ocean has a surface area of approximately 1.65×10^8 km^2.

The Atlantic Ocean has a surface area of approximately 1.06×10^8 km^2.

   a State which ocean has the greater surface area.

   b Calculate the difference between the surface areas of the two oceans.

   c The total surface area of the world's oceans is 361 000 000 km^2.

      Work out the combined surface area of the other three oceans (the Indian, Southern and Arctic). Give your answer in standard form.

4 The Earth is approximately 9.3×10^7 miles from the Sun and 2.4×10^5 miles from the Moon.

Work out how much further is it from the Earth to the Sun than from the Earth to the Moon.

 Checklist of learning and understanding

Standard form

- Very large and very small numbers can be written in standard form by expressing them as the product of a value greater or equal to 1 and less than 10, and a power of 10.
- Positive powers of ten indicate large numbers and negative powers of ten indicate decimal fractions (small numbers).

Using a calculator

- The exponent function of the calculator allows you to enter calculations in standard form without entering the × 10 part of the calculation.
- When a number has too many digits to display, the calculator will give the answer in exponent form.

Calculations in standard form

- You can multiply and divide numbers in standard form by applying the rules of indices.
- You can add or subtract numbers in standard form without a calculator by writing them out in full.

Chapter review

For additional questions on the topics in this chapter, visit GCSE Mathematics Online.

1 Which of the following is correctly written in standard form?

    A 4.0×10^3 B 0.1258 C 32×10^{-3} D 1×5^2

2 Express the following numbers in standard form.

    a 45 000   **b** 80   **c** 2 345 000

    d 32 000 000 000   **e** 0.0065   **f** 0.009

    g 0.00045   **h** 0.0000008   **i** 0.00675

3 Write the following as ordinary numbers.

    a 2.5×10^3 **b** 3.9×10^4 **c** 4.265×10^5

    d 1.045×10^{-5} **e** 9.15×10^{-6} **f** 1.0×10^{-9}

    g 2.8×10^{-5} **h** 9.4×10^7 **i** 2.45×10^{-3}

4 Work these out. Use a calculator and give the answers in standard form.

    a $5 \times 10^4 + 9 \times 10^6$ **b** $3.27 \times 10^{-3} \times 2.4 \times 10^2$

    c $5(8.1 \times 10^9 - 2 \times 10^7)$ **d** $(3.2 \times 10^{-1}) - (2.33 \times 10^{-3})$ (to 3 sf)

5 Simplify the following without using a calculator and give the answers in standard form.

    a $(1.44 \times 10^7) + (4.3 \times 10^7)$ **b** $(4.9 \times 10^5) \times (3.6 \times 10^9)$

    c $(3 \times 10^4) + (4 \times 10^3)$ **d** $(4 \times 10^6) \div (3 \times 10^5)$

 6 There were 17 million families in the UK in 2006.

    a The mean number of children per family was 1.8

    How many children were there in the UK?

    Give your answer in standard form.   *(2 marks)*

    b The total income of families in the UK was £5.6×10^{11}.

    What was the mean income per family?

    Give your answer to an appropriate degree of accuracy.   *(3 marks)*

                                                  © AQA 2013

7 The Sun has a mass of approximately 1.998×10^{27} tonnes.

    The planet Mercury has a mass of approximately 3.302×10^{20} tonnes.

    a Work out which has the greater mass.

    b How many times heavier is the greater mass than the smaller?

8 The UK has an approximate area of 2.4×10^5 km^2.

    Australia has an area of approximately 7.6×10^6 km^2.

    a Find the difference in the areas of the two countries. Give your answer in standard form.

    b Calculate the combined area of the two countries. Give your answer in standard form.

    c How many times could the map of the UK fit on to the map of Australia if they were drawn at the same scale?

Find answers at: cambridge.org/ukschools/gcsemaths-studentbookanswers

16 Further algebra

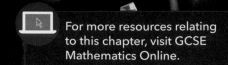
Using mathematics: real-life applications

Situations that involve motion, including acceleration, stopping distance, velocity and distance travelled (displacement) can be modelled using quadratic expressions and formulae.

"At the site of a crash, I measure the length of the tyre skid marks and apply an equation to work out the speed at which vehicles were moving before the accident."

(Police road accident investigator)

Before you start ...

Ch 7	Check that you remember how to simplify expressions.	**1**	Simplify: $3x + 6y + 2xy - 2x$
Ch 7	Make sure you can multiply out brackets.	**2**	Expand: $2x(x - y)$
Ch 7	Make sure you can factorise binomial expressions.	**3**	Factorise fully: $27xy - 9x$
Ch 7	You should be able to recognise an identity.	**4**	Is the identity symbol used correctly in each example? Give reasons why or why not. **a** $3(2a^2 - 4) \equiv 6a^2 - 12$ **b** $2x + 4 \equiv 7x - 8$
KS3 Ch 7	You should be able to express situations using algebra.	**5**	3 is added to a number and this new number is multiplied by 6 more than another number. Which expression represents this situation? A $(3 + y)x + 6$ B $(3 + y)(x + 6)$
KS3 Ch 1, 7	Make sure you remember the rules for multiplying negative and positive quantities.	**6**	Simplify: **a** 6×-5 **b** -3×-7 **c** $-2a \times b$ **d** $-y \times -y$ **e** $-2a \times -5a$

Assess your starting point using the Launchpad

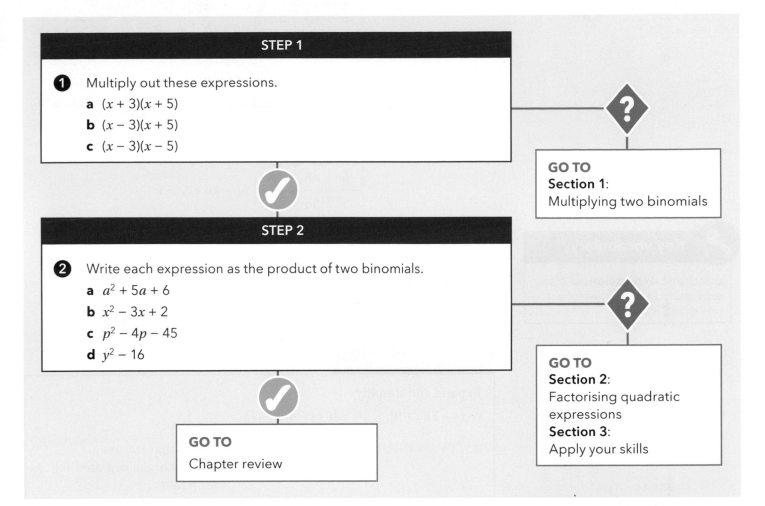

STEP 1

1 Multiply out these expressions.

a $(x + 3)(x + 5)$

b $(x - 3)(x + 5)$

c $(x - 3)(x - 5)$

GO TO
Section 1:
Multiplying two binomials

STEP 2

2 Write each expression as the product of two binomials.

a $a^2 + 5a + 6$

b $x^2 - 3x + 2$

c $p^2 - 4p - 45$

d $y^2 - 16$

GO TO
Section 2:
Factorising quadratic expressions
Section 3:
Apply your skills

GO TO
Chapter review

Section 1: Multiplying two binomials

A **binomial** is an expression that contains two terms.

For example:

$x + 2$ $3x^2 + 4$ $2x^2 - 5y^3$

A **binomial product** is the product of two binomials.

To multiply two brackets together each term in the first bracket must be multiplied by each term in the second bracket.

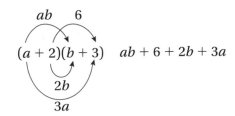

$$(a + 2)(b + 3) \quad ab + 6 + 2b + 3a$$

You can also use a grid to make sure you have multiplied all the terms.

Key vocabulary

binomial: an expression consisting of two terms
binomial product: the product of two binomial expressions, for example $(x + 2)(x + 3)$

Tip

Writing numbers in expanded notation to do long multiplication is similar to finding a binomial product.

14×27 can be written as

$(10 + 4) \times (20 + 7)$
$= 10 \times 20 + 10 \times 7 + 4 \times 20 + 4 \times 7$
$= 200 + 70 + 80 + 28$
$= 378$

Find answers at: cambridge.org/ukschools/gcsemaths-studentbookanswers

×	a	2
b	ab	$2b$
3	$3a$	6

$\left.\right\} ab + 2b + 3a + 6$

The product of two binomials gives you four terms.

When you multiply out brackets you need to take care with the minus signs.

$(a - 2)(b + 3)$

×	a	-2
b	ab	$-2b$
3	$3a$	-6

$\left.\right\} ab - 2b + 3a - 6$

When the product contains like terms you collect these to simplify the expression.

The expression $x^2 + 8x + 15$ is a **quadratic expression**, because the highest power of x in the expression is x squared (x^2).

The general form of a quadratic expression is $ax^2 + bx + c$.

Key vocabulary

quadratic expression: an expression in which the highest power of x is x^2

WORKED EXAMPLE 1

Expand and simplify:

a $(x - 2)(x + 9)$ **b** $(x - 4)(x - 7)$

a $(x - 2)(x + 9) = x^2 + 9x - 2x - 18$ — Notice that you get a positive and a negative like term here.

$= x^2 + 7x - 18$ — Collect like terms.

b $(x - 4)(x - 7) = x^2 - 7x - 4x + 28$ — Notice that the like terms are both negative here.

$= x^2 - 11x + 28$ — Collect like terms.

Perfect squares

A perfect square is any number that is the square of a rational number, and the square root of the square number is a rational number. (A rational number is a whole number or a number that can be written as a fraction.)

In the case of a square of a binomial, the square root will also be a binomial.

1, 4, 9, 16, 25 and 36 are perfect squares (square numbers).

a^2, x^2, $(xy)^2$ and $(2x)^2$ are all perfect squares.

A term such as $16x^2$ is a perfect square because it is equivalent to $(4x)^2$.

A term such as $5y^2$ is not a perfect square because only the y is a perfect square, the 5 is not.

When a binomial is multiplied by itself the product is called a **perfect square**.

Key vocabulary

perfect square: a binomial product of the form $(a \pm b)^2$

Expanding and simplifying a perfect square always produces the same pattern.

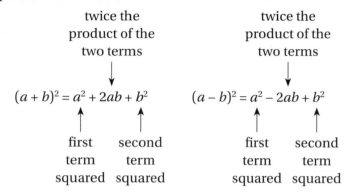

$$(a + b)^2 = a^2 + 2ab + b^2 \qquad (a - b)^2 = a^2 - 2ab + b^2$$

Perfect squares produce a pattern that can be used to expand them without doing any working.

EXERCISE 16A

1 Expand and simplify $(x + 1)(x + 3)$.

Choose your answer from the following options.

A $x^2 + x + 4$ B $x^2 + x + 3$ C $x^2 + 4x + 4$ D $x^2 + 4x + 3$

2 $(x + 2)(x - 5) = x^2 - 3x + c$

What is the value of c?

Choose from the following options.

A -10 B -7 C 7 D 10

3 Expand and simplify:

  a $(x + 2)(x + 5)$ **b** $(x - 2)(x - 5)$ **c** $(x + 2)(x - 5)$

  d $(x - 2)(x + 5)$ **e** $(x + 3)(x - 4)$ **f** $(x + y)(x + y)$

4 Expand and simplify:

  a $(x - 5)(x - 1)$ **b** $(a - 7)(a - 4)$ **c** $(m + 4)(m - 5)$

  d $(p - 6)(p + 4)$ **e** $(x - 7)(x + 6)$ **f** $(x + 11)(x - 3)$

  g $(x - 11)(x - 7)$ **h** $(x + 8)(x - 3)$ **i** $(x - 12)(x - 6)$

5 Expand and simplify:

  a $(2x + 4)(3x + 3)$ **b** $(3x + 4)(5x + 2)$ **c** $(2x - 5)(3x + 1)$

  d $(4y - 3)(5y + 1)$ **e** $(3a - 5)(2a - 1)$ **f** $(2b - 5)(b - 3)$

  g $(2y - 3)(3y - 5)$ **h** $(2x + 4)(2x - 6)$ **i** $(5x - 3)(4x - 1)$

6 Expand and simplify these perfect squares:

  a $(x + 5)^2$ **b** $(x - 5)^2$

  c Write a sentence describing how to multiply out a perfect square.

7 Expand each of these perfect squares:

  a $(x + 2)^2$ **b** $(x + 7)^2$ **c** $(x - 3)^2$

  d $(x - 9)^2$ **e** $(2x + 1)^2$ **f** $(1 - 3x)^2$

Find answers at: cambridge.org/ukschools/gcsemaths-studentbookanswers

8 If $A = 3x + 2$ and $B = 2x - 1$ work out:

    a AB   **b** $A^2 + B^2$ **c** $(A - B)(A + B)$

9 Find the area, in terms of x, of each of these squares.

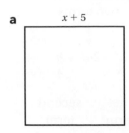 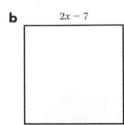

    a $x + 5$ **b** $2x - 7$

    c Calculate the area of each square in **a** and **b** when $x = 8$.

The difference of two squares

Work through Exercise 16B to find a shortcut for expanding binomials in the form of $(a + b)(a - b)$.

EXERCISE 16B

1 Expand each of the following binomials.

    a $(x + 1)(x - 1)$ **b** $(a + 2)(a - 2)$

    c $(3 + x)(3 - x)$ **d** $(5 - y)(5 + y)$

2 How many terms are there in your answers to question 1? Give a reason why this happens.

3 What is special about each term in the binomials you expanded in question 1?

4 Write down a rule that you can use to quickly find the answer to any similar expansion.

5 Copy this expansion and fill in the gaps.

$(x + y)(x - y)$

$= x^2 + \square - xy - \square$

$= \square - \square$

6 The example in question 5 shows that $(x + y)(x - y) \equiv x^2 - y^2$.

This is called the difference of two squares.

    a Which are the two squares?

    b How can you recognise when a binomial expansion is a difference of two squares?

    c Is $(3 + y)(y - 3)$ a difference of squares? Give a reason why or why not.

Section 2: Factorising quadratic expressions

Expanding a binomial such as $(x + 3)(x + 4)$ gives you a quadratic expression.

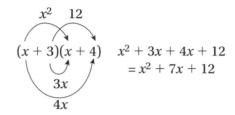

Tip

Do you remember how to factorise an expression by taking out a common factor?

Revise that section in Chapter 7 if you are not sure.

Factorising means 'putting the brackets back into the expression.'

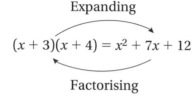

In this section you will learn how to factorise quadratic expressions in the form of $x^2 + bx + c$.

In this expression x is the variable, b is the **coefficient** of x and c is a **constant**.

Factorising a quadratic expression is the inverse of finding the product of (multiplying) two binomials.

In general:

$$(x + a)(x + b) = x^2 + (a + b)x + ab$$

This pattern can be used to develop a strategy for factorising trinomials.

Work out the signs before you factorise by looking at the signs in the trinomial.

If the **constant is positive**, the brackets will have the same sign.

- If the middle term (the x term) is positive, both brackets will have positive signs.
- If the middle term is negative, both brackets will have negative signs.

If the **constant is negative**, the brackets will have different signs.

- When the signs are different, the middle term is the difference between the two factors.
- The largest number in the factor pair will have the same sign as the middle term in the expression.

Key vocabulary

coefficient: the number in front of a variable in a mathematical expression. In the term $5x^2$, 5 is the coefficient and x is the variable.

constant: in algebra, a constant is a number on its own

Problem-solving framework

Factorise $x^2 - 4x - 12$

Steps for solving problems	What you would do for this example
Step 1: Make two sets of brackets and write an x in each. You can put x in each bracket because to get x^2 you need to multiply x by x. The constant is negative. To get a negative product you have to multiply a negative number by a positive number. This means one bracket will have a negative sign and the other will have a positive sign.	$x^2 - 4x - 12$ $= (x + \boxed{})(x - \boxed{})$
Step 2: The constant is -12. You need factors of 12 that have a difference of 4 to make the middle term $4x$.	Factor pairs of 12 are: 1×12 2×6 3×4
Step 3: Which factor pair meets the conditions? (Which factor pair will give you -4 if you add the numbers together and give you -12 if you multiply them?)	There is a difference of 4 between 2 and 6. $-2 + 6 = 4$ $-6 + 2 = -4$ -6 and $+2$ are the pair you need to satisfy the conditions. $-6 + 2 = -4$ and $-6 \times 2 = -12$ So, the 6 goes in the bracket with the negative sign. The 2 goes in the bracket with the positive sign. $x^2 - 4x - 12 = (x + 2)(x - 6)$
Step 4: Check your answer.	Expand the binomial: $(x + 2)(x - 6) = x^2 - 4x - 12$ Yes, this is the expression you started with.

When you factorise any expression, the first step should be to check for, and remove, common factors.

Once you have done this, you factorise the brackets as before.

WORKED EXAMPLE 2

Factorise $4x^2 - 12x - 40$

$4x^2 - 12x - 40 = 4(x^2 - 3x - 10)$ Take out the common factor of 4.

$4x^2 - 12x - 40 = 4(x - 5)(x + 2)$ Factorise the expression.

You can always check by multiplying out the brackets.

EXERCISE 16C

1 Find two numbers that meet each set of conditions:

    a Have a sum of 5 and a product of 6.

    b Add to give 8 and multiply to give 7.

    c Have a product of -8 and a sum of 2.

    d Multiply to give 24 and add to give -10.

    e Produce -24 when multiplied, and sum to 5.

    f Have a sum of 3 and a product of -18.

2 Factorise each of the following.

    a $x^2 + 14x + 24$ **b** $x^2 + 3x + 2$ **c** $x^2 + 7x + 12$

    d $x^2 + 12x + 35$ **e** $x^2 + 12x + 27$ **f** $x^2 + 7x + 6$

    g $x^2 + 11x + 30$ **h** $x^2 + 10x + 16$ **i** $x^2 + 11x + 10$

    j $x^2 + 8x + 7$ **k** $x^2 + 24x + 80$ **l** $x^2 + 13x + 42$

3 Factorise each of the following.

    a $x^2 - 8x + 12$ **b** $x^2 - 9x + 20$ **c** $x^2 - 7x + 12$

    d $x^2 - 6x + 8$ **e** $x^2 - 12x + 32$ **f** $x^2 - 14x + 49$

    g $x^2 - 8x - 20$ **h** $x^2 - 7x - 18$ **i** $x^2 - 4x - 32$

    j $x^2 + x - 6$ **k** $x^2 + 8x - 33$ **l** $x^2 + 10x - 24$

4 Factorise these expressions fully:

    a $2x^2 + 6x + 4$ **b** $6x^2 - 24x + 18$ **c** $5x^2 - 5x - 10$

    d $2x^2 + 14x + 20$ **e** $2x^2 + 4x - 6$ **f** $3x^2 - 30x - 33$

5 What are the factors of $y^2 - 1$?

Choose from the following options.

    A $(y-1)(y-1)$ B $(y-1)(y+1)$ C $(y+1)(y+1)$ D $(y-\frac{1}{2})(y+\frac{1}{2})$

The difference of two squares

Earlier you saw that multiplying out binomials in the form $(a+b)(a-b)$ gives a product that is the difference of two squares.

$$(a-b)(a+b) = a^2 + ab - ab - b^2$$
$$= a^2 - b^2 \text{ (simplifying)}$$

When you are asked to factorise a quadratic of the form $a^2 - b^2$, you can apply what you know about the difference of two squares to find the factors.

WORKED EXAMPLE 3

Factorise

a $x^2 - 4$ **b** $x^2 - 36$ **c** $9 - a^2$ **d** $100 - y^2$

a $x^2 - 4 = x^2 - (2)^2$
$\qquad\quad = (x + 2)(x - 2)$

> Express both terms as squares.
>
> Apply the identity:
> $a^2 - b^2 \equiv (a + b)(a - b)$

b $x^2 - 36 = x^2 - (6)^2$
$\qquad\qquad = (x + 6)(x - 6)$

> Express both terms as squares.
>
> Apply the identity:
> $a^2 - b^2 \equiv (a + b)(a - b)$

c $9 - a^2 = 3^2 - (a)^2$
$\qquad\quad = (3 + a)(3 - a)$

> Express both terms as squares.
>
> Apply the identity:
> $a^2 - b^2 \equiv (a + b)(a - b)$

d $100 - y^2 = (10)^2 - y^2$
$\qquad\qquad = (10 + y)(10 - y)$

> Express both terms as squares.
>
> Apply the identity:
> $a^2 - b^2 \equiv (a + b)(a - b)$

Tip

You can also think of factorising a difference of two squares as taking the square root of each term and writing these in brackets, one with a negative sign and one with a positive sign. The order in which you write down the brackets doesn't matter.
$(a - b)(a + b) = (a + b)(a - b)$

Mathematically a difference of two squares such as $x^2 - 4$ is a special case of the quadratic expression $x^2 + bx + c$.

In a difference of two squares, the coefficient of x is 0, so there is no x term ($x \times 0 = 0$) and the constant (c) is a negative number.

Using the difference of two squares in number problems

You can use the difference of two squares to subtract square numbers, such as $86^2 - 14^2$ without using a calculator, and without working out the square values, which can be very large numbers.

WORKED EXAMPLE 4

Work out $86^2 - 14^2$

$86^2 - 14^2 = (86 + 14)(86 - 14)$

> Write the subtraction as the product of its factors.

$\qquad\qquad = 100 \times 72$

> Add and subtract the values in each bracket.

$\qquad\qquad = 7200$

> Find the product.

This method can also be used to find one of the shorter sides in a right-angled triangle.

WORK IT OUT 16.1

In this right-angled triangle, the hypotenuse measures 13 cm and one of the shorter sides measures 5 cm.

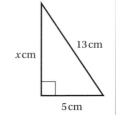

Use the difference of squares and Pythagoras' theorem to calculate the length of the unknown side.

Which of these options is correct?

What mistakes are there in the other options?

Option A	Option B	Option C
$13^2 - x^2 = 5^2$	$x^2 = 13^2 - 5^2$	$x^2 = 13^2 - 5^2$
$169 - x^2 = 25$	$x^2 = (13 + 5)(13 - 5)$	$x^2 = (13 - 5)(13 - 5)$
$x^2 = 194$	$x^2 = 18 \times 8$	$x^2 = 8 \times 8$
$x = \sqrt{194}$	$x^2 = 144$	$x^2 = 64$
$x = 13.9$ cm	$x = \sqrt{144}$	$x = \sqrt{64}$
	$x = 12$ cm	$x = 8$ cm

Tip

You should remember Pythagoras' theorem from KS3.

The theorem states that for a right-angled triangle, the square of the length of the hypotenuse (longest side) is equal to the sum of the squares of the lengths of the other two sides.

So in the triangle shown, $a^2 = b^2 + c^2$.

You will need to know the theorem from memory.

See Chapter 35 for more information and practice.

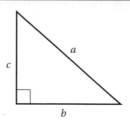

EXERCISE 16D

1 Factorise each of the following.

   a $x^2 - 36$ **b** $p^2 - 81$ **c** $w^2 - 16$

2 Using $(a - b)(a + b) = a^2 - b^2$, work out the value of the following.

   a $100^2 - 97^2$ **b** $50^2 - 48^2$ **c** $639^2 - 629^2$

   d $98^2 - 45^2$ **e** $83^2 - 77^2$ **f** $1234^2 - 999^2$

3 Use the difference of two squares method to find the value of a in each triangle.

Leave the answer in square root form.

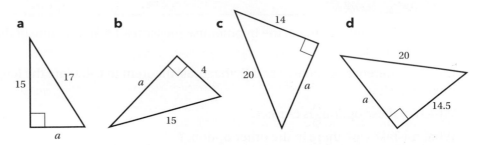

a

b

c

d

Section 3: Apply your skills

You can use what you have learned about expanding, simplifying and factorising algebraic expressions to work out the value of unknown quantities in different types of problems.

These skills also give you the tools to describe problems algebraically so that you can solve them efficiently.

EXERCISE 16E

Answer these questions to review what you have learned in this chapter.

1 Decide whether each statement is true or false.

a $(x + 11)(x - 5) = x^2 + 6x - 55$

b $x^2 + 2x + 4$ is a perfect square.

c $(a - 8)^2 = a^2 - 64$

d $69^2 - 11^2$ can be solved by calculating $(69 + 11)(69 - 11)$.

2 Write an expression for the area of each shape.

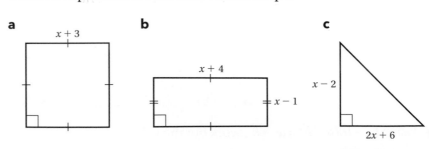

a

b

c

> ### Tip
>
> Remember:
> Area of a square = side × side
> Area of rectangle = length × breadth
> Area of triangle = $\frac{1}{2}$ × base × height

3 The cost of rubber matting for a children's play area is £19.50 per square metre.

The rectangular play area is $(x + 4)$ metres wide and $(x + 7)$ metres long.

a Write an expression for the area to be covered by rubber matting.

b Write an expression for the cost of the rubber matting.

c Given that $x = 12$, find the cost of the rubber matting.

4 A carpet fitter has a square piece of carpet with sides of x metres.

He plans to cut a 60 cm wide strip off the square carpet and place it along the adjacent side of the square as shown in the diagram.

The area marked with a cross will be cut off and discarded.

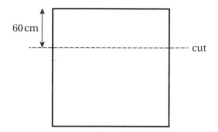
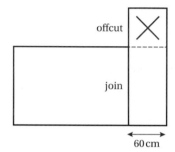

a Express the length and breadth of the rectangular carpet that the carpet fitter intends to make, in terms of x.

b Write an expression for the area of the rectangular carpet.

c What type of expression is this?

d Form an expression and work out the difference in the areas of the original square carpet and the new rectangular carpet.

5 The area of each rectangle and an expression for the length of one side are given.

Use this information to find an expression for the length of each missing side.

a Area $= 8a + 12$

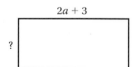

b Area $= 10mn + 15$

c Area $= (2y)^2 - 49$

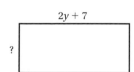

d Area $= x^2 + x - 30$

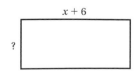

Find answers at: cambridge.org/ukschools/gcsemaths-studentbookanswers

6 Copy and fill in the blanks.

a $(x + 5)(x + 7) = x^2 + \boxed{}x + \boxed{}$ b $(x + \boxed{})(x + 6) = x^2 + 9x + \boxed{}$

c $(x + 4)(x - \boxed{}) = x^2 - 2x - \boxed{}$ d $(2x + 3)(x + \boxed{}) = 2x^2 + 7x + \boxed{}$

e $(\boxed{}x + \boxed{})(2x + 5) = 4x^2 + 12x + \boxed{}$

7 Factorise:

a $x^2 - 11x + 24$ b $x^2 - 25x + 24$

c Write another two quadratic expressions with a first term of x^2 and a constant term of 24.

8 Use $a^2 - b^2 = (a + b)(a - b)$ to evaluate $1999^2 - 1998^2$.

9 The area of a quadrilateral is expressed as $x^2 - 25$.

Say whether or not this quadrilateral can be a square.

Checklist of learning and understanding

Expanding binomials

- A binomial expression is one that contains two terms.
- Expand means remove the brackets and multiply out the terms.
- After you expand binomials you simplify further by collecting any like terms.
- A binomial multiplied by itself is a perfect square.

  $(a + b)^2 \equiv a^2 + 2ab + b^2$

  $(a - b)^2 \equiv a^2 - 2ab + b^2$

- A binomial in the form of $(a - b)(a + b)$ gives a product that is a difference of two squares.

  $(a - b)(a + b) = a^2 - b^2$

Factorising

- Factorising is the inverse operation to multiplying out brackets
- You can factorise by taking out a common factor.

  $6ab + 3ad \equiv 3a(2b + d)$

- You can factorise a quadratic expression by writing it as a product of its two binomial factors.

  $x^2 - x - 6 \equiv (x + 2)(x - 3)$

- The rules for multiplying positive and negative signs are important when you factorise trinomials.

Chapter review

 For additional questions on the topics in this chapter, visit GCSE Mathematics Online.

1 Expand and simplify:

a $(x-2)^2 + (x-4)^2$

b $(x-2)^2 + (x+2)^2$

Tip

Expand and simplify each bracket first and then simplify by collecting like terms.

2 Copy and fill in the blanks:

a $(x+3)(x-\square) = x^2 - 2x - \square$

b $(x+3)(x+\square) = x^2 + 10x + \square$

c $(x+2)(x-\square) = x^2 - x - \square$

d $(x+6)(\square + \square) = x^2 + 11x + 30$

e $(x+4)(\square + \square) = x^2 + 10x + 24$

3 a Expand $3(x-6)$ *(1 mark)*

b Factorise $5y - 10$ *(1 mark)*

c Expand and simplify $3(4w+1) - 5(3w-2)$ *(3 marks)*

© AQA 2012

4 a Find an expression for the area of a rectangular field if the length is $(x+1)$ metres and the width is $(x-5)$ metres.

b Write an expression in simplest terms for the perimeter of the field.

5 Use the difference between two squares to simplify the expression $(x+8)^2 - (x-8)^2$.

6 Write an expression in its simplest form for the area of the shaded part of this rectangle.

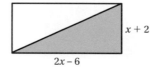

$x+2$

$2x-6$

7 The sides of a triangle are $(x+8)$ cm, $(x+6)$ cm and $(x-1)$ cm.

If the square of the longest side is equal to the sum of the squares of the other two sides, the triangle is right-angled.

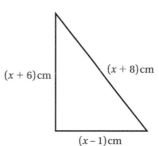

$(x+6)$ cm

$(x+8)$ cm

$(x-1)$ cm

a Which is the longest side in this triangle? How do you know?

b What is the square of the longest side?

c Find the sum of the squares of the other two sides.

d Use your answers to parts **b** and **c** to work out the value of x that makes this a right-angled triangle.

Find answers at: cambridge.org/ukschools/gcsemaths-studentbookanswers

17 Equations

In this chapter you will learn how to ...

- solve linear equations and apply them in context.
- solve quadratic equations.
- set up and solve simultaneous equations.
- use graphs to find approximate solutions to equations.

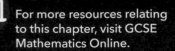 For more resources relating to this chapter, visit GCSE Mathematics Online.

Using mathematics: real-life applications

Accounting involves a great deal of mathematics. Accountants set up computer spreadsheets to calculate and analyse data. Programs such as Microsoft Excel® work by applying different equations to values in columns or cells, so you need to know what equations or formulae to use to get the results you need.

"Although the computer does the actual calculations, I have to insert different equations to tell it what operations to perform and in which order to perform them. It is important to check that the equations are producing the correct answers, though." *(Accountant)*

Before you start ...

KS3 Ch 7	Check you can write an equation to represent a problem mathematically.	**1** One of the equations below correctly represent this problem. Identify this equation and then write the correct equation. 'I think of a number, multiply it by 6 and add 1. The answer is 37. What is my number?' A $6x + 1 = 37$ B $y \times 6 = 37 - 1$ C $6a = 36$ D $6x + 1 + 37 = 0$
KS3 Ch 1	You should be able to recognise and apply inverse operations.	**2** Complete the following statements. **a** $7 + \square = 0$ **b** $\square - 8 = 0$ **c** $-4a + \square = 0$ **d** $5 \times \square = 1$ **e** $\frac{1}{6} \times \square = 1$ **f** $\square \times 12x = x$
KS3 Ch 16	You need to know how to factorise quadratic expressions.	**3** Match each expression to its factors. **a** $x^2 - 5x + 6$ **b** $x^2 + 3x$ **c** $x^2 - 25$ **d** $x^2 - 5$ A $x(x + 3)$ B $(x + 5)(x - 5)$ C $(x - 2)(x - 3)$ D $(x + \sqrt{5})(x - \sqrt{5})$

Assess your starting point using the Launchpad

STEP 1

1 Match each equation in the first box to its solution in the second box.

> **Equations**
> **a** $x + 7 = 19$ **b** $x - 6 = 11$ **c** $2x + 5 = 7$
> **d** $8x = -24$ **e** $2 - 3x = 8$

> **Solutions**
> A $x = 1$ B $x = 17$ C $x = -2$
> D $x = 12$ E $x = -3$

f How can you check whether a solution is correct?

2 Solve.

a $9a - 7 = 7a + 3$ **b** $3(x + 5) = 2(x + 6)$

3 When 16 is added to twice Jack's age, the answer is 44.
Write an equation and solve it to find Jack's age?

GO TO
Section 1:
Linear equations

STEP 2

4 If $x^2 - 2x - 3 = 0$, which pair of values is the solution?
A $x = 3$ or $x = -1$ B $x = -3$ or $x = 1$

5 What are the possible values of x given that $x^2 - 16 = 0$

GO TO
Section 2:
Quadratic equations

STEP 3

6 **a** How many whole number solutions can you find for $x + y = 6$?
b Which of those solutions are correct if $x + y = 6$ and $x - y = 4$?

GO TO
Section 3:
Simultaneous equations

GO TO
Step 4:
The Launchpad continues on the next page …

Find answers at: cambridge.org/ukschools/gcsemaths-studentbookanswers

Launchpad continued ...

STEP 4

 7 A company hires out meeting rooms.

The total cost, y, can be worked out using the equation $y = 15x + 40$, where x represents the number of hours the room is hired for.

The graph of this equation is the straight line shown here.

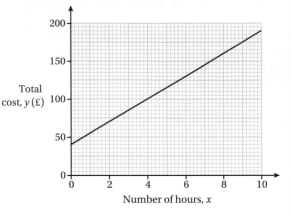

Total cost, y (£)

Number of hours, x

a Use the graph to find the cost of hiring a meeting room for 4 hours.

b What is the value of x when y is 175?

c What is the value of y when x is 5?

GO TO
Section 4:
Using graphs to solve equations

GO TO

Chapter review

Section 1: Linear equations

An equation is a mathematical statement that contains an equal sign. For example:

$$x + 2 = 5 \qquad 3 + x = 5 \qquad 3 + 2 = x \qquad 2x + 3 = 6$$

The **unknown** can be represented by any letter but x and y are used most often.

The same letter can represent different values in different equations.

For example, in the equation $x + 1 = 4$, the value of x is 3, but in the equation $x + 2 = 3$, the value of x is 1.

If the highest power of the unknown is 1 the equation is a **linear equation**.

Solving an equation involves working out the value of the unknown letter.

In simple equations like $x + 3 = 7$, you can solve for x without needing to do any working. This is called solving by inspection.

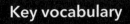 **Key vocabulary**

unknown: part of an equation that is represented by a letter

linear equation: an equation where the highest power of the unknown is 1, for example $x + 3 = 7$

In more complex equations, you can find the solution by carrying out inverse operations on both sides of the equation.

WORKED EXAMPLE 1

Solve each equation for x.

a $2x + 8 = 14$ **b** $2(x + 1) = 10$

a $2x + 8 = 14$

$2x + 8 - 8 = 14 - 8$ Subtract 8 from both sides.

$2x = 6$

$\dfrac{2x}{2} = \dfrac{6}{2}$ The term $2x$ means $2 \times x$, so divide each side by 2 to find x.

$x = 3$ Check your answer $x = 3$ by substitution: $2 \times 3 + 8 = 6 + 8 = 14$

b $2(x + 1) = 10$

$\dfrac{2(x + 1)}{2} = \dfrac{10}{2}$ Get rid of $\times 2$ by dividing both sides by 2.

$x + 1 = 5$

$x + 1 - 1 = 5 - 1$ Subtract 1 from both sides.

$x = 4$ Check your answer $x = 4$ by substitution: $2 \times (4 + 1) = 2 \times 5 = 10$

Tip

The examples here show each step in detail to help you understand the process of solving an equation. In your own work you might find it more efficient to combine steps or leave out some of the working. Check your answer mentally or calculate on paper to avoid errors.

EXERCISE 17A

1 Choose the correct solution for x in the equation $2x + 3 = 17$.

   A $x = 10$ B $x = 7$ C $x = 20$ D $x = -7$

2 Solve each equation by inspection.

Check your answers by substitution.

   a $x + 11 = 8$ **b** $x - 6 = 11$ **c** $-2x = 16$

   d $x + 7 = 29\frac{1}{2}$ **e** $3x = -24$ **f** $6x - 21 = 3$

3 Solve each equation by writing down at least two steps. Check your answers.

   a $2a - 5 = 7$ **b** $3b + 4 = 19$ **c** $5d - 7 = 23$

   d $3e - 2 = 16$ **e** $5h + 21 = 11$ **f** $6a + 17 = -1$

   g $3a - 16 = -31$ **h** $4b + 12 = -16$ **i** $2t - 8 = 5$

4 Solve each equation. Do this without expanding the brackets.

   a $2(x + 3) = 8$ **b** $3(x - 2) = 15$

   c $4(b - 1) = 12$ **d** $5(p + 1) = 10$

   e $3(x - 3) = 18$ **f** $2(y + 4) = 14$

   g $2(3x + 4) = 0$ **h** $2(y - 3) = -8$

   i Give a reason why not expanding the brackets in these equations means that you can solve them in fewer steps.

Tip

When you are asked to solve an equation for x, you cannot give an answer in the form of $-x = 3$ or $-x = -4$. If you end up with a negative unknown, divide both sides of the equation by negative 1 to get a positive value $(-) \div (-) = (+)$.

 Find answers at: cambridge.org/ukschools/gcsemaths-studentbookanswers

Choose the correct solution for x in $3(x + 1) = 4(x - 2)$.

A $x = -11$ B $x = -5$ C $x = 11$ D $x = 5$

6 Consider the equation $2(x + 1) - 3(x - 2) = 6$.

     a Why does it make sense to expand the brackets before solving the equation in this example?

     b Expand the brackets, collect like terms on the left of the equation and then solve it for x.

Equations with the unknown on both sides

Some equations have the unknown in expressions on both sides of the equation.

In these equations you take steps to get all the terms containing the unknown on to the same side of the equation.

The expressions might also contain brackets. If that is the case, you need to expand the brackets first.

Tip

Remember you can combine steps in your own working. These worked examples show all the steps in detail.

WORKED EXAMPLE 2

Solve for x.

     a $5x - 5 = 3x + 1$ b $2y + 17 = 5 - 6y$ c $2(3x - 1) = 2(x + 1)$

a
$$5x - 5 = 3x + 1$$
$$5x - 5 - 3x = 3x + 1 - 3x$$
$$2x - 5 = 1$$
$$2x - 5 + 5 = 1 + 5$$
$$2x = 6$$
$$x = 3$$
$$5 \times 3 - 5 = 3 \times 3 + 1$$
$$10 = 10$$

Subtract $3x$ from each side.

Add like terms.

Add 5 to both sides.

Simplify.

Divide both sides by 2.

Check by substitution:

$5 \times 3 - 5 = 10$

$3 \times 3 + 1 = 10$

b
$$2y + 17 = 5 - 6y$$
$$2y + 17 + 6y = 5 - 6y + 6y$$
$$8y + 17 = 5$$
$$8y + 17 - 17 = 5 - 17$$
$$8y = -12$$
$$\frac{8y}{8} = \frac{-12}{8}$$
$$y = \frac{-3}{2}$$

Add $6y$ to both sides (this helps you get rid of negative signs).

Add like terms.

Subtract 17 from both sides.

Simplify.

Divide both sides by 8.

Reduce the fraction to its simplest terms.

c
$$2(3x - 1) = 2(x + 1)$$
$$6x - 2 = 2x + 2$$
$$6x - 2 - 2x = 2x + 2 - 2x$$
$$4x - 2 = 2$$
$$4x - 2 + 2 = 2 + 2$$
$$4x = 4$$
$$x = 1$$

Expand the brackets paying attention to the signs.

Subtract $2x$ from both sides.

Add like terms.

Add 2 to each side.

Divide both sides by 4.

EXERCISE 17B

1 Solve the following equations. Check each answer by substitution.

a $13x + 1 = 11x + 9$ **b** $5t - 4 = 3t + 6$

c $4y + 3 = 2y + 8$ **d** $5y + 1 = 3y + 13$

e $3y + 10 = 5y + 3$ **f** $12x + 1 = 7x + 11$

g $5x - 2 = 3x + 6$ **h** $5x + 12 = 20 - 11x$

i $8 - 8a = 9 - 9a$ **j** $5x + 3 = 2(x + 2)$

2 Solve these equations by expanding the brackets first.

a $2(x + 1) + 4(x + 2) = 22$ **b** $3(x + 1) = 2(x + 2)$

c $5(t + 3) = 3(2t + 1)$ **d** $7(x + 2) = 4(x + 5)$

e $4(x - 2) + 2(x + 5) = 14$ **f** $3(x + 1) = 2(x + 1) + 2x$

g $-2(x + 2) = 4x + 9$ **h** $4 + 2(2 - x) = 3 - 2(5 - x)$

3 Solve this equation in x.

$3(x - 1) = 4(x + 2)$

Choose your answer from the options given.

A $x = -11$ B $x = -5$ C $x = 11$ D $x = 5$

4 Look at these two equations and answer parts **a** and **b**.

i $2(x + 8) - 3x = x + 16$ **ii** $4(3 + x) + 4x = 4(2x + 3)$

a If an equation is true for any value of x, it is an identity.

Which of these two equations is an identity? Give a reason for your answer.

b Is there a solution for the other equation? Give a reason for your answer and find the solution if there is one.

Setting up and solving linear equations

You can use algebra to set up and then solve your own equations.

When you set up an equation you must say what the letters stand for.

WORKED EXAMPLE 3

The sum of two numbers is 54. If one number is 14 more than the other number, find the two numbers.

Let x be the value of one unknown

> Let x be the value of one of the unknown numbers

$\therefore$ value of second number is $x + 14$

> The other number is 14 more than x.

$x + (x + 14) = 54$

> The total of the two numbers is 54.
>
> Use this information to form an equation.

$x + x + 14 = 54$
$2x + 14 = 54$
$\quad\quad 2x = 40$
$\quad\quad\quad x = 20$

> Subtract 14 from both sides.
>
> Divide both sides by 2.

If $x = 20$
Value of second number is
$x + 14 = 20 + 14$
$\quad\quad\quad = 34$

> Use the value of $x = 20$ to find the value of $x + 14$.

The two numbers are 20 and 34
Check: $20 + 34 = 54$

> Check the total is 54.

You can solve problems like this without writing equations. However, writing equations will help you to be more efficient.

When the problem involves a shape it is useful to draw a sketch and label it to help you set up the equation.

WORKED EXAMPLE 4

 In a triangle, the largest angle is four times the size of the smallest angle.

The third angle is 24° bigger than the smallest angle.

Write an equation and solve it to find the size of each angle in this triangle.

What type of triangle is this?

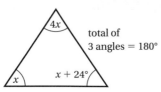

> Draw a sketch diagram.
>
> Mark the angles using the information given in terms of x.

Let x be the value of the smallest angle.
Then the largest angle is $4x$
and the third angle is $x + 24°$

Continues on next page . . .

$x + 4x + (x + 24°) = 180°$

The angles of a triangle total 180°. Use this fact to form an equation.

$x + 4x + x + 24° = 180°$
$6x + 24° = 180°$
$6x = 156°$
$x = 26°$

Simplify and solve the equation.

Collect like terms.

Subtract 24 from both sides.

Divide both sides by 6.

If $x = 26°$
$x + 24° = 26° + 24°$
$= 50°$
$4x = 4 × 26°$
$= 104°$

Use this fact to calculate the values of the other two angles.

$26° + 50° + 104° = 180°$

Check that the total of the three angles is equal to 180°.

This is an obtuse angled triangle.

This triangle has one angle that is greater than 90°.

2 The length of a rectangle is three times its width.

If the perimeter is 24 centimetres, find the area of the rectangle.

$P = 2(L + W)$

$A = L × W$

Draw a sketch and label it.

If x represents the width
Length is $3x$

You need to find the lengths of the sides to work out the area.

Perimeter $= 2(x + 3x) = 24$

Form an equation in x to represent the perimeter.

$2 ×$ (width + length) $= 24$ cm

$2(x + 3x) = 24$
$x + 3x = 12$
$4x = 12$
$x = 3$ cm

Solve for x.

Divide both sides by 2.

Collect like terms.

Divide both sides by 4.

Width $= 3$ cm
Length $= 3 × 3 = 9$ cm
Area of rectangle $= 3 × 9$
$= 27$ cm^2

Find the values of width and length given that $x = 3$.

Calculate the area.

Area = width × length

Make sure to provide the correct units for the answers.

Tip

Make sure you know what the unknown is and state what letter you are using to represent it.
We tend to let x be the unknown, but you can choose any letter as long as you define it.

Find answers at: cambridge.org/ukschools/gcsemaths-studentbookanswers

EXERCISE 17C

1 For each of the following, write an equation and solve it to find the unknown number.

   a Three times a certain number is 348. What is the number?

   b Seven less than a number is −2. What is the number?

   c Six greater than a number is −4,. What is the number?

   d Two less than four times a number is 66. What is the number?

   e Two consecutive numbers have a sum of 63. What are the numbers?

   f Three less than twice a number is −2. What is the number?

2 Form an equation and solve it to answer each question.

   a When 16 is added to twice Melissa's age, the answer is 44.

   How old is Melissa?

   b Stephen buys 8 identical pens.

   He receives 80p change from £20.00.

   How much does a pen cost?

   c Multiplying a number by 2 and then adding 5 gives the same answer as subtracting the number from 23.

   What is the number?

   d Mustafa is twenty years older than his daughter.

   His daughter has worked out that in five years' time, she will be half her dad's age.

   How old is she now?

3 A square has sides of $3x$ cm. A parallelogram has sides of $2x$ cm and $(x + 9)$ cm.

   a Write an expression for the perimeter of the square.

   b Write an expression for the perimeter of the parallelogram.

   c The two quadrilaterals have the same perimeter.

   Form an equation and solve it to find the length of one side of the square.

4 The area of this rectangle is $10\,\text{cm}^2$.

   Calculate the value of x and use it to find the length and width of the rectangle.

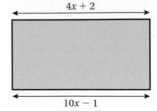

$4x + 2$

$10x − 1$

Section 2: Quadratic equations

A quadratic equation has at least one term with a **variable** that is squared (x^2) and no variables with a power higher than 2.

When you square root a number, there is a positive and negative answer.

For example, $\sqrt{9} = 3$ **or** -3. This is written as $\pm\sqrt{9} = \pm 3$

Because you are dealing with a squared variable, quadratic equations have two solutions, known as **roots**. (Some have only one, others have none and in some cases, only one of the roots is valid.)

When you are asked to solve a quadratic equation you need to give a **solution** that contains both roots.

The solution to the equation $x^2 = 9$ is $x = \pm 3$

Look at this diagram showing a graph plotted from a quadratic equation. It shows why a quadratic can have a maximum of two solutions.

This diagram shows the quadratic function $y = x^2 + 4x - 5$. It cuts the x-axis in two places marked as the positive root and the negative root.

These are the points at which $y = 0$, so you can solve for x by writing the equation as $0 = x^2 + 4x - 5$.

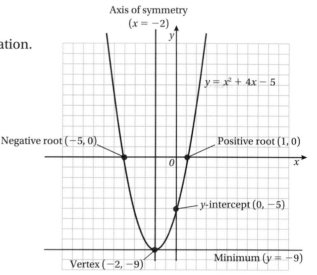

Axis of symmetry ($x = -2$)

$y = x^2 + 4x - 5$

Negative root $(-5, 0)$ Positive root $(1, 0)$

y-intercept $(0, -5)$

Vertex $(-2, -9)$ Minimum $(y = -9)$

Factorising to solve quadratic equations

The general form of a quadratic equation is $x^2 + bx + c = 0$ (when the coefficient of x^2 is 1).

Zero factor principle

The only way to get a product of 0 is to multiply by 0.

For example, if $7 \times a = 0$, then you know that $a = 0$

This means that if $(x - 1)(x - 2) = 0$ then either $(x - 1) = 0$ or $(x - 2) = 0$.

If $x - 1 = 0$, then $x = 1$.

If $x - 2 = 0$, then $x = 2$.

This is the zero factor principle.

Tip

Make sure you remember these three methods of factorising quadratic expressions:

$x^2 - 6x \equiv x(x - 6)$ taking out a common factor
$x^2 + 5x + 4 \equiv (x + 1)(x + 4)$ writing a trinomial as a product of binomials
$x^2 - 100 \equiv (x + 10)(x - 10)$ applying the difference of two squares identity

Read through Chapter 16 again if you have forgotten anything.

WORKED EXAMPLE 5

Solve:

a $x^2 - 3x + 2 = 0$ **b** $x^2 - 4 = 0$ **c** $x^2 - 6x = 0$

a $x^2 - 3x + 2 = 0$

     $(x - 1)(x - 2) = 0$ Factorise the left-hand side.

     Either $x - 1 = 0$ or $x - 2 = 0$ Apply the zero factor principle.

     $\therefore x - 1 = 0$ Solving each factor for x.
     $x = 1$ Add 1 to both sides.
     or
     $\therefore x - 2 = 0$ Add 2 to both sides.
     $x = 2$

     $x = 1$ or $x = 2$ State the solution.

b $x^2 - 4 = 0$

     $(x + 2)(x - 2) = 0$ Factorise using the difference of squares identity.

     Either $(x + 2) = 0$ or $(x - 2) = 0$ Apply the zero factor principle.

     $x + 2 = 0$ Solve the equations.
     $\therefore x = -2$ Subtract 2 from both sides.
     $x - 2 = 0$
     $\therefore x = 2$ Add 2 to both sides.

     $x = -2$ or $x = 2$ State the solutions.

c $x^2 - 6x = 0$

     $x(x - 6) = 0$ Factorise by taking out a common factor of x.

     Either $x = 0$ or $(x - 6) = 0$ Apply the zero factor principle.

     $x - 6 = 0$ In this case you already have one value for x so you need only solve one equation.
     $\therefore x = 6$ Add 6 to both sides.

     $x = 0$ or $x = 6$ State the solution.

After working through these examples you should be able to see a clear set of steps for solving a quadratic equation in the form of $x^2 + bx + c = 0$.

Step 1

If necessary, take all the terms to the left-hand side so the right-hand side is 0.

Step 2

Factorise the left-hand side:

- check for common factors
- check for difference of squares
- write trinomials as a binomial product.

Step 3

Write each factor equal to 0.

Solve the equations to find the roots.

EXERCISE 17D

1 From the options below, choose the correct factors of $x^2 + 2x - 15$.

A $(x+3)(x-5)$ B $(x-3)(x-5)$ C $(x+3)(x+5)$ D $(x-3)(x+5)$

2 Solve these equations.

a $x^2 - 5x = 0$ b $x^2 - x = 0$ c $4x^2 + 8x = 0$

d $8x^2 - 2x = 0$ e $5x^2 + 2x = 0$ f $2x^2 + x = 0$

3 Solve these equations.

a $x^2 - 16 = 0$ b $100 - x^2 = 0$ c $x^2 - 1 = 0$

d $9x^2 - 36 = 0$ e $4x^2 - 1 = 0$ f $9x^2 - 4 = 0$

4 Find the solutions of each equation.

a $x^2 + 9x + 18 = 0$ b $x^2 - 10x + 9 = 0$

c $x^2 + 2x - 8 = 0$ d $x^2 - 9x + 20 = 0$

e $x^2 - 4x - 12 = 0$ f $9x^2 + 3x - 6 = 0$

5 Solve these equations.

a $x^2 - x = 12$ b $(x+3)^2 = 25$

c $2x^2 + x = 0$ d $4x^2 = 3x$

e $x^2 + 4x = 5$ f $x^2 + 6x - 13 = 14$

g $-18 - 3x = -x^2$ h $3x^2 - 21x + 36 = 0$

Setting up and solving quadratic equations

As with linear equations, you can set up and solve quadratic equations.

Always define the letters you are using in your equation.

When you use quadratic equations to model real-life situations you might find that one of the solutions is not possible.

For example, if x is the length of the side of a box in metres, and you get the roots $x = 2.5$ or $x = -1.75$ you can ignore the value of -1.75 as this cannot be the length of an object.

Tip

If the problem involves square units then you can probably use a quadratic equation to solve it.

WORKED EXAMPLE 6

A rectangle with an area of 28 cm² has one side 3 cm longer than the other.

How long are each of the shorter sides?

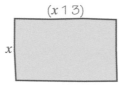

Shorter side = x
Longer side = $x + 3$

Draw a diagram and label the sides.

$A = x(x + 3)$

Area of a rectangle is length × breadth.

$x(x + 3) = 28$
$x^2 + 3x = 28$
$x^2 + 3x - 28 = 0$

Use the information in the question.

Expand the brackets.

Subtract 28 from each side to get 0 on the right-hand side to form a quadratic equation equal to zero.

$(x + 7)(x - 4) = 0$
Either $(x + 7) = 0$ or $(x - 4) = 0$
$x + 7 = 0$
$\therefore x = -7$
$x - 4 = 0$
$\therefore x = 4$

Factorise.

Apply the zero factor principle.

Solve the equations

Subtract 7 from both sides

Add 4 to both sides.

$x = -7$ or $x = 4$
Length of shorter sides = 4 cm

State the solution to the problem.

In this problem you can ignore the $x = -7$ solution because -7 cm is not a possible length for the side of a rectangle.

EXERCISE 17E

1 Form and solve a quadratic equation for each of the following questions and find the value(s) of the unknown numbers.

a The product of a certain whole number and four more than that number is 140.

What could the number be?

b The product of a certain whole number and three less than that number is 108.

What could the number be?

c The difference between the square of a number and three times the original number is 10.

What are possible values of the number?

d The product of two consecutive positive even numbers is 48.

What are the numbers?

2 The base of a triangle is 4 cm longer than twice its height.

The area of the triangle is 48 cm².

Form and solve a quadratic equation and state a valid answer for the height of the triangle.

Tip

Remember the area of a triangle is half the length of the base × height.

3 A rectangular hall has a floor area of 210 m².

The length of the hall is 1 m more than twice its breadth.

What are the dimensions of the hall?

Section 3: Simultaneous equations

Simultaneous equations are used to solve problems involving two conditions that are met at the same time.

For example, $x + y = 4$ and $3x - y = 2$

This is a pair of equations in two unknowns that are both true.

You can use the fact that both these equations are true to solve them at the same time (simultaneously).

Key vocabulary

simultaneous equations: a pair of equations with two unknowns that can be solved at the same time

Find answers at: cambridge.org/ukschools/gcsemaths-studentbookanswers

WORKED EXAMPLE 7

There are 30 rose bushes in a nursery. Some are red and others are white.

There are twice as many white rose bushes as red.

How many rose bushes of each colour are there?

Let w = **number** of white rose bushes
and r = **number** of red rose bushes
$r + w = 30$
$w = 2r$

To solve this you need to set up two equations.

There are 30 rose bushes altogether.

The number of white bushes is twice the number of red bushes.

Form two equations.

$r + w = 30$

r	0	10	20	30
w	30	20	10	0

Draw up a table for each equation to show some values of r and w.

$w = 2r$

r	0	5	10	15
w	0	10	20	30

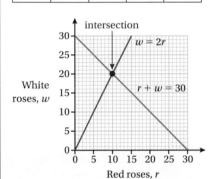

Draw the graph of each set of values. You get two lines that intersect in one place only.

Point of intersection is $(10, 20)$
so $r = 10$ and $w = 20$
There are 10 red rose bushes and
20 white rose bushes.
$r + w = 30$
$10 + 20 = 30$
$w = 2r$
$20 = 2 \times 10$

The point of intersection (r, w) is the simultaneous solution of the two equations.

State the solution.

Check the solutions by substitution in both equations.

You can draw graphs to solve simultaneous equations but this method takes a long time and it might not be very accurate, especially if the solution values are fractions.

There are two methods of solving simultaneous equations using algebra: substitution and elimination.

The method you choose depends on how the equations are written.

Solving simultaneous equations by substitution

Problem-solving framework

Solve these simultaneous equations.

$x - 2y + 1 = 0$ and $y + 4 = 2x$

Steps for solving problems	What you would do for this example
Step 1: Number the equations (1) and (2).	$x - 2y + 1 = 0$ (1) $y + 4 = 2x$ (2)
Step 2: Rearrange one equation so x or y is on its own on the left-hand side.	Equation 2 seems simpler, so rearrange it to get: $y = 2x - 4$ (2)
Step 3: Substitute the right-hand side of the rearranged equation into the other equation.	Substitute $(2x - 4)$ in place of y in (1). $x - 2(2x - 4) + 1 = 0$
Step 4: Solve the new equation (which now only has one unknown).	$x - 2(2x - 4) + 1 = 0$ $x - 4x + 8 + 1 = 0$ $-3x + 9 = 0$ $-3x = -9$ $x = 3$
Step 5: Substitute the solution into either of the original equations to find the other unknown.	Substitute $x = 3$ into (2) and solve. $y + 4 = 2(3)$ $y + 4 = 6$ $y = 6 - 4$ $y = 2$
Step 6: Write the solution.	The solution is $x = 3$ and $y = 2$

 Tip

This method is suitable when one of the equations already has x or y on its own on one side of the equation or when you can easily rearrange one of the equations to have x or y on its own.

EXERCISE 17F

1 Solve the following pairs of simultaneous equations by substitution. Check that your solutions satisfy **both** equations.

a $y = x - 2$
$\quad y = 3x + 4$

b $y = 2x + 6$
$\quad y = 4 - 2x$

c $y = x + 1$
$\quad x + y = 3$

d $y = x - 2$
$\quad 3x + y = 14$

e $y = 2x + 1$
$\quad x + 2y = 12$

f $y = 1 - 2x$
$\quad x + y = 2$

2 Which of the following options is a correct solution for $y = 2x$ and $2x + 3y = 24$?

A $x = 3, y = 2$ B $x = -3, y = 2$ C $x = 3, y = 3$ D $x = 3, y = 6$

3 Solve each pair of simultaneous equations by substitution.

a $y = 3x - 5$
$\quad y = 6x - 11$

b $y = 2x - 3$
$\quad y = 3x - 5$

c $x = 2y - 1$
$\quad 2x + y = 11$

4 Solve these simultaneous equations.

a $x + 2y = 11$
$\quad 2x + y = 10$

b $x - y = -1$
$\quad 2x + y = 4$

c $5x - 4y = -1$
$\quad 2x + y = 10$

d $3x - 2y = 29$
$\quad 4x + y = 24$

e $3x + y = 6$
$\quad 9x + 2y = 1$

f $3x - 2 = -2y$
$\quad 2x - y = -8$

Solving simultaneous equations by elimination

In this method you add or subtract the equations to get rid of one of the unknown variables.

You might need to multiply or divide one equation by a factor before you do this.

Problem-solving framework

Solve the simultaneous equations $2x + y = 8$ and $x - y = 1$.

Steps for solving problems	What you would do for this example
Step 1: Number the equations (1) and (2).	$2x + y = 8 \qquad (1)$ $x - y = 1 \qquad (2)$
Step 2: Decide whether you can add or subtract to get rid of a variable.	(1) has a variable of y and (2) has a variable of $-y$. If you add the equations, these terms will cancel out. Add (1) + (2). $(2x + y) + (x - y) = 8 + 1$ $2x + y + x - y = 9$ $3x = 9$
Step 3: Solve the combined equation (which now only has one unknown).	$3x = 9$ $x = 3$
Step 4: Substitute the solution into either of the original equations to find the other unknown.	Substitute $x = 3$ into (2). $3 - y = 1$ $-y = 1 - 3$ $-y = -2$ $y = 2$
Step 5: Write the solution.	The solution is $x = 3$, $y = 2$

Problem-solving framework

Solve this pair of simultaneous equations.

$x + 3y = 7 \qquad x + y = 5$

Steps for solving problems	What you would do for this example
Step 1: Number the equations (1) and (2).	$x + 3y = 7 \qquad (1)$ $x + y = 5 \qquad (2)$
Step 2: Decide whether you can add or subtract the equations to get rid of a variable.	Addition will not eliminate one of the variables here so you need to subtract. Subtract (2) from (1). $(x + 3y) - (x + y) = 7 - 5$ $x + 3y - x - y = 2$ $2y = 2$
Step 3: Solve the combined equation (which now has one unknown).	$2y = 2$ $y = 1$
Step 4: Substitute the solution into either of the original equations to find the other unknown.	Substitute $y = 1$ into (2). $x + 1 = 5$ $x = 4$
Step 5: Write the solution.	The solution is $x = 4$, $y = 1$

Tip

If the signs are different, add to eliminate one variable.

If the signs are the same, including when they are both negative, subtract.

EXERCISE 17G

1 Solve the following pairs of simultaneous equations by elimination.
Check that each solution satisfies **both** equations.

a $x - y = 2$
$3x + y = 14$

b $2x - 3y = 3$
$x + 3y = 6$

c $3x + y = 4$
$2y - 3x = -10$

d $2x - y = 13$
$5x + y = 13$

e $x + 2y = 14$
$4x - 2y = 14$

f $-x - y = 3$
$x + 5y = -11$

g $x + y = 5$
$3x + y = 9$

h $3x + 4y = 15$
$x + 4y = 13$

i $2x - y = 7$
$4x - y = 15$

2 Solve the following simultaneous equations by elimination.

a $x + y = 2$
$3x - y = 10$

b $2x + y = 5$
$x + y = 2$

c $2x - 3y = 1$
$3x + 3y = 9$

3 Solve each pair of simultaneous equations. Choose the most suitable
method for doing this.

a $2x + y = 7$
$3x + 2y = 12$

b $-2x + 8y = 6$
$2x = 3 - y$

c $4x + 2y = 50$
$x + 2y = 20$

d $x + y = -7$
$x - y = -3$

e $y = 1 - 2x$
$5x + 2y = 0$

f $y = 2x - 5$
$y = 3 - 2x$

Setting up and solving simultaneous equations

Some problems can be described using a pair of simultaneous equations.

Once you have defined the variables and set up the equations you can use
algebra to solve them.

Tip

If a problem asks for two different pieces of information then it means there are
two unknowns and you will need two equations to solve it.

Problem-solving framework

A field contains a number of goats and chickens.

Altogether there are 60 heads and 200 legs.

How many are there of each type of animal?

Steps for solving problems	What you would do for this example
Step 1: Work out what you have to do. Start by reading the question carefully.	You have to find the number of goats, g, and the number of chickens, c.
Step 2: What information do you need? Have you got it all?	You need to know how many there are altogether. You're not told this, but you can work it out because each goat and each chicken must have one head. This means that the number of goats and the number of chickens must equal 60. $$g + c = 60$$ Now you need another equation to link the goat and chickens. You've already used the number of heads, so it must be something to do with the legs. Goats have 4 legs each, so the number of goat legs is $4 \times g$. Chickens have 2 legs each, so the number of chicken legs is $2 \times c$. There are 200 legs in total so: $4g + 2c = 200$
Step 3: Decide what maths you can use.	There are two unknowns so you should use simultaneous equations.
Step 4: Set out your solution clearly. Check your working and that your answer is reasonable.	Let the number of goats be g and the number of chickens be c. $$g + c = 60 \quad (1)$$ $$4g + 2c = 200 \quad (2)$$ $g = 60 - c$ Make g the subject of equation (1). Substitute $(60 - c)$ for g in (2) and solve: $$4(60 - c) + 2c = 200$$ $$240 - 4c + 2c = 200$$ $$240 - 2c = 200$$ $$240 - 200 = 2c$$ $$40 = 2c$$ $$20 = c$$ Substitute $c = 20$ into equation (1) to find g. $$g + 20 = 60$$ $$g = 40$$ Check your result by substituting c and g into original equation (2). $$4(40) + 2(20) = 200$$ $$160 + 40 = 200$$ Yes, this works.
Step 5: Check that you've answered the question.	There are 20 chickens and 40 goats.

EXERCISE 17H

1 George spent £2.40 on sweets and Sanjita spent £2.10 on sweets.

George bought six fizzers and four toffees.

Sanjita bought three fizzers and five toffees.

Work out the cost of each type of sweet.

2 A number x is multiplied by 4 and 1 added. This is the same value as the number x multiplied by 2 and 9 added. What is the value of x?

Choose your answer from the following options.

A $x = 9$ B $x = 4$ C $x = 3$ D $x = -4$

3 In a shop, Sam was given £1.65 as change.

The change was made up of 5p coins and 10p coins only.

He was given eighteen coins in total.

How many of each coin did he get?

4 Two children have a total of 264 stickers between them.

One child has 6 fewer stickers than 5 times the other child's stickers.

How many do they each have?

5 The sum of two numbers, a and b, is 120.

When b is subtracted from $3a$, the result is 160.

Find the values of a and b.

6 Two numbers have a sum of 76 and a difference of 48.

What are the numbers?

7 A taxi company charges a flat fee plus a set amount per mile.

A journey of 10 miles costs £7.

A journey of 15 miles costs £9.

What is the cost of a journey of 8 miles?

Section 4: Using graphs to solve equations

If you have a graph you can use it to solve an equation or to answer questions based on the equations.

If there are two equations, you need two graphs. In Section 3 you used a pair of graphs to find the solution to a pair of simultaneous equations.

> **Tip**
>
> You will work with graphs and equations again in Chapter 28 and Chapter 37.

Find answers at: cambridge.org/ukschools/gcsemaths-studentbookanswers

WORKED EXAMPLE 8

This is the graph of the equation $4x + y = 2$.

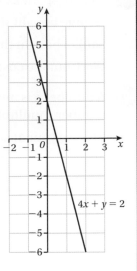

1 Use the graph to estimate the value of y when:

    a $x = 0$ **b** $x = 1$ **c** $x = 2$.

2 What is the value of x when $y = -4$?

Each point on the graph represents a value of x and y that work in this equation.

To find the solutions for different values of x or y, you need to use the value you have been given as one of the coordinates of a point. If you take a line from this point to the graph you can estimate the value of the other coordinate.

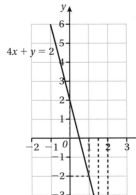

When $x = 0$, $y = 2$

When $x = 1$, $y = -2$

When $x = 2$, $y = -6$

When $y = -4$, $x = 1\frac{1}{2}$

The solutions are shown on the graph in different colours.

EXERCISE 17I

1 From the graph, estimate the solutions for $y - 2x = 1$ and $x + y = 10$

Choose your answer from the options below.

A $x = 4, y = 6$ B $x = 3, y = 7$

C $x = 7, y = 3$ D $x = 3, y = 6$

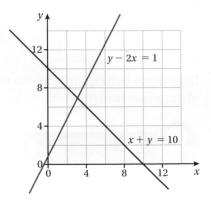

2 This graph represents the distance travelled by a cyclist over time.

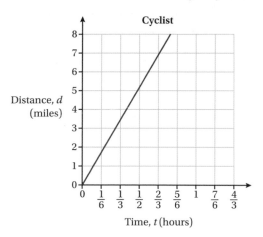

Cyclist

Distance, d (miles)

Time, t (hours)

a Use the graph to estimate how far the cyclist has travelled after 30 minutes.

b How long did it take the cyclist to cover a distance of 8 miles?

c The equation $s = \dfrac{d}{t}$ can be used to work out the speed, s, of the cyclist. Use values for d and t from the graph to estimate the speed at which the cyclist was travelling.

3 This graph shows the distance covered over time by a motorist in a car.

a Estimate how long it took the driver to travel 70 km.

b How far did the driver travel in the first 20 minutes?

c By using two points on the graph, estimate the speed at which the driver was travelling.

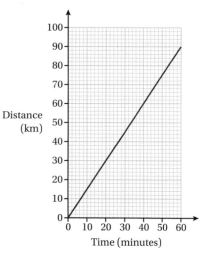

Distance (km)

Time (minutes)

4 Use this graph of the equation $y = 3x - 2$ to estimate the value of y for the following values.

a $x = 0$ **b** $x = 1$ **c** $x = 2$

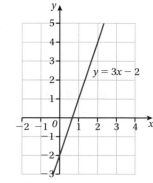

$y = 3x - 2$

Find answers at: cambridge.org/ukschools/gcsemaths-studentbookanswers

5 This graph shows how water drains from a tank at a constant rate.

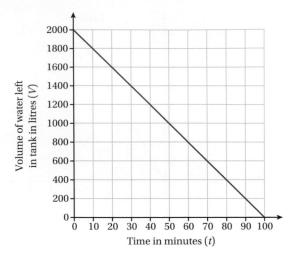

a How much water was in the tank to start with?

b How long did it take for the tank to empty?

c Zena says the equation for this graph is $y = 2000 - 20x$ and Leane says it is $y + 20x = 2000$.

Show, using different points from the graph, that they are both correct.

6 This graph shows the cost of producing goods and how much money is earned from sales (revenue).

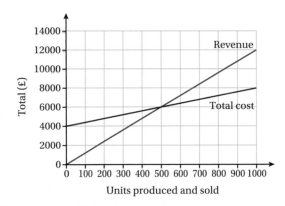

a Use the graph to estimate the point at which the costs and revenue are equal.

b The point at which costs and revenue are equal is called the break-even point.

How does this information help a business owner?

7 This diagram show the graphs of two linear equations $y = 2x$ and $y = -2x + 8$.

Use the graph to find the solution to the two equations.

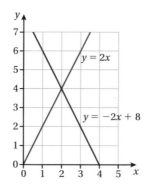

8 This graph of a quadratic equation models a stunt rider's path in the air as he does a jump.

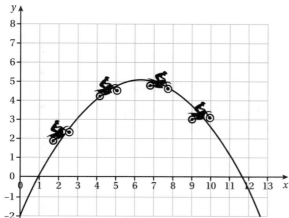

> **Tip**
>
> The solution of a quadratic equation is the value of x when $y = 0$. On a graph, these values are found where the graph intersects the x-axis.

a What do you think the axes represent in this case?

b What values on the horizontal axis represent the rider taking off and landing again?

c Why are these two values useful in terms of the equation?

d Use the graph to estimate the coordinates of the maximum height reached by the rider during this jump.

9 The graphs of two quadratic equations are given here.

Graph A

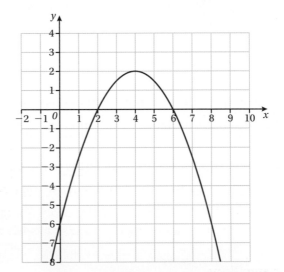

$y = x^2 - 4x - 5$

Graph B

$y = -x^2 - 2x + 8$

Use the graphs to estimate the solution of each equation.

Check your solutions by substitution.

10 This is the graph of a quadratic equation but the equation is not given.

Write down how you can use the graph to find the roots of the equation even though you don't know what the equation is.

11 Naresh is going to the USA.

He needs to buy a data package for his mobile so he can text home.

This graph shows the costs of three different options.

The number of text messages is shown on the x-axis and the related costs are shown on the y-axis in dollars.

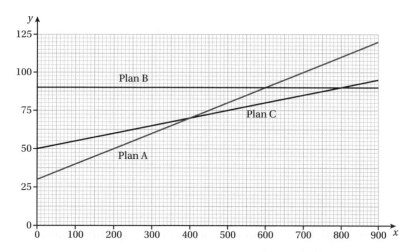

a Which plan represents a set monthly fee? How do you know?

b Estimate the point at which Plan C and Plan A cost the same.

c What is the maximum number of texts you can send on Plan A before it begins to cost more than Plan B?

d Which plan is best for Naresh if he sends more than 800 texts per month? Why?

 Checklist of learning and understanding

Linear and quadratic equations

- A linear equation has one unknown and will have one unique value as a solution.
- A quadratic equation has a square as the highest power for the variable.
- Quadratic equations in the form of $x^2 + bx + c = 0$ can be solved by factorising.
- Quadratic equations have a maximum of two roots. Sometimes there is only one root because the values are the same or a value doesn't work in the context.

Simultaneous equations

- Simultaneous equations are a pair of equations that have solutions that satisfy both equations.
- Simultaneous equations can be solved algebraically by substitution or by elimination.

Graphs and problems

- Equations are useful for setting up problems mathematically.
- You can find or estimate the solution of equations using graphs.
- You need two graphs to solve simultaneous equations. The solution is the point of intersection of the graphs.

 Find answers at: cambridge.org/ukschools/gcsemaths-studentbookanswers

Chapter review

1 Solve for x.

  a $8x + 5 = 3(2x - 11)$ **b** $x^2 = 8 - 2x$ **c** $4(x + 2) = 3(x + 1)$

  d $-x^2 = 8x + 12$ **e** $(x + 2)^2 = 36$ **f** $(x + 4)(x + 3) = 6$

2 Read each statement and decide whether it is true or false. If it is false, give a reason why.

  a $5(x - 2) = 15$, so $x = 2$.

  b The statement 'four is subtracted from a number x that has been multiplied by 5 and this is equal to the number x subtracted from 14' can be represented as $5x - 4 = 14 - x$.

  c The two solutions to the quadratic equation $x^2 - 2x - 15 = 0$ are $x = 3$ and $x = -5$.

  d $x = 2$ and $y = 1$ are the simultaneous solutions to the pair of equations $y = x + 4$ and $y = 2x + 3$.

  e The graph below represents a quadratic equation whose solutions are $x = 1$ and $x = -2$.

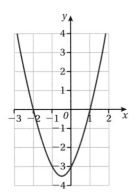

3 Solve.

  a $4a = 36$ **b** $3x + 19 = 46$ **c** $4(2x - 3) = 84$ **d** $2x + 7 = x + 9$

 4 There are n plums in Bag A.

Bag B has three times as many plums as Bag A.

Bag C has 14 more plums than Bag A.

Bag B and Bag C have the same number of plums.

Bag A   Bag B   Bag C

Use algebra to work out the number of plums in Bag A.

You must show your working.   *(4 marks)*

© AQA 2013

5 Find the solutions for $y^2 - 64 = 0$.

Choose your answer from the options below.

A $y = 32$ and $y = -32$ B $y = 8$ and $y = -8$

C $y = 4$ and $y = -4$ D $y = 16$ and $y = -16$

6 Study this graph.

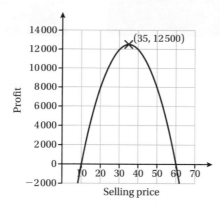

a What are the roots of the quadratic equation modelled by this graph?

b What does the graph tell you about the selling price?

7 Is $y = x + 2$ equivalent to $5y = 5x + 10$?

How can you tell this without solving the equations?

8 **a** What happens when you try to solve this pair of equations?

$x + y = 2$

$x + y = 4$

b What would their linear graphs show?

9 If you drew the graph of $y = x^2 + 2x - 4 = 0$, where would the curve cut the x-axis?

10 The sum of two numbers is 19 and their difference is 5.

a Write a set of equations in terms of x and y to show this.

b Solve the equations simultaneously to find the two numbers.

5 Find answers at: cambridge.org/ukschools/gcsemaths-studentbookanswers

18 Functions and sequences

For more resources relating to this chapter, visit GCSE Mathematics Online.

Using mathematics: real-life applications

Finding a pattern and working out how the parts of the pattern fit together is important in scientific discovery. Scientists use sequences to model and solve real-life problems, such as estimating how quickly diseases spread.

Tip

When you work with sequences you can draw diagrams, flow charts or tables to organise the patterns and make sense of them.

'When a new outbreak of a disease occurs I need to work out how quickly it is spreading. To do this I look at the sequence in which the numbers of victims are increasing. I use the sequence to predict how many people will become infected in a certain length of time.'
(Medical researcher)

Before you start ...

KS3 Ch 4	You need to know your times tables and recognise multiples of numbers.	**1**	**a** Write down the first five multiples of 7. **b** Which of these are multiples of 6? 56, 66, 86, 18, 54, 36
KS3 Ch 4	You need to be able to recognise square numbers and cube numbers.	**2**	**a** Which of these are square numbers? 1, 16, 66, 50, 25, 4, 6, 9, 49 **b** Which of these are **not** cube numbers? 9, 15, 27, 64, 1, 8, 125
KS3	You need to be able to spot and describe patterns.	**3**	**a** Describe the rule for continuing the sequence. shape 1 shape 2 shape 3 **b** How many matchsticks are needed for shape 6?

Assess your starting point using the Launchpad

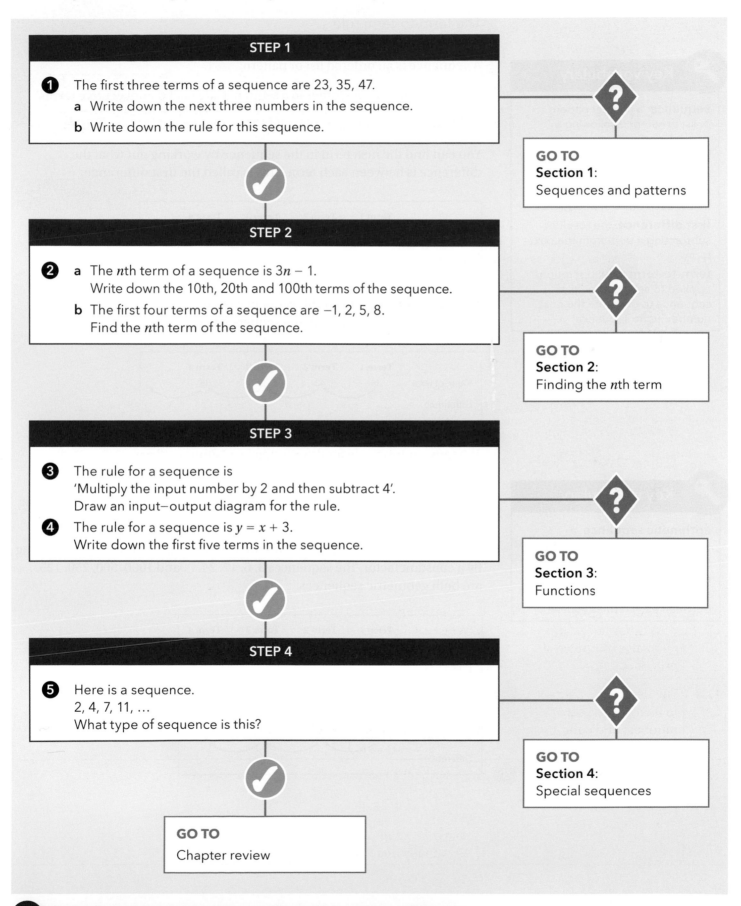

STEP 1

1 The first three terms of a sequence are 23, 35, 47.
  a Write down the next three numbers in the sequence.
  b Write down the rule for this sequence.

GO TO
Section 1:
Sequences and patterns

STEP 2

2 **a** The nth term of a sequence is $3n - 1$.
    Write down the 10th, 20th and 100th terms of the sequence.
  b The first four terms of a sequence are -1, 2, 5, 8.
    Find the nth term of the sequence.

GO TO
Section 2:
Finding the nth term

STEP 3

3 The rule for a sequence is
  'Multiply the input number by 2 and then subtract 4'.
  Draw an input–output diagram for the rule.
4 The rule for a sequence is $y = x + 3$.
  Write down the first five terms in the sequence.

GO TO
Section 3:
Functions

STEP 4

5 Here is a sequence.
  2, 4, 7, 11, …
  What type of sequence is this?

GO TO
Section 4:
Special sequences

GO TO
Chapter review

Find answers at: cambridge.org/ukschools/gcsemaths-studentbookanswers

Section 1: Sequences and patterns

The term-to-term rule

Key vocabulary

sequence: a number pattern or list of numbers following a particular order

term: each number in a sequence is called a term

consecutive terms: terms that follow each other in a sequence

first difference: the result of subtracting a term from the next term

term-to-term rule: operations applied to any number in a sequence to generate the next number in the sequence

A **sequence** is an ordered list or pattern.

Terms that follow each other in a sequence are called **consecutive terms**.

The first term in a sequence is called T(1), the second T(2), and so on.

You can find the next term in the sequence by working out what the difference is between each term. This is called the **first difference**.

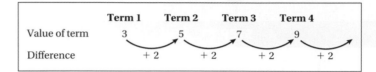

The **term-to-term rule** for this sequence is 'add two'.
$9 + 2 = 11$ so the next term in the sequence is 11.

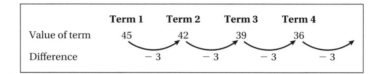

The term-to-term rule for this sequence is 'subtract three'.

3, 5, 7, 9, ... and 45, 42, 39, 36, ... are both **arithmetic sequences**.
In an arithmetic sequence, the terms are generated by adding or subtracting a constant difference.

In a **geometric sequence**, the terms are generated by multiplying or dividing by a constant factor. The sequences 3, 6, 12, 24, ... and 1000, 500, 250, 125, ... are both geometric sequences.

Key vocabulary

arithmetic sequence: a sequence where the difference between each term is constant

geometric sequence: a sequence where the ratio between each term is constant

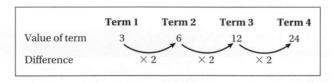

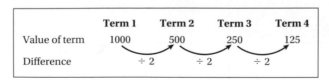

WORKED EXAMPLE 1

"I use term-to-term rules in my job. I know that each row of bricks will have three fewer bricks than the row below it, so I can work out how many bricks I need in each row."

(Bricklayer)

The first row of the wall has 57 bricks.

a Write down the term-to-term rule.

b Find the number of bricks in the next three rows.

a The term-to-term rule is 'subtract three'.

> The number of bricks decreases by 3 for each new row.

b 57 in the first row
57 – 3 = 54 in the second row
54 – 3 = 51 in the third row
51 – 3 = 48 in the fourth row

> Subtract 3 from 57 to get the next term.
> Continue to do this for the next two terms.

EXERCISE 18A

1 Write down the next three terms of each sequence.
Give a reason for each of your answers.

a 4, 7, 10, 13, …   **b** 38, 43, 48, 53, …   **c** 27, 23, 19, …   **d** 63, 57, 51, …

e 1, 2, 4, 8, …   **f** 64, 32, 16, …   **g** 4, 12, 36, …   **h** 729, 243, 81, …

2 A sequence begins 3, 9, 15, 21, …
The rule for continuing the sequence is 'add 6'.
What are the next three numbers in this sequence?

a 27, 33, 41, …   **b** 26, 32, 38, …   **c** 25, 31, 37, …   **d** 27, 33, 39, …

3 This sequence of patterns is made from bricks.

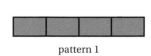

pattern 1

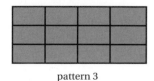

pattern 2   pattern 3

a How many bricks are needed for pattern 4?

b Describe the rule for continuing the sequence.

Find answers at: cambridge.org/ukschools/gcsemaths-studentbookanswers

4 Write down the term-to-term rule of each sequence.

a 7, 14, 21, 28, ... **b** 19, 15, 11, 7, ...

c 2, 8, 32, 128, ... **d** 84, 42, 21, ...

5 Write down the term-to-term rule and the next three terms of each sequence.

a 3.5, 5.5, 7.5, ... **b** 1.2, 2.4, 4.8, ...

c $1\frac{1}{2}$, 3, $4\frac{1}{2}$, ... **d** 8, 5, 2, ...

e 72, 36, 18, ... **f** −10, −7, −4, ...

6 A ball is dropped from a height of 96 cm.

Each time it hits the ground it bounces back to half its previous height.

a How high will it bounce on its 4th bounce?

b How many times will it bounce before it bounces to below 1 cm?

7 T(1) of a sequence is 4.

The term-to-term rule is 'add x'.

Find a value for x so that:

a every second term is an integer

b every third term is a multiple of 4

c T(2) is smaller than T(1).

Section 2: Finding the nth term

The position-to-term rule

Term-to-term rules are useful for generating the first few terms of a sequence and for finding the next term in a given sequence. They are less useful when you want to find the 50th or 100th term.

A **position-to-term** rule allows you to work out the value of any term in a sequence if you know its position in the sequence.

The sequence 1, 3, 5, 7, ... can be generated using the position-to-term rule 'position number × 2, subtract 1' by substituting the position number into the rule.

Position in sequence	Position-to-term rule 'position × 2, − 1'	Term
1	$(1 \times 2) - 1$	1
2	$(2 \times 2) - 1$	3
3	$(3 \times 2) - 1$	5
4	$(4 \times 2) - 1$	7
5	$(5 \times 2) - 1$	9
6	$(6 \times 2) - 1$	11
7	$(7 \times 2) - 1$	13
8	$(8 \times 2) - 1$	15
9	$(9 \times 2) - 1$	17
10	$(10 \times 2) - 1$	19

Tip

It can help to write out the sequence and label the difference between each term.

Tip

Look for the term-to-term rule to answer this question.

Key vocabulary

position-to-term rule: operations applied to the position number of a term in a sequence in order to generate that term

The nth term

The notation $T(n)$ refers to 'any term' in the sequence, where n is the position of the term. $T(n)$ is known as the 'nth term'.

When given the terms of a sequence, you can use the first difference to help you find the rule for the nth term by comparing the first difference with number patterns you already know.

Problem-solving framework

Find an expression for the nth term of the sequence: 5, 8, 11, 14, 17, ...

Steps for solving problems	What you would do for this example
Step 1: Identify what you have to do.	You are trying to find an expression to work out the value of any term in the sequence.
Step 2: If it is useful, draw a table.	Draw a table showing the position and the term: | n	1	2	3	4	5
---	---	---	---	---	---
$T(n)$	5	8	11	14	17	
Step 3: Start working on the problem using what you know.	Label the table with the difference between each term: | n	1	2	3	4	5
---	---	---	---	---	---
$T(n)$	5	8	11	14	17	 $+3 \quad +3 \quad +3 \quad +3$ The difference in this sequence is '$+3$'.
Step 4: Connect to other sequences and compare.	(If the difference was '$+2$' you would compare to $2n$; if it was '-4' you would compare it to $-4n$, and so on.) Add this sequence to your table: | n	1	2	3	4	5
---	---	---	---	---	---
$T(n)$	5	8	11	14	17
Multiples of 3 ($3n$)	3	6	9	12	15	 $+2$ Compare the sequence with the sequence for $3n$. Each term in the sequence is 2 more than $3n$. So the expression for the nth term of this sequence could be $3n + 2$.
Step 5: Check your working and that your answer is reasonable.	Test for $n = 5$: $(3 \times 5) + 2 = 15 + 2$ $15 + 2 = 17$ The fifth term is 17 so the expression is correct.
Step 6: Have you answered the question?	Yes. The expression for the nth term is $3n + 2$.

Find answers at: cambridge.org/ukschools/gcsemaths-studentbookanswers

Tip

If you are struggling to find the rule for an arithmetic sequence, you can use the following formula: $(a + d(n - 1))$ where a = first term, and d = common difference. The **common difference** is the constant difference between terms.

WORK IT OUT 18.1

The nth term of a sequence is $3n - 2$.
Write down the first five terms of the sequence.
Only one answer below is correct.
Give reasons why the other two are wrong.

Option A	Option B	Option C
$-2, 1, 4, 7, 10$	$1, 4, 7, 10, 13$	$-1, 1, 3, 5, 7$

EXERCISE 18B

1 This pattern is made using drinking straws.

pattern 1   pattern 2   pattern 3   pattern 4

   a Which pattern will have 32 straws?

   b How many straws will be in pattern 20?

   c What is the position-to-term rule?

2 The nth term of a sequence is $5n - 1$.
What is the 10th term of the sequence?
Choose your answer from the following options.
  A 49   B 13   C 50   D 52

3 The nth term of a sequence is $3n - 1$.

   a Write down the first six terms of the sequence.

   b Work out the 20th term.

   c Nathan says,
      "The 40th term of the sequence is double the 20th term."
      Show that he is wrong.

4 Find the value of the following terms for each position-to-term rule.

    i 1st term   **ii** 2nd term   **iii** 3rd term   **iv** 4th term
    v 10th term   **vi** 20th term   **vii** 100th term

    a $4n + 1$ **b** $4n - 5$ **c** $8n + 2$
    d $5n - \dfrac{1}{2}$ **e** $\dfrac{n}{2} + 1$ **f** $-2n + 1$

5 Here is a sequence.

    $4, 11, 18, 25, 32, \ldots$

   What is the expression for the nth term of the sequence?
   Choose your answer from the following options.
    A $4n + 7$ B $7n + 4$ C $4n - 7$ D $7n - 3$

6 A sequence begins

    $5, 9, 13, 17, \ldots$

   Find the nth term of the sequence.

7 Find the *n*th term of each sequence.

a 3, 5, 7, 9, ... **b** 3, 7, 11, 15, ... **c** −1, 4, 9, 14, ...

d 7, 12, 17, 22, ... **e** −3, 0, 3, 6, ... **f** −1, 6, 13, 20, ...

8 Here is a sequence of numbers from a science experiment.

67, 73, 79, 85, ...

Find the *n*th term of the sequence.

9 The table shows the heights of a sunflower over a three-week period. The growth rate is constant.

a How tall will the sunflower be in the *n*th week?

b How tall will the sunflower be in the 100th week?

c Give a reason why your answer to part **b** is unlikely to be true.

Week	Height
1	4.5 cm
2	6.7 cm
3	8.9 cm

10 Tammy starts with £100. She saves £4 every week.

a How much will she have after 52 weeks?

b How long will it take her to save £400?

11 In a restaurant, tables can be put together in a line to seat different numbers of people.

a How many people can sit at 6 tables in a line?

b How many people can sit at 10 tables in a line?

c Can 31 people be seated at tables arranged in a line? Give a reason for your answer.

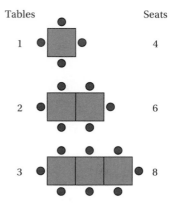

12 The first four terms of a sequence are 4, 7, 10, 13. What is the rule for this sequence? Choose from these options.

A position number 1 3 B 2 3 position number

C 3 3 position number 1 1

Section 3: Functions

A **function** is a rule for changing one number into another.

'Multiply by two', 'add three' and 'divide by 2 and then add 1' are examples of functions.

You can use algebra to write functions, for example 'multiply by 2' can be written as the expression '2*n*'.

Functions can be expressed in different ways:

$y = x + 3$ $x \rightarrow x + 3$ $f(x) = x + 3$

These all mean the same thing: take any value of *x* and add 3 to it to get a result.

The steps you take to work out the value of a function can be shown as a simple flow diagram or function machine.

A function machine shows the input, operation and output for a given rule.

Input ⟶ | rule ⟩ ⟶ Output

In a function there is only **one** possible output for each input.

 Key vocabulary

function: a set of instructions for changing one number (the input) into another number (the output)

Tip

You can think of a function as 'the answer you will get' if you apply this rule to a number.

Generating a sequence using a function

You can generate a sequence using a function.

The table shows the outputs when you input the values 1 to 10 into the function $y = 2n + 4$

$$n \longrightarrow \boxed{\times 2} \longrightarrow \boxed{+4} \longrightarrow 2n + 4$$

Input	Function	Output
1	× 2 + 4	6
2	× 2 + 4	8
3	× 2 + 4	10
4	× 2 + 4	12
5	× 2 + 4	14
6	× 2 + 4	16
7	× 2 + 4	18
8	× 2 + 4	20
9	× 2 + 4	22
10	× 2 + 4	24

So the function $y = 2n + 4$ generates the sequence
6, 8, 10, 12, 14, 16, 18, 20, 22, 24, ...

If you know the values of a sequence, you can find the function that generates the sequence by finding the position-to-term rule.

WORKED EXAMPLE 2

Here is a sequence.

3, 8, 13, 18, 23, ...

Write the function machine that generates this sequence.

(n)	1	2	3	4	5
$T(n)$	3	8	13	18	23

+5   +5   +5   +5

Draw a table showing the position and term.
Work out the difference between consecutive terms.
The terms increase by 5.

(n)	1	2	3	4	5
$T(n)$	3	8	13	18	23
$5n$	5	10	15	20	25

Compare the sequence with the sequence for $5n$.
Each term in the sequence is 2 less than the term in the sequence $5n$.

$$n \longrightarrow \boxed{\times 5} \longrightarrow \boxed{-2} \longrightarrow 5n - 2$$

The function could be 'multiply by 5, subtract 2'; test it using a term from the sequence.

$$4 \rightarrow (4 \times 5) \rightarrow 20 \rightarrow -2 \rightarrow 18 \checkmark$$

EXERCISE 18C

1 The numbers 1 to 10 are input into the function $x \rightarrow x + 3$ to make a sequence. Write down the sequence.

2 The numbers 1 to 10 are input into the function $y = x + 7$ to make a sequence. What are the last three numbers of the sequence? Choose from these options.

A 8, 9, 10   B 15, 16, 17   C 7, 14, 21   D 56, 63, 70

3 Input the numbers 1 to 10 into each function to generate a sequence.

a $x \rightarrow x - 5$ **b** $x \rightarrow 3x$ **c** $n \rightarrow n + 7$ **d** $n \rightarrow \dfrac{n}{2}$

4 Input the numbers 21 to 30 into each function to generate a sequence.

a $y = 2x$ **b** $y = x - 8$ **c** $y = \dfrac{x}{3}$ **d** $y = x + \dfrac{1}{2}$

5 The diagram shows a sequence of patterns.

a Write down the number of circles in each pattern in the sequence.

b Work out the number of circles in pattern 5.

c Complete the function below

Pattern number $(n) \rightarrow$ 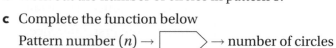 $\rightarrow$ number of circles

d How many circles will be in the 6th and 10th patterns?

6 Jess is paid £6.25 per hour. Write down a function to show how much she is paid for working n hours.

7 Zena is paid £500 plus £3 for every item she sells.

a Write down a function to show how much she is paid for selling p items.

b How much would she be paid if she sold 40 items?

Section 4: Special sequences

Some patterns and sequences of numbers are well known.
You need to be able to recognise and use the following patterns.

Special sequence	Description
Simple arithmetic progression (or linear sequences)	The **difference** between each term is constant, for example, 3, 5, 7, ... or 14, 11, 8, ...
Geometric sequences	The **ratio** between each term is constant, for example, 3, 6, 12, 24, ...
Triangular numbers	These are made by arranging dots to form equilateral triangles. 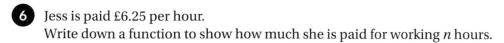 1 dot 3 dots 6 dots 10 dots 15 dots

Find answers at: cambridge.org/ukschools/gcsemaths-studentbookanswers

Square numbers	A square number is the product of multiplying a whole number by itself. For example, $3^2 = 3 \times 3 = 9$ Square numbers form the sequence: 1, 4, 9, 16, 25, 36, …
Quadratic sequences **Tip** $T(n) = n^2 + 3$ means 'the nth term of this sequence is n squared plus 3'.	These sequences are linked to square numbers. A quadratic sequence has a position-to-term rule that involves squaring one of the variables. For example, $T(n) = n^2 + 3$. <table><tr><td>n</td><td>1</td><td>2</td><td>3</td><td>4</td><td>5</td></tr><tr><td>$T(n)$</td><td>4</td><td>7</td><td>12</td><td>19</td><td>28</td></tr></table> $+3 \quad +5 \quad +7 \quad +9$ First different is not constant. $+2 \quad +2 \quad +2$ Second difference is constant. The second difference is the difference between each term of the first difference.
Cube numbers	A cube number is the product of multiplying a whole number by itself and then by itself again. 64 is a cube number because $4^3 = (4 \times 4 \times 4) = 64$ Cube numbers form the sequence: 1, 8, 27, 64, 125, …
Fibonacci sequences	The term-to-term rule for a sequence of Fibonacci numbers is 'add the previous two terms together'. The most well-known example is: 1, 1, 2, 3, 5, 8, 13, 21, …

Did you know?

Leonardo Fibonacci was an Italian mathematician who developed the number pattern 1, 1, 2, 3, 5, 8, 13, 21, … while he was trying to work out how many offspring a pair of rabbits would produce over different generations.

The Fibonacci pattern is found in many natural situations.

In the Fibonacci series, the sequence of numbers is created by adding the 1st and 2nd terms together to make the 3rd term; adding the 2nd and 3rd terms together to make the 4th term, and so on.

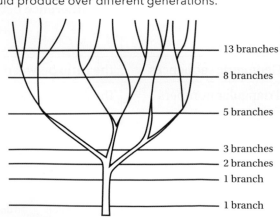

13 branches
8 branches
5 branches
3 branches
2 branches
1 branch
1 branch

EXERCISE 18D

1 **a** What type of number is 36? Choose your answer from the following options.

    A A square number   B A square and triangular number

    C A triangular number   D A prime number

    b Write down the next two terms in the sequence(s) made up of the number type(s) you identified in your answer to part **a**.

2 The pattern shows T(4), T(5), T(6) and T(7) in a sequence.

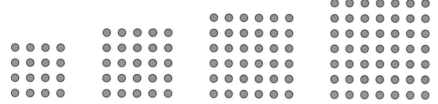

    a Describe the rule for the sequence.

    b What is the name of this sequence of numbers?

3 The photo shows pattern 5 of a sequence.

    a What type of number is shown?
       Give a reason for your answer.

    b Write down the first ten numbers in the sequence.

    c Find the first and second differences between the terms of the sequence.

    d What type of sequence is this?

pattern 5

4 A female bee has a mother and a father.

A male bee has a mother but no father.

The diagram shows the family tree of a male bee.

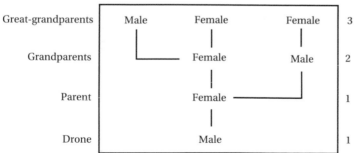

    a How many great-great-grandparents does the male bee have?

    b The family tree shows four generations of bee.
       Copy and complete the tree so that it shows six generations.

      A Write down a sequence for the number of bees in each generation.

      B How many bees are there in the ninth generation?

      C Describe the rule for this sequence.

      D What type of sequence is this?

Find answers at: cambridge.org/ukschools/gcsemaths-studentbookanswers

5 Which of the following pairs of numbers appears in the Fibonacci sequence?

    A 22, 34   B 56, 89   C 89, 144   D 256, 357

6 **a** The first two terms of a Fibonacci sequence that follows the rule of 'each term being the sum of the previous two terms' are 3, 4. Write down the first ten terms of the sequence.

    b The first two terms of a different Fibonacci-type sequence that follows the rule 'add the first term to double the second term are' −2, 3. Write down the first ten terms of the sequence.

    c The first two terms of another Fibonacci-type sequence that follows the rule 'double the first term then add the second term' are 2, −3. Write down the first ten terms of the sequence.

7 The 6th and 7th terms of a Fibonacci sequence are 31, 50.

    What are the first two terms in the sequence?

8 A Fibonacci-type sequence is made by subtracting the second term from double the first term.

    a If the first two terms are 6 and 3, what would the 6th and 7th terms be?

    b If the first two terms are 3 and 6, what would the 6th and 7th terms be?

    c If the 6th and 7th terms are 45 and -83, what would the first two terms be?

9 Find the following terms using each rule for the nth term.

    i 1st term   **ii** 2nd term   **iii** 3rd term   **iv** 5th term
    v 10th term   **vi** 20th term   **vii** 50th term

    a $n^2 + 5$ **b** $n^2 - 3$ **c** $2n^2 + 1$ **d** $2n^2 - 7$

10 The nth term of a sequence is $n^3 + 1$.

    Write down the first six terms of the sequence.

11 The nth term of a sequence is $n^2 + n$.

    Write down the first ten terms of the sequence.

12 Compare your answer to question 10 with your answer from question 3.

    a What is the expression for finding the nth triangular number?

    b Find the 10th and 25th triangular numbers.

Checklist of learning and understanding

Sequences

- Sequences can be formed using a term-to-term rule. Each term is generated by applying the same rule to the previous term.

- The position-to-term rule is used to find the value of any term, known as the nth term, in a sequence using its position in the sequence.

Functions

- A function is an expression or rule for changing one number (the input) into another number (the output).

- A sequence can be generated by inputting an ordered set of numbers into a function.

Special sequences

- It is important to be able to recognise familiar sequences such as square numbers, cube numbers, triangular numbers and Fibonacci numbers.

- In a quadratic sequence the first difference between the terms is not constant but the second difference is, and the pattern is linked to square numbers.

  Chapter review

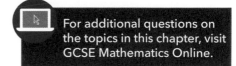
For additional questions on the topics in this chapter, visit GCSE Mathematics Online.

1 For each sequence:
   a write down the missing terms
   b find the nth term
   c find the 25th term.
   A 1.5, 2, ☐, 3, 3.5, ☐, ...   B ☐, 28, 24, ☐, 4, 8, ☐, ...
   C $\frac{1}{2}, \frac{1}{4},$ ☐, $\frac{1}{16}, \frac{1}{32},$ ☐, ...   D 5, ☐, 17, 23, 29, ☐, ...

2 Which of the following sequences uses the same rule as the Fibonacci sequence? Choose your answer from the following options.
   A 2, 4, 8, 14, ...   B 0, 2, 4, 6, 8, ...   C 2, 8, 16, 32, ...   D 2, 2, 4, 6, 10, ...

3 What is the next term of this quadratic sequence?
   Choose your answer from the following options.
      −4, −1, 4, 11, ...
   A 25   B 20   C 24

4 PolyPond manufacture square fish ponds.
   They only do one style that increases in size as shown in the diagram.

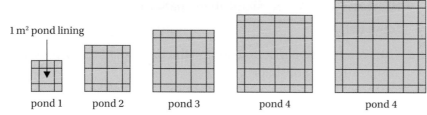

1 m² pond lining

pond 1   pond 2   pond 3   pond 4   pond 4

The price of each pond is £100 + £10 per square metre of pond lining.
   a What is the price for pond 6?
   b What is the rule for calculating the price of any pond?

5 The nth term of a sequence is $4n + 8$.
   a Work out the 6th term.
   b Which term has a value of 56?
   c Is 35 a term in this sequence? Give a reason for your answer.

```
            1
          1   1
        1   2   1
      1   3   3   1
    1   4   6   4   1
  1   5   10  10  5   1
```

6 Pascal's triangle is shown on the left.

Each number is the sum of the two numbers above it, except for the edges which are all 1.

a Copy and complete Pascal's triangle to the 10th row.

b i Find the total for each row.

ii Describe the rule for the sequence of totals.

c A sequence of diagonal numbers from Pascal's triangle is highlighted.

1, 3, 6, 10, …

i What is the name for the numbers in this sequence?

ii Find the nth term of the sequence.

7 The table shows the number of people infected by a virus over a four-day period.

Day	1	2	3	4
Number of people infected	8	13	18	23

The infection rate is constant.

a How many people will be infected on day 5?

b How many people will be infected on the nth day?

c There are 126 people.

How long will it be before everyone is infected?

8 This sequence of shapes is made from square tiles.

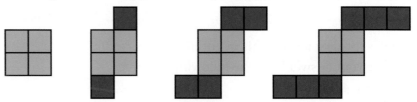

a Write down the number of tiles in each shape as a sequence.

b How many tiles are needed for the fifth shape?

c Complete this function machine for calculating the number of tiles used to make any shape in the pattern:

input $(n) \rightarrow$  $\rightarrow$ output

d Use your function machine to find the number of tiles needed for the 20th, 25th and nth shape.

9 Tamsyn gets 28 days holiday every year.

She gets an additional half day for each overnight survey.

a How much holiday will she get in one year if she does b overnight surveys?

Write a function for calculating how much holiday she will get if she does b overnight surveys in a year.

b Tamsyn did 16 overnight surveys last year.
How much holiday did she get?

19 Basic probability

In this chapter you will learn how to ...

- use the language of probability and the 0 to 1 probability scale.
- calculate the probability of events happening or not happening.
- carry out experiments, record outcomes and use results to predict future probabilities.

> For more resources relating to this chapter, visit GCSE Mathematics Online.

Using mathematics: real-life applications

Data are collected by many professionals and used to find the probability of particular things happening. For example, in a fertility clinic data collected over a period of many years can be used to draw a graph that shows the probability that a woman of a particular age will be successful at becoming pregnant.

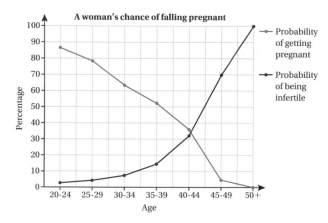

"A 20-year old woman has an 86% chance of becoming pregnant and only a 3% chance of being infertile. This means there is a high probability that she will get pregnant if she is trying to have a baby."

(Fertility doctor)

Before you start ...

Ch 5, 6, 13	You need to be able to calculate with fractions, decimals and percentages.	**1** Choose the correct answer without doing the calculations. **a** $\frac{1}{2}+\frac{1}{4}$ A $\frac{2}{3}$ B $\frac{2}{6}$ C $\frac{3}{4}$ **b** 0.2×0.3 A 0.5 B 0.06 C 0.6 **c** 20% of 40 A 0.8 B 8% C 8
Ch 5, 6, 13	You should be able to find equivalent fractions, decimals and percentages.	**2** Choose the correct sign: $<, =, >$ **a** $\frac{12}{25}\ \square\ 8\%$ **b** $0.8\ \square\ 8\%$ **c** $\frac{24}{50}\ \square\ 0.5$

Tip

In probability calculations you will need to work with fractions, decimals and percentages, often interchangeably. Remember:

- a fraction is a number in the form $\frac{a}{b}$
- you can change fractions to decimals and decimals to fractions (see Chapter 6).

Find answers at: cambridge.org/ukschools/gcsemaths-studentbookanswers

Assess your starting point using the Launchpad

STEP 1

1 Match events **A** to **D** with these probabilities.

a A probability of 0.

b A 100% probability of happening.

c A probability of about 0.5.

d A probability of about 80%.

    A Getting heads when you toss a coin.

    B May following June this year.

    C Choosing a letter of the alphabet and not getting a vowel.

    D Getting a number from 1 to 6 when you roll an ordinary dice.

GO TO
Section 1:
The probability scale

STEP 2

2 Wilf has six green sweets, two red sweets and three yellow sweets in a packet.

He puts his hand into the packet and chooses the first sweet he touches.

What is the probability that it will be green?

GO TO
Section 2:
Calculating probability

STEP 2

3 A doctor keeps records of how many patients who have the flu vaccination actually get the flu. Over a three-year period, he found that out of 2500 people who had the vaccination, three still got the flu.

a Estimate the probability that people who had the vaccination will get the flu.

b If 7300 people have the flu injection, how many would you expect to get the flu?

GO TO
Section 3:
Experimental probability
Section 4:
Mixed probability problems

GO TO
Chapter review

Section 1: The probability scale

The **probability** of something happening (or not happening) is a measure of how likely it is.

For example:

- there is a good chance it will rain tomorrow
- I'm certain that it's going to rain tomorrow
- it is impossible for Arsenal to win the league this year
- there's a fifty-fifty chance that she will make the team.

Impossible means there is no chance that something will happen.

Certain means it will definitely happen.

A **fifty-fifty** or **even chance** means that it is just as likely to happen as it is not to happen.

Defining probability

An **event** is the mathematical word for the thing (or things) that happens.

An **outcome** is a single result of an experiment.

Tossing a coin is an event. There are two possible outcomes:

outcome 1: heads   outcome 2: tails

If you flipped the coin in the hope of getting heads, then heads is a favourable outcome.

The chance of an event happening is called the probability of the event.

Mathematicians use the short form P(E) to represent 'the probability of the event.'

Expressing probability in numbers

Probability can be described in numbers using a scale from 0 to 1.

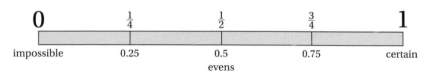

For example:

- The probability that the day immediately after a Friday will be a Tuesday is 0. It is impossible.
- The probability that the day immediately after a Sunday will be a Monday is 1. It is certain.
- The probability of getting heads when you flip a fair coin is 0.5. You have an equal or even chance of getting heads or tails.

The smaller the fraction, the less likely it is that the event will happen.

An event with a probability of 0.5 or $\left(\frac{1}{2}\right)$ is more likely to happen than an event with a probability of 0.25 or $\left(\frac{1}{4}\right)$ or 0.1 or $\left(\frac{1}{10}\right)$.

Key vocabulary

event: the thing to which we are trying to give a probability
outcome: a single result of an experiment

Tip

Remember that E in this notation means the event. So if the event is 'getting heads when you toss a coin', then you would write P(heads) or P(H) as the short form of 'the probability of getting heads'.

Tip

You cannot get a negative number or an answer greater than 1 when you calculate probability. If you do, then you know you have made an error.

 Find answers at: cambridge.org/ukschools/gcsemaths-studentbookanswers

Probability as a percentage

The same probability can be given as a decimal, fraction or percentage.

Some probabilities make more sense when given in a particular form.

For example, the probability of winning a car in a free online competition is calculated to be:

$$0.00038\% \text{ and also } \frac{1}{266\,144}$$

Both express the same probability but writing it as a fraction shows what a small probability there is of winning.

EXERCISE 19A

1 Jacinda has three red scarves, two yellow scarves and a black scarf.

She takes a scarf without looking, hoping for the black one.

a Describe the event in this example.

b List the possible outcomes.

c State whether Jacinda has a high or low probability of a favourable outcome. Give a reason for your answer.

d State which outcome has the highest probability. Give a reason for your answer.

2 Zara has 10 black, 5 white, 6 red and 3 green sweets in a packet.

She offers the packet to her friend Paula who takes a sweet without looking.

a What colour is Paula most likely to pick?

b Which colour has the lowest chance of being picked?

c What is the probability that she picks a red sweet?

d What is the probability that the sweet is white or green?

3 Write the probability of each event as a fraction, a decimal and a percentage.

a You'll get heads when you toss a coin.

b You'll get a 7 when you roll a normal dice.

c You'll win a raffle when you have not bought a ticket.

d You'll win a raffle with 1000 tickets sold when you have bought a ticket.

e A newborn baby will be a girl.

f You'll get an odd number when you roll a dice.

g You will see a famous person this week.

h It will rain tomorrow.

Tip

If a probability question involves dice, assume that it refers to a normal (unbiased), six-sided dice with the sides numbered 1 to 6, unless the question tells you otherwise.

4 Work with a partner. Discuss whether the following statements are true or false. Give reasons for your answers.

a It can either rain or be sunny, so there is a 50% chance of rain tomorrow.

b It hasn't rained for over three weeks now, so it is certain to rain this week.

c You have to be very lucky to get doubles when you roll two dice.

d If a woman has already given birth to three boys, she has an excellent chance of having a girl next time round.

e It is unlikely that I will ever be able to have a credit card because I have a bad credit history.

f Two football teams playing against each other have an equal chance of winning.

Section 2: Calculating probability

Equally likely, random outcomes

When you flip a fair coin there are two possible outcomes: head and tails.

You have the same chance of getting heads as you have of getting tails. The outcomes are **equally likely**.

This does not mean that if you flip a coin six times in a row you will get three heads and three tails. Although the outcomes are equally likely, they are also **random**.

However, the more times you flip the coin, the closer you will get to an equal number of heads and tails.

Theoretical probability

When the outcomes of an event are equally likely you can calculate the probability of each event using the formula:

probability of an event = $\dfrac{\text{number of favourable outcomes}}{\text{total number of outcomes}}$

Tip

A fair, or unbiased, coin, spinner or dice is one that is symmetrical, not damaged or unbalanced in ways that make it fall more often on one side than the other. Each outcome is equally likely to occur.

Key vocabulary

equally likely: having the same probability of happening
random: not predetermined

WORK IT OUT 19.1

A teacher puts the names of six students: April, Basil, Candy, David, Eliza and Fatimah into a container. He chooses one at random. Calculate the probability that the teacher draws the following: **a** Basil **b** a girl's name **c** a name other than Basil. Which of these solutions is correct? Why are the others incorrect?

Solution A	Solution B	Solution C
a $P(\text{Basil}) = \frac{1}{5} = 0.2$	**a** $P(\text{Basil}) = \frac{1}{6} = 0.17$	**a** $P(\text{Basil}) = \frac{1}{6} = 1.7\%$
b $P(\text{girl}) = \frac{3}{6} = \frac{1}{2} = 0.5$	**b** $P(\text{girl}) = \frac{4}{6} = \frac{2}{3} = 0.67$	**b** $P(\text{girl}) = \frac{4}{6} = 6.7\%$
c $P(\text{not Basil}) = 1 - 5 = -4$	**c** $P(\text{not Basil}) = 1 - \frac{1}{6} = \frac{5}{6} = 0.83$	**c** $P(\text{not Basil}) = \frac{5}{6} = 8.3\%$

Find answers at: cambridge.org/ukschools/gcsemaths-studentbookanswers

The probability of an event not happening

The sum of all the possible outcomes of an event is 1.

If the probability of a given outcome is P(E), then the probability of that outcome **not** happening is

$$1 - P(E)$$

In Work It Out 19.1, each name has a $\frac{1}{6}$ probability of being chosen.

The probability of choosing Basil is $\frac{1}{6}$

$$P(\text{not Basil}) = 1 - \frac{1}{6} = \frac{5}{6}$$

Mutually exclusive events

Events that cannot happen at the same time are known as **mutually exclusive**.

For example, if you drew one card from a standard pack of playing cards:

- drawing a card that is a king and a queen is mutually exclusive
- drawing a card that is red and the number two is possible so is not mutually exclusive.

To find the probability of a favourable outcome from mutually exclusive events, you add the probabilities of each of the possible favourable outcomes.

What is the probability that the teacher in Work It Out 19.1 chooses either April or Basil?

In this example, the two events cannot take place at the same time. The two events are mutually exclusive.

You add together the probabilities of the two outcomes:

$$P(\text{April}) + P(\text{Basil}) = P(\text{April } or \text{ Basil})$$
$$\frac{1}{6} + \frac{1}{6} = \frac{2}{6} = \frac{1}{3}$$

EXERCISE 19B

1 Calculate the theoretical probability of each outcome.

Order the outcomes from most likely to least likely.

a Tossing a coin and getting tails.

b Rolling a dice labelled 1 to 6 and getting 2.

c Randomly picking a red counter from a bag that contains 3 green, 1 red and 5 blue counters.

d Rolling two dice and getting seven as the total score.

2 An unbiased six-sided dice is rolled.

Choose the correct probability for each outcome.

a P(rolling a 4)

    A $\frac{1}{5}$ B $\frac{1}{6}$ C $\frac{5}{6}$ D 1

b P(rolling an odd number)

    A 0   B $\frac{1}{2}$ C $\frac{3}{4}$ D 1

c P(not getting a 2 or a 3)

    A 0   B $\frac{1}{2}$ C $\frac{1}{3}$ D $\frac{2}{3}$

3 For each of the following events:

    i identify all the possible outcomes

    ii state whether the outcomes are equally likely or not and give a reason why.

a A fair dice is rolled.

b 100 raffle tickets are placed in a barrel and one is drawn at random.

c A drawing pin is dropped to see whether it lands point up or point down.

d A coin is drawn from a bag containing twelve £1 coins and twenty-five 50p coins.

e A student from your class is chosen to speak at a school assembly.

f Tossing two coins at the same time.

4 A couple have three children.

They have an equal chance of having a boy or a girl.

What is the probability that their first child is a girl?

5 A wallet contains three £1 coins and four £2 coins.

What is the probability that the first coin taken at random from the wallet is:

a £1?   **b** not £1?   **c** 50p?

6 In a game, a dart is thrown at a board made of 20 sectors.

It is equally likely to hit any of the numbers from 1 to 20.

Work out the probability that the dart will land on:

a an even number   **b** a number < 13   **c** a multiple of 6

d 26   **e** a number that is not 19.

Tip

Remember: a sector is the part of a circle between two radii.

7 Tiles with each of the 26 letters of the alphabet are placed in a bag.

A tile is drawn at random.

What is the probability of getting:

a a vowel?

b a consonant?

c a letter from the word 'SQUARE'?

d a letter from the name John or a letter from the name Ali?

e a letter from the name Nicky or a letter from the name Sue?

Find answers at: cambridge.org/ukschools/gcsemaths-studentbookanswers

8 Two people are competing in a competition.

There are three possible outcomes: win, draw or lose.

Does this mean that the probability of one person winning is $\frac{1}{3}$?
Give a reason for your answer.

Section 3: Experimental probability

Predicting outcomes

The probability of getting heads when you toss a coin is $\frac{1}{2}$.

In real life, if you toss a coin twice, it doesn't always land once on heads and once on tails.

In the same way, if you roll a dice it can land on any of the numbers from 1 to 6. If you roll the dice six times, you wouldn't always get 1, 2, 3, 4, 5 and 6.

Experiments with coins, counters, dice, spinners or playing cards involve a number of trials.

For each trial, the outcome is recorded to see how often the favourable outcome occurred.

Work through the following exercise that is an experiment to record the outcomes when you toss two coins at the same time.

EXERCISE 19C

Work in pairs. You need two identical coins and a small container. Shake the coins in the container and then drop them on to your desk. Do this 40 times each (80 times in total).

a This table shows the three possible outcomes in this event. Copy it into your exercise book.

Possible outcomes	Predicted frequency	Tally	Actual frequency
Heads, Heads (HH)			
Heads, Tails (HT)			
Tails, Tails (TT)			

b Predict how many times you think each outcome will occur in 80 throws. Write your prediction in the table.

c Do the experiment. Take turns to drop the coins and use tallies to record the outcomes.

d Total the tallies and write the actual frequency of each outcome (in other words, how many times each outcome happened).

e How do your results compare with your predictions?

f How many times would you expect to get two heads if you dropped these two coins 10 000 times? Give a reason for your answer.

In this experiment you found the relative frequency of different outcomes.

Relative frequency is the number of times you get a favourable outcome (for example 'two heads') out of all the outcomes. It is useful for estimating probability.

$$\text{Relative frequency} = \frac{\text{number of favourable outcomes}}{\text{total number of outcomes}}$$

If the favourable outcome is 'two heads' and two heads came up 32 times in the experiment, the relative frequency of heads is:

$$\text{Relative frequency (HH)} = \frac{32}{80} = 0.4$$

Two heads came up 40% of the time.

Increasing the number of trials gives a relative frequency that is closer to the theoretical probability of the event.

Predictions based on evidence from real life

People collect data (empirical evidence) about all sorts of things to make predictions about what might happen in the future.

For example, an insurance company collects data about the age of drivers who have car accidents. They find that drivers aged from 17 to 23 years have a higher relative frequency of being involved in an accident.

The company estimates the probability of drivers getting into an accident and uses this to work out how much to charge for their premiums.

Here are some examples of where probabilities based on evidence are used.

- In weather forecasting.
- In market research to predict what people might buy.
- By medical professionals to work out the risk of different people contracting a disease.
- By sports teams to work out the chance of a team or player winning their match.
- By insurance companies to work out life expectancy and health-related problems.
- By industry to work out the probability that a manufactured part might be faulty.

WORK IT OUT 19.2

A laboratory tested 500 batches of tablets and found four to be contaminated.

What is the probability that a batch of tablets produced in this laboratory is:

a contaminated?

b not contaminated?

Which of these options gives the correct answers? What is wrong with the answers in the other option?

Option A	Option B
a P(contaminated) $= \frac{4}{500} = 0.8\%$ **b** P(not contaminated) $= \frac{496}{500} = 92\%$	**a** P(contaminated) $= \frac{4}{500} = 0.008$ **b** P(not contaminated) $= 1 - 0.008 = 0.992$

EXERCISE 19D

1 Two groups of students drop a drawing pin and record how many times it lands point up or point down.

The results are:

	Point up	Point down
Group A	32	50
Group B	50	44

What is the experimental frequency of the drawing pin landing point up? Choose from the following options.

A $\dfrac{50 + 44}{32 + 50}$ B $\dfrac{32 + 50}{2}$ C $\dfrac{50 + 44}{50 + 44}$ D $\dfrac{32 + 50}{82 + 94}$

2 During the month of November it rained on 20 days.

If you chose a day at random in November, what is the probability that it rained on that day?

Choose from the options below.

A 0 B 1 C $\dfrac{1}{3}$ D $\dfrac{2}{3}$

3 A coin is tossed 60 times. It lands heads up 35 times.

What is the experimental probability of getting heads from this experiment?

4 Nathan threw balls of paper from his desk into the bin.

The paper balls landed in the bin 175 out of 200 throws.

What is the experimental probability that the paper will land in the bin the next time Nathan throws?

5 Nina and Maria made up a game with an eight-sided dice. The sides of the dice are labelled 6, 24, 9, 29, 15, 7, 18 and 12.

They take turns to roll the dice.

Nina wins the roll if the dice shows a multiple of 2.

Maria wins the roll if the dice shows a multiple of 3.

a Is this a fair game? Give a reason for your answer.

b What is the theoretical probability that the dice will show a multiple of 3?

6 Paul has six red T-shirts, a green T-shirt and a yellow T-shirt.

He says the probability of picking a red T-shirt at random is $\dfrac{6}{3}$ because there are three possible colours and six red T-shirts to choose from.

Paul's reasoning is incorrect. What words would you use to tell him where he had gone wrong?

7 Mrs Noonan drives a taxi on the same route every morning.

Over a period of 290 days, she has been stopped by a train crossing the road 58 times.

Calculate the experimental probability that she will be stopped by the train crossing on her morning route.

8 A pharmacist kept a record of the brand of painkiller bought by 80 customers in a month. These are her results:

Brand	Stopthepayne	Make-it-go-away	Painless	Generic
Frequency	27	22	20	11

a Based on this data, what is the experimental probability of a customer buying:

  i a generic painkiller?

  ii a 'Stopthepayne' painkiller?

b Do you think this data is enough to predict the brand of painkiller that would be chosen by most customers in Britain? Give a reason for your answer.

9 Another pharmacist only stocks the 'Make-it-go-away' brand and the generic brand.

He estimates that three times as many customers choose the 'Make-it-go-away' brand over the generic brand.

a A total of 381 customers chose the 'Make-it-go-away' brand.

Estimate how many customers chose the generic brand.

b Copy and complete this table.

Brand	Number sold	Relative frequency
Make-it-go-away	381	
Generic		
Total		

c Use the data in your table to estimate the probability that the next person who buys a painkiller will choose:

  i the 'Make-it-go-away' brand

  ii the generic brand.

10 Amy kept a record of the weather forecast for ten days and compared it with the actual weather on each day.

These are her results:

Day	Forecast	Actual weather	Was the forecast correct?
1	Rain	Rain	Yes
2	Some showers	Sunny and warm	No
3	Cloudy	Cloudy	Yes
4	Sunny and warm	Sunny and warm	Yes
5	Some showers	Sunny and warm	No
6	Some showers	Some showers	Yes
7	Cloudy and windy	Cloudy and windy	Yes
8	Rain	Rain	Yes
9	Sunny and warm	Some showers	No
10	Sunny and warm	Sunny and warm	Yes

a Calculate the experimental probability that the weather forecast is correct.

b What is the chance that the weather forecast is wrong?

c Amy is going for a hike the next day.

The weather forecast for that day is rain.

Should she take rain gear with her? Give reasons why or why not.

11 Mica lives in Edinburgh. She uses predictions from a specialist weather website and finds its forecasts to be accurate 99% of the time.

This is the meteogram she downloaded on the 24 March.

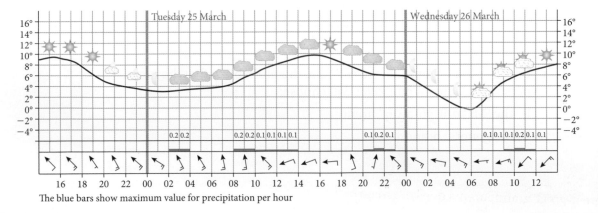

The blue bars show maximum value for precipitation per hour

Tip

You can do this activity using any weather forecasting website. You could compare two or more websites to see which one has the highest probability of being correct for your area.

a What information is shown on the graph?

b Mica can only work when it is not raining. Should she schedule her work for Tuesday?

c Choose a website to download the meteogram or long-term forecast for your area.

Decide how you will test the reliability of the data and work out how accurate it is for your area.

Organising outcomes – tables and frequency trees

Tables and simple diagrams can be used to record and organise information.

Frequency trees can be useful for doing this as well.

WORKED EXAMPLE 1

A doctor is interested in whether patients know the difference between having a cold and having the flu.

Out of 42 patients, 11 said they had a cold and 31 said they had the flu.

Only 19 of those who said they had the flu actually had flu,

Four of those who said they had a cold actually had the flu.

Construct a two-way table and a frequency tree to show this information.

Two-way table

Self diagnosis	Actual diagnosis	
	Cold	Flu
Cold	7	4
Flu	12	19

Frequency tree

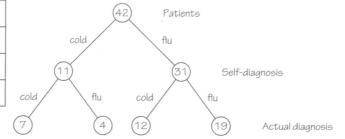

When you have organised data in two different ways, check that the numbers in your two-way table are the same as the numbers at the end of each branch of your frequency table.

Frequency trees

A frequency tree shows the actual frequency of different events.

Frequency trees allow you to understand and make sense of complicated probabilities.

The branches of the tree show the paths or decisions.

The 'leaves' show the actual number of data for each path.

Both the two-way table and the frequency tree in Worked Example 1 show the same information, but the frequency tree is clearer. It shows how many patients thought they had a cold or flu without you having to add the data in the table.

 Tip

Frequency trees are organisational tools and they are often used in computer programming (they are sometimes called binary trees). They are not the same as probability tree diagrams, that you will deal with in Chapter 24.

Find answers at: cambridge.org/ukschools/gcsemaths-studentbookanswers

EXERCISE 19E

1 A hotel chain keeps track of which customers make use of its in-house spa facilities.

Here are the results.

Gender	Use the spa	Don't use the spa
Female	780	232
Male	348	640

a Copy and complete this frequency tree to show this data.

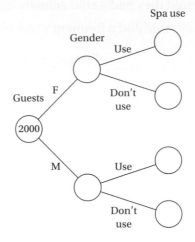

b Are male or female guests more likely to use the spa? Justify your answer.

2 Of 60 patients visiting a doctor's rooms, 42 are convinced they will need prescription medication.

The others think they probably won't need a prescription.

Of those who think they will need a prescription 13 do not actually need one.

Altogether, 36 patients need a prescription.

Copy and complete the frequency tree to show the actual numbers.

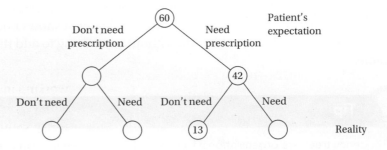

3 Eighty volunteers take an HIV-test to help the medical researchers work out how accurate the test is.

Of the volunteers, 17 people are HIV-positive, the rest are not.

The results show that one of the HIV-positive people gets a negative result on the test.

Two of the HIV-negative people get a positive result.

Draw a frequency tree to show the actual results.

Section 4: Mixed probability problems

In real life, people tend to use probability informally to explain things and to predict what will happen in the future. For example:

- "It is never sunny here in February."
- "Most people prefer to wear sandals in summer."
- "We are only selling 10 000 tickets so you have an excellent chance of winning the car."
- "Young people who haven't had a driving licence for very long have more accidents than older drivers."

Understanding probability allows you to think more critically about statements like these.

You can work out more accurately what the probability is of different things happening.

WORKED EXAMPLE 2

Zunaid read on a travel website that September was a good time to holiday in Italy because there was little chance of rain and the chance of sunny weather was high.

He went on the Internet and found the average weather for the first four weeks (28 days) of September.

Sunny days	Cloudy days	Rainy days
11	9	8

Was this claim correct?

The relative frequency of rainy days was $\frac{8}{28} = \frac{4}{14}$ or 28.6%. This is not such a low chance of rain. The relative frequency of sunny days was $\frac{11}{28} =$ 39.3%. This is less than an even chance of sun.

No, the claim is incorrect.

> Once you have finished your working make sure you answer the question.

Problem-solving framework

Sometimes the way a problem is worded can be confusing, but the actual calculations in probability are generally fairly simple additions or multiplications.

When you have to solve a word problem involving basic probability you can do this by organising your work and following the steps as shown in the example below.

Nazim is throwing a ball randomly at a wall on the side of a building.

The side of the building is 2 m high and 10 m wide.

There are three windows on the side of the building, each window is 2 m wide and 1 m high.

What is the probability that Nazim will hit a window when he throws the ball at the wall?

Express your answer as a percentage.

Steps for solving problems	What you would do for this example
Step 1: What are you trying to work out?	The probability of Nazim hitting any of the windows.
Step 2: What do you need to work out before you can find this?	The area of the wall and the area of the windows. Area of wall $= 10\,\text{m} \times 2\,\text{m} = 20\,\text{m}^2$ Area of windows $= 3 \times (2\,\text{m} \times 1\,\text{m}) = 3 \times 2\,\text{m}^2 = 6\,\text{m}^2$
Step 3: Apply the formula and calculate the probability. Convert the answer to a percentage.	$P(\text{hits window}) = \dfrac{6}{20} = \dfrac{3}{10}$ $\dfrac{3}{10} \times 100 = 30\%$
Step 4: Make sure you have answered the question and set out the solution clearly in the correct format.	There is a 30% probability that Nazim will hit a window.

EXERCISE 19F

1 A coin is tossed 20 times.

Busi claimed the coin was unfair because it landed on tails only 5 out of the 20 times.

She says the probability of getting tails when you toss a coin is 0.5, so if you toss the coin 20 times you should get $20 \times 0.5 = 10$ tails.

Was she correct? Give a reason for your answer.

2 Grey College has a sports tournament against St George's College every year.

The weather on the day of the tournament can be described as sunny and dry, cloudy and humid or rainy.

Grey College keeps a record of the weather on the day and whether the College won or drew the tournament. Here are its results for the past 30 years.

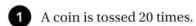

Weather	Wins	Draws	Tournaments played
Sunny and dry	4	1	7
Cloudy and humid	3	2	10
Rainy	3	3	13
Total	10	6	30

a What is the relative frequency of rain on tournament days?

b A student from Grey College says they have a better chance of winning if it is sunny.

Is this a correct statement? Give a reason for your answer.

c A student from St George's says they have an almost even chance of winning the tournament, no matter what the weather.

Is this a correct statement? Give a reason for your answer.

d Calculate the experimental probability that Grey College will draw a tournament.

3 An eight-sided dice has sides coloured red, blue, green, black and white.

If the probability of the dice landing on red is $\frac{1}{4}$, choose the true statement from the following options.

A Four sides are red.   B One out of five sides is red.

C Two sides must be red.   D There are more red sides than black sides.

4 Two coins are tossed 100 times in a trial.

The experimental probability of getting two heads is found to be $\frac{3}{10}$.

What does this mean? Choose the correct statement.

A Every third toss resulted in two heads.   B Two heads came up three times.

C Two heads came up 30 times.   D The coins are biased.

5 The chart below is a ten-day weather forecast in April for Cardiff.

Today	Sun 8	Mon 9	Tue 10	Wed 11	Thu 12	Fri 13	Sat 14	Sun 15	Mon 16
Rain	Showers	Sunny	Sunny	Sunny	Sunny	Partly cloudy	Mostly sunny	Cloudy	Scattered showers
Chance of rain:									
100%	80%	10%	0%	0%	0%	0%	0%	10%	30%

a What is the probability that it will rain on:

i Sunday 8 April   **ii** Sunday 15 April?

b Write down what you understand by 100% probability of rain.

c Rhys wants to go hiking on Monday 9 April.

Should he pack rain clothes? Give a reason for your answer.

d The 10-day forecast for Plymouth for this period shows a 0% probability of rain every day.

Does this mean it definitely won't rain in Plymouth in this period? Give a reason why or why not.

Find answers at: cambridge.org/ukschools/gcsemaths-studentbookanswers

Tip

A false-positive in a drug test means that a person who is not using drugs tests positive for drug use.

6　A local educational authority wants to introduce random drug testing in secondary schools.

It claims the tests have a very small false-positive rate of one half of one per cent.

a Express one half of one per cent as a decimal.

b A school has a total of 800 students.

Some parents claim that four students at the school could incorrectly test positive for drug use.

Are the parents concerns valid? Give a reason why or why not.

c There were 3 831 937 secondary school students included in the drug testing.

How many of them would you expect to be incorrectly accused of being drug users?

7　In a drugs test, 1% of the athletes tested are actually using prohibited drugs.

If an athlete is using prohibited drugs, 90% of the time he or she will fail the drug test.

Of the athletes who are **not** using prohibited drugs, 10% will also fail the drug test even though they are not using drugs.

a Copy and complete this table to show how many athletes will pass or fail the drug test for every 1000 athletes tested.

Status	Test positive (i.e. fail drug test)	Test negative (i.e. pass drug test)	Total
Athletes who are using illegal substances			10
Athletes who are not using illegal substances			990
Total			1000

b Represent the same information on a frequency tree.

c An athlete tests positive for the illegal substance.

What is the probability that she is not actually using the substance? Give your answer as a percentage.

d Another athlete tests negative for the illegal substance. Is it certain that he is not using them? Give a reason for your answer.

8 Eighty people are asked if they can tell the difference between butter and margarine.

The results are: 37 say they can, 24 say no and 19 say they are not sure.

The interviewer then carries out a blind taste test.

Of those who said they could tell the difference, 14 got it wrong.

Of those who said no, 9 got it right.

Of those who said they were not sure, 14 got it wrong.

Draw a frequency tree to show the outcomes of this experiment.

9 Lee and Haroon want to know what the probability is of getting two heads when you toss two coins one after the other.

Lee says it is 25% and Haroon says it is $33\frac{1}{3}$%.

They decide to do an experiment in which they toss five different sets of two coins and record the outcomes.

a List all the outcomes possible when you toss two coins.

b Complete this table to show the results of Lee and Haroon's experiment.

Set of coins	Number of tosses	Number of times we got two heads	Running total of two heads	Percentage of two heads (running total)
Two 10p coins	25	6	6	$\frac{6}{25} \times 100 = 24$
Two 50p coins	25	8		
Two £1 coins	25	5		
Two £2 coins	25	7		
Two 20p coins	25	9		

c What type of probability have they recorded?

d According to their results, what is the relative frequency of getting two heads?

e Do their results settle their argument? Give reasons why or why not?

10 Lee finds a computer program that simulates coin tosses.

He does a trial tossing the two coins 1000 times.

The computer produces this graph of his results.

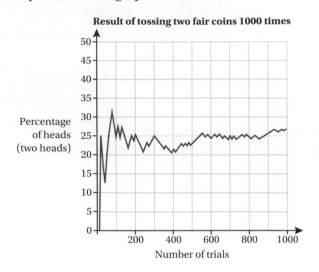

Result of tossing two fair coins 1000 times

a What does the graph show?

b What does the yellow line on the graph represent?

c Why does the other line vary up and down?

d What happens to the line showing the results as the number of trials increases?

e How does this graph help to settle the argument between Lee and Haroon?

 ## Checklist of learning and understanding

Range of probabilities

- The probability scale ranges from 0 to 1. Impossible events have a probability of 0 and certain events have a probability of 1. It is not possible to have a negative probability (< 0) or a probability greater than 1.
- Probabilities between 0 and 1 can be expressed as fractions, decimals or percentages.

Theoretical probability

- Probability of an event $= \dfrac{\text{number of favourable outcomes}}{\text{total number of outcomes}}$

Sum of probabilities and complementary events

- The sum of probabilities will always total 1.
- The probability of an event happening is equal to 1 minus the probability that the event will not happen. $P(\text{not } E) = 1 - P(E)$.

Experimental probability and relative frequency

- Experimental probability tells you how often a favourable outcome occurs in an experiment.

  Experimental probability $= \dfrac{\text{relative frequency of favourable outcomes}}{\text{number of possible outcomes}}$
- Tables and frequency trees can be used to organise the outcomes of different experiments.

- Statistical data can be used to give relative frequencies of particular events. The relative frequency of an event can be used to predict future outcomes.

Mutually exclusive events

- Mutually exclusive events cannot happen at the same time. For example, you cannot throw a 1 and a 5 at the same time when you roll one dice.

 Chapter review

 For additional questions on the topics in this chapter, visit GCSE Mathematics Online.

1. The probability of choosing a green sweet from a packet is found to be 0.3. There are 20 identical sweets in the packet. How many of them are green? Choose your answer from the options below.

   A 3   B 6   C 6.6   D 30

2. Sharon is playing a game and she needs to roll a six on a dice to start.

   What is the probability of her rolling a six on her first go? Choose the correct answer from the given options.

   A $\frac{1}{6}$ B $\frac{5}{6}$ C $\frac{6}{6}$ D 0

3. A box contains 30 red, 40 white, 2 brown and 8 green beads.

   One bead is chosen at random.

   What is the probability that it will be:

   a white?   **b** not green?   **c** brown or green?

4. A bag contains only red counters and blue counters.

   There are 6 more red than blue.

   A counter is chosen at random from the bag.

   The probability it is blue is $\frac{1}{4}$.

   How many red counters are in the bag?   *(3 marks)*

   © AQA 2013

5. Imogen rolled a dice 200 times. She recorded her results in this table.

Result	1	2	3	4	5	6
Frequency	28	20	20	40	36	56
Experimental probability						

   a Copy the table and complete it by calculating the experimental probability of each result.

   b What is the relative frequency of rolling an odd number?

   c The theoretical probability of rolling a four is $\frac{1}{6}$.

   Compare this with Imogen's data. Suggest why the two probabilities might be different.

6 Will interviews 64 people to get their opinions about sending texts when in company.

Of those interviewed, 44 say it is rude to send texts in company.

Will then observes the people at a large event.

Of those who said it was rude to send texts in company, 13 sent texts when at the table with others.

Of those who said it was acceptable, 9 did not send texts when in company.

Complete the frequency tree to show this data.

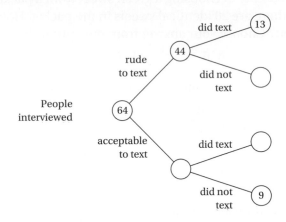

7 A company tests a new brand of soap and produces the following data.

Number of participants	Developed a rash	Did not develop a rash
2500	180	2320

a Use these results to work out the probability of using this soap and developing a rash.

b The company decides to print the following warning statement on the soap:

'7% of people who use this soap might develop a rash.'

i Is the statement correct?

ii Suggest why the company would use a percentage rather than giving the number of people who developed a rash.

iii If 100 people used this soap, how many of them would you expect to develop a rash?

iv Give a reason why the word 'expect' is used in part **iii** above.

20 3D objects

In this chapter you will learn how to ...

- apply what you already know about the properties of 3D objects.
- work with 2D representations of 3D objects.
- construct and interpret plans and elevations of 3D objects.

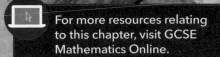

For more resources relating to this chapter, visit GCSE Mathematics Online.

Using mathematics: real-life applications

Buildings, engine parts, vehicles and packaging are all carefully planned and designed before they are built or made. Most design work starts on paper or screen using two-dimensional images to represent the final three-dimensional objects.

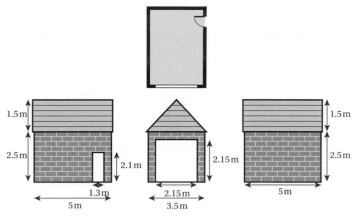

"No one will buy an apartment that isn't built yet if they don't know what it is going to look like. When we sell a development we show people floor plans as well as elevations from all four sides. Sometimes we also have a 3D scale model of the development." *(Estate agent)*

Before you start ...

KS3 Ch 8	You must be able to identify and name some common 3D objects.	**1** Name each of these 3D objects. **a** **b** **c** **d**
Ch 8	You should know the basic properties of polygons and other 3D objects.	**2** True or false? Correct the false statements. **a** A cube has 4 faces. **b** A cube has 12 edges. **c** A cuboid has 8 vertices.
KS3 Ch 32	You must be able to accurately construct lines and angles using your ruler and a pair of compasses.	**3** Construct and bisect a right angle ABC.

Find answers at: cambridge.org/ukschools/gcsemaths-studentbookanswers

Assess your starting point using the Launchpad

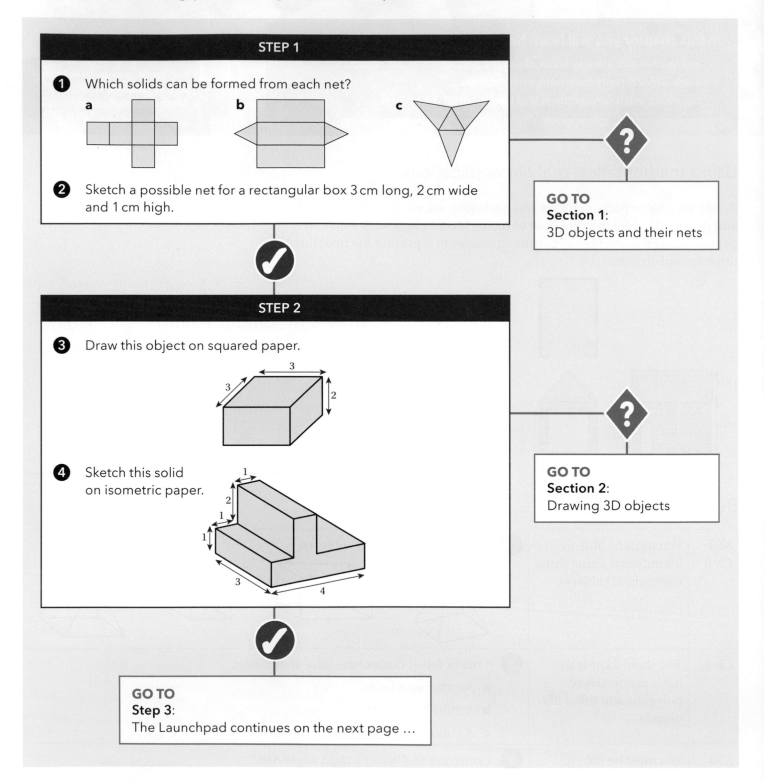

STEP 1

1 Which solids can be formed from each net?

a   b   c

2 Sketch a possible net for a rectangular box 3 cm long, 2 cm wide and 1 cm high.

GO TO
Section 1:
3D objects and their nets

STEP 2

3 Draw this object on squared paper.

3
3
2

4 Sketch this solid on isometric paper.

1
2
1
1
3
4

GO TO
Section 2:
Drawing 3D objects

GO TO
Step 3:
The Launchpad continues on the next page …

Launchpad continued ...

STEP 3

5 Which is the plan view for this square-based pyramid?

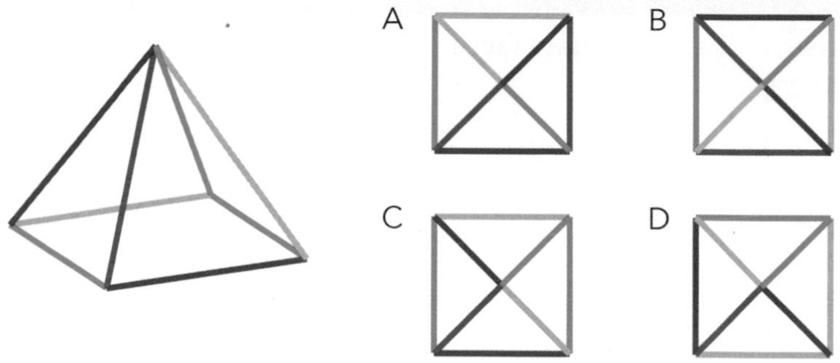

A

B

C

D

6 Draw the plan view, front and right side elevation of each shape on squared paper.

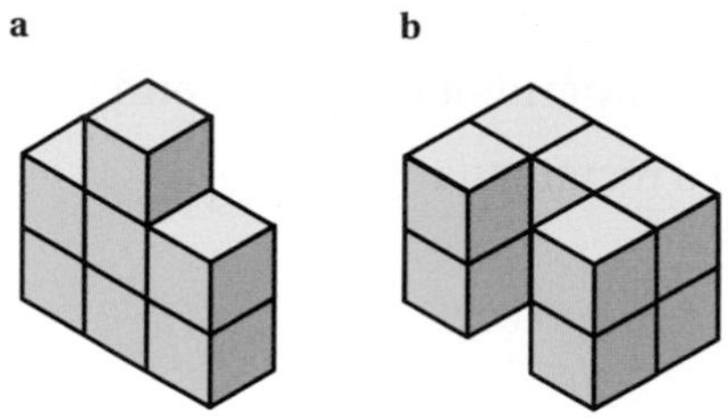

a

b

? GO TO
Section 3:
Plan and elevation views

✓ GO TO
Chapter review

Section 1: 3D objects and their nets

A polyhedron is a 3D shape made up of flat faces. The plural of polyhedron is polyhedra.

The table summarises the main properties of different polyhedra.

Polyhedron	Faces	Vertices	Edges
Cube (square prism)	6 square faces	8	12
Cuboid (rectangular prism)	2 congruent rectangular end faces 2 congruent side rectangular faces 2 congruent rectangular top and bottom faces	8	12
Triangular prism	2 congruent triangular end faces 3 rectangular faces	6	9
Pentagonal prism	2 congruent pentagonal end faces 5 rectangular faces	10	15
Triangular pyramid	1 triangular base 3 triangular faces that meet at an apex	4	6
Square-based pyramid	1 square base 4 triangular faces that meet at an apex	5	8

Tip

Shapes are **congruent** if all their corresponding measurements are equal. You will learn more about congruent shapes in Chapter 34.

Cylinders, cones and spheres are also 3D shapes but they are not classified as polyhedra because they are not formed of flat faces that are polygons.

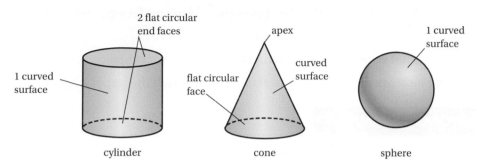

Nets of 3D objects

A **net** is a 2D representation of a 3D shape. You can fold up a net to make the 3D shape.

For printed packaging the design is printed on to the net, and then the net is folded up to make the box itself.

A cube has six square faces. There are 11 possible ways of arranging the faces to make the net of a cube.

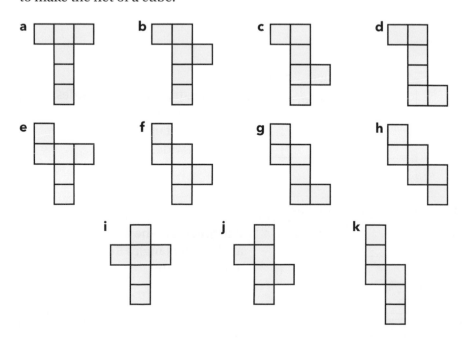

Did you know?

The parts of a car body are cut from sheets of steel or aluminium. The way in which multiple nets can be placed on the sheet metal prevents wastage and helps a company to be efficient.

Find answers at: cambridge.org/ukschools/gcsemaths-studentbookanswers

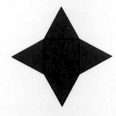

You can use the properties of a 3D shape to help you recognise nets and identify the shapes they will make.

This net shows that the object has one square face and four triangular faces.

It is the net of a square-based pyramid.

When this net is folded up, the triangular faces will meet at a common point.

You can also use the properties to sketch or construct the net of a shape.

Tip

When you draw a net, always start in the middle of the page to give yourself space to construct all the faces.

WORKED EXAMPLE 1

Construct an accurate net of this rectangular prism.

2 cm   3 cm   5 cm

	side	
front	bottom	back
	side	
	top	

You know that a cuboid has six rectangular faces, so your net will have six faces.

Draw a rough sketch to start with.

To construct an accurate net you need to use the measurements given on the diagram.

Use a ruler and pencil to draw the net.

5 cm
3 cm

Draw the bottom face first. This is a rectangle 3 cm wide and 5 cm long.

2 cm   5 cm   2 cm
3 cm

Next construct two of the sides that join on to the bottom. These are both rectangles 3 cm long and 2 cm wide.

2 cm
2 cm   5 cm   2 cm
3 cm
2 cm

Construct the other two sides that join on to the bottom. These are both rectangles 5 cm long and 2 cm wide.

Continues on next page …

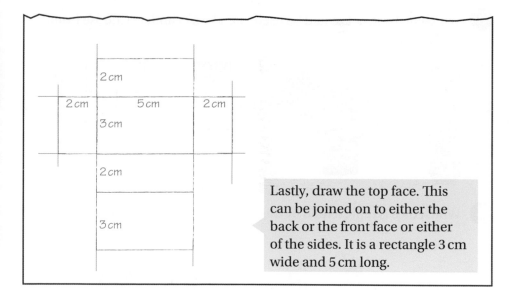

Lastly, draw the top face. This can be joined on to either the back or the front face or either of the sides. It is a rectangle 3 cm wide and 5 cm long.

Tip

More on construction is covered in Chapter 32.

EXERCISE 20A

1 Describe each object fully by referring to its properties. State whether it is a polyhedron or not, giving a reason for your decision.

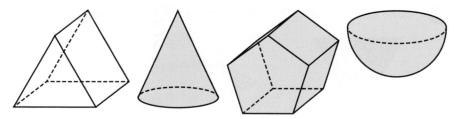

2 Which 3D shape can be created from the net shown below? Choose from the options given.

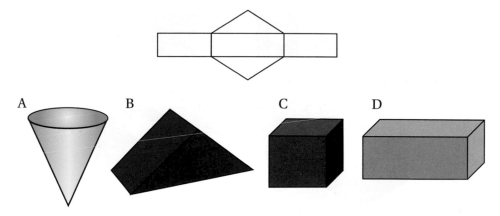

A   B   C   D

3 Which of these nets could be used to make a cylinder? Choose from A, B C or D.

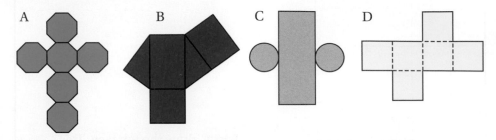

A B C D

4 Which dice is represented by this net? Choose from the options given.

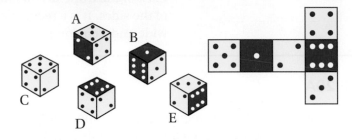

A B C D E

5 Name the 3D shapes that can be formed from each net.

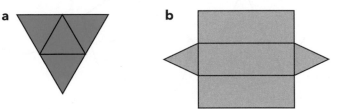

a b

6 The six faces of a cube are shown.

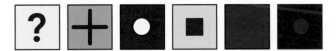

Here are three different views of the cube.

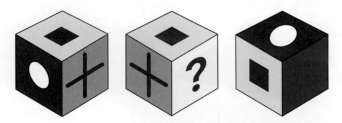

Here is the net of the cube. Only one of the faces has been recorded.

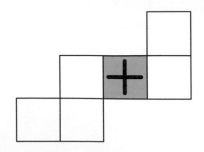

Copy and complete the net.

7 Here are some possible arrangements of five square faces.

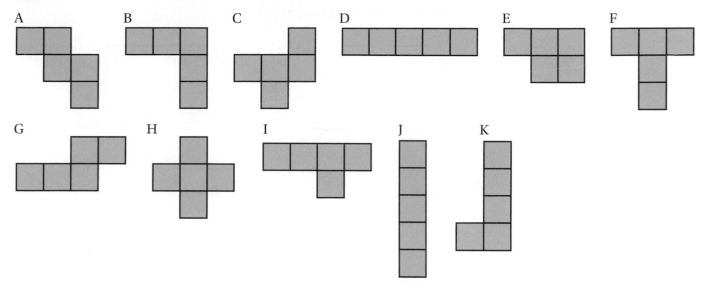

a Which of these nets cannot be folded up to form an open box?

b Draw one more net for an open box. Make sure your net is not just a turned or flipped over version of the ones shown here.

Section 2: Drawing 3D objects

You need to be able to draw 3D objects and to interpret and make sense of drawings of 3D objects from different perspectives.

There are a number of ways of drawing 3D objects to show their features in 2D.

Prisms and cylinders using end faces

Draw prisms and cylinders by visualising the position of their end faces and drawing these first.

When you draw a cylinder you use ovals for the faces to get a more realistic drawing.

Then join the end faces by drawing lines to represent the edges.

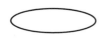
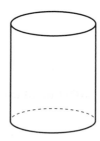
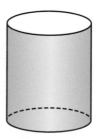

First draw the two circular end faces by drawing ovals.

Then draw in two lines to join the end faces.

Shading can make the cylinder look more realistic.

For prisms make sure you match up the corresponding vertices.

To draw a cuboid (rectangular prism):

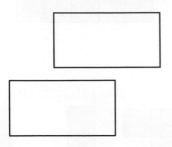 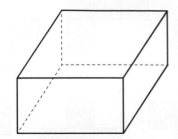

First draw two
rectangular faces.

Then draw lines to
join the vertices.

To draw a triangular prism:

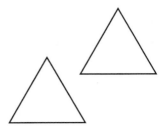 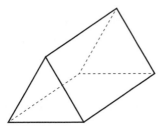

First draw the two
triangular end faces.

Then draw lines to
join the vertices.

The same process can be used for any shaped prism.

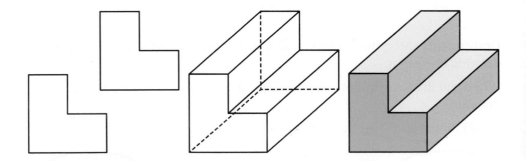

Prisms and pyramids from parallel lines

You can draw square and rectangular prisms and square-based pyramids using two pairs of parallel lines as a starting point.

To draw a prism:

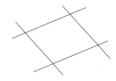 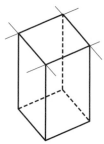

Begin by drawing two pairs of parallel lines that intersect.

Then draw three lines of equal length down (or up) from the intersections. Complete the shape by joining the ends to make a prism.

To draw a square-based pyramid:

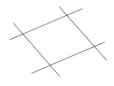 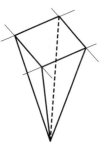 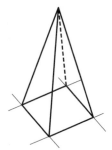

Start by drawing two pairs of parallel lines.

Mark a point and draw lines from three intersections of the parallel lines to the point.

You can also draw the point above (or to the side) of the parallel lines.

Drawing shapes on squared or isometric grids

Three-dimensional (3D) objects can be drawn on squared or isometric grids.

The grid might be made from dots or from faintly printed lines.

The diagram shows a cube and a cuboid drawn on a square grid.

The vertical lines on the grid are used to represent the vertical edges of the 3D object.
You draw along the lines at an angle on the paper to represent the horizontal edges of the 3D object.

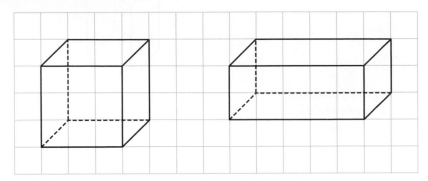

Key vocabulary

isometric grid: special drawing paper based on an arrangement of triangles

This diagram shows the same objects drawn on an **isometric grid**.

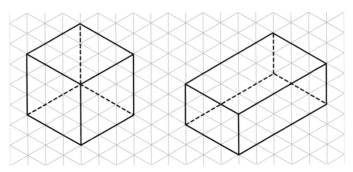

When you draw shapes on both square and isometric grids you use broken lines to show the edges that would not be seen if you viewed the shape from that angle.

You can use squared or isometric grids to draw 3D objects using the end faces or parallel lines method. The grid makes it easier for you to make sure that the end faces are the same size.

The diagrams show a cuboid drawn on a square grid and a hexagonal prism drawn on an isometric grid.

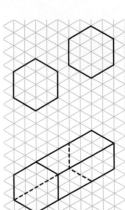

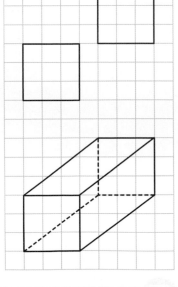

Tip

Be very careful to join up corresponding vertices.

Isometric drawings

Isometric drawings are used to visually represent three-dimensional objects in two dimensions in technical and engineering drawings.

This diagram shows the design of an engineering component on isometric paper.

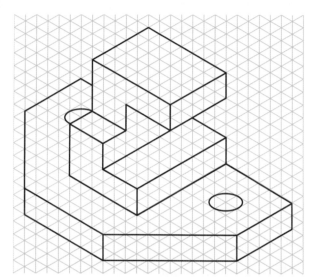

Isometric paper is very useful for drawing solids built from cubes.

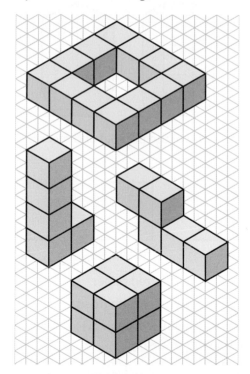

WORK IT OUT 20.1

Students were asked to draw this view of a shape on an isometric grid.

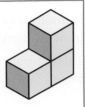

This is how they started their sketches.

Student A	Student B	Student C

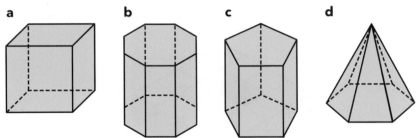

Which student is likely to end up with the correct view of the shape?

What are the others doing incorrectly?

EXERCISE 20B

1   Draw the following objects without using a grid.

    a   **b**   **c**   **d**

2   The diagram shows one of the parallel end faces of three different prisms.

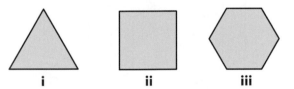

    a Sketch each prism on squared paper.

    b Use isometric paper to draw each prism.

    c Compare the two drawings of each prism. What effect does the grid you use have on your drawing?

3   Draw the following shapes on an isometric grid.

    a   **b**   **c**

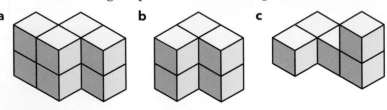

4 The diagrams show different shapes made from cubes. There are no cubes missing from the layers you cannot see.

State how many cubes you need to build each shape.

a
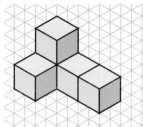

b
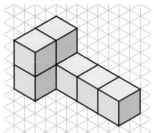

c
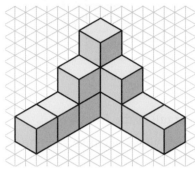

d
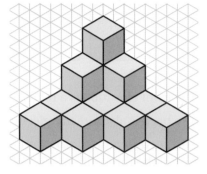

Section 3: Plan and elevation views

A **plan view** shows a 3D object from directly above.

You can also view objects from the front, sides or back.

The **front elevation** is the view from the front of the object.

The **side elevation** is the view from the side of the object.

This diagram shows the plan view, front elevation and the left side elevation of a shape built out of cubes.

 Key vocabulary

plan view: the view of an object from directly above

elevation view: the view of an object from the front, side or back

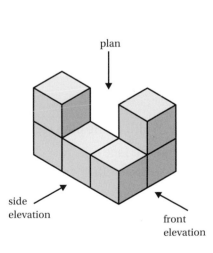

side elevation

front elevation

plan

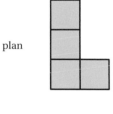

plan

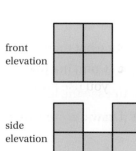

front elevation

side elevation

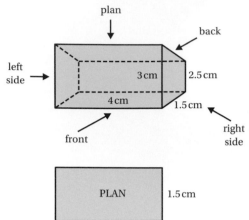

The shape in the margin is a prism with trapezium-shaped ends. The front is higher than the back.

The plan view is a rectangle. Even though the top of the object slopes down to the back, it looks like a rectangle from directly above.

The plan view is normally drawn above the front view because the two views will be the same width.

In a prism, the left and right elevations are reflections of each other. They are drawn on the left side and right side of the front elevation.

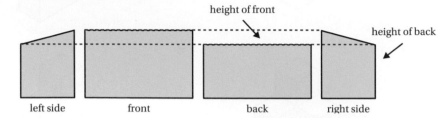

The front elevation is a rectangle.

The back is also a rectangle, but it is not at tall as the front.

You get different information from different views because each one shows two of the three dimensions of the solid.

- The plan view shows the length and width of the solid.
- The front view shows the length and height of the solid.
- The side views show the width and height of the solid.

When you draw plans or elevations you show any changes in height as solid lines. Use dotted lines to indicate any hidden edges.

WORKED EXAMPLE 2

Draw the plan, front and side elevations of this solid.

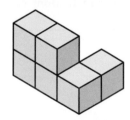

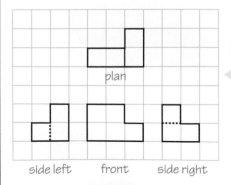

Start by drawing the plan view.

Next, draw the front view below it. It will be same width as the plan view.

Work out what the right side will look like if you view it face on.

Draw it next to the front view. It will be same height.

You can't see the left view, so you have to visualise it.

Draw it in the correct place.

When you draw views of a shape, you have to think quite carefully about what the parts you cannot see clearly will look like.

For example, look at the shape below. It is built from four cubes.

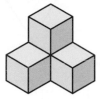

You can only see three cubes. You have to work out that the fourth one is supporting the 'top' cube.

EXERCISE 20C

1 Select the correct plan view of each object from the options given.

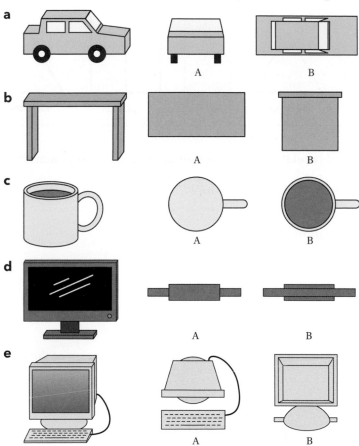

a

A   B

b

A   B

c

A   B

d

A   B

e

A   B

2 a Match each shape to its plan and elevation image.

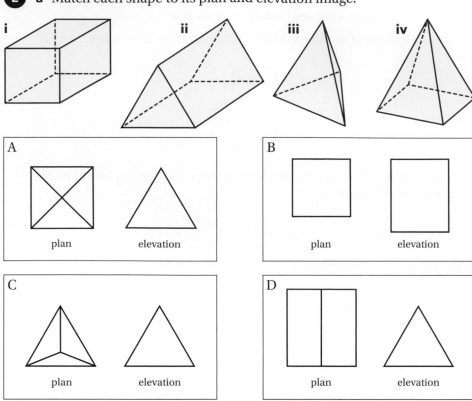

i   ii   iii   iv

A

plan   elevation

B

plan   elevation

C

plan   elevation

D

plan   elevation

b Sketch and label the elevations that are not shown for each shape.

3 For each coloured set of cubes, draw:

a a plan

b a front elevation

c a right side elevation (from the right-hand side).

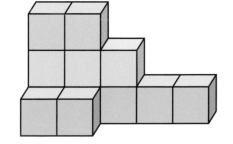

4 Draw the plan, the front elevation and the side elevation of the shape below.

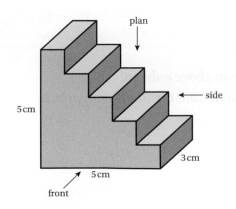

plan

side

5 cm

5 cm

3 cm

front

5 The plan view and elevations of different solids are shown.

Use these to work out what each solid looks like and draw it on an isometric grid.

a

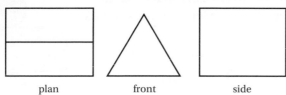

plan   front   side

b

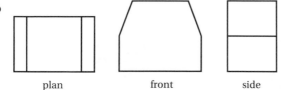

plan   front   side

c

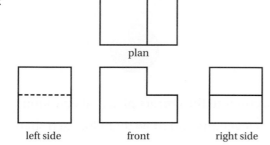

plan

left side   front   right side

 Checklist of learning and understanding

Properties of 3D shapes

- Prisms are shapes with congruent polygonal faces and a regular cross-section.
- Pyramids have a base and triangular sides that meet at an apex.
- Cylinders, cones and spheres are 3D shapes, but they are not polyhedra.
- The number and shape of the faces and the number of edges and vertices can be used to identify and name shapes.

2D representations of 3D shapes

- 3D shapes can be drawn on squared or isometric grids.
- Hidden edges are shown as dotted lines.

Plans and elevations

- A plan is a view from above a shape.
- An elevation is a view from the front, sides or back of a shape.

Find answers at: cambridge.org/ukschools/gcsemaths-studentbookanswers

For additional questions on the topics in this chapter, visit GCSE Mathematics Online.

Chapter review

1 The diagram shows the net of a 3D shape. Name the shape, choosing your answer from the options below.

A Sphere   B Cone

C Triangular prism   D Cylinder

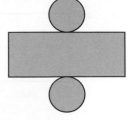

2 Give the mathematical name for the 3D object formed from each net.

a

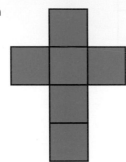

b

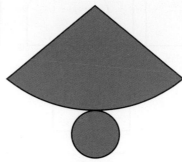

3 a Match each block of cubes to the correct plan and elevation.

b Identify any missing elevations and draw them for each shape.

i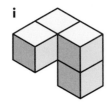

ii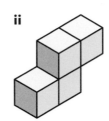

iii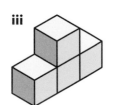

iv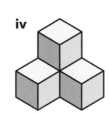

A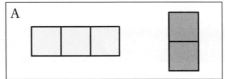

B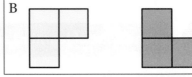

C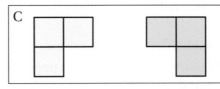

D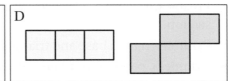

4 The plan and elevation of a solid built from cubes is shown here. Work out what the solid looks like and sketch it accurately on an isometric grid.

Plan

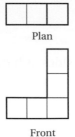

Front

Side

5 This is the left side and front elevation of a solid built from cubes.

   a Draw one possible plan view of this shape.

   b Draw a plan view that is not possible for this shape.

   c State the least and greatest number of cubes that the shape could be built from to have these elevations.

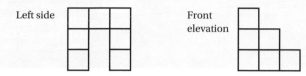

Left side   Front elevation

6 This shape is made from five cubes.

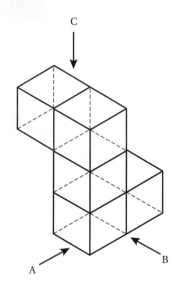

Copy these grids and draw what the shape looks like when seen from A, B and C

    From A   From B   From C

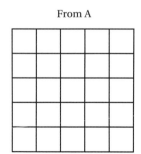
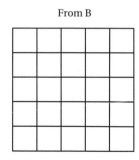
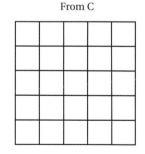

(3 marks)

© AQA 2013

21 Units and measure

In this chapter you will learn how to ...

- work with and convert standard units of measurement.
- use and convert compound units of measurement.
- work with map scales and bearings.
- construct and use scale diagrams to solve problems.

 For more resources relating to this chapter, visit GCSE Mathematics Online.

Using mathematics: real-life applications

Measurement has practical applications in many different jobs, but is it also important in everyday activities. Being able to read and work with measurements is important when you make or alter clothes, work out what materials you need to build things and weigh ingredients to make a recipe.

> **Tip**
>
> **Think units!**
>
> It is important to consider the units in which you are working. Always look back to the original question to decide on the units. With a formula, whatever units you put in must equal the units that come out.

"I use accurate measurements to work out the scale when I draw maps. The people who use maps need to understand the scale so that they can make sense of map distances."
(Cartographer)

Before you start ...

KS3 Ch 6	You must be able to multiply and divide using multiples of 10.	**1**	Work out: **a** 1000×10 **b** $10 \div 1000$ **c** $100 \div 1000$
KS3 Ch 7	You should be able to substitute numbers into a simple formula.	**2**	Use this formula to work out the pay of each person: $p = h \times r$ where p is the pay earned, h is the number of hours worked and r is the rate of pay per hour. **a** Amelia: 20 hours worked at £7 per hour. **b** Billy: 15 hours worked at £6 per hour. **c** Catrin: 40 hours worked at £5.50 per hour.
KS3	You should be able to solve problems involving direct proportion.	**3**	Six pencils cost 90p. Work out the cost of: **a** 12 pencils **b** 1 pencil **c** 4 pencils.

Assess your starting point using the Launchpad

STEP 1

1 Convert:

   a 11 569 grams into kilograms

   b $4\frac{1}{2}$ hours into seconds

   c 123 000 pence into pounds (£)

   d $5\,cm^2$ into m^2.

GO TO
Section 1:
Standard units of measurement

STEP 2

2 A car travels 16 kilometres in 20 minutes.

   a What is the average speed of the car in kilometres per hour?

   b Express this speed in m/s.

3 An object is travelling at a speed of 25 metres per second.

   Express this as a speed in kilometres per hour.

GO TO
Section 2:
Compound units of measurement

STEP 3

4 A helicopter is drawn using a scale of 1 : 100.

   On the scale drawing the length of the helicopter blade is 8 cm.

   How long is the actual blade?

5 The helicopter takes off from a point X and flies due north for 30 km to reach point Y.

   It then flies on a bearing of 150° for 15 km to reach point Z.

   a Use a scale of 1 cm to represent 10 km to make a scale drawing showing the helicopter's journey.

   b Use your diagram to find the bearing from X to Z.

   c Calculate the actual distance directly between X and Z.

GO TO
Section 3:
Maps, scale drawings and bearings

GO TO
Chapter review

Find answers at: cambridge.org/ukschools/gcsemaths-studentbookanswers

Did you know?

The USA, Liberia and Myanmar are the only three countries in the world that do not officially use the metric system of measurement. All other countries have adopted the metric system.

Section 1: Standard units of measurement

Standard metric units of measurement are used for recording length, area, volume, capacity, mass, and money.

In the metric system, units of measurement are divided into sub-units.

Each sub-unit is 10 times bigger than the one before it.

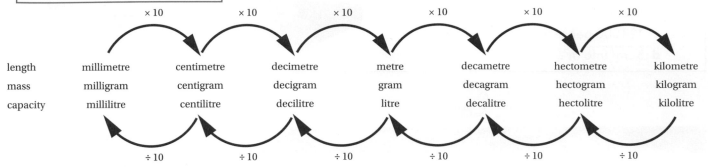

Tip

When you convert from a smaller to a larger unit there are fewer of the larger units, so you divide by a power of 10.
When you convert from a larger to a smaller unit there are more of the smaller units, so you multiply by a power of 10.

Converting between units

To convert between units in the metric system you need to multiply or divide by powers of 10.

Converting from centimetres to metres is across two sub-units.

So here you have to multiply or divide by $10^2 = 100$.

You will use the following conversions often, so it useful to remember them.

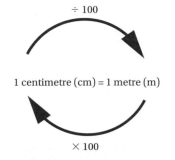

1 centimetre (cm) = 10 millimetres (mm)

1 metre (m) = 100 centimetres (cm)

1 kilometre (km) = 1000 metres (m)

1 kilogram (kg) = 1000 grams (g)

1 tonne (t) = 1000 kilograms (kg)

1 litre (l) = 1000 millilitres (ml)

1 litre (l) = 1000 cubic centimetres (cm³)

1 cubic centimetre (cm³) = 1 millilitre (ml)

WORK IT OUT 21.1

In a sponsored swim the total number of lengths swum is 94.

Each length is 25 metres.

How many kilometres were swum in total?

Which of the answers below is correct?

Option A	Option B	Option C
Total number of metres = 25 × 94 = 2350 metres Conversion: 100 metres = 1 km 2350 ÷ 100 = 23.5 km swum in total.	Total number of metres = 25 × 94 = 2350 metres Conversion: 100 metres = 1 km 2350 × 100 = 235 000 km swum in total.	Total number of metres = 25 × 94 = 2350 metres Conversion: 1000 metres = 1 km 2350 ÷ 1000 = 2.35 km swum in total.

Converting areas and volume

Area is measured in square units, such as mm² (square millimetres), cm², m² or km², so any conversion factor also has to be squared.

For example, the two squares below have the same area.

The conversion factor from m² to cm², and vice versa, is 10 000.

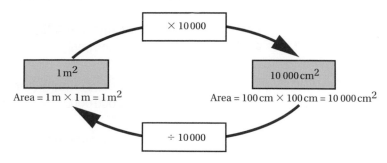

WORKED EXAMPLE 1

Convert each measure to the units given.

a 10 m² to cm² **b** 8.6 km² to m² **c** 3500 mm² to cm²

a 10 m² to cm²
$= 10 \times 10\,000 = 100\,000\,\text{cm}^2$

> Conversion factor = 10 000.

b 8.6 km² to m²
$= 8.6 \times 1\,000\,000 = 8\,600\,000\,\text{m}^2$

> Conversion factor = 1 000 000.

c 3500 mm² to cm²
$= 3500 \div 100 = 35\,\text{cm}^2$

> Conversion factor = 100.

Volume is measured in cubic units such as mm³ (cubic millimetres), cm³ or m³ so any conversion factor also has to be cubed.

For example, the two cubes below have the same volume.

The conversion factor from m³ to cm³, and vice versa, is 1 000 000.

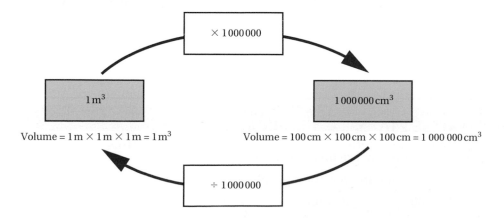

When referring to the volume of liquids, the term capacity is used. Capacity is generally measured in litres or millilitres.

WORKED EXAMPLE 2

Convert each measurement to the units given.

a $6.3\,m^3$ to cm^3 **b** $96\,500\,000\,cm^3$ to m^3 **c** $750\,cm^3$ to mm^3

a $6.3\,m^3$ to cm^3
$= 6.3 \times 1\,000\,000 = 6\,300\,000\,cm^3$

> Conversion factor = $1\,000\,000$.

b $96\,500\,000\,cm^3$ to m^3
$= 96\,500\,000 \div 1\,000\,000 = 96.5\,m^3$

> Conversion factor = $1\,000\,000$.

c $750\,cm^3$ to mm^3
$= 750 \times 1000 = 750\,000\,mm^3$

> Conversion factor = 1000.

It is easy to make mistakes if you try to calculate with measurements in different units, so it makes sense to convert them all to the same unit before doing any calculations.

WORKED EXAMPLE 3

A builder is putting a cornice around the ceiling of a room. This is a decorative strip that hides the join between the walls and the ceiling.

A plan of the room is shown to the right.

How many metres of cornice does the builder need?

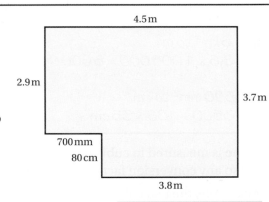

$80\,cm \div 100 = 0.8\,m$
$700\,mm \div 1000 = 0.7\,m$
Total distance around room:
$2.9 + 4.5 + 3.7 + 3.8 + 0.8 + 0.7 = 16.4\,m$
The builder needs $16.4\,m$ of decorative strip.

> As the answer needs to be given in metres, it makes sense to convert all the measurements to metres.

Tip

You will use measurement conversions in Section 3, which covers scale drawings and maps.

EXERCISE 21A

1 How many cm^3 are there in $4.5\,m^3$?

Choose your answer from the following options.

A 4500   B 45 000   C 450 000   D 4 500 000

2 Look at the table in the margin. Match each measurement on the left to the equivalent measurement on the right.

10 000 mm	10 l
10 000 ml	10 g
10 kg	10 m
0.01 kg	1 mm
0.1 cm	10 000 g

3 Convert the following lengths and masses into the given units to complete the following.

a 2.5 km = ☐ m   **b** 85 cm = ☐ mm   **c** 34 m = ☐ mm

d 1.55 m = ☐ mm   **e** 0.07 m = ☐ cm   **f** 5.4 kg = ☐ g

g 0.9 kg = ☐ g   **h** 102 g = ☐ kg   **i** 14.5 g = ☐ kg

4 Add the following capacities.

Give your answers in the units indicated in brackets.

a 3.5 l + 5 l (ml)   **b** 2.3 l + 450 ml (l)   **c** 20 l + 4.5 l + 652 ml (l)

5 Sadie uses concrete slabs to form a border around a rectangular garden.

The garden is 450 cm wide and 5.5 m long.

a Draw a diagram to represent the garden.

b Calculate the perimeter of the garden in metres.

c The concrete slabs are 120 cm long.

How many will Sadie need to form the border?

d The slabs cost £4.55 each.

Work out how much it will cost Sadie to buy the slabs she needs.

e What is the cost per metre for the concrete border?

6 Convert each of the following into the required units.

a Total mass in kg of 3 bags of flour, each of mass 1200 g.

b The length in cm of a whale 7.763 m long.

c 3567 kg of lead into tonnes.

d Area of 5 m² into mm².

e 96.35 m³ of sand into cm³.

f 345 cm³ of water into litres.

Tip

1 metric tonne is equal to 1000 kg

Time

The units of time we use on a daily basis are not decimal units.

To convert units of time you have to work out how many sub-units there are in the units you are working with.

Time is sometimes given in decimal form, for example 4.8 hours.

You can convert these times back to ordinary units in different ways.

There are 60 minutes in an hour, so

     4.8 × 60 minutes = 288 minutes = 4 hours 48 minutes

Or, you can think of this as 4 hours and 0.8 hours.

     0.8 × 60 = 48, so the time is 4 hours and 48 minutes

Tip

1 year = 365 days (366 in a leap year)

1 day = 24 hours = 1440 minutes

1 hour = 60 minutes = 3600 seconds

1 minute = 60 seconds

Calculator tip

Modern scientific calculators have a mode that you can use to do sexagesimal calculation (hours, minutes and seconds). Different models work in different ways, so read the manual or check online to see how your calculator works.

In athletics and other timed sporting events the times are often given using decimal fractions of a second.

For example, in August 2009, Usain Bolt ran the 100 m in the world record time of 9.580 seconds.

In the metric system, 1 second = 1000 milliseconds.

9.580 is time recorded exact to $\frac{1}{1000}$ of a second.

This is 9 seconds and 580 milliseconds. You cannot convert it in any other way.

12-hour and 24-hour times

Tip

Add 12 to write a pm time using the 24-hour clock, for example, 10.35 pm + 12 = 22:35.

Subtract 12 to write a time between 13:00 and 23:59 using the 12-hour clock, for example, 15:40 − 12 = 3.40 pm.

The 12-hour time system uses am to show times from midnight to noon and pm for time from noon till midnight.

The 24-hour time system shows the times 00:00 to 23:59. Midnight is 00:00.

Problem-solving framework

Mr Smith is in Moscow. He needs to return to London.

The flight from Moscow to London takes 3.6 hours.

The local time in Moscow is 3 hours ahead of the UK.

The flight is scheduled for take-off from Moscow at 18:55 local time.

On arrival it takes 45 minutes to get through the airport.

Mr Smith will stop to buy a coffee, sandwich and newspaper for the train.

Trains for central London leave at 5, 27 and 46 minutes past the hour, and the journey will take 29 minutes.

There is a 7-minute walk from the train station to his hotel.

What is the earliest time that Mr Smith can expect to arrive at his hotel? Give your answer using the 12-hour system of time.

Steps for solving problems	What you would do for this example
Step 1: What have you got to do?	First work out the time of arrival in London and then work out how long it takes from there to the hotel.

Continues on next page ...

Step 2: What information do you need?	Flight departure times: 18:55 (local time)
	Time difference between London and Moscow: 3 hours
	Flight time: 3.6 hours
	Time to get through airport: 45 minutes
	Train departure times: 5 past, 27 minutes past, 46 minutes past the hour
	Length of train journey: 29 minutes
	Walk time: 7 minutes
Step 3: What information don't you need?	Assume time to buy a coffee, sandwich and newspaper is negligible
Step 4: What maths can you use?	18:55 minus 3 hours = 15:55 (London time)
	Convert 3.6 from a decimal to time in hours and minutes:
	3 hours and 0.6 × 60 = 3 hours 36 mins
	Arrival time in London: 15:55 + 3 hours 36 mins = 19:31
	Add on time in customs: 19:31 + 45 mins = 20:16
	Next possible train is 20:27
	Time at end of train journey: 20:27 + 29 mins = 20:56
	Arrival time at venue following walk: 20:56 + 7 mins = 21:03
	21:03 − 12 = 9.03 pm
	Mr Smith can expect to arrive at his hotel at three minutes past nine in the evening at the earliest.
Step 5: Have you used all the information? At this point you should check to make sure you have calculated what was asked of you.	Flight departure time ✓
	Time difference ✓
	Flight time ✓
	Time through customs ✓
	Train departure times ✓
	Length of train journey ✓
	Walk time ✓
Step 6: Is it correct?	Estimate to check:
	$3\frac{1}{2}$ hours flying + 45 mins at airport + 10 mins wait + 30 mins train + 7 mins walk = about 5 hours
	Take off the time difference leaves 2 hours
	Leave 7 pm + 2 hours = 9 pm

Tip

When you work with time, treat hours and minutes separately. If you carry over from hours to minutes, remember you are carrying 60 minutes.

 Find answers at: cambridge.org/ukschools/gcsemaths-studentbookanswers

Money

£1 = 100p

So the number of £ × 100 gives the number of pence

and the number of pence ÷ 100 gives the number of £.

The rate at which one currency is converted to another is called an **exchange rate**.

If an exchange rate is given as 1 unit of A = x units of B, you can convert currency A to currency B by multiplying by x.

For example, £1 = €1.26

So, £400 = 1.26 × 400 = €504

Currency B can be converted to currency A by dividing by x.

For example, £1 = €1.26

So, €400 = $\frac{400}{1.26}$ = £317.46

Key vocabulary

exchange rate: a number that is used to calculate the difference in value between money from one country and money from another.

EXERCISE 21B

1   The starting pistol for a road race is fired at 12:15:30.

The first runner crosses the finish line at 14:07:22.

What was the winning time for the race?

2   How many minutes are there in 10.4 hours?

Choose your answer from the following options.

   A 64 min   B 604 min   C 624 min   D 640 min

3   Sandra is exactly 16 years old.

Calculate her age in:

   a weeks   **b** days   **c** hours   **d** seconds.

4   A boat leaves port at 14:35 and arrives at its destination $6\frac{1}{2}$ hours later.

At what time does the boat arrive?

5   An area of 250 000 cm² needs to be painted.

A pot of paint can cover an area of 10 m².

How many pots of paint are needed?

6 The table gives the value of the pound (£) against four other currencies in July 2014.

British pound (£)	Euro (€)	US dollar ($)	Australian dollar (AU$)	Indian rupee (Rs)
1	1.26	1.70	1.80	102.28

a Calculate the value of 1 of each of the other currencies in pounds at this rate.

b Convert £125 to US dollars.

c How many Indian rupees would you get if you converted £45 at this rate?

d Dilshaad has 8000 Indian rupees.

What is this worth in pounds at this rate?

Section 2: Compound units of measurement

Compound measures involve more than one unit of measurement.

For example:

- rate of pay, such as pounds per hour, involves units of money and time
- unit pricing, such as pence per gram, involves units of money and mass (or capacity or volume).

You can simplify compound measures by multiplying or dividing both units by the same factor.

Tip

A forward slash symbol / is often used instead of the word 'per'. So £8.30/hour means the same as £8.30 per hour.

WORKED EXAMPLE 4

Forty litres of petrol cost £52.

a What is the cost in £/litre?   **b** Convert the cost in £/litre to pence per millilitre.

a $£\frac{52}{40} = £1.30$
  The cost is £1.30/litre

> The compound measure £/litre tells you that pounds are the first unit.

b £1.30 = 130p
  1 l = 1000 ml
  130p per 1000 ml
  $\frac{130}{1000} = 0.13$
  $\frac{1000}{1000} = 1$
  So 130p per 1000 ml = 0.13 p/ml

> You want a compound measure comparing pence and millilitres.
> Convert pounds to pence.
> Convert litres to millilitres.
> Compare the two quantities.
> You want a rate per **one** millilitre, so divide both quantities by 1000.

Speed

Speed compares the distance travelled to the time taken.

The units of speed depend on the situation.

The speed of a car or train is often given in km/h or mph (kilometres per hour or miles per hour).

An athlete's running speed might be given in m/s (metres per second).

You need to know the formula for calculating speed.

The speed is an average speed because a journey might involve faster and slower speeds over the given period.

The triangle shows the relationship between speed, distance and time.

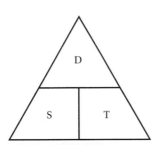

Learn this formula

$$\text{Average speed} = \frac{\text{Distance travelled}}{\text{Time taken}}$$

Tip

- To find distance: cover D with your finger. The position of S next to T tells you to multiply speed by time. Distance = Speed × Time taken
- To find time: cover T with your finger. The position of D over S tells you to divide distance by speed. Time taken = Distance ÷ Speed
- To find speed: cover S with your finger. The position of D over T tells you to divide distance by time. Speed = Distance ÷ Time taken

The units of speed given in a problem usually let you know what units to use.

For example, if the problem talks about km/h, then express distances in kilometres and time in hours to calculate the speed.

WORK IT OUT 21.2

A car travels 330 miles in $5\frac{1}{2}$ hours.

What is the average speed of the car in miles per hour (mph)?

Which of the answers below is correct?

Option A	Option B	Option C
Speed = $\dfrac{\text{Distance}}{\text{Time taken}}$ $D = 330$ miles $T = 5\frac{1}{2}$ hours = 5.5 hours $S = \dfrac{330}{5.5} = 60$ mph	Speed = Distance × Time taken $D = 330$ miles $T = 5\frac{1}{2}$ hours = 5.5 hours $S = 330 × 5.5 = 1815$ mph	Speed = Distance – Time taken $D = 330$ miles $T = 5\frac{1}{2}$ hours = 5.5 hours $S = 330 – 5.5 = 324.5$ mph

To convert speeds from one set of units to another, you need to work systematically and take care with the units.

EXERCISE 21C

1 Joe works for a minimum wage of £5.13 per hour.

He works for 14 hours.

How much does he earn in this time?

2 Henry earns £8.75 per hour.

Sireta earned £186.50 for working 22 hours.

How much more does Henry earn per hour?

3 A bricklayer lays 680 bricks in four hours.

How many does she lay per minute, to the nearest brick?

4 Bernie cycles 168 km in eight hours.

What is his average speed in kilometres per hour?

5 A car travels 531 km at an average speed of 88 km/h.

Work out the time taken.

6 Usain Bolt set an Olympic Record over 100 m at the London Olympics in 2012 with a time of 9.63 seconds.

a Express this speed in m/s.

b How fast is this in kilometres per hour?

Density and pressure

Density is the ratio between the mass and the volume of an object.

You need to know the formula for calculating the density of an object.

The triangle below helps you see the relationship between density, mass and volume.

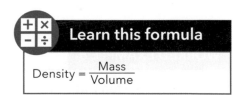

Learn this formula

$$\text{Density} = \frac{\text{Mass}}{\text{Volume}}$$

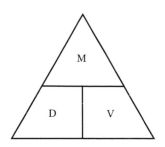

Mass = Density × Volume

$$\text{Volume} = \frac{\text{Mass}}{\text{Density}}$$

The units of density are grams per cubic centimetre (g/cm³) or kilograms per cubic metre (kg/m³).

Express the mass and the volume in the units given when you solve problems involving density.

WORKED EXAMPLE 5

A gold bar has a volume of $725\,cm^3$ and a mass of $14.5\,kg$.

What is the density of the gold bar in g/cm^3?

$$Density = \frac{Mass}{Volume}$$

Write down the formula.

$$M = 14.5\,kg = 14.5 \times 1000$$
$$= 14500\,g$$
$$V = 725\,cm^3$$

Write down the values of mass and volume (the units of density are g/cm^3 so the mass must be in g).

$$Density = \frac{14500}{725} = 20\,g/cm^3$$

The density of the gold bar is $20\,g/cm^3$

Substitute the values into the formula.

Learn this formula

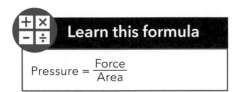

$$Pressure = \frac{Force}{Area}$$

You also need to know the formula for pressure.

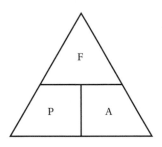

The units given for force and area give you compound units for the pressure.

For example, if force is measured in newtons and area in mm^2, the compound unit of pressure would be N/mm^2 (newtons per mm^2).

WORKED EXAMPLE 6

A brick exerts a force of $5\,N$.

Calculate the pressure exerted on the ground when the brick is in each of the following positions.

i On flat surface

Force = $5\,N$

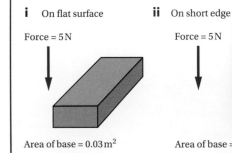

Area of base = $0.03\,m^2$

ii On short edge

Force = $5\,N$

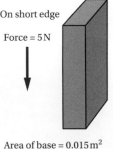

Area of base = $0.015\,m^2$

iii On long edge

Force = $5\,N$

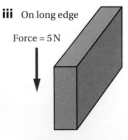

Area of base = $0.02\,m^2$

a $Pressure = \dfrac{5\,N}{0.03\,m^2}$
$$= 167\,N/m^2$$

b $Pressure = \dfrac{5\,N}{0.015\,m^2}$
$$= 333\,N/m^2$$

c $Pressure = \dfrac{5\,N}{0.02\,m^2}$
$$= 250\,N/m^2$$

Substitute the values from the diagram into the formula for pressure.

Don't forget to add the compound units for pressure.

EXERCISE 21D

1 The mass of 1 cm³ of different substances is shown in the diagram.

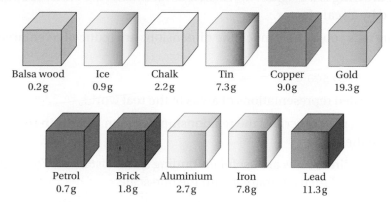

Balsa wood Ice   Chalk   Tin   Copper   Gold
0.2 g   0.9 g   2.2 g   7.3 g 9.0 g   19.3 g

Petrol   Brick   Aluminium   Iron   Lead
0.7 g   1.8 g   2.7 g   7.8 g 11.3 g

   a Calculate the density of each substance in g/cm³.

   b Express each density in g/m³ and then convert each to kg/m³.

2 The mass of an object is 15 000 kg and its volume is 958 cm³.

   What is its density, to two decimal places?

   Choose from the following options.

   A 15.66 g/cm³   B 15.6 g/cm³   C 15.66 kg   D 15.66 kg/cm³

3 A cube of material with side length 30 mm has a mass of 0.0642 kg.

   Calculate the density of the material in g/cm³.

4 Calculate the volume of a piece of wood with a mass of 0.1 kg and a density of 0.8 g/cm³.

5 Two metal blocks both exert a force of 18 N.

   Block A is a cube with side 100 cm.

   Block B is a cuboid with a base of area 6 m² in contact with the floor.

   Calculate the pressure exerted by each block in N/m².

6 A car exerts a force of 6000 N on the road.

   Each of the four wheels has an area of 0.025 m² in contact with the road.

   What pressure does the car exert on the road?

Section 3: Maps, scale drawings and bearings

A **scale drawing** is a diagram in which measurements are either reduced or enlarged by a scale factor.

The scale tells you by how much the dimensions are reduced or enlarged.

Using the map scale

Maps are scaled representations of areas of the real world.

The scale of a map describes the relationship between lengths in real life and lengths on the map.

Bar scales or **line scales** are useful for finding small distances. You measure the distance and then compare it with the line scale.

On the line scale below, each block is 1 cm long, so 1 cm on the map represents 1 km in real life.

To find a distance in real life:
- measure the map distance using a piece of paper
- make pencil marks on the paper to record the distance
- compare your marked distance with the line scale
- read off the real distance.

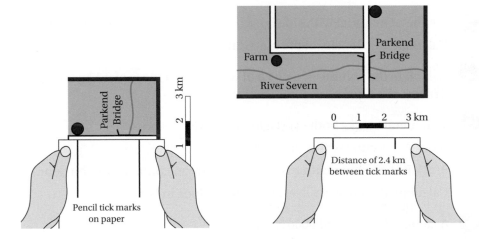

For bigger distances it is more efficient to use the **ratio scale**. You can convert any distance on a map to a real distance using the following formula:

distance on the map × scale = distance on the ground

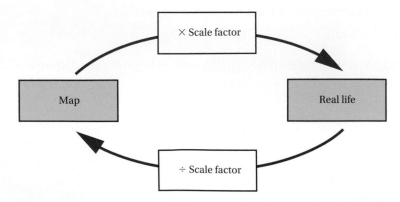

Take care with the units.

When you multiply by the scale your answer will be in the same units that you used to measure on the map.

If the question asks for different units, you will need to convert the measurement to get the units you need.

WORK IT OUT 21.3

The distance between two towns on a 1 : 25 000 map is 3.4 cm.

How many kilometres apart are these towns in reality?

Which student has worked out the correct answer?

What have the other two done incorrectly?

Student A	Student B	Student C
$\dfrac{1}{25\,000} \times \dfrac{3.4}{1}$ $= 0.000136\,\text{cm}$ $= 1.36\,\text{km}$	Map distance = 34 mm Scale = 1 : 25 000 Real distance 34 × 25 000 = 850 000 mm = 8.5 km	$3.4 \times 25\,000 = 85\,000$ The distance is 85 000 cm ÷ 100 = 850 m ÷ 1000 = 0.85 km

EXERCISE 21 E

1 Here are three line scales.

Work out what distance is represented by 1 cm in each case.

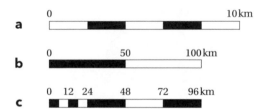

a 0 ——— 10 km

b 0 — 50 — 100 km

c 0 12 24 48 72 96 km

2 An Ordnance Survey map has a scale of 1 : 25 000.

The distance between two peaks on the map is 12.5 cm.

How far is the actual distance in kilometres?

Choose your answer from the following options.

A 0.3125 km   B 3.125 km   C 31.25 m   D 312.5 km

3 Work out the real distance (in kilometres) that a map distance of 45 mm would represent at each scale.

a 1 : 120   **b** 1 : 1200   **c** 1 : 12 000   **d** 1 : 120 000

e 1 : 1 200 000   **f** 1 : 12 000 000   **g** 1 : 120 000 000

4 Andrew says that a map drawn to a scale of 1 : 15 000 is a larger scale map than one drawn to 1 : 150 000. Is he correct?

Give reasons for your answer.

Find answers at: cambridge.org/ukschools/gcsemaths-studentbookanswers

5 The map below shows several towns.

The map has a scale of 1 : 75 000.

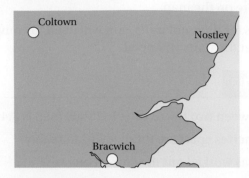

Work out the actual distance directly from Coltown to Bracwich.

6 The red line on the map shows the path of a plane flying from Edinburgh to London.

The flight took 55 minutes.

1 : 10 000 000

a Calculate the distance flown in kilometres.

b What was the plane's average speed on this flight?

7 The length of a skirt made from a sewing pattern is to be 26 cm.

The pattern is drawn to quarter scale which means it is drawn to $\frac{1}{4}$ the size of the object.

What is the length of the skirt on the pattern?

Choose your answer from the options below.

A 6 cm   B 6.5 cm   C 13 cm   D 104 cm

8 A set of toy furniture is made using a scale of 1 : 50.

Work out:

a the height of a cupboard if the toy is 5 cm high

b the width of the toy bed if the actual bed is 1.5 m wide

c the length of a table if the toy is 2.7 cm long.

9 A model of an F15 fighter jet has a scale of 1 : 32.

The real aircraft is 12.5 m long.

What is the length of the model?

10 A map of Scotland has a scale of 1 : 2 000 000.

a The distance on the map from Inverness to Glasgow is 90 mm.

What is the real distance between Inverness and Glasgow?

b The actual distance by road from Aberdeen to Dundee is 96.5 km.

How long is this road on the map?

Tip

You will use scale factors again in Chapter 33 when you deal with similar triangles and enlargements of shapes.

Constructing scale drawings

To make a scaled drawing or simple map you need to:
- find out or measure the real lengths
- decide what size your drawing is going to be so you can work out a scale
- choose an appropriate scale (if you are not given one to use) and work it out from the ratio 'length on drawing : length in real life'
- use the scale to convert the real lengths to ones you need for the scaled drawing.

WORKED EXAMPLE 7

Draw a scale plan of a rectangular park that is 115 m long and 85 m wide.

Your plan must fit into a space 7.5 cm long and 5 cm wide.

Step 1: The real measurements are 115 m and 85 m

Check that the measurements are in the same units – if not, convert so that they are.

Step 2: A scale drawing 6 cm long will fit into the given space.

Decide upon a reasonable scale that fits the paper well – not too small so you can't read it.

Step 3: Work out the scale.
Scale = length on drawing : length in real life
$$= 6\,cm : 115\,m$$
$$= 6\,cm : 11\,500\,cm$$
$$= 1 : 1917$$

Scale is a ratio and should be written as such.

In this case 6 cm : 115 cm

But they must be in the same units.

Convert the metres to centimetres.

Divide both sides by 6 to get 1 on the left.

Most scales are rounded.

1 : 1917 is a clumsy scale so try a scale of 1 : 2000

Step 4: Use the scale to convert the real distances.
Scaled length $= \dfrac{115}{2000} = 0.0575\,m = 5.75\,cm$

Scaled width $= \dfrac{85}{2000} = 0.0425\,m = 4.25\,cm$

Apply the ratio to convert the real distances to the scaled distances.

Draw a 5 cm by 7.5 cm frame.

Use your construction skills to draw an accurate rectangle 4.25 cm by 5.75 cm.

Remember to write the scale you are using on the diagram.

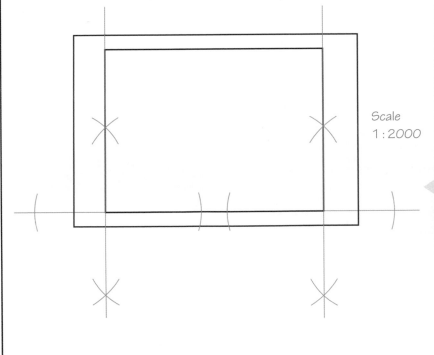

Scale
1 : 2000

To construct each vertical line accurately you need to draw a perpendicular at each corner. To do this:

1 Put your compasses on the corner and mark an arc on the base line to right and left.

2 Widen the arc of your compasses.

3 Put your compasses on one of your marks on the base line and draw an arc above and below the line.

4 Then move your compasses to your other mark on the base line and draw two more arcs above and below the line that intersect your first set.

5 Draw a line through these intersections. It should pass through the corner and be perpendicular to the base line.

6 Repeat for the other corner of the rectangle.

EXERCISE 21F

1 The floor of a school hall is 40 m long and 20 m wide.

Draw scaled diagrams to show what it would look like at each of the following scales.

a 1 : 50   **b** 1 : 500   **c** 1 : 1000

2 Measure the dimensions of your desk in centimetres.

Work out a suitable scale and draw a scaled diagram of your desk, including anything on it.

3 Jules drew this rough plan of a classroom block at her school.

She wrote the actual measurements on the plan.

Use the dimensions on the plan to draw a scaled diagram of this classroom block that fits into the width of your exercise book.

Indicate windows and doors as shown on the plan.

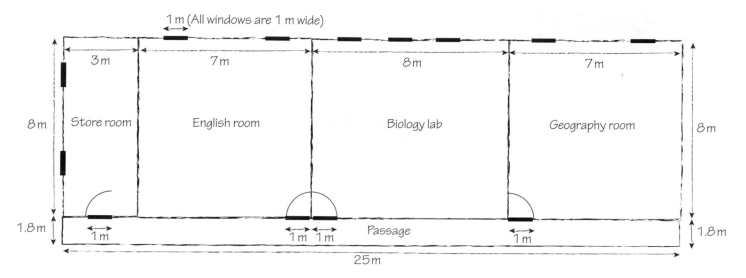

4 A plan of a house is drawn at a scale of 1 : 80.

The kitchen is 4900 mm by 3800 mm.

A sink unit is 1.2 metres long.

a What are the scaled dimensions of the kitchen?

b Calculate the scaled length of the sink unit.

Bearings

Compass directions can be given using the points shown on a compass rose. The cardinal points are north, east, south and west. The points half way between these cardinal points are north-east, south-east, south-west and north-west, with another set of 8 points defined between these eight, for example north-north-east.

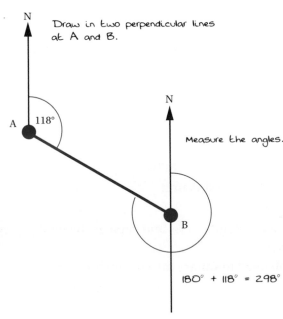

More accurate directions can be given using degrees or bearings.

Bearings are measured in degrees from 0° (north) around in a **clockwise** direction to 360° (which is back at north).

To measure bearings, you must place the baseline of your protractor in line with the compass direction north. Then you measure the angle from there to the given point.

The direction east written as a three-figure bearing is 090° as the angle from north clockwise is 90°.

Tip

You might have to draw a perpendicular to a point to make your own north line if it is not on the diagram.

WORKED EXAMPLE 8

In the diagram, find the bearings from:

a A to B **b** B to A.

N

Draw in two perpendicular lines at A and B.

A 118°

N

Measure the angles.

There are no north lines on the diagram so you have to draw them on before you can measure the bearings.

B

180° + 118° = 298°

a Bearing from A to B is 118°.
b Bearing from B to A is 298°.

EXERCISE 21G

1 Write the three-figure bearing that corresponds with each direction.

   a Due south   **b** North-east   **c** West

2 Alex is facing north-west. He makes a 270° turn clockwise.

   What direction is he now facing?

   Choose from the following options.

   A South-west   B North-east   C South-east   D West

3 Use a protractor to measure each of the following bearings on the diagram.

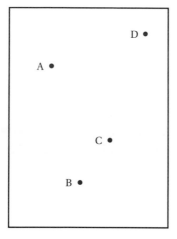

   a A to B   **b** B to A   **c** A to C

   d B to D   **e** D to A   **f** D to B

4 Beville is 140 km west and 45 km north of Lake Salina.

   Draw a scale drawing, with a scale of 1 cm to 20 km, and use it to find:

   a the bearing from Lake Salina to Beville

   b the bearing from Beville to Lake Salina

   c the shortest distance, in kilometres, between the two places.

Checklist of learning and understanding

Standard units of measurement

- You can convert between units of length, mass and capacity by multiplying or dividing by powers of ten.
- To convert squared units, you need to square the conversion factors.
- To convert cubed units, you need to cube the conversion factors.
- Units of time are not metric, so you need to use the number of parts in the sub-units when you convert units of time.

Find answers at: cambridge.org/ukschools/gcsemaths-studentbookanswers

Compound units of measurement

- Compound units of measurement involve more than one unit.
- Rates such as £/hour or cost per kilogram are compound units.
- Average speed = $\dfrac{\text{Distance travelled}}{\text{Time taken}}$
- Density = $\dfrac{\text{Mass}}{\text{Volume}}$
- Pressure = $\dfrac{\text{Force}}{\text{Area}}$

Maps, scales and bearings

- The scale of a map or diagram describes how much smaller (or bigger) the lengths on the diagram are compared to the original lengths.
- Real length = map length × scale
- The scale can be written as the ratio 'length on diagram : real length'.
- Bearings are accurate directions given in degrees from 0° to 360°. The bearing of 0° corresponds with north.
- Bearings are measured clockwise from 0° and written using three figures.

For additional questions on the topics in this chapter, visit GCSE Mathematics Online.

 Chapter review

 1 Match each statement to the correct number in the box below.

5	475	182.5	259 200

 a The number of seconds in 3 days.

 b The number of kilometres travelled in $2\frac{1}{2}$ hours by a car travelling at 73 km/h.

 c The distance in kilometres in real life of a length of 5 cm on a map with a scale of 1 : 1000.

 d The number of litres in 475 000 millilitres.

2 Write down whether the statement in each part is true or false.

 a Tony's fish tank contains 72 litres of water.

   This is 72 000 millilitres.

 b A school is 15 km from a bus stop.

   The bus travels at 40 km/hour.

   It takes half an hour for the bus to get to school.

 c The distance from Liverpool to Manchester is about 55 km.

   The scale of a map is 1 : 25 000.

   The distance on the map would be about 5.2 cm.

3 Convert 60 000 cm² to square metres.

4 How many mm² are there in 2 m²?

5 The map shows the positions of two ships A and B, and a port O.

a Ship A is north-east of O.

What is the three-figure bearing of north-east? *(1 mark)*

b Ship A sails directly to O.

In which direction does it travel? *(1 mark)*

c Measure the bearing of ship B from O. *(1 mark)*

d How far is ship B from O? *(2 marks)*

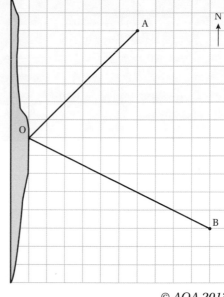

Scale: 1 square represents 10 km

© AQA 2013

6 A car is travelling at an average speed of 80 km/h for one hour on a bearing of 120°.

a Use a scale of 1 cm to 20 km to show this journey.

b After 45 km, the driver stopped for petrol.

The stop was after 40 minutes.

i Mark this spot on your diagram.

ii Calculate the speed for the part of the journey before the petrol stop.

7 The density of an object is 8 kg/m³.

Its volume is 25 m³.

Work out the mass of the object.

8 A cyclist travels due east from point A for 10 km to reach point B.

She then travels 6 km on a bearing of 125° from B to reach point C.

a Use a scale of 1 cm to 2 km to represent her journey on a scale diagram.

b Find the bearing from C to A.

c Find the direct distance from C to A in kilometres.

d It takes the cyclist 1½ hours to cycle back using the direct route from C to A.

Find her average speed:

i in km/h **ii** in m/s.

Find answers at: cambridge.org/ukschools/gcsemaths-studentbookanswers

22 Formulae

In this chapter you will learn how to ...

- use formulae to express and solve problems.
- change the subject of a formula.
- substitute numbers into formulae to find the value of the subject.
- understand and use a range of formulae, including kinematics formulae.

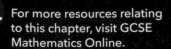 For more resources relating to this chapter, visit GCSE Mathematics Online.

Using mathematics: real-life applications

Vets use formulae to make sure they are giving animals the correct dosage of medicines for their age and mass. A poodle weighing 6 kg needs a far smaller dose of medicine than a 35 kg retriever.

"I need to make sure I give the animals I treat the correct amount of medicine. I do this by using formulae that take into account their age, mass and the ratio between any prescribed medicines." *(Veterinary surgeon)*

Before you start ...

Ch 7, 16	You need to be able to substitute values into expressions.	**1** Work out the value of $\frac{x+2y}{z}$ when: **a** $x = 7, y = 4$ and $z = 2$ **b** $x = 7, y = -2$ and $z = 2$ **c** $x = -7, y = 4$ and $z = 4$ **d** $x = -7, y = -2$ and $z = 2$
Ch 16	You should be able to solve simple equations.	**2** Solve: **a** $6x = x + 35$ **b** $5x = 64 - 3x$ **c** $2(2x + 3) = x + 7$ **d** $5x - 8 = 3x + 12$
KS 3 Ch 7, 11, 16, 17, 21	You should be familiar with some formulae already, and be able to identify the subject, variable(s) and any constants.	**3** Look at these two formulae for finding the area of shapes. $A = \frac{1}{2}bh$ $A = \pi r^2$ **a** What do the variables represent? **b** What is the constant in each formula? **c** What is the subject of each formula? **d** What tells you that the second formula applies to circles?

 Tip

Formulae often use letters for the variable that relates to the value they represent. For example, in formulae for area, A is often used to represent the **a**rea and h to represent the **h**eight. Remember the letters represent values (quantities).

Assess your starting point using the Launchpad

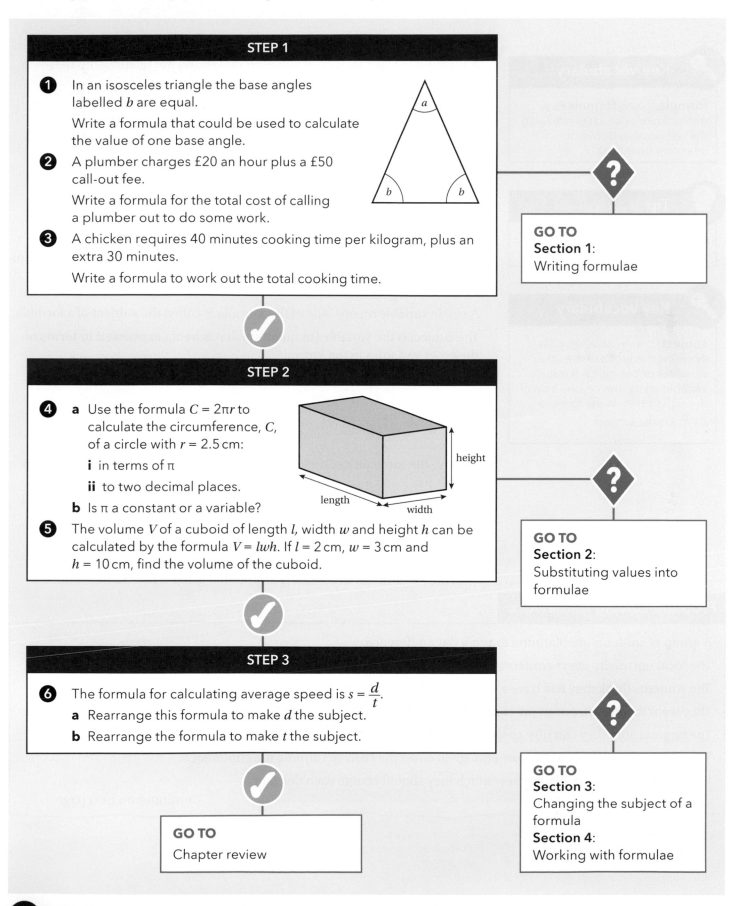

STEP 1

① In an isosceles triangle the base angles labelled b are equal.

Write a formula that could be used to calculate the value of one base angle.

② A plumber charges £20 an hour plus a £50 call-out fee.

Write a formula for the total cost of calling a plumber out to do some work.

③ A chicken requires 40 minutes cooking time per kilogram, plus an extra 30 minutes.

Write a formula to work out the total cooking time.

GO TO
Section 1:
Writing formulae

STEP 2

④ **a** Use the formula $C = 2\pi r$ to calculate the circumference, C, of a circle with $r = 2.5$ cm:

 i in terms of π

 ii to two decimal places.

 b Is π a constant or a variable?

⑤ The volume V of a cuboid of length l, width w and height h can be calculated by the formula $V = lwh$. If $l = 2$ cm, $w = 3$ cm and $h = 10$ cm, find the volume of the cuboid.

height

length

width

GO TO
Section 2:
Substituting values into formulae

STEP 3

⑥ The formula for calculating average speed is $s = \dfrac{d}{t}$.

 a Rearrange this formula to make d the subject.

 b Rearrange the formula to make t the subject.

GO TO
Chapter review

GO TO
Section 3:
Changing the subject of a formula
Section 4:
Working with formulae

Find answers at: cambridge.org/ukschools/gcsemaths-studentbookanswers

Section 1: Writing formulae

Formulae

Key vocabulary

formula (plural **formulae**): a general rule or equation showing the relationship between unknown quantities

Tip

For a reminder about variables, see Chapter 7.

Key vocabulary

subject: the variable, which is expressed in terms of the other variables or constants. It is the variable on its own on one side of the equals sign. In the formula $s = \dfrac{d}{t}$, s is the subject.

A **formula** is a special type of equation that shows the relationship between two or more unknown quantities.

For example, the formula for the area of a triangle is $A = \frac{1}{2}bh$.

To make sense of a formula you need to know what the variables represent.

In this example:

- A is the area in square units
- b is the length of the base of the triangle
- h is the perpendicular height of the triangle.

The letters A, b and h are variables. They can be replaced by different values.

In the formula $\frac{1}{2}$ is a constant. No matter what value you use for b, you have to multiply it by $\frac{1}{2}$ in the formula.

A single variable on one side of the formula is called the **subject** of a formula.

The subject is the variable (or quantity) that is being **expressed in terms of** the other variables in the formula.

In $A = \frac{1}{2}bh$, A is the subject of the formula.

Writing formulae to represent real-life situations

You use the same procedures to set up formulae as when you are setting up equations.

- List the quantities involved. Work out whether they represent the subject, a variable, a constant or a coefficient.
- Establish the relationship between each quantity. What is the subject being expressed in terms of?
- Write the formula as concisely as possible using algebraic conventions.

Problem-solving framework

A group of students are planning to run a day conference.

The local university offers conference rooms for hire at a daily rate.

The students think they will have a maximum of 60 delegates.

They want to offer refreshments costing £4 per delegate.

The largest room they can hire costs £160 for the day.

They want to charge each delegate enough to cover the costs of running the conference.

Write a formula for calculating how much they should charge each delegate.

Continues on next page ...

Steps for solving problems	What you would do for this example
Step 1: If it is useful, draw a diagram.	A diagram is not particularly useful for this question.
Step 2: Identify what you have to do.	Calculate how much to charge each delegate at the conference by writing a formula using the information given.
Step 3: Test the problem with what you already know.	You know a formula is a general rule showing the relationship between quantities.
Step 4: What maths can you use?	**1** List the quantities involved, and establish if they are the subject, a variable, a constant or a coefficient: Number of delegates, $d = 60$ (variable, as this can change). Cost of refreshments = £4 per delegate (coefficient, as this value is multiplied by how many delegates there are). Cost of the room = £160 (constant, this is fixed by the university). Cost to charge each delegate = C (subject, this is what we want to find out). **2** Establish what the relationship is between each quantity. The cost to charge each delegate is the same as the cost of having each delegate at the conference, which is the total cost divided by the number of delegates. The total cost is equal to the cost of refreshments for each delegate and the cost of the room hire. Now put this together using algebra: Cost of conference = $4d + 160$ Cost of one delegate is this value divided by the number of delegates, d. So the formula to calculate how much to charge each delegate is: $£C = \dfrac{4d + 160}{d}$ Don't forget to add the units.

EXERCISE 22A

1 The area of what shape is found using the formula $A = \frac{1}{2}bh$?

Choose your answer from the following options.

A Rectangle   B Circle   C Triangle   D Quadrilateral

2 Write a formula for:

a S in terms of C and P, where $£S$ is selling price, $£C$ is cost price and $£P$ is profit

b D in terms of n, where D is the number of degrees in n right angles

c m in terms of h, where m is the number of minutes in h hours.

3 When y is the subject and x is an unknown value, write a formula to work out y, when y is:

  a three more than x

  b six less than x

  c ten times x

  d sum of -8 and x

  e the sum of x and the square of x

  f twice x more than x plus 1

4 To cook a chicken you need to allow 20 minutes per $\frac{1}{2}$ kg and another 20 minutes.

A chicken weighs x kg.

Write a formula to show the number of minutes, m, required to cook a chicken.

Section 2: Substituting values into formulae

Key vocabulary

substitute: replacing variables with numbers

evaluate: to calculate the numerical value of something

To find the value of the subject (or any variable) in a formula you need to know the value of all the other variables.

The values are substituted into the formula to work out the missing value.

Substitute means replace the letters with the numbers you have been given.

Evaluate means calculate the numerical value of something, that is, to work something out.

WORKED EXAMPLE 1

The volume of an object can be found using the formula $V = \frac{1}{3}Ah$.

Find the volume of an object when $A = 30\ \text{cm}^2$ and $h = 6\ \text{cm}$.

$V = \frac{1}{3} \times A \times h$

$V = \frac{1}{3} \times 30 \times 6$

> Find the volume using the formula given:
>
> $V = \frac{1}{3}Ah$
>
> Substitute in the values given for A and h in the formula.

$V = \frac{1}{3} \times 30 \times 6$

$= \frac{1}{3} \times 180$

$= 60\ \text{cm}^3$

The volume of the object is $60\ \text{cm}^3$.

> Calculate the value for V.
>
> Remember to write the correct units.
>
> Volume is given in cubic units.
>
> For this example the units required are cm^3.

Tip

It is good practice to show you can correctly substitute values into a formula before calculating the answer. Write down what you need to work out and then calculate the value. Remember to include units when necessary.

Kinematics formulae

Kinematics is the study of how objects move.

In kinematics there are three important terms.

- **Velocity** – a measure of how fast an object is moving in a direction (in everyday terms this is speed).
- **Acceleration** – the rate at which the velocity of an object changes (in everyday terms this is increasing speed).
- **Displacement** – a change in the position of an object from when it started moving to where it stopped moving (in everyday terms this is distance travelled).

In science these terms have specific meanings and we say velocity, acceleration and displacement are vector quantities because they have both size and direction.

Tip

You will learn more about vectors in Chapter 30.

You will work with three kinematics formulae:

$$v = u + at$$
$$s = ut + \frac{1}{2}at^2$$
$$v^2 = u^2 + 2as$$

where

v = final velocity — velocity is measured in units of distance and time (m/s)

u = initial velocity

a = acceleration — acceleration is measured in units of distance and time (m/s/s or m/s^2)

s = displacement — displacement (distance travelled) is measured in units of length (m)

t = time taken

WORK IT OUT 22.1

Two students studying physics were given the equation $v = u + at$ and asked to calculate the value of v when:

$u = 12 \, \text{m/s}$, $a = 10 \, \text{m/s}^2$, $t = 3$ seconds.

Which student has calculated v correctly, and written the correct units for their answer?

Student A	Student B
$v = 12 + 10 \times 3$	$v = 12 + 10 \times 3$
$v = 66 \, \text{m}$	$v = 42 \, \text{m/s}$

Find answers at: cambridge.org/ukschools/gcsemaths-studentbookanswers

EXERCISE 22B

1 Calculate the volume of a cuboid with the formula $V = lbh$ when $l = 6\,\text{cm}$, $b = 3\,\text{cm}$ and $h = 4\,\text{cm}$.

Choose your answer from the following options.

A 72   B 72 cm   C 72 cm²   D 72 cm³

2 Work out the value of these expressions.

a $2a(a - 3b)$ when:

  i $a = 2$ and $b = -5$ **ii** $a = -3$ and $b = -2$ **iii** $a = \frac{1}{3}$ and $b = \frac{1}{2}$

b $x^2 - 2y$ when:

  i $x = -7$ and $y = 2$ **ii** $x = -\frac{1}{3}$ and $y = \frac{5}{6}$

3 Calculate the value of the subject in each formula.

Where units are given, include the correct units in your answer.

a $A = lw$, where $l = 6\,\text{m}$, $w = 9\,\text{m}$

b $s = \frac{d}{t}$, where $d = 72\,\text{km}$, $t = 3$ hours

c $A = \frac{1}{2}(a + b)h$, where $a = 4\,\text{cm}$, $b = 7\,\text{cm}$, $h = 9\,\text{cm}$

d $x = \sqrt{ab}$ (answer to 3 decimal places), where $a = 12$, $b = 13$

e $V = \pi r^2 h$ (answer to 3 decimal places), where $r = 3.5\,\text{cm}$, $h = 17\,\text{cm}$

f $t = a + (n - 1)d$, where $a = 10$, $n = 6$, $d = 2$

Tip

In questions working with formulae and associated units, remember to write the correct units in your answer.

4 The formula for converting temperature from degrees Fahrenheit (F) to degrees Celsius (C) is

$C = \frac{5}{9}(F - 32)$.

What is the value of C when $F = 76\,°\text{F}$ to the nearest degree?

Choose the correct answer from the following options.

A $C = 10\,°\text{C}$ B $C = 24\,°\text{C}$ C $C = 38\,°\text{C}$ D $C = 79\,°\text{C}$

5 The stopping distance of a car once the brakes are applied is given by the formula:

$d = 0.2v + 0.005v^2$

where d is the stopping distance in metres and $v\,\text{km/h}$ is the speed of the car when the brakes are applied.

Calculate the stopping distance if the brakes are applied when $v = 130\,\text{km/h}$.

6 The Greek mathematician Hero showed that the area of a triangle with sides a, b and c is given by the formula:

$A = \sqrt{s(s - a)(s - b)(s - c)}$

where $s = \frac{1}{2}(a + b + c)$.

Use Hero's formula to find the area of this triangle.

[Triangle with sides 4 cm, 9 cm, and 11 cm]

7 The simple interest payable when £P is invested at a rate of $R\%$ per year for T years is given by $I = \frac{PRT}{100}$.

Calculate the simple interest payable when £2000 is invested at 1.5% per year for 6 years.

Section 3: Changing the subject of a formula

When you need to find the value of a variable that is not the subject of the formula, you need to rearrange the formula.

A formula is a type of equation, so you can use inverse operations to rearrange the formula to make another variable (letter) the subject.

The rules for solving equations apply to formulae, so whatever you do to one side of the formula you must do to the other.

You can also substitute known values before rearranging the formula.

WORKED EXAMPLE 2

a Make r the subject of the formula $C = 2\pi r$

b Given the formula $v^2 = u^2 + 2as$, find the value of s when $u = 8$, $v = 10$ and $a = 3$.

a $C = 2\pi r$

$\dfrac{C}{2\pi} = r$ Divide both sides by 2π.

$r = \dfrac{C}{2\pi}$ Write the subject on the left-hand side.

b $v^2 = u^2 + 2as$ Rearrange the formula to make s the subject.

$v^2 - u^2 = 2as$ Subtract u^2 from both sides.

$\dfrac{v^2 - u^2}{2a} = s$ Divide both sides by $2a$.

$s = \dfrac{v^2 - u^2}{2a}$ Writing the subject on the left is the usual convention.

$u = 8, v = 10$ and $a = 3$ Substitute the values you know into the rearranged formula.

$s = \dfrac{10^2 - 8^2}{2 \times 3}$

$s = \dfrac{100 - 64}{6}$

$s = \dfrac{36}{6}$

$s = 6$

$10^2 = 8^2 + 2 \times 3s$ Alternatively, you could substitute the values into the formula first.

$100 = 64 + 6s$

$100 - 64 = 6s$

$36 = 6s$

$\dfrac{36}{6} = s$

$6 = s$

$s = 6$

EXERCISE 22C

1 $S = \dfrac{D}{T}$ is a formula for finding average speed.

Make T the subject of the formula.

Choose your answer from the options below.

   A $T = SD$ B $T = \dfrac{D}{S}$ C $T = \dfrac{S}{D}$ D $T = S + D$

 Find answers at: cambridge.org/ukschools/gcsemaths-studentbookanswers

2 These formulae have been rearranged to make the given variable the subject.

In each case, choose the correct answer from the given options.

a $A = \frac{1}{2}bh$ $b = ?$ A $\frac{A}{2h}$ B $\frac{2A}{h}$ C $2Ah$

b $V = IR$ $I = ?$ A VR B $\frac{V}{R}$ C $\frac{R}{V}$

c $V = \pi r^2 h$ $h = ?$ A πr^2 B $\frac{V}{\pi r^2}$ C $\frac{Vr^2}{\pi}$

d $A = \frac{1}{2}(a + b)h$ $a = ?$ A $\frac{2A - b}{h}$ B $\frac{2Ah}{b}$ C $\frac{2A}{h} - b$

Tip

You might recognise some of these formulae from other chapters or other subjects you are studying.

3 Rearrange the formulae to make the variable in brackets the subject.

a $y = mx + c$ (c) **b** $V = \frac{1}{2}\pi r^2 h$ (h)

c $v = u + at$ (t) **d** $A = 2\pi r^2 + 2\pi rh$ (h)

e $s = ut + \frac{1}{2}at^2$ (a) **f** $c^2 = a^2 + b^2$ (b)

4 The formula for the perimeter, P, of a rectangle, l by w, is $P = 2(l + w)$.

If $P = 20\,$cm and $l = 7\,$cm, what is the length w?

5 The area, $A\,$cm², enclosed by an ellipse is given by the formula $A = \pi ab$.

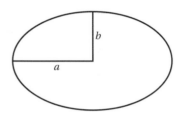

Calculate, to one decimal place, the length $a\,$cm, if $b = 3.2\,$cm and $A = 25\,$cm².

6 An object is thrown into the air at a speed of u metres per second.

Its height h metres above the ground after time t seconds of flight are related by:

$h = ut - 4.9t^2$ (ignoring air resistance)

Find the speed at which the object was thrown if it reached a height of 30 metres after 5 seconds.

7 The kinetic energy, E joules, of a moving object is given by:

$E = \frac{1}{2}mv^2$

where $m\,$kg is the mass of the object and $v\,$m/s is its speed.

a Rearrange the formula to make m the subject.

b Use the new formula to calculate the mass of the object when $E = 300$ joules and $v = 10\,$m/s.

8 The formula for the sum, S, of the interior angles in an n-sided polygon is:

$S = 180°(n - 2)$.

Rearrange the formula to make n the subject.

Use this to find the number of sides of the polygon if the sum of the interior angles is 2160°.

Section 4: Working with formulae

You are now ready to apply your skills to working with formulae on a set of general problems.

Things to remember.

- Substitute in the correct values.
- Include appropriate units in your answer.
- When writing a formula try some values to make sure it works.
- You can rearrange a formula to change the subject, but it is not always necessary when you are substituting known values.

Common formulae

Use these formulae to complete Exercise 22D.

Perimeter of a rectangle	$P = 2l + 2w$ or $P = 2(l + w)$ l = length, w = width
Area of a rectangle	$A = lw$ l = length, w = width
Area of a parallelogram	$A = bh$ b = length of base, h = perpendicular height
Circumference of a circle	$C = \pi d$ or $2\pi r$ d = diameter, r = radius
Volume of a cuboid	$V = lwh$ l = length, w = width, h = height
Surface area of a cuboid	$S = 2lw + 2wh + 2lh$ l = length, w = width, h = height
Area of a triangle	$A = \frac{1}{2}bh$ b = length of base, h = perpendicular height
Area of a trapezium	$A = \frac{1}{2}(a + b)h$ $a + b$ = sum of lengths of parallel sides, h = perpendicular height
Area of a circle	$A = \pi r^2$ r = radius
Volume of a cylinder	$V = \pi r^2 h$ r = radius, h = height
Volume of a cone	$V = \frac{1}{3}\pi r^2 h$ r = radius, h = height
Converting degrees Celsius into degrees Fahrenheit	$F = \frac{9}{5}C + 32°$
Converting degrees Fahrenheit into degrees Celsius	$C = \frac{5}{9}(F - 32)$

Find answers at: cambridge.org/ukschools/gcsemaths-studentbookanswers

EXERCISE 22D

1 State whether each statement is true or false.

Correct any false statements to make them true.

a $A = \frac{1}{2}bh$. When $b = 4.5\,\text{cm}$ and $h = 8\,\text{cm}$, then $A = 18\,\text{m}^2$.

b When the formula to calculate speed, $S = \frac{D}{T}$, is rearranged to make T the subject, it becomes $T = \frac{D}{S}$

c A formula to calculate the number n half way between two numbers x and y can be written as $n = \frac{x+y}{2}$

d In the formula to calculate the area of a circle, $A = \pi r^2$, π is a constant and A and r are the variables.

2 Use the appropriate formula from the table to complete these problems.

a Calculate the perimeter, P, of a rectangle if the length $l = 6.5\,\text{m}$ and width $w = 8\,\text{m}$.

b Calculate the height, h, of a parallelogram that has an area $A = 45\,\text{cm}^2$ and a base $b = 2.5\,\text{cm}$.

c Calculate the surface area, S, of a cuboid if the length $l = 20\,\text{cm}$, the width $w = 3.5\,\text{cm}$ and the height $h = 7.2\,\text{cm}$.

d Work out the area, A, of a circle with a radius $r = 12.3\,\text{cm}$.

e Work out the height, h, of a cone that has a volume $V = 45\,\text{cm}^3$ and a radius $r = 5\,\text{cm}$.

3 **a** Work out the Fahrenheit temperature, F, when $C = 8\,°\text{C}$.

b Calculate the Centigrade temperature, C, when $F = 72\,°\text{F}$.

c Freezing point is $0\,°\text{C}$. What is the equivalent temperature in Fahrenheit?

4 The formula $d = \frac{8m}{5}$ converts the distance, d, travelled in m miles into kilometres.

Use the formula to convert 25 miles into kilometres.

Choose the correct answer from the options below.

A 40 km   B 200 km   C 4 km   D 400 km

5 You are given the formula $s = ut + \frac{1}{2}at^2$.

Find the value of s when $u = 10$, $t = 5$ and $a = 0.27$.

6 Ohm's law states that the voltage, V in volts, is the product of the current, I in amps, and the resistance, R in ohms. So the formula is $V = IR$. Give your answers to these questions to three significant figures.

a Calculate the voltage, V in volts, when $I = 25$ milliamps and $R = 330$ ohms.

b Calculate the current, I in milliamps, when $V = 9$ volts and $R = 330$ ohms.

c Calculate the resistance, R in ohms, when $V = 9$ volts and $I = 18$ milliamps.

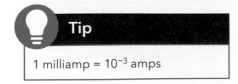

Tip

1 milliamp $= 10^{-3}$ amps

7 Use the formula $A = 4\pi r^2$ to find A to one decimal place when:

    a $r = 3$ **b** $r = 25.6$

8 In general, temperature decreases with height above sea level.

This formula shows how temperature and height above sea level are related.

$T = \dfrac{h}{200}$, where T is the temperature decrease in °C and h is the height increase in metres.

    a If the temperature at a height of 500 m is 23 °C, what will it be when you climb to 1300 m?

    b What increase in height would result in a 5 °C decrease in temperature?

9 A large wooden crate had to be moved by a car.

The crate had to be placed on its base of 150 cm long by 50 cm wide.

Which of the following cars could be used? Which would be the best to use?

Tip

Calculate the length of each car boot.

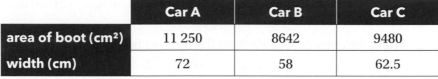

	Car A	Car B	Car C
area of boot (cm²)	11 250	8642	9480
width (cm)	72	58	62.5

10 Two friends are planning a holiday together.

One prefers resorts where the average temperatures are below 27 °C.

The other wants temperatures of at least 20 °C.

Convert the following temperatures from Fahrenheit to Celsius for three possible holiday locations. Which locations would be acceptable to both friends?

    A Sunshine Beach: 84.2 °F

    B Palm Tree Bay: 77 °F

    C Silver Sands: 80.6 °F

Tip

The formula for converting temperatures from Celsius, C, to Fahrenheits, F, is $F = 1.8C + 32$.

11 Driver A covers a distance of 87 miles in 1.4 hours travelling on a motorway.

Driver B covers a distance of 174 miles in 2.4 hours on the same motorway.

Work out the average speed of each driver.

Which driver is likely to have broken the 70 mph speed limit?

Find answers at: cambridge.org/ukschools/gcsemaths-studentbookanswers

Checklist of learning and understanding

Writing formulae

- A formula is a general rule or equation showing the relationship between quantities.
- You can use formulae to represent real-life problems as long as you define the variables you are using.

Substituting values into formulae

- To evaluate a formula, you need to know the value of all but one of its variables.
- Substitute the given values into the formula to find the unknown variable.

Changing the subject of a formula

- In any formula we can 'change the subject' by rearranging the formula in the same way as we rearrange equations.

For additional questions on the topics in this chapter, visit GCSE Mathematics Online.

Chapter review

1 Write a formula showing the total number of hours, h, worked in a 5-day week for x weeks at y hours a day.

Select the correct formula from the options below.

A $h = 5xy$ B $h = 5x + y$ C $h = \dfrac{5x}{y}$ D $h = 5 + x + y$

2 Substitute values into these formulae to work out the value of the unknown variable.

a Find v when $v = u + at$ and $u = 50$, $a = 10$ and $t = 2$.

b Find s when $s = ut + \dfrac{1}{2}at^2$ and $u = 0$, $a = 6$ and $t = 10$.

c Find v when $v^2 = u^2 + 2as$ and $u = 5$, $a = 6$ and $s = 12$.

3 The area of a circle is $A = \pi r^2$.

Rearrange the formula to calculate the radius of a circle with area $25\,\text{cm}^2$ (leave π in your answer).

4 The cost, £C, of hiring a room is given by the formula:

$$C = 12n + 250$$

where n is the number of people attending the function.

a Rearrange the formula to make n the subject.

b How many people attended the function if the cost of hiring the reception room was:

i £730?   **ii** £1090?   **iii** £1210?   **iv** £1690?

5 Rearrange the following formulae to make the letter in the brackets the subject.

a $A = \pi ab$ (a) **b** $P = 2a + 2b$ (a) **c** $\sqrt{ab} = c$ (b)

d $a\sqrt{b} = c$ (b) **e** $\sqrt{(b + c)} = c$ (b) **f** $\sqrt{(x - b)} = c$ (b)

g $\sin \theta = \dfrac{o}{h}$ (o) **h** $\dfrac{x}{\sqrt{y}} = c$ (y)

 6 Make t the subject of the formula $w = 3 + \sqrt{t}$ *(2 marks)*

23 Volume and surface area

In this chapter you will learn how to …

- calculate the volume and surface area of cuboids.
- calculate the volume and surface area of prisms.
- calculate the volume and surface area of cylinders.
- solve volume and surface area problems involving composite shapes.

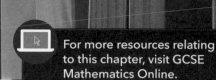

For more resources relating to this chapter, visit GCSE Mathematics Online.

Using mathematics: real-life applications

Freight costs are dependent upon the volume of material being transported. Freight rates are calculated using the container volume measured against the length of the container. The longer the container the higher the freight cost.

"To transport a container full of apples from Felixstowe, England to Le Havre in France, I have to let the freight operator know the volume of apples I have to transport as well as the dimensions of the crates. I am then quoted a transport cost."

(Apple producer)

Before you start …

Ch 8, 20	You need to be able to recognise and identify solid objects.	**1** Name each object as accurately as possible from the description. **a** A 3D object with six identical square surfaces. **b** A 3D solid with two parallel circular faces. **c** An object with a square base and triangular side faces that meet at an apex. **d** A 3D object with a circular base and one vertex. **e** A 3D object with many flat surfaces that are polygons. **f** A polyhedron with two triangular and three rectangular faces.
Ch 11	You must be able to calculate the area of plane shapes.	**2** What is the formula for the area of a circle? **3** What is the area of a right-angled triangle with sides of 3 cm, 4 cm and 5 cm?
Ch 8, 20	You should understand and use the properties of solids.	**4** A shape has 6 faces, 8 vertices and 12 edges. **a** What could it be? **b** What additional information do you need to name the shape more accurately?

Find answers at: cambridge.org/ukschools/gcsemaths-studentbookanswers

Assess your starting point using the Launchpad

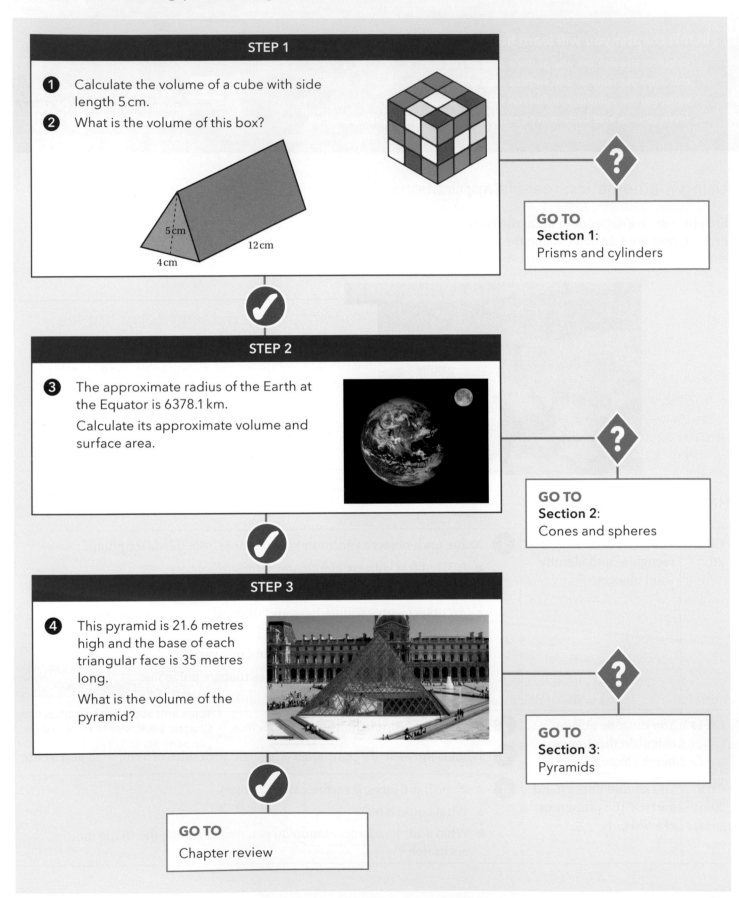

STEP 1

① Calculate the volume of a cube with side length 5 cm.

② What is the volume of this box?

5 cm
12 cm
4 cm

GO TO
Section 1:
Prisms and cylinders

STEP 2

③ The approximate radius of the Earth at the Equator is 6378.1 km.

Calculate its approximate volume and surface area.

GO TO
Section 2:
Cones and spheres

STEP 3

④ This pyramid is 21.6 metres high and the base of each triangular face is 35 metres long.

What is the volume of the pyramid?

GO TO
Section 3:
Pyramids

GO TO
Chapter review

Section 1: Prisms and cylinders

A prism is a 3D object with:

- two parallel end faces that are the same size and shape
- a uniform cross-section along its length.

The diagram below shows examples of **right prisms**.

One of the end faces is known as the base of the object. The sides are rectangles perpendicular to the base.

A cube (square prism)   A rectangular prism   A triangular prism

 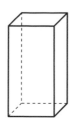 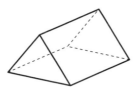

Key vocabulary

right prism: a prism with sides perpendicular to the end faces (base)

Volume

The volume of an object is the three-dimensional space that it takes up. Volume is given in cubic units, such as mm³, cm³ and m³ (for solids).

You find the volume of any right prism by finding the area of its cross-section (which is the same as its base) and multiplying this by its length. This is the same for a cylinder: you find its volume by multiplying the area of its circular base by its length.

Learn this formula

Volume of a prism
= area of cross-section × length

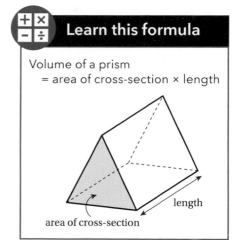

length

area of cross-section

Surface area

Surface area is the total area of the faces of a three-dimensional object.

Sketching a rough net of the object can help you to see what faces to include when you calculate the surface area.

The net of a cuboid shows that the surface area includes the area of six faces.

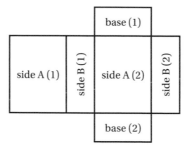

base (1)

side A (1) | side B (1) | side A (2) | side B (2)

base (2)

The surface area is calculated by adding the area of each of its faces. The opposite faces match, so

surface area = 2(area of side A) + 2(area of side B) + 2(area of base)

A cube has six identical square faces.
You can use the following formulae for volume and surface area:

Volume of a cube = x^3

Surface area of a cube = $6x^2$

Tip

You learnt about nets of solids in Chapter 20. Revise that section if you need to.

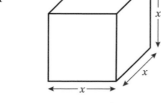

x

x

x

 Find answers at: cambridge.org/ukschools/gcsemaths-studentbookanswers

WORKED EXAMPLE 1

Calculate the volume and surface area of this cuboid.

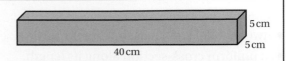

5 cm
5 cm
40 cm

Volume of cuboid = 40 × 5 × 5 = 1000 cm³

> The volume of a cuboid is found using the formula: volume = length × width × depth.
>
> The answer is given as units³ as it has three dimensions.

Surface area of cuboid = 4 × (40 × 5) + 2 × (5 × 5)
$$= 800 + 50$$
$$= 850 \text{ cm}^2$$

> The surface area of a cuboid is the total area of each of its faces.
>
> It has four faces that measure 40 cm × 5 cm and two faces that measure 5 cm × 5 cm.

Prisms with cross sections of other shapes

The same general formula is used to find the volume and the surface area of any prism, or a cylinder.

Volume of a prism = area of cross-section × length

For example, this is a triangular prism. The base is a triangle.

Area of triangle $= \frac{1}{2}bh$

Volume of a prism = area of cross-section × length

Volume of triangular prism $= \frac{1}{2}bh \times L$

Surface area of triangular prism = 2(area of triangular base) + area of three side faces

$$= 2(\frac{1}{2} \times b \times h) + (a \times L) + (c \times L) + (b \times L)$$

Prisms with a trapezium base

Area of trapezium base $= \frac{1}{2}(a + b) \times h$

Volume of prism $= \frac{1}{2}(a + b) \times h \times l$

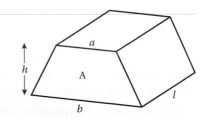

WORK IT OUT 23.1

What is the volume of soil that can be contained in this skip?

Which of the following is the correct calculation?

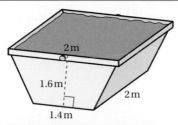

Calculation A	Calculation B	Calculation C
Area of the trapezium	Area of the trapezium	Area of the trapezium:
Area $= \frac{1}{2}(a + b) \times h$	Area $= \frac{1}{2}(a - b) \times h$	Area $= \frac{1}{2} \times b \times h$
Area $= \frac{1}{2} \times 3.4 \times 1.6 = 2.72\,\text{m}^2$	Area $= \frac{1}{2} \times 0.6 \times 1.6 = 0.48\,\text{m}^2$	Area $= \frac{1}{2} \times 1.4 \times 1.6 = 1.12\,\text{m}^2$
Volume =	Volume =	Volume =
area of the trapezium × length	area of the trapezium × length	area of the trapezium × length
Volume $= 2.72 \times 2 = 5.44\,\text{m}^3$	Volume $= 0.48 \times 2 = 0.96\,\text{m}^3$	Volume $= 1.12 \times 2 = 2.24\,\text{m}^3$

Cylinders

Cylinders are not prisms, but you find their volume and surface area in the same way as you do with prisms.

Volume of a cylinder $= \pi r^2 \times h$

The net of a prism shows that the curved surface forms a rectangle when it is flattened out. The length of the rectangle is equivalent to the circumference of the circular base.

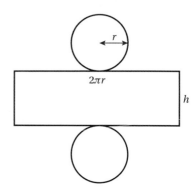

The surface area of a cylinder is calculated using the formula:

$S = 2\pi rh + 2\pi r^2$

Find answers at: cambridge.org/ukschools/gcsemaths-studentbookanswers

WORKED EXAMPLE 2

A road roller has a roller on the front that is filled with water to make it heavy.

The tank of water in the roller has a radius of 0.95 m and a length of 2.4 m.

Find the volume of water in the roller.

> Try to remember this formula:
>
> volume is the area of the cross-section times the length.

Volume of water = area of circle × length

Volume = $\pi r^2 \times l$

Volume of water = 3.14 × 0.95 × 0.95 × 2.4

$\qquad\qquad\qquad$ = 6.80124 m³

$\qquad\qquad\qquad$ = 6.8 m³ (to 1 dp)

Rearranging the formula

Tip

You will learn more about rearranging formulae in Chapter 22.

You can find the length of a prism if you know the volume and area of the base by changing the subject of the formula. For example:

The volume of a triangular prism is 100 cm³ and the area of the end face is 25 cm².

How long is the prism?

Volume = area of the triangle × length

so $V \div A = L$

$100 \div 25 = L = 4$ cm

In the same way, you can find the radius or diameter of the base of a cylinder when you know the other dimensions by changing the subject of the formula.

EXERCISE 23A

1 Calculate the volume of a cube of side 10 cm. Choose the correct answer from the options below.

A 10 cm³ $\qquad$ B 40 cm³ $\qquad$ C 100 cm³ $\qquad$ D 1000 cm³

2 Calculate the volume and surface area of each object. (Each object is a closed object.)

a

6 cm
12 cm

b

5 cm
4 cm
8 cm
6 cm

c

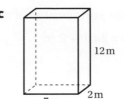

12 m
7 m
2 m

d

5 cm
6 cm

e

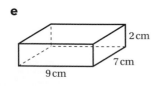

2 cm
9 cm
7 cm

f

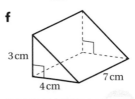

3 cm
4 cm
7 cm

3 1 litre = 1000 cm^3.

What is the capacity, in litres, of the aquarium below?

60 cm

1 m   30 cm

4 The volume of a cube is 144 m^3. What is the length of each side? Choose the correct length from the options below.

A 5.24 m   B 12 m   C 36 m   D 576 m

5 The dimensions of a swimming pool are 50 m long and 25 m wide.

The water is 2 m deep.

What is the capacity of water in the swimming pool?

6 What is the volume of this triangular prism? Give your answer to two decimal places.

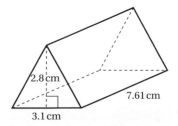

2.8 cm

7.61 cm

3.1 cm

7 What is the surface area of one side of this roof?

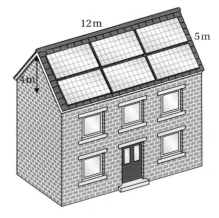

12 m

5 m

4 m

8 Calculate the volume of the object in the diagram.

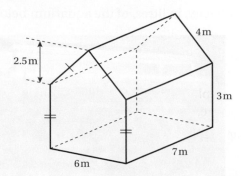

9 A piece of wood has a cylindrical hole drilled through the middle, as shown in the diagram.

Calculate the volume of the wood.

Section 2: Cones and spheres

Cones

The formula for the volume of a cone is

$\frac{1}{3}$ × area of circular base × h

where h is the perpendicular height from the base to the apex of the cone.

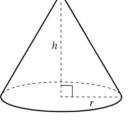

The area of the base can be found using the formula for the area of a circle, πr^2.

Volume of a cone $= \frac{1}{3}\pi r^2 h$

> 💡 **Tip**
>
> In some problems involving cones you might need to use Pythagoras' theorem to find the perpendicular height using the radius and the slant height. You will deal with Pythagoras' theorem a lot in maths.

WORKED EXAMPLE 3

Find the volume of a cone of radius 12 cm with a perpendicular height of 14 cm.

$\text{Volume} = \frac{1}{3}(\pi r^2)h = \frac{1}{3}(3.14 \times 12 \times 12) \times 14$
$= 2110.08\,\text{cm}^3$

The formula for the volume of a cone is made up of the area of the circle at the end times the height divided by three as there are three cones in the equivalent cylinder. You will remember the formula for the area of a circle which is πr^2.

The area of the curved surface of a cone is $\pi r l$, where r is the radius of the base, and l is the **slant height** of the cone.

Therefore, the surface area (S) of the cone is:

S = area of curved surface + area of base

$= \pi r l + \pi r^2$

Spheres

A sphere is any perfectly round object.

The volume of a sphere is equal to $\frac{4}{3}\pi r^3$, where r is the radius of the sphere.

The surface area of a sphere is equal to $4\pi r^2$, where r is the radius of the sphere.

Many objects include spheres or parts of spheres in their structure.

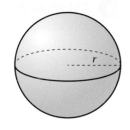

Tip

When working with π (pi), you might be asked to give your answer in terms of π. This means you leave π in your answer but do the other working.

WORKED EXAMPLE 4

The radius of the Earth is approximately 6378.1 km. Give your answers in standard form to four significant figures.

a Find the approximate volume and surface area of the Earth.

b Water covers 70% of the Earth's surface. What is the surface area of land?

a $V = \frac{4}{3} \times \pi \times 6378.1^3$

　　$= 1\,086\,832\,412\,000 \, \text{km}^3$

　　$= 1.087 \times 10^{12} \, \text{km}^3 \; (4 \, sf)$

Surface area $= 4 \times \pi \times 6378^2$

　　　　　　$= 511\,201\,962.3 \, \text{km}^2$

　　　　　　$= 5.112 \times 10^8 \, \text{km}^2 \; (4 \, sf)$

The volume of a sphere is given by the formula:

$V = \frac{4}{3}\pi r^3$

The surface area of a sphere is given by the formula: $4\pi r^2$

b 30% of the Earth's surface area is land.

0.3 × 511 201 962.3

$= 153\,360\,588.7 \, \text{km}^2$

$= 1.534 \times 10^8 \, \text{km}^2 \; (4 \, sf)$

Once you have found the surface area of the Earth you can find 30% by multiplying the whole by 0.3

Tip

In calculations with such large values answers are usually given in standard form (see Chapter 15).

EXERCISE 23B

1 Calculate the volume and surface area of each object. (The objects are all closed.)

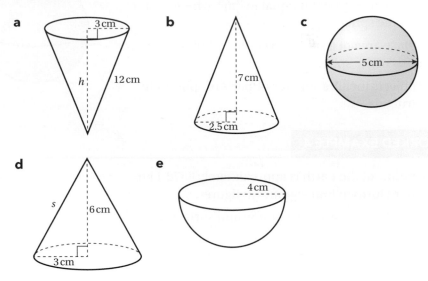

a 3 cm, h, 12 cm

b 7 cm, 2.5 cm

c 5 cm

d s, 6 cm, 3 cm

e 4 cm

2 The Earth's moon has a mean radius of 1738 km.

Find its approximate volume. Take π to be 3.14

3 Find the surface area of a sphere with radius 20 cm. Take π to be 3.14
Choose from the options below.

A $1256\,\text{cm}^2$ B $1675\,\text{cm}^3$ C $5024\,\text{cm}^2$ D $1256\,\text{cm}^3$

4 The table below gives some standard diameters of spherical balls used in different sports. Calculate the surface area of each ball. Assume they are round and ignore any dimples on the surface.

	Sport	Standard diameter
a	snooker	52.5 mm
b	tennis	6.35 cm
c	football	15 cm
d	golf	42.7 mm
e	bowling	21.6 cm
f	basketball	25.4 cm
g	hockey	3 cm
h	baseball	74 mm
i	cricket	7 cm

5 A factory needs to calculate the volume and surface area of plastic cones.

The dimensions of the cones are given in the table.

Calculate each volume and surface area.

	Radius, (r cm)	Slant height, (s cm)
a	5	10
b	18	34
c	7	21
d	16	22
e	60	64
f	9	26
g	30	52

6 A conical tent has a circular base with a diameter of 3 m, and a slant height of 3 m.

Calculate the volume of the tent.

Composite solids

In real life, objects are often made up of more than one shape.

This is the winning design for the air traffic control tower at Newcastle airport. The design incorporates cut-off conical shapes around a cuboid-shaped cement tower.	This is the design of the North Gate bus station in Northampton. You can see that many different solids have been used in the design.

Tip

It is useful to use a system for checking that you have included all the surfaces when you are finding the surface area of a composite shape.

To find the total surface area of a composite solid you need to find the area of each part separately then add them together.

The area of some faces will overlap and not form part of the 'outside' area of the solid. You need to be careful to use only the parts of the solid that form the surface area of the shape.

WORKED EXAMPLE 5

Calculate the total volume and surface area of the object shown to the right.

Give your final answers to two decimal places.

The object consists of a cone and a cylinder.

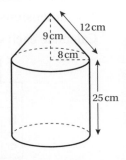

Volume

Volume of cone $= \frac{1}{3}(\pi r^2) \times h$

$\qquad = \frac{1}{3} \times \pi \times (8)^2 \times 9$

$\qquad = 603.19 \text{ cm}^3$

> You must split the object into two separate objects in order to be able to do the calculation.

Volume of cylinder $= \pi r^2 h$

$\qquad = \pi \times (8)^2 \times 25$

$\qquad = 5026.55 \text{ cm}^3$

Total volume $= 5629.74 \text{ cm}^3$

Surface area

Conical top is a cone without a base.
Curved surface area $= \pi r s$

$\qquad = \pi \times 8 \times 12$

$\qquad = 301.59 \text{ cm}^2$

> Remember that the surface area of the cone will not include the base as it is part of the cylinder below it and joined to it.

Cylinder with one base only.
S = area of base + area of curved side

$\qquad = \pi \times (8)^2 + 2 \times \pi \times 8 \times 25$

$\qquad = 1457.70 \text{ cm}^2$

> The surface area of the cylinder will only include one base at the bottom as the top is joined to the cone.

Total surface area $= 1759.29 \text{ cm}^2$

Frustum of a cone

A frustum is what is left if the top of a cone has been removed. It is a truncated cone.

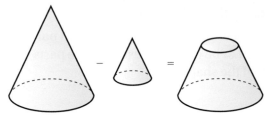

To find the volume of the frustum you find the volume of the whole cone and subtract the part that is missing.

Volume of a cone $= \frac{1}{3}(\pi r^2)h$

You can find the surface area of the frustum of a cone in a similar way. First find the surface area of the whole and subtract the surface area of the part of the cone that is missing.

Surface area of a cone $= = \pi r l + \pi r^2$, where l is the slant height.

Remember to add on the area of the circles at the top and the bottom if needed.

WORKED EXAMPLE 6

Calculate the surface area and volume of the polystyrene coffee cup in the picture.

The cup is $\frac{2}{3}$ of the size of a cone. Take pi to be 3.14

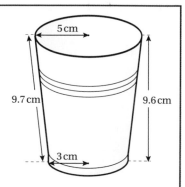

Surface area

Original cone slant height is $9.7 \div 2 \times 3 = 14.55\,cm$
Surface area of original cone $= \pi r l$
$\qquad = 3.14 \times 5 \times 14.55$
$\qquad = 228.44\,cm^2$
Surface area of cut-off part $= \pi r l$
$\qquad = 3.14 \times 1.5 \times (14.55 - 9.7)$
$\qquad = 22.84\,cm^2$
Surface area of cup $= 228.44 - 22.84 = 205.6\,cm^2$

You divide by $\frac{2}{3}$ because it is $\frac{2}{3}$ of the cone. Remember to find the surface area of the whole and subtract the surface area of the missing part which is $\frac{1}{3}$ of the original part leaving $\frac{2}{3}$.

Volume

Height of cup is $9.6\,cm$, which is $\frac{2}{3}$ the original cone height
Height of original cone $= 9.6 \div 2 \times 3 = 14.4\,cm$
Volume of original cone $= \frac{1}{3}(\pi r^2)h$
$\qquad = \frac{1}{3} \times 3.14 \times 5^2 \times 14.4$
$\qquad = 376.8\,cm^3$
Height of cut-off part $= 14.4 - 9.6 = 4.8\,cm$
Volume of cut-off part $= \frac{1}{3} \times 3.14 \times 3^2 \times 4.8$
$\qquad = 45.22\,cm^3$
Volume of cup $= 376.8 - 45.22 = 331.58\,cm^3$

EXERCISE 23C

1 Find the surface area of each solid. Give your answers to the nearest cm² or mm².

a

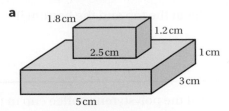

b

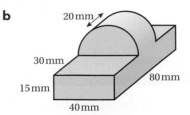

2 Calculate the volume of each solid.

a

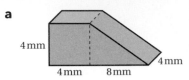

b

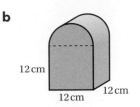

c

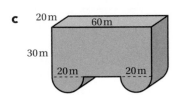

d

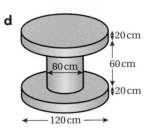

3 A sphere of diameter 1.6 m is cut through the centre to form two hemispheres.

Calculate the surface area of each hemisphere.

4 A flower container as shown in the diagram needs painting with preservative.

The tub is $\frac{1}{4}$ of the size of a full cone with the same top radius.

The slant height of the full cone is 219.3 cm.

a Calculate the outside surface area of one container, including the base, to the nearest whole number.

b A gardener has five of these flower tubs to preserve.

What preservative coverage will she need to preserve all five tubs, including the base, at least once?

Section 3: Pyramids

Pyramids are named according to the shape of their base.

The volume of a pyramid is $\frac{1}{3}$ of the volume of a prism with the same base area and height.

Volume of a pyramid $= \frac{1}{3} \times$ area of base $\times$ perpendicular height

The surface area of a pyramid is the total area of the base plus the area of each triangular side.

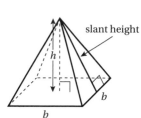 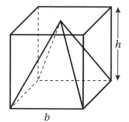

WORKED EXAMPLE 7

Calculate the volume and the surface area of the square-based pyramid.

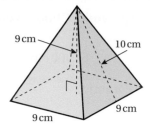

Volume of pyramid $= \frac{1}{3} \times$ area of base $\times h$

$= \frac{1}{3} \times 9 \times 9 \times 9 = 243\,\text{cm}^3$

Use the formula for the volume of a pyramid and substitute in the given values.

Surface area of pyramid $= b \times b + 4 \times (\frac{1}{2} \times \text{slant height} \times b)$

$= (9 \times 9) + 4 \times (\frac{1}{2} \times 10 \times 9)$

$= 81 + 180 = 261\,\text{cm}^2$

Surface area of pyramid = area of square base + 4 × area of triangular sides

Height of triangular side is the slant height of 10 cm shown in the diagram.

EXERCISE 23D

1 The six pyramids below have either square or triangular bases.

Calculate the volume and the surface area of each one.

a
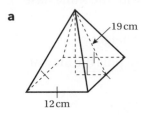
19 cm

12 cm

b
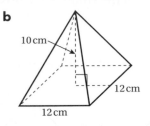
10 cm

12 cm

12 cm

c
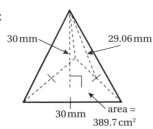
30 mm

29.06 mm

30 mm

area = 389.7 cm²

d
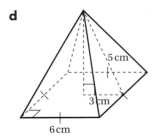
5 cm

3 cm

6 cm

e
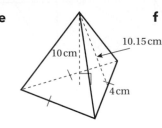
10 cm

10.15 cm

4 cm

f
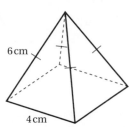
6 cm

4 cm

Tip

Pythagoras' theorem states that for a right-angled triangle, the square of the length of the hypotenuse, a, is equal to the sum of the squares of the lengths of the other two sides (b and c).

$$a^2 = b^2 + c^2$$

2 A pyramid is 16 cm tall and has a square base with side 7.5 cm.

Calculate the volume of the pyramid. Choose your answer from the options below.

A 40 cm³ B 300 cm³ C 900 cm³ D 2700 cm³

3 This is a photo of the Great Pyramid.

It has a square base.

Calculate the volume of the Great Pyramid.

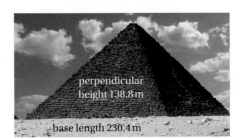
perpendicular height 138.8 m

base length 230.4 m

4 Pyramid A has a square base of side 6 m and perpendicular height 8 m.

Pyramid B has an equilateral triangle with side 6 m as a base and perpendicular height 8 m.

Find the difference in the volumes of the pyramids.

5 The wooden sculpture shown is a triangular-based pyramid.

The base is an equilateral triangle with side 1 m. The height of the sculpture is 2 m.

Calculate the volume of wood in the sculpture.

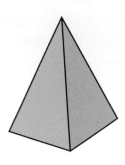

6 An obelisk is a square-based column with a pyramidal structure on the top.

Calculate the volume and surface area of the obelisk in the photograph.

It is 30 m high, the square base has an area of 5 m² and the pyramid itself is 1.5 m high.

Checklist of learning and understanding

Volume

- Volume is the amount of space a 3D object occupies.
- Volume is calculated in cubic units.
- The volume of a prism and a cylinder is the area of base × length.
- Volume of a cone = $\frac{1}{3}$ × area of base × height.
- Volume of a sphere = $\frac{4}{3}\pi r^3$.
- Volume of a pyramid = $\frac{1}{3}$ × area of base × height.

Surface area

- The surface area of a solid is the combined areas of all the external faces.

Chapter review

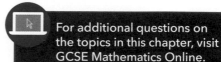
For additional questions on the topics in this chapter, visit GCSE Mathematics Online.

1   Calculate the area of canvas used to make this tent.

Assume the shape is a triangular prism and that there is no base sheet.

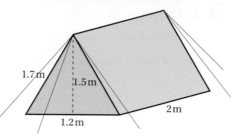

2   Each of these solids has been built from cubes with side length 2 cm.
Find the total surface area of each solid.

a

b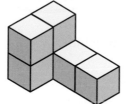

c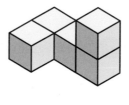

3   Calculate the volume of the model house in the diagram.

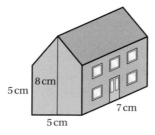

Find answers at: cambridge.org/ukschools/gcsemaths-studentbookanswers

4 This sculpture is made of a cube with a cylinder cut out through the middle of it.

Calculate the volume of the sculpture.

3 m

5 The dimensions of a cube are whole numbers. The volume of the cube is 64 cm³.

Which of the following whole numbers could be a side length?

A 4 cm   B 10 cm   C 8 cm   D 16 cm   E 5 cm

6 Calculate:

a the volume of the tin in the diagram

b the surface area of the printed label.

7 The diagram shows two cylinders.

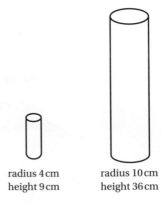

radius 4 cm
height 9 cm

radius 10 cm
height 36 cm

How many times bigger is the volume of the large cylinder than the small cylinder?

You must show your working.

(4 marks)

24 Further probability

In this chapter you will learn how to …

- use a range of sample space diagrams to list outcomes of combined events.
- apply the addition rule and use various representations to solve probability problems.

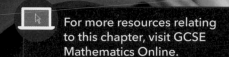

For more resources relating to this chapter, visit GCSE Mathematics Online.

Using mathematics: real-life applications

Medical researchers have developed a range of tests to detect drug use, blood-alcohol levels, disease markers and genetic and birth defects in unborn children. The probability that the test results are accurate is very high, but it is seldom 100%.

"An incorrect test result can be devastating. People can be convicted of drink-driving or more serious crimes, risk surgery or decide to terminate a pregnancy based on test results, so it is really important to understand the probability of a good test giving a bad result."

(Medical statistician)

Before you start …

Ch 5, 6	You'll need to be able to calculate effectively with fractions and decimals.	**1**	These calculations are all incorrect. What should the answers be? **a** $\frac{1}{8} + \frac{1}{4} = \frac{1}{12}$ **b** $\frac{2}{3} + \frac{1}{5} = \frac{2}{15}$ **c** $1 - \frac{3}{5} = -\frac{2}{5}$ **d** $\frac{2}{3} \times \frac{2}{5} = \frac{2}{15}$ **e** $0.3 \times 0.6 = 1.8$
KS3 Ch 19	You should be familiar with the vocabulary of basic probability.	**2**	Select the correct term from the box for each definition. event outcomes random sample space relative frequency **a** The ratio of number of times an event is recorded to the total number of trials conducted. **b** The results of an experiment. **c** An outcome of an experiment, such as getting heads when you toss a coin. **d** Having an equal likelihood of happening. **e** The list of all possible outcomes.
Ch 19	Check that you can list all the possible outcomes of an experiment.	**3**	Copy and complete each list of possible outcomes. **a** Two students are to be chosen at random from a group of males and females: FF, FM, … **b** Two coins are to be tossed at the same time: HH, … **c** Two cards are selected from a set of three cards labelled A, B and C and placed next to each other in the order they are drawn: AB, AC, …

Assess your starting point using the Launchpad

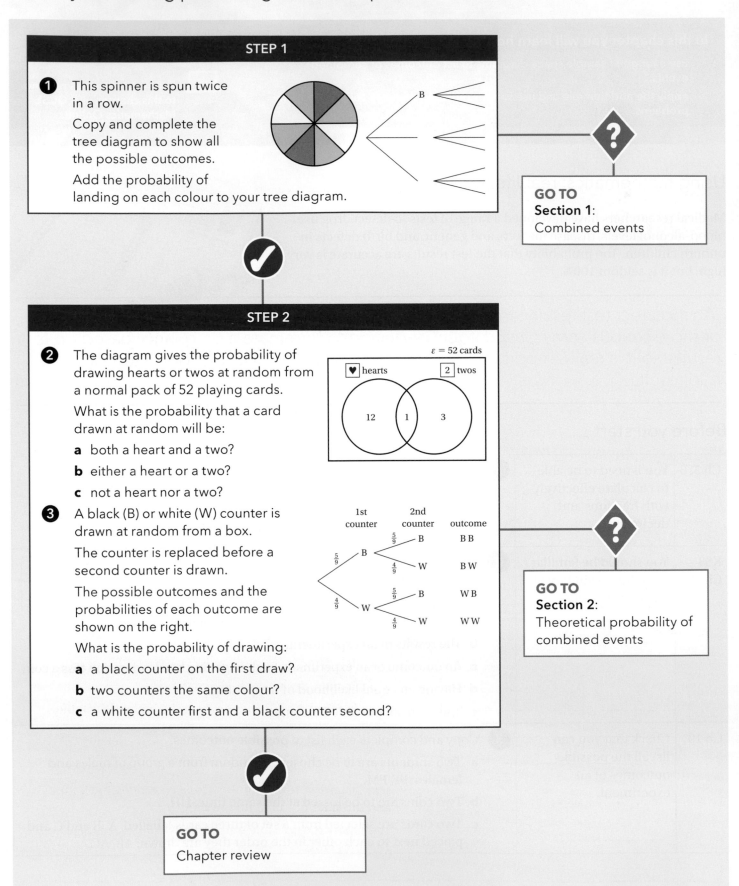

STEP 1

1 This spinner is spun twice in a row.

Copy and complete the tree diagram to show all the possible outcomes.

Add the probability of landing on each colour to your tree diagram.

GO TO
Section 1:
Combined events

STEP 2

2 The diagram gives the probability of drawing hearts or twos at random from a normal pack of 52 playing cards.

$\varepsilon = 52$ cards

♥ hearts   2 twos

12   1   3

What is the probability that a card drawn at random will be:

a both a heart and a two?

b either a heart or a two?

c not a heart nor a two?

3 A black (B) or white (W) counter is drawn at random from a box.

The counter is replaced before a second counter is drawn.

The possible outcomes and the probabilities of each outcome are shown on the right.

1st counter   2nd counter   outcome

$\frac{5}{9}$ B
$\frac{5}{9}$ B — $\frac{5}{9}$ B   B B
$\frac{4}{9}$ W   B W
$\frac{4}{9}$ W — $\frac{5}{9}$ B   W B
$\frac{4}{9}$ W   W W

What is the probability of drawing:

a a black counter on the first draw?

b two counters the same colour?

c a white counter first and a black counter second?

GO TO
Section 2:
Theoretical probability of combined events

GO TO
Chapter review

Section 1: Combined events

Two or more events can happen at the same time.

For example, if you toss a coin and roll a dice then you get heads (H) or tails (T) and a number from 1 to 6.

These are called **combined events** because there is a combination of outcomes.

You need to find efficient ways of identifying all the possible outcomes so that you can find the probability of different combinations of outcomes.

The diagram shows the **sample space** for tossing a coin and rolling a dice at the same time.

The sample space must include all possible outcomes of the combined events.

The sample space in the diagram can be represented as an ordered list like this:

H, 1   H, 2   H, 3   H, 4   H, 5   H, 6   T, 1   T, 2   T, 3   T, 4   T, 5   T, 6

Tables and grids

Listing the sample space can take a long time.

Two-way tables and grids let you work faster and also let you see quickly whether you have left out, or repeated any outcomes.

> ### Key vocabulary
>
> **combined events**: one event followed by another event producing two or more outcomes
>
> **sample space**: a list or diagram that shows all possible outcomes from two or more events

WORKED EXAMPLE 1

Represent the sample space for tossing a coin and rolling a dice using:

a a table   **b** a grid.

a *Table*

Coin \ Dice	1	2	3	4	5	6
Heads	H1	H2	H3	H4	H5	H6
Tails	T1	T2	T3	T4	T5	T6

Draw a two-way table with the numbers on a dice along the top and the sides of a coin down the side.

Then list the possible outcomes in the body of the table.

b *Grid*

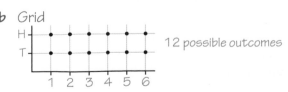

12 possible outcomes

Draw a grid with the numbers on a dice along the bottom and the sides of a coin up the side.

Then mark the possible outcomes as dots where the gridlines cross.

Find answers at: cambridge.org/ukschools/gcsemaths-studentbookanswers

Using tables to list probabilities of favourable outcomes

In some cases you don't have to list all the possible outcomes.

For example, this table shows how many ways there are to get a total score of 7 when you roll two ordinary dice.

Number on dice	1	2	3	4	5	6
1	2	3	4	5	6	7
2	3	4	5	6	7	
3	4	5	6	7		
4	5	6	7			
5	6	7				
6	7					

Once you get to a sum of 7 you can stop because the next sum will be greater than that.

The table shows there are six ways of getting a score of 7: (1, 6), (2, 5), (3, 4), (4, 3), (5, 2) and (6, 1).

Even though you haven't filled in the empty blocks, you can still see that there are 36 possible outcomes. So the probability of getting 7 is $\frac{6}{36}$ or $\frac{1}{6}$.

EXERCISE 24A

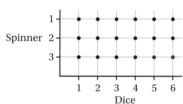

1 The grid represents the possible outcomes when you roll a dice and spin a triangular spinner marked 1, 2 and 3.

  a What is the probability of getting a total of 4? Choose the correct option below.

    A 3   B $\frac{1}{6}$ C $\frac{1}{4}$ D 0.4

  b What is the probability of getting a score of 4 or higher? Choose the correct option below.

    A 1   B $\frac{4}{5}$ C $\frac{5}{6}$ D 0.14

2 Use a grid to represent the sample space for:

  a tossing two coins

  b choosing a letter at random from the word CAT and tossing a coin

  c picking a counter from each of two bags containing one red, one blue and one yellow counter.

3 **a** Draw a table to show:

    i all possible combinations of scores when you roll two dice

    ii the sample space for tossing a coin and spinning a spinner with sectors A, B, C and D.

  b For each table drawn, make up five probability questions that could be answered from the tables. Exchange questions with a partner and answer each other's questions.

4 Two cards are taken at random from a normal pack of 52 cards.

Copy and complete this two-way table to show all the possible outcomes for drawing red or black cards.

First card / Second card	Diamonds (red)	Hearts (red)	Clubs (black)	Spades (black)
Diamonds (red)	RR			
Hearts (red)	RR			
Clubs (black)	RB			
Spades (black)	RB			

a How many possible outcomes are there?

b What is the probability of drawing two black cards?

c What is the most likely probability?

Venn diagrams

Venn diagrams show the mathematical relationships between sets of data.

Different events (sets of outcomes) are represented by circles inside a rectangular frame that in turn represents the sample space (universal set).

The Venn diagram below shows even numbers and multiples of 3 between 1 and 16.

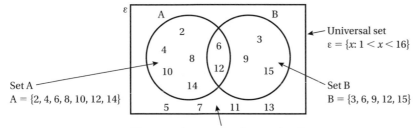

Universal set
$\varepsilon = \{x: 1 < x < 16\}$

Set A
$A = \{2, 4, 6, 8, 10, 12, 14\}$

Set B
$B = \{3, 6, 9, 12, 15\}$

These numbers are in ε, but not A or B.

ε is the universal set. In this case it the whole numbers between 1 and 16.

The circles A and B represent sets as shown in the diagram.

There are seven elements in set A. This can be written as n(A) = 7, which means 'the number of elements in set A is 7'.

There are five elements in set B, so n(B) = 5.

Elements that are common to both sets are written in the overlapping section of the circles to show that they belong to both sets.

Any elements of the universal set but **not** part of set A or set B are written inside the rectangle but outside the circles.

Intersection, union and complement of sets

Venn diagrams can also represent operations between sets. The three important operations for probability work are shown below.

The shaded area represents the intersection between set A and set B. The intersection of two sets is the elements that are common to (shared by) both sets.

$A \cap B = \{6, 12\}$

$n(A \cap B) = 2$

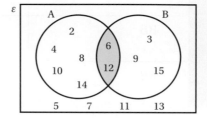

The shaded area here represents the union of set A and set B. This is the combined elements of both sets with no elements repeated.

$A \cup B = \{2, 3, 4, 6, 8, 9, 10, 12, 14, 15\}$

$n(A \cup B) = 10$

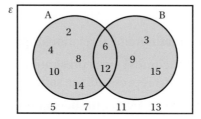

The complement of a set refers to all the elements in the universal set other than the ones in the given set.
The complement of set A is shaded below.

$A' = \{3, 5, 7, 9, 11, 13, 15\}$

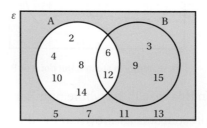

Set notation

Sometimes the information about sets is described in a specific way using set notation.

For example:

A = {integers greater than zero but less than 20}

This is quite a lot to write out, so it makes sense to use a shorter notation.

A = {integers > 0 but < 20}

C is the set of prime numbers greater than 10 but less than 20. You can write this as:

C = {11, 13, 17, 19}.

WORKED EXAMPLE 2

Draw a Venn diagram to represent the following information:

ε = {a, b, c, d, e, f, g, h}

A = {a, b, c, e}

B = {c, d, e, f, g}

c and e are elements of A and B, so A ∪ B = {c, e}

Start by comparing the sets to find the intersection and any elements that are in the universal set but not in A or B (the complement of A and B or (A ∪ B)'.

h is not in A or B, so (A ∩ B)' = h

In other words, h is outside the two circles.

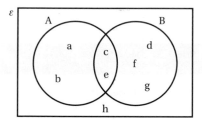

Draw the diagram and label it correctly.

In some problems you might be given information and have to define the sets yourself. In some cases you might not be able to list the separate elements of the sets so you write the number of elements in each set.

WORKED EXAMPLE 3

In a survey, 25 people were asked to say if they liked chocolate and if they liked ice cream.

Fifteen people said they liked ice cream and eighteen said they liked chocolate.

Draw a Venn diagram and use it to work out the probability that a person chosen at random from this group will like both chocolate and ice cream.

ε = {number of people surveyed}, so, n(ε) = 25
C = {people who like chocolate}, so, n(C) = 18
I = {people who like ice cream}, so, n(I) = 15
n(C) + n(I) = 18 + 15 = 33
But there were only 25 people surveyed, so 8 people must have said they liked both chocolate and ice cream (since 33 − 25 = 8). This tells you that: n(C ∩ I) = 8

Start by defining the sets and writing the information in set language.

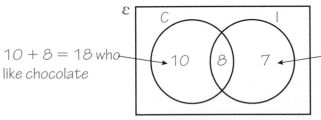

10 + 8 = 18 who like chocolate

8 + 7 = 15 who like ice-cream

Use the figures to draw your Venn diagram.

P(person likes both) = $\dfrac{\text{number of people who like both}}{\text{number of people surveyed}}$

 = $\dfrac{8}{25}$ = 0.32

Finally, calculate the probability.

Tip

You don't know the names of the people, so you can't list them in the diagram. You do know how many of each response there was, so you can just write the number of people in the diagram.

EXERCISE 24B

1 Use this Venn diagram to answer the following questions.

Choose the option to correctly complete the statements given.

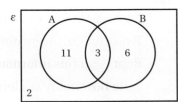

a n(A) = ☐

    A 9   B 6   C 11   D 14

b n(A ∪ B) = ☐

    A 14   B 20   C 22   D 23

c n(A ∩ B) = ☐

    A 2   B 3   C 9   D 20

2 ε = {integers from 1 to 20 inclusive}, A = {6, 7, 8, 9, 10, 11, 12} and
B = {factors of 24}.

    a Draw a Venn diagram to show this information.

    b Use your Venn diagram to find:

       i $A \cap B$ **ii** $A \cup B$ **iii** n(A)   **iv** n(A′)   **v** B′

3 The Venn diagram shows the different sports chosen by students from one particular class.

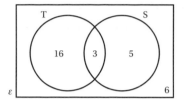

T represents students who play tennis and S represents those who take swimming.

    a How many students are in the class?

    b How many students play tennis?

    c How many students play tennis and swim?

    d If a student is chosen at random from the class, what is the probability that he or she will take swimming?

4 Nadia has 20 pairs of shoes.

Six pairs are sports shoes, four pairs are red. Only one of the pairs of sports shoes is red.

Draw a Venn diagram to show this information.

Work out the probability that a pair of shoes chosen at random from her shoe collection will be neither red nor sports shoes.

5 A factory employs 100 people.

Forty-seven of the employees have to work with moving machinery. If these people have long hair they have to tie it back.

Thirty-five employees have long hair and, of these, some work with moving machinery.

Twenty-three employees neither have long hair nor work with moving machinery.

Draw a Venn diagram to show this information.

Use your diagram to work out the probability of a random employee having to tie his or her hair back at work.

6 Twenty students walked into a classroom.

Of these students, 13 were wearing headphones and 15 were sending texts.

Four students were not wearing headphones nor sending texts.

Represent this information on a Venn diagram.

State how many students were wearing headphones while sending texts when they walked into class.

Find answers at: cambridge.org/ukschools/gcsemaths-studentbookanswers

Tip

Tree diagrams show probabilities, not actual responses. This is the main difference between them and the frequency trees you worked with in Chapter 19.

Tree diagrams

A tree diagram is a branching diagram that shows all the possible outcomes (sample space) of one or more activity.

To draw a tree diagram:

- draw a dot to represent the first activity
- draw branches from the dot to show all possible outcomes of that activity only
- write the outcomes at the end of each branch
- draw a dot at the end of each branch to represent the next activity
- draw branches from this point to show all possible outcomes of that activity
- write the outcomes at the end of the branches.

These two diagrams both show the possible outcomes for throwing a dice and tossing a coin at the same time. Both diagrams are correct.

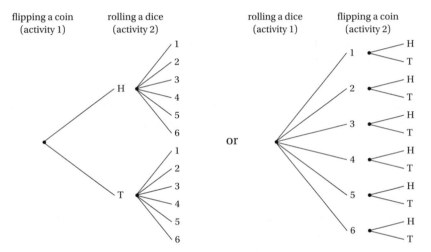

Once you've drawn a tree diagram you can list the possible outcomes by following the paths along the branches.

Listing the combinations lets you work out the probability of different events.

WORKED EXAMPLE 4

Draw a tree diagram to show that when the probability of having a boy or a girl is equal, there are eight possible combinations of boys and girls in a three-child family. Then work out the probability of having three children with the same gender.

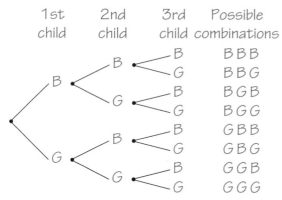

Draw a dot for the first-born child.

Draw and label two branches, one B and one G.

Repeat this at the end of each branch for the second and third child.

List the possible combinations.

You can see from the diagram that there are 8 possible combinations of boys and girls.

There is only one outcome that produces 3 girls so:

$P(3 \text{ girls}) = \frac{1}{8}$

Similarly:

$P(\text{all the same gender}) = \frac{2}{8} = \frac{1}{4}$

You can use the diagram to find different probabilities.

 Did you know?

This tree diagram assumes that a boy or a girl is equally likely for each pregnancy. In reality the probability of having a boy or a girl varies by family and by country. In China, the probability of having a boy is much higher than in other countries (for various reasons). Worldwide, the probability of having a boy is a little higher than having a girl. The UN estimates that in 2013 there were 107 boys born for every 100 girls born.

EXERCISE 24C

1 Here are two groups of jelly beans.

Draw a tree diagram to show the sample space for taking a different coloured jelly bean at random from each group of jelly beans.

2 Sandy has a bag containing a red, a blue and a green pen.

Copy and complete this tree diagram to show the sample space when she takes a pen from the bag at random, replaces it, and then takes another pen.

3 Draw a tree diagram to show the sample space when three coins are tossed one after the other.

State the number of ways there are to get two heads and a tail.

4 Customers of a gift-wrapping service can choose striped, checked, metallic, spiral or plain brown wrapping paper.

They then choose white, silver, black or pink ribbon.

a Draw a tree diagram to show all the possible combinations of paper and ribbon.

b How many possible combinations are there?

Choose from the following options.

A 2　　　　　　B 4　　　　　C 9　　　　　　　D 20

c What is the probability that a customer will choose metallic paper and a silver ribbon?

d What is the probability of choosing metallic or brown paper with a black ribbon?

5 In a knockout quiz, the winner goes on to the next round.

Hassan takes part in a four-round quiz and he estimates that he has an equal chance of winning or losing each round.

a Using W to represent win and L to represent lose, draw a tree diagram to show all possible outcomes for Hassan.

b How many possible outcomes are there?

c What is the probability that he will win the first round given his own estimate of his chances?

Section 2: Theoretical probability of combined events

You can use sample space diagrams (tables, grids, tree diagrams and Venn diagrams) to find the probabilities of combined events.

Once you have identified all the possible outcomes, you mark the ones that are favourable and use these to find the probability of different outcomes.

You work this out using the formula:

$$P(\text{event happens}) = \frac{\text{number of ways the event can happen}}{\text{number of possible outcomes}}$$

WORKED EXAMPLE 5

Jay has six cards with the numbers 0, 0, 2, 2, 3 and 7 on them.

He picks a number, returns it and then picks another at random.

a Draw a grid to show the sample space.

b Use the grid to find the probability that Jay will pick:

  i two numbers that are the same

  ii two numbers that add up to 7.

a

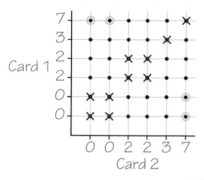

The grid shows there are 36 possible outcomes.

b i $P(\text{two numbers the same}) = \dfrac{10}{36}$

$$= \dfrac{5}{18}$$

or 0.28 (to 2 dp)

The successful outcomes are marked with a cross on the grid.

  ii $P(\text{sum of } 7) = \dfrac{4}{36}$

$$= \dfrac{1}{9}$$

The successful outcomes are circled on the grid.

EXERCISE 24D

1 A coin is tossed twice. What is the probability of getting two tails?

Choose from the options below.

A $\dfrac{1}{2}$ B $\dfrac{1}{4}$ C $\dfrac{3}{4}$ D $\dfrac{1}{3}$

2 In a restaurant diners can have their meal served with a choice of chips, baked potato or rice, as well as a choice of green salad, coleslaw or mixed vegetables.

  a Draw up a tree diagram and complete it to show the sample space for the possible side dish combinations.

  b What is the probability of choosing rice and salad? (Assume each choice is equally likely.)

  c What is the probability of choosing rice and potatoes?

3 One box contains a red, a yellow and a blue marble, the other box contains a red, a green and a purple marble.

   a Draw up a table to show the sample space if you choose one marble at random from each box.

   b What is the probability of choosing two red marbles?

   c What is the probability of choosing a red and a purple marble?

   d Is it possible to end up with one yellow marble and one blue marble? Give a reason for your answer.

4 Linda and Annie each take a coin at random out of their pockets and add the totals together.

Linda has two £1 coins, a 50p coin, a £2 coin and three 20p coins in her pocket.

Annie has three £2 coins, one £1 coin and three 50p coins.

   a Draw up a two-way table to show all the possible outcomes for the sum of the two coins.

   b What is the probability that the coins will add up to exactly £2.50?

   c What is the probability of the coins adding up to less than £2?

   d What is the probability that the coins will add up to £3 or more?

Different types of events

The type of event determines whether you add or multiply the probabilities.

Mutually exclusive events and the addition rule

P(A or B) = P(A) + P(B), where A and B are mutually exclusive events.

This is called the addition rule for mutually exclusive events.

For example, a bag contains 3 red, 2 yellow and 5 green sweets in it and you choose one sweet at random.

You cannot pick a red sweet and a yellow sweet at the same time, so the events P(red) and P(yellow) are mutually exclusive.

You can work out the probability of choosing *either* a red *or* a yellow sweet.

There are 3 red and 2 yellow sweets, so $\frac{5}{10}$ of the sweets are either red or yellow.

$$P(\text{red or yellow}) = P(\text{red}) + P(\text{yellow}) = \frac{3}{10} + \frac{2}{10} = \frac{5}{10} = \frac{1}{2}$$

Tip

You should remember from Chapter 19 that mutually exclusive events cannot happen at the same time.

Tip

Questions with 'either–or' events usually involve mutually exclusive events so they can be solved by adding the probabilities.

Events that are not mutually exclusive

When you list the elements in the union of sets you do not repeat shared elements (those in the intersection).

In set language, we can write this as $n(A \cup B) = n(A) + n(B) - n(A \cap B)$. The elements in the intersection of sets are not mutually exclusive and this affects your probability calculations.

$$P(A \ or \ B) = P(A) + P(B) - P(A \ and \ B)$$

WORKED EXAMPLE 6

The Venn diagram shows the possible outcomes when a six-sided dice is rolled. Set A = {prime numbers} and set B = {odd numbers}. Use the diagram to find the probability of rolling a number that is either odd or prime.

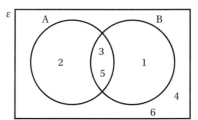

$P(A \ or \ B) = P(A) + P(B) - P(A \ and \ B)$

$P(A) = \dfrac{3}{6}$

$P(B) = \dfrac{3}{6}$

$P(A \ and \ B) = \dfrac{2}{6}$

> The total number of outcomes is the denominator.
>
> It is easier to add and subtract the fractions if you don't simplify the fractions first.

$So, P(A \ or \ B) = \dfrac{3}{6} + \dfrac{3}{6} - \dfrac{2}{6} = \dfrac{4}{6} = \dfrac{2}{3}$

> You can see this is true by looking at the diagram.
>
> The combined elements of A and B are 1, 2, 3 and 5, giving you $\dfrac{4}{6}$ numbers falling into one or the other of these sets.
>
> We don't want to add the numbers that fall into the intersecting part twice which is why we subtract $n(A \cap B)$ in the formula.

Key vocabulary

independent events: events that are not affected by what happened before

Independent events

When the outcome of one event does not affect the outcome of the others, the events are **independent**.

For example, rolling a dice and tossing a coin are independent events. The score on the dice doesn't affect whether you get heads or tails.

Tree diagrams are useful for solving problems involving independent events. You write the probabilities of the events on the branches.

Here is the tree diagram showing possible outcomes for throwing a dice and tossing a coin at the same time (H is used for a head and T is used for a tail).

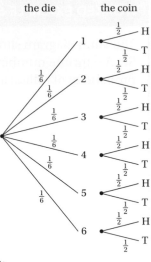

The probability of combined events on a tree diagram

Tip

It can be helpful to use a colour to mark the route along the branches to show which events you are dealing with.

To find the probability of one particular combination of outcomes, multiply the probabilities on consecutive branches.

For example, the probability of throwing a 5 and getting heads is $\frac{1}{6} \times \frac{1}{2} = \frac{1}{12}$

This is called the multiplication rule and it works for independent events only.

$$P(A \text{ and } B) = P(A) \times P(B)$$

Combining the rules

To find the probability when there is more than one favourable combination or when the events are mutually exclusive:

- multiply the probabilities on consecutive branches
- add the probabilities (of each favourable combination) obtained by multiplication,

  for example, throwing 1 or 2 and getting heads is

  $$\left(\frac{1}{6} \times \frac{1}{2}\right) + \left(\frac{1}{6} \times \frac{1}{2}\right) = \frac{1}{12} + \frac{1}{12} = \frac{2}{12} = \frac{1}{6}$$

WORKED EXAMPLE 7

Two coins are tossed together. Draw a tree diagram to find the probability of getting:

a two tails **b** one head and one tail.

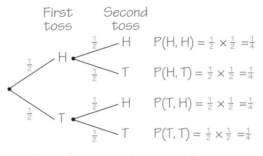

Draw the tree diagram first.

a P(TT) = P(T on 1st toss) × P(T on 2nd toss)

$$= \frac{1}{2} \times \frac{1}{2} = \frac{1}{4}$$

Multiply the probabilities on consecutive branches.

b P(HT or TH) = P(HT) + P(TH)

$$= \left(\frac{1}{2} \times \frac{1}{2}\right) + \left(\frac{1}{2} \times \frac{1}{2}\right)$$

$$= \frac{1}{4} + \frac{1}{4} = \frac{1}{2}$$

Add the probabilities obtained by multiplication.

Dependent events

When the outcome of one event affects the outcome of the other, the events are said to be **dependent**.

Here are 4 red and 2 yellow sweets.

 Key vocabulary

dependent events: events in which the outcome is affected by what happened before

One sweet is removed at random before a second sweet is removed. What is the probability of the second sweet being red?

The answer to this depends on what colour the first sweet was. If the first sweet was red then the probability on the second branch that the second sweet was red is $\frac{3}{5}$, because there are only 5 sweets left and only 3 of those are red.

 1 red eaten

If the first sweet was yellow then the probability on the second branch that the second sweet was red is $\frac{4}{5}$. There are still only 5 sweets left to choose from, but this time 4 of them are red.

 1 yellow eaten

Find answers at: cambridge.org/ukschools/gcsemaths-studentbookanswers

For dependent events you can find the probability by adapting the multiplication rule to accommodate the dependent event.

P(A *and then* B) = P(A) × P(B *given that* A *has occurred*)

This example shows how you can use modified tree diagrams to work this out.

WORKED EXAMPLE 8

A box contains three yellow, four red and two purple marbles.

A marble is chosen at random and not replaced before choosing the next one.

Three marbles are chosen (without replacement), what is the probability of choosing:

a three red marbles?   **b** a yellow, a red and a purple marble in that order?

a These are the only outcomes we need

another red out so only 2 left
only 7 marbles left to choose from

1 red out already so 3 left
only 8 marbles left altogether

$P(RRR) = \frac{4}{9} \times \frac{3}{8} \times \frac{2}{7} = \frac{1}{21}$

> Draw only the part of the tree diagram that you need.
>
> Work out the probability by multiplying the probabilities on consecutive branches.

b We need Y/R/P   still 4 red but only 8 to choose from

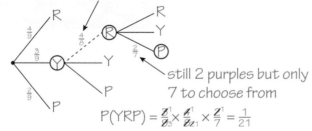

still 2 purples but only 7 to choose from

$P(YRP) = \frac{3}{9} \times \frac{4}{8} \times \frac{2}{7} = \frac{1}{21}$

> Draw only the part of the tree diagram that you need.
>
> Work out the probability by multiplying the probabilities on relevant branches.

EXERCISE 24E

1 Which of these rules would you use to find the joint probability of two independent events?

A P(A) + P(B)   B P(A) × P(B)   C P(A) × P(B *given* A)

2 In a class of 28 students, 12 take physics, 15 take chemistry and 8 take neither physics nor chemistry.

a Draw a Venn diagram to represent this information.

b What is the probability that a student chosen at random from this class:

i takes physics but not chemistry?

ii takes physics or chemistry?

iii takes physics and chemistry?

3 Nico chooses one consonant and one vowel at random from the names of towns on road signs he passes.

The next road sign is DUNDEE.

a Draw up a sample space diagram to list all the options that Nico has.

b Calculate P(D *and* E).

c Calculate P(D *and* (E *or* U)).

d Calculate P(*not* (N *and* U)).

4 A bag contains 3 red counters, 4 green counters, 2 yellow counters and 1 white counter.

Two counters are drawn from the bag one after the other, without being replaced.

Calculate:

a P(2 red counters)   **b** P(2 green counters)

c P(2 yellow counters)   **d** P(white *and then* red)

e P(white *or* yellow *in any order, but not both yellow*)

f P(white *or* red *in any order, but not both red*)

g P(white *or* yellow *first and then any other colour*).

5 Mohammed has four tiles from a word game with the letters A, B, C and D on them.

He draws a letter at random and places it on the table. He then draws a second letter and a third, placing them down next to the previously drawn letter.

a Work out the probability that the letters he has drawn spell the words:

  i cad   **ii** bad   **iii** dad

b Work out the probability that he will not draw the letter B.

c Work out the probability of drawing the letters in alphabetical order.

6 In a standard pack of cards, A = {hearts} and B = {kings}. If a card is picked at random, work out:

a P(A)   **b** P(B)   **c** P(A *and* B)   **d** P(A *or* B)

7 Ruth has a bag containing 18 fruit drop sweets.

Ten are apple flavoured and eight are blackberry flavoured.

She chooses a sweet at random and eats it.

Then she chooses another sweet at random.

a Calculate the probability that:

  i both sweets are apple flavoured

  ii both sweets are blackberry flavoured

  iii the first is apple and the second is blackcurrant

  iv the first is blackberry and the second is apple.

b Add up your answers from part **a**. Give a reason why you should get an answer of 1 if you worked out the probabilities correctly.

Find answers at: cambridge.org/ukschools/gcsemaths-studentbookanswers

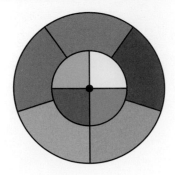

8 Adrianna has a colour wheel with four colours on the inside and five colours on the outside as shown. She turns the wheel to find possible combinations of two colours.

  a Draw a sample space to show all the possible colour combinations on this wheel.

  b Work out P(blue *and* brown).

  c Work out P(yellow *or* orange).

  d Adrianna doesn't like green or orange.

   If she picks a combination at random, what is the chance that she will get a combination with either or both of these colours?

9 The labels were accidentally knocked off three students' lockers.

The labels say Raju, Sam and Kerry.

The tree diagram shows the possible ways of replacing the labels.

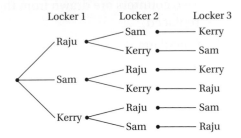

  a Copy the diagram and write the probabilities next to each branch.

  b Are these events dependent or independent? Give a reason for your answer.

  c How many correct ways are there to match the name labels to the lockers?

  d How many possible ways are there for the labels to be replaced on the lockers?

  e If the labels were randomly stuck back on to the lockers, what is the chance of getting the names correct?

  f Work out the probability of getting the labels on lockers 2 and 3 correct given that the first one is correctly labelled Kerry.

Checklist of learning and understanding

Representing combined events

- The sample space of an event is all the possible outcomes of the event.
- When an event has two or more stages it is called a combined event.
- Lists, tables, grids, tree diagrams and Venn diagram can be used to represent combined events.

Calculating probabilities for combined events

- For mutually exclusive events, P(A *or* B) = P(A) + P(B).
- For independent events, P(A *and* B) = P(A) × P(B).
- When independent events are mutually exclusive, you need to add the probabilities obtained by multiplication.
- For dependent events, P(A *and then* B) = P(A) × P(B *given that* A *has occurred*).

Chapter review

 For additional questions on the topics in this chapter, visit GCSE Mathematics Online.

1 Choose the most appropriate method and represent the sample space in each of the following.

a A coin is tossed and an 8-sided dice, with faces numbered 0 to 7, is rolled at the same time.

b Boxes A, B and C contain pink and yellow tickets. A box is selected at random and a ticket is drawn from it.

c The number of ways in which three letters P, A and N might be arranged to form a three-letter sequence.

d In a class of 24 students, 10 take art, 12 take music and 5 take neither.

2 Two normal six-sided dice are rolled simultaneously. Draw a sample space for this information and hence calculate the probability of rolling:

a double 2   **b** at least one 4

c a total greater than 9   **d** a total of 6 or 7.

3 The letters from the word MANCHESTER are written on cards and placed in a bag.

a One letter is drawn at random. Work out the probability of drawing a vowel.

b A letter is drawn from the bag, noted and replaced and then another letter is drawn.

Copy and complete this tree diagram to show all the probabilities.

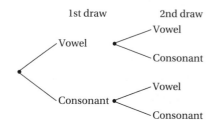

c Use the tree diagram to work out the probability of drawing:

i two vowels   **ii** two consonants

iii a vowel and a consonant   **iv** at least one consonant.

d Give a reason why drawing the letters can be considered independent events in this case.

e How could you change the experiment to make the events dependent?

4 The probability of rolling a six on a biased dice is $\frac{1}{5}$

The dice is rolled twice.

a Copy and complete the tree diagram.

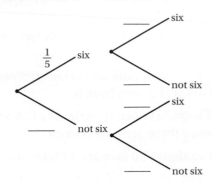

(2 marks)

b Work out the probability of rolling exactly one six.　　*(2 marks)*

© *AQA 2013*

5 There are 50 students in a year group.

Thirty have brown eyes, nine have fair hair and three have both brown eyes and fair hair.

Represent this information on a Venn diagram.

Use the Venn diagram to work out the probability that a student chosen at random from this group:

a has neither brown eyes nor fair hair

b has brown eyes but not fair hair.

6 The probability of the sun shining on a given day of the weekend is given as 0.3

What is the probability of it being sunny on both Saturday and Sunday?

Choose from the options below.

A 0.6　　　　　　B 0.9　　　　　　C 0.03　　　　　　D 0.09

7 An unbiased cubical dice has six faces numbered 4, 6, 10, 12, 15 and 24.

The dice is thrown twice and the highest common factor (HCF) of the scores is recorded.

a Draw a probability diagram to show the possible outcomes.

b Calculate the probability that:

　i the HCF is 2

　ii the HCF is greater than 2

　iii the HCF is not 7

　iv the HCF is 3 or 5.

25 Inequalities

In this chapter you will learn how to …

- use the correct symbols to express inequalities.
- understand and interpret inequalities.
- solve linear inequalities in one variable and represent the solution set on a number line.

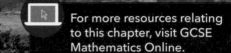

For more resources relating to this chapter, visit GCSE Mathematics Online.

Using mathematics: real-life applications

Inequalities are one way of showing the ranges of values that have to be met and considered in running a successful business. For example, a business might want wastage to be less than a certain figure, or profit to be greater or equal to a particular amount.

"I work in quality control in food standards. One of my jobs is to check that the quality and size of the ingredients match the details shown on the labels."   *(Quality controller)*

Before you start …

Ch 17	You must be able to solve linear equations.	**1**	**a** If $3x + 2 = 2x + 5$, then $x = ?$ **b** If $4(n + 3) = 6(n - 1)$, then $n = ?$
Ch 1, 4	You should be confident with ranking numbers in ascending or descending order.	**2**	Write this set of numbers in numerical ascending order: $-2 \qquad 50 \qquad -27 \qquad \dfrac{1}{3} \qquad 1.25 \qquad 2\%$
Ch 1, 4	You need to remember the rules for operations with negative integers.	**3**	Evaluate the following: **a** $5 \times (-2)$ **b** $-5 \times (-2)$ **c** $12 \div 6$ **d** $12 \div (-6)$ **e** $7 - (-1)$

Find answers at: cambridge.org/ukschools/gcsemaths-studentbookanswers

Assess your starting point using the Launchpad

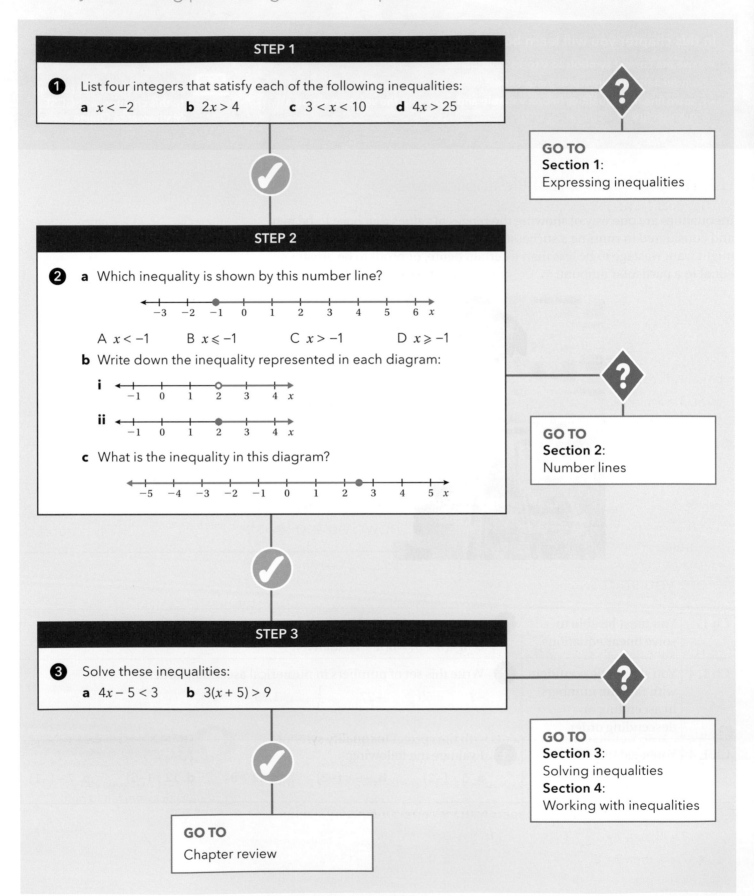

STEP 1

❶ List four integers that satisfy each of the following inequalities:

a $x < -2$ **b** $2x > 4$ **c** $3 < x < 10$ **d** $4x > 25$

GO TO
Section 1:
Expressing inequalities

STEP 2

❷ **a** Which inequality is shown by this number line?

A $x < -1$ B $x \leqslant -1$ C $x > -1$ D $x \geqslant -1$

b Write down the inequality represented in each diagram:

i

ii

c What is the inequality in this diagram?

GO TO
Section 2:
Number lines

STEP 3

❸ Solve these inequalities:

a $4x - 5 < 3$ **b** $3(x + 5) > 9$

GO TO
Section 3:
Solving inequalities
Section 4:
Working with inequalities

GO TO
Chapter review

Section 1: Expressing inequalities

An **inequality** is a mathematical sentence that uses symbols, such as $<$, $\leqslant$, $>$ or $\geqslant$, in place of an equals sign.

The expressions on either side of the symbol are not equal.

The most common inequality symbols are:

> $>$ greater than
>
> $<$ less than
>
> $\geqslant$ greater than or equal to
>
> $\leqslant$ less than or equal to.

Two inequality symbols are used to give a range of values.

For example,

$2 < x < 6$ means 2 is *less than x* and *x is less than* 6.

Another way to read this statement is to say *x* lies between 2 and 6.

Addition and subtraction of inequalities

If you add the same number to both sides of an inequality, then the resulting inequality is still true.

If you subtract the same number from both sides of an inequality, then the resulting inequality is still true.

Multiplication and division of inequalities

If you multiply or divide both sides of an inequality by a positive number, then the resulting inequality is still true.

If you multiply or divide both sides of an inequality by a negative number, then you must **reverse** the inequality sign to make the resulting inequality true.

For example:

$7 > 3$

if you multiply both sides by -2 then the result is:

$-14 < -6$

EXERCISE 25A

1 Copy and complete the statements with the correct inequality symbol.

  a $7 > 3$, then $4 + 7 \,\square\, 4 + 3$ **b** $8 < 13$, then $8 - 5 \,\square\, 13 - 5$

  c $-5 < -1$, then $-5 + 3 \,\square\, -1 + 3$ **d** $-4 > -11$, then $-4 - 6 \,\square\, -11 - 6$

2 Copy and complete the statements with the correct inequality symbol.

  a $7 > 3$, then $2 \times 7 \,\square\, 2 \times 3$ **b** $8 < 13$, then $2 \times 8 \,\square\, 2 \times 13$

  c $7 > 3$, then $7 \div 2 \,\square\, 3 \div 2$ **d** $8 < 13$, then $8 \div 2 \,\square\, 13 \div 2$

Tip

Remember that you read inequalities from left to right.

3 Copy and complete the statements with the correct inequality symbol.

a $7 > 3$, then $(-2) \times 7 \square (-2) \times 3$ **b** $8 < 13$, then $(-2) \times 8 \square (-2) \times 13$

c $7 > 3$, then $7 \div (-2) \square 3 \div (-2)$ **d** $8 < 13$, then $8 \div (-2) \square 13 \div (-2)$

4 List the whole number values for x if $x > 6$ and $x \leqslant 8$. Choose from the following options.

A 6, 7   B 6, 7, 8   C 6, 7   D 7, 8

5 For each inequality, list four whole numbers that satisfy the inequality.

a $x > 14$ **b** $x \geqslant 6$ **c** $x \leqslant -2$

d $x + 3 \geqslant 7$ **e** $x - 4 \leqslant 5$

6 If $x > 6$ how many values can x take?

7 If $3 < x < 8$, how many whole number (integer) values can x take?

How many values can x take if you include decimal values or fractions?

8 What whole number values are given by $6 > x > 2$?

Section 2: Number lines

You can use a **number line** to illustrate an inequality.

When drawing and illustrating values on a number line you use an open dot (small circle) if the starting value is not included. You use a solid dot if the starting point is included.

The expression $x \leqslant 11$ means numbers less than 11 including 11. So a number line representing $x \leqslant 11$ shows values starting from and including 11 with a solid dot at 11.

The expression $x > 11$ means numbers greater than 11. So a number line representing $x > 11$ starts at 11 but the open dot is taken to signify that 11 is not included.

EXERCISE 25B

1 Choose the correct inequality represented by this diagram.

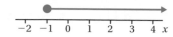

A $x > -1$ B $x < -1$ C $x \geqslant -1$ D $x \geqslant -2$

2 Draw number lines to indicate each of the following inequalities.

a $x > 4$ **b** $x \leqslant (-1)$ **c** $x \geqslant (-5)$ **d** $3 \leqslant x \leqslant 10$

e $(-3) \leqslant x \leqslant 10$ **f** $(-10) \leqslant x \leqslant (-3)$

3 Write the inequalities that are shown in the number line diagrams.

a

b

c

d

e

4 Write an inequality to describe each of these diagrams.

a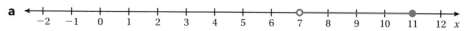

b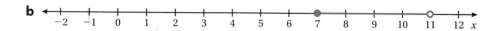

c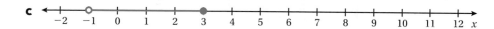

d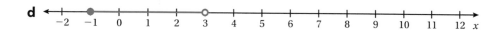

Section 3: Solving inequalities

Solving a linear inequality means finding all of the values for x that satisfy that inequality.

You can solve inequalities using the same methods that you used for linear equations.

However, you must apply the rules that you learned in Section 1.

WORKED EXAMPLE 1

Solve for x. Show your solutions on a number line.

a $4x - 5 < 3$ **b** $\dfrac{5x - 3}{2} \geqslant 11$ **c** $-5 \leqslant 3x + 4 \leqslant 13$

a $4x - 5 < 3$
$\quad 4x < 8$
$\quad\; x < 2$

> Add 5 to both sides.
> Dividing both sides by 4.
> Draw number line.

b $\dfrac{5x - 3}{2} \geqslant 11$
$\quad 5x - 3 \geqslant 22$

> Multiply both sides by 2 to cancel out the denominator.
> Add 3 to both sides.

$\quad\;\; 5x \geqslant 25$
$\quad\;\;\; x \geqslant 5$

> Divide both sides by 5.
> Draw number line.

c $\quad -5 \leqslant 3x + 4 \leqslant 13$
$\quad -5 - 4 \leqslant 3x \leqslant 13 - 4$
$\quad\;\; -9 \leqslant 3x \leqslant 9$
$\quad\;\; -3 \leqslant x \leqslant 3$

> Subtract 4 from each expression.
>
> Divide all the terms by 3.
> Draw number line.

EXERCISE 25C

1 Choose the answer that satisfies the inequality $12 - x \geqslant 18$.

    A $x \leqslant 6$ B $x \geqslant 6$ C $x \geqslant -6$ D $x \leqslant -6$

2 Solve:

    a $x + 3 \geqslant 7$ **b** $x - 7 \leqslant 4$ **c** $x + 12 > 9$

    d $x - 2 < 3$ **e** $x + 4 \geqslant -8$ **f** $x - 10 > -6$

    g $x - 5 > -12$ **h** $2x \geqslant 6$ **i** $3x > -15$

    j $3(x + 5) \geqslant 9$ **k** $2(5x - 2) > 5$ **l** $2(x - 3) \leqslant 5$

    m $\dfrac{x + 3}{2} \leqslant \dfrac{3 - x}{2}$ **n** $-5x + 3 \geqslant 78$

3 Solve:

    a $4x \leqslant 20$ **b** $-10x \geqslant 130$ **c** $-12x > -42$

    d $\dfrac{-x}{2} \leqslant 5$ **e** $\dfrac{-x}{5} > 4$ **f** $3 - 2x > 5$

    g $2 - 5x \leqslant -8$ **h** $4(7 - x) < 5$

4 Solve:

    a $5(x - 2) - 2(3x + 1) > 0$ **b** $5(2x - 3) < 4(x + 3)$

    c $3(x + 4) - 4(x + 2) > 0$ **d** $2(3x - 7) - 5(2x + 3) \leqslant 0$

Tip

Remember, if you multiply or divide both sides of an inequality by a negative number, then you must reverse the inequality sign to make the resulting inequality true.

Section 4: Working with inequalities

WORK IT OUT 25.1

Solve for x:

$2x - 5 < 1$

Which is the correct solution? Identify the errors made in the incorrect solutions.

Option A	Option B	Option C
$2x - 5 + 5 < 1 + 5$	$2x - 5 + 5 > 1 + 5$	$2x - 5 - 5 < 1 - 5$
$2x < 6$	$2x > 6$	$2x < -4$
$\dfrac{2x}{2} < \dfrac{6}{2}$	$\dfrac{2x}{2} > \dfrac{6}{2}$	$\dfrac{2x}{2} < -4$
$x < 3$	$x > 3$	$x < -2$

EXERCISE 25D

1 Solve each inequality and draw a number line to show the range of values each inequality can take.

   a $x + 1 > 5$ **b** $2x - 1 < 6$ **c** $\dfrac{x + 1}{2} \geqslant -4$

   d $-2x + 1 \leqslant 6$ **e** $1 - 5x \geqslant 21$ **f** $3d + 5 \leqslant 5d + 7$

2 The values for x are whole numbers and satisfy the inequality $0 < x < 10$.

   Copy and complete the Venn diagram with the correct values for x.

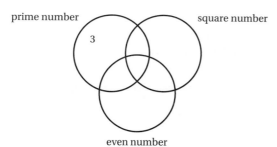

3 To solve the following problems, first write the statements as inequalities.

   Then solve for the variable.

   a When 5 is added to twice p, the result is greater than 17. What values can p take?

   b When 16 is subtracted from half of q, the result is less than 18. What values can q take?

   c The sum of $4d$ and 6 is greater than the sum of $2d$ and 18. What values can d take?

   d A number a is increased by 3 and this amount is then doubled. If the result of this is greater than a, what values can a take?

Find answers at: cambridge.org/ukschools/gcsemaths-studentbookanswers

4 **a** Richard works part-time for £12 an hour. He saves 25% of what he earns.

How many hours will he need to work in order to save at least £75 in a week?

b Lara works for £p an hour and saves 25% of what she earns.

Write an inequality that expresses the number of hours she will need to work in order to save at least £75 in a week.

 Checklist of learning and understanding

Describing inequalities

- Inequalities use the symbols >, <, ⩾, ⩽ and indicate a range of values.
- Inequalities can be illustrated on a number line:

  A closed dot (●) indicates that the starting value is included.

  An open dot (○) indicates that the starting value is not included.

Addition and subtraction rules of inequalities

- If $a > b$, then $a \pm c > b \pm c$; likewise, if $a < b$, then $a \pm c < b \pm c$.

Multiplication and division rules of inequalities

- Multiplying or dividing by a positive number: if $a > b$ and $c > 0$, then

  $ac > bc$ and $\dfrac{a}{c} > \dfrac{b}{c}$

- Multiplying or dividing by a negative number: $10 > 8$, but if you multiply by -2 then $-20 < -16$; if you divide by -2 then $-5 < -4$. You must reverse the sign in each case. In other words: if $a > b$ and $c < 0$, then $ac < bc$ and $\dfrac{a}{c} < \dfrac{b}{c}$

Solving inequalities

- Linear inequalities in one variable can be solved as equations. The answer indicates a range of values for the variable.

 For additional questions on the topics in this chapter, visit GCSE Mathematics Online.

Chapter review

1 Which set shows all the integer values of x that satisfy $-10 < 5x \leqslant 10$?

A $-2, -1, 0, 1, 2$ B $-1, 0, 1, 2,$ C $-1, 0, 1$ D $-2, -1, 0, 1$

2 Which of the following statements are true?

A $x + 11 > x - 11$

B $x \geqslant 12$ means that a number x is greater than 12

C This number line shows the inequality $x \leqslant -1$:

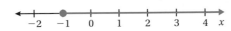

3 **a** Solve $4x - 7 \leqslant 13$ *(2 marks)*

b Show $3 < x \leqslant 8$ on the number line.

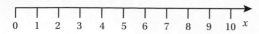

(2 marks)

© AQA 2013

4 A whole number, x, is such that $-3 \leqslant x < 5$.

A whole number, y, is such that $-4 \leqslant y \leqslant 2$.

Write down the greatest possible value of:

a $x + y$ **b** $x - y$ **c** xy

5 I am thinking of an integer. I double it and add 1. The result is less than -7.

What is the largest integer I can be thinking of?

6 If x is an integer, list all the values of x such that $-1 < 2x \leqslant 8$.

7 Frozen chickens will be sold by a major chain of supermarkets only if they weigh at least 1.2 kg and not more than 3.4 kg.

a Represent this region on a number line.

b Write an inequality to represent this region.

26 Ratio

In this chapter you will learn how to ...

- work with equivalent ratios.
- divide quantities in a given ratio.
- identify and work with fractions in ratio problems.
- apply ratio to real contexts and problems, such as those involving conversion, comparison, scaling, mixing and concentrations.

For more resources relating to this chapter, visit GCSE Mathematics Online.

Using mathematics: real-life applications

Ratio is used in many different real-life situations. Converting between different currencies, working out which packet of crisps is the best value for money, mixing large quantities of cement and scaling up a recipe to cater for more people all involve reasoning using ratios.

"Every day customers bring me paints to match. I have to understand how changing the ratio of base colours affects the colour of the paint and how to scale the quantities up and down for larger or smaller amounts of paint. If I get it wrong, customers will have patches of different colours and their walls will look quite strange."

(Paint technician)

Before you start ...

Ch 5	You need to be able to identify and simplify fractions.	**1**	**a** In a class of 35 students, 21 are boys. What fraction of the class is girls? **b** What fraction of this shape is shaded? Write your answer in its simplest form.
Ch 5	You need to be able to find a fraction of a quantity.	**2**	Find $\frac{2}{3}$ of 42.
Ch 5	You need to be able to find an original amount given a fraction.	**3**	There are 51 parents of students in the audience at a school play. These parents make up $\frac{3}{4}$ of the audience. How many people are in the audience?

Assess your starting point using the Launchpad

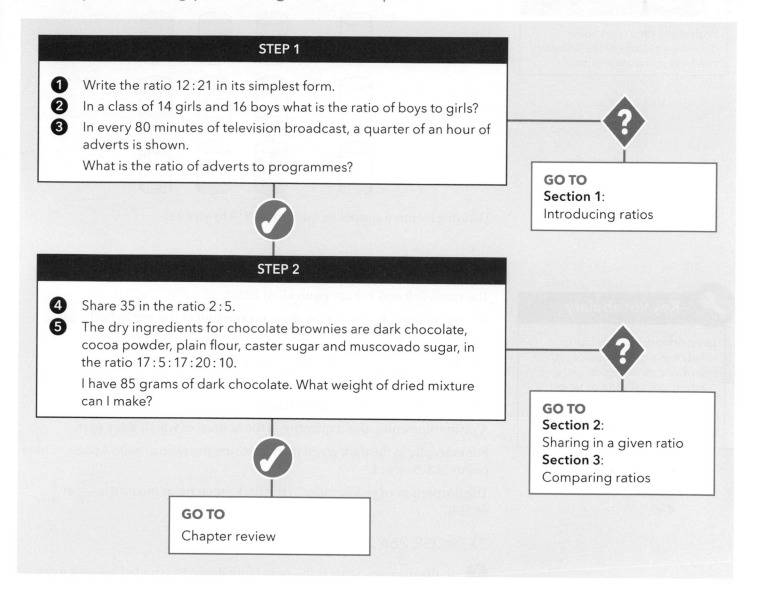

STEP 1

❶ Write the ratio 12 : 21 in its simplest form.

❷ In a class of 14 girls and 16 boys what is the ratio of boys to girls?

❸ In every 80 minutes of television broadcast, a quarter of an hour of adverts is shown.

What is the ratio of adverts to programmes?

GO TO
Section 1:
Introducing ratios

STEP 2

❹ Share 35 in the ratio 2 : 5.

❺ The dry ingredients for chocolate brownies are dark chocolate, cocoa powder, plain flour, caster sugar and muscovado sugar, in the ratio 17 : 5 : 17 : 20 : 10.

I have 85 grams of dark chocolate. What weight of dried mixture can I make?

GO TO
Section 2:
Sharing in a given ratio
Section 3:
Comparing ratios

GO TO
Chapter review

Section 1: Introducing ratios

Ratio describes how parts of equal size relate to each other.

For example, most colours of paint can be mixed from the four base colours: blue, yellow, red and white.

> **🔑 Key vocabulary**
>
> **ratio:** a comparison of different parts or amounts in a particular order

To mix a batch of green paint, you need to know how much of the base colours to mix.

A ratio of yellow to blue paint of 1 : 3 means one unit of yellow for every three units of blue. This would give a very dark green.

A ratio of yellow to blue paint of 5 : 1, means five units of yellow for every one unit of blue. This would give a much lighter green.

 Find answers at: cambridge.org/ukschools/gcsemaths-studentbookanswers

Tip

With many ratio questions, drawing a picture of the situation can help you work it out.

The diagram shows a ratio of yellow to blue of $3:9$.

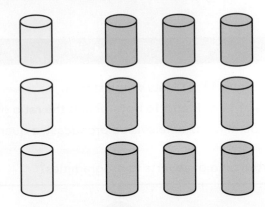

Dividing by three simplifies the ratio of $3:9$ to give $1:3$.

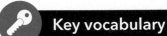

The ratios $3:9$ and $1:3$ are **equivalent** ratios.

The yellow paint makes up the same **proportion** of the mix in both cases.

The difference between ratio and proportion

A ratio compares two or more quantities with each other.

A proportion compares a quantity to the 'whole' of which it is a part.

For example, in the dark green paint mixture, the ratio of yellow paint to blue paints is $3:9$ or $1:3$.

The proportion of yellow paint in the dark green paint mixture is $\frac{3}{12}$ or $\frac{1}{4}$ or 25%.

Key vocabulary

proportion: the number or amount of a group compared to the whole, often expressed as a fraction, percentage or ratio

equivalent: having the same value. Two ratios are equivalent if one is a multiple of the other.

EXERCISE 26A

1 In the diagram, what is the ratio of unshaded to shaded squares in its simplest form?

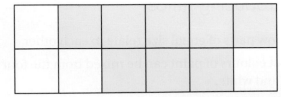

Choose your answer from the options below.

A 1:3   B 1:2   C 4:12   D 2:1

2 Three-quarters of a school go on an end-of-year trip to an adventure park.

What is the ratio of those that go to those that do not go?

Choose the correct answer from the options below.

A 3:1   B 3:4   C 3:7   D 4:1

3 On a school trip, 36 girls and 45 boys went with 9 teachers.

   a Write down the ratio of boys to girls.

   b Write down the ratio of students to teachers.

   c Write down the ratio of students to people on the trip.

   d The school policy is that each teacher can be responsible for no more than 10 students.

     State whether this requirement has been met on this trip.

4 Write down the ratio of shaded squares to unshaded squares in each diagram.

Write the answers in their simplest form.

  a 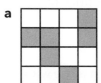   **b** 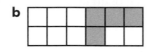   **c**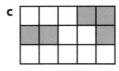

5 Write down the ratio of shaded squares to total squares in each diagram.

Write the answers in their simplest form.

  a 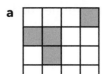   **b** 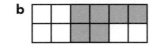   **c**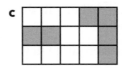

6 The ratio of shaded to unshaded squares in this diagram is $1 : 3$.

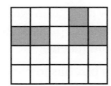

How many more squares need to be shaded to make the ratio $2 : 3$?

7 The distance between the post office and the bank is represented as 5 cm on a map.

In real life this distance is 20 m. Write the scale of the map as a ratio.

8 On a scale drawing of a cruise ship, a cabin is 8 cm from the restaurant.

On the actual ship the distance is 76 m.

Express the distances as a ratio.

9 A TV programme lasts 90 minutes.

The crew recorded 60 hours of footage.

What is the ratio of used footage to recorded footage?

> **Tip**
>
> Ratios do not include units. To compare measured amounts you need to make sure they are written in the same units.

 Find answers at: cambridge.org/ukschools/gcsemaths-studentbookanswers

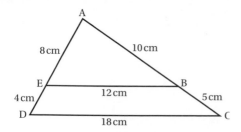

10 a Use the diagram to find the ratio of:

    i side AB to side AC   **ii** side EB to side DC   **iii** side AE to side AD.

b What does this ratio tell you about triangles ABE and ACD?

c What does it tell you about lines EB and DC?

d Write down the ratio of angle AEB to angle ADC.

11 A jam recipe uses 55 g of fruit to make 100 g of jam. The rest is sugar.
Write down the ratio of fruit to sugar.

12 An adult ticket for the cinema is one-and-a-half times the price for a child's ticket.

What is the ratio of the price of an adult ticket to the price of a child's ticket?

13 In a school, $\frac{3}{5}$ of sixteen-year-olds have a mobile phone.
What is the ratio of sixteen-year-olds with mobiles to those without?

Section 2: Sharing in a given ratio

WORKED EXAMPLE 1

Three siblings inherit £32 000 from their mother. In her will she stated that they should receive the money divided according to how many children they each have.

Simon has one daughter, Oliver has three daughters and Lucy four sons.

How should the money be shared between them?

Simon, Oliver and Lucy have children in the ratio 1 : 3 : 4

In total there are 8 boxes, in which we have to share £32 000.

Each box gets $\frac{£32\,000}{8}$ = £4000

So:

Simon receives £4000

Oliver receives 3 × £4000 = £12 000

Lucy receives 4 × £4000 = £16 000

(This method also shows that Simon gets $\frac{1}{8}$ of the total amount, Oliver gets $\frac{3}{8}$ and Lucy gets $\frac{1}{2}$)

£4000 + £12 000 + £16 000 = £32 000

Simon Oliver Lucy

Draw a diagram where each box represents the number of parts of the whole each individual should receive.

Each box has to have the same quantity in it.

Work out the amount that each person receives in the correct ratio.

The final step is to double check that the shared quantities sum to the original amount.

Tip

The box method shown in Worked Example 1 is useful for working out problems on shares in a given ratio.

EXERCISE 26B

1 Share 144 in each of the given ratios.

    a 1:3   **b** 4:5   **c** 11:1

    d 2:3:1   **e** 1:2:5   **f** 2:7:5:4

2 A tropical fruit smoothie is made with strawberries, pineapple and banana in the ratio of 3:1:1.

    Using a total of 300 grams of fruit, what weight of strawberries is used?

    Choose from the options below.

    A 60 g   B 100 g   C 180 g   D 200 g

3 Chocolate butter icing is made using icing sugar, cocoa powder and butter in the ratio of 2:3:1.

    A recipe asks for 120 g of cocoa powder.

    How much butter icing will this make?

    Choose your answer from the following options.

    A 40 g   B 80 g   C 240 g   D 720 g

4 To make mortar you mix sand and cement in the ratio of 4:1.

    a How much sand is needed to make 25 kilograms of mortar?

    b What fraction of the mix is cement?

5 The inner circle of a £2 coin is made of copper and nickel in the ratio 3:1.

    The inner circle weighs 6 grams.

    How much copper is used to make the centres of ten £2 coins?

6 Flaky pastry is made by mixing flour, margarine and lard in the ratio 8:3:3.

    a How much of each ingredient is needed to make 350 g of pastry?

    b What fraction of the pastry is made by the margarine and lard together?

7 The sides of a rectangle are in the ratio of 2:5.

    Its perimeter is 112 cm.

    a What are the dimensions of the rectangle?

    b Use these dimensions to calculate its area.

8 Orange squash is made by mixing one part cordial to five parts water.

    How much squash can you make with 750 ml of cordial?

9 Two-stroke fuel is made by mixing oil and petrol in the ratio of 1:20.

    How much oil needs to be mixed with 10 litres of petrol to make two-stroke fuel?

10 In a recipe for tiffin, the ratio of biscuit to dried fruit to butter to cocoa powder is 5:6:2:2.

    How much of each ingredient is needed to make 600 g of tiffin?

Find answers at: cambridge.org/ukschools/gcsemaths-studentbookanswers

11 In a music college the ratio of flute to oboe to string to percussion players is $7:2:15:1$.

The college has 175 students.

How many students play the oboe?

12 The ratio of red to green to blue to black to white pairs of socks in a drawer is $2:3:7:1:4$.

There are eight pairs of white socks.

How many pairs of socks are there altogether?

13 Potting compost is made by mixing loam, peat and sand in the ratio of $7:3:2$.

A gardener uses 4.5 kg of peat to make potting compost.

How much potting compost does she make?

Section 3: Comparing ratios

Tip

The scale of maps is given as a ratio in the form of $1:n$. For example, $1:25\,000$

When you want to compare ratios, it is often useful to write them in the form $1:n$, where n represents a number.

WORKED EXAMPLE 2

Red and white paint can be mixed to make pink paint.

Which of the mixes below will give the lightest shade of pink?

Mix A 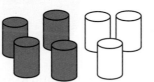   **Mix B**    **Mix C**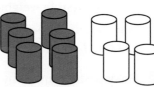

A 4:3
B 3:2
C 6:4

Work out the ratios of red to white paint for each of the mixes.

A $\frac{4}{4}:\frac{3}{4} = 1:0.75$

B $\frac{3}{3}:\frac{2}{3} = 1:0.67$

C $\frac{6}{6}:\frac{4}{6} = 1:0.67$

Change these to the form $1:n$ by dividing both parts of the ratio by the first part.

Give the answers as decimals to make the comparison simpler.

Mix A has the greatest amount of white paint per unit of red paint (0.75 tins of white for 1 tin of red), so this will be lightest shade of pink.

Check that you have answered the question.

Ratios in the form of $1:n$ are also useful for converting from one unit to another.

For example, the ratio of inches to centimetres is $1:2.54$.

This means that 1 inch is equivalent to 2.54 cm.

So, 2 inches = 2×2.54 cm and
12 inches = 12×2.54 cm.

This is a linear relationship and it can be shown as a straight-line graph.

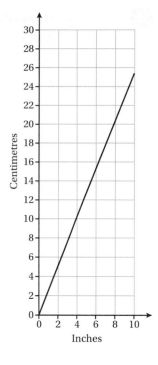

EXERCISE 26C

1 A model car's bonnet is 2.8 cm wide.

In real life the bonnet measures 1.96 m.

What is the ratio of the model to real life in the format $1:n$?

Choose the correct option below.

A $1:0.7$ B $1:196$ C $1:70$ D $1:2.8$

2 Different types of coffee are made by mixing espresso shots, hot water and milk in specified ratios.

Espresso	$1:0:0$
Double espresso	$2:0:0$
Flat white	$1:2:1$
Cappuccino	$1:0:2$
Latte	$1:0:4$

Put the drinks in order of strength of coffee with the weakest first.

3 When Jules was going on holiday he used this graph to convert between pounds and euros.

  a What is the ratio of pounds to euros?

     Express this in the form $1:n$.

  b What is the ratio of euros to pounds?

     Express this in the form $1:n$.

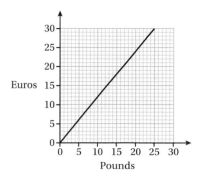

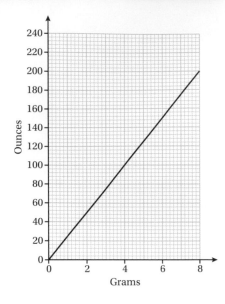

4 This graph shows the relationship between ounces and grams.

   a What is the ratio of ounces to grams?

      Express this in the form $1 : n$.

   b What is the ratio of grams to ounces?

      Express this in the form $1 : n$.

5 The ratio of fluid ounces to millilitres is $1 : 28$.

   a Draw a conversion graph to show this relationship.

   b What is the ratio of millilitres to fluid ounces in the form $1 : n$?

6 Daisy is aged 5, Patrick is aged 8 and Iona is aged 12.

They share a packet of sweets in the same ratio as their ages. There are no sweets left over.

Iona gets 21 more sweets than Daisy.

   a How many sweets were there in the packet to begin with?

   b What fraction of the sweets did Patrick get?

7 The ratio of kilometres to miles is approximately $8 : 5$.

A car travels at 60 miles per hour for 30 minutes.

How many kilometres does it travel?

8 These are the ingredients for a sausage casserole that serves 6 people.

> **Sausage casserole** *(serves 6)*
>
> 12 sausages
>
> 3 tins of tomatoes
>
> 450 g potatoes
>
> 9 tsp mixed herbs
>
> 600 ml vegetable stock

Find the quantities of ingredients needed to serve sausage casserole to 4 people. Show all the steps in your working.

9 Gill and her sister Bell share a box of chocolates.

Bell gets $\frac{1}{3}$ of the box.

Gill shares her chocolates with her best friend Katy in the ratio $4 : 3$.

Katy gets 12 chocolates.

How many chocolates were there in the box?

10 A quarter of a box of chocolates are white chocolates.

The ratio of dark to milk chocolates is $2 : 5$.

There are 7 white chocolates.

How many more milk chocolates than dark chocolates are there?

Golden ratios

The golden ratio has been studied and used for centuries. Artists, including Leonardo da Vinci and Salvador Dali often produced work using this ratio. The ratio can also be seen in buildings, such as the Acropolis in Athens. The golden ratio is said to be the most aesthetically pleasing way to space out facial features.

The diagram shows how the golden ratio can be worked out using the dimensions of a 'golden' rectangle. The large rectangle ACDF is similar to BCDE. Hence the ratio of $a:a+b$ is equivalent to $b:a$.

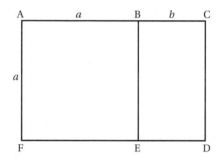

An approximate numerical value for this ratio can be found by measuring.

EXERCISE 26D

How golden are your hands?

Measure the distances A, B and C.

Now calculate these ratios and write them in the form $1:n$.

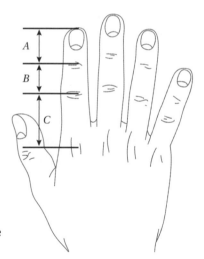

 Distance B : Distance C

 Distance A : Distance B

 Length of your hand : Distance from your
 wrist to your elbow

Can you see anything special about these ratios?

The closer your results are to 1.1618 the more golden is your hand!

The Fibonacci sequence follows the golden ratio.

If you calculate the ratio of consecutive numbers in the Fibonacci sequence you will find that the ratio gets closer and closer to the actual golden ratio $\frac{1+\sqrt{5}}{2}$ =as you get further along the sequence.

EXERCISE 26E

Tip

To answer the questions about triangles, pentagons and rectangles in Exercise 26E you might need to look again at Chapter 8. For the question on circles, you could refer to Chapter 10.

1 What is the ratio of the side length of a square to its perimeter in the form $1:n$?

2 What is the ratio of the diameter of a circle to its circumference in the form $1:n$?

3 The three angles of a triangle are in the ratio $3:3:4$. What information can you give about the triangle?

4 The ratio of the five angles in a pentagon are $1:1:1:1:1$. What information does this tell you about the pentagon?

Give a reason for your answer.

5 The ratio of the angles in a triangle is $1:2:1$. What information can you give about the triangle?

6 Grace and Oliver share a box of chocolates.

Oliver gets $\frac{3}{7}$ of the chocolates.

Grace then shares her chocolates between herself and her sister, Val, in the ratio $3:1$.

Grace gets 9 chocolates.

How many chocolates were in the box?

Choose from the options below.

A 21   B 28   C 40   D 60

7 Gareth and Fergus share a box of chocolates.

Gareth gets $\frac{3}{5}$ of the box.

The ratio of white to milk to dark chocolates in Fergus's share is $1:2:1$. He gets 4 white chocolates.

The ratio of milk to dark to white chocolates in Gareth's share is $2:1:5$.

How many of each type of chocolate were in the box?

 Checklist of learning and understanding

Notation

- The order in which a ratio is written is important. A ratio of $2:5$ means 2 parts to 5 parts. Each part is equal in size.

Simplifying ratios

- Two ratios are equivalent if one is a multiple of the other.
- Ratios can be simplified by dividing both parts of the ratio by a common factor.
- Expressing ratios in the form $1:n$ makes it easy to compare ratios.

Sharing in a given ratio

- The box method can be used to tackle problems that involve sharing a quantity in a given ratio.
  To share quantity Q in the ratio $a:b:c$, divide the quantity evenly into $a+b+c$ boxes.

Chapter review

For additional questions on the topics in this chapter, visit GCSE Mathematics Online.

1 Write down the ratio of vowels to consonants in the English alphabet.

2 Write down the ratio of prime numbers to square numbers between (and including) 1 and 20.

Give your answer in its simplest form.

3 Share 360 in the ratio $3:5:1$.

4 Using the graph below, express the ratio of miles to kilometres in the form $1:n$.

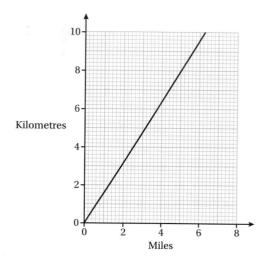

5 A juice drink is made using 2 parts cordial to 4 parts water.

Callum makes up 300 ml of juice drink, but he adds an extra 50 ml of water.

Now what is the ratio of cordial to water?

Choose your answer from the following options.

A $1:2$ B $1:3$ C $2:5$ D $50:300$

6 In a car park, cars are either silver, blue, red, black or yellow.

Three quarters of the cars are not silver.

The proportion of blue to red to black to yellow cars is $6:2:3:1$.

There are 6 more black cars than yellow cars.

How many cars of each colour are in the car park?

Tip

Don't forget about the silver cars!

7 A toy is made from red bricks and yellow bricks.

Number of red bricks : number of yellow bricks = $5:2$

There are 210 more red bricks than yellow bricks.

How many red bricks are in the toy?

(3 marks)

© AQA 2012

Find answers at: cambridge.org/ukschools/gcsemaths-studentbookanswers

27 Proportion

In this chapter you will learn how to ...

- understand proportion and the equality of ratios.
- solve problems involving direct and inverse proportion, including using graphs and algebra to do this.
- understand that 'x is inversely proportional to y' is equivalent to 'x is proportional to $\frac{1}{y}$'.
- interpret equations that describe direct and inverse proportion.

 For more resources relating to this chapter, visit GCSE Mathematics Online.

Using mathematics: real-life applications

Proportional reasoning is very common in daily life. You use proportional reasoning when you mix ingredients for a recipe, convert between units of measurement or work out costs per unit. It is an area of maths where you can use many different methods to solve particular problems.

Tip

Review the sections in Chapter 26 on equivalent ratios and fractions to prepare for this chapter.

"I test out new dishes on my family. Then I have to scale up the recipes in proportion so that they taste just as good. Sometimes it might be for just a few people at one table in my restaurant, at other times it might be for a whole room of wedding guests." *(Chef and restaurant owner)*

Before you start ...

KS3 Ch 5	You need to know how many minutes there are in fractions of an hour.	**1** How many minutes are there in: **a** half an hour? **c** a third of an hour?	**b** a quarter of an hour? **d** a fifth of an hour?
KS3 Ch 5	You need to be able to find what fraction of an hour a given time is.	**2** What fraction of an hour is: **a** 5 minutes? **c** 54 minutes?	**b** 24 minutes?
KS3 Ch 7, 17	You should know how to substitute values into formulae.	**3** $g = 3b$ **a** What is the value of g when $b = 7$? **b** What is the value of b when $g = 72$? **c** What is b when $g = 1.2$?	

Assess your starting point using the Launchpad

STEP 1

1. A recipe for chocolate muffins makes 12 muffins. It uses 180 g of dark chocolate.

   How much chocolate is needed to make 30 muffins?

2. A car is travelling at 80 km per hour.

   How far would it travel in 75 minutes?

3. €1 = $1.40

   What is the price in euros of a T-shirt that costs $24?

GO TO
Section 1:
Direct proportion

STEP 2

4. The cost of carpeting a hallway is proportional to the area of the hall.

   One hallway measuring 15 m² costs £97.50.

   a Find a formula for the cost, c, of carpeting a hallway with area, a.

   b How much would it cost to carpet an area of 32 m²?

   c What area can be carpeted for £328.90?

GO TO
Section 2:
Algebraic and graphical representations

STEP 3

5. Ten people have enough food for a six-day camping trip.

   a How long would the food last if there were only five people?

   b Two more people join the group unexpectedly.

   How long would the food last now?

GO TO
Section 3:
Inverse proportion

GO TO
Chapter review

Find answers at: cambridge.org/ukschools/gcsemaths-studentbookanswers

Section 1: Direct proportion

When two quantities vary but remain in the same **ratio** they are said to be in **direct proportion**.

A simple example would be the quantity and price of petrol.

The more petrol a driver puts into the car, the more it costs.

In problems involving variables in direct proportion, you might be given a rate such as price per litre.

If not, it might be helpful to find this rate – this is called the unitary method.

Consider the following problem.

A car travels 12 miles in 15 minutes.

a At what speed is the car travelling?

b How far would the car go in 75 minutes?

c How long would it take the car to travel 80 miles?

Think of how you would find the answers to these questions.

One approach is to assume that distance and time are directly proportional to each other, which allows you to develop a **mathematical model** of the problem.

Assuming that distance and time are directly proportional to each other, you can write down a range of combinations of time and distance that would represent the same speed.

Then you can use these to answer the questions. The diagram shows some combinations.

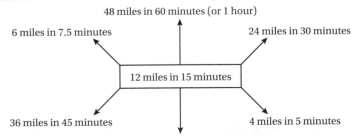

a Having scaled the quantities up and down, you can see that the car covers 48 miles in an hour so its speed is 48 miles per hour.

b The car would travel 36 miles in 45 minutes and 24 miles in 30 minutes. Therefore it would travel 60 miles in 75 minutes.

c The car would travel 4 miles in 5 minutes. Multiply both of these quantities by 20 to find that it would do 80 miles in 100 minutes (or 1 hour and 40 minutes).

These are not the only combinations you could write down or the only ones that you could use to answer the original questions.

Key vocabulary

ratio: the relationship between two or more groups or amounts, showing how much bigger one is than another

direct proportion: two values that both increase in the same ratio

Key vocabulary

mathematical model: a representation of a real-life problem that uses assumptions to simplify the situation so that it can be solved mathematically

Tip

Very often when working with proportion problems it helps to write down a proportion fact you know and consider what would happen if one side is halved, doubled, tripled, multiplied by 10, and so on.

These notes will often help you to solve the original problem. For example, if you know that six eggs make two cakes, then half the number of eggs, three, will make just one cake.

EXERCISE 27A

1 A Bluefin tuna fish can travel 3 km in 20 minutes.

List some other distance–time facts about the fish.

Assume that it always travels at a constant rate.

2 Two dogs eat 120 grams each of dried food twice a day.

How much food is needed to feed the dogs for 10 days?

Choose your answer from the options below.

A 4.8 kg   B 2.4 kg   C 1.2 kg   D 240 g

3 A lorry travels 48 kilometres in 40 minutes.

At what speed is the lorry travelling?

Choose from the following options.

A 1.2 km/h   B 48 km/h   C 68 km/h   D 72 km/h

4 Each day a cat eats 40 grams of dried cat food.

At this rate, how many grams would it eat in a fortnight (two weeks)?

5 Patrick works for four hours and gets paid £22.

What is his rate of pay per hour?

6 Jelly beans cost £1.20 for 100 g.

a How much would 50 g cost?

b How much would 300 g cost?

c How much would 1 kg cost?

d What weight of jelly beans could you buy with £4.20?

7 Ben uses his mobile to make a 12-minute international call, costing him £4.20.

a How much would it cost him to make an international call for 18 minutes?

Danny makes an international call for 20 minutes and it costs him £6.40.

b Whose phone is the best value, Ben's or Danny's? Why?

8 The following ingredients for pancakes serves eight people.

100 g plain flour   2 eggs   300 ml semi-skimmed milk

a Copy and complete this table.

Ingredients	8 people	4 people	16 people	12 people	20 people
plain flour	100 g				
eggs	2				
semi-skimmed milk	300 ml				

b Rakin has 2 litres of milk, 500 g of plain flour and 9 eggs. What is the greatest number of people he can serve?

 Find answers at: cambridge.org/ukschools/gcsemaths-studentbookanswers

Tip

Calculator allowed.

9 a A TGV train travels at 320 kilometres per hour. Assuming that the train is going at its full speed, how far does it travel in:

  i 2 hours?   **ii** 30 minutes?   **iii** 15 minutes?

  iv 1 minute?   **v** 10 seconds?

b The equator is approximately 40 000 km long.

If it were possible, how long would it take to travel around it in a TGV train?

10 A cheetah can reach speeds of up to 120 kilometres per hour.

At this speed, how far would it travel in 15 seconds?

Unitary method

Tip

This is very much like an equivalent ratio problem in Chapter 26.

WORKED EXAMPLE 1

Danny bought a T-shirt in Florida for $18 on his debit card.

When he returned home the charge on Danny's debit card statement was £10.71.

He also bought a pair of jeans for $32.

Assuming the bank uses the same exchange rate, what would this charge appear as on his debit card statement?

From the price of the T-shirt
$18 = £10.71

$$÷18 \left(\begin{array}{c} \$18 = £10.71 \\ \$1 = 0.595 \end{array} \right) ÷18$$

$$×32 \left(\begin{array}{c} \$1 = £0.595 \\ \$32 = £19.04 \end{array} \right) ×32$$

So the charge on Danny's debit card statement should say £19.04.

In this example scaling up and down is too inefficient and it is better to use the unitary method.

Start by finding the exchange rate of dollars to pounds.

Divide both sides by 18.

Now use this rate to find the cost in pounds of $32.

EXERCISE 27B

1 £1 = $1.68

How many dollars is £25 worth?

Choose from the options below.

  A $17   B $42   C $14.88   D $25

2 A tin holding 2.5 litres of paint costs £14.50.

How much would a 750 ml tin cost?

Choose from the options below.

  A £43.50   B £8.70   C £5.80   D £4.35

3 Copy and complete this table:

Pounds (£)	1	2	5	15				124.53
Dollars ($)	1.68				26.88	71.40	80.50	

4 Before going to Australia, Finley exchanges £175 into Australian dollars.

He gets an exchange rate of £1 = AU$1.81.

How many dollars does he get?

5 Amber exchanges $44 into pounds.

The exchange rate is £1 = $1.68.

How many pounds does she receive?

6 Paint is sold in a variety of tins.

The price per litre remains the same.

Find the cost of each of these tins of paint:

a 750 ml	**b** 1 litre	1.5 litres = £18	**c** 5 litres	**d** 25 litres

7 Lucy exchanges £50 for €60.50.

a What is the exchange rate from pounds to euro?

b What is the exchange rate from euro to pounds?

8 When planning a holiday in Switzerland, Ethan compares two resorts.

The exchange rate from pounds to Swiss francs is £1 = CHF1.48.

Which resort is a better deal? State the price difference in pounds.

	Accommodation	Food	Ski rental	Flights
Bun di Scuol	£340	£65	£300	£69
Flims-Laax-Falera	CHF444	CHF148	CHF164.28	CHF213.12

Find answers at: cambridge.org/ukschools/gcsemaths-studentbookanswers

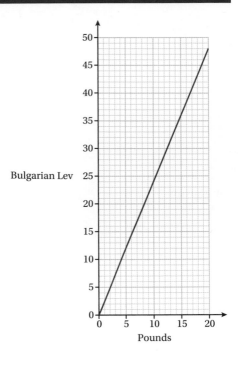

9 The graph shows how to convert between pounds and Bulgarian Lev (ЛВ).

  a Work out the exchange rate from pounds to Lev.

  b Work out the exchange rate from Lev to pounds.

10 Use the following exchange information to answer the questions below.

UK pounds	Euro	Kenyan shilling	Indian rupee
£1	€1.21	KSh145	Rs 102

Mongolian tughrik	New Zealand dollars	Brazilian real
₮3000	$1.95	R$3.77

  a Aaron exchanged £350 into euro.

  Work out how many euro he got.

  b Aaron had KSh40 600.

  Work out how much this is in pounds.

  c In Kenya, Aaron went on a safari drive.

  He reserved this before going at a cost of £185. He paid in Kenya.

  Work out how much it cost in Kenyan shillings.

  d When he left India, Aaron exchanged 5202 Indian rupees into Mongolian tughrik.

  Work out how many tughrik he got.

  e Aaron paid €11 for a hostel in France, KSh1305 in Kenya, Rps500 in India, ₮6500 in Mongolia, $15 in New Zealand and R$20 in Brazil.

  Write these prices in order of expense with the cheapest first.

11 What information would you need to collect to compare the 'crowdedness' of two school playing fields? How would you carry out the comparison?

Section 2: Algebraic and graphical representations

Direct proportion problems can also be represented graphically or generalised through the use of algebra.

This allows you to solve problems concerning the same relationship, either by reading information off a graph or by using an algebraic formula.

WORK IT OUT 27.1

Which of these graphs shows a pair of variables that are directly proportional to each other?

Give a reason for your answer.

Give reasons how you can tell that the variables in the other graphs are not directly proportional to each other.

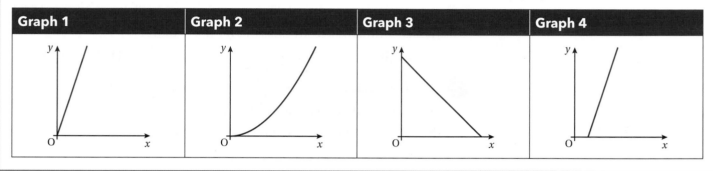

| Graph 1 | Graph 2 | Graph 3 | Graph 4 |

The graph of a directly proportional relationship has a fixed gradient and goes through the origin.

The mathematical symbol $\propto$ means that two values are proportional.

For example, if you pay per minute to use your mobile phone the total time of the call, t, is proportional to the cost of the call, c. Hence $t \propto c$.

This means that for a fixed value k (often called the constant of proportionality), you can write a formula linking the time and cost:

$c = kt$

If you pay 75p for a 15-minute call, you can calculate the value of k by substituting the known values into the formula.

$c = kt$

$75 = k \times 15$

$5 = k$

So the formula linking the cost in pence, c, and time in minutes, t, is $c = 5t$.

 Tip

Be careful with units in questions. In this example the cost is in pence and time in minutes. To use the formula you will need to make sure that all the quantities are in pence and minutes and convert any that are not.

WORK IT OUT 27.2

Which of these formulae represent variables that are directly proportional to each other?

For each one give a reason why or why not.

Formula 1	Formula 2	Formula 3	Formula 4
$y = 3x + 5$	$10w = h$	$\frac{s}{t} = 7$	$d^2 = 4f$

EXERCISE 27C

1 Two variables r and s are directly proportional. When $r = 4.5$, s is 15.75.

Which formula correctly links the variable r and s?

A $r = 3.5s$ B $3.5r = s$ C $r = 70.875s$ D $70.875r = s$

2 This is a distance–time graph for two runners, A and B.

   a Write down how far runner A travelled after 30 minutes.

   b Write down how long it took runner B to travel 18 km.

   c State which runner is going fastest.

   d What is the speed of each runner?

   e What assumptions have been made when drawing this graph?

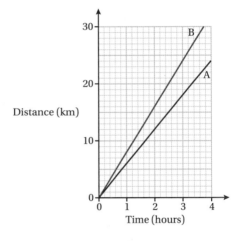

3 The graph shows the cost of telephone cable.

   a What is the cost per metre?

   b Copy and complete this formula: cost = _____ × length.

   c Write a formula linking the cost, c, in pounds and length of wire, l, in metres.

4 The graph shows the number of new cars a factory can make.

The number of cars being produced is directly proportional to the number of days that the factory stays open.

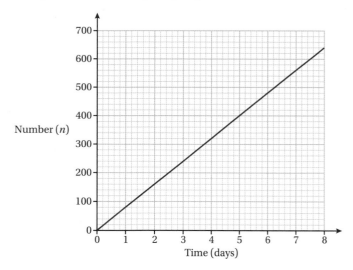

How many cars would you expect the factory to make in 20 days?

What assumptions have you made?

5 The length of an object's shadow is directly proportional to the object's height.

a Use this diagram to help show why this is true.

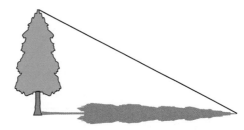 

b At one specific time in the day, a man of height 1.8 m has a shadow of 1.35 m.

i What fraction of the man's height is the length of his shadow?

ii The Angel of the North is 20 m tall.

How long would its shadow be at the same time?

iii The shadow of a stone at Stonehenge at this time is 502.5 cm.

How tall is the stone?

6 Two variables p and q are directly proportional. When $p = 6.5$, q is 52.

a Find the value of q when p is 3.8

b Find the value of p when q is 14.8

7 Wheelchair ramps are designed with a specific steepness allowing their safe use.

One such ramp has a horizontal distance of 4 m and a height gain of 60 cm.

Write a formula for the horizontal distance, *d*, in terms of the height gain, *h*.

Section 3: Inverse proportion

In some cases one quantity decreases as the other one increases.

For example, if you increase your speed, the time it takes to travel a fixed distance is reduced.

If you add more workers to a job, the time it takes to complete the job goes down. These types of relationship are inversely proportional.

WORK IT OUT 27.3

A rectangle has a fixed area of 24 cm².

Its length, *x*, and height, *y*, can vary.

Which of the graphs below represents this situation?

Give reasons for your answer.

Graph 1	Graph 2	Graph 3	Graph 4

For the rectangle with a fixed area in Work It Out 27.3, its length and height are in **inverse proportion**.

When one of these dimensions increases, the other must decrease for the area to remain the same.

Generally, if *x* is inversely proportional to *y*:

where ∝ is the 'proportional to' symbol and *k* is the 'constant of proportionality'

$$y \propto \frac{1}{x}$$
$$y = \frac{k}{x}$$

The value of *y* gets smaller as the value of *x* gets bigger.

Key vocabulary

inverse proportion: a relation between two quantities such that one increases at a rate that is equal to the rate that the other decreases

EXERCISE 27D

1 It takes 3 builders 4 days to build a wall.

How many builders would take 2 days to build the same wall?

Choose from the options below.

A 12 builders B 6 builders C 4 builders D 3 builders

2 It takes 4 people 3 days to paint the school hall.

  a State the number of person-days this is.

  b Work out how long it would take 2 people to paint the hall.

  c Work out how long it would take 6 people.

  d The job needs to be completed in a day.

    How many people are needed?

  e What assumptions have you made?

3 While on holiday, Karen budgets to buy five souvenirs at $2.40 each.

  a What is the total amount Karen intends to spend on souvenirs?

  b How many souvenirs costing $0.80 each could she buy with her budget?

  c Karen needs eight souvenirs of equal value. How much should she pay for each souvenir to keep within her budget?

4 Speed, s, miles per hour and travel time, t, hours are inversely proportional.

The faster you travel the less time a journey takes.

For a journey between Cambridge and Manchester this can be represented by $s = \dfrac{180}{t}$.

  a It takes James four hours to make the journey.

    At what speed is he travelling?

  b How long will it take to do the journey at 60 miles per hour?

  c Megan takes 2 hours 15 minutes to make the journey.

    At what speed is she travelling?

5 A water tap is running at a constant rate of r litres per minute, filling a pond in m minutes.

The greater the flow of water the less time it takes to fill up the pond.

This can be represented as $r = \dfrac{600}{m}$

  a Copy and complete the table.

m (minutes)	10	20	30	40	50	60	70	80	90	100
r (litres per minute)										

  b Draw a graph to represent this situation.

Checklist of learning and understanding

Direct proportion

- Two quantities that are directly proportional to each other increase and decrease at the same rate. For example, if one is tripled so is the other, if one is halved so is the other.
- Direct proportion between two variables x and y can be represented as $y = kx$, where k is the constant of proportionality. The constant of proportionality can be found by substituting known values into the formula.
- The graph of two directly proportional variables is a straight line graph of the form $y = mx$, where m is positive. It looks like the graph below.

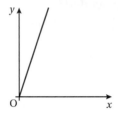

Inverse proportion

- If two quantities are inversely proportional to each other then as one increases the other decreases. For example, if one is tripled the other is divided by three, if one is halved the other is doubled.
- Inverse proportion between two variables x and y can be represented as $y = \dfrac{k}{x}$, where k is the constant of proportionality. The constant of proportionality can be found by substituting known values into the formula.
- The graph of two inversely proportional variables is of the form $y = \dfrac{m}{x}$, where m is positive. It looks like the graph below.

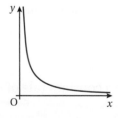

Chapter review

 For additional questions on the topics in this chapter, visit GCSE Mathematics Online.

1 Wine gums cost 90p for 200 grams.

   a How much would 800 grams cost?

   b What weight of wine gums would you get for £2.75?

2 This stir-fry recipe serves 6 people.

   120 g chicken

   300 g vegetables

   15 tbsp of soy sauce

Siobhan has 300 grams of chicken, 500 grams of vegetables and 60 tablespoons of soy sauce.

What is the greatest number of people she can serve with this recipe?

3 Here are some of the ingredients for a pie.

   Minced lamb   450 g

   Potatoes   900 g

   Carrots   75 g

   Stock   300 ml

Oliver has only 300 g of minced lamb.

How much of the other ingredients should he use?   *(3 marks)*

© AQA 2012

4 A T-shirt costs £24 or €30.

Which is the correct exchange rate of euros into pounds?

A £1 = €1.25   B €1 = £0.80   C £1 = €0.80   D €1 = £1.25

5 The graph shows the cost of buying electrical wire.

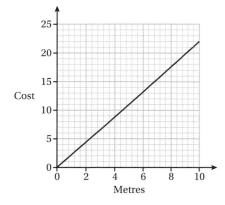

Write a formula for the cost, c, in terms of the number of metres bought, m.

6 It takes three hairdressers an hour to style the hair of models for a fashion show.

How long would it take nine hairdressers?

 Find answers at: cambridge.org/ukschools/gcsemaths-studentbookanswers

28 Graphs of linear functions

In this chapter you will learn how to ...

- use a table of values to plot graphs of linear functions.
- identify the main features of straight-line graphs and use them to sketch graphs.
- sketch graphs from linear equations in the form $y = mx + c$.
- find the equation of a straight line using the gradient and points on the line.

For more resources relating to this chapter, visit GCSE Mathematics Online.

Using mathematics: real-life applications

This is a photograph of a building nicknamed *The Gherkin*, in London. The curves and lines of the building were designed using complex equations and their graphs. Architecture is just one of many professions in which people plot and use graphs in their work.

Tip

Review the sections in Chapter 26 on equivalent ratios and fractions to prepare for this chapter.

"When designing a new building, I use graphs to help identify and describe the structural properties the building needs to have."

(Architect)

Before you start ...

KS3 Ch 17	You should remember how to generate terms in a sequence using a rule.	**1** Use the rule $T(n) = 3n - 2$ to complete this table.	<table><tr><td>**Term number**</td><td>1</td><td>3</td><td>5</td><td>10</td></tr><tr><td>**Term**</td><td></td><td></td><td></td><td></td></tr></table>
KS3	You should be able to give the coordinates of points on a grid.	**2** Look at the grid below. **a** Write down the coordinates of points A, D and E. **b** What point has the following coordinates? **i** (−2, 2)　　　**ii** (0, −6) **c** What is the name given to the point (0, 0)?	
Ch 16	You must be able to manipulate and solve equations.	**3** Solve for x. **a** $4 - 3x = 13$　　**b** $\frac{x}{7} = 6$　　**c** $-3(5x + 2) = 0$ **4** If $y = 2x + 5$: **a** find y when $x = -2$　**b** find x when $y = 8$.	
KS3	You should remember how to change the subject of a formula.	**5** Make y the subject of each equation. **a** $-2x - y + 1 = 0$　　**b** $2x + 3y = 6$　　**c** $x - 2y = -2$	

Assess your starting point using the Launchpad

STEP 1

1 Complete the table of values for each function.

a $x - y = 2$

x	−2	−1	0	1
y				

b $x + y = 4$

x	−2	0	1	2
y				

c $2x + y + 2 = 0$

x	−3	−2	0	1
y				

d $x - 2y + 2 = 0$

x	−2	0	2	4
y				

2 The graphs of two of the functions from question 1 are shown here.

Match each graph to its equation.

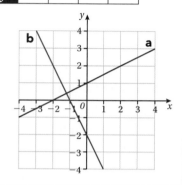

GO TO
Section 1:
Plotting graphs

STEP 2

3 **a** Sketch the graph of $y = 2x + 4$ without plotting a table of values.

  b Find the gradient and y-intercept of the resulting straight line.

4 Find the equation of the straight line that passes through the points (1, 4) and (3, 7).

5 A line cuts the x-axis at 4 and the y-axis at 5. What is its gradient?

GO TO
Section 2:
Gradient and intercepts
of straight-line graphs

STEP 3

6 Which of these lines are parallel to each other?

A $y = -3x + 3$ B $y = 7 - 3x$ C $y = 3x + 7$

D $y = \frac{1}{3}x + 3$ E $y = 7 - 2x$

7 A line is parallel to the line $y = \frac{1}{2}x$ and passes through the point (2, 4). What is its equation?

GO TO
Section 3:
Parallel lines
Section 4:
Working with straight-line
graphs

GO TO

Chapter review

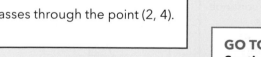
Find answers at: cambridge.org/ukschools/gcsemaths-studentbookanswers

Section 1: Plotting graphs

Straight-line and curved graphs show relationships.

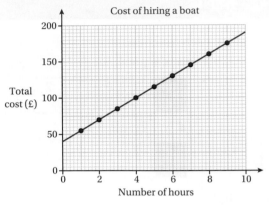

Cost of hiring a boat

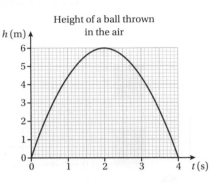

Height of a ball thrown in the air

Key vocabulary

function: a set of instructions for changing one number (the input) into another number (the output)

coordinates: an ordered pair (x, y) identifying position on a grid

Think of a graph as a picture of a **function**. The graph shows what happens when you apply a rule to x to get a value of y.

Each pair of x and y values, (x, y), form the **coordinates** of a point on the line.

Functions that produce straight lines when you plot matching x- and y-values are called linear functions.

Plotting graphs of linear functions

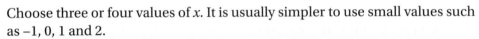

Choose three or four values of x. It is usually simpler to use small values such as -1, 0, 1 and 2.

Draw a table and apply the function to each value of x to find the corresponding values of y.

Plot the (x, y) coordinates on a set of axes to draw the graph.

Tip

When you worked with functions and sequences in Chapter 18 you used a rule to find the terms in a pattern or sequence. You will apply these skills again in this section.

Tip

When you draw a graph, continue the line in both directions through the points. Don't just join the three plotted points together as they are just three of the infinite number of points on the line.

WORKED EXAMPLE 1

Draw a table of values and plot the graph of $y = 2x + 1$.

x	-1	0	1	2
y	-1	1	3	5

Choose some values for x.

Substitute each x-value into the equation to find the matching y-value.

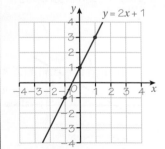

Plot at least three points using the coordinates in the table.

Points $(-1, -1)$, $(0, 1)$ and $(1, 3)$ have been plotted here.

Draw a straight line through the points.

Label the graph with the equation.

EXERCISE 28A

1 Draw a table of values for each function and plot the graph.

a $y = x$
(where x ranges from -2 to 1)

b $y = x + 2$
(where x ranges from -2 to 1)

c $y = 3x - 5$
(where x ranges from 0 to 3)

d $y = 6 - x$
(where x ranges from 0 to 8)

e $y = 2x + 1$
(where x ranges from -2 to 1)

f $y = x - 1$
(where x ranges from -2 to 1)

g $y = -2x + 3$
(where x ranges from -2 to 1)

h $y = 4 - x$
(where x ranges from 0 to 6)

i $y = 3x - 2$
(where x ranges from -1 to 2)

2 What is the minimum number of points you need to plot a straight line accurately?

Give reasons for your answer.

3 Which point lies on the line $y = 3x - 4$?

Choose the correct answer from the options below.

A $(3, -4)$ B $(3, 5)$ C $(3, 4)$ D $(3, -1)$

Section 2: Gradient and intercepts of straight-line graphs

The main characteristics of a straight-line graph are:

- the **gradient**, or slope of the graph
- the **x-intercept** (where it crosses the x-axis)
- the **y-intercept** (where it crosses the y-axis).

You can use these characteristics to sketch graphs without drawing up a table of values.

Gradient

Gradient is a measure of how steep a line is.

On a graph, the gradient is the vertical distance travelled (difference between the y-coordinates) divided by the horizontal distance travelled (difference between the x-coordinates):

$$\text{Gradient of a line} = \frac{\text{change in } y\text{-values}}{\text{change in } x\text{-values}}$$

or, more simply,

$$\text{gradient} = \frac{\text{vertical rise}}{\text{horizontal run}}$$

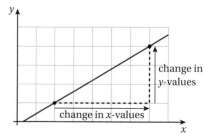

> **Key vocabulary**
>
> **gradient**: a measure of the steepness of a line
> $$\text{Gradient} = \frac{\text{change in } y\text{-values}}{\text{change in } x\text{-values}}$$
> **y-intercept**: the point where a line crosses the y-axis when $x = 0$
>
> **x-intercept**: the point where a line crosses the x-axis when $y = 0$

WORKED EXAMPLE 2

Calculate the gradient of each line.

a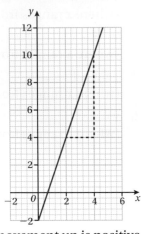

b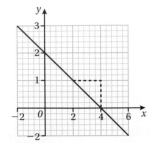

movement down is negative

movement up is positive

a Gradient $= \dfrac{change\ in\ y\text{-}values}{change\ in\ x\text{-}values} = \dfrac{6}{2} = 3$

> Use the formula to work out the gradient.

b Gradient $= \dfrac{change\ in\ y\text{-}values}{change\ in\ x\text{-}values} = \dfrac{-1}{2}$

> Notice that the change in y-values is negative in this case.

You don't need to draw the graph to find the gradient of a line.

You can calculate the gradient if you know the coordinates of any two points on the line.

WORKED EXAMPLE 3

Calculate the gradient of the line that passes through the points (1, 4) and (3, 8).

$\dfrac{difference\ in\ y\text{-}values}{difference\ in\ x\text{-}values} = \dfrac{(point\ 2\ y\text{-}value - point\ 1\ y\text{-}value)}{(point\ 2\ x\text{-}value - point\ 1\ x\text{-}value)}$

$= \dfrac{(8-4)}{(3-1)}$

$= \dfrac{4}{2}$

$= 2$

The gradient of the line that passes through the points (1, 4) and (3, 8) is 2.

> Going from left to right, (1, 4) will come before (3, 8) on the line. Let (1, 4) be 'point 1' and (3, 8) be 'point 2'.
>
> Substitute the x-values and y-values into the formula.

 Tip

You might see this written as
$\dfrac{difference\ in\ y\text{-}values}{difference\ in\ x\text{-}values} = \dfrac{(y_2 - y_1)}{(x_2 - x_1)}$
where point 1 is (x_1, y_1) and point 2 is (x_2, y_2). The small '1' and '2' tell you which point the x- and y-values belong to.

EXERCISE 28B

1 Calculate the gradient of each line. Leave your answer as a fraction in its lowest terms if necessary.

a
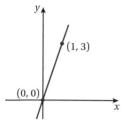

b
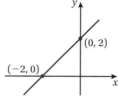

c
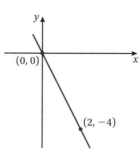

d
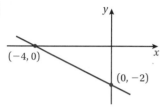

e
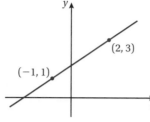

f
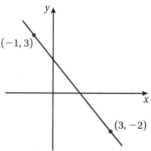

2 Find the gradient of the line that passes through points A and B in each case.

a A(1, 2) and B(3, 8)   **b** A(0, 6) and B(3, 9)

c A(−1, −4) and B(−3, 2)   **d** A(3, 5) and B(7, 12)

3 What is the gradient of the straight line $2y = 6x + 1$?

Choose your answer from the following options.

A 1   B 2   C 3   D 6

The *x*-intercept and *y*-intercept

All points on the *x*-axis have a *y*-value of 0. All points on the *y*-axis have an *x*-value of 0.

The points where a graph crosses the *x*-axis and *y*-axis are called the *x*-intercept and the *y*-intercept.

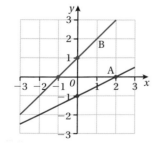

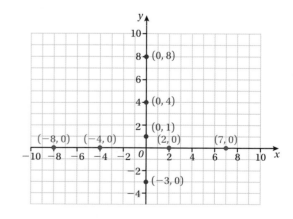

For example, in the diagram:

- line A has an *x*-intercept at (2, 0) and a *y*-intercept at (0, −1)
- line B has an *x*-intercept at (−1, 0) and a *y*-intercept at (0, 1).

Find answers at: cambridge.org/ukschools/gcsemaths-studentbookanswers

Using the gradient and y-intercept to sketch graphs

The general form of a linear equation is $y = mx + c$.

In this form, the equation gives you important information about the graph.

The value of the **coefficient** m is the gradient of the graph.

The value of the **constant** c is the y-intercept.

In the equation $y = -x + 2$, the coefficient of x is -1 and the constant is 2.

The gradient is -1 and the line crosses the y-axis at the point $(0, 2)$.

This is the graph of $y = -x + 2$.

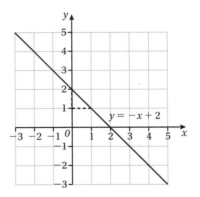

Key vocabulary

coefficient: the number before a variable

constant: a number on its own

Tip

When the equation is in the form $y = mx + c$, you can identify the gradient and y-intercept without plotting the graph. If a linear equation is not written in this form you can rearrange it so that it is. More on rearranging formulae is covered in Chapter 22.

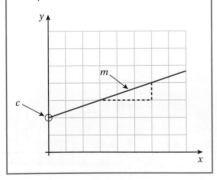

WORK IT OUT 28.1

Find the gradient and y-intercept of the linear function $y = -2x + 4$.

Do not plot a graph. Write down which direction the line moves across the page.

Which of the answers below is correct?

Why is the other one incorrect?

Option A	Option B
$y = -2x + 4$	$y = -2x + 4$
2 is the coefficient of x.	-2 is the coefficient of x.
4 is the constant.	4 is the constant.
So, the gradient is 2 and the y-intercept is 4.	So, the gradient is -2 and the y-intercept is 4.
The gradient is positive so the graph goes up to the right.	The gradient is negative so the graph goes down to the right.

Using the x-intercept and y-intercept to sketch a graph

When you know where the graph cuts the axes, you can sketch the graph of the line.

You find the x-intercept by substituting $y = 0$ into the equation and you find the y-intercept by substituting $x = 0$ into the equation.

WORKED EXAMPLE 4

Find the x- and y-intercepts and use them to sketch the graph of $y + 2x = 6$.

When $\quad x = 0$
$$y + 2(0) = 6$$
$$y = 6$$
$(0, 6)$ is the y-intercept

> To find the y-intercept let $x = 0$.
>
> This is the point where the line $y + 2x = 6$ cuts the y-axis

When $\quad y = 0$
$$0 + 2x = 6$$
$$2x = 6$$
$$x = 3$$
$(3, 0)$ is the x-intercept

> To find the x-intercept let $y = 0$.
>
> This is the point where the line $y + 2x = 6$ cuts the x-axis

$(3, 0)$ is the x-intercept and $(0, 6)$ is the y-intercept.

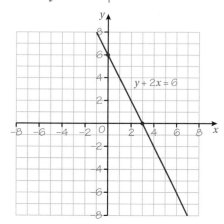

> Plot the two points and join them to draw the graph.
> Label the line.

EXERCISE 28C

1 Plot the graph of each function. Write a description of each one, giving the y-intercept and gradient, stating whether this is positive or negative.

a $y = 3x - 2$ **b** $y = -2x + 3$ **c** $y = \frac{1}{2}x - 1$ **d** $y = x - 1$

2 Rearrange each equation so it is in the form $y = mx + c$. Sketch each of the lines.

a $2y - 3x$ **b** $6x + 2y + 10 = 0$ **c** $3y - 6x + 12 = 0$

d $2y - x + 18 = 0$ **e** $6y - 2x + 18 = 0$ **f** $2x - 3y + 12 = 0$

3 Match each graph to the correct linear equation.

a $y = x + 1$ **b** $y = 3 - x$ **c** $y = 9 - 3x$

d $y = x + 4$ **e** $y = -2x + 20$

A

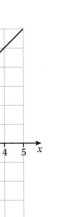

B

C

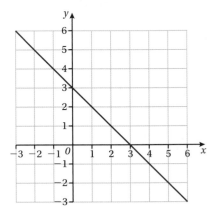

D

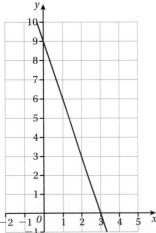

E

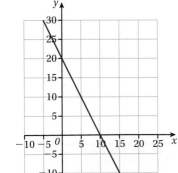

4 Sketch the graph of each line by calculating the coordinates of the x- and y-intercepts.

Write down the gradient of each graph.

a $2x + y = 4$ **b** $3x + 4y = 12$ **c** $x + 2y = 1$ **d** $3x + y = 2$

e $x - y = 4$ **f** $x - y = 1$ **g** $4x - 2y = 8$ **h** $3x - 4y = 12$

Finding the equation of a line using two points on the line

If you have the coordinates of two points on a line you can use them to find the gradient.

Once you have the gradient, you can find the y-intercept by substituting values (x, y) into the equation $y = mx + c$ and solving it to find c.

You can then write the equation of the line in the form: $y = mx + c$

WORKED EXAMPLE 5

Find the equation of the line passing through points $(3, 11)$ and $(6, 7)$.

In point $(3, 11)$, $x = 3$ and $y = 11$
In point $(6, 7)$, $x = 6$ and $y = 7$

Find the gradient of the line first.

Identify the values of the x coordinates and the y coordinates for each point.

$\dfrac{(11 - 7)}{(3 - 6)}$

Gradient $= \dfrac{\text{change in } y\text{-values}}{\text{change in } x\text{-values}}$

$\dfrac{11 - 7}{3 - 6} = \dfrac{4}{-3}$

Gradient $= \dfrac{-4}{3}$

Calculate the value of the gradient.

Take care with negative values.

$y = \dfrac{-4}{3}x + c$

The general equation of a straight line is $y = mx + c$, where m is the value of the gradient.

$7 = \dfrac{-4}{3} \times 6 + c$
$7 = -8 + c$
$15 = c$
$y = \dfrac{-4}{3}x + 15$

Substitute one of the given points on the line into the general equation.

$(6, 7)$ is a given point on the line. Substitute in the equation and calculate the value of c, the y-intercept.

$11 = \dfrac{-4}{3} \times 3 + 15$
$11 = -4 + 15$
$11 = 11$

Check that $(3, 11)$ lies on the line.

$y = \dfrac{-4}{3}x + 15$

This is the equation of the line passing through points $(3, 11)$ and $(6, 7)$.

WORKED EXAMPLE 6

Find the equation of a line that has the same gradient as the line $y = \frac{1}{2}x - 3$ and passes through the point $(-1, 2)$.

Gradient, $m = \frac{1}{2}$

The line has an equation of the form:

$y = \frac{1}{2}x + c$

> The general equation of a straight line is $y = mx + c$, where m is the value of the gradient and c is where the line cuts the y-axis, the y-intercept.
>
> The line has the same gradient as the line $y = \frac{1}{2}x - 3$

$y = \frac{1}{2}x + c$

$2 = (\frac{1}{2} \times -1) + c$

$c = 2 + \frac{1}{2}$

$c = \frac{5}{2}$

> Substitute the values you know into the equation to find the value of c.

$y = \frac{1}{2}x + \frac{5}{2}$

> This is the equation of the new line, that has the same gradient as $y = \frac{1}{2}x - 3$ and passes through the point $(-1, 2)$.

EXERCISE 28D

1 For each equation, find c if the given point is on the line.

a $y = 3x + c$ $(1, 5)$ **b** $y = 6x + c$ $(1, 2)$

c $y = -2x + c$ $(-3, -3)$ **d** $y = \frac{3}{4}x + c$ $(4, -5)$

2 Which of the following options is the equation for the line that passes through the points $(0, 3)$ and $(-3, 0)$?

A $y = x + 3$ B $y = -x - 3$ C $y = 3x + 1$ D $y = -x + 3$

3 Find the equation of the line passing through each pair of points.

a $(0, 0)$ and $(6, -2)$ **b** $(0, 0)$ and $(-2, -3)$

c $(-2, -5)$ and $(-4, -1)$ **d** $(-2, 9)$ and $(3, -1)$

4 **a** A line passes through the point $(2, 4)$ and has gradient 2.

Find the y-coordinate of the point on the line when $x = 3$.

b A line passes through the point $(4, 8)$ and has gradient $\frac{1}{2}$.

Find the y-coordinate of the point on the line when $x = 8$.

c A line passes through the point $(-1, 6)$ and has gradient -1.

Find the y-coordinate of the point on the line when $x = 4$.

Tip

Find the equation of the line before you try to find the coordinates of points on it.

Section 3: Parallel lines

Lines with equal gradients are parallel to each other.

The three lines on the graph are parallel to each other.

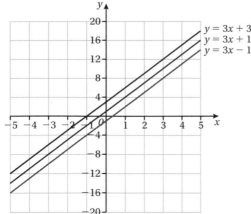
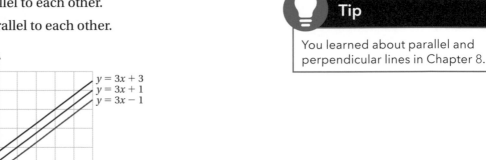

> **Tip**
>
> You learned about parallel and perpendicular lines in Chapter 8.

The equations of the lines show they each have a gradient of 3.

WORK IT OUT 28.2

In which option have parallel lines been correctly grouped together?

Option A	Option B	Option C
$y = 4 - 2x$	$y = \frac{1}{3}x + 1$	$y = x - 1$
$y + 2x = 5$	$3y + x = 1$	$y + x = 1$
$y = -2x + 1$	$y = 3x + 1$	$y = 1 - x$
$y = 3x + 1$	$2y = x + 1$	$x = y + 1$
$y - 3x = -1$	$2y - x = 3$	$x - y = 1$
$y = 2 + 3x$	$y = \frac{1}{2}x - 1$	$x = 1 - y$

If equations written in the form $y = mx + c$ have identical values for m, they have the same gradient. Lines with the same gradient are parallel.

EXERCISE 28E

1 Identify the parallel lines in each set.

a $y = 3x - 5$ $y = x - 5$ $3x + 7 = y$ $6x - y = -1$

b $y = 2x + 3$ $y = 3x + 2$ $2x - y = -6$

   $2y = x + 3$ $y = 2x - 3$

c $y + 3 = x$ $x + y = 3$ $y = 3x - 1$ $y + x = 8$

2 Find the equation of the line that:

a is parallel to the line $y = 2x - 3$ and passes through the point $(1, 5)$

b is parallel to the line $y = 3x - 1$ and passes through the point $(-1, 2)$.

3 a The line $y = (2a - 3)x + 1$ is parallel to $y = 3x - 4$.

Find the value of a.

b The line $y = (3b + 2)x - 1$ is parallel to $y = bx - 4$.

Find the value of b.

4 Find the equation of the blue line.

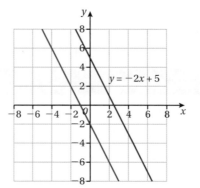

5 The vertices (corners) of a quadrilateral have coordinates A(1, 6), B(3, 14), C(15, 16) and D(13, 8).

a Find the gradient of the line AB.

b Find the equation of the line AB.

c Prove that ABCD is a parallelogram.

6 Investigate lines that are parallel to the x- and y-axes.

How are the equations for these graphs different to those for sloping graphs?

Give reasons for your answer.

Tip

You learned about the properties of quadrilaterals in Chapter 8.

Section 4: Working with straight-line graphs

You need to be able to interpret straight-line graphs.

Interpreting straight-line graphs means you can:

- work out the equation of the line
- calculate the gradient of a line using given information
- use straight-line graphs to model and solve problems, including solving simultaneous equations.

The point of intersection of any two straight-line graphs is the solution to the simultaneous equations (of the lines).

> **Tip**
>
> You learned about simultaneous equations in Chapter 17.

WORKED EXAMPLE 7

a Sketch the graphs of $x + 3y = 6$ and $y = 2x - 5$.

b What are the coordinates of the point of intersection of the two graphs?

c Show, by substitution, that these values of x and y are the simultaneous solution to the two equations

a Sketch the graphs.
$x + 3y = 6$
Let $x = 0$
$3y = 6$
$y = 2$
Let $y = 0$
$x = 6$
Plot $(0, 2)$ and $(6, 0)$.

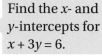 Find the x- and y-intercepts for $x + 3y = 6$.

$y = 2x - 5$
y-intercept $= -5$
gradient $= 2$
Plot the line $y = 2x - 5$ using the gradient and the y-intercept.

Use the equation of the line for $y = 2x - 5$.

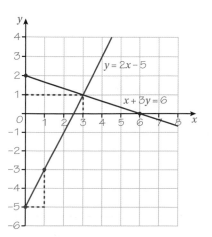

Continues on next page . . .

b The point of intersection is (3, 1).

> Read this from the graph.

c Let $x = 3$ and $y = 1$
Substitute in $x + 3y = 6$:
$3 + 3(1) = 6$.
Substitute in $y = 2x - 5$:
$1 = 2(3) - 5$
$1 = 6 - 5$
$1 = 1$
The values of x and y work for both equations, which shows that they are the solution to the simultaneous equations $x + 3y = 6$ and $y = 2x - 5$.

EXERCISE 28F

1 This table of values has been generated from a function.

x	−2	−1	0	1	2	3
y	−4	−3	−2	−1	0	1

a Which of these functions would produce the values in the table?
Choose from the options below.

   A $y = -x + 2$ B $y = 2x - 1$ C $y = -2x + 4$ D $y = x - 2$

b Plot the graph of this function.

c Draw a line parallel to your graph that crosses the y-axis at (0, 3) and write its equation.

2 Find equations that satisfy the following statements.
Write them in the form $y = mx + c$.

a A linear equation that does not pass through the first quadrant.

b Two lines whose gradients differ by 2.

c An equation of a straight line that passes through (2, 3) and has a gradient of 3.

Tip

When a plane is divided up by an x-axis and a y-axis, each area is called a quadrant. They are numbered as below.

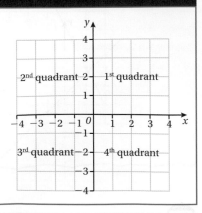

3 Calculate the gradient of the line shown in the diagram.

Write down the equation of the line.

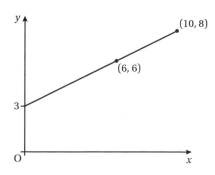

4 Sketch each of the following graphs.

a $y = 3x + 2$ **b** $y = -2x - 1$ **c** $2y = x + 8$

d $x - y = -3$ **e** $y + 4 = x$ **f** $3x + 4y = 12$

> **Tip**
>
> Sketch means draw a basic diagram to represent each equation showing the direction and intercept on the y-axis.

5 Find the equation of the line that passes through each pair of points.

a $(5, 6)$ and $(-4, 10)$ **b** $(3, 4)$ and $(-2, 8)$ **c** $(-2, 6)$ and $(1, 10)$

6 **a** Find the equation of the line with gradient -4 that passes through the point $(0, -6)$.

     b Find the equation of the line with gradient -4 that passes through the point $(3, 8)$.

     c Find the equation of the line that passes through the points $(-4, 8)$ and $(-6, -2)$.

7 The line passing through the points $(-1, 6)$ and $(4, b)$ has gradient -2. Find the value of b.

8 **a** Is the gradient of this straight line 0.5 or -0.5? Write down the equation of the line.

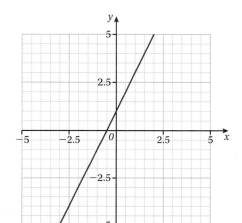

     b Write down the equation of this line.

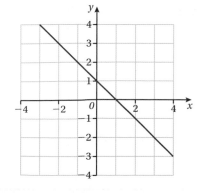

Find answers at: cambridge.org/ukschools/gcsemaths-studentbookanswers

9 Find the equations of the four straight lines that would intersect to make this rhombus.

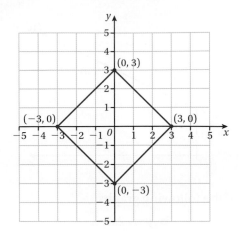

 Checklist of learning and understanding

Plotting graphs

- You can use the equation of a line to generate a table of x- and y-values.
- Choose any three (x, y) values, plot them and join the points to draw the graph.

Characteristics of graphs

- The general form of a straight-line graph is represented by $y = mx + c$, where m is the gradient and c is the point where the line cuts the y-axis.
- You can find the equation of a straight line if you have two points on it or one point and the gradient.
- The gradient of a line can be found if you are given two points (x_1, y_1) and (x_2, y_2) that lie on the line:
$$\text{gradient} = \frac{\text{change in } y\text{-values}}{\text{change in } x\text{-values}} = \frac{y_2 - y_1}{x_2 - x_1}$$
- The x-intercept is where a line crosses the x-axis and $y = 0$; the y-intercept is where a line crosses the y-axis and $x = 0$ or the value of c in the general equation $y = mx + c$.
- You can sketch graphs using the gradient and y-intercept or using the x- and y-intercepts.

Parallel graphs

- Parallel lines have the same gradient so the value of m is equal when the equations are written in the form $y = mx + c$.

Chapter review

For additional questions on the topics in this chapter, visit GCSE Mathematics Online.

1 Draw these lines on the same grid.

a $y = x + 1$ **b** $y = 2x + 5$ **c** $y + 2 = 4x$

2 Write the equation of each line.

a
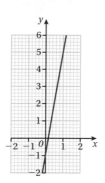

b
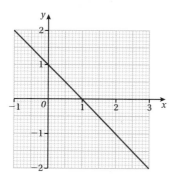

c
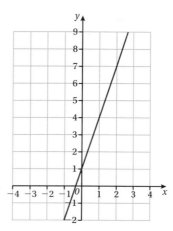

d
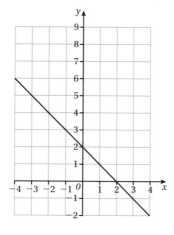

3 Which of the following lines are parallel to each other?

A $y = \frac{1}{2}x + 1$ B $2y - x = 4$ C $y = 2x - 5$ D $y = 0.5x + 3$

4 Find the equation of a line parallel to $y = \frac{1}{2}x + 1$ passing through the point $(-1, 2)$.

5 **a** Work out the equation of line AB.   *(3 marks)*

b Work out the equation of the line passing through $(2, -3)$ and parallel to the line $y = 3x + 4$ *(2 marks)*

© *AQA 2013*

6 Find the equation of the line that passes through the points $(2, 4)$ and $(6, -12)$.

Choose from the following options.

A $y = -4x + 12$ B $y = 4x + 12$ C $y = \frac{2}{3}x + 12$ D $y = -\frac{2}{3}x + 12$

7 **a** Draw a graph of the two lines $y = 3x - 2$ and $y + 2x = 3$.

Find their point of intersection.

b Show by substitution that this is the simultaneous solution to the two equations.

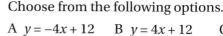 **Find answers at: cambridge.org/ukschools/gcsemaths-studentbookanswers**

In this chapter you will learn how to …

- construct and interpret graphs in real-world contexts.
- interpret the gradient of a straight line graph as a rate of change.

For more resources relating to this chapter, visit GCSE Mathematics Online.

Using mathematics: real-life applications

All sorts of information can be obtained from graphs in real-life contexts. The shape of a graph, its gradient and the area underneath it can tell us about speed, time, acceleration, prices, earnings, break-even points or the values of one currency against another, among other things.

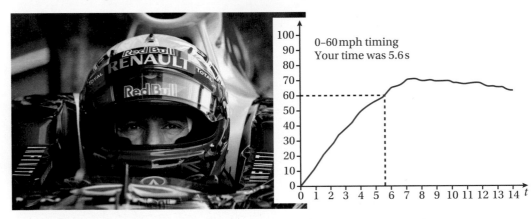

"My car needs to perform at its optimum limits. We generate and analyse diagnostic graphs to calculate the slight changes that would increase power, acceleration and top speed." *(Racing driver)*

Before you start …

Ch 27	You will need to be able to distinguish between direct and inverse proportion.	**1**	Which of these graphs shows an inverse proportion? How do you know this? 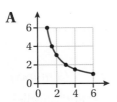 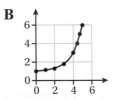 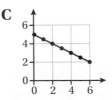
Ch 28	You'll need to be able to calculate the gradient of a straight line.	**2**	Calculate the gradient of AB. 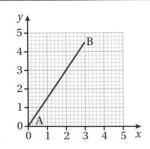

Assess your starting point using the Launchpad

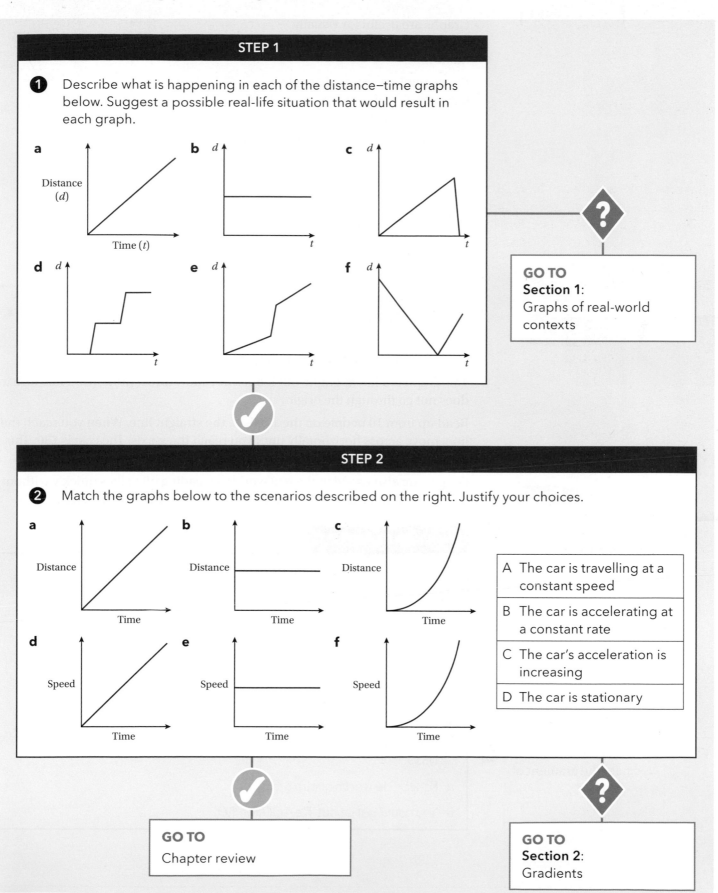

STEP 1

1 Describe what is happening in each of the distance–time graphs below. Suggest a possible real-life situation that would result in each graph.

a Distance (d) / Time (t)

b d / t

c d / t

d d / t

e d / t

f d / t

GO TO
Section 1:
Graphs of real-world contexts

STEP 2

2 Match the graphs below to the scenarios described on the right. Justify your choices.

a Distance / Time

b Distance / Time

c Distance / Time

d Speed / Time

e Speed / Time

f Speed / Time

A	The car is travelling at a constant speed
B	The car is accelerating at a constant rate
C	The car's acceleration is increasing
D	The car is stationary

GO TO
Chapter review

GO TO
Section 2:
Gradients

Find answers at: cambridge.org/ukschools/gcsemaths-studentbookanswers

Section 1: Graphs of real-world contexts

Graphs are useful for visually representing the relationships between quantities.

For example, a group of people have tickets to see a play at the costs shown in the graph below.

The tickets include transport and seats in the theatre.

This graph shows lots of information.

The horizontal axis (or x-axis) shows the number of people attending. The vertical axis (or y-axis) shows the total cost.

The cost depends on the number of people attending. However, there is a cost of £10 for 0 people attending. This is a group charge.

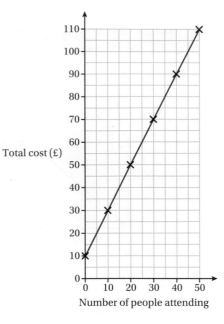

There are six marked points on the graph.

This graph is a linear graph, but it does not show direct proportion because it does not go through the origin.

Read up from 10 people on the x-axis to the straight line. When you reach the line, move across horizontally until you reach the y-axis. The cost is £30. This means that 10 people will need to pay £30 to attend the play.

Graphs are also useful in the real world for reading off values quickly without having to do the whole calculation. They serve as conversion charts.

WORKED EXAMPLE 1

This graph shows the amounts of Indian rupees you would get for different amounts of US dollars at an exchange rate of US$1 : Rs 45. This relationship is a direct proportion.

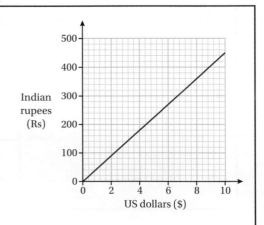

a Use the graph to estimate the dollar value of Rs 250.

b Use the graph to estimate how many rupees you could get for US$9.

a Rs 250 is worth about $5.50.

b You could get about Rs 400 for $9.

Distance–time graphs

Graphs that show the connection between the distance an object has travelled and the time taken to travel that distance are called distance–time graphs.

Time is normally shown along the horizontal axis and distance on the vertical.

The graphs normally start at the origin because at the beginning no time has elapsed (passed) and no distance has been covered.

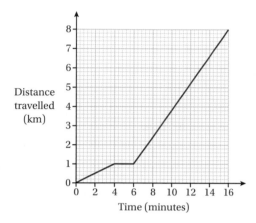

Look at the graph. It shows the following journey:

- a cycle for 4 minutes from home to a bus stop 1 km away
- a 2 minute wait for the bus
- a 7 km journey on the bus that takes 10 minutes.

The line of the graph remains horizontal while the person is not moving (waiting for the bus) because no distance is being travelled.

The steeper the line, the faster the person is travelling.

WORKED EXAMPLE 2

The graph shows the relationship between the length and the breadth of a hall.

Find the formula for this relationship.

Reading the points off the graph, we have $(4, 10), (5, 8), (8, 5)$ and $(10, 5)$.

The area of the hall is constant, at $4 \times 10 = 40$ m.

This graph shows an inverse proportion.

The formula is length $= \dfrac{40}{\text{breadth}}$

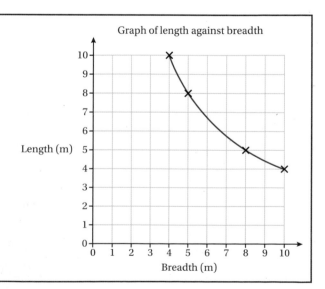

Graph of length against breadth

Because it shows a real-world context, the graph in the example above is only valid for that particular range of values.

 Find answers at: cambridge.org/ukschools/gcsemaths-studentbookanswers

1 Choose one of the options below to complete the sentence:

A distance–time graph shows a stationary object. Which option describes the gradient of this graph?

A Negative   B Positive   C Zero   D Doesn't exist

2 This graph shows the movement of a taxi in city traffic during a four-hour period.

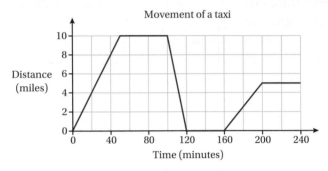

Movement of a taxi

a Using the information from the graph, describe the taxi's journey.

b For how many minutes was the taxi waiting for passengers in this period?

Give a reason how you can tell?

c What was the total distance travelled?

d Calculate the taxi's average speed during:

   i the first 20 minutes   **ii** the first hour

   iii from 160 to 210 minutes   **iv** for the full period of the graph.

3 This distance–time graph represents Monica's journey from home to a supermarket and back again.

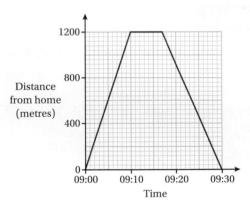

a How far was Monica from home at 09:06 hours?

b How many minutes did she spend at the supermarket?

c At what times was Monica 800 m from home?

d On which part of the journey did Monica travel faster, going to the supermarket or returning home?

4 A swimming pool is 25 m long. Jasmine swims from one end to the other in 20 seconds.

She rests for 10 seconds and then swims back to the starting point.

It takes her 30 seconds to swim the second length.

  a Draw a distance–time graph for Jasmine's swim.

  b How far was Jasmine from her starting point after 12 seconds?

  c How far was Jasmine from her starting point after 54 seconds?

5 A hurricane disaster centre has a certain amount of clean water. The length of time the water will last depends on the number of people who come to the centre.

  a Calculate the missing values in this table.

No. of people	120	150	200	300	400
Days the water will last	40	32			

  b Plot a graph of this relationship.

Section 2: Gradients

Speed in distance–time graphs

The steepness (slope) of a graph gives an indication of the rate of change.

A straight line graph indicates a constant rate of change.

For distance–time graphs, the rate of change is equivalent to speed.

The steeper the graph, the greater the speed.

An upward slope and a downward slope represent movement in opposite directions.

The distance–time graph shown is for a person who walks, cycles and then drives for three equal periods of time.

> **Tip**
>
> You worked with kinematic formulae in Chapter 22. Revise that section if you need to.

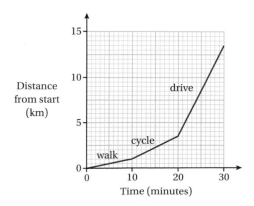

For each period, speed is given by the formula:

$$\text{speed} = \frac{\text{distance travelled}}{\text{time taken}}$$

Using gradient triangles to interpret changing gradients

Looking at the gradient of a graph along with the axis labels gives a large amount of detail – even when, as in this case, there is no scale given.

Consider these graphs:

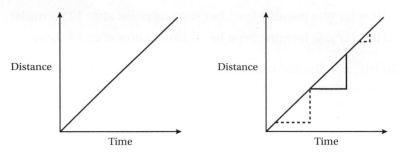

In this case, as time moves on the distance covered increases. So the car is moving.

Gradient triangles are drawn on the graph. It doesn't matter where these triangles are drawn, each is similar to the others, so the sides represent the same gradient (rise/run).

This shows that the car is moving at a constant speed.

If the the car is speeding up, or accelerating, we can show this on a speed–time graph. The speed is increasing at a steady rate over time. If we plot speed against time, this shows acceleration.

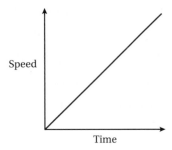

EXERCISE 29B

1 The following graphs show what is happening to the level of water in a tank.

Describe what is happening in each case. Justify your answers using gradient triangles.

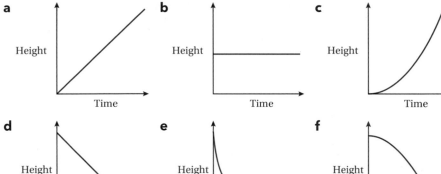

a Height / Time
b Height / Time
c Height / Time
d Height / Time
e Height / Time
f Height / Time

2 The following graphs show what is happening to the price of oil.

Describe what is happening in each case, giving reasons for your answers using gradient triangles.

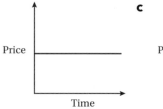

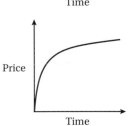

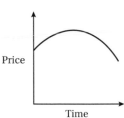

a Price / Time
b Price / Time
c Price / Time
d Price / Time
e Price / Time
f Price / Time

3 The following is a speed–time graph of a parachute jump.

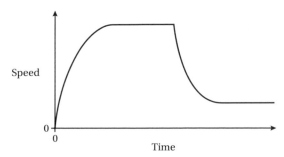

Describe what is happening to the speed and acceleration of the parachutist throughout the jump.

Checklist of learning and understanding

Graphs of real-world contexts

- Real-world graphs show the relationship between variables.

Gradient

- Distance–time graphs show the connection between the distance an object has travelled and the time taken to travel that distance. If speed is constant the gradient is constant.
- Gradient triangles can be used to estimate the changes in the gradient.
- A speed-time graph shows acceleration.
- If acceleration is constant then the gradient is constant.

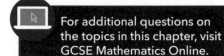

For additional questions on the topics in this chapter, visit GCSE Mathematics Online.

Chapter review

1. The speed–time graph below represents the journey of a train between two stations. The train slowed down and stopped after 15 minutes because of engineering work on the railway line.

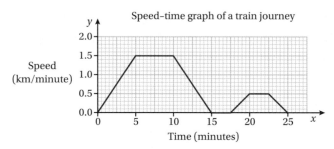

Speed-time graph of a train journey

a Calculate the greatest speed, in km/h, that the train reached.

b Calculate the deceleration of the train as it approached the place where there was engineering work.

c Calculate the distance the train travelled in the first 15 minutes.

d For how long was the train stopped at the place where there was engineering work?

e What was the speed of the train after 19 minutes?

f Calculate the distance between the two stations.

2 The distance–time graph represents a journey Alf makes.

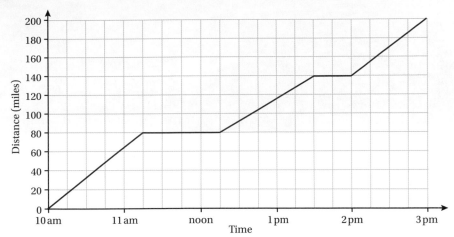

Alf claims that he stopped for less than one-quarter of his total journey time.

Is he correct?

You must show your working. *(3 marks)*

© *AQA 2013*

3 The graph shows how the population of a village has changed since 1930.

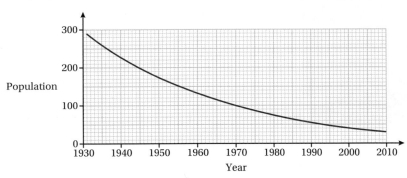

a Copy the graph using tracing paper and find the gradient of the graph at the point (1950, 170).

b What does this gradient represent?

30 Vector geometry

In this chapter you will learn how to ...

- represent vectors as a diagram or column vector.
- add and subtract vectors.
- multiply vectors by a scalar.

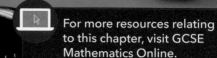 For more resources relating to this chapter, visit GCSE Mathematics Online.

Using mathematics: real-life applications

Vectors are used in navigation to make sure that two ships don't crash into each other. They are used to model objects sliding down slopes with varying amounts of friction. They can be used to work out how far an object can tilt without tipping over, and much more.

"When landing at any airport I have to consider how the wind will blow me off course. Over a set amount of time I expect to travel through a particular vector but I have to add on the effect the wind has on my flight path. If I don't do this accurately I woulds struggle to land the plane safely." *(Pilot)*

Before you start ...

KS3	You need to be able to plot coordinates in all four quadrants.	**1**	Draw a set of axes going from −6 to 6 in both x- and y-directions. Plot the points A(2, 3), B(−3, 4) and C(−2, −3).
KS3	You need to be able to add, subtract and multiply negative numbers.	**2**	Calculate. **a** $3 - 7$ **b** $-4 + 11$ **c** $-5 - 18$ **d** -4×7 **e** -3×-9
KS3 Ch 17	You need to be able to solve simple linear equations.	**3**	Solve. **a** $12 = 4m - 36$ **b** $2k + 15 = 7$ **c** $-6 + 5d = -41$
KS3 Ch 17	You need to be able to solve simultaneous linear equations.	**4**	Solve. $3x + 2y = 8$ and $4x - 3y = 5$

Assess your starting point using the Launchpad

STEP 1

① Write down the column vector for $\overrightarrow{HG}$.

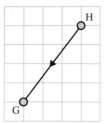

② Draw the triangle ABC where $\overrightarrow{AB} = \begin{pmatrix} 3 \\ -5 \end{pmatrix}$ and $\overrightarrow{CA} = \begin{pmatrix} 2 \\ 7 \end{pmatrix}$.

GO TO
Section 1:
Vector notation and representation

STEP 2

③ $\mathbf{j} = \begin{pmatrix} -1 \\ 3 \end{pmatrix}$ $\qquad$ $\mathbf{k} = \begin{pmatrix} 2 \\ 1 \end{pmatrix}$ $\qquad$ $\mathbf{l} = \begin{pmatrix} -4 \\ -2 \end{pmatrix}$

Write the following as single vectors.
a $\mathbf{j} + \mathbf{k}$ $\qquad$ **b** $2\mathbf{k} - \mathbf{l}$

④ Find the values of f and g.
$\begin{pmatrix} 10 \\ g \end{pmatrix} - 4 \begin{pmatrix} f \\ -3 \end{pmatrix} = \begin{pmatrix} -2 \\ 18 \end{pmatrix}$

⑤ In the diagram,
$\overrightarrow{AC} = \begin{pmatrix} 14 \\ 2 \end{pmatrix}$ and $\overrightarrow{AB} = \begin{pmatrix} 9 \\ 12 \end{pmatrix}$

Find:
a $\overrightarrow{CA}$
b $\overrightarrow{CA} + \overrightarrow{AB}$

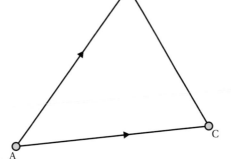

⑥ Which of these vectors are parallel?

$\begin{pmatrix} -3 \\ 4 \end{pmatrix} \begin{pmatrix} 9 \\ 16 \end{pmatrix} \begin{pmatrix} 15 \\ -20 \end{pmatrix} \begin{pmatrix} -3 \\ 2 \end{pmatrix}$

GO TO
Section 2:
Vector arithmetic
Section 3:
Mixed practice

GO TO
Chapter review

Find answers at: cambridge.org/ukschools/gcsemaths-studentbookanswers

Section 1: Vector notation and representation

A **vector** describes movement from one point to another, it has a direction and a magnitude (size).

Vectors can be used to describe many different kinds of movement. For example: **displacement** of a shape following translation, displacement of a boat during its journey, the velocity of an object, and the acceleration of an object.

A vector that describes the movement from A to B can be represented by:

- an arrow in a diagram

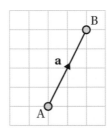

- $\overrightarrow{AB}$ (arrow indicates direction)

- **a** (if handwritten this would be underlined, <u>a</u>)

- a column vector $\begin{pmatrix} x \\ y \end{pmatrix}$

If you were to travel along this vector in the opposite direction, from B to A, you would represent this vector as:

- $\overrightarrow{BA}$

- **–a**

- $\begin{pmatrix} -2 \\ -4 \end{pmatrix}$

Column vectors

In a column vector, **x** represents the **horizontal** movement; **y** represents the **vertical** movement.

	Movement	
	x	**y**
Positive	right	up
Negative	left	down

In the diagram, $\overrightarrow{AB} = \begin{pmatrix} 2 \\ 4 \end{pmatrix}$

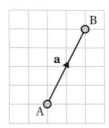

EXERCISE 30A

1 Match up equivalent representations of the vectors.

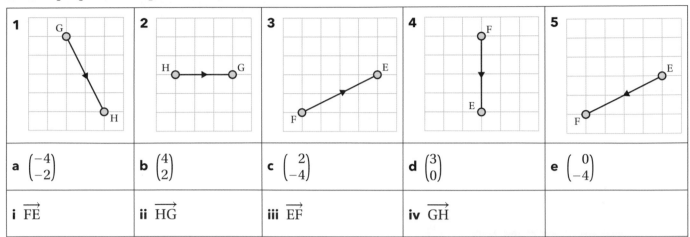

1	2	3	4	5
a $\begin{pmatrix} -4 \\ -2 \end{pmatrix}$	**b** $\begin{pmatrix} 4 \\ 2 \end{pmatrix}$	**c** $\begin{pmatrix} 2 \\ -4 \end{pmatrix}$	**d** $\begin{pmatrix} 3 \\ 0 \end{pmatrix}$	**e** $\begin{pmatrix} 0 \\ -4 \end{pmatrix}$
i $\overrightarrow{FE}$	**ii** $\overrightarrow{HG}$	**iii** $\overrightarrow{EF}$	**iv** $\overrightarrow{GH}$	

2 Use the diagram to find the column vector, $\overrightarrow{DC}$.
Choose your answer from these options.

A $\begin{pmatrix} 4 \\ -2 \end{pmatrix}$ B $\begin{pmatrix} 2 \\ -4 \end{pmatrix}$

C $\begin{pmatrix} -4 \\ 2 \end{pmatrix}$ D $\begin{pmatrix} -2 \\ 4 \end{pmatrix}$

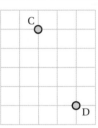

3 Which one of the following diagrams represents $\overrightarrow{BA} = \begin{pmatrix} -3 \\ -2 \end{pmatrix}$?

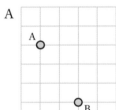

4 Use the diagram to answer the following questions.

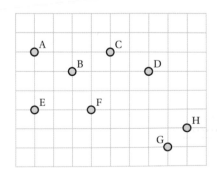

a Write the column vector for

   i $\overrightarrow{AB}$ **ii** $\overrightarrow{DC}$ **iii** $\overrightarrow{BC}$

   iv $\overrightarrow{DF}$ **v** $\overrightarrow{HF}$ **vi** $\overrightarrow{BH}$

b What do you notice about $\overrightarrow{AB}$ and $\overrightarrow{DC}$?

c What do you notice about $\overrightarrow{AB}$ and $\overrightarrow{BH}$?

Find answers at: cambridge.org/ukschools/gcsemaths-studentbookanswers

5 Draw a pair of axes going from −8 to 8 in both x- and y-directions.

Plot the point A (2, −1).

Then plot points B, C, D, E, F and G where:

$$\overrightarrow{AB} = \begin{pmatrix} 2 \\ 7 \end{pmatrix} \qquad \overrightarrow{AC} = \begin{pmatrix} -3 \\ 7 \end{pmatrix} \qquad \overrightarrow{AD} = \begin{pmatrix} -6 \\ 3 \end{pmatrix}$$

$$\overrightarrow{AE} = \begin{pmatrix} 5 \\ 3 \end{pmatrix} \qquad \overrightarrow{AF} = \begin{pmatrix} -3 \\ -1 \end{pmatrix} \qquad \overrightarrow{AG} = \begin{pmatrix} 2 \\ -1 \end{pmatrix}$$

6 **a** A is the point with coordinates (3, −4).

B is the point with coordinates (−1, 2).

Find the column vector that describes the movement from A to B.

b Give the coordinates of two more points, E and F, where the vector from E to F is the same as $\overrightarrow{AB}$.

7 **a** K is the point with coordinates (−2, −1).

L is the point with coordinates (−8, 9).

Find the column vector that describes the movement from K to L.

b Use your answer to find the coordinates of the midpoint of KL.

> **Tip**
>
> The midpoint of the line KL is halfway along the line from K to L.

8 These vectors describe how to move between points A, B, C and D.

$$\overrightarrow{AB} = \begin{pmatrix} 2 \\ 1 \end{pmatrix} \qquad \overrightarrow{BC} = \begin{pmatrix} 1 \\ 0 \end{pmatrix} \qquad \overrightarrow{DA} = \begin{pmatrix} -1 \\ 2 \end{pmatrix}$$

Draw a diagram showing how the points are positioned to form the quadrilateral ABCD.

9 The vector $\begin{pmatrix} 12 \\ -8 \end{pmatrix}$ describes the displacement from point A to point B.

a What is the vector from point B to point A?

b Point A has coordinates (3, 5).

What are the coordinates of point B?

Section 2: Vector arithmetic

Addition and subtraction

The diagram shows $\overrightarrow{AB} = \begin{pmatrix} 2 \\ 4 \end{pmatrix}$, $\overrightarrow{BC} = \begin{pmatrix} 4 \\ -2 \end{pmatrix}$, and $\overrightarrow{AC} = \begin{pmatrix} 6 \\ 2 \end{pmatrix}$

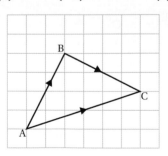

Moving from A to B and then from B to C is the same as moving directly from A to C. In other words, you can take a 'shortcut' from A to C by adding together $\overrightarrow{AB}$ and $\overrightarrow{BC}$.

$\overrightarrow{AC}$ is known as the **resultant** of $\overrightarrow{AB}$ and $\overrightarrow{BC}$.

$\overrightarrow{AB} + \overrightarrow{BC} = \overrightarrow{AC}$

$\begin{pmatrix} 2 \\ 4 \end{pmatrix} + \begin{pmatrix} 4 \\ -2 \end{pmatrix} = \begin{pmatrix} 6 \\ 2 \end{pmatrix}$

The diagram shows $\overrightarrow{AB}$ and $\overrightarrow{CB}$.

To find $\overrightarrow{AC}$ you need to travel along $\overrightarrow{CB}$ in the opposite direction.

So, **subtract** $\overrightarrow{CB}$.

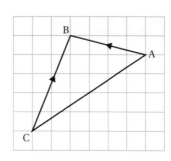

$\overrightarrow{AB} - \overrightarrow{CB} = \overrightarrow{AC}$

$\begin{pmatrix} -4 \\ 1 \end{pmatrix} - \begin{pmatrix} 2 \\ 5 \end{pmatrix} = \begin{pmatrix} -4-2 \\ 1-5 \end{pmatrix} = \begin{pmatrix} -6 \\ -4 \end{pmatrix}$

Multiplying by a scalar

Multiplying a vector by a **scalar** results in repeated addition.

This is the same as multiplying the x-component by the scalar, k, and the y-component by the same scalar, k.

$\overrightarrow{AB} = \begin{pmatrix} 4 \\ -1 \end{pmatrix}$ and $\overrightarrow{CD} = \begin{pmatrix} 12 \\ -3 \end{pmatrix}$

$\overrightarrow{CD} = 3\overrightarrow{AB}$

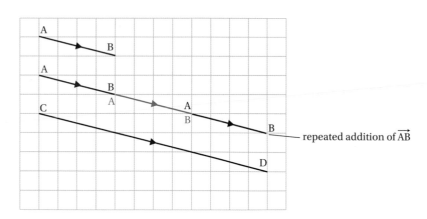

repeated addition of $\overrightarrow{AB}$

$3 \times \begin{pmatrix} 4 \\ -1 \end{pmatrix} = \begin{pmatrix} 4 \\ -1 \end{pmatrix} + \begin{pmatrix} 4 \\ -1 \end{pmatrix} + \begin{pmatrix} 4 \\ -1 \end{pmatrix}$ ———— repeated addition

$= \begin{pmatrix} 3 \times 4 \\ 3 \times -1 \end{pmatrix}$ ———— multiplying the x-component by the scalar k

———— multiplying the y-component by the scalar k

$= \begin{pmatrix} 12 \\ -3 \end{pmatrix}$

Multiplying a vector by a scalar, k, results in a **parallel vector** with a magnitude multiplied by k.

Vectors are parallel if one is a multiple of the other.

WORK IT OUT 30.1

Which of the following vectors are parallel?

$$\mathbf{a} = \begin{pmatrix} 3 \\ -1 \end{pmatrix} \qquad \mathbf{b} = \begin{pmatrix} 4 \\ -3 \end{pmatrix} \qquad \mathbf{c} = \begin{pmatrix} 9 \\ -3 \end{pmatrix} \qquad \mathbf{d} = \begin{pmatrix} 6 \\ 2 \end{pmatrix} \qquad \mathbf{e} = \begin{pmatrix} -6 \\ 2 \end{pmatrix}$$

Option A	Option B	Option C
Vectors **a** and **c**	Vectors **d** and **e**	Vectors **a**, **c** and **e**

EXERCISE 30B

1 Which pair of the following four vectors are parallel? Choose your answer from the options below.

$$\mathbf{p} = \begin{pmatrix} -1 \\ 2 \end{pmatrix} \qquad \mathbf{q} = \begin{pmatrix} -2 \\ -4 \end{pmatrix} \qquad \mathbf{r} = \begin{pmatrix} 4 \\ 8 \end{pmatrix} \qquad \mathbf{s} = \begin{pmatrix} 0 \\ 3 \end{pmatrix}$$

A **p** and **q** B **r** and **s** C **p** and **s** D **q** and **r**

2 $$\mathbf{p} = \begin{pmatrix} -3 \\ 2 \end{pmatrix} \qquad \mathbf{q} = \begin{pmatrix} 5 \\ -1 \end{pmatrix} \qquad \mathbf{r} = \begin{pmatrix} -3 \\ -2 \end{pmatrix} \qquad \mathbf{s} = \begin{pmatrix} 4 \\ -7 \end{pmatrix}$$

   a Write each of these as a single vector.

      i **p** + **q**   **ii** **s** − **r**   **iii** 4**p**

      iv −3**s**   **v** **p** + **q** + **r**   **vi** 2**p** + **q** − 2**s**

   b Which of the results from parts **i** to **vi** are parallel to the vector $\begin{pmatrix} 3 \\ -2 \end{pmatrix}$?

3 Give three vectors parallel to $\begin{pmatrix} 2 \\ -3 \end{pmatrix}$.

4 Find the values of x, y, z and t in each of the following vector calculations.

   a $\begin{pmatrix} x \\ 3 \end{pmatrix} + \begin{pmatrix} 5 \\ y \end{pmatrix} = \begin{pmatrix} 9 \\ 3 \end{pmatrix}$ **b** $\begin{pmatrix} 10 \\ y \end{pmatrix} - \begin{pmatrix} x \\ -3 \end{pmatrix} = \begin{pmatrix} -2 \\ 8 \end{pmatrix}$ **c** $\begin{pmatrix} x \\ -3 \end{pmatrix} + \begin{pmatrix} -6 \\ y \end{pmatrix} = \begin{pmatrix} 11 \\ -8 \end{pmatrix}$

   d $z\begin{pmatrix} x \\ 12 \end{pmatrix} = \begin{pmatrix} 7 \\ -24 \end{pmatrix}$ **e** $z\begin{pmatrix} -12 \\ y \end{pmatrix} = \begin{pmatrix} 3 \\ -8 \end{pmatrix}$ **f** $\begin{pmatrix} 2 \\ -4 \end{pmatrix} + z\begin{pmatrix} 5 \\ y \end{pmatrix} = \begin{pmatrix} 17 \\ 14 \end{pmatrix}$

   g $\begin{pmatrix} x \\ -4 \end{pmatrix} - z\begin{pmatrix} -5 \\ -3 \end{pmatrix} = \begin{pmatrix} 20 \\ 5 \end{pmatrix}$ **h** $z\begin{pmatrix} 3 \\ 4 \end{pmatrix} + t\begin{pmatrix} 2 \\ -2 \end{pmatrix} = \begin{pmatrix} 18 \\ 10 \end{pmatrix}$

5 In the diagram, $\overrightarrow{AB} = \begin{pmatrix} 20 \\ 16 \end{pmatrix}$

The ratio of AC : CB is 1 : 3.

Write the column vector for:

   a $\overrightarrow{AC}$ **b** $\overrightarrow{BC}$

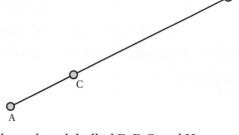

6 The four vertices of a quadrilateral are labelled E, F, G and H.

The following vectors describe how to move between some of the vertices.

$$\overrightarrow{EF} = \begin{pmatrix} 3 \\ -1 \end{pmatrix} \qquad \overrightarrow{HG} = \begin{pmatrix} 6 \\ -2 \end{pmatrix} \qquad \overrightarrow{EH} = \begin{pmatrix} 0 \\ 1 \end{pmatrix}$$

   a What can you say about sides EF and HG?

   b Predict what kind of quadrilateral EFGH is.

   c Draw the quadrilateral and find $\overrightarrow{GF}$.

Tip

You can multiply a vector by a fractional scalar if you need to divide. If you need a reminder on fractions see Chapter 5; if you need a reminder of how to calculate ratios, see Chapter 26.

7 ABCD is a quadrilateral.

$\overrightarrow{AB} = \overrightarrow{DC}$ and $\overrightarrow{DA} = \overrightarrow{CB}$

What kind of quadrilateral is ABCD?

How do you know this?

Section 3: Mixed practice

It is important that you understand what calculations are needed when given a problem involving vectors.

Test your knowledge using the exercise.

EXERCISE 30C

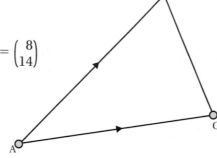

1 In the diagram, $\overrightarrow{AC} = \begin{pmatrix} 10 \\ 2 \end{pmatrix}$ and $\overrightarrow{AB} = \begin{pmatrix} 8 \\ 14 \end{pmatrix}$

Find:

a $\overrightarrow{CA}$

b $\overrightarrow{CA} + \overrightarrow{AB}$

2 Two triangles have vertices ABC and DEF.

The coordinates of the vertices are:

A(0, 0), B(3, 2), C(2, 5) and D(1, 1), E(7, 5), F(5, 11).

a Compare the vectors:

  i $\overrightarrow{AB}$ and $\overrightarrow{DE}$

  ii $\overrightarrow{AC}$ and $\overrightarrow{DF}$

b What does this tell you about the triangles ABC and DEF?

3 In a game of chess different pieces move in different ways.

- A king can move one square in any direction (including diagonals).
- A knight moves two squares horizontally and one square vertically or two squares vertically and one horizontally.

A chessboard is eight squares wide and eight squares long.

What vectors can the following pieces move?

a King

b Knight

4 The vector from A to B is $\begin{pmatrix} 1 \\ 3 \end{pmatrix}$.

The vector joining C to D is parallel to $\overrightarrow{AB}$.

D is three times the distance from C as B is from A.

What is the vector from C to D? Choose your answer from these options.

A $\begin{pmatrix} 4 \\ 6 \end{pmatrix}$ B $\begin{pmatrix} -1 \\ -3 \end{pmatrix}$ C $\begin{pmatrix} 1 \\ 9 \end{pmatrix}$ D $\begin{pmatrix} 3 \\ 9 \end{pmatrix}$

 Find answers at: cambridge.org/ukschools/gcsemaths-studentbookanswers

5 A ship travels 8 km east and 10 km north.

Write a column vector to describe how the ship has travelled.

6 The vector from E to F is $\begin{pmatrix} -6 \\ 2 \end{pmatrix}$ and the vector from F to G is $\begin{pmatrix} 5 \\ 1 \end{pmatrix}$.

What is the vector from:

a E to G?   **b** G to F?

c E to the midpoint of EF?   **d** G to the midpoint of EF?

7 The vector from A to B is $\begin{pmatrix} 1 \\ -2 \end{pmatrix}$.

The vector joining C to D is parallel to AB, D is five times the distance from C as B is from A.

What is the vector from C to D?

Tip

Remember that the midpoint of EF is half the distance from E to F. What does this mean about how far you move horizontally and vertically to get from E to the midpoint of EF?

Checklist of learning and understanding

Notation

- Vectors can be written in a variety of ways: $\overrightarrow{AB}$, **a**, $\begin{pmatrix} 1 \\ 2 \end{pmatrix}$

Addition and subtraction

- To add or subtract vectors simply add or subtract the x- and y-components.

$$\begin{pmatrix} 3 \\ 2 \end{pmatrix} + \begin{pmatrix} 2 \\ -4 \end{pmatrix} = \begin{pmatrix} 5 \\ -2 \end{pmatrix} \qquad \begin{pmatrix} -1 \\ 4 \end{pmatrix} - \begin{pmatrix} 5 \\ -6 \end{pmatrix} = \begin{pmatrix} -6 \\ 10 \end{pmatrix}$$

Multiplication by a scalar

- To multiply by a scalar you can use repeated addition, or multiply the x-component by the scalar and the y-component by the scalar.

$$3\begin{pmatrix} -2 \\ 1 \end{pmatrix} = \begin{pmatrix} -2 \\ 1 \end{pmatrix} + \begin{pmatrix} -2 \\ 1 \end{pmatrix} + \begin{pmatrix} -2 \\ 1 \end{pmatrix} = \begin{pmatrix} -6 \\ 3 \end{pmatrix}$$

$$3\begin{pmatrix} -2 \\ 1 \end{pmatrix} = \begin{pmatrix} -6 \\ 3 \end{pmatrix}$$

- Multiplying a vector by a scalar quantity produces a parallel vector; you can identify that vectors are parallel if one vector is a multiple of the other. Parallel vectors can be part of the same line and described using a ratio.

Chapter review

For additional questions on the topics in this chapter, visit GCSE Mathematics Online.

1 What is the difference between coordinate $(-2, 3)$ and vector $\begin{pmatrix} -2 \\ 3 \end{pmatrix}$?

2 Match the parallel vectors.

$\mathbf{a} = \begin{pmatrix} -6 \\ 2 \end{pmatrix}$ $\mathbf{b} = \begin{pmatrix} 1 \\ 3 \end{pmatrix}$ $\mathbf{c} = \begin{pmatrix} 3 \\ -1 \end{pmatrix}$ $\mathbf{d} = \begin{pmatrix} 7 \\ 21 \end{pmatrix}$

$\mathbf{e} = \begin{pmatrix} -2 \\ 4 \end{pmatrix}$ $\mathbf{f} = \begin{pmatrix} -6 \\ 12 \end{pmatrix}$ $\mathbf{g} = \begin{pmatrix} -1 \\ 2 \end{pmatrix}$

3 Calculate.

a $\begin{pmatrix} 1 \\ -2 \end{pmatrix} + \begin{pmatrix} -2 \\ -1 \end{pmatrix}$ **b** $\begin{pmatrix} 0 \\ -3 \end{pmatrix} - \begin{pmatrix} -2 \\ 4 \end{pmatrix}$ **c** $-3\begin{pmatrix} 2 \\ -1 \end{pmatrix}$

4 In triangle OEF, N is the midpoint of EF and M the midpoint of ON.

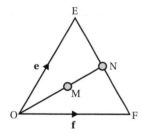

$ON = \mathbf{e} + \frac{1}{2}(-\mathbf{e} + \mathbf{f})$

What is the vector from E to M?

A $-\frac{3}{4}\mathbf{e} + \frac{1}{2}\mathbf{f}$ B $\mathbf{e} + \mathbf{f}$ C $\frac{1}{2}(\mathbf{f} - \mathbf{e})$ D $\frac{1}{4}(\mathbf{f} - \mathbf{e})$

5 In the diagram, M is the midpoint of AB.

Find:

a $\overrightarrow{AB}$

b $\overrightarrow{AM}$

c $\overrightarrow{MO}$

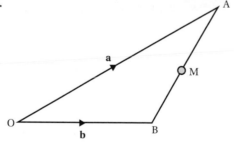

31 Transformations in a plane

For more resources relating to this chapter, visit GCSE Mathematics Online.

Using mathematics: real-life applications

You can see examples of reflections, rotations, and translations all around you. Patterns in wallpaper and fabric are often translations, images reflected in water are reflections and the blades of a wind turbine are a good example of rotation.

Tip

Tracing paper is very useful for work with transformations. Don't be afraid to ask for it in an exam.

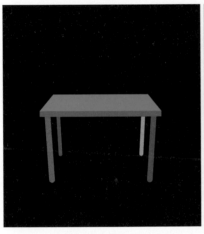

"I use transformations all the time when I program computer graphics. Transformations allow me to position objects, shape them and change the view I have of them. I can even change the type of perspective that is used to show something."

(Computer programmer)

Before you start …

Ch 9	You need to know what angles of 90°, 180° and 270° look like and also the directions clockwise and anticlockwise.	**1** How many degrees is each angle? State whether each arrow is showing clockwise or anticlockwise movement.	**a** **b** **c**
Ch 28	You need to know how to plot straight-line graphs in the form $x = a$, $y = a$ and $y = x$.	**2** Draw the graph for each equation. **a** $y = 2$ **b** $y = x$ **c** $x = -1$ **d** $y = -x$	
Ch 30	You need to know what a vector is and how they describe movement.	**3** **a** What is the difference between the coordinate (3, 2) and the vector $\binom{3}{2}$? **b** What is the difference between the vectors $\binom{-1}{3}$ and $\binom{3}{1}$?	

Assess your starting point using the Launchpad

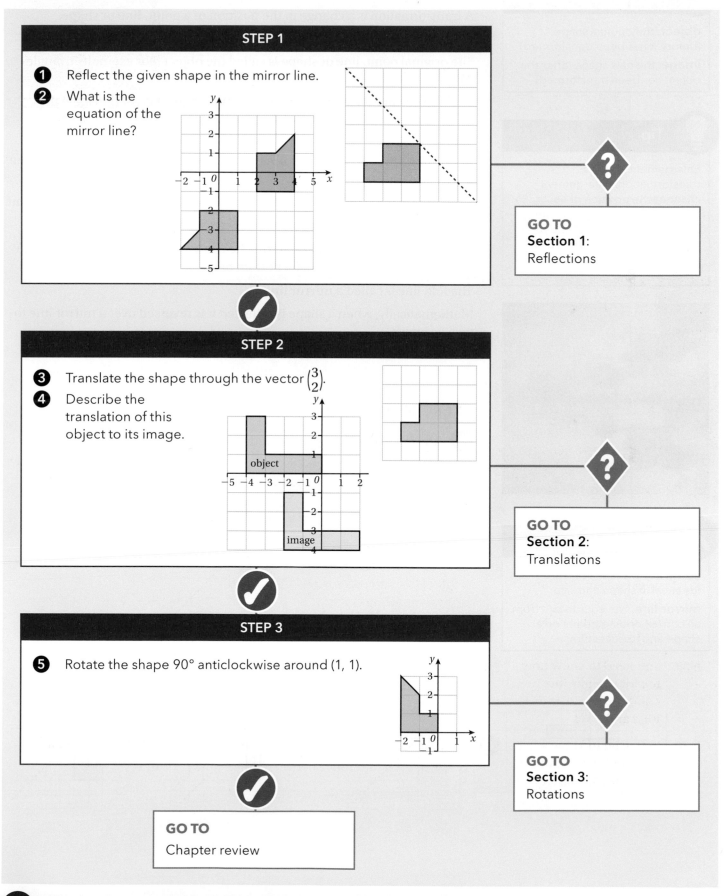

STEP 1

① Reflect the given shape in the mirror line.

② What is the equation of the mirror line?

GO TO
Section 1:
Reflections

STEP 2

③ Translate the shape through the vector $\begin{pmatrix} 3 \\ 2 \end{pmatrix}$.

④ Describe the translation of this object to its image.

object

image

GO TO
Section 2:
Translations

STEP 3

⑤ Rotate the shape 90° anticlockwise around (1, 1).

GO TO
Section 3:
Rotations

GO TO
Chapter review

🖱 **Find answers at: cambridge.org/ukschools/gcsemaths-studentbookanswers**

Key vocabulary

object: the original shape (before it has been transformed)

image: the new shape (after the object has been transformed)

Tip

Enlargement is also a transformation. Enlargement changes the position of an object and also its size. Under enlargement an object and its image are similar. You will deal with similar figures in more detail in Chapter 33.

Key vocabulary

congruent: shapes that are identical in shape and size

mirror line: line equidistant from all corresponding points on a shape and its reflection

Section 1: Reflections

A transformation is a change in the position of a point, line or shape.

When you transform a shape you change its position or its size.

The original point, line or shape is called the **object**. For example, triangle ABC.

The transformation is called the **image**. The symbol ′ is used to label the image. For example, the image of a triangle with vertices ABC is a triangle with vertices A′B′C′.

Reflection, rotation and transformation change the position of an object, but not its size.

Under these three transformations an object and its image will be **congruent**.

You can see the reflection of clouds and trees in the photograph.

If you draw a line horizontally across the centre of the image and fold it, the top half will fit exactly on to the bottom half.

The fold line is called a **mirror line**.

Mathematically, when a shape is reflected it is reversed over a mirror line to give its image.

EXERCISE 31A

1 The following shape is reflected in the dotted line.

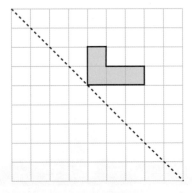

Which diagram shows the correct reflection?

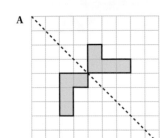

A

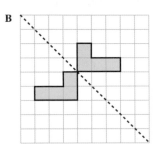

B

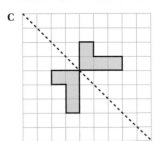

C

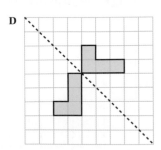

D

2 The following images are painted on three pieces of square paper.

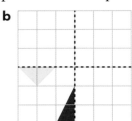 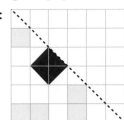 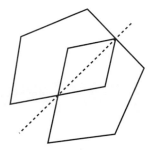

a   b   c

While the paint is still wet, the paper is folded along the dotted lines.

Draw what each image looks like.

3 In the diagram, the line of reflection has been marked.

Copy the shape and join corresponding points in the two halves of the diagram.

What do you notice?

4 Copy each grid and reflect each shape in the given mirror line.

a   b   c

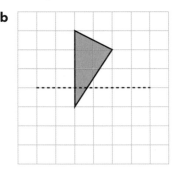 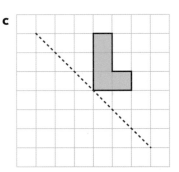

In a reflection, the object and the image are the same distance from the mirror line.

If you join a pair of corresponding points the line formed is cut in half by the mirror line and they meet at 90°.

The mirror line is the **perpendicular bisector** of any pair of corresponding points.

Tip

You can turn your book around so that diagonal mirror lines look vertical or horizontal. Often our brains find this easier than working diagonally.

Key vocabulary

perpendicular bisector: a line perpendicular to another that also cuts it in half

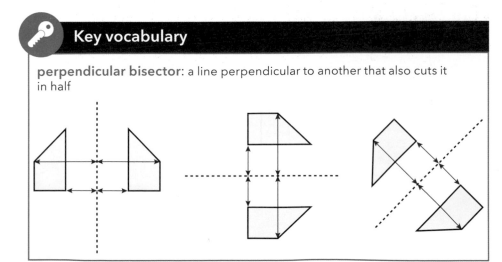

Find answers at: cambridge.org/ukschools/gcsemaths-studentbookanswers

WORK IT OUT 31.1

This Z shape is reflected in the line $y = -1$.

What is its image?

Which one of these answers is correct?

What has gone wrong in each of the others?

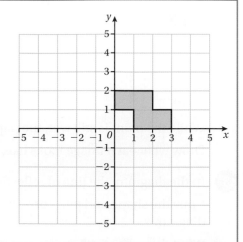

Option A	Option B	Option C

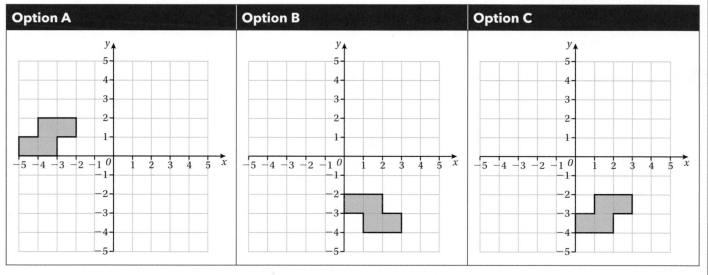

EXERCISE 31B

1 The following shape is reflected in the line $y = -x$.

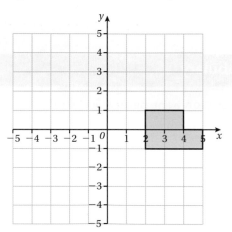

Which diagram shows the correct reflection of the shape at the bottom of the opposite page?

A

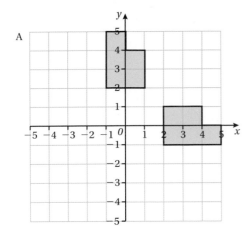

B

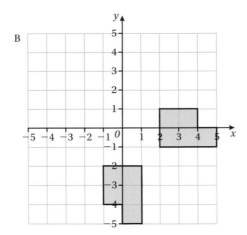

C

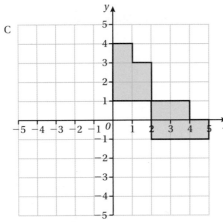

D

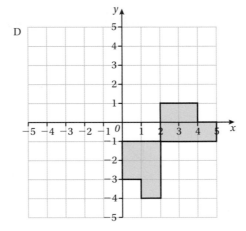

2 Copy the grid. Reflect the triangle in the line $x = 1$.

Then reflect both the triangle and the resultant image in the line $y = -1$.

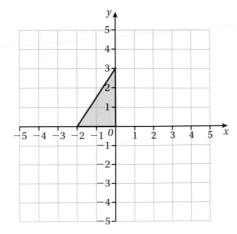

3 Copy the grid. Reflect this shape in the line $y = x$, and then reflect the shape and the resultant image in the line $y = -x$.

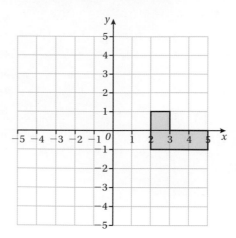

4 Copy the grid. Carry out the ten reflections listed below to reveal the picture.

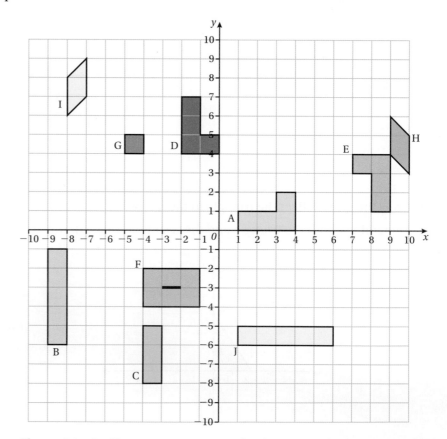

a Shape A in the line $y = x$

b Shape B in the x-axis

c Shape C in the line $y = -2$

d Shape D in the line $y = 4$

e Shape E in the line $x = 7$

f Shape F in the line $y = -x$

g Shape G in the line $x = -4$

h Shape H in the line $x = 1.5$

i Shape I in the line $y = 6$

j Shape J in the line $y = x$

Describing reflections

You need to be able to draw a mirror line on a diagram.

When describing reflections, you must give the equation of the mirror line when the reflection is shown on a coordinate grid.

The mirror line is the perpendicular bisector of two corresponding points in a reflection.

So if you can't 'spot' a mirror line, you can join two corresponding points and construct the perpendicular bisector to find it.

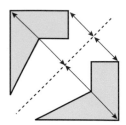

 Tip

To check a reflection, trace the **object**, the **image** and the mirror line. If you fold the tracing paper along the mirror line, the shapes should match up exactly.

EXERCISE 31C

1   What is the equation of the mirror line in the reflection below?

Choose from the following options.

A $x = -2$ B $x = 2$ C $y = -2$ D $y = 2$

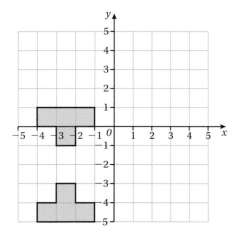

2 Find the equation of the mirror line in each reflection.

a

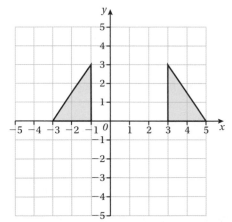

b

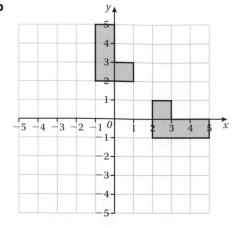

c

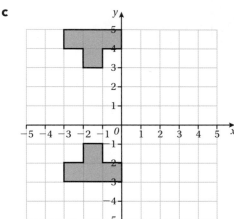

d

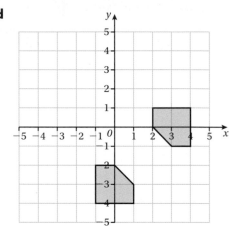

3 **a** Fully describe each of the following reflections.

i Shape A to shape E.

ii Shape C to shape G.

iii Shape A to shape C.

iv Shape H to shape D.

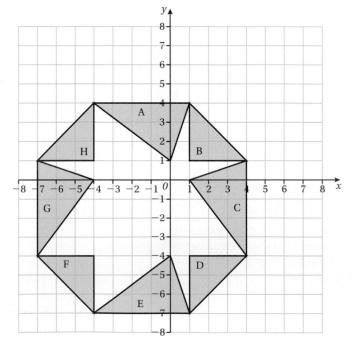

b Challenge another student to describe a reflection of two triangles you choose from the diagram.

4 Trace each pair of shapes and construct the mirror line for the reflection.

a

b

c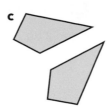

Section 2: Translations

A translation is a slide along a straight line. (Think about pushing a box across a floor.)

The translation can be from left to right (horizontal), up or down (vertical) or both (horizontal and vertical).

The image is in the same **orientation** as the object and every point on the shape moves exactly the same distance in exactly the same direction. Translated shapes are congruent to each other.

Translations are described on a coordinate grid using column vectors.

A column vector shows horizontal displacement over vertical displacement.

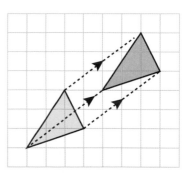

🔑 **Key vocabulary**

orientation: the position of a shape relative to a grid

WORKED EXAMPLE 1

Describe the translation ABC to A′B′C′ by means of a column vector.

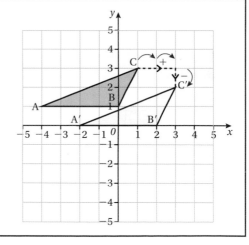

Look at point C and point C′.

> Take any point on the object and find the corresponding point on the image.

To get from C to C′ move:
2 units to the right = +2
and
1 unit down = −1

> Work out how the point has been translated horizontally and vertically.

The translation is $\begin{pmatrix} 2 \\ -1 \end{pmatrix}$

> Write this as a vector.

💡 **Tip**

Drawing on a grid to show the movements of a shape can help you to avoid unnecessary mistakes.

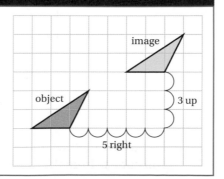

EXERCISE 31D

1 Copy each shape and translate it as directed.

a Translate 6 right and 2 up.   **b** Translate 3 left and 1 down.   **c** Translate 3 down and 4 right.

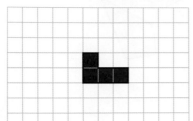 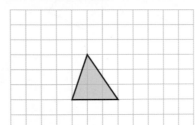 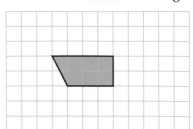

WORK IT OUT 31.2

This T shape is translated through a vector of $\begin{pmatrix} -2 \\ 4 \end{pmatrix}$. Draw its image.

Which one of these answers is correct?

What has gone wrong in each of the others?

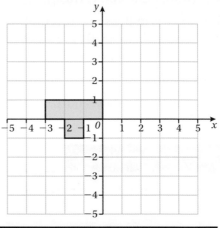

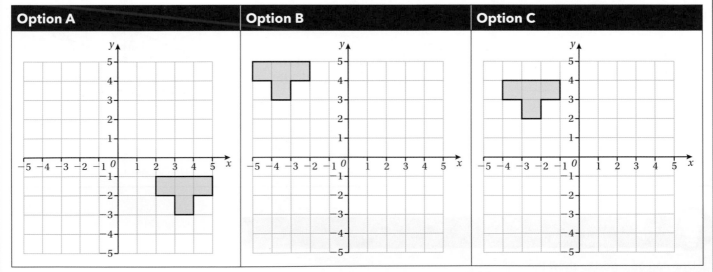

EXERCISE 31E

1 Copy and translate each shape using the given vector.

a $\begin{pmatrix} 3 \\ -2 \end{pmatrix}$ **b** $\begin{pmatrix} -1 \\ 2 \end{pmatrix}$ **c** $\begin{pmatrix} 0 \\ 4 \end{pmatrix}$

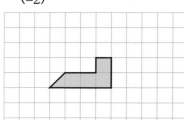 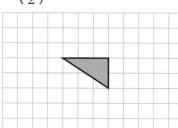 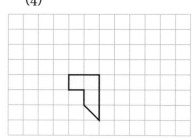

2 **a** Copy and translate each shape by the given vector.

    i Translate shape A $\begin{pmatrix} -1 \\ -3 \end{pmatrix}$ **ii** Translate shape B $\begin{pmatrix} 1 \\ 5 \end{pmatrix}$

    iii Translate shape C $\begin{pmatrix} 2 \\ -1 \end{pmatrix}$

  b Give the name of the shape you have put together.

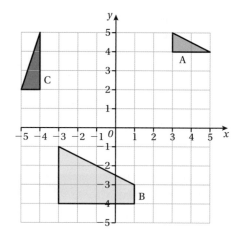

3 Copy and translate each piece of this jigsaw using the vectors on the right.

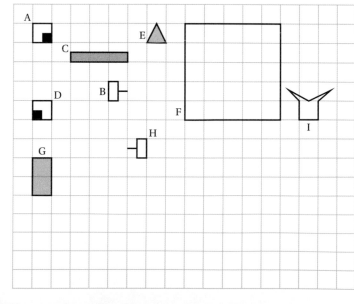

A $\begin{pmatrix} 12 \\ -8 \end{pmatrix}$

B $\begin{pmatrix} 12 \\ -5 \end{pmatrix}$

C $\begin{pmatrix} 10 \\ -9 \end{pmatrix}$

D $\begin{pmatrix} 14 \\ -4 \end{pmatrix}$

E $\begin{pmatrix} 7 \\ -9 \end{pmatrix}$

F $\begin{pmatrix} 3 \\ -7 \end{pmatrix}$

G $\begin{pmatrix} 13 \\ -5 \end{pmatrix}$

H $\begin{pmatrix} 5 \\ -2 \end{pmatrix}$

I $\begin{pmatrix} -1 \\ -2 \end{pmatrix}$

Describing translations

Tip

Make sure you count from the object to the image and write this as a column vector (not a coordinate).

You should be able to use vectors to describe a translation. Remember to count between corresponding points on the two shapes.

WORK IT OUT 31.3

a Which transformations below are reflections and which are translations?

b How did you make your decision?

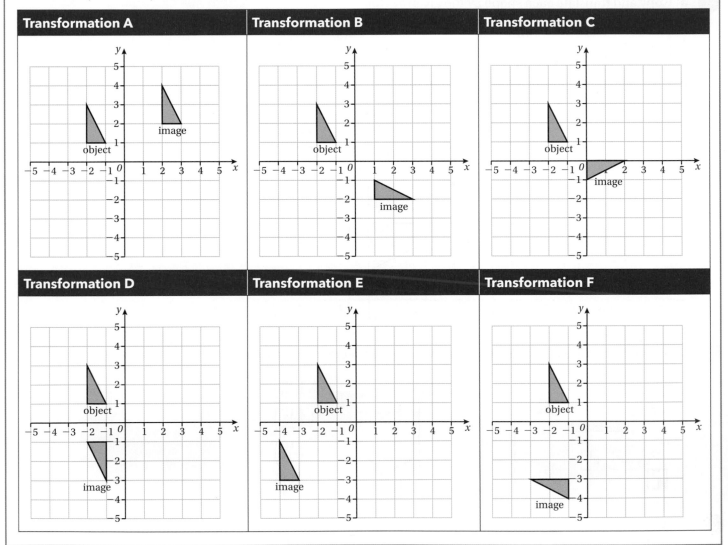

EXERCISE 31F

1 Which vector correctly describes the translation from shape B to shape A shown in the grid on the right?

A $\begin{pmatrix} 2 \\ -4 \end{pmatrix}$ B $\begin{pmatrix} -4 \\ 2 \end{pmatrix}$ C $\begin{pmatrix} 4 \\ -2 \end{pmatrix}$ D $\begin{pmatrix} -2 \\ 4 \end{pmatrix}$

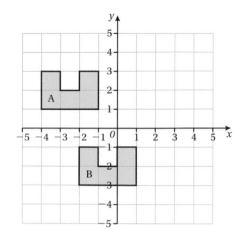

2 Here are some completed translations.

The objects are shown in grey and the images are in colour.

Write column vectors to describe the translation from each object to its image.

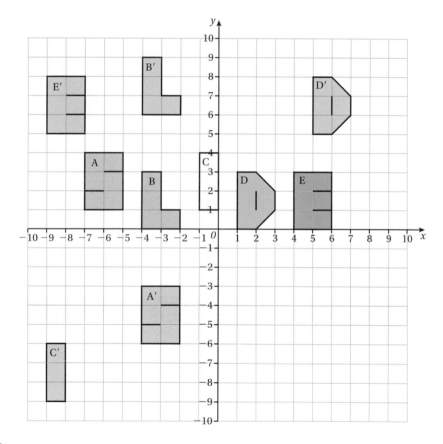

3 Work on a grid.

In any position on your grid, draw the four objects A, B, C and D that have been used to make up the image shown on the right.

Make up translation instructions for moving the four objects into position to form the image.

Exchange with a partner and perform the translations to make sure their instructions are correct.

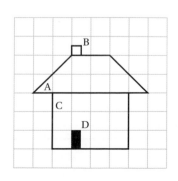

Find answers at: cambridge.org/ukschools/gcsemaths-studentbookanswers

Section 3: Rotations

A rotation is a turn. An object can turn clockwise or anticlockwise around a fixed point called the centre of rotation.

The centre of rotation might be inside, on the edge of or outside the object.

A rotation changes the orientation of a shape, but the object and its image remain congruent.

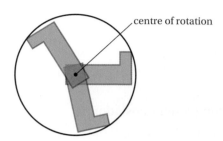

centre of rotation

To carry out a rotation you need to know the centre of rotation as well as the angle and direction of rotation.

In this book, all rotations will be in multiples of 90°.

WORK IT OUT 31.4

This L shape is rotated anticlockwise, with centre of rotation (0, 1) through an angle of 90°. What is its image?

Which one of these answers is correct?

What has gone wrong in each of the others?

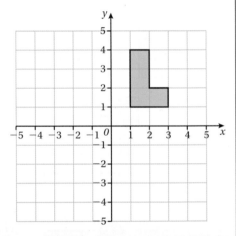

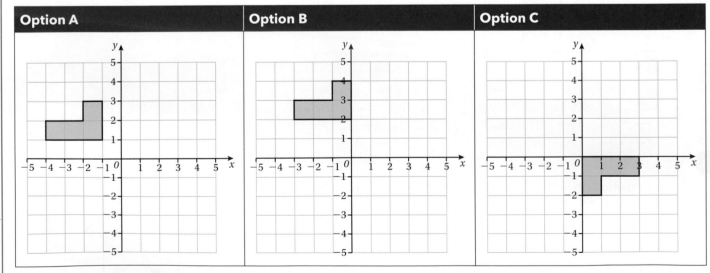

Option A	Option B	Option C

EXERCISE 31G

1 Copy and rotate each shape as directed.

   a Rotate 90° clockwise.   **b** Rotate 180°.   **c** Rotate 90° anticlockwise.

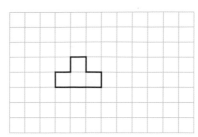 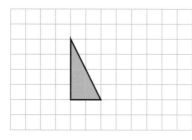 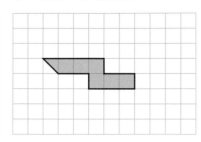

2 Copy and rotate each shape as directed about the marked centre of rotation.

   a Rotate 180°.   **b** Rotate 90° clockwise.   **c** Rotate 90° anticlockwise.

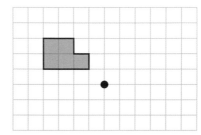 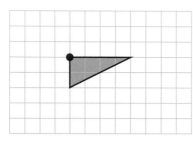 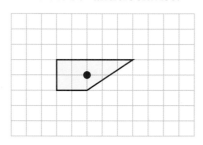

3 Which of the following diagrams shows a rotation?

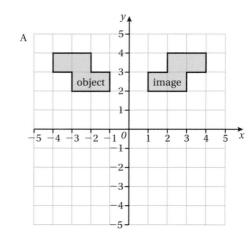 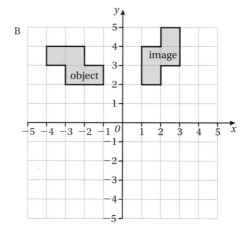

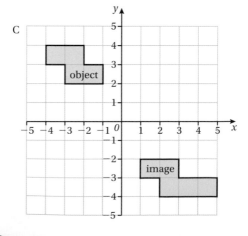 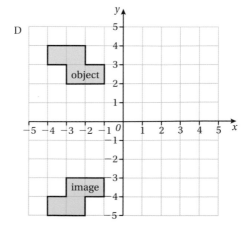

Find answers at: cambridge.org/ukschools/gcsemaths-studentbookanswers

4 Copy and rotate the triangle 180° about the origin.

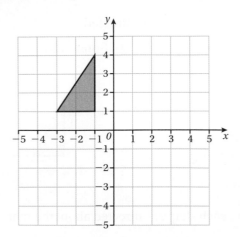

5 Copy and rotate the shape 90° clockwise around the point (1, 1).

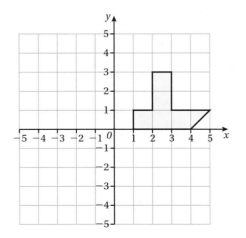

6 Copy and rotate the shape 90° anticlockwise around the point (−2, 1).

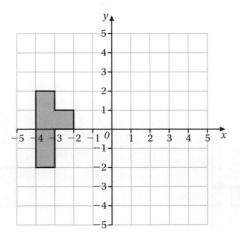

7 Copy and rotate the shape 90° anticlockwise around the point (2, 1).

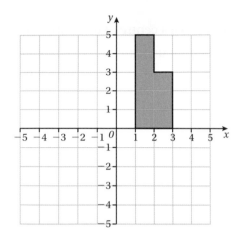

8 Copy the grid. Rotate each shape as directed.

Shape A: 90° anticlockwise around the point (−1, −1).
Shape B: 180° around the point (2, 3).
Shape C: 90° clockwise around the point (1, 0). Label this new shape D.
Shape D: 180° around the point (−3.5, 2).
Shape E: 180° around the point (3, 1).

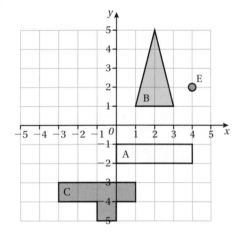

9 The following image was designed by drawing a triangle and rotating this around the origin in multiples of 90°.

What do you notice about the coordinates of the vertices of the triangle?

Would this work if you rotated an image around a different point? Write down your reasons why.

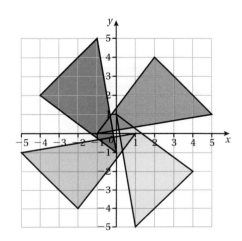

Describing rotations

To describe a rotation you give a centre of rotation, angle and direction.

You can find the centre of rotation using tracing paper and trial and error.

Trace the object and rotate the tracing paper using different centres of rotation.

Spotting the centres of rotation improves with practice.

WORK IT OUT 31.5

a Which of these transformations are reflections, which are rotations and which are translations?

b How did you make your decision?

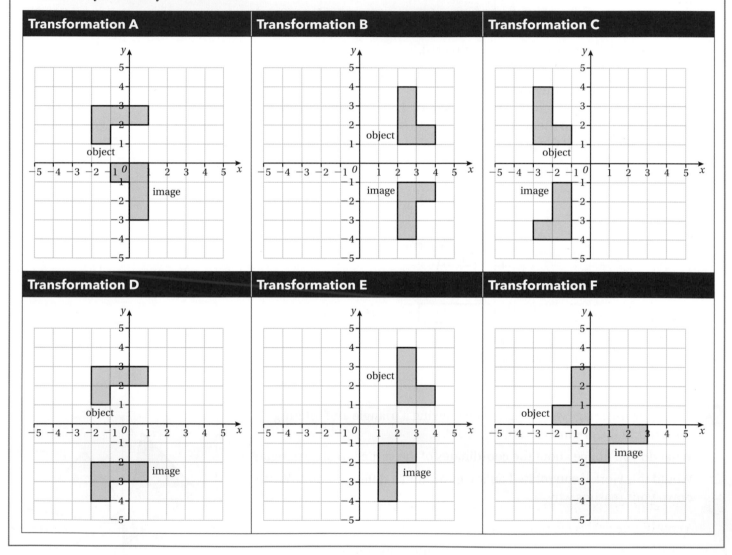

EXERCISE 31H

1 Which of the following correctly describes the rotation in the diagram?

A Rotation of 90° anticlockwise, centre (0, 4).

B Rotation of 180°, centre (0, 4).

C Rotation of 90° anticlockwise, centre (0, 5).

D Rotation of 90° clockwise, centre (0, 5).

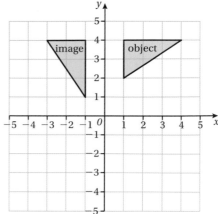

2 Describe each of the following rotations.

a

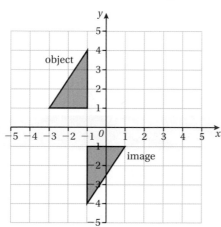

b

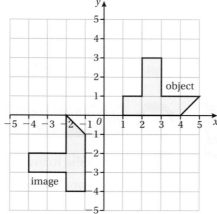

c

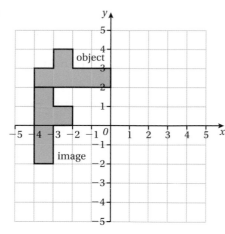

d

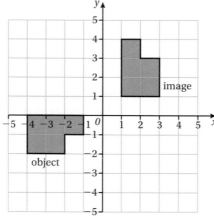

3 This section of wallpaper has been designed using rotations.

A coordinate grid is overlaid on top of the pattern.

Identify and describe as many different rotations as you can.

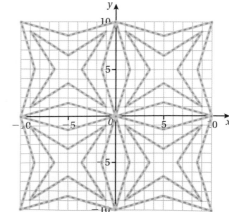

Find answers at: cambridge.org/ukschools/gcsemaths-studentbookanswers

Checklist of learning and understanding

Reflections

- Reflections change the orientation of a shape or object but the image remains congruent.
- To describe a reflection the equation of the mirror line must be given.
- The mirror line is the perpendicular bisector of any two corresponding points on the image and the object.

Translations

- Translations leave the orientation of the shape unchanged but move it horizontally and/or vertically.
- Translations are described using vectors.

Rotations

- A rotation is a turn around a centre of rotation. Rotations are described by giving the coordinates of the centre of rotation, and the angle and direction of the rotation.

For additional questions on the topics in this chapter, visit GCSE Mathematics Online.

 Chapter review

 1 Which of the following statements are true?

Give reasons for your answers.

a The images constructed by reflecting, rotating or translating are congruent with the objects.

b The images constructed by reflecting, rotating or translating are similar to the objects.

c The images constructed by reflecting, rotating or translating are in the same orientation to the objects.

d The images constructed by reflecting, rotating or translating have the same angles as the objects.

2 Describe fully the transformation from:

a shape A to shape B   **b** shape B to shape C

c shape C to shape A.

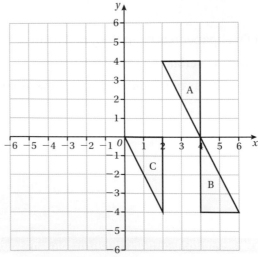

3 The triangle below is used to create a tessellating pattern.

The pattern is produced using multiple translations and one rotation.

Write down how this could be done.

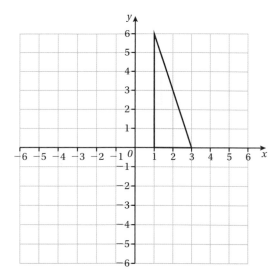

4

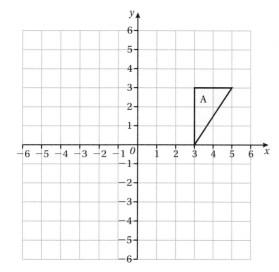

Rotate shape A, 90° clockwise around the point (1, 2). Label it B.

Reflect shape B in the line $y = x$. Label it C.

Translate shape C through the vector $\begin{pmatrix} -1 \\ 1 \end{pmatrix}$. Label it D.

5 **a** Translate the shape by the vector $\begin{pmatrix} 2 \\ 3 \end{pmatrix}$. *(2 marks)*

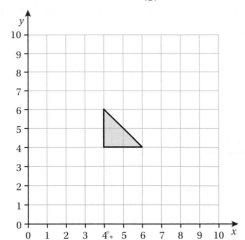

b Describe fully the single transformation that takes shape A to shape B. *(3 marks)*

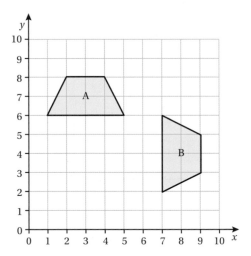

© AQA 2013

6 Describe how the figure in the diagram can be drawn using only transformations of shapes A, B, C and D.

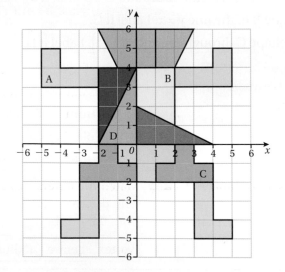

32 Construction and loci

In this chapter you will learn how to ...

- use a ruler, protractor and pair of compasses effectively.
- use a ruler and a pair of compasses to bisect lines and angles and construct perpendiculars.
- use construction skills to construct geometrical figures.
- construct accurate diagrams to solve problems involving loci.

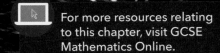

For more resources relating to this chapter, visit GCSE Mathematics Online.

Using mathematics: real-life applications

Draughtspeople and architects need to draw accurate scaled diagrams of the buildings and other structures they are working on. Although the drawings are complicated, they still use ordinary mathematical instruments like pencils, rulers and pairs of compasses to draw them.

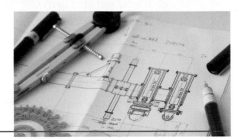

"I prepare technical drawings and plans that are given to me by an architect. I use a CAD program, but I always start with a drawing board and plans that I draw using my ruler, set squares and pair of compasses."

(Draughtsperson)

Before you start ...

KS3	You need to be able to measure and draw angles accurately using a protractor.	**1**	Read the correct measurement for each angle. **a** **b**
		2	Use a ruler and a protractor to draw a reflex angle the same size as this one.
KS3	You should be able to convert between units of length.	**3**	Choose the correct answers. **a** 1 m is equivalent to: A 10 mm B 100 mm C 1000 mm D none of these measurements **b** Half of 8.7 cm is: A 43 mm B 435 mm C 43.5 mm D none of these measurements
KS3 Ch 8	You must know and be able to use the correct names for parts of shapes, including circles.	**4**	Match the letters **a** to **e** on the diagrams with the correct mathematical names from the box below. vertex centre radius side diameter

Find answers at: cambridge.org/ukschools/gcsemaths-studentbookanswers

Assess your starting point using the Launchpad

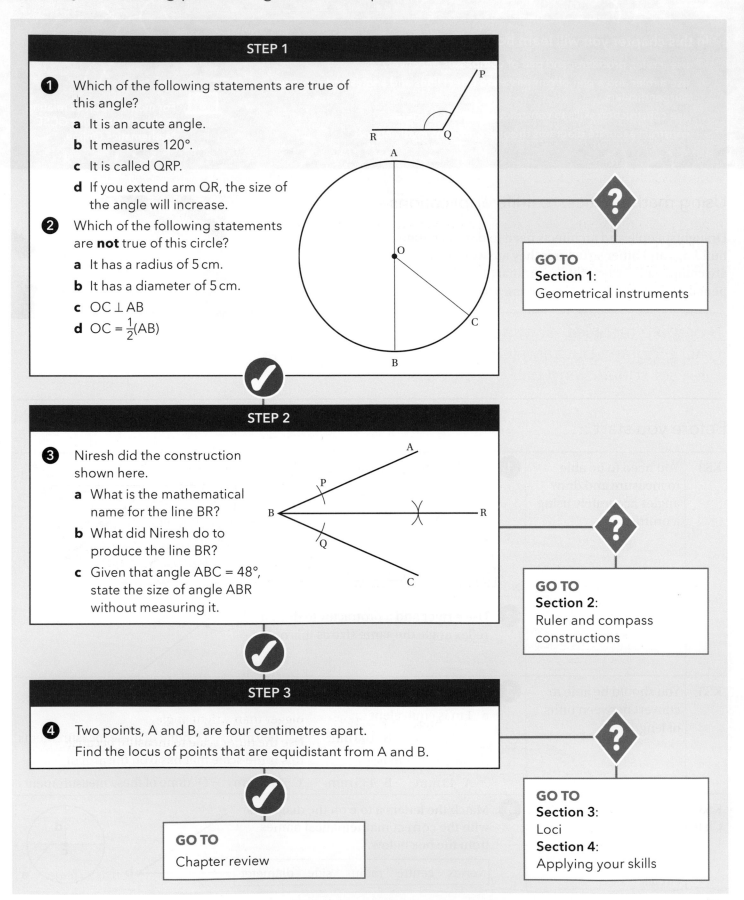

STEP 1

1 Which of the following statements are true of this angle?

  a It is an acute angle.

  b It measures 120°.

  c It is called QRP.

  d If you extend arm QR, the size of the angle will increase.

2 Which of the following statements are **not** true of this circle?

  a It has a radius of 5 cm.

  b It has a diameter of 5 cm.

  c OC ⊥ AB

  d OC = $\frac{1}{2}$(AB)

GO TO
Section 1:
Geometrical instruments

STEP 2

3 Niresh did the construction shown here.

  a What is the mathematical name for the line BR?

  b What did Niresh do to produce the line BR?

  c Given that angle ABC = 48°, state the size of angle ABR without measuring it.

GO TO
Section 2:
Ruler and compass constructions

STEP 3

4 Two points, A and B, are four centimetres apart.
Find the locus of points that are equidistant from A and B.

GO TO

Chapter review

GO TO
Section 3:
Loci
Section 4:
Applying your skills

Section 1: Geometrical instruments

Measuring and drawing angles

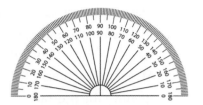

Protractors like the one in the diagram have two scales.

These are for measuring angles facing different directions.

To avoid measuring on the wrong scale, estimate the size of the angle before you measure.

Use your knowledge of acute, right and obtuse angles to estimate as accurately as possible.

WORKED EXAMPLE 1

a Estimate and then measure the size of each red angle.

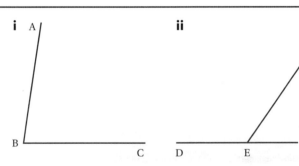

a i Estimate about 80°.

Angle ABC = 82°

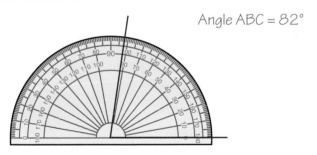

This is an acute angle but it is close to 90°.

Use the inner scale to measure because this is the scale that has 0 on the arm of the angle.

ii Estimate about 130°.

Angle DEF = 125°

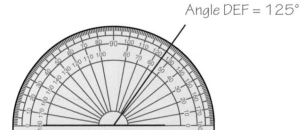

This is an obtuse angle. It is about one-third bigger than a right angle.

Use the outer scale to measure because this is the scale that has 0 on the arm of the angle.

Continues on next page …

b Use your protractor to draw angle ABC = 76°.

b

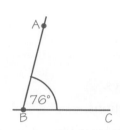

	Draw a line using your ruler.
	Mark B, the vertex in angle ABC.
	Place your protractor with its centre on B and baseline on the line you drew.
	Measure and mark 76°.
	Remove the protractor.
	Draw a line from B through the 76° marking.
	Label the angle correctly.

💡 Tip

If the arms of the angle are too short to read the scale correctly use a ruler and a pencil to extend them. This doesn't change the size of the angle but it allows you to read the measurement more accurately. If you cannot draw on the angle (because it is in a book) you can extend the arm with the straight edge of a sheet of paper.

Parts of a circle

🔑 Key vocabulary

radius (plural **radii**): distance from the centre to the circumference of a circle. One radius is half of the diameter of the circle.

circumference: distance round the outside of a circle

semicircle: half of a circle

chord: a straight line that joins one point on the circumference of a circle to another point on its circumference. The diameter is a chord that goes through the centre of the circle.

Make sure you know the names of the parts of a circle as you will need to use them in your work on construction.

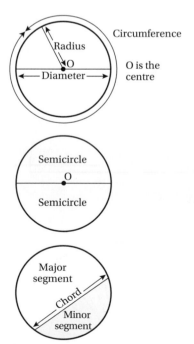

WORKED EXAMPLE 2

a Draw a circle with a **radius** of 4.5 cm.

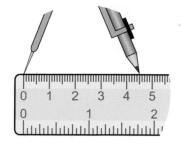

Place the pair of compasses alongside a ruler and open it to 4.5 cm.

Draw a circle.

4.5 cm

b Make an accurate copy of this figure.

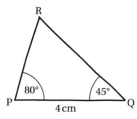

R

80° 45°

P   4 cm   Q

P   4 cm   Q

First draw the base line of 4 cm and label this PQ.

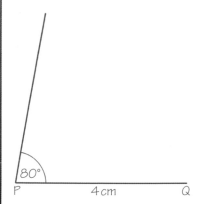

80°

P   4 cm   Q

Use the protractor to measure the angle 80° from point P and draw a line.

Continues on next page …

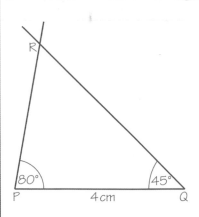

From point Q measure the angle 45° and draw a line from Q extending out so that is crosses the other line.

Where the two lines cross is point R. This is the apex of the triangle.

c Construct an equilateral triangle with side lengths 6 cm.

First draw the base line of 6 cm with a ruler and label it AB.

Then set your compasses to 6 cm and draw an arc above that line, setting the point of your compasses at A.

Repeat this from the other side at point B.

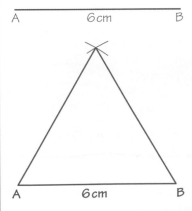

Where the two arcs join is the apex of the triangle. Use this point to complete the triangle.

This process has constructed a triangle with three equal side lengths and three equal angles, each 60°.

The method in Worked Example 2c can be used for triangles with sides of different lengths by setting your pair of compasses to whatever the lengths of the sides are.

EXERCISE 32A

1 The diameter of a circle is 15 cm.

What is the radius of the circle?

Choose from the following options.

A 7.5 cm   B 10 cm   C 15 cm   D 30 cm

2 Use a ruler and protractor to draw and label the following angles.

   a PQR = 25°   **b** DEF = 149°   **c** XYZ = 90°

3 Write down how could you use a protractor marked from 0° to 180° to measure an angle of 238°.

4 **a** Draw a line MN that is 8.4 cm long.

     i   At M, measure and draw angle NMP = 45°.

     ii At N, measure and draw angle RNM = 98°.

   b Give a reason why the lengths of MP and NR do not matter in this diagram.

5 Use a pair of compasses to construct:

   a a circle of radius 4 cm

   b a circle of diameter 12 cm

   c a circle of diameter 2 cm, that shares a centre, O, with another circle of radius 5 cm.

6 Draw a line AB that is 70 mm long.

Construct the circle for which this line is the diameter.

7 Draw a circle of radius 3.5 cm and centre O.

Use a ruler to draw any two radii of the circle. Label them OA and OB.

Join point A to point B to form triangle AOB.

Measure angles AOB, OBA and BAO.

Write the measurements on your diagram.

8 Accurately draw the shapes in the following diagrams.

a 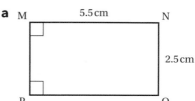   **b**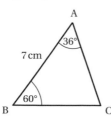

9 Write a step-by-step set of instructions for using only a ruler and a pair of compasses to construct:

   a an equilateral triangle ABC with sides of 6.4 cm

   b a semicircle with a radius of 30 mm.

Find answers at: cambridge.org/ukschools/gcsemaths-studentbookanswers

Section 2: Ruler and compass constructions

Bisecting a line

Key vocabulary

bisect: divide exactly into two halves

You can use a ruler and a pair of compasses to **bisect** any line without measuring it.

WORKED EXAMPLE 3

Bisect a line AB by construction.

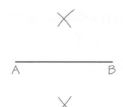

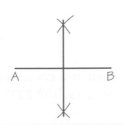

Draw a line and mark points A and B on it.

Open the pair of compasses to any width that is greater than half the line.

Place the point of the compasses on A and draw arcs above and below the line.

Keep the compasses open to the same width and place the point on B.

Draw arcs above and below the line so that they cut the first set of arcs.

Use a ruler to join the points where the arcs intersect.

Tip

Remember perpendicular means 'at right angles to'.

Key vocabulary

midpoint: the centre of a line; the point that divides the line into two equal halves

perpendicular bisector: a line perpendicular to another that also cuts it in half

The point where the constructed line cuts AB is called the **midpoint** of AB.

The distance from A to this point is equal to the distance from B to this point.

The constructed line is perpendicular to AB, so it is called the **perpendicular bisector** of AB. All points along the constructed line will be an equal distance from both point A and point B.

Constructing perpendiculars

You can use your pair of compasses to construct a line perpendicular to any point on a given line or to construct a perpendicular line from a point above or below a given line.

Construct a perpendicular at a given point on a line

WORKED EXAMPLE 4

Construct XY ⊥ AB at a point X on a line.

Tip

Remember ⊥ is the symbol that means 'perpendicular to'.

Draw a line about 12 cm long and label it AB.

Open your compasses to a width of about 4 cm.

Mark on a point, X.

Place the point of your compasses on X.

Draw two arcs to cut AB on either side of X.

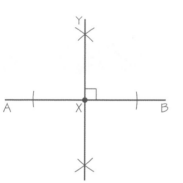

Construct the perpendicular bisector of the line segment between the arcs.

Draw a line through the intersecting arcs.

Label one end of it Y to produce XY and mark the right angle.

Construct a perpendicular from a point to a line

WORKED EXAMPLE 5

Construct PX perpendicular to line AB from point P.

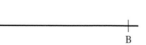

Continues on next page . . .

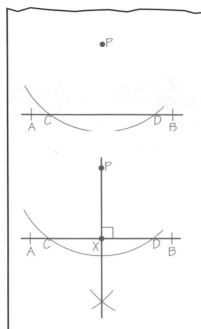

Place the point of your compasses on P.
Draw an arc that cuts AB in two places.

Label these points of intersection C and D.

Open the pair of compasses to a width more than half the distance between C and D.

Place the point on C and draw an arc on the opposite side of the line to point P.

Place the point on D and draw an arc that intersects the one you just drew. Draw a line from the intersecting arcs to P.

Label PX and mark the right angle.

Tip

You should remember from your work on parallel and perpendicular lines in Chapter 8 that the shortest distance from any point to a line is a perpendicular from the point to the line.

Bisecting an angle

An angle bisector divides any angle into two equal halves.

WORKED EXAMPLE 6

Construct an equilateral triangle with equal angles of 60°.

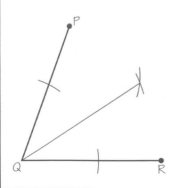

Draw a straight line and label it QR.

Open your compasses to the width of QR and draw an arc from point Q above the line.

Repeat this from point R.

Using a ruler draw a line from point Q to the intersecting arcs.

Repeat from point R.

This constructs an equilateral triangle with equal angles of 60°.

Tip

Remember if you bisect a 90° angle you will then have two angles of 45°.

EXERCISE 32B

1 Define the term 'bisect'.

Choose from the options below.

A To draw a perpendicular line.   B To double.

C To find the midpoint.   D To cut into two halves.

2 Draw each of the following line segments.

Find the midpoint of each line by construction.

a AB = 9 cm   **b** MN = 48 mm   **c** PQ = 6.5 cm

3 **a** Draw any three acute angles. Bisect each angle without measuring.

b How could you check the accuracy of your constructions?

4 Measure and draw the angles shown.

Using only a ruler and a pair of compasses, bisect each angle.

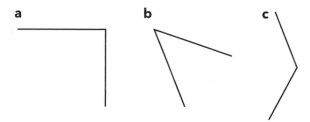

5 Draw any triangle ABC.

a Construct the perpendicular bisector of each side of the triangle.

b Draw a circle with its centre where the perpendicular bisectors meet.
Use the distance to vertex A as the radius.

c What do you notice about this circle?

6 Construct equilateral triangle DEF with sides of 7 cm.

a Bisect each angle of the triangle by construction. Label the point
where the angle bisectors meet as O.

b Measure DO, EO and FO. What do you notice?

7 Draw MN = 80 mm. Insert any point A above MN.

a Construct AX ⊥ MN.

b Draw AB // MN.

8 Construct an equilateral triangle with side lengths of 5 cm.

Section 3: Loci

Key vocabulary

locus (plural **loci**): a set of points that satisfy the same rule

A **locus** is a set of points that obey a certain rule.

You can think of a locus as the path that shows all the possible positions for a point.

The locus of points at a given distance from a fixed point forms a circular path.

You can use a pair of compasses to construct this locus.

WORKED EXAMPLE 7

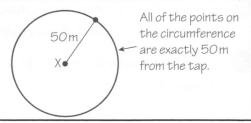

A tap is located at point X.

Draw the locus of points that are exactly 50 metres from the tap.

Your diagram does not need to be to scale.

All of the points on the circumference are exactly 50 m from the tap.

In Worked Example 7, the locus of points that are less than 50 m from the tap is the region inside the circle.

If you are asked to construct this type of locus, you should shade the interior of the circle.

This shows that all the points inside the circumference meet the conditions of the locus.

You should show the circumference as a broken line to indicate that it is **not** included in the locus.

> The locus of a point at distance, r, from a fixed point, O, is a circle with centre O and radius r.

Tip

If a line is included in the locus you draw it as a solid line. If the line is not included, but just shows the edge of the locus you draw it as a broken, or dashed, line.

WORKED EXAMPLE 8

India lives at point A. Joby lives at point B.

They want to meet exactly midway between their homes.

Draw a diagram to show where they could meet.

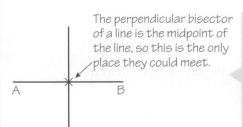

The perpendicular bisector of a line is the midpoint of the line, so this is the only place they could meet.

Draw a line to join the points.

Construct the perpendicular bisector of this line.

The point where the lines cross is exactly midway between their homes.

In Worked Example 8 any point on the perpendicular bisector is the same distance from A and B.

If India and Joby wanted to meet at a point that was the same distance from their home, they could meet anywhere along that line.

However, the question asked you to find the point exactly midway between A and B.

The midpoint of line AB is the only point that meets that condition.

The locus of points equidistant from two fixed points is the perpendicular bisector of the line joining the two points.

The locus of points a fixed distance, d, from a line is the pair of parallel lines that are d cm away from the given line.

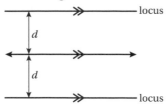

Tip

Remember a line continues to infinity in both directions, so it has no end points.

The locus of points at a fixed distance, d, from a line segment is a pair of parallel lines d cm away from the line segment, as well as the semicircles of radius d cm at the ends of the line segment.

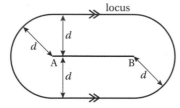

The locus of points that is equidistant from the arms of the angle ABC is the line BP shown below.

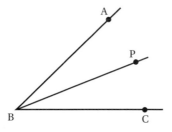

The locus of points that is equidistant from two intersecting lines is their angle bisector.

EXERCISE 32C

1 Loci are common in architecture and also in the line markings on sports fields.

Identify and describe some of the loci in the two photographs in the margin.

2 A tractor is used to trim the hedge around the perimeter of a rectangular field.

The tractor drives at a constant distance of 2 m from the hedge.

Describe the shape produced by the locus of the tractor's path.

Choose your answer from the options below.

A Circle   B Rectangle with rounded corners

C Rectangle   D Square

3 In words, describe the point, path or area that each locus will produce.

a Points that are 200 km from a shop at point X.

b Points that are more than 2 km but less than 3 km from a straight fence 1 km long.

c Points that are equidistant from the two baselines of a tennis court.

d Points that are equidistant from the four corners of a soccer field.

e Points that are within 1 km of a railway line.

4 Accurately construct the locus of points 4 cm from a point D.

5 Draw angle MNO = 50°.

Accurately construct the locus of points equidistant from MN and NO.

6 Draw line PQ of length 4 cm long.

Construct the locus of points 1 cm from PQ.

7 PQ is a line segment of 5 cm.

X is a point exactly 4 cm from P and exactly 2.5 cm from Q.

Show by construction the possible locations of point X.

8 Draw a rectangle ABCD with AB = 6 cm and BC = 4 cm.

a Construct the locus of points that is equidistant from AB and BC.

b Shade the locus of points that is less than 1 cm from the centre of the rectangle.

c Construct the locus of points that is exactly 1 cm outside the perimeter of the rectangle.

Section 4: Applying your skills

You need to be able to combine the construction techniques you have learned to construct accurate diagrams of shapes and to construct loci to show different situations.

In many cases you will need to decide which construction technique to use.

Many of the loci problems that you will have to solve will be presented in context.

You might be asked to draw scaled diagrams to solve these problems.

The scale might be given, for example, 1 cm : 10 km.

If you are not given a scale, always state the scale that you have used.

Problem-solving framework

A, B and C represent three towns.

A mobile phone tower is to be erected in the area.

The tower is to be equidistant from towns A and B and within 30 km of town C.

Show by accurate construction on a scale diagram all possible sites for the tower.

Use a scale of 1 cm : 10 km.

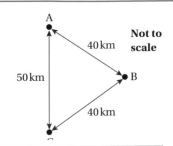

Steps for solving problems	What you would do for this example
Step 1: Work out what you have to do. Start by reading the question carefully.	You have to find the locus of points equidistant from A and B and the locus of points that is less than 30 km from C. The solution is where these loci overlap.
Step 2: What information do you need? Have you got it all?	You have to draw a scale diagram. The distances and the scale are given. The conditions for the loci are given.
Step 3: Decide what maths you can use.	First work out the lengths you have to construct using the scale. The scale is 1 cm : 10 km. So: $\dfrac{40\,\text{km}}{10}$ is represented by 4 cm $\dfrac{50\,\text{km}}{10}$ is represented by 5 cm Next use these lengths to construct a triangle using your ruler and pair of compasses. Once you have the triangle you can find the loci by construction.
Step 4: Set out your solution clearly. Check your working and that your answer is reasonable.	The tower could be built at any position along the thick red line.
Step 5: Check that you've answered the question.	You have shown the overlapping loci and written a statement to answer the question.

EXERCISE 32D

1 A scale drawing is made of a town.

The scale is 10 m : 1 cm.

The post office is 54 m from the nursery.

What is the distance between the two on the scale drawing?

Choose your answer from the options below.

A 0.54 cm   B 5.4 cm   C 54 cm   D 5.4 m

2 Draw line AB of length 5.2 cm.

Construct the perpendicular bisector of AB, which crosses AB at E.

Mark the point D 44 mm along the perpendicular bisector from E.

Mark point F on DE such that DF = FE = 22 mm.

Construct MN // AB and passing through point F.

3 Construct a parallelogram with sides of 46 mm and 28 mm and a longest diagonal of length 60 mm.

Measure and write in the length of the other diagonal.

4 Accurately construct a square of side 45 mm.

5 **a** Construct a quadrilateral ABCD such that angle ABC = 90°,
AB = DC = 2.2 cm
and AD = BC = 5 cm.

b What kind of quadrilateral is this?

6 On a map, the position of buried treasure is known to be 10 metres from point Y and 12 metres from point Z.

Y and Z are 15 metres apart.

Draw a scale diagram and mark with an X all the places where the treasure might be buried.

Use a scale of 1 cm to 2 m.

7 A monkey is in a rectangular enclosure which is 10 m by 17.5 m.

The monkey is able to stretch through the fence around its enclosure and reach a distance of 25 cm.

a Draw a scale diagram to show the locus of points that the monkey can reach outside its enclosure.

b Show on your diagram where you should place a safety barrier to make sure that visitors cannot touch the monkey.

Give a reason for your answer.

Checklist of learning and understanding

Geometry constructions

- A protractor is used to measure and draw angles.
- You can use a ruler and a pair of compasses to construct perpendicular lines and to bisect lines and angles.
- The perpendicular bisector of any line cuts the line at its midpoint.
- The shortest distance from a point to a line is always the perpendicular distance.

Loci

- A locus is a set of points that meet the same conditions.
- The locus of points can be a single point, a line, a curve or a shaded area.
- Loci can be used to solve problems involving equal distances and overlapping areas.

Chapter review

For additional questions on the topics in this chapter, visit GCSE Mathematics Online.

1   **a**   Use a protractor to measure angles *a* and *b* on this clockface.

     b   Draw two angles which are the same size as *a* and *b*.

     c   Bisect the two angles you have drawn by construction.

2   Draw a line AB of length 6.5 cm.

     a   Find its midpoint by construction.

     b   Indicate the locus of points that is equidistant from A and B on your diagram.

Find answers at: cambridge.org/ukschools/gcsemaths-studentbookanswers

3 Town X is due north of town Y.

They are 20 km apart.

Town Z is 25 km from town X and 35 km from town Y.

a Draw a scale diagram to show the location of town Z in relation to the other two towns.

Use a scale of 1 cm : 5 km.

b A railway runs between towns X and Y such that it is equidistant from both towns.

Indicate the position of the railway on your diagram.

c The electricity supply from town X is carried on a cable that is the same distance from XZ and XY along its length.

Indicate on your diagram where this cable would be.

 4 The scale drawing shows a post which is 1.5 metres from the fence.

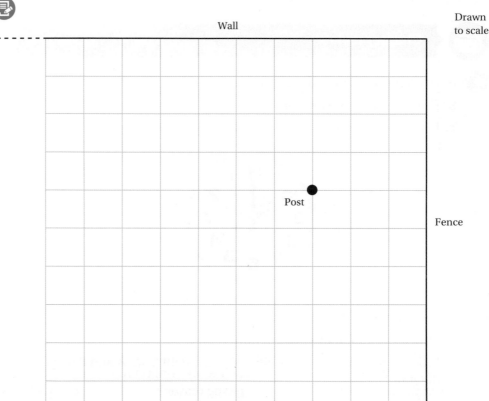

Wall

Drawn to scale

Post

Fence

a How far is the post from the wall? *(1 mark)*

b A pony is tied to the post by a rope.

The pony can reach 2.5 metres from the post.

On the scale drawing, show accurately the area that the pony can reach. *(2 marks)*

c Work out the scale of the drawing as a ratio.

Give your answer in its simplest form. *(3 marks)*

33 Similarity

In this chapter you will learn how to ...

- identify similar triangles and prove that two triangles are similar.
- work with scale factors to enlarge shapes on a grid.
- find the scale factor and centre of enlargement of a transformation.
- apply the concept of similarity to calculate unknown lengths.

For more resources relating to this chapter, visit GCSE Mathematics Online.

Using mathematics: real-life applications

When you enlarge a photo, project an image on to a screen or make scaled models you are dealing with similarity. Many toys and other objects are scaled, but similar, versions of larger objects from real life.

"I work with scale drawings and scale models all the time. The models are mathematically similar to the real aircraft so the clients can see what they are buying. We made these scale models to display at an international air show."

(Aircraft designer)

Before you start ...

Ch 9	You need to be able to label angles correctly.	**1** a Which angle is a right angle? b What size is angle DOA? c What size is angle BOD?	(diagram with angles 120°, 80°, points D, C, O, A, B)
KS3	You need to know the criteria for when two triangles are congruent.	**2** Prove that the triangles below are congruent, giving reasons.	(triangles: DEF with 6.5 cm, 8.8 cm, 10 cm, 60°, 40°; ABC with 8.8 cm, 6.5 cm, 80°)
Ch 17	You need to know how to solve simple equations using inverse operations.	**3** Solve: a $3x = 24$	b $15 = 6h$ c $6.25 = 25k$
Ch 26	You need to be able to recognise numbers in equivalent ratios.	**4** Which pairs of numbers are in the same ratio as $3:2$? A $6:5$ B $4:6$ C $0.15:0.1$ **5** Given that $\dfrac{x}{15} = \dfrac{4}{90}$, find x.	

Find answers at: cambridge.org/ukschools/gcsemaths-studentbookanswers

Assess your starting point using the Launchpad

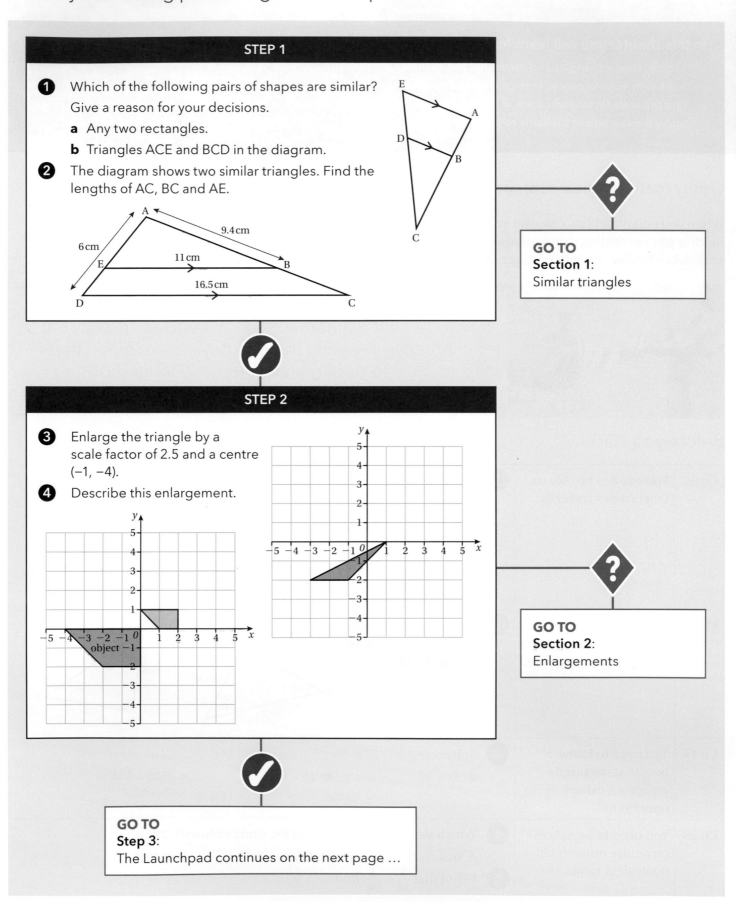

STEP 1

1 Which of the following pairs of shapes are similar? Give a reason for your decisions.

   a Any two rectangles.

   b Triangles ACE and BCD in the diagram.

2 The diagram shows two similar triangles. Find the lengths of AC, BC and AE.

GO TO
Section 1:
Similar triangles

STEP 2

3 Enlarge the triangle by a scale factor of 2.5 and a centre (−1, −4).

4 Describe this enlargement.

GO TO
Section 2:
Enlargements

GO TO
Step 3:
The Launchpad continues on the next page ...

Launchpad continued …

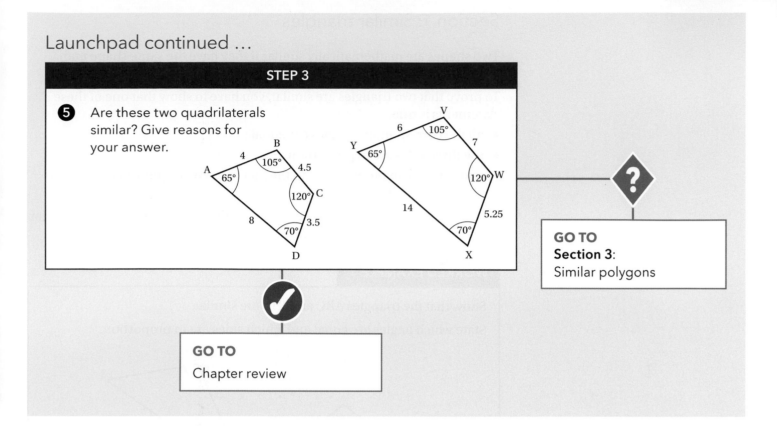

STEP 3

5 Are these two quadrilaterals similar? Give reasons for your answer.

GO TO
Chapter review

GO TO
Section 3:
Similar polygons

Section 1: Similar triangles

Two shapes are mathematically similar if they have the same shape and proportions but are different in size.

To prove that two triangles are similar, you have to show that one of these statements is true:

- all the corresponding angles are equal
- the three sides are in proportion
- two sides are in proportion and the included angles (between these two sides) are equal.

You must name triangles with the corresponding vertices in the correct order when you are saying they are similar.

WORKED EXAMPLE 1

Show that the triangles ABC and RTS are similar.

State which angles are equal and which sides are in proportion.

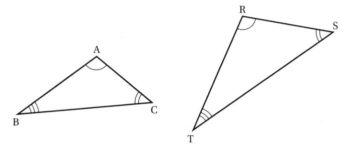

Triangle ABC is similar to triangle RTS because angle A = angle R, angle B = angle T and angle C = angle S.
The three sides are in proportion, so $\frac{AB}{RT} = \frac{AC}{RS} = \frac{BC}{TS}$.

Finding unknown lengths using proportional sides

In similar triangles the lengths of any pair of corresponding sides are in the same ratio.

You can use the ratio of corresponding sides to find the lengths of unknown sides in similar figures.

Problem-solving framework

In the diagram, triangle ABC is similar to triangle QRP.

Find the length of x.

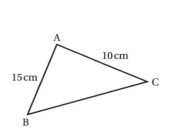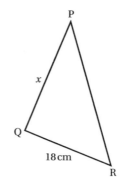

Steps for solving problems	What you would do for this example
Step 1: Identify the similar triangles in the problem and write them down with the vertices in the correct order.	Triangle ABC is similar to triangle QRP.
Step 2: Write down what you know.	That the triangles are similar. Two sides of triangle ABC. One side of triangle QRP.
Step 3: Find the ratio between the sides.	AB corresponds to QR, so the ratio is 15 : 18.
Step 4: Write a proportion with the unknown side.	$\dfrac{AC}{QP} = \dfrac{15}{18} = \dfrac{10}{x}$
Step 5: Solve the proportion.	$x = \dfrac{18 \times 10}{15} = 12\,cm$
Step 6: Have you answered the question?	$x = 12\,cm$

EXERCISE 33A

1 Each diagram below contains a pair of similar triangles.

Identify the matching angles and the sides that are in proportion.

Write down your reasons using the correct angle vocabulary.

a
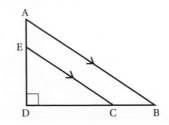

b
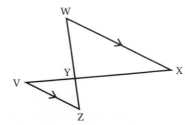

c
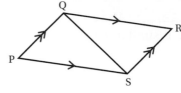

d
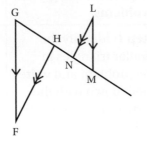

2 Are the following pairs of triangles similar? Give reasons for your answers.

a
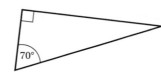

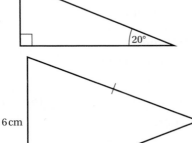

b
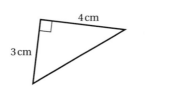

c
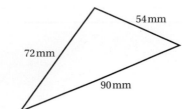

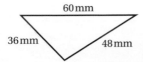

3 State whether each of the statements below is true or false.

Write down your reasons and give a counter-example for any statement you believe is false

a All isosceles triangles are similar.

b All equilateral triangles are similar.

c All right-angled triangles are similar.

d All right-angled triangles with an angle of 30° are similar.

e All right-angled isosceles triangles are similar.

f No pair of scalene triangles are ever similar.

4 Each diagram below contains three similar triangles.

Identify the matching angles and sides in each group of triangles. Give reasons for your answer.

a

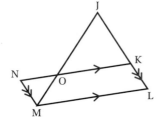

b

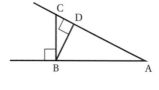

5 The two shapes below are similar.

Find the missing lengths c and d.

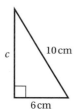

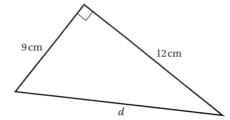

6 The two shapes below are similar.

Find the missing lengths e and f.

Find answers at: cambridge.org/ukschools/gcsemaths-studentbookanswers

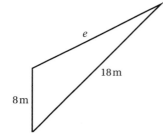

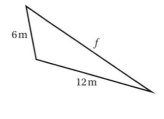

7 Find the lengths of AE, CE and AB.

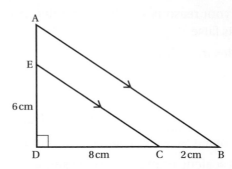

8 Find the lengths of YZ and XY.

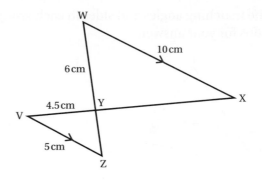

9 Copy the diagram. Put the lengths in the correct positions on the diagram to complete the similar shapes.

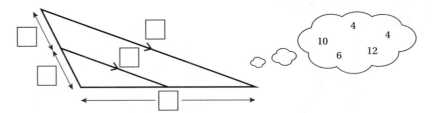

10 Copy the diagram. Put the lengths in the correct positions to complete the similar shapes.

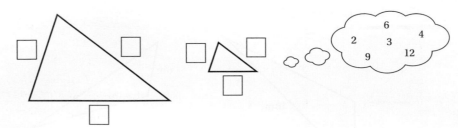

Section 2: Enlargements

An enlargement is a transformation that changes the position of a shape as well as its size.

Under enlargement, an object and its image are similar shapes, because their angles remain unchanged.

In mathematics, you use the word enlargement for all transformations that produce similar images even if the image is smaller than the original object.

To construct an enlargement of a shape, you multiply the length of each side by the scale factor.

Before you enlarge a shape, consider its new dimensions.

Has it got bigger?
Has it stayed the same size?
Has it got smaller?

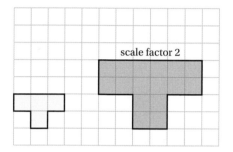

scale factor 2

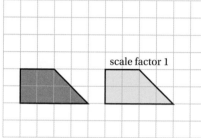

scale factor 1

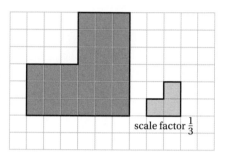

scale factor $\frac{1}{3}$

WORKED EXAMPLE 2

Draw an enlargement of triangle ABC by a scale factor of 2.

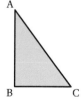

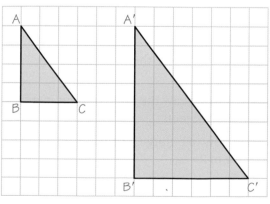

The image of triangle ABC is triangle A'B'C'.

The length of A'B' is twice the length of AB, the length of A'C' = 2AC and length of B'C' = 2BC.

Notice that triangle ABC is similar to triangle A'B'C' and that the sides are in proportion

EXERCISE 33B

1 Enlarge each shape by the scale factor given.

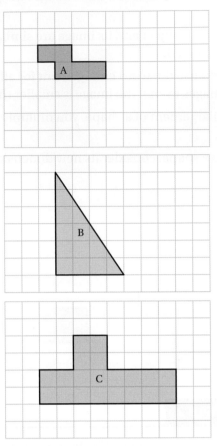

a Enlarge A by a scale factor of 3.

b Enlarge B by a scale factor of 0.5.

c Enlarge C by a scale factor of $1\frac{1}{2}$.

The centre of enlargement

You need two pieces of information to accurately draw an enlargement: the scale factor and the centre of enlargement.

The centre of enlargement is the point from where the enlargement is measured.

When you use a centre of enlargement, you draw the enlargement in a certain position in relation to the original object.

The table on the next page shows you how to enlarge a shape from a given centre of enlargement by a scale factor of 2.

Step 1: Find the distance from the centre of enlargement to a point on the object. You can draw a ray from the centre to the point.	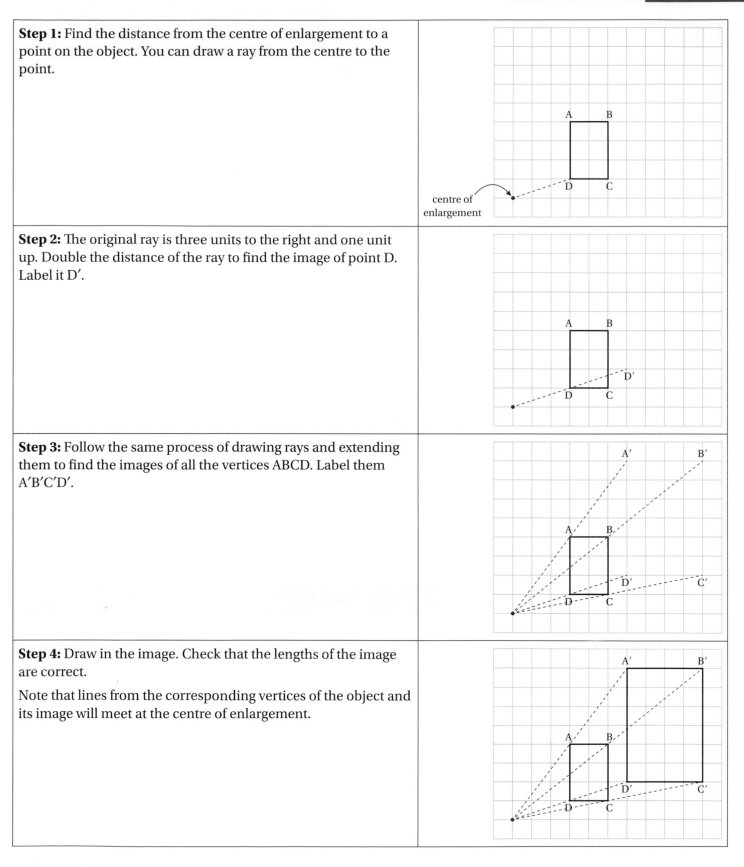
Step 2: The original ray is three units to the right and one unit up. Double the distance of the ray to find the image of point D. Label it D′.	
Step 3: Follow the same process of drawing rays and extending them to find the images of all the vertices ABCD. Label them A′B′C′D′.	
Step 4: Draw in the image. Check that the lengths of the image are correct. Note that lines from the corresponding vertices of the object and its image will meet at the centre of enlargement.	

The procedure is the same for a centre of enlargement in any position, even for a centre of enlargement inside the shape itself.

WORK IT OUT 33.1

This triangle is enlarged from centre (−3, 4) with a scale factor of 2. Draw its image.

Which one of these answers is correct?

Why are the others wrong?

How many marks would you give the incorrect answers if you were the teacher? Why?

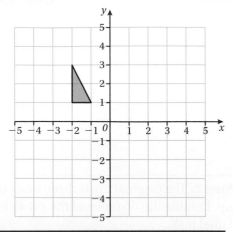

Option A	Option B	Option C

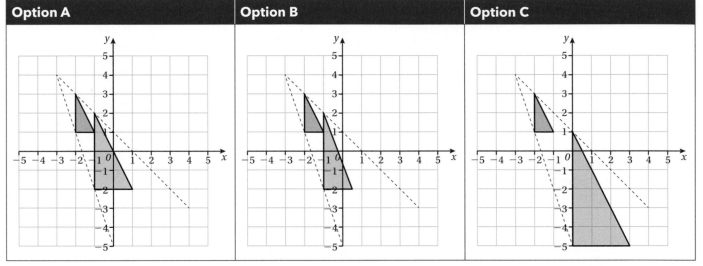

Tip

Sketch the new shape before you construct the enlargement. Draw one ray to identify the new position of the shape. After drawing the enlargement add in additional rays to check that it is in the correct position.

Fractional scale factors

If the scale factor is a fraction, the image will be smaller than the object.

WORKED EXAMPLE 3

Enlarge the triangle on the grid by a scale factor of $\frac{1}{2}$ through the given centre of enlargement.

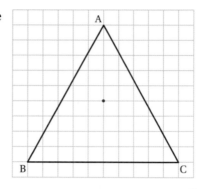

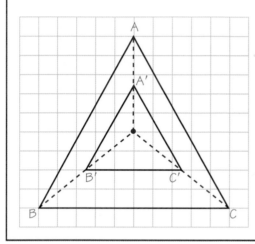

In this case, the rays from each vertex of the object are halved to find the position of the image.

EXERCISE 33C

1. Enlarge each shape as directed.

   Use the point C as the centre of enlargement.

   a Enlarge shape R by a scale factor of 3.

   b Enlarge shape S by a scale factor of 2.

   c Enlarge shape T by a scale factor of $\frac{1}{2}$.

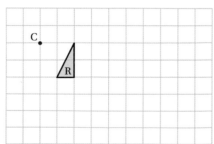

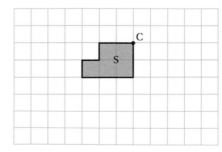

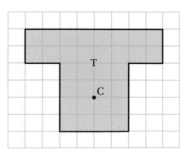

2 Enlarge the given shape by a scale factor of 3.
Use the origin as the centre of enlargement.

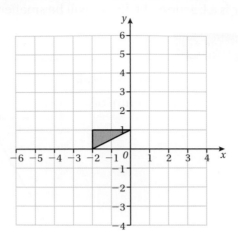

3 Enlarge the given shape by a scale factor of 2.
Use (−4, 3) as the centre of enlargement.

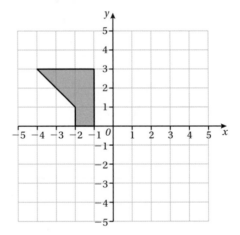

4 Enlarge the given shape by a scale factor of $\frac{1}{3}$.
Use (−5, 2) as the centre of enlargement.

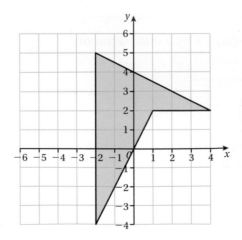

5 Enlarge the given shape by a scale factor of $1\frac{1}{2}$.
Use $(0, 1)$ as the centre of enlargement.

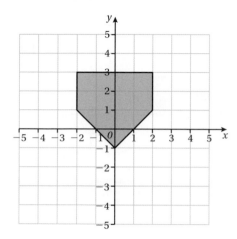

Properties of enlargements

You need to remember the following properties of an enlargement.
- The centre of enlargement can be anywhere: inside the object, on a vertex or side of the object or outside the object.
- A scale factor greater than 1 will enlarge the object. A scale factor smaller than 1 will reduce the size of the object although this is still called an enlargement.
- The object and its image are similar under enlargement. Sides are in the ratio $1 : k$, where k is the scale factor.
- The area of an object and its image will be in the ratio $1 : k^2$, where k is the scale factor.
- An object and its image have the same angles.
- For positive scale factors an object and its image have the same orientation.

Describing enlargements

To describe an enlargement you need to give:
- the scale factor
- the centre of enlargement.

The ratio of sides gives the scale factor.

To find the centre of enlargement you need to draw lines from corresponding vertices of the object and its image to find the point where they meet.

WORK IT OUT 33.2

What scale factors have been used to enlarge this shape?

Which one of these students' answers is correct?

What feedback would you give each student to make sure they don't make the same mistakes again?

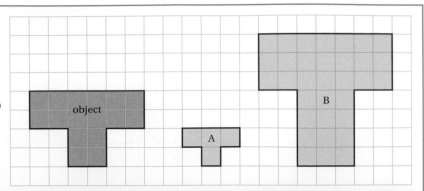

Student A	Student B	Student C
A scale factor of 2 has been used to produce shape A. The top of shape A is 3 squares across, multiply this by 2 to get 6, the length of the top of the object. B can't be an enlargement. Its top is 7 squares and the object is 6. You can't do that using multiplication. Maybe it's 1?	Since the sides have halved in length to get A, the scale factor is $\frac{1}{2}$. Shape B isn't an enlargement. The sides have been increased by different numbers of squares.	To get shape A you have to take away one square along the bottom and along each side edge. So the scale factor is -1. Shape B is a scale factor of $1\frac{1}{2}$ because 2 squares have become 3 squares.

EXERCISE 33D

1 Which of the photos below show an enlargement of the original?

How can you tell?

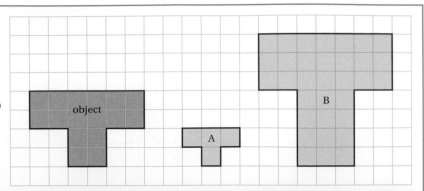

A

B

C

2 Triangle ABC is enlarged to give triangle A′B′C′.

Angle BCA is 80°. What is angle B′C′A′?

Choose from the following options.

A 40°   B   80°   C 160°   D It is impossible to say.

3 Which of the following houses are enlargements of house A?

For each enlargement state the scale factor.

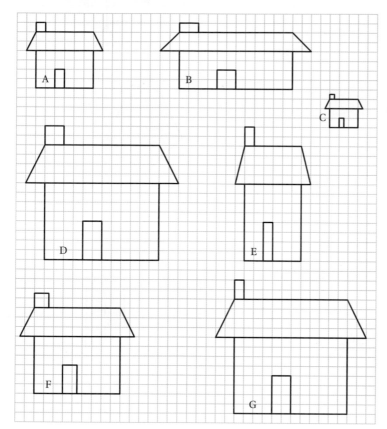

4 These diagrams each show an object and its image after an enlargement.

Describe each of these enlargements by giving both the scale factor and the coordinates of the centre of enlargement.

a

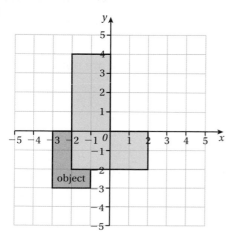

b

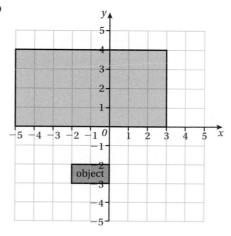

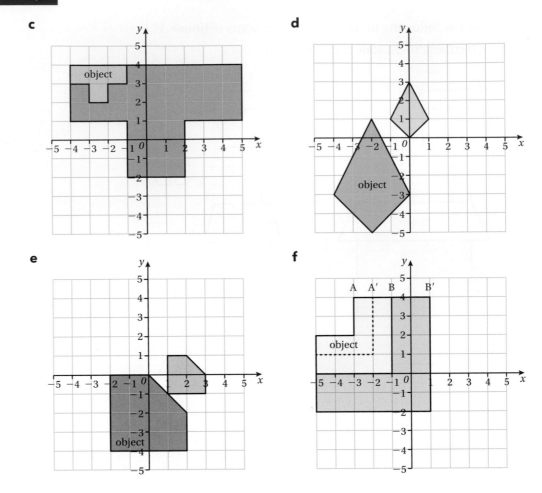

Section 3: Similar polygons

Two polygons are similar if:

- the angles in one polygon are equal to the angles in the other polygon

and

- the ratios of the sides from one polygon to the other are kept the same.

For polygons other than triangles, equal angles alone are not sufficient to prove similarity.

WORKED EXAMPLE 4

Which of the quadrilaterals, B to D, are similar to A?

A 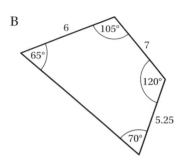   B 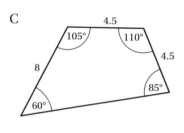   C   D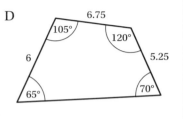

B has the same size angles as A, but the sides are not in proportion.

For example, $\frac{4}{6} \neq \frac{4.5}{7}$. So B is not similar to A.

The angles in C are different to the angles in A, so C is not similar to A.

D has corresponding angles equal to those in A.

Test to see whether the sides are in the same proportion: $\frac{4}{6} = \frac{4.5}{6.75} = \frac{3.5}{5.25}$ D is similar to A.

D is an enlargement of A with a scale factor of 1.5

EXERCISE 33E

1 A triangle with side lengths 3 cm, 4 cm and 5 cm is enlarged.

Which of the following could be this enlarged shape's side lengths?

A 5 cm, 12 cm, 13 cm   B 4 cm, 6 cm, 5 cm

C 6 cm, 8 cm, 15 cm   D 15 cm, 9 cm, 12 cm

2 State whether each statement below is true or false.

Write down your reasoning.

a All squares are similar.

b All hexagons are similar.

c All rectangles are similar.

d All regular octagons are similar.

3 Sketch the following pairs of shapes and decide if they are similar.

Write down your reasoning.

a Rectangle ABCD with AB = 5 cm and BC = 3 cm.
Rectangle EFGH with EF = 10 cm and FG = 6 cm.

b Rectangle ABCD with AB = 5 cm and BC = 3 cm.
Rectangle EFGH with EF = 10 cm and GH = 9 cm.

c Square ABCD with AB = 4 cm.
Square EFGH with EF = 6 cm.

4 The two shapes below are similar.

Find the missing lengths *a* and *b*.

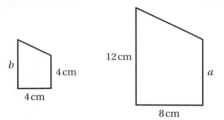

5 The two shapes below are similar.

Find the missing lengths of the sides in the second shape.

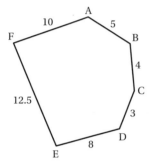
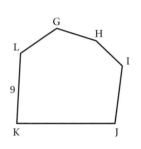

6 The shape below has been enlarged by a scale factor of 1.5 to create the image GHIJKL.

AB = 5 cm and BC = 7 cm.

Find the lengths of the missing sides in the second shape.

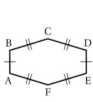
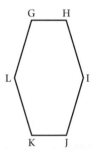

7 Emily drew the diagram below as a plan for a display.

The actual size of each side will be 10 m.

a What is the scale factor of enlargement of the plan?

b Write the scale as a ratio.

Checklist of learning and understanding

Similar triangles

- Two triangles are similar if all three corresponding angles are equal. Similar triangles are the same shape and their corresponding sides are in proportion.
- The proportion between corresponding sides of similar triangles can be used to solve problems in geometry.

Enlargements

- An enlargement is a transformation that changes the position and size of a shape.
- Enlargements are described by a scale factor and centre of enlargement.

Similar shapes

- If shapes are enlarged, similar shapes are created with all their sides in proportion. The proportionality between lengths can be used to solve geometry problems.

Chapter review

 For additional questions on the topics in this chapter, visit GCSE Mathematics Online.

1 Which of the following are always similar?

    A Isosceles triangles   B Equilateral triangles

    C Right-angled triangles   D Scalene triangles

2 **a** Prove that triangle VWX is similar to triangle VYZ.

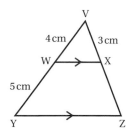

    b Find the length of XZ.

3 A tree is 3 m high and its shadow has a length of 7.5 m.

At the same time of day, a building casts a shadow that is 16.25 m long.

Use similar triangles to calculate the height of the building.

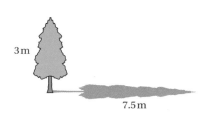

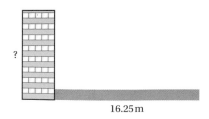

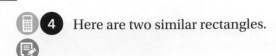

4 Here are two similar rectangles.

Not drawn
accurately

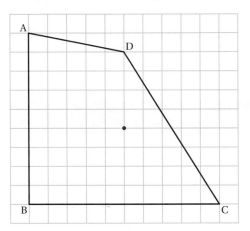

3 cm

10 cm

15 cm

Work out the area of the larger rectangle. *(5 marks)*

© AQA 2013

5 Draw an enlargement of ABCD by $\frac{1}{2}$.

Use the given point as the centre of enlargement.

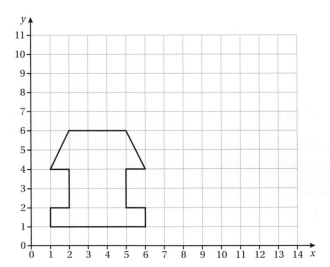

6 Draw an enlargement of the shape by a scale factor of 1.5.

Use the origin as the centre of enlargement.

7 Are any two regular hexagons similar shapes?

Give reasons for your answer.

8 Are any two rhombuses similar shapes?

Give reasons for your answer.

34 Congruence

In this chapter you will learn how to ...

- show that two triangles are congruent using the cases SSS, ASA, SAS, RHS.
- apply congruency in calculations and simple proofs.

For more resources relating to this chapter, visit GCSE Mathematics Online.

Using mathematics: real-life applications

Congruent triangles are used in construction to reinforce structures that need to be strong and stable.

"When designing any bridge I have to allow for reinforcement. This ensures that the bridge stays strong and doesn't collapse under heavy traffic. Any bridge I design has many congruent triangles."

(Structural engineer)

Before you start ...

Ch 8	You need to know how to label angles and shapes that are equal.	**1** Here are two identical triangles. **a** Write down a pair of sides that are equal in length. **b** What angle is equal in size to angle BAC? **c** Write down another pair of angles that are equal in size.
Ch 9	You need to know basic angle facts.	**2** Match up the correct statement with the correct diagram. **a** Vertically opposite angles are equal. **b** Alternate angles are equal. **c** Corresponding angles are equal.
Ch 8,9	You should be able to apply angle facts to find angles in figures and to justify results in simple proofs.	**3** Decide whether each statement is true or false. **a** Angle DBE = 40° (alternate to angle ADB) **b** Angle BEC = 50° (complementary to angle ADB) **c** Triangle ABD, triangle BDE and triangle BCE are equilateral. **d** Angle BDE = angle BED = 70°
Ch 8	You need to know and be able to apply the properties of triangles and quadrilaterals.	**4** What is the value of x? Choose the correct answer. A 60° B 30° C 45° D 50°

Find answers at: cambridge.org/ukschools/gcsemaths-studentbookanswers

Assess your starting point using the Launchpad

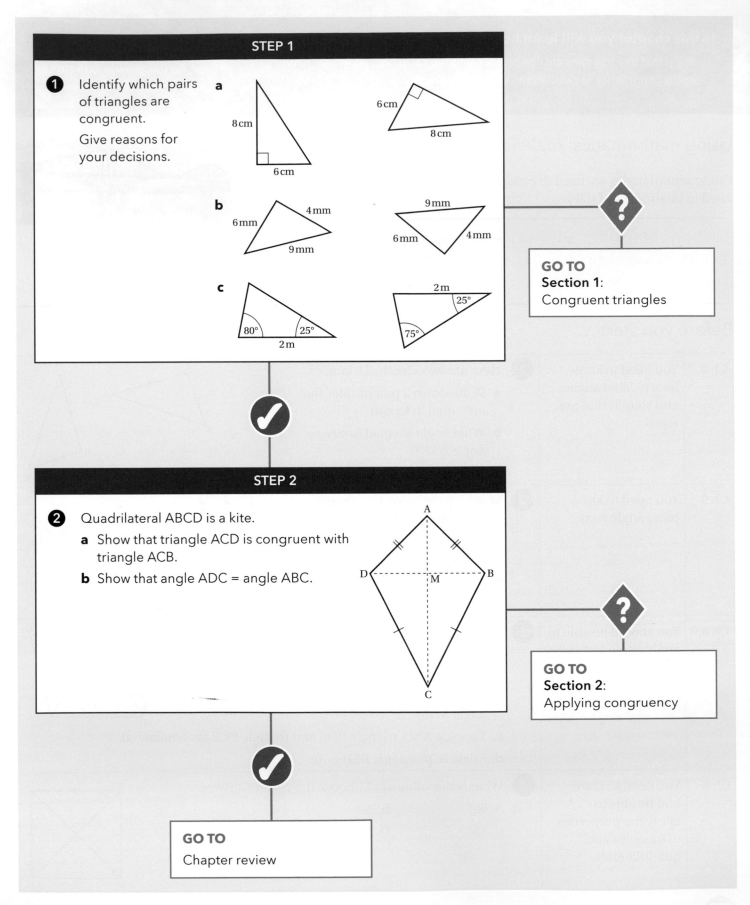

STEP 1

1 Identify which pairs of triangles are congruent.

Give reasons for your decisions.

a 8 cm, 6 cm / 6 cm, 8 cm

b 4 mm, 6 mm, 9 mm / 9 mm, 6 mm, 4 mm

c 80°, 25°, 2 m / 2 m, 25°, 75°

?

GO TO
Section 1: Congruent triangles

STEP 2

2 Quadrilateral ABCD is a kite.

a Show that triangle ACD is congruent with triangle ACB.

b Show that angle ADC = angle ABC.

?

GO TO
Section 2: Applying congruency

GO TO
Chapter review

Section 1: Congruent triangles

Congruent triangles are identical in shape and all corresponding measurements are equal.

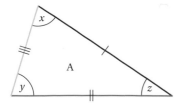 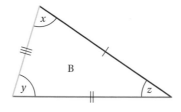

When the triangles are in different orientations you need to think carefully about the corresponding sides and angles.

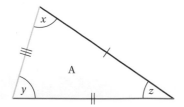 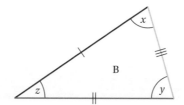

Key vocabulary

congruent: shapes that are identical in shape and size

Tip

You worked with congruent shapes in different orientations when you dealt with reflections and rotations in Chapter 31.

Tip

If you place two congruent triangles on top of each other the angles and sides will match up. The matching sides and angles are the corresponding sides or angles.

Two triangles are congruent if one of the following sets of conditions is true.

Side Side Side or **SSS:** the three sides of one triangle are equal in length to the three sides of the other triangle.	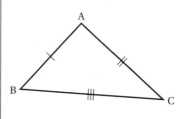 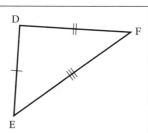
Angle Side Angle or **ASA**: two angles and one side of one triangle are equal to two angles and the corresponding side of the other triangle.	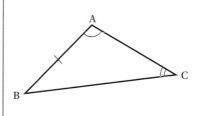 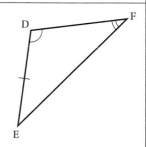

Side Angle Side or **SAS**: two sides and the included angle of one triangle are equal to two sides and the included angle of the other triangle.	
Right angle Hypotenuse Side or **RHS**: the hypotenuse and one other side of a right-angled triangle are equal to the hypotenuse and one other side of the other right-angled triangle.	

Tip

It is important to write the letters of the vertices of the two triangles in the correct order.

When we write that triangle ABC is congruent to triangle DEF, it means that:

angle A = angle D, angle B = angle E, angle C = angle F

and

AB = DE, AC = DF and BC = EF.

The conditions in the table above and on the preceding page are the minimum conditions for proving that triangles are congruent. No other combinations of side and angle facts are sufficient to tell you whether a triangle is congruent or not.

For example, the triangles in each pair in the table below are not congruent.

Two triangles with all their angles equal can still be very different sizes.	
The condition Side Angle Side (SAS) must be the included angle (between the two sides). Otherwise, you do not know if they are congruent or not. The third side might have a different length in the two triangles.	

Although a pair of triangles with one of these sets of information might still be congruent, the conditions given are not sufficient proof that they are.

WORK IT OUT 34.1

Here are three proofs for congruence for the pair of triangles.

Which one uses the correct reasoning?

Why are the others incorrect?

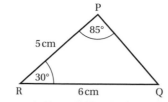 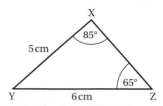

Option A	Option B	Option C
In triangle PQR and triangle XYZ: PR = XY = 5 cm angle P = angle X = 85° RQ = YZ = 6 cm so triangle PQR is congruent to triangle XYZ (SAS).	In triangle PRQ and triangle XYZ: In triangle PRQ, angle Q = 65° (sum of angles in a triangle) angle Q = angle Z = 65° RQ = YZ so the triangles are congruent.	In triangle PRQ and triangle XYZ: PR = XY = 5 cm RQ = YZ = 6 cm In triangle XYZ, angle Y = 30° (sum of angles in a triangle), so triangle PRQ is congruent to triangle XYZ (SAS).

EXERCISE 34A

1 Match up each of the congruency descriptions (SSS, ASA, SAS, RHS) with each pair of triangles below:

a

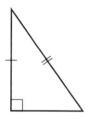

b

 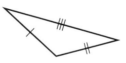

c

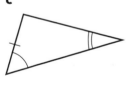

d

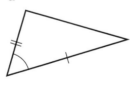 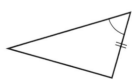

2 Triangles ABC and EFG are congruent.

Angle ABC = 35° and angle FGE = 90°

What is angle CAB?

Choose from the options below.

A 35°   B 55°   C 90°   D It's impossible to say.

3 For each pair of triangles below, state whether the triangles are congruent or not, or whether there is not enough information.

a
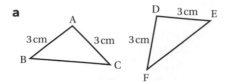

b
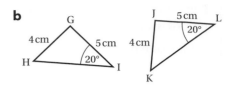

c
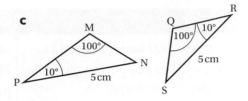

d
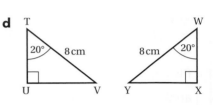

4 Sophia says that triangle ABC is congruent to triangle CDE.

Is she correct?

Give reasons for your answer.

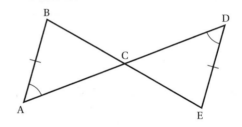

5 Write down two different reasons for congruence of triangles DEF and DGF.

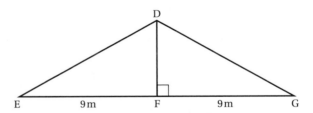

6 In the diagram, PQ is parallel to SR and QT = TR = 2 cm.

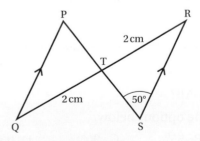

Show that triangle PQT is congruent to triangle SRT.

7 Are triangles ABE and CBD in the figure congruent? Give reasons for your answer.

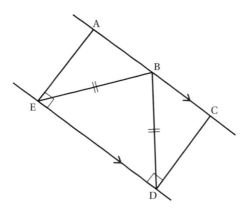

8 Triangle ABD is isosceles.

AC is the perpendicular height.

Which triangles are congruent?

Give reasons for your answer.

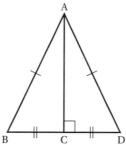

9 In the figure below, PR = SU.

Is triangle PQR congruent to triangle SQU? Give reasons for your answer.

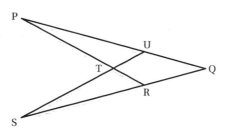

10 ABCD in the figure is a kite.

Henry thinks this shape doesn't have any congruent triangles because none of the sides are marked as equal.

a say why he is wrong.

b list each pair of congruent triangles in the shape.

Give reasons for your answer.

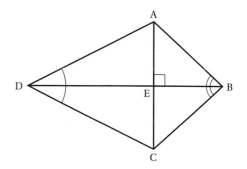

11 Quadrilateral ABCD is a rhombus.

Show that:

a triangle AED is congruent to triangle CEB

b triangle AEB is congruent to triangle CED.

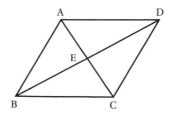

Section 2: Applying congruency

Problem-solving framework

In a problem-solving situation, you will need to combine what you have learnt previously with your new skills to solve problems.

The following steps are useful for solving geometry problems.

Steps for solving problems	What you would do for this example
Step 1: Read the question carefully to decide what you have to find.	In the diagram, AM = BM and PM = QM. **a** Give reasons why triangle AMP is congruent to triangle BMQ. **b** Show that AP // BQ. 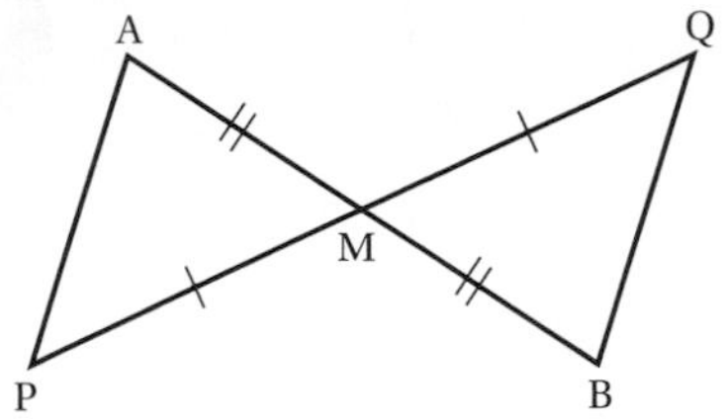
Step 2: Write down any further information that might be useful.	The two triangles also have vertically opposite angles, that are equal.
Step 3: Decide what method you will use.	You are given two pairs of equal sides and you can see that the included angle is also equal, so use SAS to prove congruence.
Step 4: Set out your working clearly.	**a** In triangles AMP and BMQ: AM = BM (given) PM = QM (given) Angle AMP = angle BMQ (vertically opposite angles are equal at M) So triangle AMP is congruent to triangle BMQ (SAS). **b** Angle APM = angle BQM (matching angles of congruent triangles). Hence APM and BQM are alternate angles and AP // BQ.

WORKED EXAMPLE 1

In the diagram, triangle DEF is divided by GF into two smaller triangles.

Show that FG is perpendicular to DE.

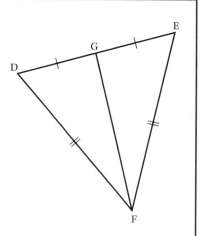

In triangle FGD and triangle FGE, side FG is common to both triangles.
DG = GE   DF = EF
So the triangles are congruent (SSS).
Angle DGF = angle EGF and the two angles lie on a straight line.
So each angle = 90°, and FG is perpendicular to DE.

EXERCISE 34B

1 In the diagram below, show that KL = ML.

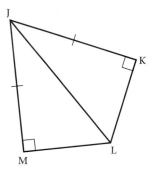

2 Use the facts given in the diagram to:

a show that angle ABE = angle EDC

b show that quadrilateral ABCD is a parallelogram.

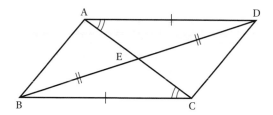

3 In the quadrilateral, SP = SR and QP // RS. Angle QRP = 56°.

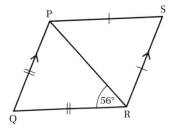

Calculate the size of angle PSR and give your reasons.

 Find answers at: cambridge.org/ukschools/gcsemaths-studentbookanswers

4 In the diagram, PQ = PT and QR = TS.

Holly says that triangle PRS is an equilateral triangle.

Jacob says it is an isosceles triangle.

Who is right? Say why.

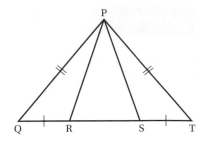

5 In the figure below, show that:

a triangle AEB is congruent to triangle CEB

b angle EAD = angle ECD.

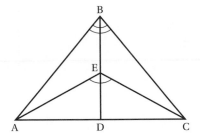

6 A farmer has two sons. He gives them a field each.

One son gets field ABC and the other son gets field CDA.

a is each field the same size? Give reasons for your answer.

b one of the sons thinks his corner at 'B' is smaller than his brother's corner at 'D'. Show that he is wrong.

AD = BC and AD // BC.

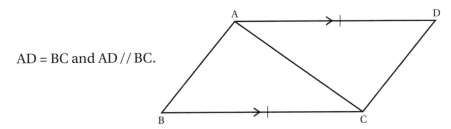

Checklist of learning and understanding

Congruent triangles

- You can prove that two triangles are congruent using one of the four cases of congruence:
  - Side Side Side or SSS: the three sides of one triangle are equal in length to the three sides of the other triangle.
  - Angle Side Angle or ASA: two angles and one side of one triangle are equal to the corresponding two angles and one side of the other triangle.
  - Side Angle Side or SAS: two sides and the included angle of one triangle are equal to two sides and the included angle of the other triangle.
  - Right angle Hypotenuse Side or RHS: the hypotenuse and one side of a right-angled triangle are equal to the hypotenuse and one side of the other right-angled triangle.

Chapter review

For additional questions on the topics in this chapter, visit GCSE Mathematics Online.

1 State whether these pairs of triangles are congruent.
Give reasons for your answers.

a
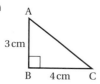

b

c
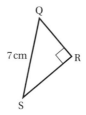

2 Peter says these triangles are congruent because the hypotenuse is the same. Why is he wrong?

3 These two triangles are congruent.

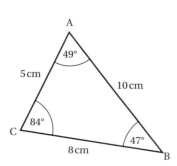

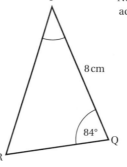

Not drawn accurately

a What is the size of angle P?
Choose your answer from the following options.

   A 47°   B 49°   C 84°   D none of these   *(1 mark)*

b What is the length of PR?
Choose your answer from the following options.

   A 5 cm   B 8 cm   C 10 cm   D none of these   *(1 mark)*

© AQA 2013

4 In the figure below, show that angle QTS = angle QRP.

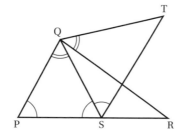

5 Use triangle congruence to show that angle EBC = angle ECB in the diagram below.

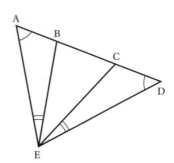

6 In the figure below, triangle ABD lies between two parallel lines.
BC = CA = AD

Lucy thinks that angle EAD is three times bigger than angle ABC.

Is she correct? Give reasons for your answer.

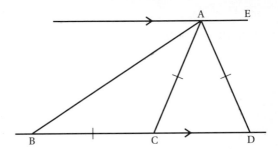

7 Use congruent triangles to show that angle QPR = angle STR.

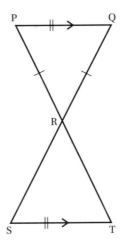

8 Show that WX = XV in the diagram.

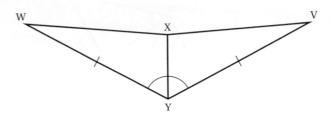

35 Pythagoras' theorem

In this chapter you will learn how to ...

- develop full knowledge and understanding of Pythagoras' theorem.
- apply Pythagoras' theorem in 2D problems.
- link the maths to real-life skills for industry.

 For more resources relating to this chapter, visit GCSE Mathematics Online.

Using mathematics: real-life applications

Builders, carpenters, garden designers and navigators all use Pythagoras' theorem in their jobs. It is a method based on right-angled triangles that helps them to work out unknown lengths.

"I use Pythagoras' theorem to help me navigate the ship ... I need to know how far away we are from port and I use the theorem to calculate this..."
(Navigation officer)

Calculator tip

Make sure you know how to square a number and calculate a square root using your calculator.

Tip

When answering questions about Pythagoras' theorem it might be useful to draw a diagram if one isn't provided.

Before you start ...

Ch 1 and 4	You need to be confident with calculating squares and square roots.	**1** a Which are correct? i $\sqrt{100} = \sqrt{10}$ ii $\sqrt{100} = 10$ iii $\sqrt{100} = \pm10$ iv $10^2 = 100$ b Which are correct? i $4^2 = 4 \times 2 = 8$ ii $3^3 = 3 \times 3 \times 3 = 27$
Ch 9	You need to recognise different types of angle and be able to define them.	**2** a Which is a right angle? Identify the other angles. i ii iii iv v b How many degrees are there in three right angles?
Ch 8	You'll need to apply the properties of different types of triangles to solve problems.	**3** What is the area of triangle ABC? **4** What do you know about angles x and y in this triangle?

Assess your starting point using the Launchpad

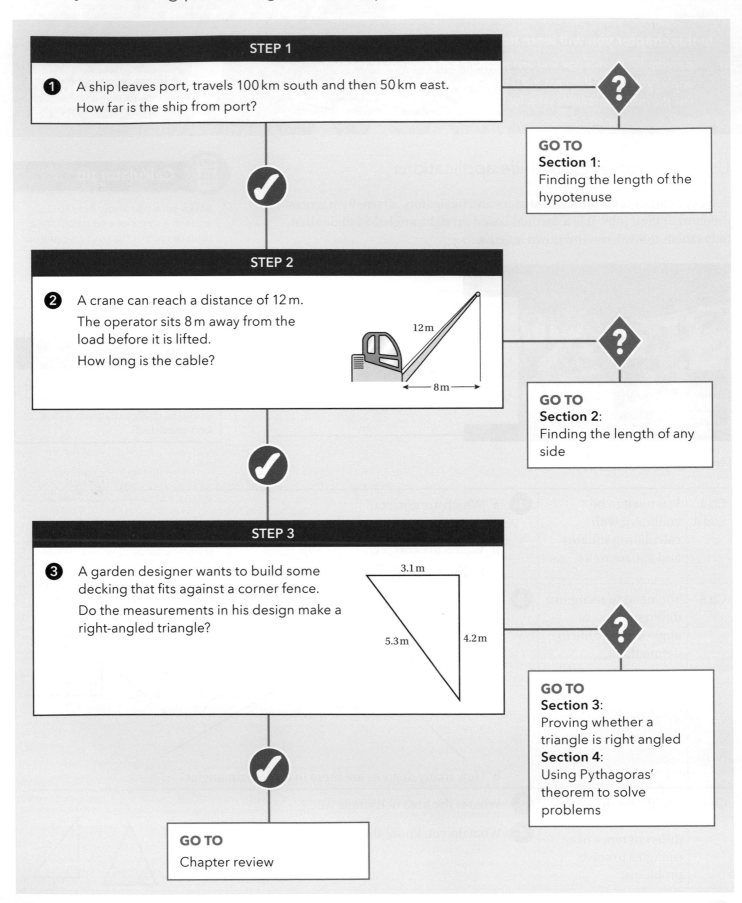

STEP 1

1 A ship leaves port, travels 100 km south and then 50 km east.
How far is the ship from port?

GO TO
Section 1:
Finding the length of the hypotenuse

STEP 2

2 A crane can reach a distance of 12 m.
The operator sits 8 m away from the load before it is lifted.
How long is the cable?

12 m

8 m

GO TO
Section 2:
Finding the length of any side

STEP 3

3 A garden designer wants to build some decking that fits against a corner fence.
Do the measurements in his design make a right-angled triangle?

3.1 m

5.3 m   4.2 m

GO TO
Section 3:
Proving whether a triangle is right angled
Section 4:
Using Pythagoras' theorem to solve problems

GO TO
Chapter review

Section 1: Finding the length of the hypotenuse

Here is a picture of a tilted square.

One way to find the area of a tilted square is by dividing the square into right-angled triangles and a square, then adding the areas together to find the area of the square.

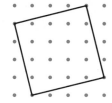

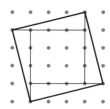

The tilted square in this example has four triangles.

Each triangle has a base of four squares and a height of one square, so its area is:

$$\frac{1}{2}b \times h = \frac{1}{2} \times 4 \times 1 = 2 \text{ squares}$$

So the area of the four triangles is $4 \times 2 = 8$ squares.

The square in the middle has an area of $3 \times 3 = 9$ squares.

The area of the tilted square is $8 + 9 = 17$ squares.

What is Pythagoras' theorem?

Pythagoras' theorem describes the relationship between the lengths of the sides of a right-angled triangle.

The **theorem** states:

*In a right-angled triangle, the square of the length of the **hypotenuse** is equal to the sum of the squares of the two shorter sides.*

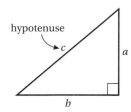

For this triangle, the theorem can be expressed using the formula:

$$a^2 + b^2 = c^2$$

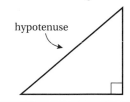
Tip

Naming conventions for a right-angled triangle:

always use capital letters for a vertex

hypotenuse is called c

side b is opposite angle B

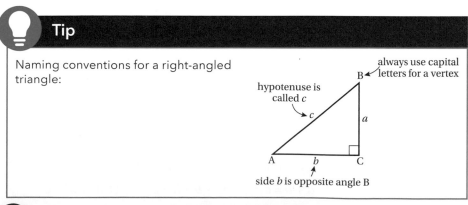

EXERCISE 35A

1 In this diagram, three squares have been drawn on the sides of a right-angled triangle.

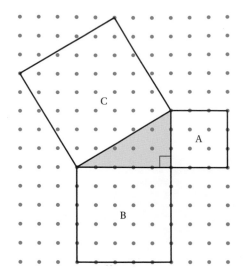

Find and record the area of each square in a table like the one below.

Draw some different right-angled triangles and repeat the process.

Make sure that the square labelled C is opposite the right angle.

Area of square A	Area of square B	Area of square C

What do you notice about the relationship between the different areas?

WORK IT OUT 35.1

A right-angled triangle has two shorter sides of 3 cm and 4 cm.

Calculate the length of the hypotenuse.

Which of these students has got the correct answer to the question?

Why are the others wrong?

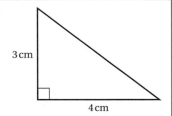

Student A	Student B	Student C
$a^2 + b^2 = c^2$	$a^2 + b^2 = c^2$	$a^2 + b^2 = c^2$
$3 \times 2 = 6$	$3 \times 3 = 9$	$3 \times 3 = 9$
$4 \times 2 = 8$	$4 \times 4 = 16$	$4 \times 4 = 16$
$6 + 8 = c^2$	$9 + 16 = c^2$	$9 + 16 = c^2$
$14 = c^2$	$25 = c^2$	$25 = c^2$
$c = \sqrt{14} = 3.74$ cm	$c = \sqrt{25} = 5$ cm	$c = 25$ cm
(to 2 dp)		

EXERCISE 35B

1 **a** Calculate:

   i 25^2 **ii** 5.3^2 **iii** 167^2 **iv** 136^2 **v** 14.5^2

   b Calculate, working to two decimal places:

   i $\sqrt{3}$ **ii** $\sqrt{7}$ **iii** $\sqrt{4}$ **iv** $\sqrt{17}$ **v** $\sqrt{61}$

2 Which of the following is the correct formula for Pythagoras' theorem?

   A $a^2 + b^2 = c$ B $a + b = c$ C $\frac{1}{2}b \times h = c$ D $a^2 + b^2 = c^2$

3 Find the length of the hypotenuse in each of the following triangles.

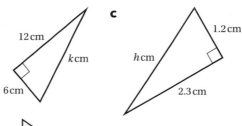

a
6 cm
x cm
8 cm

b
12 cm
k cm
6 cm

c
1.2 cm
h cm
2.3 cm

d
1.5 cm
p cm
0.6 cm

e
4 m
t m
6 m

4 **a** Jamie calculates that the hypotenuse of this triangle is 14 cm.

Without calculating the length yourself, write down why this must be wrong.

b He recalculates and gets 7 cm for the length of the hypotenuse.

Write down how you know that this is wrong.

c What range of answers could Jamie have given where you wouldn't know straight away that his answer was wrong?

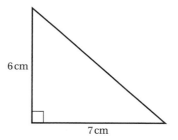

6 cm

7 cm

Section 2: Finding the length of any side

If you know the lengths of any two sides of a right-angled triangle, you can use them to find the length of the third side.

In the formula $a^2 + b^2 = c^2$, c is the hypotenuse and a and b are the two shorter sides.

The formula can be rearranged to make a or b the subject of the formula:

$$a^2 = c^2 - b^2 \qquad\qquad b^2 = c^2 - a^2$$

WORK IT OUT 35.2

This is the design of an access ramp for the front entrance to a building.

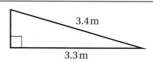

3.4 m

3.3 m

What is the vertical height of the step?

Which of these calculations is correct for this design?

Why are the others wrong?

Calculation A	Calculation B	Calculation C
$c^2 - b^2 = a^2$	$c^2 - b^2 = a^2$	$c^2 - b^2 = a^2$
$3.4^2 - 3.3^2 = a^2$	$3.3^2 + 3.4^2 = c^2$	$3.4^2 - 3.3^2 = a^2$
$3.4 \times 2 = 6.8$	$3.3 \times 3.3 = 10.89$	$3.4 \times 3.4 = 11.56$
$3.3 \times 2 = 6.6$	$3.4 \times 3.4 = 11.56$	$3.3 \times 3.3 = 10.89$
$6.8 - 6.6 = a^2$	$10.89 + 11.56 = c^2$	$11.56 - 10.89 = a^2$
$0.2 = a^2$	$22.45 = c^2$	$a^2 = 0.67$
$a = \dfrac{0.2}{2}$	$a = \sqrt{22.45}\,\text{m} = 4.74\,\text{m}$	$a = \sqrt{0.67}\,\text{m} = 0.82\,\text{m}$
$a = 0.1\,\text{m}$	(to 2 dp)	(to 2 dp)

 Tip

Always think about whether the answers are realistic and reasonable. The ability to recognise whether values are reasonable will help you to spot mistakes.

Find answers at: cambridge.org/ukschools/gcsemaths-studentbookanswers

EXERCISE 35C

1 Find the length of the missing side in each of these triangles.

a

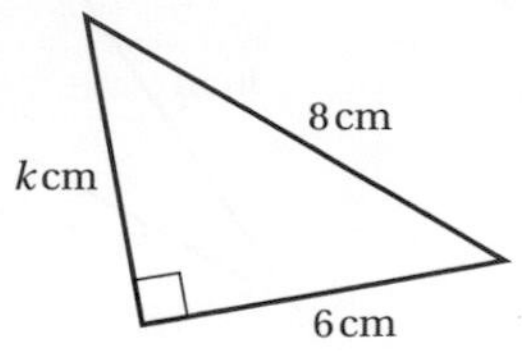

8 cm
k cm
6 cm

b

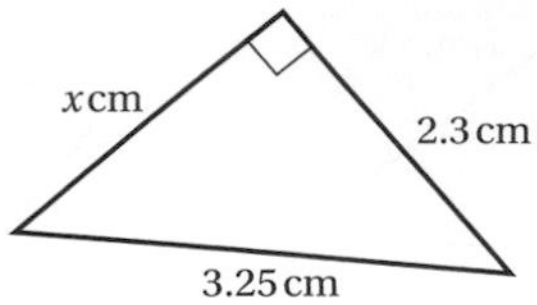

x cm
2.3 cm
3.25 cm

c

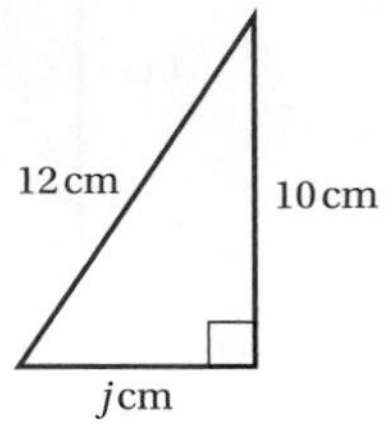

12 cm
10 cm
j cm

d

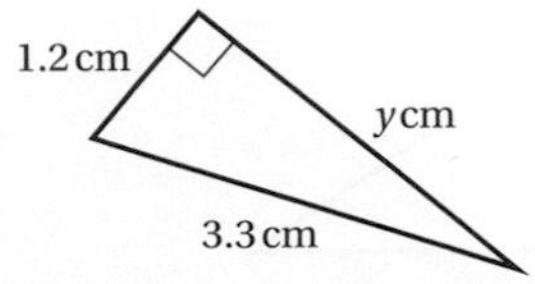

1.2 cm
y cm
3.3 cm

e

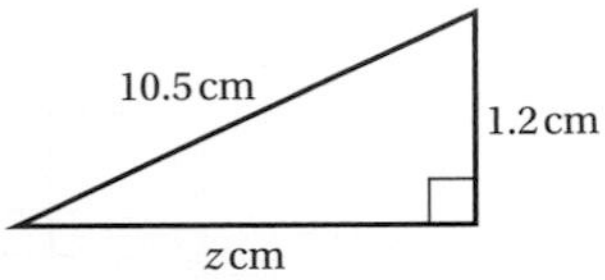

10.5 cm
1.2 cm
z cm

2 In the triangle ABC, what is the length AC?

Choose your answer from the following options.

A 10 cm   B 100 cm

C $\sqrt{6} + \sqrt{8}$ D $8^2 - 6^2$

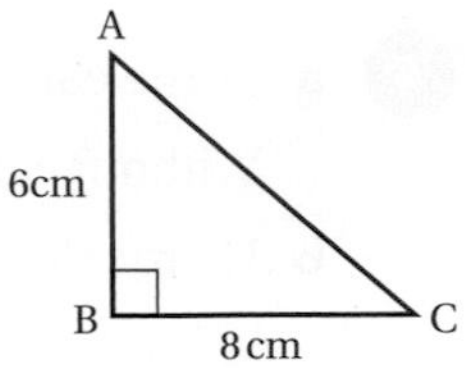

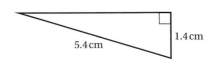

A
6 cm
B
8 cm
C

3 Jamil says that the missing side in this triangle is 5.5 cm long.
Without calculating the length, write down why he must be wrong.

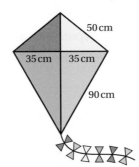

1.4 cm
5.4 cm

4 This kite is made up of two isosceles triangles, as shown in the diagram.

50 cm
35 cm   35 cm
90 cm

Work out the length of the rod that holds the kite together from top to bottom.

5 The front of a tent has the dimensions shown in the diagram.
It is a scalene triangle.
The height is 8 m.
Work out the length of the base.

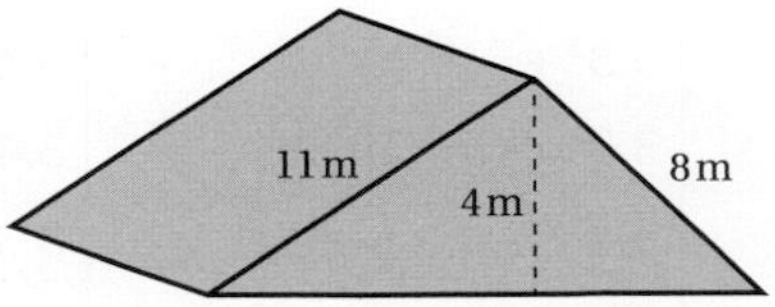

11 m
4 m
8 m

6 Match the options A–D to the correct triangle **a–d**.

a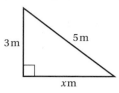

A $2.56 + 0.25 = 2.81$

$x = \sqrt{2.81}$ m

b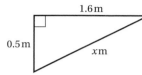

B $x^2 = 6^2 + 2.5^2$

c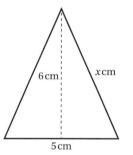

C $6^2 - 4^2 = x^2$

d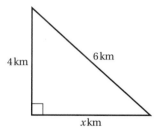

D $x = 4$ m

7 A girl swims across a river in a straight line.

The distance she swims is 20 m from one shore to the other.

The distance along the bank she has travelled is 10 m.

The banks are parallel.

Work out how far apart the banks are.

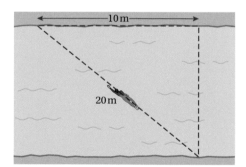

Tip

Note that there are different types of right-angled triangle:

Scalene right-angled triangle
- one right angle
- two other unequal angles
- no equal sides

Isosceles right-angled triangle
- one right angle
- two other equal angles, always 45°
- two equal sides

You can apply Pythagoras' theorem to both types of right-angled triangle.

 Find answers at: cambridge.org/ukschools/gcsemaths-studentbookanswers

Section 3: Proving whether a triangle is right angled

"I use 'Pythagorean triples' in my job. Using the 3, 4, 5 rule I know whether the window frame is a true right angle or not. If it is a right angle the window will fit properly." *(Window fitter)*

If a triangle contains a right angle, then both sides of Pythagoras' theorem will be equal. In other words $a^2 + b^2$ will equal c^2.

This fact is crucial to many people in their jobs.

For example, carpenters need to make rectangular window frames.

If the sides of the triangle at the corner of the frame have lengths in the ratio of $3:4:5$, then the angle is a right angle because $3^2 + 4^2 = 5^2$.

Many people know this as the '3, 4, 5 rule'.

Key vocabulary

Pythagorean triple: three non-zero positive integers, (a, b, c), for which $a^2 + b^2 = c^2$

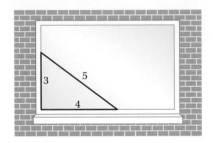

The side lengths 3, 4, 5 are known as a **Pythagorean triple**.

WORK IT OUT 35.3

Is this triangle right-angled?

Which of these answers is correct?

Where have the others gone wrong?

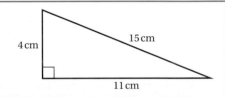

Option A	Option B	Option C
$4 + 11 = 15$ So $a^2 + b^2 = c^2$ Yes, the triangle is right-angled.	$a^2 + b^2 = 4^2 + 11^2$ $\quad = 4 \times 2 + 11 \times 2$ $\quad = 8 + 22 = 30$ $c^2 = 15^2 = 15 \times 2 = 30$ $a^2 + b^2 = c^2$ Yes, the triangle is right-angled.	$a^2 + b^2 = 4^2 + 11^2$ $\quad = 16 + 121 = 137$ $c^2 = 15 \times 15 = 225$ $a^2 + b^2 \neq c^2$ No, the triangle is not right-angled.

EXERCISE 35D

1 Use Pythagoras' theorem to help you decide which of the following triangles is right angled.

a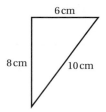
6 cm
8 cm
10 cm

b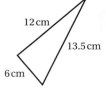
12 cm
13.5 cm
6 cm

c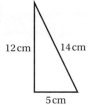
12 cm
14 cm
5 cm

d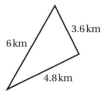
3.6 km
6 km
4.8 km

e
24 cm
25 cm
7 cm

2 The lengths of the sides of a number of different triangles are given below.

In each case, state whether the triangles are right angled.

a 1, 1, 1   **b** 5, 7, 9   **c** 5, 12, 13

d 8, 10, 6   **e** 1, 2, 2

3 A builder uses 3, 5, 4 triangles to make right angles.

a Write down the dimensions of three other right-angled triangles where the sides are in the ratio $3:4:5$.

b Some other Pythagorean triples occur regularly. Carry out an investigation to find at least five common triples.

4 A farmer's field has straight sides of length 25 m and width 15 m.

There is a 35 m long drainage pipe lying diagonally across the field from corner to corner.

Is the field a rectangle with right angles at the corners?

Write down your reasoning.

Find answers at: cambridge.org/ukschools/gcsemaths-studentbookanswers

Section 4: Using Pythagoras' theorem to solve problems

You will apply Pythagoras' theorem regularly in geometry and trigonometry, especially where you need to find missing sides in figures with right angles.

WORKED EXAMPLE 1

Find the length of side x and then calculate the perimeter of this composite shape.

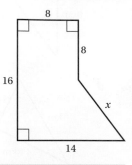

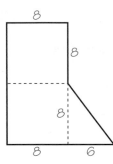

Divide the shape up to make a right-angled triangle.

$$8^2 + 6^2 = x^2$$
$$64 + 36 = x^2$$
$$100 = x^2$$
$$x = 10\,cm$$
$$Perimeter = 16 + 14 + 8 + 8 + 10 = 56\,cm$$

Now you can use Pythagoras' theorem to find x.

EXERCISE 35E

In each of the following show your working and give reasons where necessary.

The figures are not to scale and all dimensions are in centimetres.

1 Find the length of x in this figure.

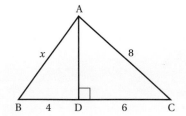

2 Work out the lengths of:

  a BE   **b** BD   **c** BC

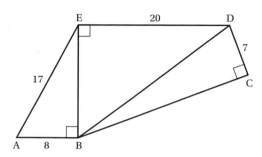

3 Find the length of AB in this diagram.

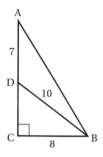

4 Calculate the length of:

  a AC

  b BC

  c EC

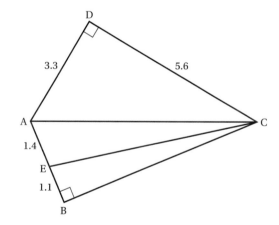

5 ABCD is a trapezium.

  a Calculate the perpendicular height EB.

  b Find the area of the trapezium.

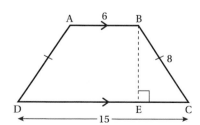

a Find the length of side AD.

b Calculate the perimeter of this shape.

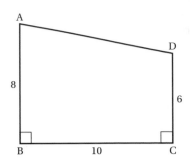

Pythagoras' theorem is also very useful for solving a range of problems involving real-life contexts.

Shortest and longest route problems are a good example.

Problem-solving framework

Sally wants to cross a 100-metre by 60-metre rectangular football field diagonally from one corner to the other. There is a game playing so she has to go round the edge.

Calculate how much further she has to walk.

If you get a question like this you can use the following steps to approach it:

Steps for solving problems	What you would do for this example
Step 1: If it is useful to have a diagram, sketch one and add the information. This might help you visualise the problem.	 60 m 100 m
Step 2: Identify what you have to do.	Find the difference between the length of the diagonal and the length of the two sides added together.
Step 3: Test the problem with what you know. Can you use a ruler? What type of angle is it?	You could use a ruler, but you would have to draw a very accurate diagram to scale. As you have a right-angled triangle and side lengths you can use Pythagoras' theorem.
Step 4: What maths can you use?	Use Pythagoras' theorem to work out the length of the diagonal: $100^2 + 60^2 = c^2$ $10\,000 + 3600 = c^2$ $13\,600 = c^2$ $c = \sqrt{13\,600} = 116.6\,\text{m}$ If she walked straight across the diagonal the distance would be 116.6 m. She has to go round the outside which is $100 + 60 = 160\,\text{m}$, so she must walk $160 - 116.6 = 43.4\,\text{m}$ further.

Continues on next page ...

Step 5: Check your workings and that your answer is reasonable.	A diagonal pitch length of 116.6 m seems reasonable given the sides are 60 m and 100 m.
Step 6: Have you answered the question?	You were asked to find how much further she would have to walk. You have found this to be 43.4 m.

This type of problem-solving is common in many shape and space questions.

It is useful to understand the process that you will go through to begin to solve the problem.

These steps can be used to solve lots of problems.

EXERCISE 35F

1 Computer gaming designers use x- and y-coordinates to place characters or objects in a game.

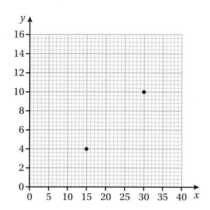

One player is at coordinate (30, 10) and the other at (15, 4).

Work out how far apart the two players are.

2 The size of a screen on a television or computer (for example, 15 inches) is usually given as the length of the diagonal.

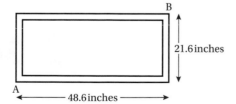

The diagram shows the length and breadth of a screen. How would the size of this screen be given?

3 Zoe is going to buy a new television. It is an 80-inch television (measured along its diagonal length).

Her current television has a 52-inch screen.

Both are the same height, 40 inches.

a How much wider is Zoe's new television than her current one?

b Zoe needs to place the television in a 58-inch gap between the chimney and the wall. Will the new television fit in this space?

Find answers at: cambridge.org/ukschools/gcsemaths-studentbookanswers

4 The diagram shows the side view of a shed.
Calculate the height from the ground to the top of the roof of the shed.

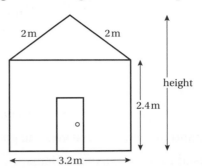

Tip

Think of the trapezium as a composite shape. How can you divide it up to solve the problem?

5 Show how you could use Pythagoras' theorem to find the length of side BD in this trapezium.

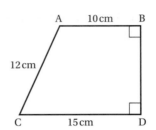

6 The height of a ship's mast above the boom is 8 m.

The longest side of the main sail is 11.4 m.

a How far does the boom of the sail swing out?

The shortest side of the smaller sail has a length of 1.5 m.

b How long is the longest side of the smaller sail?

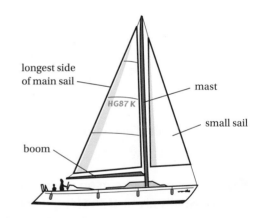

Checklist of learning and understanding

Pythagoras' theorem

- Pythagoras' theorem only applies to right-angled triangles.
- The theorem states that the square of the hypotenuse of a right-angled triangle equals the sum of the squares of the other two sides. It can be written as:
  $$a^2 + b^2 = c^2$$
- The formula can be rearranged to find either of the other two sides:
  $$a^2 = c^2 - b^2$$
  $$b^2 = c^2 - a^2$$
- You can use the theorem to find the length of the hypotenuse (the longest side). The theorem can also be used to prove there is a right angle within a triangle or to find a missing length within a right-angled triangle.

- Always draw a diagram and label it. Also write out the formula you are using to fully show what you have done.
- Pythagorean triples are three lengths that satisfy the formula and therefore prove you have a right angle; learn the common ones, such as 3, 4, 5 and 5, 12, 13.

Chapter review

 For additional questions on the topics in this chapter, visit GCSE Mathematics Online.

1 Which of the following statements are true?

    a Using Pythagoras' theorem you can find any angle within a right-angled triangle.

    b If you know one length in a right-angled triangle, you can find the other two.

    c You can show that 3, 4, 5 is a Pythagorean triple using Pythagoras' theorem.

    d The hypotenuse is always the longest side in a right-angled triangle.

 2 Work out the length x. Give your answer to 1 decimal place. *(4 marks)*

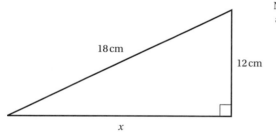

Not drawn accurately

18 cm

12 cm

x

(4 marks)

© AQA 2013

3 What is the perimeter of this kite?

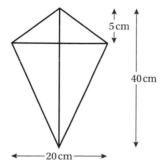

5 cm

40 cm

20 cm

4 A traditional five-bar gate measures 4 m wide.

It is 1.5 m high at its highest point, where the diagonal pieces of wood meet.

What is the length of each diagonal piece of wood used in the gate?

In this chapter you will learn how to …

- use trigonometric ratios to find lengths and angles in right-angled triangles.
- find and memorise exact values of important trigonometric ratios.

For more resources relating to this chapter, visit GCSE Mathematics Online.

Using mathematics: real-life applications

Trigonometry means 'triangle measurements' and it is very useful for finding the lengths of sides and sizes of angles of triangles. Trigonometry is used to work out lengths and angles in navigation, surveying, astronomy, engineering, construction and even in the placement of satellites and satellite receivers.

"I use a theodolite to work out the height of mountains. You basically point it at the top of the mountain. The theodolite uses the principles of trigonometry to measure angles and distances." *(Geologist)*

Before you start …

Ch 35	You should be able to use Pythagoras' theorem to find lengths in triangles.	**1** Find the length of x in each triangle: **a** triangle with sides 7, x (hypotenuse), and base 16 **b** triangle with sides 7, x, and base 5
Ch 12	You must be able to work with approximate values and round to a specified number of places.	**2** What is $\sqrt{53}$ to two decimal places? **3** If $c^2 = 94.34$, what is c to three significant figures?
Ch 26, 27	You need to be able to use ratio and proportion to calculate sides in similar triangles.	**4** Find the length of AC if the ratio of sides $\dfrac{AB}{AC} = \dfrac{5}{3}$ and AB = 35 cm.

Assess your starting point using the Launchpad

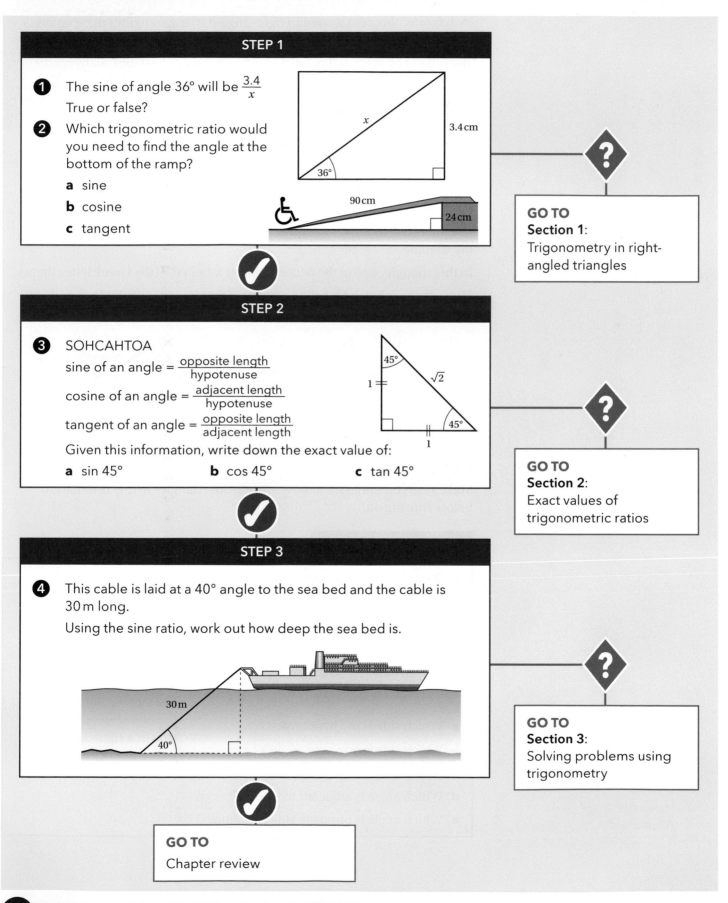

STEP 1

1 The sine of angle 36° will be $\frac{3.4}{x}$
True or false?

2 Which trigonometric ratio would you need to find the angle at the bottom of the ramp?

  a sine

  b cosine

  c tangent

GO TO
Section 1:
Trigonometry in right-angled triangles

STEP 2

3 SOHCAHTOA

sine of an angle $= \dfrac{\text{opposite length}}{\text{hypotenuse}}$

cosine of an angle $= \dfrac{\text{adjacent length}}{\text{hypotenuse}}$

tangent of an angle $= \dfrac{\text{opposite length}}{\text{adjacent length}}$

Given this information, write down the exact value of:

  a sin 45°   **b** cos 45°   **c** tan 45°

GO TO
Section 2:
Exact values of trigonometric ratios

STEP 3

4 This cable is laid at a 40° angle to the sea bed and the cable is 30 m long.

Using the sine ratio, work out how deep the sea bed is.

GO TO
Section 3:
Solving problems using trigonometry

GO TO
Chapter review

Section 1: Trigonometry in right-angled triangles

Pythagoras' theorem is used in right-angled triangles to find missing sides when two sides are known.

The ratio of corresponding pairs of sides in similar triangles is always the same.

These facts are important in understanding and using trigonometry.

Naming the sides of right-angled triangles

The hypotenuse is the longest side of a right-angled triangle, opposite the right angle.

The other two (shorter) sides are named in relation to the acute angles in the triangle.

In this triangle, one of the acute angles is labelled θ (the Greek letter theta).

The sides can then be labelled opposite (that is, opposite angle θ) and adjacent (that is, adjacent to angle θ).

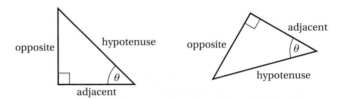

This system of naming the sides is fundamental to working with trigonometry.

Make sure you understand how it works for triangles in any orientation before moving on.

WORKED EXAMPLE 1

In the right-angled triangle XYZ shown here:

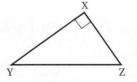

a Which side is the hypotenuse? YZ

b Which side is opposite angle Y? XZ

> Remember the hypotenuse is the longest side in a right-angled triangle.

c Which side is adjacent to angle Z? XZ

d Which angle is adjacent to side XY? Angle Y

e Which angle is opposite side XZ? Angle Y

The trigonometric ratios

This diagram shows three similar right-angled triangles.

The green sides are opposite angle θ and the blue sides are adjacent to it.

The ratio of $\dfrac{\text{opposite}}{\text{adjacent}}$ sides is $\dfrac{1}{2}$ for all these similar triangles.

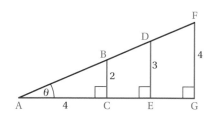

$$\frac{BC}{CA} = \frac{2}{4} = \frac{1}{2}$$

$$\frac{DE}{EA} = \frac{3}{6} = \frac{1}{2}$$

$$\frac{FG}{GA} = \frac{4}{8} = \frac{1}{2}$$

$$\therefore \frac{\text{OPPOSITE}}{\text{ADJACENT}} = \frac{1}{2}$$

In similar triangles like the set above, the ratios $\dfrac{\text{opposite}}{\text{hypotenuse}}$, $\dfrac{\text{adjacent}}{\text{hypotenuse}}$ and $\dfrac{\text{opposite}}{\text{adjacent}}$ are equal in all the triangles.

These ratios are called the trigonometric ratios (shortened to trig. ratios) and they are named as follows:

- the sine ratio, $\sin \theta$, is the ratio of the side opposite the angle to the hypotenuse
- the cosine ratio, $\cos \theta$, is the ratio of the side adjacent to the angle to the hypotenuse
- the tangent ratio, $\tan \theta$, is the ratio of the side opposite the angle to the side adjacent to the angle

$$\sin \theta = \frac{a}{c} = \frac{\text{opposite}}{\text{hypotenuse}}$$

$$\cos \theta = \frac{b}{c} = \frac{\text{adjacent}}{\text{hypotenuse}}$$

$$\tan \theta = \frac{a}{b} = \frac{\text{opposite}}{\text{adjacent}}$$

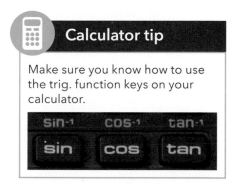

Calculator tip

Make sure you know how to use the trig. function keys on your calculator.

sin⁻¹ cos⁻¹ tan⁻¹
sin cos tan

The three ratios have the same value for a particular angle no matter how long the sides are.

For example, $\sin 30°$ is $\dfrac{1}{2}$ or 0.5 for any right-angled triangle. This means that the length of the opposite side is half the length of the hypotenuse if the angle you are working with is 30°.

You can find the ratio for any angle using your calculator.

WORKED EXAMPLE 2

1 For triangle ABC, find the value of:

a $\sin A$

b $\cos A$

c $\tan A$

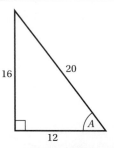

a $\sin A = \dfrac{opposite}{hypotenuse} = \dfrac{16}{20} = \dfrac{4}{5}$

> Identify the trigonometric ratio to use and then substitute in the lengths given.

b $\cos A = \dfrac{adjacent}{hypotenuse} = \dfrac{12}{20} = \dfrac{3}{5}$

> Identify the trigonometric ratio to use and then substitute in the lengths given.

c $\tan A = \dfrac{opposite}{adjacent} = \dfrac{16}{12} = \dfrac{4}{3}$

> Identify the trigonometric ratio to use and then substitute in the lengths given.

2 Use your calculator to find the value of each of these trig. ratios. Give your answers to three significant figures where necessary.

a $\cos 32°$ **b** $\sin 18°$ **c** $\tan 80°$

a $\cos 32° = 0.848$

> Check you know how to find the cos of an angle and the inverse of it using your calculator.

b $\sin 18° = 0.309$

> With each of these three ratios, enter the angle given and press sin, cos or tan.

c $\tan 80° = 5.67$

> Check to make sure you round appropriately to the given degree of accuracy.

EXERCISE 36A

1 For the following triangles, which trigonometric ratio could be used?
Calculate the missing lengths giving your answer to two decimal places.

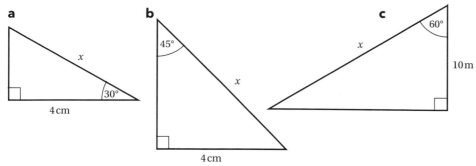

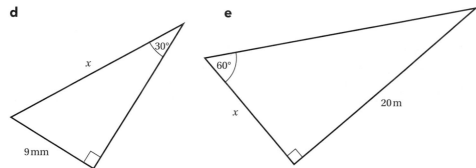

2 Using your calculator, find the sine of the following angles.
Give your answers to two decimal places.

    a 26°   **b** 49°   **c** 66°

    d 2°   **e** 101°   **f** 19°

3 Using your calculator, find the cosine of the following angles.
Give your answer to three decimal places.

    a 13°   **b** 47°   **c** 110°

    d 87°   **e** 15°   **f** 36°

4 Using your calculator, find the tangent of the following angles.
Give your answer to one decimal place.

    a 25°   **b** 73°   **c** 3°

    d 49°   **e** 17.65°   **f** 88°

Finding unknown sides

Finding unknown sides or angles is called solving the triangle.

You can use the three trigonometric ratios to do this.

If you know an angle (other than the right angle) and one side in a right-angled triangle, you can use trig. ratios to form an equation. You can then solve it to find the missing lengths.

You will not be told which ratio to use. You have to pick the right one based on the information that you have about the triangle.

You can remember the ratios using the mnemonic SOH-CAH-TOA and the formula triangles:

SOH: Sin $x = \dfrac{\text{Opposite}}{\text{Hypotenuse}}$ CAH: Cos $x = \dfrac{\text{Adjacent}}{\text{Hypotenuse}}$ TOA: Tan $x = \dfrac{\text{Opposite}}{\text{Adjacent}}$

> **Tip**
>
> If you have two sides of a right-angled triangle you can find the other side using Pythagoras' theorem.

WORKED EXAMPLE 3

a In triangle ABC, angle B = 90°, AC = 15 cm and angle C = 35°.

Calculate the length of AB to one decimal place.

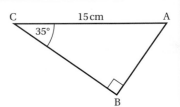

Given: angle C = 35°
AB is opposite angle C
CA = 15 cm and is the hypotenuse

$\sin 35° = \dfrac{opp}{hyp}$

$\sin 35° = \dfrac{AB}{15}$

> Use the ratio with opposite and hypotenuse.
>
> sine ratio = $\dfrac{\text{opp}}{\text{hyp}}$

AB = sin 35° × 15

> Multiply both sides by 15 to get AB on its own.

AB = 8.6 cm

> Use your calculator to find the value of sin 35°.

b In triangle XYZ, angle Z is a right angle and angle X = 71°.
Side YZ = 7.9 cm

Calculate the length of XZ to one decimal place.

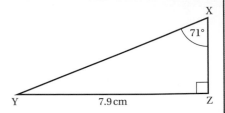

Given: angle X = 71°
YZ = 7.9 cm = opposite side
XZ is the adjacent side

> Identify the information you have been given.

Continues on next page ...

Use the ratio with *opposite* and *adjacent*, which is TOA.

$$\tan 71° = \frac{opp}{adj}$$

$$\tan 71° = \frac{7.9}{XZ}$$

$$XZ \times \tan 71° = 7.9$$

$$XZ = \frac{7.9}{\tan 71°}$$

$$XZ = 2.7 \text{ cm (to 1 dp)}$$

> Identify the trig. ratio that uses the information you have been given.

> Fill in the information you know.

> Multiply both sides by XZ to deal with the fraction.

> Divide by tan 71° to get XZ on its own.

> Complete the calculation on your calculator.
> Give your answer to the appropriate degree of accuracy.

EXERCISE 36B

1 For each triangle, choose the appropriate trigonometric ratio and find the length of the unknown side.

Give your answers to two decimal places.

> **Tip**
>
> Draw a sketch of the triangle in the question. Circle the angle you are working with and mark the sides H, A and O to help you see which values you have and which you need.

a
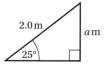

b

c

d
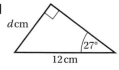

e

f

g

h
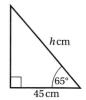

i
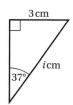

j
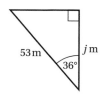

k

l
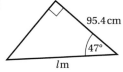

Find answers at: cambridge.org/ukschools/gcsemaths-studentbookanswers

Calculator tip

Your calculator can 'work backwards' to find the size of the unknown angle associated with a particular trigonometric ratio.

To find the angle if you have the ratio, key in the inverse trigonometric function on your calculator, $\sin^{-1}$, $\cos^{-1}$ or $\tan^{-1}$.

Finding unknown angles

To find the size of unknown angles using the trigonometric ratios you need to use the inverse function of each ratio.

On most calculators these are the second functions of the sin, cos and tan buttons.

They are usually marked $\boxed{\sin^{-1}}$, $\boxed{\cos^{-1}}$ and $\boxed{\tan^{-1}}$. You may need to use the $\boxed{\text{SHIFT}}$ key to get these functions.

WORKED EXAMPLE 4

1 Given that $\tan x$ is 5, what is the size of angle x?

Using a calculator:

$\boxed{\text{SHIFT}}$ $\boxed{\tan}$ $\boxed{5}$ $\boxed{=}$

Identify on your calculator which key combination will produce the angle size.

$\boxed{78.69006753}$

The answer will be given in full to a varying degree of decimal places according to the size of angle.

Angle x is $78.7°$

Round the final answer to an appropriate degree of accuracy.

2 Find the size of angle x in each triangle.

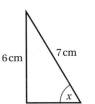
a

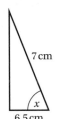
b

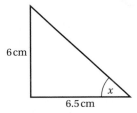
c

a $\sin x = \dfrac{\text{opp}}{\text{hyp}}$

Identify which trig. ratio to use.

$\sin x = \dfrac{6}{7} = 0.857$

Fill in the information you are given.

$\sin^{-1} 0.857 = x = 59°$

Identify on your calculator which key combination will find the size of angle from the ratio.

b $\cos x = \dfrac{\text{adj}}{\text{hyp}}$

Identify which trig. ratio to use.

$= \dfrac{6.5}{7} = 0.929$

Fill in the information you are given.

$\cos^{-1} 0.929 = x = 21.79°$

Identify on your calculator which key combination will find the size of angle from the ratio.

c $\tan x = \dfrac{\text{opp}}{\text{adj}}$

Identify which trig. ratio to use.

$= \dfrac{6}{6.5} = 0.923$

Fill in the information you are given.

$\tan^{-1} 0.923 = x = 42.7°$

Identify on your calculator which key combination will find the size of angle from the ratio.

WORK IT OUT 36.1

For a ladder to be safe it must be inclined at between 70° and 80° to the ground.

The diagram shows a ladder resting against a wall.

Is the ladder positioned safely?

Which of these calculations gives you the answer that you need?

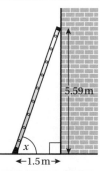

Not to scale

5.59 m

←1.5 m→

Option A	Option B	Option C
$\sin x = \dfrac{1.5}{5.59} = 0.268$	$\cos x = \dfrac{1.5}{5.59} = 0.268$	$\tan x = \dfrac{5.59}{1.5} = 3.73$
$\sin^{-1} 0.268 = 15.56°$	$\cos^{-1} 0.268 = 74.43°$	$\tan^{-1} 3.73 = 74.98°$

EXERCISE 36C

1 Which of the following angles, to two decimal places, has a tan of 0.475?

    A 61.64°   B 28.36°   C 25.41°   D 0.008°

2 Find the value of θ for each ratio:

    a $\sin \theta = 0.682$ **b** $\cos \theta = 0.891$

    c $\tan \theta = 2.4751$ **d** $\sin \theta = 0.2588$

3 Calculate the size of each marked angle.

    Give your answers to one decimal place.

a
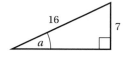

b
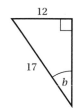

c
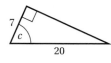

d
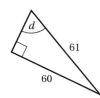

e
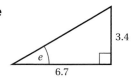

f
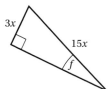

4 PQR is a right-angled triangle.

    PQ = 11 cm and QR = 24 cm

    Calculate the size of angle PRQ.

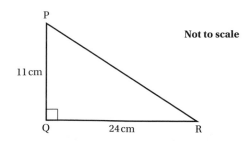

Not to scale

Find answers at: cambridge.org/ukschools/gcsemaths-studentbookanswers

5 What is the size of angle x?

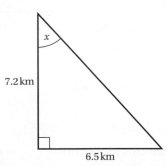

7.2 km

6.5 km

6 For each triangle, draw a sketch and calculate the missing value.

a In triangle ABC, angle B = 90°, BC = 45 units and angle C = 23°.
Calculate the length of AB.

b In triangle PQR, angle R = 90°, PQ = 12.2 cm and angle P = 57°.
Calculate the length of QR.

c In triangle EFG, angle G = 90°, EG = 8.7 cm and angle E = 49°.
Calculate the length of FG.

d In triangle XYZ, angle Y = 90°, XZ = 36 units and angle X is 25°.
Calculate the lengths of:

    i XY   **ii** YZ

7 For each triangle, draw a sketch and then calculate the required values.

a In triangle ABC, angle C = 90°, BC = 6.7 units and AB = 9.8 units.
Calculate angle A.

b In triangle DEF, angle D = 90°, DF = 13 units and EF = 17 units.
Calculate angle F.

c In triangle GHI, angle I = 90°, HI = 8.2 cm and GI = 13.7 cm.
Calculate the sizes of:

    i angle G   **ii** angle H

d In triangle JKL, angle J = 90°, JK = 85 mm and KL = 113 mm.
Calculate the sizes of:

    i angle K   **ii** angle L

e In triangle MNO, angle O = 90°, NO = 20.6 cm and MN = 29.8 cm.
Calculate:

    i angle N   **ii** angle M   **iii** the length of MO

f In triangle PQR, angle Q = 90°, PQ = 57.3 mm and QR = 45.1 mm.
Calculate:

    i angle P   **ii** angle R   **iii** the length of PR

Section 2: Exact values of trigonometric ratios

The sides of right-angled triangles are not always perfect squares. When you work out trigonometric ratios on your calculator you often get approximate (or truncated) values.

However, some values of sin, cos and tan can be calculated exactly.

You need to know the exact values of the sin, cos and tan ratios for 0°, 30°, 45° and 60° angles, as well as the values of sin and cos for 90°. There is no tan ratio for 90°.

Sine, cosine and tangent ratios for 30° and 60°

The diagram shows an equilateral triangle of side 2 cm.

Angle $y = 60°$ (angles of equilateral triangle are equal).

Angle DEF is bisected by EG, so $z = 30°$.

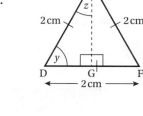

EG is the perpendicular bisector of the base. So, DG and GF are each 1 cm long.

Using Pythagoras' theorem, you can find the length of EG.

$$2^2 - 1^2 = EG^2$$
$$4 - 1 = EG^2$$
$$3 = EG^2$$
$$EG = \sqrt{3}$$

The square root of 3 is not an exact value so you leave it in surd form as it is easier to work with.

This gives us the right-angled triangle below:

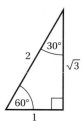

$$\sin 30° = \frac{\text{opposite}}{\text{hypotenuse}} = \frac{1}{2}$$

$$\cos 30° = \frac{\text{adjacent}}{\text{hypotenuse}} = \frac{\sqrt{3}}{2}$$

$$\tan 30° = \frac{\text{opposite}}{\text{adjacent}} = \frac{1}{\sqrt{3}}$$

$$\sin 60° = \frac{\text{opposite}}{\text{hypotenuse}} = \frac{\sqrt{3}}{2}$$

$$\cos 60° = \frac{\text{adjacent}}{\text{hypotenuse}} = \frac{1}{2}$$

$$\tan 60° = \frac{\text{opposite}}{\text{adjacent}} = \frac{\sqrt{3}}{1} = \sqrt{3}$$

Sine, cosine and tangent ratios for 45°

The diagram shows a right-angled isosceles triangle with the two equal sides 1 cm long.

The hypotenuse is $\sqrt{2}$ cm.

The base angles, x, are each 45°.

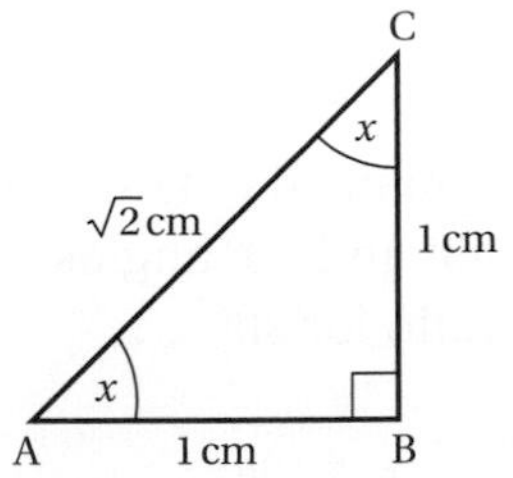

$$\sin 45° = \frac{\text{opposite}}{\text{hypotenuse}} = \frac{1}{\sqrt{2}}$$

$$\cos 45° = \frac{\text{adjacent}}{\text{hypotenuse}} = \frac{1}{\sqrt{2}}$$

$$\tan 45° = \frac{\text{opposite}}{\text{adjacent}} = \frac{1}{1} = 1$$

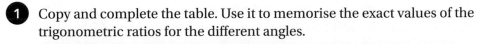

You need to know these exact values of special angles.

You can always draw the triangles to find them if you forget.

EXERCISE 36D

1 Copy and complete the table. Use it to memorise the exact values of the trigonometric ratios for the different angles.

Angle θ	sin θ	cos θ	tan θ
0°			
30°			
45°			
60°			
90°			tan 90° is undefined

2 Without using your calculator, find:

a $\sin 30° + \cos 60°$ **b** $\sin 45° + \cos 45°$ **c** $\cos 30° + \sin 60°$

Section 3: Solving problems using trigonometry

The trigonometric ratios can be applied to many different types of measurement problems.

If the question does not include a sketch, it is useful to draw one.

Make it large and clear and mark on it what you know. This will help you to identify the correct ratio to use to solve the problem.

Angles of elevation and depression

Many trigonometry problems involve lines of sight. (In other words, looking at an object from a distance away.)

Problems that involve looking up to an object can be described in terms of an **angle of elevation**. This is the angle between an observer's line of sight and a horizontal line.

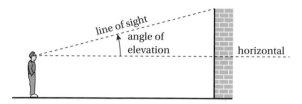

Key vocabulary

angle of elevation: when looking up, the angle between the line of sight and the horizontal

angle of depression: when looking down, the angle between the line of sight and the horizontal

When an observer is looking down, the **angle of depression** is the angle between the observer's line of sight and a horizontal line.

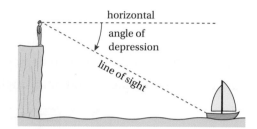

Problem-solving framework

A ship is laying cable along the sea bed.

The angle of the cable to the sea bed is 40° and the length of cable to the sea bed is 40 metres.

The ship is 50 miles offshore and travelling north-west.

What is the depth of the sea bed?

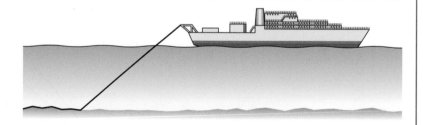

Steps for solving problems	What you would do for this example
Step 1: What have you got to do?	Use Pythagoras' theorem or trigonometry to find the depth of water.
Step 2: What information do you need?	Angle 40° and length of cable as the hypotenuse is 40 m.
Step 3: What information don't you need?	50 miles offshore and the direction of travel.

Continues on next page ...

Step 4: What maths can you use?	Use a right-angled triangle. Cannot use Pythagoras' theorem as you do not know two lengths, so use trig. ratios. Decide which trigonometric function to use: sin, cos or tan? One angle and the hypotenuse are known so need to find the opposite length. $\sin 40° = \dfrac{\text{opp}}{\text{hyp}} = \dfrac{\text{opp}}{40}$ $0.643 \times 40 = \text{opposite length} = 25.72\,\text{m}$ The sea bed is 25.7 metres deep (to 3 sf).
Step 5: Have you done it all?	Yes, the question has been answered and the correct units have been used in the answer.
Step 6: Is it correct?	Yes, double-checked and estimated. The depth must be less than 40 m. $\sin 30° = 0.5$ so half of 40 m would be 20 m.

EXERCISE 36E

1 Measure the marked angles in each diagram in degrees.

State whether each is an angle of depression or an angle of elevation.

a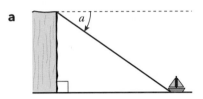

b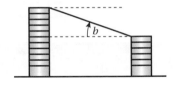

c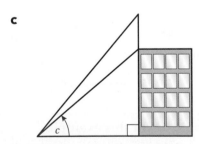

d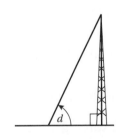

2 In diagram **a** in question 1, the boat is 800 m from the base of the cliff.
Work out the height of the cliff.

3 In diagram **d** in question 1, the distance from the top of the mast to the point where the cable is attached to the ground is 35 m.
Work out the height of the mast.

4 Calculate the angle marked x in the diagram.

Choose your answer from the options below.

A 24.62°   B 2.4°

C 0.416°   D 65.38°

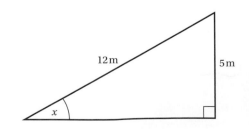

5 A mother goat stands on one side of the river with one of her kids 100 m away along the river bank. The younger of her kids swam across the river and is calling for her. Assuming there is no water current,

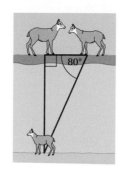

   a what distance does the mother goat need to swim straight across the river to reach her baby?

   b What distance is the line of sight from the mother and younger goat to the older kid, once the mother reaches the other side?

6 A child's playground slide is 4.2 m long and makes an angle of 63° with the horizontal.

   Calculate the height of the slide.

7 Carol is in a hot-air balloon at point C in the sky.

   CG is the vertical height of the hot-air balloon above the ground.

   David is standing on the ground at point D.

   The distance between points D and G is 27 m.

   The angle of elevation from David to the hot-air balloon is 53°.

   Calculate the length of CG.

8 Two boats are sailing a distance of 25 m apart.

   The angle of depression from the top of a lighthouse to one boat is 35° and to the other boat is 55°.

   How tall is the lighthouse?

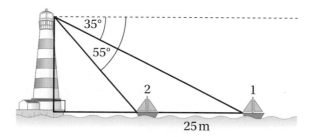

9 Mike is standing 15 m away from a flagpole.

   The angle of elevation from his line of sight to the top of the flagpole is 60°.

   a Calculate the height of the flagpole if Mike's eye is 1.6 m above ground level.

   b Mike moves another 10 m further away from the flagpole.

     How will the angle of elevation from his line of sight to the top of the flagpole change?

10 Two observers in different positions at A and B are watching a rare bird on a tree at C.

The angle of elevation from A to C is 56° and the angle of elevation from B to C is 25°.

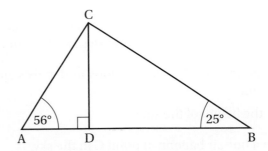

a Person B is standing 15 m from D (the base of the tree).

Calculate the height of the bird above the ground (the length CD).

b Calculate the distance of person A from D.

11 Paolo is standing at a point P, 30 m away from a mobile phone signal tower.

The angle of depression from the top of the tower to P is 56°.

Calculate the height of the tower.

12 A tree surgeon measures the angle of elevation from her point of view to the top of a tree as 20°.

She is standing 10 m away from the tree.

a If she assumes that the tree is perfectly perpendicular, how would she calculate the height of the tree?

b To check her calculation, she moves another 10 m away from the tree in a straight line, and measures the angle of elevation again.

What should the angle measurement be now if her first measurement and calculation were correct?

Checklist of learning and understanding

Trigonometric ratios

- In a right-angled triangle, the longest side is the hypotenuse. For a given angle, θ, the other two sides can be labelled opposite (to angle θ) and adjacent (to angle θ).

- The sine, cosine and tangent ratios can be used to find unknown sides and angles in right-angled triangles.

  ○ $\sin \theta = \dfrac{\text{opposite}}{\text{hypotenuse}}$

  ○ $\cos \theta = \dfrac{\text{adjacent}}{\text{hypotenuse}}$

  ○ $\tan \theta = \dfrac{\text{opposite}}{\text{adjacent}}$

- You can find the value of a ratio using the sin, cos and tan buttons on your calculator.
  To find the size of an angle, use the inverse functions $\sin^{-1}$, $\cos^{-1}$ and $\tan^{-1}$.

Exact values

- You can find the exact values of sin, cos and tan for special angles. Some exact values contain square roots.

Angle θ	$\sin \theta$	$\cos \theta$	$\tan \theta$
0°	0	1	0
30°	$\dfrac{1}{2}$	$\dfrac{\sqrt{3}}{2}$	$\dfrac{1}{\sqrt{3}}$
45°	$\dfrac{1}{\sqrt{2}}$	$\dfrac{1}{\sqrt{2}}$	1
60°	$\dfrac{\sqrt{3}}{2}$	$\dfrac{1}{2}$	$\sqrt{3}$
90°	1	0	tan 90° is undefined

 Chapter review

For additional questions on the topics in this chapter, visit GCSE Mathematics Online.

1 What is the value of cos 45°?

Choose from the following options.

A $\dfrac{1}{\sqrt{2}} = 0.707$ B $\dfrac{1}{\sqrt{3}} = 0.577$ C 1   D 0.5

2 The diagram shows a triangle ABC.

Angle A = 20°, angle C = 90° and AB = 32 m

Calculate the height BC.

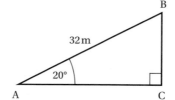

3 A ladder leans against the side of a house.

The ladder is 4.5 m in length and makes an angle of 74° with the ground.

How high up the wall will it reach? (This length is marked x in the diagram.)

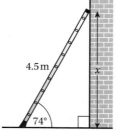

Not drawn accurately

4 The ladder from question 3 is placed 0.9 m away from the side of the house.

What angle does the ladder now make with the ground? (This angle is marked y in the diagram.)

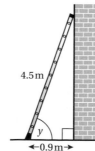

Not drawn accurately

5 The diagram shows three pieces of glass in a conservatory roof.

Not drawn accurately

H

h

35°

1.2 m

a Work out the height, *h*, of the smallest piece. (3 marks)

b Each piece of glass is the same width, 1.2 metres.

Work out the height, *H*, of the rectangular piece. (2 marks)

© AQA 2013

6 The dimensions of the lean on the Leaning Tower of Pisa are shown below.

From the information given, what is the actual height of the tower?

86°

56.27 m

7 Triangles ABC and PQR are similar.

AC = 3.2 cm, AB = 4 cm and PR = 4.8 cm

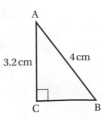

A

3.2 cm

4 cm

C

B

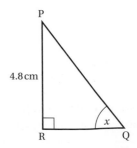

P

4.8 cm

R

x

Q

Write down why sin *x* = 0.8

604

37 Graphs of other functions and equations

In this chapter you will learn how to ...

- plot and sketch graphs of linear and quadratic functions.
- identify the main features of graphs of quadratic functions and equations.
- plot and sketch other polynomials and reciprocal functions.

For more resources relating to this chapter, visit GCSE Mathematics Online.

Using mathematics: real-life applications

Graphs are used to process information, make predictions and generalise patterns from sets of data. The nature of the data and the relationship between values reveals the shape and form of the graph.

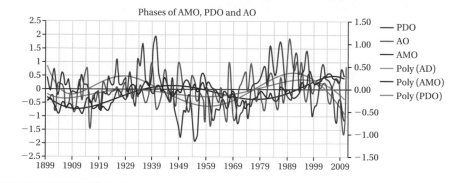

Phases of AMO, PDO and AO

"I study the earth using gravity, magnetic, electrical and seismic methods. I used this graph in a study of the Pacific and Atlantic Oceans. I need to be able to understand equations and recognise the features of graphs to understand and interpret it." *(Geophysicist)*

Before you start ...

Ch 28	You should be able to interpret equations of linear graphs.	**1**	For the graph $y = 3x + 1$: **a** identify the gradient of the graph **b** give the coordinates of the y-intercept **c** find the value of x when $y = -14$ **d** show that it is parallel to the graph $2y - 6x = -4$.
Ch 28	You must be able to generate a table of values from a function.	**2**	Given $y = 3x^2 + 1$, copy and complete the table of values: {TABLE_PLACEHOLDER}
Ch 17	You need to be able to find the roots of a quadratic equation algebraically.	**3**	What are the roots of: **a** $x^2 + 2x - 8 = 0$? **b** $x^2 + 5x = -4$?
Ch 14	You should be able to work with cubed numbers and cube roots.	**4**	Evaluate: **a** 2^3 **b** 4^3 **c** $\sqrt[3]{125}$ **d** $\sqrt[3]{-27}$

Table for question 2:

x	-2	-1	0	1	2
y					

Find answers at: cambridge.org/ukschools/gcsemaths-studentbookanswers

Assess your starting point using the Launchpad

STEP 1

1 How many points do you need to calculate to plot the graph of a linear equation?

2 Sketch the graph of the linear equation $y = 2x + 1$.

GO TO
Section 1:
Review of linear graphs

STEP 2

3   **a** Is this the graph of $y = x^2 + 1$ or $y = -x^2 + 1$?

b How can you tell?

c Is the turning point a maximum or a minimum?

d What are the coordinates of the vertex?

e For what values of x is $y = 0$?

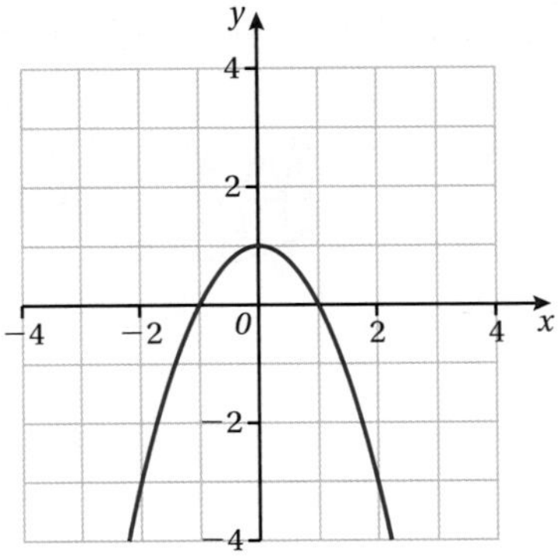

GO TO
Section 2:
Quadratic functions

STEP 3

4   **a** What type of equation is $y = x^3$?

b How many points do you need to calculate to plot the graph of $y = x^3$?

5 Given $y = \frac{1}{x}$:

a what happens when $x = 0$?

b what happens to the value of y as the value of x increases?

c when $x = 60$, what is the value of y?

GO TO
Section 3:
Other polynomials and reciprocals
Section 4:
Plotting, sketching and recognising graphs

GO TO
Chapter review

Section 1: Review of linear graphs

Graphs in the form of $y = mx$

- In the equation $y = mx + c$, the value of c tells you where the graph cuts the y-axis.
- When there is no value of c in the equation you get a graph in the form of $y = mx$.
- Graphs of the form $y = mx$ pass through the origin (0, 0) because when $y = 0$, x must be 0.
- Any linear equation of the form $y = mx$ passes through the origin with a gradient of m.
- The graphs of $y = mx$ and $y = -mx$ are shown on the right.
- If $m = 1$, the equation is written as $y = x$. If $m = -1$, the equation is written as $y = -x$.
- $y = x$ is the line that passes through the origin from left to right going up at an angle of 45°, assuming equal scales.
- $y = -x$ is the line that passes through the origin from left to right going down at an angle of 45°.

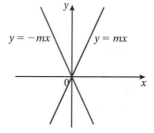

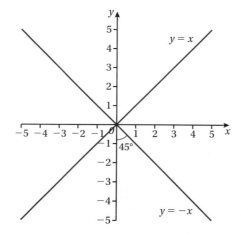

Sketching $y = ax$ ...	Examples	Notes
if a is greater than 1	$y = 3x$ $y = 7x$	The line still passes through the origin but it is steeper than $y = x$.
if a is a value between 0 and 1	$y = \frac{1}{2}x$ $y = \frac{1}{5}x$	The line still passes through the origin but it is less steep than $y = x$.
if a is a negative value	$y = -3x$ $y = -\frac{1}{2}x$	The line still passes through the origin but it will go down from left to right like $y = -x$.

Find answers at: cambridge.org/ukschools/gcsemaths-studentbookanswers

Vertical and horizontal lines

The equations of some lines are in the form of $x = a$ or $y = b$, where a and b are constant values. Equations of this form tell you that the value of x or y never changes.

For example, the graph of the equation $x = 7$ passes through the point $(7, 0)$. It also passes through all points on the grid with an x-coordinate of 7. Some of these points are $(7, -4)$, $(7, -1)$, $(7, 3)$ and $(7, 50)$.

Another example is the graph of the equation $y = 7$, that would need to pass through the point $(0, 7)$ and all other points with a y-coordinate of 7.

The graphs of $x = 7$ and $y = 7$ are shown here.

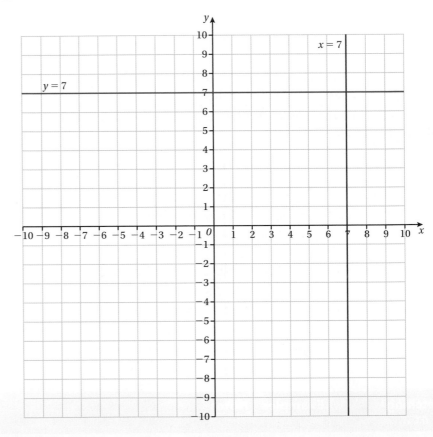

In general:

- any graph in the form of $x = a$ is parallel to the y-axis and passes through a on the x-axis
- any graph in the form of $y = b$ is parallel to the x-axis and passes through b on the y-axis
- the values of a and b in $x = a$ and $y = b$ can be positive or negative.

The axes themselves can be described using equations.

The x-axis is the line $y = 0$ and the y-axis is the line $x = 0$.

Tip

You should be able to recognise and sketch the graphs of any line in the form $x = a$ or $y = b$.

EXERCISE 37A

1 Which of the following points lies on the line $y = -2x + 3$?

A $(1, 2)$ B $(1, 1)$ C $(1, 5)$ D $(-1, 1)$

2

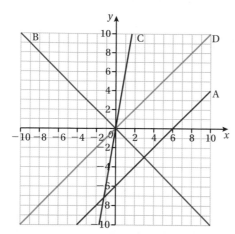

Write down which of the graphs on the grid above can be described in each of the following ways.

a The x-coordinate of each point is equal to the y-coordinate.

b The gradient is negative.

c The general form of the graph is $y = mx$.

d The y-coordinate is 6 times the x-coordinate.

e The y-coordinate is 6 less than the x-coordinate.

3 Give the equation of each line on the grid in question 2.

4

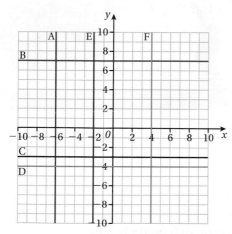

a Write down the equation of each of the lines A to F.

b What is the equation of the line parallel to D that passes through point $(0, 7)$?

5 Draw the following graphs on a grid numbered from −6 to 6 on each axis.

a $x = -3$ **b** $y = 5$ **c** $y = -3$ **d** $x = 5$

Find answers at: cambridge.org/ukschools/gcsemaths-studentbookanswers

6 Name the type of quadrilateral enclosed by the four lines you drew in question 5.

Give reasons for your answer.

7 **a** Write down the equations of two lines that divide the quadrilateral formed in question 5 into two identical rectangles.

b What is the name of a line that divides shapes into two identical halves?

Choose from the options below.

A Mirror line   B Perpendicular bisector   C Line of best fit

c It is possible to draw two other lines that divide the quadrilateral into two equal halves.

i Draw these lines on your diagram.

ii Work out the equation of each line.

Section 2: Quadratic functions

A **quadratic** expression has the form $ax^2 + bx + c$, where $a \neq 0$.

Two quadratic expressions are $2x^2 + 4x - 1$ and $3x^2 + 7$, but $2x - 1$ is a linear expression as it has no x^2 term.

The graph of a quadratic function is a curve called a **parabola**.

The path of moving objects such as this basketball can be modelled as a parabola.

The simplest equation of a parabola is $y = x^2$.

This is the graph of $y = x^2$.

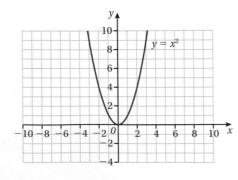

You can plot the graph of a quadratic function by drawing up a table of values.

WORKED EXAMPLE 1

Plot the graph of the function $y = x^2 + 2$.

Draw up a table of x- and y-values that satisfy the equation $y = x^2 + 2$.

x	-3	-2	-1	0	1	2	3	4	5
y	7	0	-5	-8	-9	-8	-5	0	7

To make the graph as accurate as possible, you need to make sure you include at least five points (the more the better), and both positive and negative values of x.

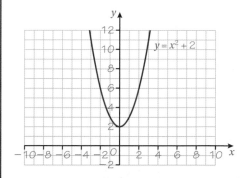

Plot all the points on a grid and join them to produce a smooth curve that extends through and beyond the points you have plotted.

Label the curve.

 Tip

The shape of a parabola can extend upwards to a maximum point or downwards to a minimum point. The equation of the graph tells you which of these shapes it will be.

EXERCISE 37B

1. **a** Complete a table of values of x from -3 to 3 for each equation.
   Draw the graphs on the same grid.

   i $y = x^2$ **ii** $y = -x^2$

   b How are the graphs different?

   c How does the sign of the x^2 term affect the shape of the graph?

2. $y = -2x^2 + 3$. State the value of y when $x = -5$.
   Choose from the options below.

   A $y = 53$ B $y = -47$ C $y = -53$ D $y = 47$

3. **a** Complete a table of values of x from -3 to 3 for each function.
   Draw the graphs on the same grid.

   i $y = 3x^2$ **ii** $y = \frac{1}{3}x^2$ **iii** $y = 4x^2 + 1$ **iv** $y = -2x^2 + 3$

   b What does the constant value in the equations of graphs **iii** and **iv** tell you about the graphs?

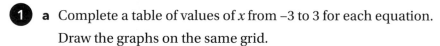 **Find answers at: cambridge.org/ukschools/gcsemaths-studentbookanswers**

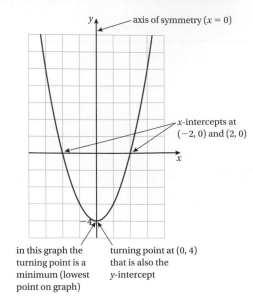

in this graph the turning point is a minimum (lowest point on graph)

turning point at (0, 4) that is also the y-intercept

Features of parabolas

Quadratic graphs have features you can use to sketch and interpret them.

The main features of a parabola are:

- the axis of symmetry – a line that divides the parabola into two symmetrical halves
- the y-intercept where the curve cuts the y-axis – a parabola can only have one y-intercept
- the turning point or vertex of the graph – this is the point at which the graph changes direction
- the x-intercepts where the curve cuts the x-axis – a parabola can have 0, 1 or 2 x-intercepts depending on its position.

The graph either has a minimum turning point or a maximum turning point.

If the x^2 term is positive, the turning point will be a minimum (this is the lowest point of the graph).

If the x^2 term is negative, the turning point will be a maximum (this is the highest point of the graph).

WORKED EXAMPLE 2

For each parabola write down:

i the turning point and whether it is a minimum or maximum

ii the axis of symmetry

iii the y-intercept

iv the x-intercepts.

a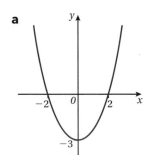

b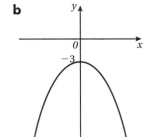

c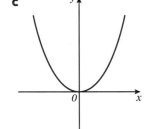

Parabola **a**

i Turning point at $(0, -3)$; minimum

ii Axis of symmetry: $x = 0$

iii y-intercept at $(0, -3)$

iv x-intercepts at $(-2, 0)$ and $(2, 0)$

Parabola **b**

Turning point at $(0, -3)$; maximum

Axis of symmetry: $x = 0$

x-intercept at $(0, -3)$

There are no x-intercepts.

Parabola **c**

Turning point at $(0, 0)$; minimum

Axis of symmetry: $x = 0$

x-intercept at $(0, 0)$

One x-intercept at $(0, 0)$

x-intercepts and roots of a quadratic equation

The *x*-intercepts of a parabola are the roots of the quadratic equation that defines the graph.

You can find the roots graphically by reading their values off the graph.

You can also solve the quadratic equation to find its roots. The roots are the points at which its graph crosses the *x*-axis (or the *x*-intercepts). This is useful when you have to sketch the graph.

EXERCISE 37C

1 For each parabola, write down:

   i the turning point and whether it is a minimum or maximum

   ii the axis of symmetry

   iii the *y*-intercept

   iv the *x*-intercepts.

a
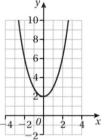

b
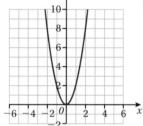

c
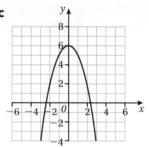

d
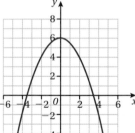

e
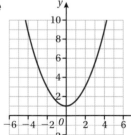

f
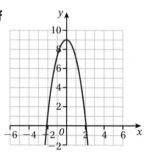

2 Graphs A to E are shown on the same grid.

Use the diagram to work out whether each statement is true or false.

  a Graph A has two *x*-intercepts.

  b Graphs A and B have minimum turning points.

  c Graph B has *y*-intercepts at (−2, 0) and (2, 0).

  d Graphs B and C have the same *x*-intercepts.

  e The equation of graph D will have a positive x^2 term.

  f Graph E has a maximum turning point at (0, −2).

  g The equation of graph D has a constant of 2. This tells you the *y*-intercept is (0, 2).

  h All of these graphs are symmetrical about $x = 0$.

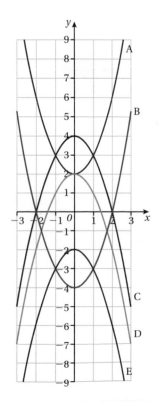

Sketching quadratic graphs

You can use the features of a parabola to sketch graphs without drawing up a table of values.

A sketch shows the general features of a graph but it does not have to be drawn on graph paper. How to sketch a parabola:

- Make sure the equation is in the general form $y = ax^2 + c$, where a is the coefficient of x and c is a constant.
- Check the sign of a to decide whether the graph goes up to a maximum turning point (negative) or down to a minimum turning point (positive).
- Work out the y-intercept. This is given by c in the equation.
- Calculate the x-intercepts by substituting $y = 0$ and solving for x. If there are no x-intercepts you will have to find the coordinates of one point on the graph.
- Mark the y-intercept and x-intercepts (if they exist) and use the shape of the graph as a guide to draw a smooth curve.
- Label your graph.

Tip

Draw a smooth curve to join the points and try to make your graph as symmetrical as possible.

WORKED EXAMPLE 3

Sketch the graph of $y = 3x^2$

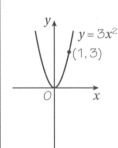

Coefficient of x is 3, which is positive, so graph goes down to a minimum turning point.

There is no constant, so graph goes through the origin $(0, 0)$.

When $y = 0$ $x = 0$. There is only one solution for x, so find a point on the graph.

When $x = 1$, $y = 3(1)^2 = 3$

So, $(1, 3)$ is a point on the curve.

Sketch and label the graph.

WORKED EXAMPLE 4

Sketch the graph of $y = -x^2 + 4$

Coefficient of x is -1, so graph goes up to a maximum turning point.

Constant is 4, so y-intercept is $(0, 4)$.

x-intercepts when $y = 0$

$$0 = -x^2 + 4$$

$$\therefore x^2 - 4 = 0$$

This is a difference of two squares.

$$(x + 2)(x - 2) = 0$$

$$x + 2 = 0 \text{ or } x - 2 = 0$$

$$x = -2 \text{ or } x = 2$$

So, intercepts are $(-2, 0)$ and $(2, 0)$.

Sketch and label the graph.

An alternative way of finding the solution for x:

$$x^2 - 4 = 0$$

so $x^2 = 4$

which gives the solution for x:

$$x = \pm 2$$

EXERCISE 37D

1 Sketch and label these graphs on the same grid.

a $y = x^2$ **b** $y = 2x^2$ **c** $y = \frac{1}{2}x^2$

d $y = -2x^2$ **e** $y = -\frac{1}{2}x^2$

2 Write down how the value of the **coefficient** of x^2 affects the wideness of the parabola's shape.

3 Solve each equation algebraically to find the x-intercepts of each graph. Do not draw the graphs.

a $y = x^2 - 4$ **b** $y = x^2 - 9$

4 Sketch the following graphs on the same grid.

a $y = x^2 - 3$ **b** $y = 3x^2 - 4$

c $y = -x^2 - 2$ **d** $y = -3x^2 + 12$

5 Noor sketched these graphs but she didn't write the equations on them.

Use the features of each graph to work out what the correct equations are.

a
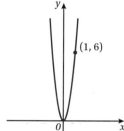

b
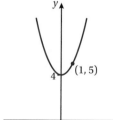

c
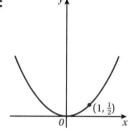

d
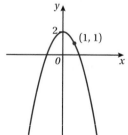

e
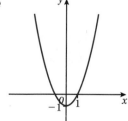

f
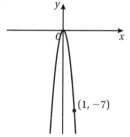

Find answers at: cambridge.org/ukschools/gcsemaths-studentbookanswers

Section 3: Other polynomials and reciprocals

A **polynomial** is an expression with many terms.

If the highest power of x is 3, the expression is called a cubic expression.

For example, $2x^3$ and $2x^3 + x^2 + 3$ are both cubics.

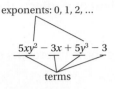

A polynomial   Not polynomial

You can use a table of values to plot the graph of a cubic equation. The simplest equation of a cubic graph is $y = x^3$.

All cubic graphs have a similar shape. The diagram shows the basic shape of cubic graphs in the form of $y = ax^3$.

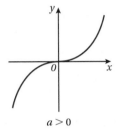 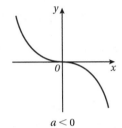

The shape on the left occurs when a is positive. This is called an increasing curve.

The shape on the right occurs when a is negative. This is called a decreasing curve.

The larger the value of a, the steeper the curve.

This is a table of values for $y = x^3$ for values of x from −3 to 3.

x	−3	−2	−1	0	1	2	3
y	−27	−8	−1	0	1	8	27

To draw an accurate graph you plot all of the calculated points and draw a smooth curve through and beyond them.

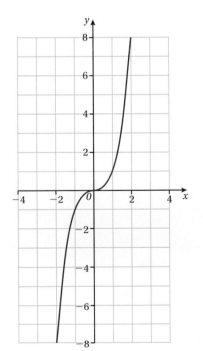

Note that the curve passes through the origin but it is not symmetrical.

When you sketch a cubic graph you need to show its general shape and its important features. You still use a table of values, but you don't need to work out as many points as you need for an accurate graph.

EXERCISE 37E

1 Complete a table of values for whole number values of x from -3 to 3 for the graph $y = -x^3$.

Write down how this graph differs from the graph of $y = x^3$.

2 Use a table of values to sketch the following pairs of cubic graphs.

Plot each pair on the same grid, but use a separate grid for each pair.

a $y = -2x^3$ and $y = 2x^3$

b $y = \frac{1}{2}x^3$ and $y = -\frac{1}{2}x^3$

3 Work with a partner to compare the pairs of graphs you drew in question 2.

Write down how you could sketch the graph of $y = -4x^3$ if you were given the graph of $y = 4x^3$.

4 Complete a table of values for whole number values of x from -3 to 3 for these equations.

Draw a graph of each curve.

a $y = x^3 + 1$

b $y = x^3 - 2$

5 Look at the graphs and their equations in question 4.

What information does the constant give you about the graph?

6 The red line is the graph $y = x^3$.

Write down the equations of graphs A and B.

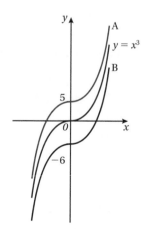

> **Tip**
>
> Remember that when you cube a negative number you will get a negative result.
>
> For example,
> $(-1)^3 = -1 \times -1 \times -1 = -1$

Reciprocal functions

The product of a number and its **reciprocal** is 1.

For example:

$$8 \times \frac{1}{8} = 1 \qquad \frac{2}{5} \times \frac{5}{2} = 1$$

Every number has a reciprocal except for 0, as $\frac{1}{0}$ cannot be defined.

The reciprocal of a is $\frac{1}{a}$

$$a \times \frac{1}{a} = 1$$

The general equation of a reciprocal function is $y = \frac{a}{x}$, where a is a constant value.

This equation can be rearranged to give $xy = a$.

The graphs of reciprocal functions have a usual shape. Each graph is made up of two curves that are mirror images in opposite quadrants of the grid.

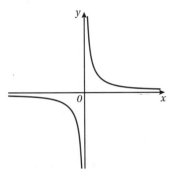

This is the table of values for the equation of $y = \frac{1}{x}$.

x	-3	-2	-1	$-\frac{1}{2}$	$-\frac{1}{3}$	0	$\frac{1}{2}$	$\frac{1}{2}$	1	2	3
y	$-\frac{1}{3}$	$-\frac{1}{2}$	-1	-2	-3	not defined	2	3	1	$\frac{1}{2}$	$\frac{1}{3}$

In order to draw a reciprocal graph accurately you need to work with some non-integer values of x.

There is no y-value when $x = 0$ because division by 0 is undefined.

To draw the graph:

* plot the (x, y) values from the table
* join the points with a smooth curve
* write the equation on both parts of the graph.

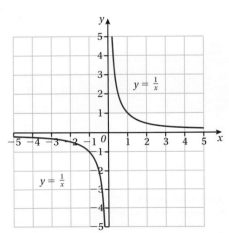

Note that as the value for x gets bigger, the value for y gets closer and closer to 0 as y becomes smaller and smaller but the graph never actually meets the x-axis.

EXERCISE 37F

1 Copy and complete each table for the given values of x. Plot the graphs on the same grid.

a $y = \dfrac{2}{x}$

x	-4	-2	-1	1	2	4
y						

b $y = \dfrac{6}{x}$

x	-6	-3	-1	1	3	6
y						

c $xy = -12$

x	-10	-8	-6	-4	-2	2	4	6	8
y									

d $y = \dfrac{8}{x}$

x	-8	-6	-4	-2	1	2	4	6	8
y									

2 Compare the graphs that you have drawn for question 1. How does the value of the constant in the equation affect the position of the graph?

3 Plot each of the following graphs on the same grid using x-values from -5 to 5.

a $y = \dfrac{1}{x}$ **b** $y = \dfrac{1}{x} + 1$ **c** $y = \dfrac{1}{x} + 3$

4 Use your graphs from question 3 to describe how the constant c in the equation $y = \dfrac{a}{x} + c$ changes the reciprocal graph of $y = \dfrac{a}{x}$.

5 Neo says that the line $y = x$ is the line of symmetry of the graph $y = \dfrac{1}{x}$. Is he correct?

Give reasons for your answer.

Section 4: Plotting, sketching and recognising graphs

You have seen that you can use the features of different types of graphs to work out what they will look like and how to sketch them.

You have also learnt that equations in different forms produce different types of graphs.

- $y = mx + c$ will produce a straight-line or linear graph.
- $y = ax^2 + c$ will produce a quadratic graph called a parabola.
- $y = ax^3$ will produce a cubic curve.
- $y = \dfrac{a}{x}$ and $xy = a$ will produce a reciprocal curve.

Find answers at: cambridge.org/ukschools/gcsemaths-studentbookanswers

EXERCISE 37G

1 Work out whether each statement is true or false. Correct any false statements.

a The points $(3, 7)$, $(0, 1)$ and $(-1, -1)$ all lie on the line $y = 2x + 1$.

b The graph of the equation $y = \dfrac{5}{x}$ cannot be evaluated for $x = 0$.

c This diagram shows the graph of a quadratic equation with roots 1 and −1.

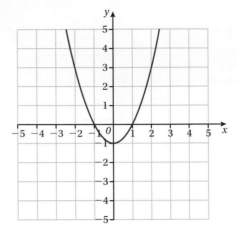

d The function $xy = 5$ is the same as $y = \dfrac{5}{x}$.

e The graph of $y = -2x^2 + 4$ goes down to a minimum turning point with a y-intercept at $(0, -2)$.

f The line $y = -x$ is a line of symmetry of $xy = 4$.

2 Sketch each of the following graphs.

a $y = x + 2$ **b** $y = 3x - 4$ **c** $y = 7 - 3x$

d $y = 3$ **e** $x = -5$

3 Draw up a table of values and plot each graph.

a $y = 2x^2$ **b** $y = x^2 - 3$ **c** $y = -x^2 + 5$

d $y = x^3 + 4$ **e** $y = \dfrac{1}{x}$ **f** $y = \dfrac{1}{x} + 1$

4 Solve the following equations algebraically.

Write down the x-intercepts of each graph.

a $y = x^2 - 16$ **b** $y = x^2 - 2x$

5 A quadratic equation has roots $x = -3$ and $x = 5$.

Give the coordinates of the points of intersection with the x-axis.

6 Match each of the following graphs with the appropriate equation from the list.

a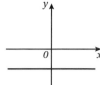

b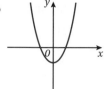

c

d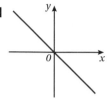

e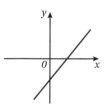

f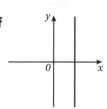

g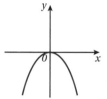

h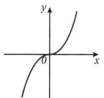

i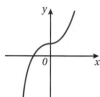

Equations:

i $y = x^2 - 2$ **ii** $y = 3x - 4$ **iii** $xy = 1$

iv $y = -x$ **v** $y = 2x^3$ **vi** $y = 3x^3 + 3$

vii $x = 4$ **viii** $y = -4$ **ix** $y = -x^2$

 Checklist of learning and understanding

Linear functions

- Linear functions produce straight-line graphs.
- The general form of the linear function is $y = mx + c$.
- Graphs $x = a$ are vertical lines parallel to the y-axis.
- Graphs $y = b$ are horizontal lines parallel to the x-axis.
- Lines of the form $y = mx$ go through the origin.

Quadratic functions

- Graphs of quadratic equations, such as $y = ax^2$ and $y = ax^2 + c$, are called parabolas.
- When a is positive, the graph goes down to a minimum point. When a is negative, the graph goes up to a maximum point. The y-intercept is given by c.
- Parabolas have a turning point, that can be a minimum or maximum depending on the shape of the graph.

Polynomials and reciprocals

- To draw graphs of polynomials, first calculate a table of values that satisfy the equation for a range of values of x.
- A cubic function is a curve defined by $y = ax^3$.
- A reciprocal function is a graph made up of two curves in opposite quadrants defined by $y = \dfrac{a}{x}$ or $xy = a$.

 Find answers at: cambridge.org/ukschools/gcsemaths-studentbookanswers

For additional questions on the topics in this chapter, visit GCSE Mathematics Online.

Chapter review

1 **a** Copy and complete this table for $y = 2x + 1$.

Plot the points to draw a straight-line graph.

x	−2	−1	0	1	2	3
y						

b Use the graph to find:

i the value of y when $x = -1.5$ **ii** the value of x when $y = 6$.

2 **a** Complete the table of values for $y = x^2 - 3$ *(2 marks)*

x	−2	−1	0	1	2
y					

b Draw the graph of $y = x^2 - 3$ for values of x from −2 to 2.   *(2 marks)*

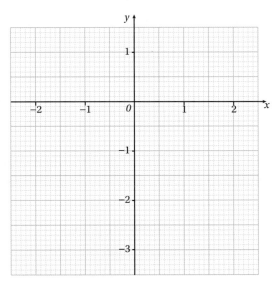

c Use your graph to work out the values of x when $y = 0.5$ *(2 marks)*

© AQA 2012

3 **a** Copy and complete this table for $y = 2x^2 - 5$.

Plot the points to draw the curve of the parabola.

x	−2	−1	0	1	2
y			−5	−3	

b Give the coordinate of the minimum point of the curve (the turning point).

c What line is the axis of symmetry for this graph?

d Estimate the roots of the equation $2x^2 - 5 = 0$.

4 Match the equations $y = x^3$ and $y = \dfrac{1}{x}$ with the correct graph.

a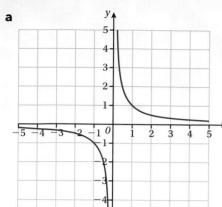

b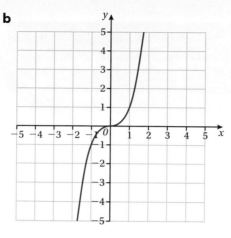

5 Draw a sketch diagram of $y = x^3 - 5$ and $y = \dfrac{1}{x} + 2$.

6 The roots of the quadratic equation $x^2 + 2x - 3 = 0$ are $x = 1$ and $x = -3$.

What are the coordinates of the points at which the equation $y = x^2 + 2x - 3$ cuts the x-axis?

Find answers at: cambridge.org/ukschools/gcsemaths-studentbookanswers

38 Growth and decay

Using mathematics: real-life applications

Many real-life situations involve growth (increase) or decay (decrease) as time passes. Population numbers, growth of bacteria, disease infection rates, world temperature patterns and the value of money or possessions might all increase or decrease over time.

"My computer program calculates interest on a daily basis. This means whatever is in the account gains interest, not just the initial investment." *(Investment broker)*

Before you start ...

Ch 6, 13	You must be able to convert percentages to decimals.	**1** Write each of the following as a decimal: **a** 5% **b** 190% **c** 0.4% **d** 12.5%	
Ch 13	You must be able to find a percentage of a quantity using multiplication.	**2** Find, using multiplication only: **a** 68% of £300 **b** 2% of $80 **c** 4.5% of £56 **d** 114% of $650 **e** 99.5% of £1540	
Ch 13	You must be able to increase or decrease a quantity by a given percentage by multiplying by a suitable decimal.	**3** Carry out the following increases and decreases using only multiplication: **a** increase $44 by 22% **b** increase £35 by 5.5% **c** decrease £13 by 44% **d** decrease $170 by 8%	

Assess your starting point using the Launchpad

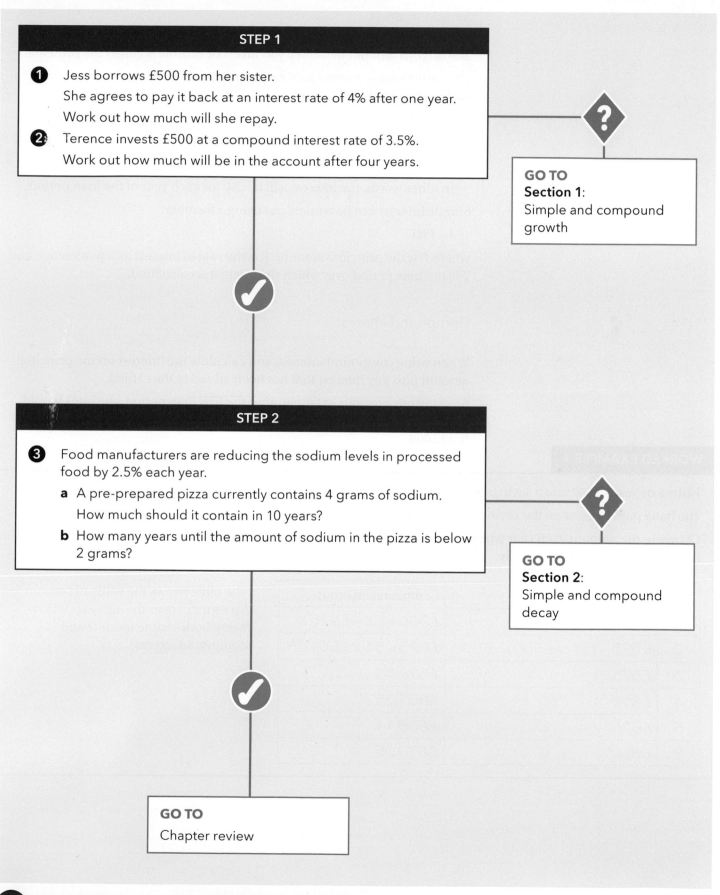

STEP 1

1 Jess borrows £500 from her sister.
She agrees to pay it back at an interest rate of 4% after one year.
Work out how much will she repay.

2 Terence invests £500 at a compound interest rate of 3.5%.
Work out how much will be in the account after four years.

GO TO
Section 1:
Simple and compound growth

STEP 2

3 Food manufacturers are reducing the sodium levels in processed food by 2.5% each year.

a A pre-prepared pizza currently contains 4 grams of sodium.
How much should it contain in 10 years?

b How many years until the amount of sodium in the pizza is below 2 grams?

GO TO
Section 2:
Simple and compound decay

GO TO
Chapter review

Find answers at: cambridge.org/ukschools/gcsemaths-studentbookanswers

Section 1: Simple and compound growth

Simple interest

The original amount of money you invest or borrow is called the principal.

Simple interest is interest paid on the principal. The same interest is paid for each time period.

For example:

£1000 is borrowed at an interest rate of 5% per year.

Each year the interest charged is 5% × £1000 = £50.

In other words, the interest will be £50 for each year of the loan period.

Simple interest can be worked out using a formula:

$I = PRT$

where P is the principal amount, R is the rate of interest as a percentage and T is the time period over which the interest is calculated.

Compound interest

When using compound interest, you calculate the interest on the principal amount plus any interest that has been added to the capital.

So using our previous example, after the first loan period, the bank would work out the interest you owe based on £1050 (principal plus interest) not £1000.

WORKED EXAMPLE 1

Fatima deposits £500 into a savings account for six years.

The bank pays interest on the savings at 5% per year.

Compare the amount each year when the interest is calculated using simple interest to the amount when the interest is compounded annually.

Year	Simple interest	Compound interest
1	£500 + 5% = £525	£500 + 5% = £525
2	£525 + (5% of £500) = £550	£525 + 5% = £551.25
3	£575	£578.81
4	£600	£607.75
5	£625	£638.14
6	£650	£670.05

The table shows the value of the investment over the six years when using both simple interest and compound interest.

WORK IT OUT 38.1

Three students attempt the question below.

Decide who has got the correct answer and also who has used the most efficient method to find it.

The population of Europe is growing at a rate of 0.2% per year.

The current population is 739 million.

What will the population be in three years' time?

Student A	Student B	Student C
Find 0.2%:	Year 1:	Increase by 0.2% means there is 100.2%, do this three times in a row.
0.2% of 739 000 000	Find 0.2% of 739 000 000	739 000 000 × 1.002 × 1.002 × 1.002
= 0.002 × 739 000 000	= 0.002 × 739 000 000	= 739 000 000 × 1.002^3
= 1 478 000	= 1 478 000	= 743 442 874
The same growth for 3 years:	Add it on: 740 478 000	
3 × 1 478 000 = 4 434 000	Year 2:	
Add it on:	Find 0.2% of 740 478 000	
739 000 000 + 4 434 000	= 0.002 × 740 478 000	
= 743 434 000	= 1 480 956	
	Add it on: 741 958 956	
	Year 3:	
	Find 0.2% and add it on	
	1 483 918 + 741 958 956	
	= 743 442 874	

Tip

Always show your working for these types of questions so that your teacher can see how you have calculated your answer. Write down what you type into the calculator so you can check it several times.

Working with compound interest and growth rates is like working with function machines.

Each time an output is produced it goes back to becoming an input and the process is repeated.

For example, the population of starlings in a park is 80 and it increases at a rate of 10%. Predict how many starlings there will be after five years.

To increase a quantity by 10% we multiply by 1.1 (100% + 10% = 110% or 1.1)

Tip

The number we multiply by is called the multiplier. So here we are multiplying by 1.1, which means that 1.1 is the multiplier.

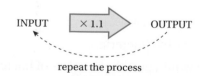

INPUT   × 1.1   OUTPUT

repeat the process

Find answers at: cambridge.org/ukschools/gcsemaths-studentbookanswers

The first input is 80.

$$80 \times 1.1 = 88$$

$$88 \times 1.1 = 96.8$$

Notice that if our model was to stop here you would round sensibly. However, you use the unrounded value to ensure the following year's prediction is more accurate.

$$96.8 \times 1.1 = 106.48$$

$$106.48 \times 1.1 = 117.128$$

$$117.128 \times 1.1 = 128.8408$$

So we would predict that there will be 129 starlings after five years.

This could be re-written as:

$$80 \times 1.1 \times 1.1 \times 1.1 \times 1.1 \times 1.1 = 80 \times 1.1^5$$

EXERCISE 38A

1. Copy and complete this table for simple interest at the given rate.

Investment(£)	Interest rate (%)	1 year	2 years	6 years	n years
250	2				
1500	4.5				
	3	£51.50			

2. Patrick invests £300 in an account with a compound interest rate of 2%. Calculate how much is in the account after:

   a 1 year   b 3 years   c 8 years.

3. Leona invests £400 at a compound interest rate of 4%.

   How much interest (to the nearest penny) will she earn in three years? Choose from the following options.

   A £449.95   B £448   C £49.95   D £48

4. A company grows in size each year by 10%.

   In 2014, the company employs 726 people.

   How many did it employ in 2012?

   Choose from the following options.

   A 580   B 588   C 600   D 660

5. An amount of £1000 is invested with a compound interest rate of 3%.

   Plot a graph showing how much money is in the account over the first 10 years of the investment.

6. A colony of bacteria grows by 4% every hour.

   At first the colony has 100 bacteria.

   Which calculation would give the number of bacteria after 24 hours?

   A $100 \times 4 \times 24$ B 100×4^{24} C 100×1.04^{24} D $100 \times 0.04 \times 24$

7 The population of Ireland is growing at an annual rate of 1.7%.

In 2014 the population was 4.6 million.

a Assuming that this growth rate remains constant, predict how many people will be living in Ireland in 2024.

b How many new inhabitants are there in 2024?

c Use this model to show how many people there were in Ireland in 2012.

Write down the reasons for your answers.

8 The Bank of England's target inflation rate is 2%.

This tells you how much the cost of living, food, fuel and rent is likely to go up each year.

In 2015, a month's rent is given as £450.

Assuming that the bank targets are correct, predict how much a month's rent is likely to be in 20 years' time.

9 Gavin is saving for a new bike.

The model he wants cost £255. So far he has saved £200.

Gavin's dad has offered to pay him 8% interest each month on this amount.

How long is he going to have to wait for the bike?

Show clear working to give reasons for your answer.

10 Population growth models help predict the spread of invasive species.

Zebra mussels are one such species.

Their population can increase by 1900% each year.

Two zebra mussels are found in a freshwater lake.

Should biologists be worried that this will have a significant impact over the next 10 years?

Give detailed reasoning in your answer.

11 Two investors are investing for five years and have a choice.

They can either have 6% simple interest or 5.5% compound interest.

a Which should they choose?

b Would the answer change if they were investing for four years?

12 Jenny is saving for her first car. She needs a deposit of £2775.

Each month she saves £200 in an account offering 1% interest a month.

a Work out if Jenny has enough money after a year to buy a car.

b If not, how much extra money does she need?

c How many more months will this take her to save?

13 Between 1980 and 2010 the price of a chocolate bar went from 25p to 65p.

a By what percentage did the cost rise?

b Predict how much the bar will cost in 2040. (Assume the cost keeps increasing at the same rate.)

c What is the annual percentage increase?

d In what year does the chocolate bar first cost more than £1?

 Find answers at: cambridge.org/ukschools/gcsemaths-studentbookanswers

14 Jon invests an inheritance of £100 000 at a rate of 5% for 10 years.

    a How much more money does he earn using compound interest compared to simple interest?

    b What simple interest rate would be needed to achieve the same earnings?

15 A two-bedroomed house cost £195 000 last year and now costs £216 450.

    Assuming the price keeps rising at the same rate, how much will this house cost in three years' time?

16 Which of the following investment models gives the highest earnings?

Model A	Model B	Model C
Year 1: 5% interest	Years 1–3	Years 1–3
Year 2: 4% interest	4% compound interest	4.1% simple interest
Year 3: 3% interest		

17 A colony of bacteria grow by 5% every hour.

    How long does it take for the colony to double in size?

Section 2: Simple and compound decay

When the value of something goes down it has depreciated.

For example, a brand new car will show a **depreciation** in value of about 30% in the first year of ownership alone.

WORKED EXAMPLE 2

A new computer depreciates by 30% per year.

It cost £1200 new.

What will it be worth in two years' time?

Method 1
Value after 1 year = £1200 – (30% of £1200)
                  = £1200 – £360
                  = £840
Value after 2 years = £840 – (30% of £840)
                  = £840 – £252
                  = £588

> Each year the value decreases by 30%.

Method 2
Value after 1 year = 70% of £1200 = £840
Value after 2 years = 70% of £840 = £588

> Each year its new value is 70% (100% – 30%) of its value in the previous year.

When the number of items in a population declines over time, it is called decay rather than depreciation.

For example, if the population of squirrels is in decay, it means that each year there are fewer and fewer animals in the population.

If the rate of decline is 10%, each year 10% of the squirrels disappear, leaving 90%. So from one year to the next the number of animals is $n \times 0.9$, where n is the number of animals you are starting with each year.

WORK IT OUT 38.2

Three students attempt the question below.

Decide who has got the correct answer and also who has used the most efficient method to find it.

For every 1000 m you go up in the Earth's atmosphere, the atmospheric pressure decreases by 12%. This is called the lapse rate.

The sea-level atmospheric pressure is 100 300 pascal (Pa).

What is the atmospheric pressure for a skydiver at an altitude of 4000 metres?

Student A	Student B	Student C
12% of 100 300	Decrease by 12% leaves 88%	Decrease by 12% leaves 88%, do this four times in a row.
$= 0.12 \times 100\,300$	88% of 100 300	$100\,300 \times 0.88 \times 0.88 \times 0.88 \times 0.88$
$= 12\,036$	$= 0.88 \times 100\,300$	$= 100\,300 \times 0.88^4$
$4 \times 12\,036 = 48\,144$	$= 88\,264$	$= 60\,149.444608\,\text{Pa}$
$100\,300 - 48\,144$	88% of 88 264	60 149.4 Pa (to 1 dp)
$= 52\,156\,\text{Pa}$	$= 77\,672.32$	
	88% of 77 672.32	
	$= 68\,351.6416$	
	88% of 68 351.6416	
	$= 60\,149.444608\,\text{Pa}$	

EXERCISE 38B

1 A computer depreciates in value by 3% every six months.

Originally the computer cost £799.

How much is it worth, to the nearest penny, 24 months later?

Choose your answer from the options below.

A £719.10   B £727.09   C £729.22   D £707.35

2 After losing 15% of its value a car is worth £4250.

What was it worth originally?

Choose your answer from the options below.

A £5000   B £4887.50   C £4265   D £3612.50

3 A car depreciates in value each year by 8%.

A new compact car costs £11 000. How much will it be worth in:

a 1 year?   **b** 3 years?   **c** 8 years?

Find answers at: cambridge.org/ukschools/gcsemaths-studentbookanswers

4 Copy and complete this table:

Initial cost (£)	Depreciation rate (%)	1 year	2 years	6 years
400	2			
2 500	15			
50 000	3.5			

5 A pesticide is absorbed by the soil (i.e. it decays) at a rate of 7% a year.

A farmer used 2 kg of pesticide on a field in 2000.

Work out how much pesticide remains in the soil in the field in 2014.

6 The height of the water in a tank reduces by 15% every 5 minutes.

Which of the following graphs shows this?

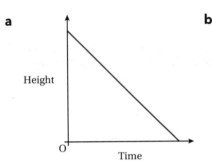

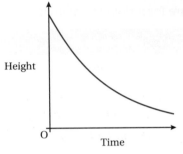

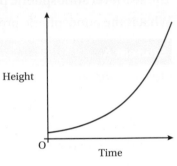

7 At the start of an experiment there are 8000 bacteria in a population.

A lethal pathogen is introduced to the population causing a reduction of 1600 in an hour.

a What is the percentage decrease in population?

b Assuming the same rate of decrease, how many bacteria would you expect to be alive after 8 hours?

c How long will it be until fewer than 100 bacteria are alive?

8 For every 1000 m higher that you climb, the atmospheric pressure decreases by 12%.

The sea-level atmospheric pressure is 100 300 pascal (Pa).

Work out the pressure at a height of 39 km above sea level.

9 The population of Bulgaria is decreasing at a rate of 0.6% per year.

In 2014, the population was 7.4 million people.

a How many people are expected to be living in Bulgaria in 2020?

b How many years until the population gets to below 7 million?

10 The cost of mobile phones has been falling.

Three years ago the latest model cost £400.

Today the latest model costs £342.95.

Assuming the price keeps falling at this rate, how long will it be until the current model costs less than two-thirds of today's price?

Checklist of learning and understanding

Simple and compound growth

- Simple growth, such as interest, is a fixed rate of growth, calculated on the original amount.
- The formula $I = PRT$ can be used to calculate simple interest.
- Compound growth, such as compound interest, is calculated on the principal for the first period and then compounded by calculating it on the principal plus any interest paid or due for each previous period.
- You can work out compound growth using a multiplier for each period.

Simple and compound decay

- A drop in value of an object over time is called depreciation.
- A decline in a population is called decay.
- Simple and compound decay are found by subtraction or by working out the percentage remaining.

Chapter review

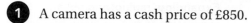

For additional questions on the topics in this chapter, visit GCSE Mathematics Online.

1 A camera has a cash price of £850.

Nasief buys it on credit and pays a 10% deposit, with the balance to be paid over two years at a simple interest rate of 10%.

Calculate:

  a the amount of his deposit

  b the balance owing after deducting the deposit

  c the amount of interest paid in total over two years

  d the monthly payment amount for 24 equal monthly instalments

  e the difference between the cash price and what Nasief actually paid.

2 David invests £5000 in a savings account.

The account pays 3.2% compound interest per year.

Work out the value of his investment after 3 years.   *(4 marks)*

Give your answer to the nearest penny.   © *AQA 2013*

3 Salma invests £2300 in an account that pays 6% interest compounded half-yearly.

Work out how much money she will have after two years.

4 A car valued at £8500 depreciates by 30% in the first year, 20% in the second year and a further 12% in the third year.

Calculate how much is it worth after three years.

5 Each year the education department arranges a quiz.

There are 140 students in the competition to start with.

During each round, half of the quiz contestants are eliminated.

How many students are still participating after Round 4?

 Find answers at: cambridge.org/ukschools/gcsemaths-studentbookanswers

Glossary

A

Adjacent: next to each other. In shapes, sides that intersect each other are adjacent.

Alternate angles: the angles on parallel lines on opposite sides of a transversal

Angle of depression: when looking down, the angle between the line of sight and the horizontal

Angle of elevation: when looking up, the angle between the line of sight and the horizontal

Arithmetic sequence: a sequence where the difference between each term is constant

B

Binomial: an expression consisting of two terms

Binomial product: the product of two binomial expressions; for example, $(x + 2)(x + 3)$

Bisect: to divide exactly into two halves

Bivariate data: data that is collected in pairs

C

Categorical data: data that has been arranged in categories

Chord: a straight line that joins one point on the circumference of a circle to another point on its circumference. The diameter is a chord that goes through the centre of the circle.

Circumference: distance round the outside of a circle

Coefficient: the number in front of a variable in a mathematical expression. In the term $5x^2$, 5 is the coefficient and x is the variable.

Co-interior angles: the angles within the parallel lines on the same side of the transversal

Combined events: one event followed by another event producing two or more outcomes

Common denominator: a number into which all the denominators of a set of fractions divide exactly

Congruent: shapes that are identical in shape and size

Conjugate: binomial expressions with the same terms but opposite signs

Consecutive: following each other in order and without a gap. For example 1, 2, 3 or 35, 36, 37.

Consecutive terms: terms that follow each other in a sequence

Constant: a number on its own

Continuous data: data that can have any value

Conversion factor: the number that you multiply or divide by to convert one measure into another smaller or larger unit

Coordinates: an ordered pair (x, y) identifying a position on a grid

Correlation: a relationship or connection between data items

Corresponding angles: angles that are created at the same point of the intersection when a transversal crosses a pair of parallel lines

Cyclic quadrilateral: any quadrilateral with all four vertices on the circumference of a circle

D

Degree of accuracy: the number of places to which you round a number

Dependent events: events in which the outcome is affected by what happened before

Dependent variable: the variable that is being measured in an experiment

Depreciation: the loss in value of an object over a period of time

Direct proportion: two values that both increase in the same ratio

Discrete data: data that can be counted and can only have certain values

Displacement: a change in position

E

Elevation view: a view of an object from the front, side or back

Error interval: the difference between the upper and lower bounds

Equalities: having the same amount or value

Equally likely: having the same probability of occurring

Equivalent: having the same value. Two ratios are equivalent if one is a multiple of the other.

Estimate: an approximate answer or rough calculation

Evaluate: to calculate the numerical value of something

Event: the thing to which you are trying to give a probability

Exchange rate: a number that is used to calculate the difference in value between money from one country and money from another

Expanding: multiplying out an expression to get rid of the brackets

Exponent: the number that says how many times a letter or number is multiplied by itself. It is another name for power or index.

Expression: a group of numbers and letters linked by operation signs

Exterior angles: angles produced by extending the sides of a polygon

F

First difference: the result of subtracting a term from the next term

Formula (plural **formulae**): a general rule or equation showing the relationship between unknown quantities

Function: a set of instructions for changing one number (the input) into another number (the output)

G

Geometric sequence: a sequence where the ratio between each term is constant

Gradient: a measure of the steepness of a line

$$\text{Gradient} = \frac{\text{change in } y\text{-values}}{\text{change in } x\text{-values}}$$

H

Hypotenuse: the longest side of a right-angled triangle; the side opposite the 90° angle

I

Identity: an equation that is true no matter what values are chosen for the variables

Image: the new shape (after the object has been transformed)

Independent events: events that are not affected by what happened before

Index: a power or exponent indicating how many times a base number is multiplied by itself

Index notation: writing a number as a base and index, for example 23

Inequality: a mathematical sentence in which the left side is not equal to the right side

Integers: whole numbers in the set {… −3, −2, −1, 0, 1, 2, 3, …}. When they have a negative or positive sign they can be referred to as **directed numbers**.

Interior angles: angles inside a two-dimensional shape at the vertices or corners

Inverse proportion: a relation between two quantities such that one increases at a rate that is equal to the rate that the other decreases

Irrational number: a number that cannot be written in the form of $\frac{a}{b}$ or as a terminating or repeating decimal

Irregular polygon: a polygon that does not have equal sides and equal angles

Isometric grid: special drawing paper based on an arrangement of triangles

L

Line of symmetry: a line that divides a plane shape into two identical halves, each the reflection of the other

Linear equation: an equation where the highest power of the unknown is 1, for example $x + 3 = 7$

Locus (plural loci): a set of points that satisfy the same rule

M

Mathematical model: a representation of a real-life problem; assumptions are used to simplify the situation so that it can be solved mathematically

Midpoint: the centre of a line; the point that divides the line into two equal halves

Mirror line: a line equidistant from all corresponding points on a shape and its reflection

Mutually exclusive: events that cannot happen at the same time

N

Number line: a line marked with positions of numbers showing the valid values of a variable

O

Object: the original shape (before it has been transformed)

Orientation: the position of a shape relative to the grid

Outcome: a single result of an experiment or situation

Outlier: data value that is much larger or smaller than others in the same data set

P

Parabola: the symmetrical curve produced by the graph of a quadratic function

Parallel vectors: vectors with the same direction. When drawn next to each other they are parallel lines, even if they go in opposite directions.

Perfect square: a binomial product of the form $(a \pm b)^2$

Perimeter: the distance around the boundaries (sides) of a shape

Perpendicular bisector: a line perpendicular to another that also cuts it in half

Plan view: the view of an object from directly above

Plane shape: a flat, two-dimensional shape

Polygon and more

Polygon: a closed plane shape with three or more straight sides

Polyhedron: a solid shape with flat faces that are polygons

Polynomial: an expression made up of many terms with positive powers for the variables

Population: the name given to a data set

Position-to-term rule: a function for finding the value of any term in a sequence using its position

Prime factor: a factor that is also a prime number

Product: the result of multiplying numbers and/or terms together

Proportion: the number or amount of a group compared to the whole, often expressed as a fraction, percentage or ratio

Pythagorean triple: three non-zero positive integers (a, b, c) for which $a^2 + b^2 = c^2$

Q

Quadratic: an expression with a variable to the power of 2 but no higher power

Quadratic expression: an expression in which the highest power of x is x^2

R

Radius (plural radii): distance from the centre to the circumference of a circle. The radius is half of the diameter of the circle.

Random: not predetermined

Ratio: the relationship between two or more groups or amounts, explaining how much bigger one is than another

Rational number: a number that can be expressed in the form of $\frac{a}{b}$ (or as its equivalent as a terminating or repeating decimal)

Reciprocal: the value obtained by inverting a fraction. Any number multiplied by its reciprocal is 1.

Reflection: an exact image of a shape about a line of symmetry (mirror line)

Regular polygon: a polygon with equal straight sides and equal angles

Representative sample: a smaller quantity of data that represents the characteristics of a larger population

Right prism: a prism with sides perpendicular to the end faces (base)

Roots: the individual values of x in a quadratic equation when $y = 0$

Rotation symmetry: symmetry by turning a shape around a fixed point so that it looks the same in different positions

Round to significant figures (sf): round to a specified level of accuracy from the first significant figure

Rounding: writing a number with zeros in the place of some digits

S

Sample: a small set of data from a population

Sample space: a list or diagram that shows all possible outcomes from two or more events

Scalar: a numerical quantity (it has no direction)

Scale factor: a number that scales a quantity up or down

Second difference: the difference between each term in the first difference

Semicircle: half of a circle

Sequence: a number pattern or list of numbers following a particular order

Set: a collection. The brackets { } are shorthand for 'the set of'. For example, {2, 4, 6, 8} is the set of the numbers 2, 4, 6, 8, which represents the even numbers.

Significant figure: the first non-zero digit when you read a number from left to right (see also **round to significant figures (sf)**)

Simultaneous equations: a pair of equations with two unknowns that can be solved at the same time

Solution: all possible values of x in an equation. Depending on the quadratic equation, x can have one, two or possibly no solutions.

Subject: the variable which is expressed in terms of other variables or constants. It is the variable on its own on one side of the equals sign. In the formula $s = \dfrac{d}{t}$, s is the subject.

Substitute: to replace variables with numbers

Surd: if $\sqrt[n]{a}$ is an irrational number, then $\sqrt[n]{a}$ is called a surd

T

Term: a combination of letters and/or numbers. Each number in a sequence is called a term.

Term-to-term rule: operations applied to any number in a sequence to generate the next number in the sequence

Theorem: a statement that can be demonstrated to be true by accepted mathematical operations

Transversal: a straight line that crosses a pair of parallel lines

Trinomial: an expression with three terms

Truncation: cutting off all digits after a certain point without rounding

U

Unknown: part of an equation which is represented by a letter

V

Variable: a letter representing an unknown number

Vector: a quantity that has both magnitude and direction. For example, displacement (30 m south), velocity (30 m/s forwards) or acceleration due to gravity (9.8 m/s² down).

Vertically opposite angles: angles that are opposite one another at an intersection of two lines. Vertical in this context means 'of the same vertex or point' and not up and down.

X

x-intercept: the point where a line crosses the x-axis when $y = 0$

Y

y-intercept: the point where a line crosses the y-axis when $x = 0$

Index

Acknowledgements

Questions from AQA past question papers © AQA.

These questions are indicated by .

Questions from Cambridge IGCSE® Mathematics reproduced with permission of Karen Morrison and Nick Hamshaw.

The authors would like to thank Fran Wilson for her work on GCSE Mathematics Online.

Cover © 2013 Fabian Oefner www.fabianoefner.com; p1 (top) Henry Gan/Photodisc/Thinkstock; p1 Denis Kuvaev/Shutterstock; p15 (top) cherezoff/iStock/Thinkstock; p15 Chad McDermott/Shutterstock; p17 © Detail Nottingham/Alamy; p36 (top) marekuliasz/iStock/Thinkstock; p36 Brian A. Jackson /Shutterstock; p58 (top) Yuriy S/iStock/Thinkstock; p58 Tyler Olson/Shutterstock; p70 (top) SDivin09/iStock/Thinkstock; p70 Chameleons Eye/Shutterstock; p83 (top) Andrey Popov/iStock/Thinkstock; p83 Leah-Anne Thompson/Shutterstock; p85 William West/Staff/Getty Images; p88 © Jumana el Heloueh/Reuters/Corbis; p95 (top) agsandrew/iStock/Thinkstock; p95 wavebreakmedia/Shutterstock; p110 (top) Monarx3d/iStock/Thinkstock; p123 kilukilu/Shutterstock; p129 Ieva Geneviciene/Shutterstock; p134 (top) Mark_Stillwagon/iStock/Thinkstock; p134 Mikio Oba/Shutterstock; p138 Dmitry Kalinovsky/Shutterstock; p145 Ryan Lewandowski/Shutterstock; p152 (top) David Chapman/Design pics/Valueline/Thinkstock; p152 itman__47/Shutterstock; p163 iceink/Shutterstock; p171 (top) imagean/iStock/Thinkstock; p171 Federico Rostagno/Shutterstock; p177 stefano spezi/Shutterstock; p189 (top) Joe McDaniel/iStock/Thinkstock; p189 Dmitry Kalinovsky/Shutterstock; p196 Pixsooz/Shutterstock; p202 (top) shutter_m/iStock/Thinkstock; p218 (top) Jeffrey Collingwood/Hemera/Thinkstock; p218 CandyBox Images/Shutterstock; p231 (top) agsandrew/iStock/Thinkstock; p231 Sergey Kamshylin/Shutterstock; p244 (top) Leigh Prather/iStock/Thinkstock; p244 Dariush M./Shutterstock; p258 (top) Alison Bradford Photography/iStock/Thinkstock; p258 Andrey_Popov/Shutterstock; p88 (top) © PhotoAlto/Alamy; p288 © Monty Rakusen/Cultura/Corbis; p291 © Roger Bamber/Alamy; p299 (top) murengstockphoto/Thinkstock; p299 (bottom) Shaiith/Thinkstock; p303 (top) Chemik11/iStock/Thinktstock p323 (top) alfimimnill/iStock/Thinkstock; p346 (top) Mike Watson Images/moodboard/Thinkstock; p346 Dorling Kindersley/Getty Images; p352 Taiga/Shutterstock; p370 (top) deyangeorgiev/iStock/Thinkstock; p370 /Shutterstock; p378 © PCN Photography/Alamy; p383 (top) Phil Ashley/Photodisc/Thinkstock; p383 govicinity/Shutterstock; p384 (top) Arvind Balaraman/Shutterstock; p384 (bottom) Isantilli/Shutterstock; p388 Dmitry Kalinovsky/Shutterstock; p389 Sergio Bertino/Shutterstock; p393 (left) courtesy of Newcastle International Airport p393 (right) © 2ebill/Alamy; p398 Chameleons Eye/Shutterstock; p400 cpphotoimages/Shutterstock; p401 (top) maury75/iStock/Thinkstock; p401 angellodeco/Shutterstock; p423 (top) Tabor Gus/Corbis; p423 © Olaf Doering/Alamy; p432 (top) Eugen Weide/Hemera/Thinkstock; p432 T. Fabian/Shutterstock; p437 Adam Gilchrist/Shutterstock; p439 Valentyn Volkov/Shutterstock; p444 (top) Kuzma/Thinkstock; p444 Michael Jung/Shutterstock; p445 terekhov igor/Shutterstock; p446 ermess/Shutterstock; p447 Maksim Kabakou/Shutterstock; p448 Rtimages/Shutterstock; p449 Christian Delbert/Shutterstock; p458 (top) Kerem Yucel/iStock/Thinkstock; p458 Dan Breckwoldt/Shutterstock; p476 (top) zentilia/iStock/Thinkstock; p476 Zryzner/Shutterstock; p486 (top) sutichak/iStock/Thinkstock; p486 Michael Winston Rosa/Shutterstock; p493 Herbert Kratky/Shutterstock; p496 (top) ninjacpb/iStock/Thinkstock; p498 Pal Teravagimov/Shutterstock; p519 (top) Huskyomega/iStock/Thinkstock; p519 Franz Pfluegl/Shutterstock; p521/522 Yulia Glam/Shutterstock; p531 (top) UMB-O/Shutterstock; p531 (bottom) Vector House/Shutterstock; p535 Gemenacom/Shutterstock; p537(top) Comstock/Stockbyte/Thinkstock; p537 © Andrzej Gorzkowski Photography/Alamy; p552 Lucy Clark/Shutterstock; p559(top) Pietro Ballardini/iStockEditorial/Thinkstock; p559 Ross Strachan/Shutterstock; p571 (top) stevanovicigor/iStock/Thinkstock; p571 © Emma Smales/VIEW/Corbis; p578 racorn/Shutterstock; p585 © Rob Wilkinson/Alamy; p586(top) Digital Vision/Photodisc/Thinkstock; p586 GECO UK/Science Photo Library; p604 Svetlana Jafarova/Shutterstock; p605 (top) shaunnessey/iStock/Thinkstock; p605 © Jenny E. Ross/Corbis; p610 herreid/Thinkstock; p624(top) shutter_m/iStock/Thinkstock; p624 Pressmaster/Shutterstock.